Survey Methods in Social Investigation

by

SIR CLAUS MOSER

*Director, Central Statistical Office and
Visiting Professor of Social Statistics, London School of Economics and
Political Science*

and

G. KALTON

Leverhulme Professor of Social Statistics, University of Southampton

SECOND EDITION

HEINEMANN EDUCATIONAL BOOKS

LONDON

Heinemann Educational Books Ltd.

LONDON EDINBURGH MELBOURNE AUCKLAND TORONTO
SINGAPORE HONG KONG KUALA LUMPUR
IBADAN NAIROBI JOHANNESBURG
NEW DELHI

ISBN 0 435 82603 4 (cased edition)
ISBN 0 435 82604 2 (paperback)

Published by
Heinemann Educational Books Ltd
48 Charles Street, London W1X 8AH

Printed in Great Britain by
Robert MacLehose and Co Ltd
The University Press, Glasgow

Contents

PREFACE TO THE SECOND EDITION ix

PREFACE TO THE FIRST EDITION xi

ACKNOWLEDGEMENTS xv

GUIDE FOR THE READER xvii

1. THE NATURE OF SOCIAL SURVEYS, AND SOME
   EXAMPLES
   1.1. Introduction 1
   1.2. Historical background 6
   1.3. The classical poverty surveys 7
   1.4. Regional planning surveys 11
   1.5. The Government Social Survey—now part of the
        Office of Population Censuses and Surveys 13
   1.6. Market, audience and opinion research 15
   1.7. Some other surveys 20

2. THE PLANNING OF SOCIAL SURVEYS
   2.1. Preliminary study 41
   2.2. The main planning problems 43
   2.3. Pre-tests and pilot surveys 47

3. THE COVERAGE OF SURVEYS
   3.1. Definition of the population 53
   3.2. Censuses and sample surveys 54
   3.3. The idea and the advantages of sampling 56
   3.4. The use of sampling in Great Britain 58

4. BASIC IDEAS OF SAMPLING
    4.1. Introduction   61
    4.2. Estimation and testing of hypotheses   62
    4.3. Accuracy, bias and precision   63
    4.4. Sampling distributions and standard errors   69
    4.5. Significance tests   74
    4.6. Summary of simplifications   76

5. TYPES OF SAMPLE DESIGN
    5.1. Introduction   79
    5.2. Random sampling   80
    5.3. Stratification   85
    5.4. Cluster and multi-stage sampling   100
    5.5. Sampling with varying probabilities   111
    5.6. Concluding remarks   116

6. FURTHER TYPES OF SAMPLE DESIGN
    6.1. Area sampling   118
    6.2. Multi-phase sampling   121
    6.3. Replicated sampling   124
    6.4. Quota sampling   127
    6.5. Panel and longitudinal studies   137
    6.6. Master samples   143

7. OTHER ASPECTS OF SAMPLING
    7.1. Sample size   146
    7.2. Random numbers   152
    7.3. Sampling frames   154
    7.4. Non-response   166

8. AN EXAMPLE OF A NATIONAL RANDOM SAMPLE
   DESIGN   188

9. EXPERIMENTS AND INVESTIGATIONS
    9.1. Causality   211
    9.2. Validity of experiments   214
    9.3. Controlling for the effects of extraneous variables 220
    9.4. Other designs   224
    9.5. Examples of investigations   226
    9.6. Factorial designs   230
    9.7. Sample designs for experiments and investigations   233

10. METHODS OF COLLECTING THE INFORMATION I
    —DOCUMENTS AND OBSERVATION
    10.1. Introduction   238
    10.2. The use of documentary sources   240
    10.3. Observation   244

11. METHODS OF COLLECTING THE INFORMATION II
    —MAIL QUESTIONNAIRES
    11.1. The role of direct questioning   256
    11.2. The advantages of mail questionnaires   257
    11.3. The limitations of mail questionnaires   260
    11.4. Non-response in mail surveys   262

12. METHODS OF COLLECTING THE INFORMATION III
    —INTERVIEWING
    12.1. Types of interviewing   270
    12.2. The nature of the survey interview   271
    12.3. The interviewer's task   273
    12.4. Selection and training   282
    12.5. Some practical points   291
    12.6. Informal interviewing   296

13. QUESTIONNAIRES
    13.1. General principles of design   303
    13.2. Question content   310
    13.3. Question wording   318
    13.4. Open and pre-coded questions   341
    13.5. Question order   346
    13.6. Concluding remarks   347

14. SCALING METHODS
    14.1. Introduction   350
    14.2. Types of scales   352
    14.3. Reliability and validity   353
    14.4. General procedures in attitude scaling   357
    14.5. Rating scales   358
    14.6. Thurstone scales   360
    14.7. Likert scales   361
    14.8. Guttman scales   366
    14.9. Semantic differential   373
    14.10. Concluding remarks   376

15. RESPONSE ERRORS
15.1. Response bias and response variance 378
15.2. Sources of response errors 385
15.3. Operation of response errors 388
15.4. Detection of response errors 392
15.5. Control and measurement of response errors 403

16. PROCESSING OF THE DATA
16.1. Editing 410
16.2. Coding 414
16.3. Tabulation 428

17. ANALYSIS, INTERPRETATION AND PRESENTATION
17.1. Introduction 439
17.2. Statistical description 440
17.3. Population estimates and sampling errors 442
17.4. Interpreting relationships 447
17.5. Causal models 458
17.6. Index construction 464
17.7. Presentation 467

18. CONCLUDING REMARKS 480

BIBLIOGRAPHY 489

INDEX OF NAMES AND ORGANIZATIONS 527

INDEX OF SUBJECTS 538

Preface to the Second Edition

SINCE THE First Edition of this book was published there has been a considerable increase in survey activity throughout the world, and methods have become more rigorous and well-developed. We have tried to reflect these changes in this new edition. Examples of more recent surveys have been given in many places and particularly in Chapter 1 which has been entirely rewritten. Even so, we have not hesitated to retain as examples many early surveys, since they help to illustrate the development of methods, and are often still the best examples of their type.

As to methods, changes have been made throughout the book so as to reflect the latest developments, including for instance recent research on mail questionnaires and the use of computers for processing survey data. Furthermore there are the following major additions to the First Edition: Chapter 1 has been expanded considerably with examples of a wide range of surveys and methods; the chapter in the first edition entitled Types of Sample Design has been enlarged and divided into two chapters—Chapters 5 and 6—with the second chapter containing fuller descriptions of several sample designs; a special chapter, Chapter 9, dealing with Experiments and Investigations has been added; the section in the first edition on scaling methods has been enlarged into a full chapter, Chapter 14; and Chapter 17 has two new sections, Section 17.4 on Interpreting Relationships and Section 17.5 on Causal Models.

The net effect is to make a few parts of the book harder. This reflects the fact that techniques have become more rigorous and is in line with the teaching of the subject; courses on survey methods in universities and technical colleges have become notably more sophisticated in a technical sense. We have, however, kept the harder sections down to an absolute minimum and only a small part of the book is above the technical level of the First Edition. Moreover, in order to make it easy for the reader who does not need these sections to identify them, they are printed in a smaller type.

We have been helped by a number of people in the preparation of this new edition. Our greatest debt is to Dr Tessa Blackstone who undertook most of the work needed for the up-to-date survey of surveys which appears as Chapter 1. We believe that this chapter will be valuable in its own right, and we are most grateful to Dr Blackstone.

We would also like to thank the following who have helped us either by providing information about their organization's survey practices or by commenting on various parts of the book: Miss J. Atkinson, Miss L. R. Austen, Mr B. A. Bates, Mr J. Bibby, Dr B. Cooper, Dr H. Durant, Mr B. P. Emmett, Professor L. Kish, Mr F. F. Land, Mr L. Marchant, Dr A. C. McKennell, Mrs S. B. Quinn, Mr C. Scott, Dr J. C. Scott, Dr A. P. E. L. Sealy, Mr R. Sherwood, Professor A. Stuart, Mr H. J. F. Taylor, Mr P. J. Wakeford and Mr J. H. Westergaard.

We are grateful to Miss C. Martin, Miss A. Usher and Miss M. Vaughan for their part in typing the manuscript, to Mr A. C. Jhavary and Mr A. J. Deacon who worked on the bibliography, and to Mr P. Marks who checked the calculations. Above all, we should like to thank Mrs F. H. Kalton, without whose excellent work in typing, reading and proof-reading we would not have completed the task.

Finally, we wish to thank Mr A. Hill (Chairman and Managing Director of Heinemann Educational Books Ltd.) for his interest and help throughout the production of the book, and Professor D. G. MacRae for his most helpful advice and encouragement.

C. A. MOSER

January, 1971   G. KALTON

Preface to the First Edition

THIS BOOK has grown out of a course of lectures given at the London School of Economics during the last few years. It is intended primarily as an introduction to the methodology of surveys for students in the social sciences but I hope that it may also be useful to the many whose work requires an understanding of the methods of surveys, including those who commission them and have to evaluate their results. The book is concerned primarily with what one thinks of as 'large scale' surveys rather than with case studies of individuals, small groups or institutions.

Another type of reader whose needs have been particularly in my mind is the research worker in the social sciences who wishes to conduct an *ad hoc* survey but has little idea of the principles of sampling or questionnaire design or how to go about the processing and analysing of the results. He, unlike the professional surveyor with an established organization of specialists, field workers and routine staff at his call, has to start from scratch, probably doing a good deal of the work himself and usually with very limited resources. My hope is that this book will provide research workers so placed with a groundwork of knowledge about general ideas; for instruction on practical details they can then turn to a survey manual or to a specialist for advice.

With such a potential readership in mind, I have tried not to overload the book with detail and technicalities, for the study of these without a sound understanding of general methodology can all too easily lead to the application of methods to situations for which they are ill-suited. I have tried, also, to stress the limitations of the survey approach and to caution potential users against an uncritical faith in its power. Not every research programme needs a survey, and indeed many questions can be dealt with as satisfactorily by 'desk research' as by fact-collecting. With the social survey, as with any scientific method, part of the skill lies in knowing when to use it at all.

A good deal of space is given to the subject of sampling, for this, I have found, is the aspect of surveys which is the most difficult for the non-specialist to grasp.

The discussion is in the main confined to work carried out in Great Britain and some of the examples derive from surveys with which I have been connected either at the London School of Economics or as a consultant to market research agencies. Many of the references on methodological advances, on the other hand, come from the American literature.

As the total literature on the subject now runs into thousands of items, some guidance on reading is essential. I have given, at the end of each chapter, the references that seem to me most useful on its contents. References to general textbooks are given at the end of Chapter 1.

I have cause to be grateful to a number of people who have helped me in one way or another in the writing of this book. I owe a great deal to the advice and encouragement I have received throughout from Professor R. G. D. Allen, Professor D. V. Glass and Professor M. G. Kendall, all of the London School of Economics, and I must also, more formally, thank Professor Kendall for permitting me to draw for examples on the research projects carried out under his direction within the Research Techniques Unit at the School.

I am deeply indebted to three other colleagues of mine, H. S. Booker, J. Durbin and A. Stuart, who were each good enough to read through a draft of the book and from whose many penetrating criticisms and constructive suggestions I have benefited more than I can say.

Several survey practitioners have kindly given me assistance. I am grateful to Dr H. Durant (Director of the British Institute of Public Opinion), Mr L. Moss (Director of the Government Social Survey) and Mr R. J. Silvey (Head of B.B.C. Audience Research), who read various sections of the book and made a number of valuable suggestions. Above all, I want to thank Mr T. Cauter (Director of the British Market Research Bureau) and Mr J. Downham (a senior research officer of the same organization) who both gave much precious time to the reading of a draft of the book and who offered many constructive suggestions of the utmost value. The book in its final form is of course entirely my own responsibility and, in expressing my sincere thanks to all these gentlemen, I must emphasize that none of them necessarily agree with its final form or content.

I gratefully acknowledge a grant from the Social Research Division at the London School of Economics which covered some of the typing cost and the help of Mrs D. W. Cleather and Miss J. A. Mathews (of the Typing Department) in this part of the work. Other parts of the typing were carried out by Miss J. A. Castle and Miss F. H. Johnson (of the Statistics Department) and I am grateful to them for their assistance. By far the major share of all the typing, however, has been done—and done superbly well—by Mrs E. M. Strudwick, Secretary of the Statistics Department, and I wish to express to her my sincere gratitude for the enormous amount of help she has given me.

Mr Alan Hill, of William Heinemann Ltd., has throughout been most considerate and helpful and I have much cause to be grateful to him, as also to Mr A. R. Beal of the Education Department. Mr C. R. Howe undertook the technical editing of the book and I should like to express my admiration for his skill and my thanks for the many improvements in literary presentation which he suggested.

My greatest debt of all is to my wife who, besides assisting me in many of the more tedious tasks of producing the book, helped me more than I can say by her unfailing encouragement and patience.

London School of Economics   C. A. MOSER
September, 1957

Acknowledgements

O UR THANKS are due to the Director of the Gallup Poll for permission to reproduce in slightly changed form the questionnaire on pages 332–9 (the changes, which were necessary to fit the questionnaire to the book size, were kept to the minimum); to the Editors of the *Journal of the Royal Statistical Society* for permission to reproduce from a paper by Moser and Stuart (1953) the questionnaire that appears on pages 312–4, as well as some other material, also to quote from papers by Durbin and Stuart (1951 and 1954a), and to reproduce from a paper by Gray and Corlett (1950) the material used in Table 7.3; to the Controller of Her Majesty's Stationery Office for permission to reproduce material used in Table 7.2 (Gray and Gee, 1967), and for permission to quote several extracts from *A Handbook for Interviewers* (Atkinson, 1967); to the Central Office of Information for permission to reproduce material from the Radio and Television Enquiry on pages 305–7; to John Wiley and Sons for permission to reproduce (in slightly changed form) from W. E. Deming's *Some Theory of Sampling* (1950) the diagram that appears on page 68; to the Cambridge University Press for permission to print in Chapter 7 an extract from *Tables of Random Sampling Numbers* by Kendall and Smith (1939); to the University of Oxford Institute of Statistics for permission to reproduce in Chapters 7 and 8 two tables from *British Incomes and Savings* (Lydall, 1955); to the Director of the Institute for Social Research, University of Michigan, for permission to give in Chapter 12 extracts from a conference report published by the Institute (Survey Research Center, 1951); to the American Marketing Association for permission to quote extensively from an article by Durbin and Stuart (1954b) which appeared in the *Journal of Marketing*; to International Business Machines for permission to reproduce the punched card on page 420; to the McGraw-Hill Book Company for permission to quote in

Chapter 17 a paragraph from *Methods in Social Research* by Goode and Hatt (1952); to the U.S. Social Science Research Council for permission to quote in Chapter 17 two paragraphs from Appendix A of *Pre-Election Polls of 1948* (Mosteller and others, 1949); to the Director of the United Nations Statistical Office for permission to give in Chapter 17 extensive extracts from *Recommendations for the Preparation of Sample Survey Reports* (*Provisional Issue*) (United Nations Statistical Office, 1964); to the Editor of *The Times* for permission to quote in Chapter 18 from the fourth leader that appeared on August 3rd 1955; to the Editor of the *Incorporated Statistician* for permission to reproduce material used in Tables 7.3 and 7.6; to the Oxford University Press for permission to reproduce the attitude scale on page 363; to the University of Illinois Press for permission to reproduce the scales on page 373; and to the Editor of the *American Journal of Sociology* for permission to reproduce the figure on page 461.

Guide for the Reader

A FEW parts of this book are rather more difficult than the rest, involving a greater use of mathematical notation, and these parts have been so arranged that they can be passed over without a loss of continuity. The parts involved are: the ends of Sections 5.3, 5.4 and 5.5; the latter part of Chapter 8; the end of Section 15.1; the end of Section 17.4; and the whole of Section 17.5. At the start of each of these parts there is a distinguishing mark ●, and the more difficult material is also indicated by the use of a smaller print.

CHAPTER 1

The Nature of Social Surveys, and some Examples

1.1. Introduction

IT WOULD be pleasant to be able to open this chapter with a straightforward definition of what is meant by a 'social survey'. In fact such a definition would have to be so general as to defeat its purpose, since the term and the methods associated with it are applied to an extraordinarily wide variety of investigations, ranging from the classical poverty surveys of sixty years ago to Gallup Polls, town-planning surveys, market research, as well as the innumerable investigations sponsored by research institutes, universities and government.

As regards purpose, the range is equally wide. A survey may be occasioned simply by a need for administrative facts on some aspect of public life; or be designed to investigate a cause-effect relationship or to throw fresh light on some aspect of sociological theory. When it comes to subject matter, all one can say is that surveys are concerned with the demographic characteristics, the social environment, the activities, or the opinions and attitudes of some group of people.

We can thus see that a satisfactory definition would have to be couched in much more general terms than that introduced by Wells (1935) when he defined a social survey as a 'fact-finding study dealing chiefly with working-class poverty and with the nature and problems of the community'. This might have covered the classical community and poverty studies but would hardly be adequate, the first part at any rate, for the modern forms of survey mentioned above.

But although we shall use the term 'social survey' in a wider sense than that of Wells' definition, we shall not attempt to cover all types of social investigation. The methods described in this book are most relevant to the type of approach one associates with official surveys, market and opinion research, and, to a considerable extent, with sociological research. This does not necessarily mean the use of standardized, formal methods and the coverage of large representative samples. A researcher wishing to investigate certain aspects of family life may choose to confine himself to a handful of families, studying them intensively, rather than to make a more superficial examination of a large-scale sample.

These two approaches usually serve different ends and use different methods: the intensive study of a few cases will tend to dig deeper, but may lose something in generality; it will probably use less formal interviewing techniques than the other, and in the analysis of results will give more prominence to non-quantified material. This is an important difference, but the methodology used for such 'field studies' or 'field experiments' is in many respects so similar to that of the social survey proper that we shall refer to them from time to time.

We hope, in fact, that the distinction between different kinds of surveys will be made clear by the context, and we will now refer briefly to some major aspects in which surveys differ from each other. These are purpose, subject matter, coverage, and source of information.

The purposes of surveys

The purpose of many surveys is simply to provide someone with information. That someone may be a government department wanting to know how much people spend on food; a business concern interested in finding out what detergents people are using; a research institute studying the housing of old-age pensioners. Whether the 'client' in each case is well-advised to want these facts, or to seek them through a survey, need not worry us here. We are only concerned with noting that to him, as well as to the surveyor, the survey has a clear *descriptive* purpose.

To a social scientist, a survey may equally have a purely descriptive purpose, as a way of studying social conditions, relationships and behaviour. The sort of information needed may be how families of different size, composition and social status spend their incomes; how people are reacting to the latest productivity drive; what relationship there appears to be between education and the possibility of moving up the social ladder. In this early fact-finding stage of much work in the social sciences there is virtually no limit to the range of topics covered by surveys.

It must not be thought, however, that the purpose of surveys, whether in social research or elsewhere, is always so straightforward. Many enquiries aim to *explain* rather than to describe. Their function may be theoretical—to test some hypothesis suggested by sociological theory—or severely practical—to assess the influence of various factors, which can be manipulated by public action, upon some phenomenon. But, whichever be the case, the purpose is to explain the relationships between a number of variables. This may lead to extreme complexities in interpretation. The problems of 'causal' surveys are so important that we devote a separate chapter to them.

The usefulness of surveys (descriptive or explanatory) in social research is often debated, and one does sometimes suspect social scientists of being excessively eager to use them—to leap into the field as soon as they have a problem, collect data, tabulate answers, write a report and regard the research as finished. It is the ill-considered launching of surveys, leading to the waste of much time and money and the accumulation (often) of unwanted data, that has given rise to the scepticism with which some sociologists regard 'door-knocking' research.

It must be stressed that fact-collecting is no substitute for thought and desk research, and that the comparative ease with which survey techniques can be mastered is all the more reason why their limitations as well as their capabilities should be understood. Sound judgement in their use depends on this. It is no good, for instance, blindly applying the formal standardized methods generally used in official or market research enquiries to many of the more complex problems in which sociologists are interested.

Sometimes good judgement requires the deliberate sacrifice of quantitative precision for the greater depth attainable by more intensive methods of attack. An example will make this clear. There has been much discussion of the problem of 'early leaving' from grammar schools—pupils leaving before the end of the grammar-school course. To get the facts about this the Central Advisory Council for Education (England) (1954) conducted a national sample survey, collecting a wealth of information about the problem: its dimensions, its association with social background, and so forth. One of the vital questions arising from this survey was *why* children from 'working-class' backgrounds do so much less well at grammar schools than others. The official report put forward several possible explanations, among them the subtle influence of the parents' own attitude to education, the tradition and facilities of the home, and the character of the neighbourhood.

Now to assess the influence of these factors on a child's achievement at his grammar school calls, not for another national sample survey, but for intensive study, preferably over a number of years, of a few carefully selected schools. There would have to be interviews, possibly along informal lines, with children, parents, teachers and employment officers; and the interviewers would have to be chosen as much for their understanding of education as for their more routine professional skill.

Whether one could rightly call such further enquiry a social survey (rather than, for example, a field study) is a matter of terminology. What we want to emphasize is simply that there are types of field research that do not call for the apparatus of the large-scale sample survey.

To say this is not to underrate the usefulness of such surveys for many research programmes. In fact in the majority of such programmes they are invaluable *at some stage*. One occasionally hears a survey criticized on the grounds that it did not test a hypothesis or relate to any underlying theory. While there is often substance in this, the criticism is irrelevant to many surveys such as, for instance, the examples of straightforward factual enquiries mentioned before. Even these should always be preceded by carefully thought-out decisions about what is, and what is not, worth asking. But only in a trivial sense could it be said that this amounts to a set of hypotheses; in the narrower sense, implying the testing of a postulated relationship between two or more variables, the formulation of hypotheses is irrelevant to—and impossible for—many fact-collecting enquiries.

We must, after all, remember that the social sciences are still at an early stage of knowledge regarding human behaviour and social environment. To insist that a sociologist must not collect facts until he has a hypothesis would merely encourage the use of arbitrary hypotheses, which can be as bad as indiscriminate fact-collecting. The sociologist should look upon surveys as one way, and a supremely useful one, of exploring the field, of collecting data *around* as well as directly *on* the subject of study, so that the problem is brought into focus and the points worth pursuing are suggested. With such pilot information as a guide, a series of hypotheses can be formulated and tested by further empirical investigation.

Surveys thus have their usefulness both in leading to the formulation of hypotheses and, at a more advanced stage, in putting them to the test. Their function in a given research depends on how much is already known about the subject and on the purpose for which the information is required.

The subject matter of surveys

Even the highly selective set of examples of surveys given in the remainder of this chapter shows that there are few aspects of human behaviour that have not at some time attracted the social surveyor's attention. A full catalogue of them is out of the question here, but it will be helpful to distinguish four broad types of subject matter:[1]

[1] We should make clear that since this book is concerned broadly with social rather than economic surveys, little will be said about surveys of shops, business firms or similar economic units.

the demographic characteristics of a set of people;
their social environment;
their activities;
their opinions and attitudes.

By demographic characteristics we mean matters such as family or household composition, marital status, fertility, age, and so on. Some surveys, for example the Family Census conducted for the Royal Commission on Population, described by Glass and Grebenik (1954), are entirely on the demographic aspects of life, but almost all surveys include some questions in this field.

Social environment is taken to cover all the social and economic factors to which people are subject, including occupation and income as well as housing conditions and social amenities. These are subjects which cover, in the widest sense, the question 'How do people live?' The classical poverty surveys addressed themselves almost exclusively to answering this, as do many modern surveys.

Data on demographic factors and social environment are factual and their collection presents relatively few problems. They are less open to error (if definitions have been clear) than information on behaviour and opinions, because they are more objective. Furthermore, their accuracy can more often be checked.

Then there is the type of survey primarily concerned with 'what people do'—their behaviour and activities. By this is not meant occupation (which forms part of social environment) but, for instance, use of leisure, travelling habits, expenditure patterns, television-viewing, radio-listening and newspaper-reading. Much of the work of the Government Social Survey[1] lies in this field, and so does a good deal of market research.

Finally there is the type of survey concerned with people's opinions and attitudes. Opinion polls, as the name suggests, deal mainly with these; in many other surveys they are of marginal importance. Opinion questions have their own peculiar problems, and these are examined in a subsequent chapter.

Coverage of surveys and sources of data

Surveys differ markedly in the way they cover a given population— this term being used in the statistical sense to mean the aggregate of persons or objects under investigation. Thus one can speak of the population of people over twenty years of age in England and Wales; the population of miners in South Wales; the population of people travelling to work on the London Underground; the population of desks in a building.

[1] The Government Social Survey is now part of the Office of Population Censuses and Surveys.

The coverage of a survey can range from a few case-studies to a complete enumeration, from carefully selected samples to arbitrary collections of volunteers; so it is clear that in considering coverage a surveyor must settle first the extent to which he wishes to generalize from his findings. There are surveys in which representativeness is of minor importance, but in most the intention is to draw population inferences. This intention, when it exists, must be recognized explicitly and the survey designed accordingly.

In social surveys as here interpreted the main methods of data collection are observation, mail questionnaire and personal interview. Surveys also generally make some use of documentary information, but studies based predominantly on statistical data, documents and historical records are not dealt with here.

1.2. Historical background

The historian of social surveys in Great Britain has a relatively easy task. His main subject matter is encompassed within about the last eighty years, and there is no lack of records and documentary sources to guide him. He could, it is true, go further back and open his story with Cobbett or Defoe or even the Domesday Book, but it would be more sensible to begin with Eden, Mayhew and Booth. Of these Mayhew's (1861–62) fascinating book *London Labour and the London Poor* makes particularly entertaining reading and has been enjoying a considerable literary vogue in recent years; but it is Booth who should be considered the father of scientific social surveys.

In the eighty-odd years since Booth began his enquiry into the *Labour and Life of the People of London* (Booth, 1889–1902) great changes have occurred, both in the amount and character of survey activity and in the public interest shown in it. At the turn of the century two pioneers—Booth and Rowntree—were conducting large-scale surveys, stimulated by their concern about the living conditions of a large section of the population. During the next twenty years one or two others, notably Bowley, followed their example. By the late twenties and early thirties social surveys were being conducted in London, Tyneside, Sheffield, Southampton, Merseyside and many other cities. These, while differing in details of scope and method, all followed the broad pattern established by the pioneers. Subsequently, surveys began to be used in conjunction with town planning and various government activities, and the techniques were adapted to the needs of market and public opinion research. Today a government organization is wholly occupied undertaking social surveys, market research has become a large-scale industry, social scientists regard the social survey as one of their basic techniques, and courses on survey methodology are given in many universities.

A brief historical account of these developments will be a useful preliminary to the description of present-day methods, which is the main purpose of this book. With this in mind, surveys will be mentioned either for their methodological interest or for the importance of their results. It also needs saying that the examples relate almost exclusively to Britain. Needless to say there is a great deal of survey activity in other countries, notably the United States. For the latter, a useful general reference is the symposium on *Survey Research in the Social Sciences* edited by Glock (1967), with discussions of the role of surveys in sociology, political science, psychology, economics, anthropology, education, social work, and public health and medicine.

1.3. The classical poverty surveys

Charles Booth's[l] monumental survey was begun in 1886 and published, in a seventeen-volume edition, in 1902. Booth, a rich Liverpool shipowner, had been deeply disturbed by the poverty and living conditions of the working class, and set out to obtain 'two series of facts—first, the relative destitution, poverty or comfort of the home and, secondly, the character of the work from which the various bread-winners in the family derived their livelihood' (Booth, 1889, i, p. 13). His main problem was how to collect the information about the huge working-class population of London. 'The root idea with which I began to work', he says, 'was that every fact I needed was known to someone, and that the information had simply to be collected and put together.' He consequently applied what Beatrice Webb later termed the 'method of wholesale interviewing', collecting the information from School Attendance Officers—the people who possessed the most detailed knowledge of the parents of school-children and their living conditions. Booth's approach is best illustrated by the following quotation:

Of the wealth of my material I have no doubt. I am indeed embarrassed by its mass and by my resolution to make use of no fact to which I cannot give a quantitative value. The materials for sensational stories lie plentifully in every book of our notes; but, even if I had the skill to use my material in this way—that gift of the imagination which is called 'realistic'—I should not wish to use it here. There is struggling poverty, there is destitution, there is hunger, drunkenness, brutality and crime; no one doubts that it is so. My object has been to show the numerical relation which poverty, misery and depravity bear to regular earnings and comparative comfort, and to describe the general conditions under which each class lives. (Booth, 1889, i, p. 5.)

On the basis of his data Booth put each family into one of eight classes, of which four were below and four above the poverty line. His definitions of the various classes were vague: 'My "poor" may be described as living under a struggle to obtain the necessaries of life and make both ends meet, while the "very poor" live in a state of chronic want' (Booth, 1889, i, p. 33). It was to be left to Rowntree to give these concepts greater precision. The study, as a whole, was largely descriptive and sacrificed some generality through its exclusion of families without schoolchildren. Nevertheless, its startling results drew attention to the extent and severity of poverty and, as Beatrice Webb has shown, its political results were considerable. It was a pioneering contribution to the science of social study.

A decade after the start of Booth's investigation, Rowntree set out on his first survey of York, published under the title *Poverty: a Study of Town Life* (Rowntree, 1902). His approach varied in three important methodological aspects from that of Booth.

First, he set out to obtain information about the housing, occupation and earnings of *every* wage-earning family in York.

Secondly, he obtained his information *directly* from the families by using interviewers.

Thirdly, and most important, Rowntree gave greater precision to the concept of poverty, originating the distinction between 'primary' and 'secondary' poverty. If a family had 'total earnings insufficient to obtain the minimum necessaries for the maintenance of merely physical efficiency', it was regarded as living in 'primary' poverty (Rowntree, 1902, p. 86). If its 'earnings would be sufficient for the maintenance of merely physical efficiency were it not that some portion of it then is absorbed by other expenditure, either useful or wasteful', then it was deemed as living in 'secondary' poverty (Rowntree, 1902, p. 87). The cost of minimum requirements of food and clothing etc. was ascertained, it being assumed that the food would be purchased as cheaply as possible and selected with a careful consideration for nutritive values. This was called the poverty-line standard. It excluded any clothing not deemed essential, and did not allow for 'expenditure needful for the development of the mental, moral and social sides of human nature' (Rowntree, 1902, p. 87). Rowntree purposely made his poverty-line standards precise and very stringent, so that they might be generally acceptable as a minimum.

The method of defining 'secondary' poverty was more debatable. The number of households in which poverty was evidenced by obvious want and squalor, by the appearance of the children and from talks with the neighbours was noted; and from this total the number deemed to be living in primary poverty was subtracted. Those remaining were regarded as being in 'secondary' poverty. This calculation contained a crucial subjective element, but some distinction between the two types of poverty was undoubtedly valuable.

More than a decade elapsed before the next important survey was begun. In 1912, Bowley made a study of working-class conditions in Reading, the first of the Five-Towns surveys which also covered Northampton, Stanley, Warrington and Bolton and was published as *Livelihood and Poverty* (Bowley and Burnett-Hurst, 1915). Bowley's great methodological contribution was his use of sampling, which came to act as a decisive stimulus to social surveys. Nearly all the later poverty surveys followed this example. Both in this early survey and its follow-up study ten years later—*Has Poverty Diminished?* (Bowley and Hogg, 1925)—Bowley took care with the selection of the sample and the possible introduction of bias through refusals and non-contacts. Bowley confined himself to 'primary' poverty but used a more realistic standard, based on actual spending habits, than Rowntree. He also took into account, as his predecessors had not, the varying food needs of children of different ages.

In the early thirties survey activity increased. Ford's investigation in Southampton, begun in 1928 and published under the title *Work and Wealth in a Modern Port* (Ford, 1934) largely followed the methods of Bowley, keeping the two types of poverty separate and indeed introducing a third type—'potential' poverty. This denied the usual assumption that all family income was pooled, and was based on the income of the head of the household.

The year 1928 also saw the beginning of the monumental *New Survey of London Life and Labour*, published in a series of volumes (Smith, 1930–35). This was planned as a sequel to Booth's survey of forty years earlier and one part of it—the street survey—was aimed to provide a direct comparison with Booth's results. The other part was an enquiry among a sample of one in fifty of all persons living in private houses or as families.

In 1934 a survey of Merseyside was published, with D. Caradog Jones as its editor, under the title *The Social Survey of Merseyside* (Jones, 1934). An interesting feature was the special study of sub-normal groups. A social survey of Sheffield, published as a series of pamphlets by the Sheffield Social Survey Committee (1931–33), set out to give a historical and contemporary picture of social life in Sheffield. Different pamphlets dealt with subjects such as milk supply, housing, licensing, unemployment, adult education, juvenile employment and welfare, transport, and the standard of living.

Of the many other investigations of working-class poverty only three need be referred to, two of them initiated by Rowntree. In 1935 he directed a second survey of York, which was published as *Poverty and Progress* (Rowntree, 1941). In this he abandoned his previous poverty standard as being too stringent and unrealistic, and replaced it by his well-known 'Human Needs Standard', developed in 1918 and brought up to date in 1937 (Rowntree, 1937). He did not repeat his attempt to measure 'secondary' poverty. The survey report contained an illuminating analysis of the causes of poverty and the periods of life at which it was most acute, and also had sections on housing, health, education and leisure-time activities. In an interesting supplementary chapter Rowntree attempted to measure the accuracy of sampling; all the survey schedules were arranged in street order and the results of different sizes of samples—1 in 10, 1 in 20, 1 in 30, 1 in 40 and 1 in 50—were compared. Practical sampling difficulties arising from non-response were of course by-passed in this analysis.

In 1950 Rowntree, this time in collaboration with G. R. Lavers, conducted yet another follow-up survey of York, *Poverty and the Welfare State* (Rowntree and Lavers, 1951a). The book received a good deal of public attention, both because it was the first post-war survey wholly concerned with working-class poverty, and also because its findings suggested that the magnitude of the problem, which had been so startling in 1900 and even in 1935, had been reduced almost to vanishing point.

One or two comments on the methodology of this survey should be made. First, there is the question of how representative York was of urban Britain. Rowntree and Lavers affirmed their belief in the views expressed in *Poverty and Progress*:

> On the whole, we may safely assume that from the standpoint of the earnings of the workers, York holds a position not far from the median, among the towns of Great Britain. If on the one hand there is no important industry employing a large number of highly skilled and highly paid workers, on the other hand there are no large industries (though unfortunately there are isolated small businesses) where wages are exceptionally low. (Rowntree and Lavers, 1951a, p. 6).

The crucial part of this statement is the last; it implies that there is a small spread around the average earnings, with few very high and few very low earnings. In this case, one would expect less poverty here than in towns where there are substantial numbers of low-wage workers. This does not affect the validity of the comparison of the results for the three York surveys, but cautions against the tendency, which was evident in public discussion of the last survey, to regard the problem of poverty as having disappeared.

Secondly, it is fair to point out that the poverty line, as adapted for this survey, is open to some criticism.[1] The determination of the

---

[1] We cannot discuss here the concept of the poverty line *per se*, but must refer to the difficulty of relating this line to *actual* living conditions. Many commodities not allowed for in the classical poverty line calculations are in effect felt, by consumers, to be as necessary as food and rent. A discussion of the problem is given by Townsend (1954, 1962a).

non-food amounts was arbitrary and there has been some suggestion that the line was unduly low and the amount of poverty consequently understated (see, for instance, *Poverty: Ten Years after Beveridge* by Political and Economic Planning, 1952).

As a final comment, it is regrettable that the authors did not avail themselves of the improvements in survey methods, and particularly in sampling techniques, which had taken place since the previous York survey.

More recent work has cast doubts on the results of the Third York Survey. Abel-Smith and Townsend (1965) in *The Poor and the Poorest* show that affluence was by no means universal in mid-twentieth-century Britain. This study led to two new surveys into aspects of poverty. One was *Circumstances of Families* published by the U.K. Ministry of Social Security (1967), which sought to establish whether families with children were receiving an adequate subsistence income, taking the minimum requirements under the National Assistance Acts as a basis for comparison. The other is a large-scale national survey conducted by Abel-Smith and Townsend; at the time of writing only one part of the survey's findings, that concerned with large families, has been published (Land, 1969).

1.4. Regional planning surveys

Because of their historical place in the development of surveys, it is worth devoting a brief section to surveys in the field of town planning and reconstruction, which were important by the middle of the thirties. Housing development had formerly been carried out in an unplanned and chaotic manner, resulting in ugly and sprawling cities. This was the background and stimulus to surveys such as that initiated in Birmingham in 1935 by the Bournville Village Trust (1941) and published under the title *When We Build Again*. The aim of the survey was to study the housing situation in and around Birmingham; the location of work and the workers' journey to it; the number of open spaces and parks, and other amenities of the city and its surroundings.

Surveys prior to 1939 in this field had had a different emphasis. That of *Becontree and Dagenham* carried out by Young in 1931–33 was inspired by the hope that 'people, after studying the facts, will be better able to consider what should be done in the development of an estate such as Becontree, and that a report such as this should help in the formulation of policies to deal with the housing of working-class people in general' (Young, 1934, p. 18). The central interest of *Watling—A Survey of Social Life on a New Housing Estate* (Durant, 1939), conducted by Ruth Glass (then Ruth Durant) in 1932, was again different. Her enquiry was focused on two questions.

Had the new estate of Watling grown into a community, in the sense of 'a territorial group of people with a common mode of living, striving for common objectives'? And, secondly, what part was the community centre playing in local life?

Social surveys in town planning did not, however, come into their own until after the Second World War, when the need for widespread planned reconstruction gave them crucial importance. One of the most interesting of these was *Report on Luton* by Grundy and Titmuss (1945), a report on the town's population and housing, and on the social aspects of its public services.

Also interesting was *Middlesbrough: Survey and Plan* (Lock and others, 1947), which gave special weight to·sociological factors. The feature of greatest methodological interest here was the use of a more precise concept of neighbourhoods. These were defined, demarcated and graded in terms of a multiple index of living conditions, based on six factors: net population density, number of houses per acre, percentage of houses with a rateable value less than £11, percentage of non-owner occupiers, percentage of chief wage-earners with incomes of less than £5 per week, and number of retail shops per 1,000 people. A book on *The Social Background of a Plan* relating to this survey was published by Ruth Glass (1948). The Midlands have also been the scene of a useful group of surveys completed in the forties: the planning survey of Herefordshire, *English County* (West Midland Group on Post-War Reconstruction and Planning, 1946), the survey of Birmingham and the Black Country entitled *Conurbation* (West Midland Group on Post-War Reconstruction and Planning, 1948) and that of Wolverhampton entitled *Midland City* (Brennan, 1948).

More recently there have been an increasing number of surveys for planning purposes, and a greater willingness on the part of planning authorities to let themselves be influenced by survey results. Part of the growing importance of survey work in town planning is due to the 1966 Town and Country Planning Act, which lays down that all local authorities have a statutory duty to carry out surveys at regular intervals. The Development Corporations have also commissioned surveys. For example, the Economist Intelligence Unit has been doing a sample survey for Harlow every two years, and the Opinion Research Centre has been doing surveys among people living in Milton Keynes.

The Centre for Urban Studies (1964) at University College has developed a bibliography entitled *Land Use Planning and the Social Sciences* which refers to the various surveys. The Centre has also carried out surveys itself, evaluating the success of town planning schemes and their effects on the lives of the inhabitants of the areas concerned. Examples of these are the sample surveys of the population of Lansbury and of the London County Council housing estates in South-West Hertfordshire, published in *London: Aspects of Change* (Glass and others, 1964).

Survey work in regional planning is frequently directed less towards social than economic questions, such as industrial linkages, involving questionnaires to firms. Some surveys cover both fields, for example *Central Lancashire New Town Proposal: Impact on Northeast Lancashire* carried out by a firm of economic consultants for the U.K. Ministry of Housing and Local Government (1968). Others impinge on the field of population studies, such as the survey of industrial mobility and population migration in the North East by House and Knight (1965).

Finally, mention should be made of the U.K. Royal Commission on Local Government in England (1969) which sponsored a national sample survey on people's attitudes to their local community. Included in this survey were some interesting questions on what people knew about local government.

1.5. The Government Social Survey—now part of the Office of Population Censuses and Surveys

Probably more surveys are done for and by the government than in any other sphere. This has not always been so, and is due in large measure to the work of the Government Social Survey. Founded in 1941, the Government Social Survey has probably become the leading organization of its type, and has exerted an unquestionable influence in raising the standard of survey methods and in persuading policy-makers in government to pay attention to survey results.

The Survey has been through a variety of organizational phases. It started as, and for long remained, part of the Central Office of Information, and was then an independent department under the Treasury from 1967 to 1970, when it was merged with the General Register Office for England and Wales into a single Office of Population Censuses and Surveys. The idea behind this latest move is that surveys and censuses concerned with individuals, families and households should be planned and conducted on an integrated basis, and in association with the Central Statistical Office, which will share responsibility for planning the policy of the Office. Survey work for the government will (and should) continue to grow, and will, as in the past, rest in large measure on the highly experienced staff of the Government Social Survey, now within the new Office. One imagines that the present tradition will continue, whereby the Survey will, subject to resources, undertake enquiries requested by government departments and other official bodies, such as Royal Commissions, but the precise procedures for settling plans and priorities in the new Office are only now being worked out.

The range of subject matter covered by the Survey is extremely wide. The Central Statistical Office, the Board of Trade, the General Register Office, the Department of Health and Social Security and the Ministry of Housing and Local Government have been some of the Survey's main clients, but virtually every Government department has used it. In addition, practically every Royal Commission and official committee of recent years has conducted social enquiries, usually through the Survey. Detailed lists are given by Gray and Corlett (1950) and by Moss (1953), under whose direction over many years the Survey was built up. The Survey also maintains a regular *List of Published Reports and Papers*, and items from the 1969 list include: for the Department of Education and Science a survey of attitudes of undergraduates towards teaching; for the Ministry of Housing and Local Government a housing survey in England and Wales; for that Ministry and the Department of Health and Social Security a survey of social welfare for the elderly; for the Department of Employment and Productivity a survey of workers' employment, and one on labour mobility; for the Road Research Laboratory a survey on drivers' understanding of road traffic signs; for the Schools Council a study among young school-leavers; and so forth. Many dozens of other, equally varied, examples could be quoted, many of them—such as the studies on predicting the success of Borstal training by Mannheim and Wilkins (1955)—of great methodological interest. There is also an impressive list of technical papers by the Survey's staff.

It is worth mentioning separately four *series* of enquiries. One was the Survey of Sickness (for the General Register Office) which for six years provided useful data on the nation's health until, in 1952, it became a casualty of a government economy campaign. Another series still continuing is that on family expenditure. This has included reports on expenditure on gambling, laundry, holidays, household textiles, house repairs and domestic service, meals in restaurants, hairdressing and cosmetics; and a number of general reports. The importance of these enquiries lies in the use of their results for the estimates of national income and expenditure, and for the retail price index. They are referred to again below. A third continuing enquiry is the National Food Survey carried out for the Ministry of Agriculture, Fisheries and Food. This provides valuable information on the adequacy of the diet available to families of different size and composition, in different parts of the country and in various social groups (see U.K. National Food Survey Committee, 1968). In addition, preparatory work has been going on for a new system of multi-purpose household surveys on a continuous basis. These will cover a range of social and economic data about households and provide a continuous and flexible survey instrument for the government. They began in the last part of 1970.

Enough has been said to show the importance of the Government Social Survey's work in undertaking *ad hoc* and continuous surveys for official purposes. It is safe to say, even though such statements are hard to substantiate, that the Survey has had a great effect in improving the level of information and understanding that goes into policy deliberations in government, both in the administrative departments and in official committees. The Survey has also come to participate increasingly in social and economic research, in association with universities and research institutes.

References to the Survey's work, and to other surveys done for the government, will be found throughout this chapter and later parts of the book, including references to its more important technical publications, for example the paper on its sampling methods by Gray and Corlett (1950).

1.6. Market, audience and opinion research

Market research[1]

Market research in its widest sense has been a feature of commerce for decades. Whether through its executives, salesmen or professional advisers, every firm tries to study its market and its marketing methods. But since the 1930's the approach has become much more scientific. The market research survey, using substantially the methods described in this book, has in turn given much of the stimulus to their development.

Market research in its modern form is enjoying a great vogue in Great Britain, and, no doubt, with modern mass-production of consumer goods and the increasing competition between brands, its importance will grow rather than decrease. Already many firms have market research departments, and some employ their own field staff. But this latter scale of operation is mostly confined to the largest firms and most consumer surveys are still done by specialist research agencies. There are many of these, and professional standards are generally high.

Such agencies are usually engaged simultaneously on surveys commissioned by a number of clients, covering different populations,

[1] This brief sketch should be supplemented by reading the (introductory) chapter by Downham, Shankleman and Treasure in *Readings in Market Research* edited by Edwards (1956). In addition, the publications of the Market Research Society, and above all its Journal, should be referred to for further details. The Society also issues a list of organizations providing market research services in Great Britain.

B

products and types of question. Their association with clients is of varying degrees of closeness and is at its most useful when the agency is able to go beyond merely submitting survey reports, and can advise the management, for instance, on the value of particular types of research, on the meaning of the research results, and on their implications for the firm's marketing and distribution policy. Market research surveys proper find their most obvious role in the study of the public's buying habits, in assessing the effects of different forms of promotion, in brand research, and so forth. In all this they fill important gaps in the manufacturer's knowledge, supplementing information gleaned from such sources as sales statistics and the reports of sales representatives.

The manufacturer naturally knows his total sales, and usually how this is split up between wholesalers and retailers. But he may know little about the purchases and views of individual retailers, let alone the eventual consumers. And without market research he will know nothing about retailers' stocks. Hence the importance of the so-called 'retail audit technique', by which details of stock levels, of counter sales and so on are obtained at regular intervals from a panel of retailers.[1] The technique is discussed by Treasure (1953) and by Melhuish (1954).

Manufacturers often wish to know more about what *types* of people are buying or not buying their product, what they think of its quality, its presentation, its price; and how their attitudes are changing. Such knowledge is invaluable for guiding advertising policy, and many of the research organizations are in fact linked to advertising agencies.

Special problems arise with new products. A manufacturer may wish to test out a proposed product in various forms, colours, flavours and so on, and can avail himself of techniques of experimental design to assess the likely popularity of various alternatives. When the final choice is reduced to a few possibilities, the market researcher often tests their comparative sales appeal by placing them on the market, perhaps at varying prices, in different test areas.

Where the problem is to find the best form of an advertisement, market research methods can be used to assess the relative effectiveness of several alternatives. Equally important is the question of *where* advertising space is to be bought, for, clearly, the more people who read a particular publication, and the better-off they are, the more valuable is the advertising space. Readership surveys are used for this purpose, the best known being those conducted by the Joint Industry Committee for National Readership Surveys

[1] The use of panels—which are important in market research—is discussed in Section 6.5 below.

(JICNARS).[1] There is also substantial activity in relation to television viewing, and a parallel body, the Joint Industry Committee for Television Advertising Research (JICTAR), which conducts surveys to measure television audiences (see p. 248).

A certain amount of secretiveness regarding their work is to be expected of market research bodies, since theirs is a highly competitive business. Even so, there are now many conferences, meetings and journals to which market research practitioners contribute papers, and it is a fair bet that market researchers contribute as much as any other group to developments in survey methods. The Journal of the Market Research Society illustrates this.

BBC Audience Research

In 1936 the British Broadcasting Corporation set up a Listener Research Department to collect information about the listening habits and tastes of the British public, an attempt to establish some kind of substitute in the world of radio for the box-office of the theatre. When television came in, the Department changed its name to Audience Research.

To ascertain the amount of listening and viewing, a national quota sample (see Chapter 6) of 2,250 men and women is asked each day which of the programmes broadcast the previous day they have listened to (or viewed); *opinions* on these programmes are not sought. Interviewers use the 'aided-recall' method, i.e. they remind respondents of the programmes in question. This enables the BBC to estimate what percentage of the population (aged five and over) listens to (or views) their various programmes of the previous day's broadcasts. Apart from the usefulness to the producers of knowing trends in audience size, these surveys produce much information of interest about the factors affecting listening numbers: time of broadcast, season, competing broadcasts, nature of broadcast preceding and following it, regularity of broadcast, content, general quality, publicity, and so on.

Even ignoring the fundamental difficulty of radio research, that of distinguishing between 'listening to' a programme and merely 'hearing' it as a sort of background noise,[2] sheer size of audience is not the best, certainly not the only, criterion of a programme's quality. The BBC accordingly has volunteer panels of some 6,000 listeners and viewers whose opinions on programmes are regularly sought and analysed.

[1] The Market Research Society (1954a) has published an account of the development, application and problems of readership surveys.
[2] Audience Research does not regard a person as having 'listened' to a programme if he heard less than half of it (news bulletins apart). 'Background listening' is accepted unless the respondent has not even a vague memory of the programme.

One can never of course be confident that volunteer panels are representative of the particular population one is interested in, and the only safeguards—both used by the BBC—are to ensure that different age, sex and social class groups are correctly represented and that checks of representativeness, for example comparing results with those from *ad hoc* surveys, are made whenever possible. A description of the Department's work is given in *BBC Audience Research in the United Kingdom* (British Broadcasting Corporation, 1966), a booklet available on request from the Audience Research Department of the BBC.

Public opinion polls

Opinion questions figure in the Government Social Survey's work, in market research, in audience research, indeed in surveys of practically every kind; but in this section we will concentrate on some survey bodies that conduct regular surveys of public opinion.

One of these bodies is Social Surveys (Gallup Poll) Ltd, which was founded in 1936 as the British Institute of Public Opinion and is one of the international chain of Gallup Institutes—see Durant (1954) for a discussion of its methods. Its monthly survey findings on questions of the day and its forecasts of general and by-election results are regularly published in the *Daily Telegraph*.

Until 1959 the Gallup Poll was the only regular public opinion survey in Britain, but there are now also three other monthly polls and a quarterly one: National Opinion Polls Ltd (NOP) runs a monthly survey and publishes the results in the *Daily Mail*; Opinion Research Centre conducts a monthly survey and reports findings in the *Sunday Times* and a number of evening newspapers; Louis Harris (Research) Ltd has recently established a monthly survey, which is reported in the *Daily Express*; and Marplan Ltd publishes its results quarterly in *The Times*. The existence of several polls provides the stimulus of competition, and thus encourages developments in opinion poll methodology. One aspect in which the polls differ noticeably is their sample designs: quota sampling is used in two of the polls—those of Gallup Poll and the Opinion Research Centre—while random sampling is used in the others;[1] the sample sizes and the numbers of areas in which survey interviews are conducted also differ considerably.

Election forecasts, although the most publicized of polling activities, are in a sense the least valuable; there is, after all, little point in knowing approximately today what will be known accurately tomorrow—apart from the fact that forecasts of any kind appeal to our sporting instincts and that it is of some value to the parties to

---

[1] See Section 6.4 for a discussion of the differences between these methods.

know the *trends* in opinion. To the pollster, the value of election forecasts is that they offer one of the few opportunities of demonstrating that their methods are sound. No wonder, then, that a failure like that of the 1948 U.S. election forecasts (see Mosteller and others, 1949), or that of the 1970 British general election forecasts, creates such concern.

What happened in 1948 was that the figures from the polls showed such close running as not to justify a prediction one way or another. But past prediction successes and the general mood of the day beguiled the pollsters into making an over-confident, and undoubtedly unwarranted, prediction. Unfortunately, this failure then made them over-cautious in forecasting the 1952 election when, looked at after the event, their poll results showed convincing evidence of the impending Eisenhower victory. But success in predicting elections is in many ways an unfair criterion of the value of survey methods generally, for this sort of forecasting faces special problems, notably the uncertainty of the voting turnout and of what the 'undecided voter' will do. British general elections have in the past been somewhat easier to predict than American because a larger proportion of the electorate have turned out to vote, because there have been fewer undecided voters and because the Register of Electors provides a complete list of persons entitled to vote whereas no comparable list exists in the United States; until 1970 the general election prediction record of British polls had been good.

In the 1970 general election, all the polls — with the exception of the Opinion Research Centre's — pointed to a resounding Labour victory, whereas in the event a Conservative government was returned. There may of course have been a strong swing in the days between the last poll and the election, but most commentators rule this out as the main explanation. It may also be that the size of the predicted Labour majority encouraged apathy amongst Labour voters or even led some marginal voters to move to the Conservatives (a tendency opposite to the more conventional 'bandwaggon theory', and more plausible with the British 'back the loser' psychology). But on the face of it, a more likely explanation of the failure of most of the polls is that they did not allow for 'determination to vote', that is to say turnout; and it is no excuse to say that the figures are meant only to reflect current opinion, not to predict voting, since their inevitable use is for the latter. In addition, in what was perhaps an unusually subtle election situation, the nature of the questions and the treatment of the 'Don't knows' were probably too superficial. These are old problems and it is hard to avoid the conclusion that the polls could and should have used more sophisticated techniques. The 1970 experience has shaken confidence in opinion polls and perhaps in surveys generally. It is important that it should be subjected to the kind of high-level investigation which followed the 1948 failure in the United States (see Mosteller and others, 1949). The aim of everyday opinion surveys is modest and unobjectionable. All political policies directly or indirectly affect the public, who in turn have views on them. Whether these views are well- or ill-informed, strong or mild, emotional or rational, only good can come from the law-maker and the administrator knowing what they are, and opinion surveys endeavour to inform them. An article by Taylor (1970) discusses the political effects of public opinion polls.

1.7. Some other surveys

We must now try to illustrate the miscellaneous surveys, past and present, which do not fit into any of the classifications of the previous five sections. They range from major Government-commissioned national enquiries to small groups of cases studied by the individual sociologist, anthropologist or psychologist. They cover all types of subject matter and use in varying form all the techniques available to the surveyor.

It is difficult to do justice to such a range, and all we can do is to mention a few selected surveys on each of a few selected subjects. The choice is arbitrary, as are the dividing lines between topics.

(a) *Population*. Pride of place in this field must go to the biggest survey of all, the Population Census, which has normally been carried out every ten years, except that the sample census in 1966 has recently made it into a five-yearly event. The Census is conducted on an enumerator basis (not, as in some countries, postal), and the Census volumes describe the methods used (see also Benjamin, 1970).

A Family Census was conducted for the Royal Commission on Population in 1946, and published under the title *The Trend and Pattern of Fertility in Great Britain* (Glass and Grebenik, 1954). Its purpose was to fill the main gaps in our knowledge of fertility and family-building habits, and to this end a sample of over a million married women was questioned. The report sets a high standard in its detailed discussion of all aspects of the survey's methods, including the sampling. The same Royal Commission sponsored an enquiry on family limitation (Lewis-Faning, 1949), in which information on habits of birth control and attitudes to it was obtained from a sample of married women patients in the general wards of hospitals; the interviewing was done by doctors.

Since then the Population Investigation Committee has carried out two major surveys into patterns of fertility. The results of the first, the Marriage Survey in 1959 and 1960, were published in articles

by Rowntree and Pierce (1961) and Pierce and Rowntree (1961); the
second, a national sample survey of 2,300 marriages which enquired
into fertility and birth-control practice in Great Britain, has not yet
been published.

In 1967 the Government Social Survey carried out on behalf of
the Registrar-General the Family Intentions Survey, a major survey
of family-size expectations of married women. This work is important from the point of view of improving population forecasting.
Among smaller-scale studies of fertility one can mention Cartwright's
(1970) *Parents and the Family Planning Services*. A new official
survey of family-planning practices is to be carried out by the
Government Social Survey.

Migration, another aspect of population change, has also been
subjected to survey work, including the Government Social Survey's
enquiries into labour mobility in the late 1940's and in the 1960's.
On international migration, there is the large-scale international
passenger transport survey, carried out for the Board of Trade,
which members of the public encounter when they are interviewed
in airport lounges and the like (U.K. Board of Trade, 1969).

(b) *Housing.* Inadequate housing perhaps causes more widespread
distress than any other social problem, and there is a substantial
literature on the subject, some of it involving surveys. The Rowntree
Trust sponsored a number of surveys in the late fifties, including
Donnison and others' (1961) *Housing since the Rent Act* and Cullingworth's (1965) *English Housing Trends*. The exposure of various
malpractices by slum landlords, which came to be known as Rach-
manism in the early sixties, resulted in the setting up of the Milner
Holland Committee on London's housing (U.K. Committee on
Housing in Greater London, 1965). Several surveys were commissioned by the Committee, covering landlords, a very difficult group to
survey from the point of view of both sampling and response, and
tenants. One of these surveys was carried out by Glass and Westergaard (1965) of the Centre for Urban Studies, and is summarized in a
study entitled *London's Housing Needs*.

More recently the Centre has undertaken a large survey for the
London Borough of Camden, published as the *Report on the Housing
Rents Study by the Centre for Urban Studies* (London Borough of
Camden, 1969). This consisted of a sample survey in the private
sector of three thousand households, and a census of all council
tenants' households, covering between thirteen and fourteen thousand
households. A smaller-scale study of this kind was done by the
Greater London Council as a basis for deciding on its rent policy.
A national study excluding London was undertaken by the U.K.

National Board for Prices and Incomes (1968) to help them to decide whether rent increases could be approved. This study illustrates the difficulties differential response rates can cause.

Survey methods have been used to discover the housing needs of special groups such as old people (Hole and Allen, 1962, 1964) and the disabled (Sainsbury, 1970); Sainsbury carried out intensive interviews with the disabled, investigating their problems with respect to finance and employment as well as housing. Surveys have also been used to assess the quality of new housing such as high-rise flats. An example of a study of this kind is the Centre for Urban Studies' survey of the occupants of tall flats in Pimlico (Glass and others, 1964).

(c) *Community studies*. Sociologists and social anthropologists have carried out many general community studies of urban and rural life. Readers interested in early work in this area may like to refer to the work of Brennan, who carried out a sociological survey of southwest Wales in the early fifties (Brennan and others, 1954) and prior to this did a study of a town in the Midlands (Brennan, 1948) based on surveys. Another early study using survey methods is Kuper and others' (1953) *Living in Towns*, which contains a series of studies of life in urban communities in the Midlands. Studies of rural life do not generally use formal survey methods to the same extent as those covering large population units like cities. A complete census of an area is often taken, and in collecting the information there is usually more scope for the skill and insight of the individual investigator than for interviewers and questionnaires. Nevertheless some such studies have made use of social surveys, such as Stewart's (1948) *The Village Surveyed* and Rees' (1951) *Life in a Welsh Countryside*.

The best source for a description of community studies undertaken since that time is Frankenberg's (1966) *Communities in Britain*, which summarizes the findings from a number of studies. Of the studies of urban communities, Stacey's (1960) *Tradition and Change: a Study of Banbury* should be mentioned. More than ten years later the author returned to Banbury to record the changes that had taken place since the original study. Among other community studies are the surveys carried out on urban housing estates, such as Willmott's (1963) study of Dagenham, and the work of Spencer (1964) in Bristol.

(d) *Family life*. This is an area which sometimes presents difficulty for the conventional survey approach. Aspects of intimate social relations, decisions about family size, the way children are brought up, and other such matters are perhaps more likely to be resisted than many other survey subjects. These are also areas in which it is difficult to distinguish between objective appraisal and subjective interpretation in replies to a questionnaire. Nevertheless, since the mid-fifties there have been some interesting surveys of aspects of family life in Britain.

A recent survey of child upbringing, based on a sample of seven hundred one-year-olds in Nottingham, is that of Newson and Newson (1963, 1965). It collected information about infant feeding, toilet training, and discipline, and studied the role fathers play in caring for their children. The study demonstrated the value of using interviewers rather than health visitors for this kind of purpose. The authors subsequently produced a further book entitled *Four Years Old in an Urban Community* (Newson and Newson, 1968) which is based on a follow-up of the same sample. They intend to study these children for some years, in order to provide information on such questions as the relationship between early upbringing and later schooling.

The Institute of Community Studies in Bethnal Green has carried out some more general studies of family life, such as Townsend's (1957) *The Family Life of Old People* and two studies of family relationships in the contrasting areas of Bethnal Green (Young and Willmott, 1957) and Woodford (Willmott and Young, 1960). A more recent study was Rosser and Harris's (1965) *The Family and Social Change*, which amongst other things looked at the incidence of close contacts with kin in a sample of families in Swansea. Another study in Swansea was Bell's (1968) *Middle Class Families*, which combined a survey with a more anthropological approach, involving both participant observation in the community and a detailed investigation of the number of known kin in a small number of families. The social networks of families were investigated in a rather different way by Bott (1957), whose study of roles within the family, and the way these were associated with relationships with kin, is a good example of a survey with a small number of cases treated in great depth. Gavron (1966) took a larger sample of mothers of young children in order to investigate the problems women face while housebound with very young children. Marsden's (1969) survey *Mothers Alone* studies the serious difficulties faced by mothers who lack the support of a husband.

(e) *Sexual behaviour*. There have been no surveys of sexual behaviour in Britain comparable to the Kinsey Reports in the United States, but two studies, both by Schofield, are worth mentioning. One dealt with *The Sexual Behaviour of Young People* (Schofield, 1965a) and gives the findings from interviews with a large random sample of teenagers.[1] The other was his study of homosexuality (Schofield,

---

[1] This study provides an amusing example of an unclassifiable response to a survey question. When asked 'Are you a virgin?', one girl replied 'Not yet'.

1965b), with an interesting research design covering samples of homosexuals in prisons, homosexual patients undergoing hospital treatment, and other homosexuals, with control groups for the last two groups.

Some of the fertility surveys mentioned in (a) above included questions on contraceptive techniques and attitudes to birth control.

(f) *Family expenditure.* Family expenditure is one of the most obvious fields for the use of traditional survey methods. At the official level these studies originate primarily from the need to revise the weighting basis of retail price indices. Such was the case with the U.K. Ministry of Labour and National Service's (1940–41) survey of the *Weekly Expenditure of Working-Class Households in the United Kingdom in 1937–38* and the enquiry into household expenditure conducted in 1953–54 by the same Ministry (1957) in collaboration with the Central Statistical Office. This latter enquiry combined two methods of data collection, interviewing and record-keeping, questions relating to the household as a whole being dealt with by the interviewer, while records of personal expenditure were completed by the individuals.

The Household Expenditure Survey was followed by the Family Expenditure Survey (U.K. Ministry of Labour, 1961–1967; U.K. Department of Employment and Productivity, 1969, 1970) which has been in continuous operation since 1957. A paper by Kemsley and Nicholson (1960) describes some of the experimental work connected with the two surveys. The survey now has an annual sample of over 10,000 addresses with a rotating sample design. A detailed account of the sampling, fieldwork and coding procedures currently used is given by Kemsley (1969).

In the Family Expenditure Survey individuals are asked to keep a record of expenditure over a particular fortnight. In relation to purchases of durable goods, such as cars and refrigerators, this is a short period, so that there is a relatively high degree of variability in the estimates of expenditure on such goods. In their survey concentrating on purchases of consumer durables, Audits of Great Britain Ltd approach a large number of households and make up to four visits to each at intervals of three months to note products acquired since the last visit.

Many other institutes and researchers have worked on the subject of family expenditure. A pre-1939 investigation of the cost of living of middle-class families was carried out by Massey (1942). This was based on a sample of some 3,000 civil servants, government officials and teachers, and was arranged to be broadly comparable with the official 1937–38 enquiry. The Oxford University Institute of Statistics carried out a series of surveys on the expenditure and nutrition of small samples of households. A summary of these surveys is given by Schulz (1952). Subsequently Lydall (1955), at the same Institute, conducted a number of interview surveys on the difficult subject of savings; his findings threw a good deal of new light on income distribution, asset structure and so forth. A survey of personal savings conducted in 1955 by the Central Statistical Office with the help of the Government Social Survey and in consultation with the Institute is described by Erritt and Nicholson (1958).

The Department of Applied Economics at Cambridge used household budget surveys as part of its project on the social accounts of Cambridgeshire. This work has been described by Utting and Cole (1953, 1954).

(g) *Nutrition.* A noteworthy nutrition survey was Orr's (1936) *Food, Health and Income.* Unlike most previous and later investigators, Orr concerned himself with optimum, not minimum, dietary requirements. He asked what proportion of the population had a diet adequate for perfect health. To this end he divided the population into six income groups and studied family budget and diet records from twelve regional surveys. Other data on pre-war nutrition are given in a report by the Rowett Research Institute (1955).

In 1941 the Oxford University Institute of Statistics began a series of surveys designed to assess the cost of a 'human needs' diet, which would supply a family of five persons—an unskilled male worker, wife and three children under 14 years of age—with the minimum adequate nutrition. This work followed closely the lines of enquiry adopted with respect to the cost of food by Rowntree (1937) in *The Human Needs of Labour.* Food prices were collected from shops and stores, mainly at Oxford but also in London and Reading. An article by Schulz (1949) summarizes the results up to 1949, and reports on later surveys have been published in the Institute's Bulletin.

The major official survey is the National Food Survey (U.K. National Food Survey Committee, 1968) mentioned on page 14. This was introduced during the Second World War, but gradually its emphasis has shifted from nutritional to economic considerations. A distinctive feature is that housewives are asked to record for one week both the cost and the quantities of the food which enters their households. The Ministry of Agriculture, Fisheries and Food uses this dual information in forecasting the demand for agricultural products.

The National Food Survey seeks the quantity of food acquired by the household, rather than the amount eaten by each individual. The U.K. Ministry of Health's (1968) *Pilot Survey of the Nutrition of*

Young Children in 1963 was carried out to gain experience of the problems of recording individual diets. This is being followed by extensive surveys of the nutrition of children under school age and of expectant mothers.

(h) *Health*. In the past the major concern in the statistical study of health was with mortality, but nowadays the study of morbidity is becoming increasingly important. A number of countries have at one time or another studied morbidity through national health surveys, the most notable of these being the continuing U.S. National Health Survey which, besides providing data on many aspects of the health status of the American people, has been the stimulus for a good deal of methodological research; a description of the Survey's programme is given by the U.S. National Center for Health Statistics (1963). In Britain the Government Social Survey's monthly Survey of Sickness, which began in the Second World War, was terminated in 1952; a description and appraisal of the Survey is given by Logan and Brooke (1957).

Another source of morbidity statistics is provided by general practitioners' clinical records, and many practitioners have analysed their records to chart the morbidity experience of their practice populations and the resulting demands for medical care. In 1955–56 a study was carried out jointly by the College of General Practitioners and the General Register Office in which 171 doctors in 106 practices collaborated in keeping medical information about their patients on specially designed survey record cards for a period of a year; the survey is reported in three volumes (Logan and Cushion, 1958; Logan, 1960; Research Committee of the Council of the College of General Practitioners, 1962). A pre-Second World War study involving the collaboration of 6,000 general practitioners was that of Hill (1951); this was mainly concerned with workloads and pay, and the practitioners were asked to keep records of surgery attendances and home visits for a period of one month. More recently, Shepherd and others (1966) have carried out a survey of psychiatric illness in general practice with the collaboration of the doctors in forty-six general practices in London, who kept medical records for a year on a one-in-eight sample of their adult practice populations.

In the field of mental health, Morris (1969) has recently published a study of institutions for the mentally retarded and the patients in them. Another study of the mentally ill is Walker and McCabe's survey of 1,200 cases made the subject of orders under Part V of the Mental Health Act 1959, which authorizes either guardianship or detentions in hospital. So far only the preliminary findings have been published (de Reuck and Porter, 1968). Rutter and Graham (1966) report on psychiatric disorders in ten- and eleven-year-old children, based on a survey in the Isle of Wight, and Kay and others (1964) describe old-age disorders, based on a survey in Newcastle-upon-Tyne.

Another type of health enquiry is the epidemiological survey, which is a study of an explanatory rather than a descriptive nature. There have been numerous surveys of this sort: we will mention just two areas of enquiry for illustrative purposes. First, perhaps the best-known studies are those investigating the relationship between smoking and cancer; references to some of these studies are given in Chapter 9. Secondly, there are the investigations of the relationship between coronary heart disease and physical activity. Examples here are the comparisons between drivers and conductors on London double-decker buses, and between Government clerks and postmen, for deaths from coronary heart disease, reported by Morris and others (1953); and the analysis of a national necropsy survey by Morris and Crawford (1958) to compare the amount of physical activity involved in a man's last job between three groups, Group A being deaths from coronary heart disease, Group B deaths.in a high coronary-artery disease group, and Group C deaths from other conditions (the basal group). Further good examples of the epidemiological approach are given by Hill (1962), who also describes some clinical and field trials. Methods and applications of medical surveys and clinical trials are discussed by Witts (1964).

A health survey of impressive methodological achievement was originally sponsored by the Population Investigation Committee to obtain data on the social and economic aspects of childbearing, expenditure on childbirth, and the use made of maternity services. The enquiry was addressed to all women who were delivered of children in England, Wales and Scotland in a particular week in March 1946, and successful interviews were made with 90 per cent of them (Joint Committee of the Royal College of Obstetricians and Gynaecologists and the Population Investigation Committee, 1948; Douglas and Blomfield, 1958). The study has since grown into the National Survey of Health and Development and is currently sponsored by the Medical Research Council. A large number of the original babies—now adults—are still included in the investigation and records of their health, physical development, progress in school, reading, intelligence and occupational choices have been kept; information is now being collected on *their* children.

In 1947 a similar type of survey was undertaken in Newcastle-upon-Tyne, covering all the births in the city in the months of May and June. The children involved have also been followed for a number of years in order to study the diseases of childhood. The major findings are reported by Spence and others (1954) and Miller and others (1960).

In 1958 a second national survey of births—the Perinatal Mortality Survey—was carried out, again covering all the babies born in England, Wales and Scotland in a particular week in March. The survey was sponsored by the National Birthday Trust Fund and two books have been published on its results, *Perinatal Mortality* by Butler and Bonham (1963) and *Perinatal Problems* by Butler and Alberman (1968). The children are currently being followed in the National Child Development Study (1958 Cohort) and a first report on them at the age of seven has been published by Pringle, Butler and Davie (1966).

A further national survey of births—the British Births Survey—has just been conducted, covering all births in the United Kingdom in the week beginning 5 April 1970. The aim of this new enquiry, which is under the joint auspices of the National Birthday Trust and the Royal College of Obstetricians and Gynaecologists, is to examine all the factors affecting the well-being of the mother and baby in pregnancy, childbirth and the time immediately after delivery.

Finally, it is worth noting that surveys, besides being used to investigate the community's health, are also used to examine the working of the health services and the public's satisfaction with them. The British Medical Association (1953), for instance, sponsored an enquiry into general practice, one part of which was a field study of a sample of 158 general practices, the other a postal enquiry directed to the remaining 17,616 general-practitioner Principals in the National Health Service. Some 70 per cent of these co-operated. A fuller qualitative appraisal of 'good' general practices was carried out by Taylor (1954) under the sponsorship of the Nuffield Foundation. Cartwright (1964) carried out a survey of people who had been in hospital to discover their satisfaction with the care they received, and she has also carried out a survey of the public and their doctors, the results being presented in *Patients and their Doctors* (Cartwright, 1967).

(i) *Education.* Much of the early survey work on education was concerned with intelligence tests. In the forties and early fifties there were many small-scale surveys into the relationship between intelligence test performance and social background, family size and composition; and to these a paper by Burt (1950) and memoranda presented to the U.K. Royal Commission on Population (1950) serve as guides. A large-scale survey on the trend of intelligence was carried out during this period by the Population Investigation Committee and the Scottish Council for Research in Education (1949). Based on a sample of Scottish schoolchildren of a particular age group, this was designed to throw light on the question of whether national intelligence was falling. A follow-up volume by the Scottish Council for Research in Education (1953) discusses, among other things, the relationships of measured intelligence to height, weight and social background. In the last ten years there has been a great increase in research on many different aspects of education, but little of this has been concerned with intelligence tests as such. Where some evaluation of pupils' performance is required, measures of attainment and of ability have replaced them.

The wealth of interesting surveys on education makes selection particularly hard, but a few examples can be given. Some of the largest surveys have been undertaken on behalf of government committees investigating various aspects of education. The reports of three of these committees are particularly noteworthy in terms of their uses of surveys. The Crowther Report (Central Advisory Council for Education (England), 1959–1960) throws new light on the nature of early leaving in secondary education, through large surveys of National Servicemen and school leavers. The Robbins Committee (U.K. Committee on Higher Education, 1964) made very extensive use of surveys. Surveys of students in universities, technical colleges, and colleges of education, and of university teachers were undertaken, but perhaps the most interesting of the empirical studies was the sample survey of an entire age group, which presented difficult problems of sampling. The surveys for the Plowden Report on primary education (Central Advisory Council for Education (England), 1967) covered parents, teachers and children, and of these probably the most important were the National and Manchester surveys of children. Both these surveys collected material about the schools and children in the samples, and used interesting methods of analysis to predict attainment among primary school children.

In spite of the relative ease of sampling in surveys concerned with education, and the consequent wealth of examples, there have been few longitudinal studies. The value of such studies is, however, amply demonstrated by the National Survey of Health and Development referred to above (p. 27). This survey, directed by Douglas, is now investigating such matters as the occupational choices and marriage problems of part of the original sample of births in 1946, but since its inception it has produced several books and papers on education (Douglas, 1964, and Douglas, Ross and Simpson, 1968). In due course it will be interesting to compare the findings obtained in the second survey of this type—the National Child Development Study (1958 Cohort), see p. 28—with those of Douglas.

There have been many smaller-scale studies of educational

questions, some of which have been able to collect detailed and valuable information from the respondents concerned. Jackson and Marsden's (1962) study of eighty-eight members of the working class who had successfully overcome the barriers to high achievement that working-class children face is an example of this type of survey. It is also an example of a survey in which much of the information was collected retrospectively. Another small-scale study worth mentioning is Hargreaves' (1967) study of the effects of the organisation and structure of a secondary-modern school on the attitudes, values, behaviour and friendship patterns of its pupils. In this study within a single institution survey methods were combined with participant observation and sociometric techniques.

Finally, we should mention some regular surveys. The first of these is the U.K. Department of Education and Science's (1969) annual School Leavers' Survey, in which information is obtained from head teachers on the qualifications and destinations of a 10 per cent sample of all school leavers. Other examples are the national surveys of attainment carried out by the National Foundation for Educational Research on reading and mathematics in 1956 and 1960 (Pidgeon, 1960, and Jones, 1969), and the Department of Education and Science's surveys of reading ability (U.K. Ministry of Education, 1950, 1957; U.K. Department of Education end Science, 1966). Another survey of reading ability is being conducted in 1970 by the National Foundation to continue both the Department's and its own series. These surveys provide information on the extent to which standards in education are rising. An article by Peaker (1953) describes some of the sampling problems involved in the Ministry of Education's survey.

(j) *Social mobility.* Most surveys of human populations are directly or indirectly concerned with differences in environment, behaviour and attitudes between various social strata. But social scientists have also been specifically interested in movement between strata, both from the point of view of measuring the overall extent of upward or downward mobility, and with a view to understanding the causes of mobility and its consequences for the individual. The conceptual and methodological problems involved in measuring social mobility and making international comparisons have been described by Miller (1960) in an important survey article which includes an extensive bibliography. There are articles on the relationships between education and social mobility, some based on survey findings, in Halsey, Floud and Anderson's (1961) volume *Education, Economy, and Society.* Further evidence on this topic is provided in the surveys published as appendixes to the Robbins Report (U.K. Committee on Higher Education, 1964). The only British survey to date whose major focus has been social mobility is the study by research workers at the London School of Economics under the direction of Glass (1954). This provided data about the social origin, education and occupational achievement of a national sample of some 10,000 adults. Ancillary investigations included enquiries into the social prestige of occupations, the relationships between education and social mobility, child upbringing and social class, social mobility and marriage, recruitment in a number of professions, and the structure of voluntary organizations. Halsey and Floud at Oxford are planning a new survey on social mobility intended to provide information for comparisons with Glass's findings for the early fifties. It is also hoped to make comparisons with a recent large-scale American study (Blau and Duncan, 1967).

(k) *Occupations and special groups.* There have been interesting surveys of particular occupations carried out to investigate the labour market for the occupation, to study the profession from a sociological viewpoint, or to investigate the effects of the change in status of routine white-collar jobs. The growth of interest in manpower planning, and in industrial relations and industrial organization, has accentuated the demand for surveys of people in relation to their jobs. One of the earliest examples in this field is Bakke's (1933) *The Unemployed Man.* To date no other major survey specially concerned with the unemployed seems to have been published.

Surveys concerned with human relations in industry often rely on informal methods of interviewing and on observational techniques, as for example in Lupton's (1963) study *On the Shop Floor.* The reports by Liverpool University on industrial relations and morale, such as its study of dock workers (Liverpool University, Social Science Department, 1954), provide some interesting examples of early work in this field. Flanders, Pomeranz and Woodward's (1968) more recent study of the John Lewis partnership made use of standard survey methods.

A different kind of group was surveyed by Kelsall (1955), and his book *Higher Civil Servants in Britain from 1870 to the Present Day* provides a good deal of information about the social origins and education of this group. Since then the Fulton Committee has sponsored another survey of civil servants, which covers a wide range of topics including political attitudes and allegiances (Halsey and Crewe, 1969).

Many other groups of public employees have been the subject of surveys. The Government Social Survey interviewed a sample of personnel in the fire service in order to provide the Home Office with information on management at the various levels of command

(Thomas, 1969). Martin and Wilson (1969) carried out a survey on the use of manpower in the police force. Other studies such as the Home Office's *Workloads in Children's Departments* (Grey, 1969) have been concerned to discover the allocation of time between different aspects of a job. A similar study in a different profession is being attempted by the Vice-Chancellors' Committee, which is anxious to cost the different parts of higher education among university teachers. They have asked a sample of one in three university teachers to keep a diary for a week at three different times of the year. University teachers have also been studied in two other recent surveys. Halsey and Trow (1971) used the same sample as the Robbins Committee, one in four of all university teachers, in their study of the attitudes of academics to their work. The Higher Education Research Unit at the London School of Economics has been making a study of the pay and labour market of university staff, and this includes a mail survey of three thousand academics, as well as interviews with a large sub-sample (U.K. National Board for Prices and Incomes, 1970).

The medical profession has also been studied from the point of view of pay. The U.K. Royal Commission on Doctors' and Dentists' Remuneration (1960) sponsored a survey on this subject. Other surveys of doctors include Abel-Smith and Gales' (1964) *British Doctors at Home and Abroad* and Backett and others' (1953, 1954) studies of general practice. Cartwright (1967) has also studied general practitioners, with an interesting sample design. A survey of medical students was carried out for the U.K. Royal Commission on Medical Education (1968).

Moving away from specific occupations to wider groups of people, two large surveys of graduates have been undertaken recently. Rudd and Hatch (1968) took a cohort of students who began graduate work in 1957–58 and investigated the outcome of their studies in terms of qualifications, jobs and pay. Kelsall has also carried out a sample survey of recent graduates, which is in the process of publication. Various surveys of students have been undertaken in connection with student protest in the sixties. One such survey was conducted by members of the academic staff at the London School of Economics (Blackstone and others, 1970), and investigated the extent of participation in the conflict at L.S.E. in 1967; this was based on a complete coverage of the school's full-time students. A survey with definite policy aims was designed to assist the Department of Education and Science to recruit more graduates to the teaching profession (Morton-Williams and others, 1966). Teachers have been the subject of a number of surveys, including Kelsall's (1963) study of women teachers, which was based on a national sample and analysed some of the facts involved in wastage. The special problems faced by working women were investigated on a wider scale by Hunt (1968) of the Government Social Survey. The survey involved a national random sample of ten thousand households, in which attempts were made to contact all women between 16 and 64.

(l) *Leisure*. There have been many surveys concerned with leisure activities such as cinema-going, reading, gambling and so forth. In the field of television, increasing emphasis is being placed on the effects of particular sorts of programmes on the community, especially on children and young people and on the family. The Nuffield Foundation has sponsored two surveys, the results of which are published by Himmelweit and others (1958) in the book *Television and the Child*, and by Belson (1959a) in *Television and the Family*; both surveys contain some interesting aspects of methodology. As mentioned earlier, the BBC and JICTAR carry out regular surveys to measure audiences for particular programmes, and the Television Research Committee at Leicester University, in its role as 'initiator and co-ordinator of research into the part which television plays or could play as a medium of communications and fostering of attitudes', has also sponsored a number of surveys.

Two major national surveys outlining leisure patterns are *The Pilot National Recreation Survey*, carried out jointly by the British Travel Association and the University of Keele (Rodgers, 1967, 1969), which was concerned with outdoor recreation in the context of the total time spent on leisure, and the Government Social Survey's *Planning for Leisure* by Sillitoe (1969), which examined the recreation patterns of urban populations. In addition there have been numerous surveys of particular regions and resources. Examples of more specialized surveys are *Recreation and Tourism in the Loch Lomond Area* by Nicholls and Young (1968) and *Outdoor Leisure Activities in the Northern Region*, a report by the Northern Region Planning Committee (1969). In addition, the British Travel Association (1969) —now called the British Tourist Authority—regularly studies the holiday patterns of the British at home and of foreign tourists in the United Kingdom.

Among more sociologically oriented studies, we may mention Rowntree and Lavers' (1951b) book *English Life and Leisure*, which took its material from a large number of informal interviews and some 1,000 case histories, about a fifth of which are recorded. Another book giving an interesting view of leisure habits and urban life generally is Cauter and Downham's (1954) *The Communication of Ideas*. The bulk of the material came from a sample survey in Derby, which investigated elements of modern life connected with the communication and spread of ideas—education, reading, radio and television, the cinema, religion, travelling, and so forth.

A vivid picture of the leisure pursuits of working-class people is drawn in Zweig's (1948) *Labour, Life and Poverty*. Zweig developed successfully a mode of social study that owes little to the formal techniques of surveys, such as sampling, standardized interviewing and questionnaires, and a great deal to his personality, his ability to get people talking, and his skill in knitting their remarks and his observations into a coherent picture. A skilled investigator using this informal approach (which was, in a sense, originated by Mayhew) can provide a fuller, more lively picture than the complex apparatus of the representative sample survey. However, the two approaches achieve different ends and can rarely be considered as alternatives.

(m) *Travel*. Most people spend a good deal of their lives travelling, whether for commuting, business or leisure purposes, and the subject is clearly of sociological interest. An early social and economic analysis fortified in part by survey data was Liepmann's (1944) *The Journey to Work*. More recently, extensive surveys of travel in Great Britain have been sponsored by the U.K. Ministry of Transport (1967) and, with Ministry support, by a number of major local authorities, including the Greater London Council (1969). Land-use transportation studies, many involving substantial household-interview surveys, have now been carried out in almost every major conurbation (including Merseyside, the West Midlands, West Yorkshire, Tyneside and South-East Lancashire—North-East Cheshire); the Merseyside study (Merseyside Area Land-Use Transportation Study, 1969) is a particularly good example of this type. The Teesside area, though not a conurbation, has also been the subject of a detailed study, with particular emphasis on urban planning (U.K. Ministry of Housing and Local Government and Ministry of Transport, 1969). References to surveys concerned with travel to and from the United Kingdom have been made above.

(n) *Political behaviour*. Opinion polls apart, until quite recently survey techniques have not been as fully exploited in studying political behaviour in Britain as one might have expected. Among the first informative election surveys was that by Milne and Mackenzie (1954) for the constituency of Bristol North-East at the general election of 1951. Two studies relating to the 1950 election can be mentioned: Birch and Campbell (1950) used survey techniques in an analysis of *Voting Behaviour in a Lancashire Constituency*, which they conducted immediately after the election, and Benney, Gray and Pear (1956) carried out a study of voting behaviour in Greenwich before and up to the 1950 election.

A book by Bonham (1954) analysed opinion-poll and other data to study the voting behaviour of the 'middle classes'. Since then, the only other major survey study focused on the political behaviour of the middle class is Parkin's (1968) work on *Middle Class Radicalism*. This is concerned with the social characteristics of the supporters of the Campaign for Nuclear Disarmament, and is based on a sample of approximately 850 adult members and youth supporters of the movement. There have been several studies of working-class political attitudes, and in particular of working-class conservatism. Runciman (1966) investigated this in his book *Relative Deprivation and Social Justice*, and since then there have been two important studies of this phenomenon using survey methods. The first is McKenzie and Silver's (1968) work, based on interviews with samples of working-class voters. The second is the major study by Goldthorpe and others (1968a, 1968b) of the political and economic attitudes of affluent workers, more specifically employees of the motor industry in Luton.

Reference should be made to an early critical bibliography on electoral behaviour published by UNESCO (Dupeux, 1954–55) and to an expository article by Butler (1955a), who has also published analyses of every general election in Britain since 1951 (Butler, 1952, 1955b; Butler and Rose, 1960; Butler and King, 1965, 1966). A major work studying the forces shaping electoral choice during this century, *Political Change in Britain*, has recently been published by Butler and Stokes (1969). This includes a large interview survey of two thousand randomly selected electors, which provides a good example of the technique of re-interviewing the same sample over several years. The book also contains interesting examples of the way data from a survey may be interwoven with evidence from other sources to interpret human behaviour.

Two studies attempting to discover the effects of television on voting behaviour should also be mentioned. The first, based on surveys carried out in Leeds in 1959 (Trenaman and McQuail, 1961), failed to find any marked effect of television on attitudes or voting choice during the election campaign. But when the study was repeated in the same constituencies in 1964 the findings were different; exposure to television was found to relate to increased support for the Liberals (Blumler and McQuail, 1968).

Although there is now more survey work in studying general elections, survey research on local elections is still rare. Here there is more opportunity for secondary analysis by relating the voting returns to census data, since votes are counted by wards, rather than by constituencies as in parliamentary elections. Potentially, this should be a rewarding field for survey research.

(o) *Race relations and minority groups.* Until the late fifties relatively few surveys in Britain had concerned themselves specifically with race relations or minority groups. Then the wider interest in racial problems led to a rapid increase in survey activity. Among the earlier enquiries are those of Glass and Patterson, who both studied West Indians in Brixton; Glass's (1960) study made more use of formal survey techniques, whilst Patterson (1963) took a non-random sample and relied more heavily on participant observation. A few years before this, Robb (1954) carried out a survey in the East End of London on anti-semitic attitudes, and Banton (1959) investigated attitudes to racial minorities. Earlier still, in an enquiry making more marginal use of formal survey methods, Little (1948) employed anthropological techniques in a study of the coloured community in Liverpool.

The establishment of the Institute of Race Relations has led to the more extensive investigation of both prejudice and discrimination, and to studies involving the use of surveys on such questions as the education of immigrants. Readers should refer to the Institute's journal *Race* for short reports of surveys in this field. Three major studies must also be mentioned. Daniel's (1968) study for Political and Economic Planning, *Racial Discrimination in England*, is interesting for its revelations on the differences in attitudes towards white and coloured minority groups. It is also of methodological interest, since it attempts to set up an experimental situation by sending people from different ethnic minorities, with identical qualifications, to apply for the same jobs, and then tests the reactions of the employers. Rex and Moore (1967) studied race relations in a Birmingham community by means of a large sample survey of immigrants and local inhabitants, and concluded that the most important source of stress for both groups was poor housing. In investigating the incidence of prejudiced attitudes for the report *Colour and Citizenship*, Rose and others (1969) took a sample of five hundred white adults from five areas with a high concentration of immigrants, as well as a national sample of 2,250 people to serve as a control group.

(p) *Old age.* It is not surprising that the problems of old age have attracted the attention of social researchers, in view of the acute physical, social and economic hardships affecting old people. The Nuffield Foundation sponsored some early survey work in this area, such as *Old People* (Nuffield Foundation, 1947) and a follow-up enquiry to this, *The Social Medicine of Old Age* (Sheldon, 1948). In the late fifties and early sixties there were a number of studies of the economic situation in which old people found themselves, and of these Cole and Utting's (1962) *The Economic Circumstances of Old People* and Townsend and Wedderburn's (1965) *The Aged in the Welfare State* are examples. Another type of study concerned with old age is Townsend's (1962b) *The Last Refuge*, a survey of institutions rather than individuals, which shows the great variations in the standards of old people's homes.

Since the elderly are major users of the social services, the government is also interested in surveying their needs. The survey sponsored by the U.K. Ministry of Pensions and National Insurance (1966) on *Financial and other Circumstances of Retirement Pensioners* is one example. A study published two years later *Social Welfare for the Elderly* (Harris, 1968), carried out on behalf of the National Corporation for the Care of Old People with the support of government departments, is another; it examined the unsatisfied need for local authority and other services, including housing for the elderly, by collecting information from officials, recipients of existing services and a general sample of the elderly. An earlier survey sponsored by the government was designed to find out why people retire or continue at work (U.K. Ministry of Pensions and National Insurance, 1954).

(q) *Crime and deviant behaviour.* The formal survey approach is often difficult to employ in the study of juvenile delinquency and criminal behaviour. Random samples of the population are rarely appropriate, and samples must usually be drawn from those actually committed to institutions of one kind or another or from those brought before the courts. Special care also has to be taken in eliciting the information required. A good deal of empirical work in this field is in fact based on a secondary analysis of existing data such as the criminal statistics. Some researchers have collected their own material, but in a way different to the conventional survey; Parker and Allerton have used unstructured taped interviews with offenders, which provide much illuminating material and throw light on the causes of deviance (Parker and Allerton, 1962; see Parker, 1967, 1968). But all this does not mean that formal surveys can never be of use. An early study, largely statistical, of juvenile delinquents was that of Carr-Saunders, Mannheim and Rhodes (1942). The material dated from 1938, when the first 1,000 juveniles brought to court after a particular date were studied, and their social and environmental characteristics compared with those of controls coming from the same age groups and schools as the delinquents. Another important pre-war study was Cyril Burt's (1944) *The Young Delinquent*. A further investigation of young delinquents was Ferguson's (1952) *The Young Delinquent in his Social Setting*, which was based on a study of a large number of boys in Glasgow.

The problems of longitudinal surveys in this field are illustrated by Martin's (1962) *Offenders as Employees*. To discover the nature and extent of the social stigma experienced as a result of a conviction for a criminal offence, three hundred men convicted in Reading were followed for a number of years.

A number of studies have been carried out in penal institutions, several of them employing participant observation, the researcher either joining the prison staff or becoming an inmate. (This technique has also been used in the study of deviant sub-cultures outside prisons or other such institutions, such as drug-takers.) Other studies have sampled inmate populations in a more conventional way. Gibbens (1963) has studied Borstal boys, specially emphasizing psychological factors, and is now studying women offenders, interviewing every other entrant to Holloway at reception. An earlier example of a survey of a prison population is Roper's (1950, 1951) study of prisoners at Wakefield gaol. Pauline Morris's (1965) study *Prisoners and their Families* threw light on the special problems of prisoners' wives and children.

Two other studies in progress are worth mentioning. Willett and Hood are studying motoring offenders and a control group of non-offenders with the aim of discovering the effects of sentences and the characteristics of non-offenders. A very different kind of group, children in residential homes, which nevertheless in some sense falls into the category of deviants, is the subject of a study by Tizard, Akhurst and Rosen. The emphasis is on child-care practices in the homes and the major sampling unit is the institution. This is an example of a survey investigating various levels of a problem, since both the policies of the local authorities and the characteristics of the individual children will be studied.

The Home Office Research Unit has been responsible for a number of important surveys. One of the most interesting is the probation research project, whose major aim is to measure the success of probation for different types of offenders (Folkard and others, 1966; Barr, 1966; Barr and O'Leary, 1966; Davies, 1967). It has also carried out a number of studies of women offenders (Goodman and Price, 1967), including a study of girls appearing before a juvenile court, which involved interviewing the girls and their mothers. Three of the Unit's other current surveys should be mentioned. The first is a longitudinal study of juvenile offenders in Crawley, which includes a comparison with a control sample of non-delinquent children and a follow-up of the offenders until they are seventeen. The others are both concerned with the examination of penal methods: in the first, after-care units and prison welfare officers are surveyed, as well as ex-prisoners receiving after-care; the second involves a survey of prisoners selected for parole compared with those rejected, and attempts to evaluate the effectiveness of parole and its relationship to recidivism.

The Survey Research Centre at the London School of Economics has carried out a series of studies on methodological questions concerned with the study of delinquency. The Centre has tried to develop special techniques for eliciting information from boys about matters like undetected criminal activity (Belson and others, 1968). The successful application of such techniques would be an important step forward in surveys of delinquency.

Concluding remark

We again emphasize that this chapter is not to be taken as an exhaustive or critical survey of surveys. Its purpose has been simply to illustrate the evolution and range of social surveys in Great Britain and the wide variety of subject matter to which the techniques have been and are being applied.

NOTES ON READING

1. Short and readable accounts of the development of surveys are given by JONES (1948) and ABRAMS (1951), and by RUTH and DAVID GLASS (1950). MADGE (1953) critically discusses a number of enquiries. POLITICAL AND ECONOMIC PLANNING (1950) have published two broadsheets on the use of sample surveys in various fields. A much earlier book on social surveys, in the classical community-study sense, is that by WELLS (1935).

2. The student is recommended to read some of the original reports on the early surveys which have become classics in their field, combining factual usefulness with a wealth of material and a vividness of description absent from many of their modern successors.

3. This is the appropriate point for commenting on the book literature on surveys. There are a number of good textbooks on methods of social research in general, covering survey techniques. Perhaps the best of the modern texts is the book by SELLTIZ and others (1959). Other useful references are FESTINGER and KATZ (1953), GOODE and HATT (1952), MADGE (1953), RILEY (1963), DUVERGER (1964), PHILLIPS (1966), SIMON (1969), YOUNG (1966), DOBY (1967), MARK (1958) and SJOBERG and NETT (1968). A detailed account of practical survey procedures is given by PARTEN (1950), and there is a manual on survey methods by BACKSTROM and HURSH (1963). GALTUNG (1967) gives an interesting classificatory analysis of social research methods. FORCESE and RICHER (1970) and TUFTE (1970) have edited useful collections of articles on social research methodology. Shorter introductions to social research are provided by MANN (1968), SCHOFIELD (1969), STACEY (1969a) and THOMLINSON (1965). MOSTELLER and others (1949) give an authoritative post-mortem of the 1948 failure of the American pollsters and an important critical account of polling

methods; an earlier book on opinion polls is that by CANTRIL (1944). A volume edited by EDWARDS (1956) brings together a number of important British papers on market research; more recently SEIBERT and WILLS (1970) have edited a selection of papers on market research. YATES (1960), apart from the technical matter of sampling to which we refer later, deals extensively with survey problems. More specific references will be given in the appropriate chapters.

CHAPTER 2

The Planning of Social Surveys

2.1. Preliminary study

THE PLANNING of a social survey is a combination of technical and organizational decisions. At some point all the methodological questions dealt with in this book have to be answered: what population coverage to aim at; what information to seek; how to go about collecting this information; how to process and interpret the results, and so forth. None of these questions, however, can be answered on a purely technical level. The sample design is decided upon in the light of what is practically feasible as well as of what is theoretically desirable. Once decided, it in turn gives rise to numerous practical decisions of selection and organization. In considering these matters, due regard must be paid to the purposes of the survey, the accuracy required in the results, the cost, time and labour involved, and other practical considerations. Since funds are invariably limited, the aim throughout is to utilize them to best advantage.

The nature of the planning problems will depend on whether the survey is being carried out by one of the existing permanent survey bodies or whether a special organization has to be set up. In the former case, matters like interviewer selection and training, field supervision and so on are already settled routine; and even considerations such as the *type* of sampling, *type* of data collection and methods of tabulation are likely to follow well-established lines. The would-be surveyor who does not have the facilities of a running survey machine at his disposal obviously has a much bigger and more difficult task, and it is rarely possible for him to attain the efficiency of a professional organization. Nevertheless there are many in his position, and this chapter considers survey planning in the context of an *ad hoc* rather than an existing organization.

In the preparatory stages, various lines of approach should be explored. Much can be gained from talks with experts, both with those familiar with the subject matter of the survey and with survey practitioners in governmental and commercial survey organizations. In our experience, these practitioners are generous in giving time and advice to research workers, both out of a general spirit of helpfulness and a desire to maintain high professional standards in survey work. Then, of course, a study of the available literature is a necessity in any good research. A wealth of information on most aspects of our national life issues from all directions: in the official sphere, statistical data, reports, white papers and blue books appear in immense numbers and on an increasingly wide range of topics. Publications such as the *Guides to Official Sources* by the U.K. Interdepartmental Committee on Social and Economic Research (1951–61) and *The Sources and Nature of the Statistics of the United Kingdom*, edited by Kendall (1952–57) and now being brought up-to-date, are valuable, but it can still be a hard task to find out even what official information is available on any given subject. Perhaps the most helpful current guidance is to be found in the Central Statistical Office's *Statistical News*, a quarterly publication which, amongst other things, contains notes on new developments in official statistics.

In the non-official sphere the output is equally voluminous and still more difficult to keep track of. *The Register of Research in the Social Sciences* prepared by the National Institute of Economic and Social Research (1956) used to provide a valuable indication of the range of subject matter being covered and of the research bodies working in this field, but unfortunately this has ceased publication. Volume 3 of the annual publication *Scientific Research in British Universities and Colleges* from the U.K. Department of Education and Science and the British Council (1969), prepared in co-operation with the Social Science Research Council, provides brief notes on research in progress in the social sciences. It includes researches of government departments and other institutions as well as those of universities and colleges, and is a most valuable indicator of current research. Nevertheless, to find out, for example, what research is being done at present on, say, comprehensive schools or delinquency would require innumerable enquiries in different places, with no assurance that all the main researches would be unearthed. Most help will come through the Government Social Survey, not only from its lists of reports but also from its wide contacts in the research world; from the S.S.R.C. data bank at Essex University, which is in touch with a wide range of survey research; from individual government departments and research institutions which are active in survey research; but it is not an easy task. The S.S.R.C.'s regular *Newsletter* (which appears three times a year) is a very helpful source.

With all this activity, care clearly needs to be taken to avoid duplicating work being done, or in plan, elsewhere. It is a well-known feature of scientific history that the same invention, the same theoretical advance, is often made more or less simultaneously by several workers. This kind of 'coincidence', which is only a reflection of the current state of scientific knowledge and interest, frequently occurs also in the social sciences. Perhaps it is even more common here than in the natural sciences. Social research depends a good deal on what sources and data are available for study, and there is a consequent tendency for some parts of the field to be ploughed over and over again, while others remain virtually untouched. Or a certain problem—say the conditions of old people—may be in the public eye, thus stimulating a spate of investigations of it. Replication in different parts of the country or under different circumstances can, of course, be most valuable, but if all research workers knew of each other's projects and were willing to collaborate more, a good deal of effort and money could be saved and channelled into the more unexplored fields. Often re-analysis from a different standpoint of the findings in someone else's research, or a few additions to the questionnaire of a contemplated one, could obviate the need for a separate project.

2.2. The main planning problems

We now turn to discuss planning in general terms, with special reference to social surveys. The problems noted will be dealt with in detail in later chapters.

(a) *Objectives and resources.* The first task of planning is of course to lay down the survey's objectives precisely—and this means more than a vague statement of broad aims. It is not enough to say that the survey is intended to find out about 'the living conditions of old people'. One should define exactly what, for the purpose of the survey, is meant by an old person; whether the enquiry is to serve as a basis for inferences to a particular population of old people and, if so, what this population is. One should make clear whether 'living conditions' simply means a description of type of house, number of rooms, furniture and so forth, or whether income and expenditure data are wanted in order to gauge hardship. The initial statement should explain why the survey is being done, exactly what questions it means to cover, and what kinds of results are expected. Most important, especially if the survey is being done for a client, the statement needs to discuss how the information is to be used and what degree of accuracy is required.

Not the least important purpose of such a statement is that it will clarify the surveyor's own mind and thus probably lead to a more efficient enquiry (and one that will be more easily explained to respondents). Failure to think out the objectives of a survey fully and precisely must inevitably undermine its ultimate value; no amount of manipulation of the final data can overcome the resultant defects.

Once the objectives are settled, the plan of the survey is directed to achieving them with the required accuracy and within the given resources. Any widening of the scope, whether by the inclusion of further questions or the extension to population groups of marginal importance, should be permitted only if it is certain that the resources will not thereby become spread too thinly for the survey to achieve its main purposes.

The statement of objectives must specify the methods to be used and be as explicit in what is practicable as in what is desirable. At so early a stage only the roughest budget is possible; yet some estimates of cost, time and labour have to be attempted.

(b) *Coverage.* The first steps are to define the population to be studied—its geographical, demographic and other boundaries—and to decide whether it should be fully or only partially covered. In the latter, and far more usual, case the method of selecting the respondents has to be determined and this normally means a sample in the statistical sense. A whole host of questions then arise: what type of sample is to be used; what is the appropriate sampling unit (administrative district or constituency; ward or polling district; household, family or individual, etc.); what sampling frame—i.e. list, register, map—is available for the population in question and what difficulties are there in employing it for this particular sample design and unit; how big a sample is desirable to give the required accuracy and how big a sample is feasible on the available resources; if some economy is necessary, can the sample design be modified or the population restricted, say by cutting out marginal areas?

Provisions should be made in advance for dealing with non-response. Some non-response, both through refusals and non-contacts, is unavoidable but there are ways of reducing its magnitude and of estimating the effect of the non-response that remains upon the accuracy of the results. Follow-up approaches are necessary to increase response and the planner must decide how much time, labour and money it is worth spending on these.

(c) *Collection of data.* The choice of method for collecting the data is governed by the subject matter, the unit of enquiry and the scale of the survey.[1] A study of crowd behaviour would call for observational

---

[1] The 'unit of enquiry' is the unit, e.g. individual or household, about which information is required. It may or may not be the same as the sampling unit. One may pick a sample of households and collect information about the household members—the sampling unit is the household, the unit of enquiry the household member.

techniques. For a simple enquiry among an educated section of the population—say a professional group—and concerned with a subject of close interest to its members, a mail questionnaire might be adequate. A survey of the general population entailing many complicated questions would almost certainly call for personal interviewing, which might vary from the standardized, formal technique common in large-scale surveys down to informal conversations. Each method has its advantages and disadvantages.

(d) *Questionnaires*. Nine out of ten social surveys use a questionnaire of some kind, and the framing and arrangement of questions is perhaps the most substantial planning task. Practitioners have their experience, common sense and certain general principles to aid them, but they cannot rely on theoretical guidance in the same sense as they can in sampling decisions. Yet decisions on the scope of the questionnaire, its layout and printing, the definitions and instructions to go with it and on the wording and order of the questions have to be taken, however non-theoretical the basis.

(e) *Errors*. Every stage of the survey process is a potential source of error. Quite apart from sampling errors—which are the easiest to keep under control and to estimate—inaccuracies may enter through the interviewing, the questions, the editing, the coding, the tabulating and the analysis. Every practitioner is, for instance, aware of the risk of memory errors whenever questions about the past are asked, and this is only one of many kinds of 'response errors'. In planning a survey one must try to anticipate the likely sources of error and take whatever precautions are possible to minimize them.

(f) *Fieldwork*. The quality of interviewers is of obvious importance in field surveys, and there is still a good deal of discussion on the merits of different types of interviewers and methods of selecting and training them. Every survey organization must establish its policy on these questions, on the basis of its experience or internal research. The solitary research worker may have to use whatever field staff he can get.

Many organizational problems are bound up with fieldwork, more especially in recruiting field staff. There are the alternatives of employing full-time or part-time interviewers; of paying time-rates or piece-rates; of paying all interviewers equally or giving more to the more experienced workers, for difficult assignments or for especially good work; of briefing centrally or locally. The extent and method of field supervision has to be decided, and the checks to be made on the honesty and efficiency of interviewers.

(g) *Processing and analysis*. Although the fieldwork is the central stage of a survey, an enormous amount of work remains to be done after it. When the questionnaires come in, they must be scrutinized for errors, omissions and ambiguous classifications before they are ready for coding and tabulation. Finally comes the analysis (usually involving statistical calculations), the interpretation of results and the preparation of the report.

This phase, like the fieldwork itself, must be considered in the planning if smooth running of a survey is to be ensured. An editing scheme should be devised, together with code lists and some tentative ideas for tabulation plans. It pays to write down in advance a list of the tabulations that are likely to be required, for this helps to clarify the survey's objectives and acts as a check that relevant information will be collected and irrelevant information will not. But it is foolish to suggest that tabulation plans can be drawn up in their entirety in the planning stages of a survey. More often than not, and certainly if the subject is of any complexity, many of the tabulations and analyses cannot be decided on until one begins to handle the results.

The methods of analysis should also be given careful consideration at the planning stage. If a computer is to be used, the features of the computer programs to be employed must be studied. In particular, the code lists should be checked to ensure that they meet the programs' specifications. If weighting (discussed in Chapter 5) is required in the analysis, the programs should be examined to see whether they provide a facility for it, and if not, another method for achieving the weighting must be decided on.

(h) *Documents.* Once the above issues are settled the time is ripe for the final drafting and printing of documents. These include questionnaires, questionnaire instructions, interview record sheets, interviewer manuals and instructions, authorization cards, time and expense sheets.

(i) *Timing, cost and staffing.* Problems of timing and organization are so special to each survey that a general discussion serves little purpose. Decisions on the timing of the enquiry—in so far as there is room for choice—are governed by seasonal factors, the time at which the results are needed, and so on. In general it is better not to conduct the fieldwork in the holiday season when many people may be away from their homes. Also, if the sampling frame is updated periodically, as is the case with the Register of Electors, it may be preferable to wait for the next revision rather than select the sample from an out-of-date frame. But the prime consideration must be the time period to which the results are to apply, for to choose an 'unrepresentative' time for a survey may be as serious a defect as to study an unrepresentative sample. Once the date is fixed, it remains to set up a schedule for the completion of the various stages, and an estimate of their costs. These will include printing, sample selection, fieldwork (including travelling and subsistence) or mailing, processing and tabulating, preparation of the report, and overheads.

As regards the personnel to be used in social research surveys, there is much to be said for calling in several types of specialist. Various skills go to the making of a survey, and typically the sociologist, the psychologist, the statistician, and often the computer specialist all have something to contribute. This is not necessarily to argue that teamwork is always better than individual research; the former can involve hours of fruitless discussion and lead to disjointed research. But if the modern survey apparatus, as described in this book, is to be brought into action, it is well to make use of expert advice, especially regarding sampling problems and statistical analysis. And it is important that the statistician should be called in at the beginning of the survey, not at the end. The statistician is frequently requested to look at a quantity of completed questionnaires 'to see what he can make of the data'. Too often the reply must be that, because of insufficiency of numbers, flaws in the design, faults in the questions or other avoidable mistakes, very little can be made of them.[1] Equally many difficulties in the computer analysis can be avoided by an early consultation with the computer specialist. He is frequently presented with the problem of unscrambling a set of coded data in order to make it comply with a program's requirements, a problem which would never have arisen had he been asked to advise on the coding scheme at the planning stage.

2.3. Pre-tests and pilot surveys

This brief catalogue of planning problems makes one thing plain: it is exceedingly difficult to plan a survey without a good deal of knowledge of its subject matter, the population it is to cover, the way people will react to questions and, paradoxical though it sounds, even the answers they are likely to give. How is one to estimate how long the survey will take, how many interviewers will be needed, how much money it will cost, if one has not *done* some part of it? How, without trial interviews, can one be sure that the questions will be as meaningful to the average respondent as to the survey expert? How is one to decide which questions are worth asking at all?

Common sense suggests the necessity of doing a few test interviews or sending out trial forms by way of preparing for the main survey, and such informal trial and error is as much part of the preliminary study as are talks with experts and study of the literature. But it is

[1] A paper by Finney (1956) on 'The Statistician and the Planning of Field Experiments' contains much of relevance to the statistician's role in social surveys.

C

necessary to go further, and to try out systematically all the various features of the main enquiry. This may take the form, first, of a series of small 'pre-tests' on isolated problems of the design; and then, when the broad plan of the enquiry is established, of a pilot survey, a small-scale replica of the main survey.

The pilot survey is the dress rehearsal and, like a theatrical dress rehearsal, it will have been preceded by a series of preliminary tests and trials. Pre-tests and pilot surveys are standard practice with professional survey bodies and are widely used in research surveys. Specifically,[1] they provide guidance on:

(i) The adequacy of the sampling frame from which it is proposed to select the sample. The features of some much-used frames—e.g. the Register of Electors—are well known but, if a less familiar one is to be used, its completeness, accuracy, adequacy, up-to-dateness and convenience should be tested.

One might be planning to use the pay-roll of workers in a factory as the basis for drawing a sample. It is just as well then to give it a try beforehand—it may not be conveniently arranged or it may exclude some workers (e.g. those temporarily on leave) whom the survey is to include, or cards may be temporarily removed from it when required for some other purpose. Whether or not such defects can be overcome is another matter; what is vital is to be aware of them before starting on the survey.

(ii) The variability (with regard to the subject under investigation) within the population to be surveyed. This is of importance in determining an efficient sample design, and we shall see later that the very decision on sample size requires some knowledge of the variability of the population. Suppose that a survey were being designed to find out the average weekly rent paid by workers in a factory. The size of the sample needed to achieve the required precision would depend on how much variation there was in rent expenditure. Putting the point in extreme simplicity: if all the workers spent exactly £5 a week (i.e. variability between them were zero) a sample of 1 would suffice to give all the required precision; if, on the other hand, the variability of expenditures were high (i.e. rents ranging from, say, £3 to £10 per week) a relatively large sample would be required to provide a sufficiently precise estimate. Thus it is clear that in order to decide on a sampling plan it is helpful, to say the least, to possess some prior knowledge of the population to be sampled. Pilot studies, however, are rarely of much value in providing estimates of variability,

[1] A definitive statement as to which functions belong to the pre-tests and which to the pilot survey will not be attempted, since much will depend on the circumstances of the enquiry.

because they are too small to yield estimates with any worth-while precision. Usually the researcher has available some statistics for the same or a related area, and careful analysis of these will normally lead to a more useful estimate than the pilot study can produce. Still, the pilot study does provide valuable supporting evidence, and especially so when no closely related statistics can be found.

(iii) The non-response rate to be expected. The probable numbers of refusals and non-contacts can be roughly estimated from the pilot survey (and, partially, from pre-tests) and the effectiveness of various ways of reducing non-response can be compared. As a result, one data-collecting method may be chosen in preference to another, some questions may be excluded, the timing of interviews may be altered, and so on.

One may, for example, be debating whether to collect data from a widely dispersed population by mail or by interview. The former is cheaper, but will it achieve an adequate response? Prior experimentation can provide the answer. Or one may be wondering what effect payment of respondents would have on the response rate; again, preliminary study can help one to find out.

(iv) The suitability of the method of collecting the data. Alternative methods—observation, mail questionnaires, interviewers—are available, and one needs data on their relative cost, accuracy and likely response rates to make a sensible choice. The pre-tests and the pilot survey can also show whether the interviewers are doing an efficient job, whether too great a strain is placed on them or on the respondents, and whether the interviews should be subjected to more checks.

(v) The adequacy of the questionnaire. This is probably the most valuable function of the pilot survey. The questionnaire will have been previously tested informally on colleagues and friends, but the pre-tests and the pilot survey offer a way of trying it with the kind of interviewers and respondents to be used in the main survey. Several points will have to be watched—the ease of handling the questionnaire in the field, the efficiency of its layout, the clarity of the definitions and, of course, the adequacy of the questions themselves. Is the wording simple, clear, unambiguous, free from technical terms? Are there signs that some people are misunderstanding the questions or are insufficiently informed to give sensible answers, or that, perhaps for prestige reasons, they are answering inaccurately? Do the answers suggest that too much strain is being put on people's memories?

It is not easy to give rules for recognizing questions containing such weaknesses. Sometimes the true distribution of answers is known, in which case major deviations from it are a warning that something is wrong with either sample or question. Too great a bunching of answers at one extreme *may* be indicative of a leading question, or it may mean that people are giving stereotyped answers. A substantial number of 'Don't know' replies is often (though not necessarily) a bad sign—suggesting a vague question, one using uncommon words or going outside the respondents' experience. Such defects would lead also to a large number of 'Don't understand' comments which, together with other reactions in the field, should be reported by interviewers. If people surround their answers with many qualifications, it may be that the questions could be improved. If many refuse to answer a particular question, possibly the order of questions should be altered so that the offending one is introduced more delicately, or possibly it should be cut out altogether. Almost the most useful evidence of all on the adequacy of a questionnaire is the individual fieldworker's report on how the interviews went, what difficulties were encountered, what alterations should be made, and so forth. Perhaps it is even more valuable for the researcher to accompany some of the interviewers to observe a few interviews being conducted; and he will learn most if the interviewers selected for observation are not the best ones, for it is the less able interviewers who will encounter most difficulties and be unable to deal with them.

(vi) The efficiency of the instructions and general briefing of interviewers. A scrutiny of the completed trial questionnaires may show that interviewers did not put a ring round the 'not applicable' code when a question did not apply; that they omitted their own identity number from the questionnaire; that they did not comment on the course and success of each interview. Instructions were then clearly inadequate or the interviewers were doing a poor job. The pre-tests and pilot survey are of course themselves part of the interviewer training.

(vii) The codes chosen for pre-coded questions (see Chapter 13). Without the pilot survey it is often hard to decide on the alternative answers to be allowed for in the coding. One may wish to ask 'What labour-saving appliances do you have in your home?' and to print all—or as many as one can think of—the possible answers on the questionnaire. In the pilot survey, this can be asked as an 'open' question, all the replies being recorded verbatim; these may call to mind some appliances one might have overlooked.

(viii) The probable cost and duration of the main survey and of its various stages. If it appears that the survey will take too long or be too expensive, the pilot survey can be valuable in suggesting where economies can be made. The cost data will also have a bearing on the sample design.

(ix) The efficiency of the organization in the field, in the office, and in the communication between the two.

The pilot survey will certainly help to clarify many of the problems left unsolved by previous tests, but it will not necessarily throw up *all* the troubles of the main survey; the much bigger scale of this is almost a guarantee of snags and headaches of which the pilot survey gave no warning.[1] However, a pilot survey nearly always results in important improvements to the questionnaire and a general increase in the efficiency of the enquiry. It also has another use. Once the pilot survey is over, the research worker should ask himself whether, in the light of its results, the main survey is still worth carrying out as planned. There are cases in which an intelligent reading of the pilot survey evidence would lead him to take a more modest view of the main survey's potentialities; to see that some of the objectives are not worth pursuing because people are unwilling or unable to give accurate information; and to realize that he cannot cover as wide a field of enquiry or population as planned. The pilot survey is thus the researcher's last safeguard against the possibility that the main survey may be ineffective.

The size and design of the pilot survey is a matter of convenience, time and money. It should be large enough to fulfil the above functions, and the sample should ideally be of a comparable structure to that of the main survey; in practice it is rarely feasible for it to be as widespread as the main sample.

The design will be influenced by another factor. We have seen that the pilot survey can help to guide the choice between alternative methods of collecting the data, ordering the questions, wording and so forth. It should be designed, therefore, so as to ensure a strict testing of these alternatives. If two forms of a question are to be compared, each should be tried out on an equivalent (random) sample of respondents; otherwise the difference in effectiveness of the two questions would be mixed up with differences between the samples themselves. If many types of comparisons are to be made simultaneously—between interviewers, questions, non-response methods, instructions and so on—this calls for strict methods of experimental design, such as are mentioned in Chapter 9. These remarks apply equally to pre-tests.

---

[1] The surveyor unfortunately cannot foresee everything. The pilot survey for one national enquiry experienced a response rate of over 80 per cent; the main survey unluckily coincided with a widespread rail strike and with some adverse publicity for another survey and, whether for these or other reasons, achieved a response rate of less than 70 per cent.

NOTES ON READING
Readers may find useful a concise statement on the planning of surveys prepared by the U.S. BUREAU OF THE BUDGET (1952). Most of the books mentioned at the end of Chapter 1 have relevant chapters, and PARTEN (1950) is recommended for its concentration on practical details barely touched upon here. The book by BACKSTROM and HURSH (1963) gives a simple practical guide to survey research.

CHAPTER 3

The Coverage of Surveys

3.1. Definition of the population

THE METHODOLOGICAL problems of surveys fall into three broad groups: from whom to collect the information, what methods to use for collecting it, and how to process, analyse and interpret it. This chapter, and the five following it, will be concerned with the first of these, namely the coverage of surveys.

The first step always is to define the population[1] to be covered, a task that is never as easy as it sounds. Here it is useful to distinguish between the population for which the results are required, the *target population*, and the population actually covered, the *survey population*. Ideally the two will be the same, but for practical reasons there will usually be some differences between them.[2] For example the geographical delineation of the target population may comprise all of, say, England and Wales, while the survey population may exclude areas which are thinly populated, awkward to reach or for any other reason expensive from a fieldwork point of view. Areas like the Highlands of Scotland, Central Wales, or the Isle of Man are sometimes marginal to the purpose of the survey and can then reasonably be excluded; what matters is that such exclusions are deliberate and explicit so that the surveyor does not delude himself—or his client— that his coverage is wider than in fact it is. In deciding on exclusions he must always be aware of the gap he is creating between target and survey populations.

The definition of the population also involves the fixing of limits other than merely geographical. If the survey is concerned with the adult population of, say, Birmingham, where is the lower age-limit to

---

[1] The reader is reminded that this term is used in its statistical sense, i.e. to denote the aggregate of units to which the survey results are to apply. It need not, though of course it often does, refer to a population of human beings. An alternative term is 'universe'.

[2] One reason for a difference is that some members of the population in a survey are not contacted and so no information is obtained for them. Discussion of non-response is deferred until later, Section 7.4.

be drawn? Are persons in the Forces to be included? And what about people living in institutions like hotels, prisons, mental homes and hospitals? Every survey has its own problems of population definition, and these must be solved explicitly and precisely, with due regard to what is practical. The surveyor, for instance, may include the institutional population in his target population, but if he finds that all the available sampling frames exclude it, he has either to compromise by limiting his survey population to that of the frame or to sample the institutional population by other means.

3.2. Censuses and sample surveys

A population consists of a number of units of enquiry (see p. 44) and the surveyor must decide whether information is to be sought from all or only from some of these units, i.e. whether he should take a census or be satisfied with a sample. Before discussing this choice, we must digress for a moment and define the terms to be used.

There is some ambiguity about the usage of 'census'. Kendall and Buckland's (1960) *A Dictionary of Statistical Terms* says (p. 37) of 'census' that 'The word is used to denote a *complete* enumeration as distinct from the *partial* enumeration associated with a sample'. The alternative distinction between a census and a survey is taken to lie in the *nature of the information* collected. The former term is then generally confined to enquiries that are more or less straightforward counts, like censuses of population, distribution and production, the term 'survey' being applied to enquiries which go beyond simple enumerations. With this terminology, it is perfectly sensible to speak of sample censuses: for example the sample enquiry into fertility conducted in 1946 by the Royal Commission on Population was called the Family Census (Glass and Grebenik, 1954) and the 1966 Population Census of Great Britain was taken on a ten per cent sample basis. We shall broadly follow this second distinction here. It is by no means a hard-and-fast one, but, fortunately, it need not detain us, since this book is mainly concerned with the kinds of investigations which one instinctively calls surveys rather than censuses.

What matters much more is the description of the coverage of an enquiry. A survey (or census) should be called *complete* if virtually all the units in the population under study are covered and *incomplete* if a substantial number are arbitrarily excluded; the term *sample survey* (or census) should ideally be used only if the part of the population studied is selected by accepted statistical methods.[1] The

---

[1] Taken strictly, this terminology would mean that one should withhold the word 'sampling' from methods such as quota and purposive sampling, which lack the rigour demanded by theory. But this is contrary to common usage, and the distinction between theoretically sound and other common sampling methods is better made by the terms suggested on p. 80 below.

words 'sample' and 'part' of the population are not and should not be treated as synonymous. The use of the word 'incomplete' to describe the coverage of a survey also needs care. It should be reserved for cases where coverage or representation of a population is intended or implied, but where part of this population is for some reason not covered.

So much for terminology. As for the factors that decide the choice between a complete and a partial coverage, in ninety-nine out of a hundred surveys the question does not arise, the populations being so large or dispersed that complete coverage is ruled out by shortage of money, time (especially if the results are required for administrative or policy purposes), or trained manpower. In a research survey into the work and leisure of housewives on three housing estates, for instance, the number of housewives included was determined solely by the number of interviewers available to do the fieldwork.

Where the research is concerned with a very small and compact population—the children in a school, the inhabitants of a village, the workers in a small factory—it may be easy to cover all the members, so again the choice between complete and partial coverage barely arises. But for populations of intermediate size the choice could arise. Suppose that one wanted to study the leisure interests of the 3,000 families on a housing estate and that one *had* the resources to interview all the families. Would it be worth doing so? The answer would almost certainly be: 'No'.

Probability sampling methods make it possible to calculate how many families should be included in order to give results of the required precision—whatever it is—with a given chance of error (see next chapter for a discussion of this point). If this calculation shows that somewhere near 3,000 families are required, then of course a complete coverage *would* be desirable. But this is most unlikely— one would have to require unusually detailed analysis and high precision to need such numbers.[1] More likely, a few hundred families would be sufficient and, if these were selected at random (see Chapter 5), the results obtained would apply to the 3,000 families with a calculable margin of error. There would be no point in going to the expense and trouble of a complete coverage.

But if the survey results are to be generalized in this way, then the part of the population chosen for study should be selected according

[1] However, for very small populations, say a few hundred, the required sample size might well approach the population size. This arises because the precision of sample results depends primarily on the size of the sample, not the proportion of the population covered (see next chapter). In such cases complete coverage is commonly aimed at, for it is not worth while to introduce the complexities of sampling in order to obtain the marginal savings created by leaving out a small number of the population units.

to the rules of statistical theory. If it is not, statistically rigorous inferences from sample to population cannot be made and must not be attempted. It is entirely wrong to make an arbitrary selection of cases, to rely on volunteers or on people who happen to be at hand, and then to claim that they are a proper sample of some particular population. This is stressed because some social researchers still generalize uncritically from collections of cases to populations from which they were not properly chosen.

This is not intended to imply that a social enquiry, in order to be of any value, must be based on sampling methods. A sociologist may prefer to study half-a-dozen arbitrarily selected problem families very intensively, rather than to make a formal and more superficial enquiry among a larger, strictly selected sample of families. The two approaches, as has been said before, accomplish different ends and at their best are complementary. An extensive sample survey provides the quantitative material regarding the specified survey population—number of problem families, their size and composition, their main troubles and so on—the emphasis being on the aggregate, not the individual case. Then a small number of families can be picked out and studied intensively as so many case studies.

Zweig's (1948) approach is typical of another kind of investigation, which proceeds without rigorous sampling methods. A large number of casual and informal interviews are conducted and their results combined into a report with manifold personal observations of behaviour and habits. Though no claim to strict representativeness is possible, the method, skilfully employed, produces a picture of undoubted sociological interest. It would be impracticable applied to a randomly selected sample.

It is clear that, if a survey aims at a complete coverage, no problems of selection arise, while if it is to be confined to a few case studies, their choice is dictated by availability and willingness of the persons to co-operate rather than by principles of selection. If the approach is akin to that of Zweig, though an effort is indeed made to interview a widely varying set of people, again there are no formal problems of selection. There remains the large group of surveys in which the research worker wishes to select a part of the population in such a way that he will be able to draw inferences of calculable precision from it to the population. This necessitates the use of sampling and makes this a subject central to survey methodology.

3.3. The idea and the advantages of sampling

The idea of sampling is neither new nor unfamiliar in everyday life. The tea-taster trying different brands of tea, the merchant examining a handful of flour from the sack, the physician making a blood-test

—all these are employing the method of sampling. They do so with extreme confidence, because they have good reason to believe that the material they are sampling is so homogeneous or 'well-mixed' that the sample will adequately represent the whole.

These are somewhat trivial examples of sampling. The roots of modern sampling procedures are found—as Stephan (1948) has shown in an extensive historical account—in many diverse fields: demography, agriculture, commerce, economic statistics, social surveys and so forth. Isolated instances of attempts to make representative selections occur a century or more ago, but modern sampling methods have been developed chiefly in the last 40 to 50 years.

The advantages of sampling, as against complete coverage, have become obvious in recent years and need be stated only briefly. In the first place, sampling saves money. It is obviously cheaper to collect answers from 400 families than from 3,000, although the cost *per unit* of study may be higher with a sample than with a complete coverage (partly because more skilled personnel is used, partly because new costs—e.g. sample selection and calculations of the precision of sample results—have to be added, and partly because overhead costs are spread over a smaller number of units).

In the second place, sampling saves labour. A smaller staff is required both for fieldwork and for tabulating and processing the data.

Thirdly, sampling saves time. It was, in fact, for this purpose that sampling was first used with the Census of Population. In 1951, one per cent of the completed Census schedules were extracted at the analysis stage in order to prepare advance tabulations, which were then made available within 12 to 18 months.[1] The scale of these censuses is so enormous that formerly it had taken many years to bring out the results, by which time they had inevitably lost some of their interest.

Added to these practical advantages, a sample coverage often permits a higher overall level of accuracy than a full enumeration. The smaller numbers allow the quality of the field staff to be at a higher level; more checks and tests for accuracy can be afforded at all stages; more care can be given to editing and the analysis. Finally, fewer cases make it possible to collect and deal with more elaborate information from each.

These are all advantages that flow from having to deal with

---

[1] Sampling with the 1951 Census differed from that of subsequent Censuses in that the one per cent sampling was conducted from completed schedules, while later Censuses have employed ten per cent sampling at the enumeration stage. See pp. 59–60.

smaller numbers than would be involved in a complete coverage. What gives statistical sampling an advantage over any other way of choosing a part of the population is that, when the estimates of the population characteristics are made from the sample results, the precision of these estimates can also be gauged from the sample results themselves. This crucial point will be explained in the next chapter, while in Chapters 5 and 6 different ways of designing samples will be discussed. It will become evident that sample design is often a complicated task. Human populations are nothing if not heterogeneous, far different from the kind of material the tea-taster and doctor are sampling in our simple examples. And not only are human populations very heterogeneous, but they also tend not to be 'well mixed', similar types of persons being found in clusters; this tendency must be taken into account in designing samples. The other big difference between the sampler of human populations and the tea-taster—or even the agriculturist—is that the former has little effective control over his sampling units. He has to contend with people who refuse to be drawn into the sample, with others who are not available at the time of drawing, and so forth; in other words his best design can be spoilt by non-response. This problem is discussed in Chapter 7.

3.4. The use of sampling in Great Britain

The first rigorous application of modern sampling methods to social surveys in Britain occurred in 1912, when Bowley undertook the survey of Reading. His pioneering use of sampling proved a great stimulus to social surveys, which had formerly been based on non-random selection (as with Booth) or on complete surveys (as with Rowntree). The combination of economy and accuracy, characteristic of sampling, appealed to social investigators, and practically all the major surveys of the inter-war years followed Bowley's example.

The first official use of sampling in England—a sample of documents—was in Hilton's (1924) enquiry into the personal circumstances and industrial history of 10,000 claimants to unemployment benefit. Care was taken to ensure a representative sample and to avoid possible sources of bias. The sampling procedure was fully described by Hilton and, as Stephan (1948) has pointed out, it is strange that his methods were not sooner adopted by other government departments. It was not until 1937, in fact, that sampling was used in a large-scale official field investigation, in the well-known U.K. Ministry of Labour and National Service (1940–41) enquiry into working-class expenditure. The thirties also saw the beginning of BBC Listener Research and of many opinion and market research bodies, developments largely attributable to the possibilities of sampling. It was, however, the Second World War which gave the decisive stimulus, both in Britain and in America, to the use of sampling techniques, especially in government administration; and since then more and more surveys in all fields have utilized them.

There are innumerable examples of official sampling other than those mentioned in Chapter 1. Every government department uses sampling in its enquiries, and complete enumerations are exceptional. In the field of production enquiries, the 1968 Census of Production was the last of the line, and will be replaced by a scheme of monthly, quarterly and annual production surveys, employing various sampling schemes. The Ministry of Public Building and Works' surveys of the building industry's labour force, the Board of Trade's capital expenditure surveys and the Ministry of Agriculture, Fisheries and Food's earnings enquiries are other examples on the economic front. The Department of Employment and Productivity has introduced a new survey of earnings, which has a particularly interesting sampling basis. In the case of the Census of Population, the sampling (of schedules) in 1951 was followed by the combination of a complete enumeration for basic information together with a sample enumeration for other information in the 1961 Census, and by a full sample Census in 1966; the 1971 Census is once again based on a complete field enumeration. One could in addition mention any number of sample surveys, all of them based on probability designs, in the field of health, housing, education and social conditions generally, as well as in the economic areas. Sample surveys are also an almost invariable component of Royal Commissions and other government research programmes—the Robbins, Newsom, Crowther and Plowden reports on education, Todd report on medical manpower, Buchanan report on transport, Beeching report on the railways, Pilkington report on doctors' and dentists' remuneration, Allen report on the impact of rates, Milner Holland report on housing in Greater London, are a few that spring to mind.

In short, given the need in government for undertaking a new economic or social enquiry, the normal assumption will be that it should be based on a sample, and a scientifically designed one. There is plenty of experience and expertise at hand for designing samples, and almost all the arguments favour a sample approach. With such extensive official use of sampling, one may indeed ask whether there is ever a case for a complete census or survey. The population census is often cited as one requiring complete coverage and, while there is indeed a case for this, it is not the one often argued: namely that it is useful periodically to know population numbers and so forth with complete accuracy. The fact is that 'complete coverage' and 'complete accuracy' are illusory concepts, never attained in practice because of the many types of error that enter into any enquiry: errors of interviewing, response, coding, recording and tabulating among others. The main justification for a complete coverage in the population census is the need for adequate numbers for analysis in the individual regions, conurbations, towns and rural districts for which results are required. In other words, a complete coverage may be desirable to ensure that the numbers in the small areas are sufficient for their purpose, not because of any particular merit in the idea of completeness itself.

This argument applies most forcibly to the estimates of population size and other major demographic data. For some of the other figures collected—e.g. number of households having fixed baths—less accuracy might, however, suffice; if so, *these* questions might be addressed to a sample of the population, even though others are asked of everybody. This is an example of multi-phase sampling (see Section 6.2), as used in the 1961 Census and in recent United States Population Censuses. In the 1961 Census the sampling was performed in the field by the census enumerators, and unfortunately some of them failed to follow instructions; as a result they exerted an influence on the selection process and a somewhat biased sample was obtained. The problem of avoiding bias with field sampling is an extremely difficult one, but in view of the advantages of multi-phase sampling with the Census it would seem worth while to investigate and experiment further to find either a practicable alternative to field sampling, or a way to minimize and ideally eliminate the bias so far experienced with its use here.

NOTES ON READING

1. The notes on reading at the end of Chapter 5 contain the textbook references on sampling. The book by KISH (1965a) is particularly recommended for its full treatment of the many practical details of sampling, especially for human populations.

2. Among the textbooks recommended at the end of Chapter 1, SELLTIZ and others (1959), GOODE and HATT (1952) and FESTINGER and KATZ (1953) have particularly useful discussions of survey coverage.

3. Accounts of the history of modern sampling methods are given by SENG (1951) and by STEPHAN (1948).

4. Accounts of the use of sampling in Great Britain are given by MOSER (1949, 1955). The UNITED NATIONS STATISTICAL OFFICE (1949 onwards) periodically publishes summaries of sample surveys carried out all over the world.

5. BENJAMIN (1970) provides a useful description of the Population Censuses in Great Britain. The General Report of the 1961 Cencus (U.K. GENERAL REGISTER OFFICE, 1968) is well worth consulting; it contains a discussion of the bias with the sample enumeration.

CHAPTER 4

Basic Ideas of Sampling

4.1. Introduction

THE AIM in this chapter is to explain in fairly general terms the principles underlying sampling theory. We do not attempt to present the theory itself in rigorous terms, to derive formulae or to bring in all the refinements of which the sample designer should be aware.[1] In fact, we have in mind less the needs of the sample designer than those of the student or research worker who wants to know something about basic principles.

Only a few technical expressions need be used. One much-used pair of terms distinguishes between 'attributes' and 'variables'.[2] If one simply notes for each individual whether he possesses or does not possess a certain characteristic—blue eyes, a TV set, a given opinion on equal pay—this characteristic may be called an attribute. Quantification then lies in *counting* how many possess this attribute and how many do not, and the proportion (or percentage) with the attribute provides a useful description of the population. Alternatively, one may be interested in the actual magnitude of some variable characteristic for each sample member—his age, height or income, for example; then quantification involves *measuring* the magnitude of the characteristic in each case. A useful summary measure to describe the population in terms of a variable is an average of some form, usually the arithmetic mean.[3]

[1] We also confine ourselves for simplicity to 'large' samples—see p. 77 below.
[2] Other terms for the dichotomy are 'qualitative' and 'quantitative' or 'enumeration' and 'measurement' data. Attributes are also, for reasons implied in the following paragraph, called 0–1 variables. The dichotomy is an imprecise simplification of the types of measurement scales—nominal, ordinal, interval and ratio scales—but it will suffice for present purposes.
[3] Throughout this book, the terms 'average' and 'mean' will in fact refer to the arithmetic mean of a number of observations, i.e. $\bar{x} = \frac{1}{n}\sum_{i=1}^{n} x_i$ is the sum of the values of x divided by the number of items. $\sum_{i=1}^{n}$ denotes summation over the n items.

The distinction between attributes and variables is not as fundamental as is sometimes suggested. A variable can always be transformed into an attribute by a broad grouping: the variable 'age',
taking values, say, from 18 upwards, can be turned into an attribute
by dividing into, say, '18 to 45' and '46 and over'. Conversely, any
attribute can be changed into a variable by allocating the score '1' to
all who possess the attribute and '0' to those who do not. Suppose
that 40 out of 100 people have blue eyes; the proportion with this
attribute would then be 0·4. One could treat this as a variable,
scoring 0 for those who do not have blue eyes and 1 for those who
do. The average of this variable for the 100 people is

$$\frac{(60 \times 0) + (40 \times 1)}{100} = 0 \cdot 4.$$

The average of a 0–1 variable is thus the proportion of the population
scored 1. Hence the distinction between an attribute and a variable
is not basic, nor does the *logic* of sampling theory differ in the two
cases. In this chapter the ideas of sampling will be explained mainly
with reference to variables, but this is only a matter of convenience.

One other pair of terms must be explained—'statistic' and 'parameter'. The former refers to a summary value of a variable (or attribute) calculated *from a sample*, the latter to a summary value of the
variable (or attribute) *in the population* that one is trying to estimate.
Thus, if a sample of households is selected in order to estimate average expenditure on rent in a district, the sample average is a 'statistic',
and the (unknown) population average a 'parameter'.

4.2. Estimation and testing of hypotheses

It is helpful to distinguish two objectives of sample surveys:

(*a*) The main purpose is generally to *estimate* certain population
parameters—the average age of students in a college, the proportion
of workers in a factory working overtime, and so on. A sample is
selected, the relevant statistic (average or proportion) is calculated,
and this statistic is used as an estimate of the desired population
parameter. But, anticipating a later point, since all sample results are
subject to sampling errors, it is necessary to accompany this estimate
with a statement about its precision. As we shall see, this statement
is made in terms of what is called a 'standard error'.

(*b*) A second possible purpose may be to *test a statistical hypothesis*
about a population—e.g. the hypothesis that at least 80 per cent of
the households in a town have TV sets. A sample of households is
selected and the proportion possessing sets calculated; it emerges
that 77 per cent have TV sets. The question now is whether the

sample result is such as to discredit the hypothesis or whether it lends support to it. To answer this, one needs a criterion by which the deviation of the sample result from the hypothetical value can be judged; this criterion again is found in the measure of precision mentioned in the previous paragraph.

These two objectives, estimation and testing hypotheses, though they lead to distinct parts of statistical theory, are far from unconnected, and the link that concerns us here is the mechanism by which both are accomplished: the standard error. Since the first purpose—estimation—is far the more common in social surveys, most of the ensuing discussion will be illustrated in terms of it.

But two points of fundamental importance must first be emphasized. For one thing, statements based on sample results are always probability statements. A decision to cover only a sample, rather than every member, of a population means leaving the field of description and certainty and entering that of inference and probability. An extreme illustration will make this point clear. Suppose a survey in a factory employing 3,000 workers is conducted to estimate the proportion of workers who smoke cigarettes. If coverage is complete, i.e. if *every* worker is interviewed, and 1,500 are found to be cigarette smokers, one can state as a fact that the proportion of smokers in the population is 50 per cent. Yet if we interviewed only 2,998 of the workers and found 1,499, that is 50 per cent, to be cigarette smokers, the proportion in the whole population, i.e. in the 3,000 workers, would still be taken as 50 per cent, but this would be an estimate and not a statement of fact. Knowledge regarding some of the population members would be lacking; any conclusion about the population must be given in terms of probability.

Secondly, it must be emphasized that the principles outlined in this chapter rest on the assumption that a random method of selection (or, in American terminology, probability sampling—see Chapter 5) is employed. A random method is one in which each member of the population has a known (and non-zero) chance of being selected into the sample. To a sample selected by non-random methods the theory and its convenient consequences cannot be applied.

4.3. Accuracy, bias and precision

The basic ideas of sampling are best made clear by considering a small model population and confining ourselves to what is called *simple random sampling*—a method of selection whereby each possible sample of n units from a population of N units has an *equal* chance of being selected. Let us assume that the population consists of four members aged 15, 17, 18 and 22 respectively, so that the mean age of the population (μ) is 18.[1] A sample of 2 is to be drawn ($n = 2$) with the object of estimating μ.

Suppose that the draw results in the selection of the members aged 15 and 18. The sample mean (denoted by $\bar{x}$) is therefore 16·5, and this is taken as an estimate of μ, the population mean. Since, in this constructed example, we know that μ is 18, we are in a position to say that the estimate is *inaccurate*.[2] Had the selection fallen upon the two members aged 18 and 22, the estimate of μ would have been 20, which is even less accurate. Had it been the two aged 17 and 18, the estimate would have been 17·5, which is very close. The accuracy of a sample estimate refers to its closeness to the correct population value and since, normally speaking, the latter is not known, the actual accuracy of the sample estimate cannot usually be assessed, though its *probable* accuracy—which we term 'precision'—can be. This is explained below.

Let us now consider *all* the samples of size $n = 2$ that could have been selected from this population. It is assumed that sampling is *without replacement*: having selected the first member, one selects the second sample member from the remaining three (the first member is not 'replaced in' the population and given a chance to be selected a second time). Here are the six possible samples and the estimate of μ derived from each:

Possible samples of $n = 2$ (Ages of members selected)	$\bar{x}$ (i.e. estimate of μ)
15 and 17	16·0
15 and 18	16·5
15 and 22	18·5
17 and 18	17·5
17 and 22	19·5
18 and 22	20·0
Total	108·0

If we imagine this process continued indefinitely, each of the above samples will be drawn over and over again. The distribution formed by the values of $\bar{x}$ derived from this infinite number of samples is called the *sampling distribution of the mean*—a logical enough term since it is a distribution of the means obtained from an infinite number of samples. Now, with simple random sampling, each of the six samples by definition has an equal chance of being selected and,

[1] We are ignoring the possibility that this may in itself not be the 'true' value, since people may give wrong information etc. All that matters here is that it is the value we would get if the survey covered everybody.
[2] The term 'accuracy' is sometimes used to refer to the size of the standard error (see below), but for this the term 'precision' seems preferable and is used here.

therefore, in the long run occurs an equal number of times; the average of the estimates derived from all the possible samples is then $108/6 = 18$, which is equal to the population mean μ.

The average of the estimates of a population parameter derived from an infinite number of samples is called the *expected value of the estimator* (to be denoted by *m*). Notice that here we refer to an *estimator* rather than an *estimate*. For a given sample design, the estimator is the method of estimating the population parameter from the sample data; in this case the estimator is the sample arithmetic mean. An estimate is the value obtained by using the method of estimation for a specific sample. If, for the given sample design, the expected value of the estimator is equal to the population parameter —as in this case—the estimator is called *unbiased*; if not, it is called *biased*.[1] The difference between the expected value and the true population value is termed the bias. An example of a biased estimator would be the case where the larger of the two sample members is used to estimate μ. From the six possible samples, it is seen that the expected value of the larger values is $(17 + 18 + 22 + 18 + 22 + 22)/6 = 119/6 = 19\frac{5}{6}$. Since μ is only 18, this estimator has a bias of $1\frac{5}{6}$. Another example would be the case where the average of the two sample values is the estimator, but where the population member aged 15 can never be found. The possible pairs would then be 17 and 18, 17 and 22, and 18 and 22, giving values of $\bar{x} = 17 \cdot 5$, $19 \cdot 5$ and 20 respectively. The expected value—still assuming simple random sampling—is now 19, which is higher than the true mean; the bias is 1.

It is important to understand that any one sample may give an inaccurate estimate of the population value, even though the estimator is unbiased. Indeed in the first example above every one of the six estimates was inaccurate although the estimator was unbiased: *on average*, the sample estimates equalled the population mean. Conversely, a biased estimator may produce an accurate estimate for an individual sample; this was the case for two of the six samples (the samples 15 and 18, and 17 and 18) when the estimator was the larger sample value. The term bias, in the statistical sense, refers to the long run, not to the correctness of a single sample.

We now pass on to another principle illustrated by the simple model. Although the sampling was random and the sample arithmetic mean was unbiased, the estimates all differed somewhat from each other and from μ. This is not surprising, for as each estimate rests on only a sample of the observations they are almost certain to differ from each other. Now, in practice, the estimate of a population

---

[1] 'Unbiasedness' depends on the method of sampling as well as the method of estimation.

parameter is of course based on only *one* sample and, at first sight, the fact that any two samples are likely to produce different estimates makes this sound an extremely risky procedure. In fact it is not as risky as it might at first seem, since one can estimate *from any one randomly selected sample* (as long as it contains at least two items) how big these differences, or sampling fluctuations as they are called, are likely to be *on average*.

What is needed is a measure of the extent to which the estimates derived from different samples are likely to differ from each other; in other words, a measure of the spread of the sampling distribution. The most usual measure of the spread of any distribution is the standard deviation (or its square, the variance).[1] The standard deviation of the sampling distribution, calculated from the figures on p. 64, is therefore

$$\left\{ \sqrt{\begin{aligned} [(16 - 18)^2 + (16 \cdot 5 - 18)^2 + (18 \cdot 5 - 18)^2 + (17 \cdot 5 - 18)^2 \\ + (19 \cdot 5 - 18)^2 + (20 - 18)^2]/6 \end{aligned}} \right\}$$
$$= \sqrt{2 \cdot 16} = 1 \cdot 47.$$

This important measure is called the *standard error of the mean*, and it is a suitable criterion of the variability of the various sample estimates, that is of the probable accuracy or *precision* of any one estimate. We shall henceforth call it S.E.$(\bar{x})$, and its square, the sampling variance of the mean, Var$(\bar{x})$.[2]

S.E.$(\bar{x})$ can be represented by the following formula, and it can be estimated from a single sample:

$$\text{S.E.}(\bar{x}) = \sqrt{\frac{\sigma^2}{n} \cdot \frac{N - n}{N - 1}}$$

where σ = the standard deviation (of ages, say) in the population[3]
N = the number of units in the population
n = the number of units in the sample.

In fact, it proves more convenient in survey sampling to use a modified definition of the population standard deviation, S, rather

[1] If there are N values x_i—$x_1, x_2 \ldots x_N$—then the standard deviation is defined as

$$\sigma = \sqrt{\frac{\sum\limits_{i=1}^{N} (x_i - \mu)^2}{N}}$$

where μ is the arithmetic mean of the N values.
[2] The terms 'sampling error' and 'standard error' are often used interchangeably. It seems preferable to use the former to describe the *class* of errors caused by sampling, and the latter (or sampling variance, as the case may be) for the actual measures defined above.
[3] In the present constructed example σ happens to be known. Normally it has to be estimated from the sample—see p. 71.

than σ. The modification is trivial providing the population is large, for it consists of replacing the divisor N by $N-1$. Thus the modified standard deviation S is defined as

$$S = \sqrt{\frac{\sum_{i=1}^{N}(x_i - \mu)^2}{N-1}}.$$

With this definition,

$$\text{S.E.}(\bar{x}) = \sqrt{\frac{S^2}{n} \cdot \frac{N-n}{N}} = \sqrt{\frac{S^2}{n}\left(1 - \frac{n}{N}\right)}. \qquad \ldots(4.1)^1$$

If the population is very large relative to the sample, the factor $(1 - n/N)$, which is called the finite population correction (f.p.c.), approximates to unity and can reasonably be omitted. If the entire population is included in the 'sample', the f.p.c. becomes zero and so, logically, does the standard error. Generally speaking, the f.p.c. can be ignored without much loss if the sample does not exceed about 10 per cent of the population.

In the present example it clearly cannot be ignored, and we calculate the standard error from (4.1), with $N=4$, $n=2$ and

$$S^2 = \frac{(15 - 18)^2 + (17 - 18)^2 + (18 - 18)^2 + (22 - 18)^2}{3} = \frac{26}{3}.$$

Therefore

$$\text{S.E.}(\bar{x}) = \sqrt{\frac{(26/3)}{2} \cdot \frac{4-2}{4}} = \sqrt{2 \cdot 16} = 1 \cdot 47$$

which agrees with the previous result.

To summarize the distinction between accuracy, bias, and precision:

(i) The estimate derived from any one sample is *inaccurate* to the extent that it differs from the population parameter. In our notation, $(\bar{x} - \mu)$ measures the accuracy of an estimate of the mean. In practice μ is generally unknown, so that the *actual* deviation of a sample estimate from it cannot be measured. What can be measured is the *probable* magnitude of the deviation—see (iii) below.

(ii) An estimator is *unbiased* (*biased*) if the mean of the estimates derived from all possible samples equals (does not equal) the population parameter. The former is called the expected value of the estimator and is here denoted by m; $(m - \mu)$ is the measure of bias.

(iii) Even if the sample designer uses an unbiased estimator, the individual sample may result in an *inaccurate* estimate and, as noted

---

[1] This is the formula for a simple random sample, and has to be modified for more elaborate sample structures.

above, the actual extent of inaccuracy will almost certainly not be known. This would be rather an unsatisfactory situation were it not for the fact that one can estimate from the sample how *probable* it is that the degree of inaccuracy is of any particular magnitude. This is a much simplified definition of what is meant by the *precision* of an estimator, further discussed below.

Bias and precision thus relate to distinct aspects of a sampling procedure, a point which is well illustrated in diagrammatic form (Fig. 4.1), as adapted from Deming (1950, p. 20).

A Large bias; low precision	Sampling fluctuations ⌒‿‿‿‿⌒ . . .. |←—Bias—→| Pop. value	**NOTE** (1) The dots represent estimates of the population value derived from repeated application of the given survey procedures; i.e. they represent the sampling distribution of the estimates and their mean is the expected value.
B Large bias; higher precision	Sampling fluctuations ⌒‿‿⌒ . . .. |←—Bias—→| Pop. value	(2) The population value is what the survey is trying to estimate.
C No bias; low precision	Sampling fluctuations ⌒‿‿‿‿‿⌒ . . .. | Pop. value	(3) The terms 'large', 'low' etc. used in the panels are, of course, relative.
D No bias; higher precision	Sampling fluctuations ⌒‿‿⌒ . . .. | Pop. value	

FIGURE 4.1

In (A) and (B) there is large bias, the expected value of the estimator differing considerably from the population value: the difference between (A) and (B) is that in the former the estimates vary widely around their mean, as would be reflected in a large standard error, while in (B) they are more closely bunched around it. (C) and (D) are both unbiased, since the expected value is equal to the population value; they differ in that (C) has relatively lower precision. It can be taken that (D), which is unbiased and relatively precise, is the ideal, while (A) is to be avoided. In practice the choice is not as simple as this, and there are circumstances in which a sample designer might be prepared to tolerate some bias if thereby he could markedly increase precision.

The diagram shows that the standard error measures the fluctuations of the estimates around their own mean, that is around the expected value, not around the population value. If the two coincide, as in (C) and (D), it comes to the same thing; but if they do not—if the method is biased (through the selection and estimation procedure) —such bias will *not* be included in the standard error.

There is a measure, called the *mean square error*, which combines sampling variance and bias; in our notation this is

$$\text{MSE} = \text{Var}(\bar{x}) + (\mu - m)^2 \qquad \ldots (4.2)$$

showing that the variability around the population value (i.e. MSE) is equal to that around the expected value—Var $(\bar{x})$—plus the square of the bias. If the bias could be estimated, MSE would be a better measure than the standard error for assessing the efficiency of a sample estimator.

The avoidance of bias in the sampling procedure is discussed later. We must now look more closely at the question of precision. To extend the discussion of sampling distributions and standard errors we abandon the small-scale model and use a more lifelike illustration.

4.4. Sampling distributions and standard errors

Let us suppose that the population to be covered consists of the 3,000 students in a college, and that the purpose of the survey is to estimate their average age (μ). A sample of 150 students is randomly selected and their mean age $(\bar{x}_1)$ calculated. The 150 cases are then 'returned to the population' and a second sample of 150 students is drawn by the same procedure and their mean age $(\bar{x}_2)$ calculated. Both means are estimates of μ. If this process is continued for an infinite number of samples, the distribution of all the estimates is the so-called sampling distribution of the mean, which we have already encountered.

But how does this theoretical concept of the distribution of an infinite number of samples help in assessing the precision of an estimate derived from a single sample, which is all one would have in practice? To answer this, let us assume that 1,000 samples of 150 students each have been taken and a value of $\bar{x}$ was obtained from each; although this is not an infinite number of samples, the distribution for such a large number of samples will closely approximate to the sampling distribution. It might look something like column (a) in Table 4.1, showing that ten samples produced estimates between 18 and 19, ten samples gave estimates between 19 and 20, and so forth. The average of all the estimates is 23·5 which, with simple random sampling, would be very close to μ (not necessarily equal to it since only 1,000 samples were taken, not an infinite number). We see that some of the samples give results far away from this value, others are close to it; some err on the high side, some on the low. Our one real-life sample may be any one of these and we would not know where in the sampling distribution it fell, i.e. how inaccurate its estimate was. But what theoretical knowledge of the sampling distribution does tell us is what deviations from its mean—that is, to all intents and purposes, from the population parameter—are likely in the long run. In other words, it enables us to assess the probability of a deviation of any given size.

TABLE 4.1

Three hypothetical distributions of estimates of the mean age of 3,000 students, obtained from 1,000 random samples of 150 students each

Estimate of mean age	Number of samples		
	(a)	(b)	(c)
18–	10	60	—
19–	10	70	—
20–	30	80	—
21–	100	90	—
22–	190	100	200
23–	290	140	600
24–	240	130	200
25–	70	120	—
26–	50	110	—
27–	10	100	—
Total	1,000	1,000	1,000
Average	23·5	23·5	23·5
Standard Deviation	1·6	2·6	0·6

Column (a) is fairly typical of the sampling distribution of a mean, with a strong peak at the centre and a fair spread on either side. Columns (b) and (c) show other distributions that might have been obtained; in (b) the estimates derived from the samples differ very widely, in (c) they are closely bunched together. It is evident from these that the chance of any one sample estimate being close to μ depends on how widely dispersed all the estimates are, in fact on the spread of the sampling distribution. If this spread is high, as in (b), any one estimate is likely to be a long way out. If, to take the opposite extreme, the estimates are closely bunched around their mean, as in (c), no one estimate is likely to be far from μ.

What is here called the *precision* of a sample estimator thus depends on the spread of the sampling distribution, and this is conveniently measured by its own standard deviation, i.e. by the standard error. If the sample statistic in question is the mean, then the relevant distribution is the 'sampling distribution of the mean', the relevant standard error the 'standard error of the mean'; if it is a proportion, the terms are 'sampling distribution of the proportion' and 'standard error of the proportion'. We will for the moment continue to keep the discussion to the case of the mean.

The formula for the standard error of the mean was given on p. 66; leaving aside the f.p.c., we note that it is based on the two factors on which one would expect the precision of a sample estimator to depend:

(a) the value of n, i.e. *sample size*. Common sense suggests that one will get more precise results from a large than from a small sample; formula (4.1) shows that the standard error varies inversely to the square root of n—that is, to halve the standard error requires (other things being equal) four times as big a sample.

(b) the value of S (or σ), i.e. *variability in the population*. This also accords with common sense. If the 3,000 students are all aged exactly 23, any sample will estimate the population mean with complete precision. The population standard deviation, S or σ, would be zero, and so, from formula (4.1), would the standard error. If, on the other hand, the ages of the 3,000 vary over a wide range, the estimation of the population mean from one sample is much more 'chancy'; this will be reflected in a widely spread sampling distribution (say like (b) in Table 4.1) and therefore a larger standard error.

There remains one difficulty in the use of formula (4.1), that the value of S is rarely known. This problem is overcome by substituting for S the standard deviation of ages calculated from the *sample* (to be called s), and then estimating the standard error from the formula accordingly.[1] One must keep a clear distinction, though, between the true standard error and this, its estimate. We shall distinguish between the two by using capital letters for the former and lower-case letters for the latter; thus the estimators of the

---

[1] If the sample observations are $x_1, x_2 \ldots x_n$, then the estimator $\dfrac{1}{n} \sum\limits_{i=1}^{n} (x_i - \bar{x})^2$ is biased for σ^2 but $s^2 = \dfrac{1}{n-1} \sum\limits_{i=1}^{n} (x_i - \bar{x})^2$ is unbiased for S^2. It was for this reason that formula (4.1) was expressed in terms of S^2 rather than σ^2. If the samples are at all large, there is virtually no difference between dividing by n and $(n-1)$.

standard error and variance of a mean are given by s.e.$(\bar{x})$ and var$(\bar{x})$.

The question now is how estimates of standard errors are to be interpreted. Suppose that we have a sample of 150 students, that their mean age is 21 and that s (calculated as shown in the footnote) is 12; the standard error of the mean is then estimated by

$$\text{s.e.}(\bar{x}) = \sqrt{\frac{144}{150}} = 0.98$$

(ignoring the finite population correction). What does this figure tell us about the precision of the sample estimate? A standard error is the square root of the *average* squared deviations of all possible estimates from their mean; we are interested, as noted above, in the probability of deviations of a particular size occurring or, in other words, in the probability that one sample mean we happen to have obtained falls in any particular range of the sampling distribution. Before the standard error concept can be utilized, therefore, something needs to be said about the shape of sampling distributions and about what are termed confidence (or probability) levels.

The hypothetical distribution of column (a) in Table 4.1 closely approximates to the shape of what is called the *normal distribution* as shown in Fig. 4.2. It is an important fact that, with reasonably large samples, the sampling distributions of many statistics (e.g. the mean, the proportion) approximate to the normal distribution, and that this approximation holds even when the population itself is asymmetrical. That is, even if the ages of the 3,000 students were distributed quite asymmetrically (there being, say, a very large number at the young ages and small numbers at all the higher ages), the distribution of *means* from an infinite number of samples from this population would still be approximately normal in shape. The larger the samples, the closer will this approximation tend to be.

The approximation of many sampling distributions to normality is highly convenient, since the characteristics of the normal distribution are precisely known. It is distributed symmetrically about its mean, with a large number of small deviations from the mean and few large ones. If its standard deviation (let us call it σ') is calculated and perpendicular lines are drawn at a distance of σ' on either side of the mean, then we know that the area enclosed between these lines will comprise approximately 68 per cent of the total area under the curve. Similarly, the area enclosed by lines drawn at a distance of $2\sigma'$ either side of the mean is approximately 95 per cent of the whole, that between the mean and $\pm 2.6\sigma'$ approximately 99 per cent of the whole area. This is illustrated in Fig. 4.2.

What is the relevance of all this in the present context? If a particular sampling distribution is known to be approximately normal in shape, we are able to say that about 68 per cent of the sample estimates of which it is comprised will lie between its mean and one standard error, about 95 per cent between its mean and twice the standard error, and so on. Tables enable us to look up the exact figures for any limits chosen.

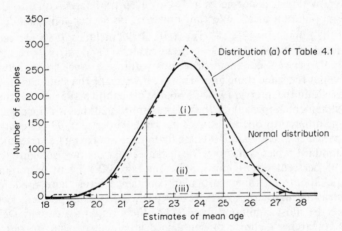

FIGURE 4.2

(i) These vertical lines are drawn at *one* standard deviation either side of the mean and enclose approx. 68 per cent of the area under the curve.
(ii) These vertical lines are drawn at *two* standard deviations either side of the mean and enclose approx. 95 per cent of the area under the curve.
(iii) These vertical lines are drawn at 2.6 standard deviations either side of the mean and enclose approx. 99 per cent of the area under the curve.

In practice, this knowledge is utilized by putting our statement about population estimates in the following form: given that the sample mean, $\bar{x}$, is an unbiased estimator of the population mean, μ, one can be '68 per cent confident' that the range

$$\bar{x} \pm \text{Standard Error of the Mean}$$

i.e.
$$\bar{x} \pm \frac{S}{\sqrt{n}} \qquad \qquad ...(4.3)$$

includes the population mean. Similarly, one's confidence would be approximately 95 per cent that the range

$$\bar{x} \pm 2\left(\frac{S}{\sqrt{n}}\right) \qquad \qquad ...(4.4)$$

includes μ, and approximately 99 per cent that

$$\bar{x} \pm 2\cdot6 \left(\frac{S}{\sqrt{n}} \right) \qquad \ldots(4.5)$$

includes μ. The ranges defined by (4.3), (4.4) and (4.5) are called *confidence intervals*. If $\bar{x} = 21$, $n = 150$, $s = 12$, we would draw the following conclusion:[1] the sample mean—an unbiased estimator of the population mean—is here 21. Since it is based on only a sample, we know that it is not necessarily—or even probably—equal to the true population mean. We can, however, be 68 per cent confident that the range $21 \pm 12/\sqrt{150}$, i.e. 20·02–21·98 includes μ; 95 per cent confident that the range 19·04–22·96 covers μ; and virtually certain —i.e. 99 per cent confident—that μ is within the range 18·05–23·95. Or to put the same thing another way: if we make the statement that μ lies within the interval 19·04–22·96, the probability is 95 per cent that the statement is correct, i.e. the chances are 1 in 20 that it is incorrect.

The different probabilities—68 per cent, 95 per cent, 99 per cent— are called *confidence levels*. (These figures are approximate; reference to standard tables will show, for instance, that the precise figure for the 95 per cent level is not 2 S.E., but 1·96 S.E.) There is nothing magic about the three particular confidence levels here used for illustration, and although these—in particular the 95 per cent level —are the most commonly used, any others might do equally well. The researcher's choice of confidence level will depend, to put it simply, on what is more important to him: a narrow range of error or a high probability of being correct.

If he wants to be able to say with high confidence that the range given does include the population mean, he will go for the 99 per cent rather than the 95 per cent level, since the former corresponds to greater confidence. The price he pays is that the range—i.e. the limits either side of the estimate—is relatively wide. If he wishes to have a narrow error band around his estimate, his confidence in stating that the band includes the population mean must be correspondingly lower. It is only reasonable that, in drawing inferences from sample to population, one should have to compromise between setting very narrow error margins around the estimate and having very high confidence that the margins will include the population parameter; one cannot expect to have it both ways.

4.5. Significance tests

Earlier in this chapter a distinction was drawn between two purposes of surveys, estimation and the testing of hypotheses, but so

---

[1] Here s is used in place of S; see p. 71. In making these calculations no account has been taken of the finite population correction.

far the treatment has been entirely in terms of the former. This is not unreasonable, since surveys are mostly concerned with estimation, but something must now be said about the reasoning involved in testing hypotheses. To illustrate this, we will take what is a typical application of hypothesis testing in surveys: the comparison of two (or more) population groups.

Two independent simple random samples of 400 individuals each are taken in towns A and B, and of these 45 per cent (180 individuals) and 52 per cent (208 individuals) respectively say they are pro-Labour politically. We may express this by saying that $p_A = 0.45$ and $p_B = 0.52$, p standing for the proportion with the given attribute. The layman might conclude at once that town B has a higher pro-Labour proportion than town A. In fact this does not necessarily follow, since both proportions are sample results and therefore subject to sampling error; the difference of 7 per cent may be no more than would be expected as a result of sampling fluctuations and, if this were so, one would call the difference 'not statistically significant'.

The test procedure is broadly as follows. We set up the so-called 'null hypothesis' that there is *no* difference between π_A and π_B, where π stands for the proportion with the attribute in the respective *populations*. The standard error of the difference between the sample proportions is then estimated (under the assumption that the null hypothesis is true) and the observed difference is compared with it. If this difference exceeds 2.6 times its standard error we conclude that the probability of a difference as large as or larger than this occurring is only about 1 per cent (for reasons analogous to those explained on pp. 72–4), so that either something very unusual has happened or the original hypothesis must be regarded as discredited. With a difference as large as this, one would probably prefer the second alternative. If the difference were, say, twice the standard error, the situation would be less clear-cut, since a difference of this size or larger would occur by chance about five times out of a hundred if the null hypothesis were true, and is therefore not so unusual an event. Whether it is unusual enough for the researcher to reject the null hypothesis is for him to decide; we shall return to this point.

To continue the above example, it can be shown that, under the assumption that the null hypothesis is true, the standard error for the difference between the two sample proportions is estimated by

$$\text{s.e.}(p_A - p_B) = \sqrt{p(1-p)\left(\frac{1}{n_A} + \frac{1}{n_B}\right)}$$

where p is a pooled estimate from the two samples of the assumed common population proportion, π.

$$p = \frac{r_A + r_B}{n_A + n_B}$$

where r_A and r_B are the numbers of individuals in each of the samples who are pro-Labour.

Here $p = \dfrac{180 + 208}{400 + 400} = 0.485$ and both n_A and n_B (the sample sizes) are 400. The standard error is estimated to be 0.035 and the observed difference of 0.07 has to be set against it. As it is twice its standard error, we would regard it as significant at the 5 per cent, but not at the 1 per cent, level.

The general topic of significance tests is beyond our scope here (see Chapter 17 for some remarks on uses and interpretation) but one other point must at least be mentioned. In drawing conclusions from a significance test, the researcher runs two risks: (1) of rejecting the null hypothesis when it is in fact true; and (2) of failing to reject the null hypothesis when it is in fact false.

In the above example, we are testing the null hypothesis that $\pi_A = \pi_B$ against an alternative hypothesis which is that π_A is not equal to π_B.[1] The first type of risk is measured by the significance level. Suppose that the null hypothesis is in fact true and that we are testing at the 5 per cent significance level; this means that five out of every hundred times we would expect to get, purely through sampling fluctuations, a difference between p_A and p_B big enough to lead us to reject the null hypothesis; in these cases we should draw the wrong conclusion. Why then does one not simply use more stringent significance levels—say the 1 per cent or even the 0.1 per cent level— so as to decrease the risk of this kind of error? The answer is that, by so doing, one would increase the risk of the second kind of error, of failing to reject the null hypothesis when it is *not* true. The statistician tries to balance the two types of error in accordance with his particular problem and with the risk attending each kind of wrong decision.[2]

4.6. Summary of simplifications

In order to introduce the ideas of sampling with a minimum of complication, a number of simplifications have been made in this chapter:

[1] A different alternative hypothesis, leading to a different procedure, would be that $\pi_A < \pi_B$.
[2] See the statistical texts recommended at the end of this chapter for full accounts of this subject.

(a) *Different statistics.* With the exception of the last section, only one type of statistical measure—the mean—has been used in the presentation. It should be understood that similar reasoning applies with other statistics. Particularly common is the estimation of a population proportion π (or a percentage), and here the standard error based on a simple random sample of size n (and ignoring the f.p.c.) is $\sqrt{\dfrac{\pi(1-\pi)}{n}}$. This can be estimated from $\sqrt{\dfrac{p(1-p)}{n}}$, where p is the proportion with the attribute in the sample.[1] Suppose that one wished to estimate what proportion of the 9,000 families in a district had motor cars and that, in a simple random sample of 400, it was found that 40 had them. Hence $p = 0.1$, $n = 400$ and

$$\text{s.e.}(p) = \sqrt{\frac{0.1 \times 0.9}{400}} = 0.015.$$

One would say that one's confidence was about 95 per cent that the range 10 per cent $\pm$ 3 per cent included π, the population percentage; or, translated into absolute numbers, that between 630 and 1,170 of the families had cars.

(b) *Sampling distributions.* We have dealt with the subject of sampling distributions very briefly. For some statistics they are known and defined exactly, for others they have been deduced only in approximate form. Furthermore, the above treatment has assumed that the sampling distribution approximates to the normal distribution. While this is often true, it is not necessarily so, and the closeness of the approximation will depend on the statistic in question, the size of the sample and the nature of the population. If the statistic is the mean, a sample of size 50 or so is generally enough—for most populations—to ensure an approximately normal sampling distribution. For estimating variances, the sample size would have to be greater to ensure such a distribution; for correlation coefficients greater still. In short, 'normality' of the sampling distribution cannot be taken for granted, although for the situations most commonly encountered in social surveys this complication need not cause much worry.[2]

---

[1] The unbiased estimator of $\text{Var}(p) = \dfrac{\pi(1-\pi)}{n}$ is in fact $\dfrac{p(1-p)}{n-1}$. For reasonably large n it matters little whether n or $(n-1)$ is used. We have therefore given in the text the better-known formula.

[2] However, to the extent that the surveyor wants to make estimates for sub-groups of the population (say, men of a particular age/social class group) rather than the population as a whole, the problem may be important. In this case the sample numbers in the relevant cells may be small enough to cast doubt on the normality assumption. See the technical literature for a discussion of alternative courses in such a situation.

(c) *Estimating procedures.* Nothing has been said about different ways of estimating a population parameter from the sample data. A mean or proportion calculated from a simple random sample is an unbiased estimator of the corresponding population parameter, but the situation is not necessarily as straightforward as this with more complex designs. The choice of estimating procedure has an important bearing on the efficiency of a sample, but the subject is beyond the scope of this book (see references at the end of the chapter).

(d) *More intricate designs.* It has been convenient to explain the theoretical background with reference to simple random sampling, and all the formulae have been based on this. In practice, as the next chapter will show, more complex designs (always incorporating an element of randomness) are usually to be preferred; and for these different and more elaborate formulae apply.

NOTES ON READING

1. Most textbooks on statistics carry chapters on sampling theory. Readers will find suitable introductions in BROOKES and DICK (1969), HILL (1966), BLALOCK (1960), McCARTHY (1957), YULE and KENDALL (1950), TIPPETT (1952) and WALLIS and ROBERTS (1956). KALTON (1966) discusses at an elementary level the ideas of statistical inference; STUART (1962) uses a simple model to discuss the principles of statistical inference and goes on to consider more complex sample designs.

2. Readers with a fair knowledge of statistics who want to study the theory of sample surveys more thoroughly are recommended to use KISH (1965a), COCHRAN (1963), YATES (1960) and HANSEN, HURWITZ and MADOW (1953). At a somewhat less advanced level, the books of SAMPFORD (1962) and YAMANE (1967) are recommended.

3. Good accounts of the basic ideas of survey sampling are the first three chapters of HANSEN, HURWITZ and MADOW (1953), the chapter by KISH in FESTINGER and KATZ (1953), Chapter 10 in McCARTHY (1957), the last chapter in SNEDECOR and COCHRAN (1967), and STUART (1962). Another good treatment is the paper by COCHRAN, MOSTELLER and TUKEY (1954), which is part of the methodological review of the Kinsey report.

CHAPTER 5

Types of Sample Design

5.1. Introduction

TWO MAJOR principles underlie all sample design. The first is the desire to avoid bias in the selection procedure, the second broadly to achieve the maximum precision for a given outlay of resources. Bias in the selection[1] can arise:

 (i) if the sampling is done by a non-random method, which generally means that the selection is consciously or unconsciously influenced by human choice;

 (ii) if the sampling frame (list, index or other population record) which serves as the basis for selection does not cover the population adequately, completely or accurately;

(iii) if some sections of the population are impossible to find or refuse to co-operate.

Any of these factors will cause systematic, non-compensating errors which are not eliminated or reduced by an increase in sample size. If the sample is taken from an inadequate list, no increase in size will correct its unrepresentativeness or eliminate the bias in the characteristics of an infinite number of samples so selected. An example is the famous 1936 *Literary Digest* débâcle. The *Digest* took a mammoth sample of 10,000,000 individuals, yet its forecast of the U.S. Presidential Election went disastrously astray because (*a*) the sample was picked from telephone directories and the like which did not adequately cover the poorer section of the electorate; and (*b*) only 20 per cent of the (mail) ballots were returned, and these probably came predominantly from the more educated sections of the population.

Bias arising from unsatisfactory frames or from non-response is

---

[1] Bias can enter through sources other than the sample selection—faulty measurement, interviewing, question wording and, as noted in the previous chapter, through the estimation procedure. Here we are concerned only with selection bias.

discussed in Chapter 7, but it is worth noting here that neither is peculiar to sampling. A 100 per cent coverage of a list covering only part of the intended population would equally be biased, and so would the 'complete' enumeration of a population in which some of the members either could not be found or refused to co-operate. Our concern in this chapter and the next one is with bias arising through the sampling method: there is only one sure way of avoiding this, namely to use a random method. Randomness lies at the base of all sound sample designs; these designs differ chiefly in the refinements introduced to minimize sampling errors for a given expenditure or, conversely, to achieve a certain precision at minimum cost. We begin, therefore, with a discussion of simple random sampling, and go on to designs which, while retaining the essential element of randomness, manage to increase precision by various restrictions and refinements. In this chapter we will take up the central techniques of sample design, namely stratification, multi-stage sampling and sampling with probability proportional to size, and Chapter 6 will discuss a variety of other techniques.

5.2. Random sampling

A *random* method of selection is one which gives each of the N units in the population to be covered a calculable (and non-zero) probability of being selected. In the American literature the term *probability sampling* is used in place of random sampling, and this has much to commend it; samples selected by methods which do not embody the feature of randomness—such as quota and purposive samples (both discussed in Chapter 6)—are called judgement samples.

The use of the term 'random' has given rise to a certain amount of confusion in the literature, due to a looseness in distinguishing between random sampling and *unrestricted random sampling*. The latter means that each possible sample of n units from a population of N units has an equal chance of being selected, which in turn implies that every member of the population has an equal chance of selection into the sample. Moreover, unrestricted random sampling is conducted 'with replacement', that is the unit selected at each draw is replaced into the population before the next draw is made; thus a unit can appear more than once in the sample.[1] Most statistical theory relates to unrestricted random sampling.

[1] There appears to be no standard terminology to distinguish between this type of sampling with and without replacement. We follow Kish (1965a) and use 'unrestricted random sampling' for the former and 'simple random sampling' for the latter. Among other approaches are those of Cochran (1963), who also uses 'simple random sampling' for sampling without replacement but suggests that 'unrestricted sampling' is just an alternative phrase for 'simple random sampling'; and of Yule and Kendall (1950), who use 'simple sampling' to mean sampling with replacement.

If unrestricted random sampling is modified to sampling without replacement, so that no unit can appear more than once in the sample, the procedure is called *simple random sampling*. With simple random sampling each possible sample of n *different* units has an equal chance of being selected, which also implies that every member of the population has an equal chance of selection into the sample.[1] Simple random sampling is preferred to unrestricted random sampling because it produces more precise estimators. The standard error of a mean for unrestricted sampling is like that for simple random sampling (equation (4.1)), except that the finite population correction is left out. As the f.p.c. is a multiplying factor which is less than one, the standard error of a simple random sample is less than that of an unrestricted sample. However, if the sampling fraction n/N is small, the difference between the two standard errors will be slight.

Both unrestricted and simple random sampling give an equal probability of selection to each member of the population, but this property is not restricted to these designs. Equal probability selection methods are widely used and Hansen, Hurwitz and Madow (1953) have coined the abbreviation *epsem* to describe them. In general, however, random samples are not necessarily *epsem* samples: all that is needed for random sampling is that the chance of selection for each member of the population is calculable and non-zero.

If the N members of the population are numbered and n of them are picked out by random numbers without replacement (see below), this will be a simple random sample; if N numbered discs are placed in a hat, mixed well, and n of them are picked out at random, this will again be a simple random sample; if a list of the N population members is arranged in a *random* order, and every $\frac{N}{n}$-th name is then picked out, this will also be a simple random sample. But in practice one often proceeds differently. One may, for instance, choose to divide the population into a number of strata (say age groups) and select a random sample from each stratum. The sample as a whole is not then a simple random one. Since some sample members must be selected from each stratum (this being the point of the stratification) a sample consisting entirely of members of one stratum could not be chosen; which illustrates that all the theoretically possible samples of n would *not* have the same chance of selection. This is a form of restricted random sampling; but the vital point is that the method of selection within each stratum is still random.

---

[1] This is evident from the list of possible samples on p. 64. The member aged 15 is picked for three of the six possible samples, so is the member aged 17 and so is each of the other two. Each population member has an equal chance $(3/6 = 1/2)$ of selection, and that chance is simply $n/N = 2/4 = 1/2$.

The importance of randomness in the selection procedure cannot be overemphasized. It is an essential part of the protection against selection bias, and the whole theoretical framework described in the last chapter rests on it. If it is not possible to assign to each population unit a calculable probability of selection, then the theory is not applicable and standard errors cannot be calculated; in other words the precision of a sample estimate cannot properly be assessed.

The layman tends to think of 'random' as being equivalent to 'haphazard' and to believe that, as long as the investigator does not exercise conscious selection and avoids obvious dangers, randomness is ensured. This is far from correct. It has been repeatedly shown that the human investigator is not a satisfactory instrument for making random selections, that he tends, however unconsciously, to 'favour' some of the population units in his selection. In the field of social surveys it is easy to see how bias can arise. Interviewers told to select a random sample of people in the street may tend to pick people of their own social type or may unconsciously go for 'average' people, thus getting a sample with too little variation in it. If instructed to select a sample of housewives at home, they may avoid the dirtier-looking houses and top-floor dwellers. One could not legitimately assign probabilities of inclusion to the people in the street or to the houses, nor assume that these probabilities were equal.

To ensure true randomness the method of selection must be independent of human judgement. There are two basic procedures:

(i) The 'lottery method'. Each member of the population is represented by a disc, the discs are placed in an urn and well mixed, and a sample of the required size is selected.

(ii) The use of random numbers (see the tables by Kendall and Smith, 1939, Fisher and Yates, 1963, and Tippett, 1927). The members of the population are numbered from 1 to N and n numbers are selected from one of the tables in any convenient and systematic way. These become the sample.

In theory both procedures are independent of human judgement and ensure randomness. However, the randomness of the lottery method depends on the assumption that the discs are well mixed so that the population can be regarded as arranged randomly. In practice, as it is difficult to achieve a satisfactory mixing of the discs, the use of random numbers generated by a random procedure is preferred (see Section 7.2).

The practicability of either procedure depends in the first instance on the size of the population. Let us suppose that a sample of 250 workers is to be selected from a factory with a labour force of 5,000, and that there is an adequate list of the workers. The workers on the list could be numbered and then random numbers could be used to make the selection, but this would be laborious. An alternative is simply to calculate the desired sampling fraction (let $k = N/n$) and select every kth worker throughout the list, starting with a randomly chosen number between 1 and k inclusive. Here $k = 5000/250 = 20$ A number between 1 and 20 is selected at random and this determines the first sample member. If this number is 6, the sample is composed of the numbers 6, 26, 46. . . . The procedure is easy and convenient. The question is, is it equivalent to simple random sampling?

Strictly speaking the answer is 'No', unless the list itself is in a random order. But no ordinary list is. Whether it is in alphabetical order or seniority order or, as is often the case with lists of the general population, in street and house number order, there is invariably some systematic arrangement. This method of selection is therefore not simple random sampling, nor does the choosing of a random starting point—although important—make it so. In general this type of sampling is called *systematic sampling*, and it differs from simple random sampling in that it does not give all possible samples of size n from the population of size N an equal chance of selection. Once the sampling fraction is determined, the random selection of the starting point determines the whole sample, i.e. if number 6 is chosen, numbers 26, 46 . . . automatically follow. There are 20 such samples that could be chosen, not the vast number that could result from the simple random method. In systematic sampling, the selection of one sample member is dependent on the selection of a previous one, while with simple random sampling from a large population the selections are virtually independent of each other.

When the list from which a systematic sample is selected can be regarded as arranged *more or less at random* or when the feature by which it is arranged is not related to the subject of the survey, the method of selection is sometimes called *quasi-random* sampling. In these cases, selecting at regular intervals from a list can be treated as approximately equivalent to simple random sampling.

Systematic sampling produces a more even spread of the sample over the population list than does simple random sampling. Usually this will lead to greater precision for the systematic sample, except when the list is randomly ordered, in which case systematic and simple random sampling have the same precision, and when the list has a periodic arrangement, in which case the systematic sample can fare badly. If the sampling interval coincides with the periodic interval of the list, or a multiple of it, a systematic sample will produce poor results.[1] But such periodicities in a list are rare and are usually easy to detect. As a result systematic sampling is widely used.

It will have been noted that the definition of randomness relates to the mode of selection, not to the resultant sample. A randomly chosen sample may look most 'unrandom' and in fact be unrepresentative (leading to inaccurate estimates). Our sample of 250 workers may by chance contain no women, even though the factory's labour force contains a fair proportion of women. So, if the survey is concerned with opinions on equal pay for men and women, this sample would hardly reflect the true state of opinion in the factory. All one can say is that 'an extraordinarily unlikely event has occurred', this sample being close to one of the tails of the sampling distribution. The surveyor has been 'unlucky', but the fact remains that if he went on taking a large number of such samples in precisely this way, then *on average* the estimates of opinion derived from them all would correspond to the true opinion in the factory.

In such a situation, there is often a temptation to reject the sample and start afresh. In a survey some years ago, the selection of towns was carried out by picking names out of a hat, and the play of chance served up a sample composed predominantly of seaside towns. For the subject under study this seemed disastrous, and it was no consolation to the surveyor to know that, if he went on selecting an infinite number of samples by this method, his results would be right on average. One could sympathize with his desire to start again, while pointing out its unsoundness and emphasizing that the chance of his getting such an extreme sample would be reflected in the confidence limits he would attach to his estimates. To reject the sample is clearly unsound because it introduces an element of judgement into the selection, and because it deprives this sample of its due probability of being selected. The proper solution to this problem— stratification—is introduced in the next section.

But it must be understood that the unrepresentativeness of a single sample does not throw doubt on the randomness of the sampling method. If the surveyor took another sample and again found far too many seaside towns in it, he would begin to have grounds for suspicion. The randomness of the process can be gauged by

---

[1] As an extreme example consider a list of married couples, listed in pairs with the husband first. A systematic sample with an even number interval (1 in 2, 1 in 4, etc.) will lead to a sample which comprises either all men or all women, where the sampling interval is a multiple of the periodic interval, the percentage of men in the sample will be either 0 or 100, depending on whether the random number chosen was odd or even. On the other hand, an odd number interval (1 in 3, 1 in 5, etc.) will lead to almost exactly 50 per cent of men and 50 per cent of women in the sample.

studying the results of repeated samples, not by the appearance of a single one.

5.3. Stratification

It is clear from the formulae of standard errors given in Chapter 4 that one way of increasing the precision of a simple random sample is to increase its size. This is not, however, the only way, and we now turn to a method for increasing precision—stratification—which is used in virtually all sample designs. One use of stratification is as a means of using knowledge of the population to increase the precision of the sample. Thus, in the example just mentioned, if the surveyor had wished to *ensure* that different types of town were adequately represented in the sample, he could have stratified by town type. Town type is then called a stratification factor.

Stratification does not imply any departure from the principle of randomness. All it means is that, before any selection takes place, the population is divided into a number of strata; *then* a random sample is selected within each stratum. If the sampling fraction is the same for every stratum, this procedure is almost certain to be an improvement on a simple random sample because it makes sure that the different strata in the population (sexes, age groups, regions, town types and the like) are correctly represented in the sample. This reduction of the play of chance is reflected in a reduction of the standard error—which, after all, is simply a measure of the influence of chance on sample composition. Thus stratified random sampling with a uniform sampling fraction tends to have somewhat greater precision than simple random sampling, and it is also generally convenient for practical reasons. But it is of course vital that the selection within strata is made randomly.[1]

Stratified sampling does not require that the sampling fraction is the same within each stratum, but this in fact is a common design. If there is such a *uniform sampling fraction*, the design is known as a *proportionate stratified sample*; the sample size from a stratum is proportional to the population size of the stratum, that is the total sample size is allocated between the strata by proportionate allocation. If there are variable sampling fractions, the sample is a *disproportionate stratified sample*. We will discuss proportionate stratified sampling first.

[1] On no account should stratified random sampling be confused with purposive sampling—in which the selection is made by human choice; one might pick a couple of seaside towns, a light-industry town etc. Such a method suffers from all the defects of leaving the selection to human judgement, and sampling theory cannot be applied to it. In stratified random sampling, although the stratification factors and the actual strata are fixed purposively, the selection of units is made at random; this makes all the difference.

The gains due to proportionate stratified sampling

Let us take as an example a college population of 3,000 students and suppose that, in order to study their views on the subject of degree reform, a random sample of 300 students is to be interviewed. A simple random sample would provide unbiased estimates of measurable precision, but it could almost certainly be bettered. A student's views on degree reform are probably related more to his special subject of study than to any other factor; common sense suggests—and theory confirms—that simple random sampling can be improved upon by ensuring that the special subject groups are correctly represented in the sample.

Suppose that the 3,000 students are distributed as in Table 5.1.

TABLE 5.1

Distribution of the 3,000 students by special subject

Economics	950
Sociology	430
Statistics	250
Political Science	390
Law	320
History	660
	——
Total	3,000

The chances are that a simple random sample would produce a proportionate distribution of the 300 students something like this, but it would not be exactly the same. Stratifying by special subject and using a proportionate allocation ensures that it is so (ignoring the influence of non-response) and will tend to increase the precision of the results. Within each of the six strata the students are selected at random; if a list of them arranged by strata is available and a uniform sampling fraction is decided on, one can simply take a systematic sample of every tenth name, starting with a random number between 1 and 10. If there is no such list but there is one (ordered in some other way) on which the stratum to which each unit belongs can be identified, one could select names at random, allotting them to their strata and continuing until all the strata are filled. Once the required number for a stratum is attained, further names selected for it are rejected.

The reason why proportionate stratification nearly always results in some gain in precision can be explained as follows. The total variation (for any particular variable or attribute) in a population may be regarded as composed of two elements: variation between strata and variation within strata. Thus, amongst the 3,000 students, those specializing in one subject will have different views from those specializing in another; and there will also be variation of opinion *within* each special group. In stratified random sampling, variation *between* strata does not enter into the standard error at all, because one ensures that this component of variation in the population is exactly reflected in the sample. There is no chance about it. Sampling, and therefore the play of chance, only takes place within strata. Consequently, since only the variation within strata enters into the standard error, the greater the proportion of the total variation in a population that is accounted for by the between-strata variation, the greater will be the gain due to stratification. The object therefore is so to arrange the strata that they differ as widely as possible from each other, and that the population within each stratum is as homogeneous as it can be. A little thought will show that this is achieved by selecting stratification factors closely related to the subject of the survey (see pp. 90–1).

In the previous chapter it was stated that the standard error of a proportion (p) based upon a simple random sample of size n is estimated by

$$\text{s.e.}(p_{\text{srs}}) = \sqrt{\frac{p(1-p)}{n}} . \qquad \ldots(5.1)[1]$$

It can be shown that the standard error of a proportion in a proportionate stratified sample is estimated by

$$\text{s.e.}(p_{\text{prop}}) = \sqrt{\frac{\sum n_i p_i(1-p_i)}{n^2}} \qquad \ldots(5.2)[2]$$

where $\sum$ = summation over all the strata
   n_i = sample number in the ith stratum
   p_i = proportion of the sample in the ith stratum possessing the attribute (in this case, proportion favouring degree reform)
   n = total sample size.

[1] For simplicity, the finite population correction will be ignored throughout this section.
[2] Strictly the formula should be written as

$$\text{s.e.}(p_{\text{prop}}) = \sqrt{\frac{1}{n^2} \sum \frac{n_i^2}{n_i-1} p_i(1-p_i)}$$

but, providing the n_i are fairly large, the simpler formula in the text is a close approximation to this. The general formula for the estimated standard error of a proportion in a stratified sample is

$$\text{s.e.}(p_{\text{st}}) = \sqrt{\frac{1}{N^2} \sum \frac{N_i^2 p_i(1-p_i)}{n_i-1}}$$

where N_i is the population number in the ith stratum and N is the total number in the population. In the case of a proportionate sample this formula simplifies to the one above.

D2

88   SURVEY METHODS IN SOCIAL INVESTIGATION

The calculations for the above example are shown in Table 5.2, the numbers in column (1) representing the sample distribution that would be obtained from taking the same proportion (1 in 10) in each stratum,[1] while those in column (2) are the (hypothetical) numbers of the sample favouring degree reform. Column (3) gives the proportions favouring degree reform, calculated by $p_i = r_i/n_i$.

TABLE 5.2

Estimation of standard error of a proportion for a proportionate stratified sample
(*Data of Table* 5.1)

Special subject	(1) n_i	(2) r_i	(3) p_i	(4) $n_i p_i (1-p_i)$
Economics	95	86	0·905	8·170
Sociology	43	22	0·512	10·736
Statistics	25	18	0·720	5·040
Political Science	39	31	0·795	6·355
Law	32	20	0·625	7·500
History	66	33	0·500	16·500
Total	300	210		54·301

(A) *To provide an estimate of the population proportion*

To estimate the proportion in the whole college who are in favour of the degree reform (π), the proportions for each stratum are worked out and then combined into a weighted average. Since in this case sampling fractions are uniform, sample numbers can be taken in place of population numbers as the weights so that p, the estimate of π, is given by $\sum n_i p_i/n$. Since $r_i = n_i p_i$, p is simply calculated as

$$p = \frac{\Sigma r_i}{n} = \frac{210}{300} = 0.700 = 70.0 \text{ per cent.}$$

Thus, with a proportionate stratified sample, the estimate of π is just the straightforward unweighted sample estimate: there is no need to calculate the various strata proportions p_i and take a weighted

[1] The application of the uniform sampling fraction to the strata populations may not give whole numbers. If it had been 1 in 15, for instance, the sample in the Economics group would have been 63.3. A convenient solution is simply to take the nearest whole number. The sampling fractions can still to all intents and purposes be regarded as uniform.

average of them. This is a considerable advantage of the proportionate allocation over the disproportionate.

(B) *Estimate of* S.E. *for a simple random sample*
   With $p = 0.700$ and $n = 300$ we have

$$s.e.(p_{srs}) = \sqrt{\frac{0.700 \times 0.300}{300}} = 0.0265.$$

(C) *Estimate of* S.E. *for a proportionate stratified random sample*
   The computation of $\Sigma n_i p_i (1 - p_i)$ is shown in column (4). With $n = 300$ we have according to formula (5.2)

$$s.e.(p_{prop}) = \sqrt{\frac{54.301}{300^2}} = 0.0246.$$

Comparison of the standard errors in (B) and (C) shows the gain of proportionate stratification. Simple random sampling acts generally as a useful basis of comparison for all varieties of random sampling, and the ratio of the variance (i.e. the square of the S.E.) of an estimator for a particular design to the variance of the estimator for a simple random sample of the same size is known as the *design effect* (Kish, 1965a), which is abbreviated to *Deff*. Here Deff is estimated by[1]

$$deff = \frac{(0.0246)^2}{(0.0265)^2} = 0.862.$$

The variance of the proportionate stratified sample is thus 14 per cent smaller than that of the same-sized simple random sample. Alternatively expressed, it means that a simple random sample of size $n = 348$ (i.e. 300/0.862) is needed to give the same precision as this proportionate stratified sample of size $n = 300$.

This illustration has been in terms of an attribute, but analogous formulae exist for variables. Suppose, for instance, that the purpose of the survey—as in the example of Chapter 4—is to estimate the mean (age) of a population. The standard error of the sample mean based on a proportionate stratified random sample of size n (ignoring the f.p.c.) is

$$S.E.(\bar{x}_{prop}) = \sqrt{\frac{\sum n_i S_i^2}{n^2}} \qquad ...(5.3)$$

---

[1] The population value of the design effect is denoted by 'Deff' and the sample estimate of it by 'deff'.

where S_i = standard deviation of the variable in question for the population in the ith stratum.
$\sum$, n_i and n as for (5.2).

To estimate (5.3), s_i, the strata standard deviations in the sample, are used in place of the S_i; the calculations will be illustrated in another context on p. 96. It is in any case clear from formulae (5.2) and (5.3) that the computation of standard errors for stratified random samples essentially means working out a standard error separately for each stratum and then combining the results into a weighted sum for the whole sample (equally, for population means and proportions, one first makes estimates for each stratum and then combines them to give an overall estimate: in the case of a proportionate stratified sample, however, this general procedure reduces to forming the straightforward sample mean or proportion, so that the calculations are very simple).

We must not give the impression that gain in precision is the only, or even the most important, reason for stratification. In the first place, the surveyor may be as interested in the results for separate strata as in those for the population as a whole. Figures for areas, town size groups, age groups and so on are likely to be of paramount importance, and stratification—if necessary, with variable sampling fractions (see below)—ensures that these sub-groups are represented in adequate numbers for the analysis. Secondly, it often helps administratively to divide the population into strata; it is convenient, for instance, to divide a national sample geographically, each area being allocated to a separate supervisor and so forth. Thirdly, many sampling frames are divided into broad groups or areas, which it is then convenient to use as strata. Fourthly, different parts of the population may call for different sampling procedures: this can be achieved by placing the different parts in separate strata. For example, a different procedure may be used to sample persons in sparsely populated rural areas from that used for the more densely populated urban areas.

The choice of stratification factors

There is no gain in precision from stratifying by a factor unrelated to the subject of the survey, for the characteristics of the different strata would not differ from each other and nothing would be gained by excluding from the sampling error the between-strata variation. Ignoring the f.p.c., the gain of a proportionate stratified sample over a simple random sample is approximately

$$\text{Var}(\bar{x}_{\text{srs}}) - \text{Var}(\bar{x}_{\text{prop}}) \doteqdot \frac{\sum n_i(\mu_i - \mu)^2}{n^2}$$

where μ_i is the population mean for the ith stratum and μ is the overall population mean.[1] This expression shows that if the strata all have the same mean, $\mu_i = \mu$, the numerator becomes zero, and there is no gain from stratification. The greater the differences between the μ_i's, the greater the gain. Note that the expression on the right-hand side cannot be negative, so that a proportionate stratified sample can never be less precise than a simple random sample. (The formula is an approximation, and the exact formula shows that it is theoretically possible for the simple random sample to be more precise by a trivial amount, but in practice this is extremely unlikely to occur.)

Thus, ideally one wishes to stratify a sample by the factors believed to be most closely related to the subject of the survey; but there are limitations on the extent to which one can put this ideal into practice. It is, for instance, only possible to stratify by a factor for which the population distribution is known and which is individually identifiable for every population member. (For a discussion of stratification *after* selection, see below.) In the above example, stratification by special subject is possible only if it is known how the 3,000 students are distributed over the special subjects *and* to which group each student belongs. That this is an important limitation in practice is made clear if one thinks of trying to stratify a sample of individuals within a town by sex and age. The distributions of these factors in the population are almost certainly known and the only difficulty is to identify the sex and age of each individual at the time the sample is drawn. If the electoral register is used as the frame, sex can usually be inferred from Christian names, so this stratification presents little problem. But age is not given on this register, so one could not incorporate an age stratification into the design.

There is also the limitation that at least one unit must be selected from every stratum, so that there cannot be more strata than the number of units in the sample. This limitation is necessary in order to obtain a valid estimator of a population mean or proportion, but if the surveyor also wants to obtain a true estimate of the precision (i.e. the S.E.) of his estimate a more stringent limitation applies: at least two units are required from each stratum,[2] so that the number

---

[1] Going back to the example on pp. 88–9, we can estimate the gain from proportionate stratification by substituting p_i for μ_i and p for μ in the above formula to give

$$\frac{\sum n_i(p_i - p)^2}{n^2} = 0.000097.$$

It is easy to check that this agrees with the result obtained directly.
[2] The reason is that the standard error depends on the standard deviations within the strata, S_i. To estimate S_i at least two units are needed; the estimator $s^2 = \frac{1}{n-1} \Sigma(x_j - \bar{x})^2$ is not defined for $n = 1$. If, however, there are strata from

of strata cannot exceed half the sample size. This limitation is rarely restrictive when sampling units within strata, because in this case often only a limited amount of information is available for forming strata and the sample is usually several times larger than the number of strata the surveyor wants to form. However, when cluster sampling or multi-stage sampling is employed (see Section 5.4) the limitation can be important. In this case there is often available a great deal of information suitable for stratification purposes, and the limitation refers not to the final number of units selected but to the number of clusters selected at the first stage of sampling, a number which can be relatively small. For example, if one selected 50 clusters at the first stage, no more than 50 strata could be formed, or only 25 or less if a true estimate of variance is to be obtained. Moreover while the gain from proportionate stratification is typically modest for sampling units, for cluster and multi-stage sampling the gain can be greater.[1]

Within these limitations, however, there is a great degree of flexibility with stratification. The formation of the strata need not be done on the basis of objective data, but can be done subjectively, for it is not the method of forming the strata, but the random sampling within strata that guarantees against selection bias. The surveyor's aim is to form homogeneous strata with regard to the survey variable; the gain he obtains depends on the extent to which, by objective or subjective means, he achieves this.

By taking combinations of stratification factors, multiple stratification can be employed. Indeed, greater precision is usually obtained by introducing another stratification factor rather than by forming more refined groups on the existing factor. Where possible, factors should be chosen which are closely related to the survey variable, but only slightly related to each other.

The question now arises as to what should be done if the survey is concerned—as all surveys are—with a number of variables and not just a single one. A stratification factor related to one variable may not be related to another; one factor may suggest itself for the income question, another for, say, television viewing, a third for gardening, and so forth. Often some factors may be chosen because they seem relevant to most questions. Otherwise one can only decide which questions have first priority and select stratification factors to suit

---

which only one unit has been sampled, they can, for purposes of obtaining an estimate of standard error, be combined with other strata: this technique, known as the collapsed strata technique, leads to an overestimate of the standard error, but the bias is usually small (see Kish, 1965a).

[1] In order to extend stratification beyond the point of having only one selection per stratum, techniques of deep stratification such as controlled selection have been developed (see Kish, 1965a). As with only one selection per stratum, with these techniques there is a problem in estimating the standard error.

these. In this situation, proportionate stratification has the advantage of giving the reassurance that stratification by a factor unrelated to a particular variable will not result in a *loss* of precision for that variable.

Disproportionate stratified sampling

The previous section described stratified sampling in which the sampling fraction was uniform over the whole population. There are, however, situations in which it is preferable to use variable sampling fractions.

One such situation arises where the populations in some strata are much more variable than those in others. Then it is evident that the strata in which the members are more mixed or variable with respect to the survey subject are more difficult to 'represent' by a sample of a given size. It would be sensible in this case to take a larger sampling fraction in the more variable strata, thereby increasing overall precision. Again, if cost per sampling unit is greater in some strata than in others, one could increase precision by taking a smaller fraction in the costlier strata. It can be shown that optimum precision for a given cost is attained if the sampling fractions in the different strata are made proportional to the standard deviations in those strata and inversely proportional to the square root of the costs per unit in the strata; in other words, if the

$$\frac{n_i}{N_i} \text{ are proportional to } \frac{S_i}{\sqrt{c_i}}$$

where n_i = sample size
N_i = population size
S_i = standard deviation
c_i = cost per unit
$\left.\begin{array}{l}\\\\\\\\\end{array}\right\}$ in the ith stratum.

If the costs per unit can be assumed to be constant throughout the strata, the optimum sampling fractions are proportional to the standard deviations. Further, if the standard deviations can be assumed to be constant throughout the strata, the optimum sampling fractions are also constant in all strata, i.e. proportionate allocation is optimum allocation if the costs and standard deviations do not differ between strata.

One of the problems of using optimum allocation in practice is that one generally does not know what the relative variability in the strata is (nor usually the relative costs). There are several ways of overcoming this difficulty. In the first place, previous surveys dealing with the same or a similar population may give guidance. Or a pilot survey may provide data from which estimates of standard deviations and costs can be derived: however, many pilot studies are too small to provide estimates of useful precision, so one may have to rely on some other means or on expert judgement. If it is difficult to estimate the strata standard deviations directly, an alternative is to relate the sampling fractions to some other measurement which is itself known or expected to be related to the standard deviations. For example, the stratum standard deviations are sometimes roughly proportional to the stratum means. The sampling fractions can then be made proportional to the stratum means, providing the relative size of these can be estimated reasonably accurately. All such sources produce approximations rather than exact figures, but these are sufficient. The reason is that small departures from the optimum allocation lead to only a slight loss of precision. If the sampling fractions are close to the 'best' fractions, there is still likely to be almost as much gain as if the 'best' fractions had been used.

This last point has a number of other implications. First, it means that complicated sampling fractions can be avoided, because rounding to simpler fractions causes little loss in precision. Secondly, it often means that it is unnecessary to use different fractions for every stratum. If the strata are separated into a small number of groups, with the strata within groups having similar fractions, little precision is lost by applying the same sampling fraction to all the strata within a group. By this procedure the analysis is simplified. Thirdly, it also means that if the optimum sampling fractions for the various strata do not differ substantially, proportionate stratification will achieve almost all the gains of optimum stratification. Kish (1965a, p. 94) suggests that generally the sampling fractions should vary by at least a factor of 2 if it is to be worth while to depart from the simplicity of proportionate stratification. There is additional labour involved in using variable sampling fractions, owing to the need to weight stratum results in order to arrive at overall estimates, and this makes it uneconomic to undertake disproportionate sampling when there is only a slight gain in precision. In particular, this is usually the case when estimating a proportion. If the costs do not differ between strata, the optimum sampling fraction is proportional to the standard deviation, S, and for a proportion S is approximately $\sqrt{\pi(1-\pi)}$. $\sqrt{\pi(1-\pi)}$ changes little for π within the range 0·1 to 0·9, as the following results show:

π	$S = \sqrt{\pi(1-\pi)}$
0·1 or 0·9	0·30
0·2 or 0·8	0·40
0·3 or 0·7	0·46
0·4 or 0·6	0·49
0·5	0·50

Thus, if the stratum percentages all lie within the range of 10 per cent to 90 per cent, the optimum sampling fractions will have less than a twofold variation. In this case it is therefore unlikely to be worth while to depart from the simplicity of proportionate allocation.

One general difficulty in choosing sampling fractions is that fractions that are best for one variable (or attribute) being studied may not be so for another. If one variable predominates in importance, this can govern the sampling fractions, but where no priority exists the problem of allocation is complex. Furthermore, while proportionate stratification as a practical rule guarantees no loss in precision over simple random sampling, this is not true for disproportionate stratification. An optimum allocation for one variable may yield an allocation that gives for another variable much lower precision than a simple random sample. This subject is discussed by Cochran (1963, Sections 5A3 and 5A4) and Yates (1960, Section 10.4). A practical discussion is given by Kish (1961) and an analytical solution is provided by Kokan and Khan (1967).

It must be pointed out that, although gain in precision is an important reason for using variable sampling fractions, it is not the only one. Results are often wanted separately for special sub-groups of the population, known technically as *domains of study*, so that it is important to have sufficient sample numbers in each domain. It is often convenient to make the domains into separate strata, or groups of strata, and the requirement of sufficient numbers in the domains may then call for variable sampling fractions. With a uniform sampling fraction a small stratum will give only a small proportion of the total sample, so that probably no meaningful results could be given for this stratum separately. If such results are required, a higher sampling fraction can be employed in the stratum; indeed, should the stratum be very small, the necessary sampling fraction could approach 1, in which case a complete coverage of that stratum may be appropriate. Adequate representation of domains of study is frequently the reason for the use of disproportionate stratified sampling in social surveys.

The question of allocation in stratified sampling is discussed more fully by Kish (1965a), Yates (1960), and Cochran (1963), among others, and an interesting account of the determination of sampling fractions in a national survey is given by Lydall (1955). The calculations of a population estimate and its standard error for disproportionate stratified sampling are illustrated below.

● To illustrate the estimation of a mean and its standard error from a stratified sample with variable fractions (and, for comparison, with a uniform sampling fraction), consider a population of 5,000 employees, stratified into three employment levels, with stratum A containing the top executives, stratum B other non-manual workers and stratum C the manual workers. The sample will comprise 200 employees, and the purpose is to estimate the mean size of their current bank account (μ) in £'s; the sample means ($\bar{x}_i$) and standard deviations (s_i) for the three groups are given in columns (3) and (4) of Table 5.3. The proportionate allocation resulting from a uniform sampling fraction is shown in column (5).

TABLE 5.3

Estimation of a mean and its standard error—stratified random samples with uniform and variable sampling fractions.
Hypothetical data

(1)	(2)	(3)	(4)	Uniform Sampling Fraction			Variable Sampling Fractions		
				(5)	(6)	(7)	(8)	(9)	(10)
Employment level	*No. of employees*	*Mean size of bank account*	*Standard deviation of size of bank account*	*Sample size*			*Sample size*		
	N_i	$\bar{x}_i$	s_i	n_i	$n_i\bar{x}_i$	$n_i s_i^2$	n_i	s_i^2/n_i	$N_i s_i^2/n_i$
A. Executives	50	300	90	2	600	16,200	10	810	2,025,000
B. Other non-manual	1,250	150	40	50	7,500	80,000	110	14·5	22,656,250
C. Manual	3,700	30	10	148	4,440	14,800	80	1·25	17,112,500
	$N=5,000$			200	12,540	111,000	200		41,793,750

(i) *Uniform sampling fraction.* The first step is to estimate the mean size of account for all employees. This is given by the sample mean, $\bar{x}$, i.e.

$$\bar{x} = \frac{\Sigma n_i \bar{x}_i}{n} = \frac{12,540}{200} = 62\cdot7.$$

Next we can estimate the standard error of the mean, still on the basis of a uniform sampling fraction. The appropriate formula (see p. 90) is

$$\text{s.e.}(\bar{x}_{\text{prop}}) = \sqrt{\frac{\Sigma n_i s_i^2}{n^2}} = \sqrt{\frac{111,000}{200^2}} = \frac{333\cdot2}{200} = 1\cdot67.$$

(ii) *Variable sampling fractions.* Alternatively, one might decide to allocate the sample disproportionately to the strata, since they appear to be of very different variability. Let us suppose for simplicity that the standard deviations for the three strata have been estimated to be roughly in the proportions A:B:C as 9:4:1 (as they in fact turned out to be in the sample). If the sampling fractions are to be in proportion to these, one would proceed as follows: Let the fraction in stratum C be $1/k$. The fractions in strata A and B then become $9/k$ and $4/k$ respectively. With a total sample of 200, this gives

$$\frac{9 \times 50}{k} + \frac{4 \times 1,250}{k} + \frac{3,700}{k} = 200$$

from which $k = 45 \cdot 75$; the sample numbers should therefore be *approximately* 10, 110 and 80. (They are recorded in column (8)). This allocation has assumed that the cost of sampling is the same in the three strata.

In order to estimate the mean size of account in the population from a stratified random sample with variable sampling fractions, the means obtained in the different strata (which we may still assume to be those in column (3)) have to be weighted by the strata population sizes:[1]

$$\bar{x} = \frac{\sum N_i \bar{x}_i}{N} = 62 \cdot 7 \text{ as before.}$$

In order to estimate the standard error of the mean, the following formula is required:

$$\text{s.e.}(\bar{x}_{\text{strat}}) = \sqrt{\frac{\sum N_i^2 s_i^2 / n_i}{N^2}}. \qquad \ldots(5.4)$$

The necessary figures are given in columns (8) to (10) of Table 5.3, and the result is

$$\text{s.e.}(\bar{x}_{\text{strat}}) = \sqrt{\frac{41,793,750}{5,000^2}} = 1 \cdot 29.$$

In terms of variances, the use of variable sampling fractions has reduced the estimated sampling variance from $1 \cdot 67^2$ to $1 \cdot 29^2$, i.e. from $2 \cdot 79$ to $1 \cdot 66$, a reduction of about 40 per cent. This was an extreme case (i.e. with very large differences in variability between the strata) and so substantial a gain would be unusual. The reader should note that no account has been taken of the finite population correction: in practice this would probably have been used here.[2]

Comparisons between strata

So far in the discussion of disproportionate stratified sampling the objective has been to estimate a mean or a proportion, either for the whole population or for some set of the strata which form a domain of study. We turn now from the *descriptive* problem of obtaining a measure for describing the population or a sub-population to the

---

[1] As mentioned earlier, with uniform sampling fractions it is convenient and valid to weight by the sample numbers rather than the population numbers, since the former are in proportion to the latter. Here we must, however, use population numbers.
[2] It would certainly have been used in stratum A (where the sampling fraction is 1 in 5) but its omission is not serious since this stratum makes by far the smallest contribution to the sampling error.

analytic problem of comparing two domain means. In terms of the above example, we might want for instance to compare the mean size of bank account for the executives in stratum A with that of the other non-manual workers in stratum B. One natural way of making the comparison is to investigate the difference between the two means, $\delta = \mu_A - \mu_B$, which is estimated by $d = \bar{x}_A - \bar{x}_B$. The optimum allocation is now to be determined in order to provide the estimator d with maximum precision within the available resources. The solution to this problem is to make the sample sizes in the strata proportional to the standard deviations in those strata and inversely proportional to the square root of the costs per unit in the strata, that is

$$n_i \text{ should be proportional to } \frac{S_i}{\sqrt{c_i}}.$$

This solution is seen to be the same as the one providing optimum precision for the estimate of the population mean, except that the N_i do not now appear. Thus here it is the sample *sizes*, not the sampling *fractions*, that are proportional to $S_i/\sqrt{c_i}$. This difference can be a source of conflict when the survey is intended both to provide an overall estimate and to compare the strata means. If the sizes of the strata differ greatly, the two rules will lead to markedly different allocations. However, since small departures from the optima lead to only slight losses in precision, it is often possible to find a compromise between the two allocations which does reasonably well for both purposes.

Since the above solution is for only two strata, the formula may be written as

$$\frac{n_A}{n_B} = \frac{S_A/\sqrt{c_A}}{S_B/\sqrt{c_B}}.$$

If costs and standard deviations are the same, then the optimum allocation is to choose $n_A = n_B$, that is to take half the sample from one stratum and the other half from the other.

The extension to more than two strata is not straightforward because there are then a number of possible comparisons that can be made. In order to determine the optimum allocation it is necessary to specify the relative importance of these comparisons. For instance, in the case of the three strata in the above example one might want to compare executives and other non-manual workers, and also other non-manual with manual workers, but one might not be interested in the comparison of executives and manual workers. In addition one might be far more interested in the first comparison than in the second. These details need to be specified before a solution can be reached. Let us suppose that equal importance is placed on the first two comparisons, and that the third comparison is of no interest. For simplicity, let the costs and standard deviations be the same for all three strata. Then, since the non-manual workers in stratum B appear in two comparisons while each of the other two groups appears in only one, one would expect to put more of the sample into stratum B. In fact a suitable allocation for this problem is to divide the sample in the ratios A:B:C as $1:\sqrt{2}:1$.

The preceding discussion demonstrates the difficulties when many comparisons are involved and shows that no general solution is possible. But one particular case deserves mention, the case where the average of the standard errors of all possible differences is to be minimized. The solution to this problem is a straight extension of the one given above for two strata, namely the n_i are proportional to $S_i/\sqrt{c_i}$. It should be noted, however, that in general this allocation can lead to greater precision for some comparisons than for others. In the special case when the costs and standard deviations are the same for all strata, this rule reduces to allocating the total sample equally between the strata.

Stratification after selection

Previously it has been noted that the possibility of stratification by a given factor depends on knowing the distribution of the population with respect to that factor and on knowing also to which stratum each population unit belongs. Ignorance of the latter is sometimes a limiting factor, even when the population distribution is known. If one wanted to stratify a sample of individuals in a town by age, one could easily get figures of the age distribution, but if there is no general population list showing the age of each individual, prior stratification would not be possible.

In such a case, one can 'stratify after selection' or 'post-stratify'. Suppose that the survey is to estimate mean income of the population (μ) and that one wants to stratify by age, but cannot do so for the reason given. A random sample is selected and each person's age ascertained at the interview. The resultant sample is then grouped by age and the mean income ($\bar{x}_i$) computed for each age stratum. The numbers (N_i) in the age groups in the population are known and the mean income for the population is estimated by

$$\bar{x} = \frac{\Sigma N_i \bar{x}_i}{N}, \text{ where } N = \text{total size of the population.} \qquad ...(5.5)$$

One would expect each age stratum to be correctly represented in the sample, but sampling fluctuations would mean that this would not hold for any one simple random sample—the purpose of proportionate stratification is in fact to ensure that it holds exactly for every such sample. A simple random sample will thus deviate somewhat from a proportionate stratified sample, and the purpose of post-stratification is to re-weight the stratum means obtained in the simple random sample so that they are represented correctly in the overall mean. Providing the simple random sample can be expected to provide a sufficient number of cases for each stratum, stratification after selection is almost as good as prior proportionate stratification. The re-weighting, however, may be something of a nuisance at the computing stage, so that the normal form of stratification is to be preferred where possible.

5.4. Cluster and multi-stage sampling

A population can generally be regarded as being made up of a hierarchy of sampling units of different sizes and types. To take our simple example of the student survey, the population in the college (and within each special subject stratum in that college) can be regarded as being composed of a number of classes, each of which is itself composed of a number of students. In the discussion so far it has been taken for granted that, within each stratum, the students would be picked separately, one by one, from the population of that stratum. In practice it is often desirable to proceed differently. One might, for example, first select a sample of classes, each single selection leading to the choice of a whole cluster of units, and then, within each of the selected clusters, one can either include all the individual units which it comprises or only a sample of them. But if this procedure is to be employed in a straightforward manner, it is necessary that each unit is a member of one and only one cluster. In practice it is likely that many students attend more than one class, in which case one might try to identify each student uniquely with just one of the classes he attends. Perhaps every student attends an economics class and no student attends more than one; if so, each student could be uniquely identified through his economics class, and the sample could be selected from the economics classes only.

The process of sampling complete groups of units is called *cluster sampling*; situations where there is any sub-sampling within the clusters chosen at the first stage are covered by the term *multi-stage sampling*. Actually the former can be regarded as the special case of multi-stage sampling, where a 100 per cent sample is taken at the second stage.

Cluster sampling

Let us begin by illustrating this special case. Suppose that a survey is to be done in a large town and that the unit of enquiry, i.e. the unit about which results are to be obtained, is the individual household. Suppose further that the town contains 20,000 households, all of them listed on convenient records, and that a sample of 200 households is to be selected. One way would be to pick the 200 from the entire list by some random method, but this would spread the sample over the whole town, with consequently high fieldwork costs and much inconvenience. One might decide therefore to concentrate the sample in a few parts of the town and, if it may be assumed for simplicity that the town is divided into 400 areas with 50 households in each, a simple course would be to select at random 4 areas (i.e. 1 in 100) and include all the households in them in the sample. The overall probability of selection is unchanged but, by selecting clusters of households, one has materially simplified and cheapened the fieldwork of the survey.

In this illustration it was the desire to lower the field costs that supposedly led to the use of a cluster sampling design. Another good reason for clustering arises when no satisfactory sampling frame for the whole population exists, so that a listing of some kind has to be made specially. It is then obviously advantageous to be able to confine the special listing to a few areas or groups. Had there been no listing of households in the above example, a sample of areas could have been taken as before, and the listings would then need to be prepared only for the four selected areas. This restriction of the listing to the selected clusters is a vital consideration in 'underdeveloped areas' where there are rarely satisfactory sampling frames, as it is also in many other places, including the United States, where adequate population lists are lacking.

Three general points about clustering should be noted. In the first place, whether or not a particular aggregate of units should be called a cluster depends on circumstances. In the above example an area was appropriately called a cluster since it contained a number of households, the household here being the unit of enquiry. In another survey, the area might be the unit of enquiry, in which case one would not call it a cluster. Equally, in another survey, the household might properly be called a cluster, if it was itself the sampling unit but if results were to relate to individual members of the household. Related to the question of whether an aggregate of units represents a cluster is the question of what constitutes the right unit of enquiry. This issue arises particularly in the study of organizations such as firms, schools and hospitals. It can be of great importance because different units of enquiry can lead to apparently markedly different findings. Thus, in a discussion of this topic, Kish (1965b) quotes an example about American high school education around 1957. With the school as the unit of enquiry, it was found that half the high schools offered no physics, a quarter no chemistry, and a quarter no geometry. However, when the student becomes the unit of enquiry, it is found that these schools accounted for only 2 per cent of all high school students. Clearly the apparent discrepancy is readily explained by the fact that generally it is the small schools which do not teach these subjects, but nevertheless the example does highlight the need to choose the appropriate unit.

A second point about clustering is that clusters need not necessarily be natural aggregates, like schools, classes, constituencies and polling districts. In area sampling (see Section 6.1) one often makes up artificial clusters by imposing grids onto maps. More commonly clustering takes advantage of existing groupings of the population. In either case clusters do not usually contain equal numbers. However, for the sake of simplicity, the present discussion will be confined to the case of equal-sized clusters.

Thirdly, in any one sample design several levels of clusters may be used. One may begin by dividing one region of England and Wales into its constituencies and pick a number of these for the sample. Within each chosen constituency, one may pick a sample of the wards comprising it; within each chosen ward a sample of its polling districts; and then finally within these a sample of households. Here, constituencies, wards and polling districts are clusters at the first, second and third sampling stages respectively of a four-stage sample.

To illustrate the working of cluster sampling (with equal-sized clusters) let us return to the example of Table 5.2, taking the *History* stratum for illustration. The population in this stratum numbered 660 students, of whom 1 in 10, i.e. 66, were randomly selected from a list; half of them, that is 33 students, were found to be in favour of degree reform. This was in fact a simple random sample within the stratum, but we will imagine for the moment that it was a clustered one: that the 660 students had first been divided into their 110 classes of 6 students each, that a sample of 11 of the 110 classes had been randomly chosen, and that all the students in each of these were included in the sample. It may be supposed that the numbers favouring degree reform in the eleven classes or clusters were: 3, 5, 2, 3, 4, 1, 4, 2, 6, 1, 2 (total 33).

To estimate the proportion for the stratum as a whole one would, of course, simply divide $33/66 = 0.5$, but it is worth noting that for equal-sized clusters the same result is achieved by working out the proportion for each cluster and then taking the average:

$$\tfrac{1}{11}(0.500 + 0.833 + 0.333 + 0.500 + 0.667 + 0.167 + 0.667 + 0.333$$
$$+ 1.000 + 0.167 + 0.333)$$
$$= \tfrac{1}{11}(5.500) = 0.5.$$

In fact, instead of thinking of the individual students, one can treat the clusters as the units of enquiry, where the variable measured for each selected cluster is the proportion of students favouring reform, $\bar{x}_i$ being the proportion for the ith cluster. The above calculation shows that the estimate of the proportion for the whole stratum is $p = \bar{x} = \Sigma\bar{x}_i/m$, where m is the number of clusters selected, here 11. Since it is a simple random sample of clusters, with the variable $\bar{x}_i$ measured for the ith cluster, the standard error of $p = \bar{x}$ is simply, from equation (4.1),

$$\text{S.E.}(\bar{x}_{\text{clust}}) = \sqrt{\left(1 - \frac{m}{M}\right)\frac{S_b^2}{m}} \qquad \ldots(5.6)$$

where there are M clusters in the population, and S_b is the standard deviation of the cluster values $\bar{x}_i$. To estimate this standard error, the estimate s_b^2 is substituted for S_b^2, where

$$s_b^2 = \frac{1}{m-1}\sum_{i=1}^{m}(\bar{x}_i - \bar{x})^2.$$

Here $m = 11$, $M = 110$ and
$$s_b^2 = \tfrac{1}{10}[(0\cdot5 - 0\cdot5)^2 + (0\cdot833 - 0\cdot5)^2 + (0\cdot333 - 0\cdot5)^2 + (0\cdot5 - 0\cdot5)^2 + \ldots + (0\cdot333 - 0\cdot5)^2]$$
$$= 0\cdot072.$$

Hence $\quad \text{s.e.}(\bar{x}_{\text{clust}}) = \sqrt{\dfrac{9}{10}\cdot\dfrac{0\cdot072}{11}} = \sqrt{0\cdot0059} = 0\cdot077.$

If the stratum result in Table 5.2 (i.e. $p = 0\cdot5$ for the history students) had been based on a simple random sample—as we supposed in Section 5.3 to have been the case—the standard error of this estimate would itself have been estimated[1] as 0·059. In other words, the clustered sample has resulted in a considerably higher standard error as compared with the simple random case. The design effect is estimated as

$$\text{deff} = \frac{(0\cdot077)^2}{(0\cdot059)^2} = 1\cdot70.$$

A design effect of greater than one is typical of real-life cluster samples, and we must now consider how this 'clustering effect' comes about.

[1] By the formula
$$\text{s.e.}(p_{\text{srs}}) = \sqrt{\left(\frac{N-n}{N}\right)\frac{p(1-p)}{n-1}},$$
where n = sample size, N = population size, p = sample proportion with the attribute—all in the one stratum.

To do this, let us make the very reasonable supposition that the division of the 660 students into 110 classes was not a random one, but that it had some relation to the characteristics of the individual students. There might have been an age criterion involved, or the division might have been connected with ability or with special interests within the field of history; the result in any case would have been to make the members within a cluster more like each other than like members of other clusters. In statistical language, there would have been a positive *intra-class correlation*.

Intra-class correlation is of the utmost importance in sample design and nearly always, in the field of social surveys, the correlation is positive. People living in a particular district of a town tend to have characteristics which make them *more* like each other than like people living in other districts; individuals in a household will on many—though not all—characteristics be more like each other than like members of other households, and so forth. The importance of this to the sample designer is that, if he selects clusters, he will tend to include or exclude (to put the point in extreme form) whole classes of units, and this increased 'riskiness' in the representativeness of the sample will be reflected in an increased sampling error. The population is 'patchy' and, whereas the simple random sample will tend to be spread over all of it, the cluster sample risks missing whole sections. If, of course, the entire population were thoroughly 'mixed', cluster sampling would be as precise as simple random sampling; but human populations tend to be anything but thoroughly mixed.

The effect on the sampling variance can be expressed as follows. If the population of MN units consists of M clusters, each of size N, and if m of these clusters are chosen and fully enumerated, then the sampling variance, for a mean or a proportion, is approximately

$$\text{Var}(C) = \text{Var}(R)[1 + (N-1)\rho] \qquad \dots(5.7)$$

where $\text{Var}(R)$ is the sampling variance for a simple random sample of the same size (mN) and ρ is the intra-class correlation. Since the design effect is $\text{Var}(C)/\text{Var}(R)$, we have

$$\text{Deff} = [1 + (N-1)\rho].$$

It is to be noted that
  (i) if $N = 1$, that is each cluster contains only one unit, $\text{Deff} = 1$, that is $\text{Var}(C) = \text{Var}(R)$. This is as expected since there is then no clustering.
  (ii) a value of $\rho = 0$ means that there is no intra-class correlation. In other words, each cluster is just as heterogeneous as the population at large. Then $\text{Deff} = 1$.

(iii) the greater the 'resemblance' of members of the same cluster, the closer will ρ approach 1 and the greater will be the design effect, which will always exceed 1.

(iv) even a small value of ρ might result in a substantial design effect, since ρ is multiplied by $(N-1)$. If ρ is small, the product $\rho(N-1)$ can be large if N is large. Suppose $\rho = 0.1$ for a certain variable and each cluster numbers 101 persons, then the variance from a sample of clusters would be 11 times that from a simple random sample of the same number of individuals.

In the present case the estimated design effect is deff $= 1.70$ and $N = 6$. Hence ρ can be estimated to be $+0.14$. In practice correlations are often of this order, but they are sometimes much higher, and are very rarely negative (ρ can never be less than $-1/N-1$).

An important principle established by this explanation is that the more heterogeneous the clusters are within themselves (i.e. the smaller ρ is), the less precision will be lost by clustering. Thus whereas, for stratification, the aim is to make the strata as homogeneous within themselves as possible, in the formation of clusters the opposite holds. This difference is accounted for by the essential difference between strata and clusters, namely that *all* the strata must be represented in the sample whereas only a *sample* of clusters is to be included.

It also follows from the formula that a large number of small clusters is better—other things being equal—than a small number of large clusters. In practice, of course, the choice of clusters is often dictated by natural groupings, but one must be prepared for the very considerable increase in sampling error that often results from clustering. As has been noted in (iv) above, the large size of the clusters (N) is partly responsible for this increase: for a fixed sample size of mN units, it limits the number of selections to m clusters. If smaller clusters could be used, more of them could be sampled. To reduce the number of units taken from selected clusters one can sample within them, that is take a two-stage sample; by this means the total sample of mN units can be spread over more clusters. It is instructive to see how this affects the design effect for a simple case. If m equal-sized clusters are selected by unrestricted sampling (i.e. with replacement) and if samples of n units are selected by simple random sampling from each primary selection, the design effect is

$$\text{Deff} = [1 + (n-1)\rho].$$

In this formula the intra-class correlation ρ is as before; being a property of the cluster, it is unaltered by the use of sub-sampling. Thus the effect of sub-sampling is to replace $(N-1)$ by $(n-1)$, which can make the design effect for the two-stage sample much less than that for the cluster sample. For instance, suppose $\rho = 0.1$, $N = 101$ and the total sample size is fixed at 1,111. For a cluster sample, this would mean the selection of 11 clusters, and, as calculated above, the design effect is 11. Suppose that with the two-stage sample $n = 11$ units were selected from each selected cluster; then 101 clusters would be selected and the design effect becomes

$$\text{Deff} = [1 + 0.1(11 - 1)] = 2.$$

Thus the design effect has been reduced by the sub-sampling from 11 to 2.

Multi-stage sampling

This last example has introduced a second stage of sampling as a modification to cluster sampling. In practice it is usually desirable and often essential to carry out the sampling in two or more stages. The population is regarded as being composed of a number of first-stage or *primary sampling units* (PSU's), each of them being made up of a number of second-stage units, and so forth. A sample—with or without stratification—is taken of the PSU's; then a sample—again with or without stratification—is taken of the second-stage units in each *selected* PSU; and so the procedure continues down to the final sampling units, with sampling ideally being at random at each stage.

The necessity for multi-stage sampling can be easily demonstrated. Suppose a random sample of 2,000 individuals is required to cover the civilian adult population of Great Britain. From a theoretical viewpoint, it would be admissible to select a simple random sample or a stratified simple random sample from a sampling frame covering the entire population. Not only would it be admissible, but, if cost and other practical considerations did not come into the picture, it could hardly be improved upon. In real life, however, these considerations are necessarily of prime importance and such a sample, thinly spread over the whole country, would be out of the question for an interview survey; almost invariably, samples for interview surveys of widely spread populations are designed on a multi-stage basis. In Britain, the PSU's for national surveys are often administrative districts (county boroughs, boroughs, urban districts, rural districts etc.) or parliamentary constituencies. In the United States counties are widely used as PSU's.

Within the selected PSU's, one may go direct to the final sampling units, such as individuals, households or addresses, in which case one would have a two-stage sample. But even to spread a sample of, say, 30 households over a town is expensive, and it would be more usual to concentrate the sample by introducing one or more intermediate sampling stages. Since individual administrative districts consist of a number of wards, each of which in turn consists of a number of polling districts, either (or both) of these types of unit can be used at intermediate stages.

Before going further, it may be useful to emphasize the respective roles of stratification and of spreading a sample over several stages. Although these two features of design fulfil quite different functions, the newcomer to the subject often has difficulty in distinguishing them. Continuing with our illustration, suppose that there are suitable lists of districts and of individuals within districts from which the sample of 2,000 adult civilians can be drawn. Let us look at four possibilities:

Design I. Simple random sample

This would involve taking the list of adults for the entire country and extracting from it a sample of the required size, either by random numbers or by some systematic procedure.[1]

Design II. Unstratified, two-stage sample

Sample I would be too thinly spread over the country to be practicable. We may decide instead to concentrate the sample in a certain number of administrative districts, selecting, say, 100 such districts from a complete list of districts. We then turn to the list of individuals for each of the selected districts, and from it select the required number (20 on average).

Design III. Stratified simple random sample

Either because the regions are believed to differ markedly from each other with regard to the subject of the survey or purely for convenience, we may decide to stratify by region (say, with a uniform sampling fraction). The first step is to allocate to each region its appropriate number of interviews. If South-West England has 7 per cent of the adult civilian population of Great Britain, 140 out of the sample of 2,000 individuals would be selected from this region. Up to this point *no sampling has taken place*. Stratification is merely a way of dividing the population into a number of sub-populations and allocating the sample between these sub-populations. Once this is done the sampling begins, and with simple random sampling within strata we would select the number of individuals required in a region from the entire list for that region.

[1] In this latter case there might in fact be an element of stratification because of the arrangement of the list.

Design IV. Stratified, two-stage sample

The stratification by region is as in Design III. But in order to concentrate the interviewing, we select a sample of administrative districts in each region and then a sample of individuals from each of the selected districts.

For purposes of illustration, the above has been confined to one stratification at the first stage and to two sampling stages. In practice the most common type of design is IV, but with several stratifications and more than two sampling stages.

The crucial advantages of multi-stage sampling are that it results in a concentration of fieldwork and consequently in a saving of time, labour and money, and that it obviates the necessity of having a sampling frame covering the entire population. As was clear from Designs II and IV, one needs a frame of the second-stage units *only for those PSU's which have been selected at the first stage.*

There are many ways of distributing a sample over various sampling stages, and in the choice between them both practical considerations and the effect on sampling errors must weigh. Suppose the survey population numbers 240,000 individuals grouped, geographically or otherwise, into 800 clusters of 300 persons each (still assuming that the clusters are of roughly equal size). A sample of 2,400 persons is to be drawn, that is the sampling fraction is 1/100. The following are a few of the ways in which the sample could be allocated:

Allocation	Number of clusters	Number of persons taken per cluster
A	800	3
B	240	10
C	120	20
D	60	40
E	40	60
F	20	120
G	8	300

These can all be looked upon as two-stage designs: in (A) a '100 per cent sample' is taken at the first stage, in (G) a '100 per cent sample' is taken at the second stage (the special case of a cluster sample). From a cost and convenience point of view, the designs get increasingly attractive as one goes from (A) to (G): the spread becomes smaller and smaller and so, broadly, does the cost per unit. But, at the same time, the designs become *less* attractive in terms of the precision achieved—in other words, the standard error increases as we move towards a smaller number of clusters which are sub-sampled at a higher rate (see p. 105). In practice, a national interview sample of 2,000–3,000 interviews would typically be spread over 80–100 of the PSU's.

The sample designer's aim is to achieve the highest precision per £1 spent, that is to find some optimum point along the scale from design (A) to design (G). The decision is not always easy, since it requires estimates of costs and variances per unit associated with the different allocations; it is a question of balancing the increased costs resulting from taking more clusters against the reduction in design effect that occurs when ρ is multiplied by a smaller value of $(n-1)$ (see p. 105). If the sampler is aiming at a given precision, the problem is to find the cheapest design that will attain it; if he must keep to a given maximum cost, the task is to find the design that will give maximum precision at that cost. In either case, the necessary estimates have to be based on previous experience, pilot surveys or guesswork. The multi-purpose problem—see p. 95—arises here too, and some priority among the variables of the survey has to be established. The reader is referred to the textbooks on sampling for a full discussion of procedures.

This discussion has been in terms of two-stage sampling, but all the principles can be generalized to more stages. As regards the standard errors for multi-stage samples, the important point to note is that each sampling stage makes its own contribution to the total sampling error. The standard error for a two-stage sample and an estimator of it are considered below.

● Consider a two-stage sample and suppose that, at the first stage, m out of a possible M districts are selected at random without replacement and that, in each of the selected districts, n out of N individuals are chosen, again by simple random sampling. Both the selection of m out of M PSU's and of n out of N second-stage units in each of the selected PSU's gives rise to sampling errors.

This is brought out by formula (5.8), which shows the sampling variance of a mean (income, let us say) based upon such a sample:

$$\text{Var}(\bar{x}) = \left(1 - \frac{m}{M}\right)\frac{S_b^2}{m} + \left(1 - \frac{n}{N}\right)\frac{S_w^2}{mn}. \qquad ...(5.8)$$

This variance is composed of two parts, the first of which—the between-district variance—has already been encountered in the discussion of cluster sampling on p. 103. But added to this variation between districts there is the second term, which arises through the second stage of sampling n of the N individuals from each selected PSU. Within each district there is a variance between its N individuals, and the average of this variance for the M districts is S_w^2, so that S_w^2 is a criterion of variation *between individuals within the PSU's*. As the sample consists of n individuals in each of m districts, making a total sample of mn individuals, S_w^2 is divided by mn and multiplied by corresponding finite population correction.

Two extremes of formula (5.8) are of interest:

(i) If *all* the PSU's are included, then $\left(1 - \dfrac{m}{M}\right)$ becomes zero, and so does the first term of the variance. This is design (A) in the scheme on p. 108, and is equivalent to a proportionate stratified random sample, in which, since they are all included in the sample, the PSU's have become strata. In order to minimize the overall variance, now consisting of only the second term in (5.8), S_w^2 must be minimized. In other words the districts (strata) should be as *internally homogeneous* as possible. This was noted before in the discussion of stratification.

(ii) At the other extreme, if all the second-stage units in each district are included, i.e. $\left(1 - \dfrac{n}{N}\right)$ is zero, only the first-stage contribution remains. This is logical; since there is now no second-stage sampling this is cluster sampling, and formula (5.8) reduces to (5.6). We have here design (G) above and, to minimize Var($\bar{x}$), we aim to minimize S_b^2. This means that districts (clusters) should be as *internally heterogeneous* as possible, which is the feature of cluster sampling noted earlier.

The general approach is that strata should be as homogeneous as possible and that, in forming clusters *within these strata*, the more mixed the membership of each cluster the better. This is a theoretical desideratum. In practice, the choice of cluster is much influenced by purely practical factors: costs, fieldwork, convenience, nature of sampling frame, groups for which data are available and so on.

Finally it is worth noting that, while the variance of a two-stage sample mean has components for each stage of sampling, between PSU's and within PSU's, a good estimate of this variance can generally be obtained from the variance between the sampled PSU's alone. If the (equal-sized) PSU's had been sampled *with replacement* an unbiased estimator of the variance of the mean would have been

$$\text{var}\,(\bar{x}) = \frac{s_b^2}{m} \qquad \qquad ...(5.9)$$

where $s_b^2 = \dfrac{1}{m-1}\,\Sigma(\bar{x}_i - \bar{x})^2$

$\bar{x}_i$ is the mean of the sample of n individuals from the ith selected PSU

and $\bar{x}$ is the mean of the whole sample.

When the PSU's are sampled without replacement this formula provides an overestimate, but, providing the sampling fraction at the first stage, m/M, is small—as is commonly the case—the amount of overestimation is slight. This is a useful result because it means that the estimate of variance is reasonably simple to calculate. Notice that formula (5.9) has the same form as the estimate of variance for a cluster sample (ignoring the f.p.c.). But while the *form* is the same the *contents* differ: with cluster sampling s_b^2 measures the variation in the *population* means of the selected PSU's while with two-stage sampling it

measures the variation in the *sample* means of the selected PSU's—
the latter reflects not only the difference between the PSU means but
also the effect of sub-sampling.

5.5. Sampling with varying probabilities

The preceding discussion was simplified by the assumption that
the clusters of sampling units were of more or less equal size. If they
are not, various complications arise, most of them beyond the scope
of this book. One approach, that of sampling with varying probabilities, is of such general importance, however, that it must at least
be mentioned.

A serious problem when the PSU's differ markedly in size is the
maintenance of control over the sample size. If the PSU's are chosen
with equal probability, then an *epsem* sample is achieved by employing
the same sampling fraction in whichever of the PSU's are selected.
This procedure means, however, that the sample size depends on
which PSU's are chosen at the first stage: with a large PSU of
20,000 persons, a second-stage sampling fraction of 1/100 yields 200
persons for the sample, while with a small PSU of 2,000 persons it
yields only 20. The researcher needs to be able to fix the sample size
within reasonable limits, so that this procedure, where the sample
size depends on which PSU's are selected by random chance, is
unsuitable when the PSU sizes differ considerably.

One method of obtaining greater control is by stratifying the
PSU's by size and selecting a sample of them in each size-group,
probably with variable sampling fractions. An alternative is the
widely used procedure of selecting the PSU's with *probability
proportional to size* (PPS). If one PSU has twice as large a population
as another, it is given twice the chance of being selected. If the *same
number* of persons is then selected from each of the chosen PSU's,
the overall probability of selection of any person will be the same.
Exact PPS sampling of the PSU's thus achieves complete control
over sample size.

PPS sampling also has a number of other advantages. In the first
place, it leads to greater precision than would a simple random
sample of PSU's and a constant sampling fraction at the second stage.
With the latter design, and when several PSU's are selected at the
first stage, a large PSU included in the sample will heavily load the
results because of the large sample of units taken from it; on the other
hand it has a fair chance of being excluded, in which case an important proportion of the population is unrepresented in the sample.
With a PPS selection a large PSU is more likely to appear in the
sample but, because only a fixed number of units is selected from it,
it cannot exert too great an effect on the total sample. Another

E

advantage of PPS selection is that equal-sized samples from each selected PSU are convenient for fieldwork; if one interviewer is assigned to each PSU, the interviewers have equal workloads. A further advantage occurs when the selected PSU's are to be studied individually, because an equal-sized sample from each PSU is generally an efficient allocation for this purpose.

A practical limitation to the use of PPS selection of PSU's is that the PSU sizes must be known. If accurate and up-to-date estimates are available, these may be used; if not, it is often better to use rough size measures rather than equal probabilities. If the PSU's are selected at the first stage with probabilities proportional to their *measures of size* rather than their true sizes, to make the design an *epsem* one the sub-samples taken from different PSU's must be allowed to vary. However, with appropriate measures of size, the variation will not be as great as that for an equal probability selection of PSU's; the closer the measures of size are to the true sizes, the less will be the variation. Variable sub-sample sizes mean of course that the overall sample size cannot be fixed exactly, but this is seldom necessary: usually the researcher needs only to control sample size within moderate limits, and sampling with probability proportional to reasonable measures of size is sufficient for this purpose.

Since in practice PSU's generally vary considerably in size, sampling with probability proportional to size, or measure of size, features in nearly all multi-stage samples. In the rest of this section we will therefore examine the two-stage selection process in greater detail, and describe a simple way of selecting PSU's with varying probabilities.

● In a two-stage sample the probability of a unit appearing in the sample is the product of the probability that its PSU is chosen at the first stage and the probability that the unit is chosen at the second stage given that its PSU was chosen at the first stage. In symbols, the probability of unit j in cluster i appearing in the sample is

$$P(U_{ij}) = P(C_i) \times P(U_{ij}|C_i) \qquad \ldots(5.10)$$

where $P(C_i)$ is the probability that the ith PSU is selected and $P(U_{ij}|C_i)$ is the probability that the jth unit in PSU i is selected at the second stage, given that PSU i was selected at the first stage.

In order to make the sample design an *epsem* one (i.e. equal probability of selection for every unit), $P(U_{ij})$ must have the same value for all units, no matter which PSU the unit belongs to. One simple way to obtain an *epsem* design is to select PSU's with equal probabilities, $P(C_i) = P_1$, and then to apply the same sampling fraction within each selected PSU, $P(U_{ij}|C_i) = P_2$. Equation (5.10), which is known as the *selection equation*, is then

$$P(U_{ij}) = P_1 \times P_2 = \text{constant.}$$

This was the scheme used in the discussion of equal-sized PSU's with $P_1 = m/M$ and $P_2 = n/N$ so that $P(U_{ij}) = mn/MN$, a constant for all units. However, if this scheme is applied to PSU's which differ greatly in size, the sample size can vary considerably, depending on which PSU's are selected for the sample. To illustrate this point, consider the following data of three administrative districts varying markedly in size:

District	Population N_i
A	20,000
B	2,000
C	8,000
Total	$T = 30,000$

A sample of individuals is to be selected in two stages; at the first stage one district is to be selected at random and at the second stage a sample of individuals is to be selected at random from the selected district. The sample design is to be an *epsem* one with $P(U_{ij}) = 1/300$. The selection equation is

$$\frac{1}{300} = \frac{1}{3} \times \frac{1}{100}$$

so that the sampling fraction at the second stage is 1/100. Thus, if district A were selected at the first stage, the sample size would be $\frac{1}{100}(20,000) = 200$; if district B, $\frac{1}{100}(2,000) = 20$; and if C, $\frac{1}{100}(8,000) = 80$. The expected sample size is $\frac{1}{300}(30,000) = 100$, but the actual size, which depends on which district is selected at the first stage, may differ considerably from this figure.

In practice, of course, several PSU's would usually be selected from a much larger number of PSU's, and this would reduce the variation. For instance, if two districts were selected at the first stage, the selection equation would become

$$\frac{1}{300} = \frac{2}{3} \times \frac{1}{200}.$$

Applying the sampling fraction $\frac{1}{200}$ to A gives a sample of 100, to B a sample of 10, and to C a sample of 40. Three possible pairs of districts could be selected at the first stage—AB, AC and BC—and these would produce samples of $100 + 10 = 110$, $100 + 40 = 140$ and $10 + 40 = 50$ individuals respectively. While the variation in sample size has been lessened, it is still greater than the surveyor is likely to tolerate for, among other reasons, he must have a reasonable degree of control on sample size in order to be able to control his budget.

A procedure which gives complete control over sample size is to select the PSU's with PPS and then take a set number of persons from each selected PSU. That this design gives every individual in the population the same chance of being selected for the sample can be demonstrated using the data in the above example. Let the overall probability still be 1/300, and let the number of second-stage units to be selected be 100. The probabilities of selection of the districts are made proportional to their sizes, that is

$$P(C_A) = \frac{20,000}{30,000}, P(C_B) = \frac{2,000}{30,000} \text{ and } P(C_C) = \frac{8,000}{30,000};$$

and, since 100 individuals are to be selected from whichever district is selected at the first stage,

$$P(U_{Aj}|C_A) = \frac{100}{20,000}, \quad P(U_{Bj}|C_B) = \frac{100}{2,000} \quad \text{and} \quad P(U_{Cj}|C_C) = \frac{100}{8,000}.$$

Thus
$$P(U_{Aj}) = P(C_A)P(U_{Aj}|C_A) = \frac{1}{300}$$

$$P(U_{Bj}) = P(C_B)P(U_{Bj}|C_B) = \frac{1}{300}$$

$$P(U_{Cj}) = P(C_C)P(U_{Cj}|C_C) = \frac{1}{300}$$

which shows that it is an *epsem* design. In general the selection equation for one PSU selected with PPS and a fixed number of individuals, n, selected at the second stage is

$$P(U_{ij}) = \frac{N_i}{T} \times \frac{n}{N_i} = \frac{n}{T} = \text{constant}$$

where N_i is the size of the ith PSU
and T is the size of the total population.

This application shows the flexibility possible in the use of the selection equation. For an *epsem* design it is not necessary that the selection probabilities are equal at each stage, but only that the product of the two probabilities is a constant value. One way to achieve a constant product is to employ equal selection probabilities at each stage; another, with several important advantages, is to sample with PPS at the first stage and then take a fixed sample size from each selected PSU at the second. But there are also other ways.

Another instance of the flexibility of the selection equation can be seen in the case where the PSU sizes are not known exactly, but only measures of size are available. Suppose, for instance, in the above example, that the total population is known to be $T = 30,000$, but the PSU sizes are unknown; however, suppose that the latter are known to differ considerably in size and their sizes are estimated to be in the ratio $A : B : C$ as $7 : 1 : 4$. The estimated sizes would then be 17,500 for A, 2,500 for B, and 10,000 for C. If the PSU's are selected with probabilities proportional to their measures of size at the first stage, to make the design an *epsem* one the selections at the second stage must be made with probabilities inversely proportional to these measures. The selection equation for a sample of m PSU's is then

$$P(U_{ij}) = \frac{mN_i'}{T'} \times \frac{n}{mN_i'} = \frac{n}{T'} \qquad \qquad ...(5.11)$$

where N_i' is the estimated size of the ith PSU
and T' is the estimated total population size.
In terms of our example $m = 1$ and the sampling fractions at the second stage, n/N_i', for the three PSU's are

$$P(U_{Aj}|C_A) = \frac{100}{17,500}, \quad P(U_{Bj}|C_B) = \frac{100}{2,500} \quad \text{and} \quad P(U_{Cj}|C_C) = \frac{100}{10,000}.$$

Applying the appropriate sampling fraction to the true size of each of the PSU's gives the sample size that would be obtained if that PSU were the one selected. Using the PSU sizes from the earlier discussion, these sample sizes are

District	Sample size
A	$\dfrac{100}{17,500} \times 20,000 = 114$
B	$\dfrac{100}{2,500} \times 2,000 = 80$
C	$\dfrac{100}{10,000} \times 8,000 = 80$

As only measures of PSU sizes rather than exact sizes have been used, the sample size is not constant whichever PSU is selected; however, the variation is slight compared with that obtained earlier for equal selection probabilities. This is so because these measures are better estimates of the true sizes than are measures giving each PSU the same size (sampling the PSU's with equal probability can be thought of as giving each PSU the same measure of size); had this not been the case, the variation would have exceeded that of the equal probability scheme. This points to the important requirement that measures of size should be reasonably good estimates of the true sizes.

Since varying probability sampling features in most present-day random samples, it is worth illustrating a selection procedure for it. If there are 20 districts in a stratum—from which 2 are to be selected with probability proportional to size or a measure of size—the 20 are listed in some order (possibly according to another stratification) and the population of each is recorded together with the cumulated population figures. Table 5.4 shows the scheme.[1]

TABLE 5.4

Scheme for selecting districts with PPS

District	Population (000's)	Cumulated Population (000's)
1	50	50
2	63	113
3	28	141
4	16	157
.	.	.
.	.	.
16	.	(say) 428
17	17	445
18	43	488
19	39	527
20	33	560

If sampling is conducted with replacement, i.e. the first district chosen is 'replaced' in the population and given a second chance of selection, the selection procedure is straightforward. Two numbers between 1 and 560 are selected from a Table of Random Numbers,

---

[1] An alternative scheme, not requiring the formation of the cumulative totals, has been developed by Lahiri (1951). For a description, see Kish (1965a).

and the districts corresponding to these numbers are included in the sample. The correspondence is obtained by reference to the column of cumulated sizes: if a random number between 1 and 50 is drawn, district 1 is selected; if a random number between 51 and 113 is drawn, district 2 is selected; and so on. If the two random numbers were, say, 451 and 479, both of them would lead to the choice of district 18 for the sample. District 18 should then be included twice in the sample, for otherwise the selection would not be PPS.

Since including a district twice in the sample can be inconvenient and since sampling with replacement is somewhat less precise, sampling without replacement is usually preferred. There are several ways of sampling with PPS without replacement. A simple and widely used method is to take a systematic selection. The cumulative total is divided by the number of selections to be made, here 560/2 to give the interval 280. A random number between 1 and 280 is drawn, say 151, to locate district 4 as the first selection; the interval 280 is added to the random number 151 to give 431, to locate district 17 as the second.

Providing no district is larger than the interval, the systematic procedure guarantees that a district is not selected more than once. A district which is larger than the interval is bound to appear once in the sample and may appear more often than that. One way to deal with such districts is to make each of them a separate stratum. The districts must appear in the sample and the sampling process consists of sampling within them; they are sometimes termed 'self-representing' districts.

5.6. Concluding remarks

In this chapter we have explained some basic aspects of sample designs in use today. We noted at the beginning that if bias in selection is to be avoided and the precision of the results is to be calculable random methods must be employed, and we return to this topic in the discussion of quota sampling in the next chapter. Randomness forms the base of the entire structure of sample design. This assured, a number of refinements are possible to meet both practical and theoretical requirements. Of these, the techniques discussed in this chapter, multi-stage sampling, with equal or varying probabilities of selection, and stratification are the most important, but in addition there are a variety of other useful methods which are described in Chapter 6. In an introductory account, all these aspects of design must inevitably be described separately, although in practice the sampler calls on them in combination. It is the purpose of Chapter 8, in which a national design is given in detail, to show how a sampler goes about this task.

One other point. We have noted repeatedly how the designer of a sample needs information about the population he is sampling to do the job most effectively. To fix sample size (see Section 7.1) he must estimate the variability in the population; in order to decide on the most appropriate sampling fractions for the various strata, he ideally needs some knowledge of their respective variability and of their respective costs; in order to decide how to distribute a sample over various sampling stages, he requires information on the variabilities within and between first-stage sampling units, and again the different cost components involved. There are often approximate methods of making these estimates, but few better than to use information available from previous sample surveys of the same, or a similar, population. Sample design is a task in which one learns from experience: in which the results of one sample can and should be used to improve the design of the next.

NOTES ON READING

1. There are several excellent textbooks which describe in detail modern methods of sample design. The best treatments of the practical aspects are KISH (1965a), YATES (1960), and HANSEN, HURWITZ and MADOW (1953). These books also give theoretical treatments of the designs and, for the reader wishing to pursue the subject at this level, we should add the books by COCHRAN (1963), RAJ (1968), MURTHY (1967), and SUKHATME and SUKHATME (1970). The two chapters in KENDALL and STUART (1968, Vol. 3) are a good short account of the mathematical theory. A more elementary book on sampling theory is by YAMANE (1967). STUART (1962) presents the basic ideas of sampling non-mathematically by using a small numerical example, and SAMPFORD (1962) discusses sample designs and analyses also without much mathematical theory, and with mainly agricultural examples; the UNITED NATIONS STATISTICAL OFFICE (1960) manual also contains mainly agricultural examples. The booklet of sampling lectures by the U.S. BUREAU OF THE CENSUS (1968b) provides a useful introduction to the subject. DEMING (1960) advocates the wide use of replication in sample design (see Section 6.3).

2. Good single-chapter introductions are those by KISH in FESTINGER and KATZ (1953), MCCARTHY in JAHODA, DEUTSCH and COOK (1951), SNEDECOR and COCHRAN (1967), LAZERWITZ in BLALOCK and BLALOCK (1968), and MCCARTHY (1957).

CHAPTER 6

Further Types of Sample Design

6.1. Area sampling

I N T H E previous chapter we discussed the two most important procedures in sample design, stratification and multi-stage sampling, and noted the importance of PPS selection in multi-stage sampling when the PSU's are unequal in size. In addition there are a number of other procedures in current use, and these will be outlined in this chapter.

We will take first of all a form of multi-stage sampling, known as area sampling, which, although seldom used in Great Britain, is the main method of sampling in the many countries without adequate population lists. The student of the American literature will encounter the term very frequently. In this method the area to be covered by a survey (e.g. a country, a county or a town) is divided into a number of smaller areas, of which a sample is selected at random; within these areas, either a complete enumeration is carried out or a further sub-sample is taken. Area sampling is basically multi-stage sampling in which maps, rather than lists or registers, serve as the sampling frame.

Suppose that a survey of living conditions is to be made in a sample of dwellings in a town and that no list of the dwellings is available to serve as a sampling frame. If there is an accurate map on which clusters of dwellings—such as blocks bounded by streets—can be identified, this can act as a convenient frame. The town area is then divided into these *blocks* (if possible, of approximately equal population), the blocks are numbered and a random sample of them is selected. The boundaries of the blocks must be well-defined, easily identifiable by the fieldworkers, and every dwelling must be clearly located in one and only one block. Where they can be used, streets, railway ,lines and rivers make good boundaries; but if there are houseboats on a river the boundary must be more precisely defined, probably as one of the river banks, so that it is clear to which block each houseboat belongs.

118

In sampling the blocks, stratification and sampling with probability proportional to a measure of size are commonly employed. With area sampling, geographical stratification is particularly widely used because the necessary stratification information is provided by the map from which the sample is selected. As the blocks are being defined and numbered on the map, they can at the same time be easily grouped into strata representing the different neighbourhoods of the town. Alternatively they can be numbered in an ordered pattern—in a serpentine manner, for example—and then a systematic sample will produce an implicit geographical stratification.

The essential requirement in forming the blocks is that they must be readily identifiable. To meet this requirement a considerable variation in their sizes has to be allowed, and, as we saw in Section 5.5, such variation causes difficulties if the blocks are selected with equal probabilities. PPS sampling overcomes these difficulties, but in order to use it a measure of size must first be assigned to each block. Sometimes data on block sizes are available, perhaps from the last Census, but they must be treated with caution. With small areas like blocks a drastic increase in size can occur in a short period of time, for example by the occupation of a new apartment building, and if no allowance is made for it this can cause serious sampling difficulties. Checks are therefore needed to ensure that past data reasonably reflect the current situation, and where they do not revised estimates should be used. The size estimates do not need to be completely accurate, but only reasonably so; it is serious inaccuracies that must be avoided. In fact, if no data are available on block sizes, rapid eye estimates, obtained by touring the town, can be used satisfactorily.

When the blocks have been defined, numbered, allocated to strata and assigned measures of size, a stratified PPS sample of them can be drawn. To obtain an *epsem* sample of dwellings the sampling fractions n/mN_i' from equation (5.11) must then be applied within the selected blocks. There are two common ways of proceeding. One is to prepare a list of all the dwellings within a selected block and to sample dwellings from the list with the sampling fraction n/mN_i'. The other is to divide the block into smaller areas of almost equal size, called *segments*, to sample the segments with the sampling fraction n/mN_i', and then to take all the dwellings from the selected segments. Each method has a number of advantages and disadvantages. For instance, segment sampling introduces another stage of clustering, which will tend to result in a larger design effect than would be the case with a sample of dwellings from the list. On the other hand, segment sampling is likely to be cheaper because there is no need to compile a list of dwellings for the whole block and because its sampled dwellings are next to each other rather than being spread round the block. Another important factor to be taken into account is that the segments may provide a more complete coverage of dwellings. An interviewer going to a small segment can take pains to ensure that all the dwellings are included, but with the listing of a large block some dwellings can more easily be missed and cannot then appear in the sample.[1]

The discussion has been in terms of a town for which it has been possible to identify and list the blocks. For a larger region or a whole country it would not be feasible to list all the blocks. Instead, extra stages of sampling would be introduced. At the first stage the country might be divided into administrative areas, for which information for stratification and for PPS sampling would be available from the Census. The selected administrative areas might then be divided into townships such that each part of an area is included in one of the townships; again, where possible, it is convenient to define the townships to coincide with recognized administrative districts for which Census data would be available. A PPS sample of townships can be taken within each selected administrative district, and then within the selected townships the procedure already described can be used. Alternatively other stages are possible. Instead of dividing a township into blocks directly, it can be divided into areas containing several blocks, sometimes called *chunks*, and a PPS sample of these can be selected. The selected chunks can then be divided into blocks and a sample of blocks selected. Census enumeration districts are sometimes employed as chunks because stratification and size data are available for them.

Thus area sampling can involve a number of stages. As far as possible the areas at each stage should be defined to coincide with areas for which statistical data are available. Information on the sizes (numbers of units) of the areas is needed so that PPS selection can be employed, and other data can be used for stratification. This usually means that the areas for the early stages are administrative districts for which Census figures are produced. At the stage of sampling blocks, there are sometimes recognized blocks for which data are available, but often this is not so and the blocks must then be delineated for the survey. In this latter case, the extra work of

---

[1] Attempts can be made to correct an inadequate list. One useful technique is the *half-open interval*. The interviewer is told not only which is the sampled dwelling but also which is the next dwelling on the list. She is instructed to conduct interviews in the sampled dwelling and any other dwellings found between it and the next one on the list. By taking account of the street ordering of the dwellings, missed dwellings can thus be unambiguously linked to one, and only one, of the listed dwellings; in this way they are given the same chance as any other dwelling of being selected for the sample.

forming the blocks, stratifying them and assigning measures of size must be carried out specifically for the survey. At the final stage of an area sample, whether it is done by a complete listing or by segment sampling, the fieldworkers must be given clear and detailed instructions to ensure that they miss none of the dwellings. A low non-coverage rate, attained only through skilful and painstaking fieldwork, is crucial for a good area sample (see Mannheimer and Hyman, 1949).

6.2. Multi-phase sampling

Briefly, multi-phase sampling is a type of design in which some information is collected from the whole sample and additional information is—either at the same time or later—collected from sub-samples of the full sample. With only one sub-sample the technique is called *two-phase sampling* or *double sampling*. Multi-phase sampling should not be confused with multi-stage sampling, with which it can indeed be combined. In the latter, different types of sampling unit (administrative districts, polling districts, individuals) are sampled at different sampling stages; in multi-phase sampling, one is concerned with the same type of sampling unit at each phase, but some units are asked for more information than others.

Multi-phase sampling is best explained by looking at an example—say a household expenditure survey. Having decided what information is wanted and selected a sample of households, one can question them on *all* the matters being covered; but this may impose a considerable burden on the respondents. The question is: Can the burden be reduced? Basic data like the size and composition of the household, occupation of its head, income, etc., may indeed be needed from every sample unit; and for other aspects, such as distribution of expenditure over the main items, one may want to analyse the results in so much detail that again the whole sample must be questioned to give the required precision. But there may be less important matters on which the surveyor does not require detailed analyses or such high precision. In regard to these, and also to factors known to be fairly constant in the population, adequate precision may perhaps be achieved by questioning a smaller sample. Finally, some information may be so costly or troublesome to collect that it is feasible to collect it from only a small part of the entire sample. In each of these situations multi-phase sampling is worth considering.

Multi-phase sampling can result in considerable economies and reduce the burden on respondents. Moreover, the information collected for the full sample can be used to improve the precision of the sub-sample results. If a sub-sample is selected after completion of data collection from the full sample, the data obtained at the first phase can be used for stratification purposes in the selection of the sub-sample; and, whether the sub-sample is subsequent to, or concurrent with, the full sample, the first-phase data can be used in the analysis to improve the precision of the sub-sample results by employing post-stratification, ratio or regression estimation techniques. The information available from the full sample can also be useful for estimating the effect of non-response in the sub-sample. Basic data about many of those who fail to co-operate in the sub-sample enquiry will have been collected and the unrepresentativeness (or otherwise) of the remainder can thus be gauged; if necessary re-weighting can then be employed to counteract the unrepresentativeness.

Suppose, for example, that we want a sample of individuals stratified by educational level, but that the necessary information is not available for the population under study. A large first-phase sample could be selected and information on their educational levels could be collected from the sampled individuals. These individuals could be allocated to strata according to their educational levels and a stratified sub-sample could then be selected. Either proportionate or disproportionate stratified sampling could be employed. Here the sub-sample is selected after the first-phase data have been collected. If the data for both phases were collected concurrently, this procedure could not be used, but in this case the second-phase sample could be allocated to strata after selection, as in post-stratification. The stratum results could then be combined in the form of a weighted average, with the weights being the estimates of the proportions of the population in each stratum obtained from the first-phase sample.

The use of two-phase sampling for the sole purpose of increasing the precision of sub-sample results is effective only if the cost of data collection is considerably lower for members of the first-phase sample than for members of the sub-sample. Part of the survey's resources are used for the first phase, leaving less available for the sub-sample—which means a smaller sample size—than would have been the case had there been no first-phase sample. If two-phase sampling is to be useful, the gain in precision resulting from the use of the first-phase data to improve the sub-sample results must outweigh the loss in precision resulting from the reduction in sub-sample size. This is likely to occur only if the cost per individual of collecting the data at the first phase is cheaper than that at the second phase by a factor of at least, say, ten. This degree of variation in costs can occur, for example, when the first-phase information is taken from some form of records or collected by mail questionnaires while the second-phase information is obtained in personal interviews.

Providing that a fairly accurate and relatively cheap screening procedure is available, two-phase sampling with disproportionate stratified sub-sampling can be useful for sampling rare populations. Suppose that a study is to investigate the characteristics of persons with a rare disease for which there is a cheap but fallible test. At the first phase a large sample could be given the test, and on the basis of the test results be separated into two strata—those with positive and those with negative reactions. For the second-phase sample, a high sub-sampling fraction could be used in the positive stratum and a low one in the negative stratum; of course, if the test were a conservative one so that it was certain that none of those with a negative reaction had the disease, sub-sampling could be confined to the positive stratum. Individuals selected for the sub-sample could then undergo a thorough examination to determine whether they had the disease and, if so, their characteristics could be recorded. Cartwright (1964) used two-phase sampling in this way to obtain a sample of persons who had been in hospital in a set period shortly before the survey was undertaken. Her first-phase sample was a two-stage stratified sample of 29,400 persons selected from the Register of Electors. A brief postal questionnaire was sent to these individuals asking whether they had been in hospital during the period of interest. All the 1,119 who replied in the affirmative were selected for interview at the second phase; in fact, at interview, 15 per cent of them were found not to have been in hospital during the specified time. Those who had been in hospital were interviewed about their views of the hospital service. In this example there were thus two strata, with a 100 per cent sub-sample taken from the positive stratum and no sub-sample taken from the negative one.

Another illustration of multi-phase sampling in this country was the survey on intelligence conducted by the Population Investigation Committee and the Scottish Council for Research in Education (1949), in which a sample of about 80,000 children was used for group intelligence tests and for the main questionnaire. A more detailed questionnaire was then addressed to a sub-sample of children born on the first three days of each month. A further sub-sample comprising those born on the first day of each alternate month was used for individual intelligence tests.

Two-phase sampling has also been used in the Population Census in this country. In 1961 certain data—basic items like sex, age, marital condition and also items like number of living rooms, baths, sinks, etc.—were collected for the whole population, and other data—e.g. occupation, place of work, age at which full-time education ceased, qualifications in science or technology—were asked of only a 10 per cent sample. Multi-phase sampling has also been used in the United States Population Censuses since 1940.

6.3. Replicated sampling

A real difficulty with complex sample designs, e.g. multi-stage stratified samples, is the laboriousness of the standard error calculations. Typically a survey report contains a very large number of numerical results, so that unless the calculations are simple the amount of work involved in calculating a standard error for each result can be prohibitive. The ease of standard error calculations is a factor to be taken into account in designing a sample.

One design which yields simple formulae for standard errors is the *paired selection* design. As Kish (1965a) describes in detail, the selection of two units per stratum in single-stage sampling or two PSU's per stratum in multi-stage sampling leads to particularly simple computing procedures for standard errors.

Another flexible approach is through *replicated* or *interpenetrating* sampling, which Deming (1960) discusses in full, with a number of illustrations. With replicated sampling, a number of sub-samples rather than one full sample are selected from the population. All the sub-samples have exactly the same design and each is a self-contained and adequate sample of the population. Replicated sampling can be used with any basic design: with stratified or non-stratified, single- or multi-stage, single- or multi-phase samples. In terms of the student survey illustration in Section 5.2, the full sample of 300 students could be made up of two sub-samples of 150 each, five sub-samples of 60 each, ten sub-samples of 30 each, or whatever combination of number and size of sub-samples is required; but, however many sub-samples are decided on, each sub-sample has to be an independent sample with the same sample design, and must be a sample covering the complete college population.

With replicated sampling, sample estimates can be calculated for each of the sub-samples, and the variation between these estimates provides a means of assessing the precision of the overall estimate. Whatever the complexity of the sample design, all the sampling error is reflected in the variation between the sub-sample estimates. If an overall sample is selected by employing c independent sub-samples, z_i is the estimate for the ith sub-sample and the overall estimate is $\bar{z} = \frac{1}{c} \sum z_i$, then the standard error of $\bar{z}$ is simply estimated by

$$\text{s.e.}(\bar{z}) = \sqrt{\frac{s_z^2}{c}} = \sqrt{\frac{\sum (z_i - \bar{z})^2}{c(c-1)}} \qquad \text{...(6.1)}$$

where $s_z = \sqrt{\dfrac{1}{c-1}\sum(z_i - \bar{z})^2}$ is an estimate of the standard deviation of the sub-sample estimates, z_i. This formula applies whatever the form of sampling procedure employed in the sub-samples. In essence, this approach considers the overall estimate as the mean of an unrestricted random sample of the c sub-sample estimates, rather than treating it—as in the usual approach—as being formed from the individual sample elements selected by the combined sub-sample design. Instead of the lengthy standard error calculations for what is typically a complex design, there are thus the relatively easy calculations involved in the standard error of a mean for an unrestricted random sample of size c, $s_z/\sqrt{c}$.

Suppose, for example, that a complex sample design of 3,000 individuals consisted of ten independent replications, and that the percentages of each sub-sample with a particular attribute were as follows: 45·7, 41·7, 43·0, 40·3, 44·7, 45·0, 46·0, 50·3, 46·3, 47·0 per cent. The overall estimate is then $\bar{z} = 45\cdot 0$ per cent and its standard error is

$$\text{s.e.}(\bar{z}) = \sqrt{\frac{1}{10 \times 9}\left[(40\cdot 3 - 45\cdot 0)^2 + (41\cdot 7 - 45\cdot 0)^2 + \ldots + (50\cdot 3 - 45\cdot 0)^2\right]}$$

$$= \sqrt{\frac{72\cdot 34}{90}} = 0\cdot 9 \text{ per cent.}$$

These calculations may constitute a substantial saving over those needed in the usual approach, but the amount of work involved can still be considerable if they have to be repeated for a large number of results. A further simplification can be obtained, at some loss of precision, by using the range of the sub-sample estimates in the estimation of the standard deviation of the z_i's. If the number of replications, c, is between 3 and 13, the range r divided by $\sqrt{c}$ can be used to estimate S_z. Then the standard error of $\bar{z}$ can be estimated by

$$\text{s.e.}(\bar{z}) = \frac{r/\sqrt{c}}{\sqrt{c}} = \frac{r}{c}.$$

In the example given, the smallest z_i is 40·3 and the largest 50·3 per cent, so that

$$\text{s.e.}(\bar{z}) = \frac{(50\cdot 3 - 40\cdot 3)}{10} = 1\cdot 0 \text{ per cent}$$

a figure which agrees reasonably well with the result from the more precise procedure above.

Besides the ease of standard error calculations, replicated sampling has two other merits. The first is practical. If the size of the total sample is too large to permit the survey results to be ready in time, one or more of the replications can be used to get out advance results.

The other merit of replicated samples lies in the light they can throw on variable *non-sampling errors* (see Chapter 15). Each of the sub-samples produces an independent estimate of the population characteristics; so if each is carried out by, for instance, a different interviewer or set of interviewers, one obtains an estimate of between-interviewer variation. Replicated, or interpenetrating, samples were first regularly used for this purpose by Mahalanobis (1946).

Here, again, it must be stressed that each of the sub-samples has to be a random sample of the whole, otherwise one cannot regard them as comparable and take the difference between them as an unbiased estimate of between-interviewer variation. It would not do, for instance, to take two sub-samples by dividing the students into two halves according to special-subject group, i.e. to put economics, sociology . . . students into one half and the remainder into the other, and then take the sub-samples one from each half. If this were done, the difference between the results for the two sub-samples would not constitute a criterion of the difference between interviewers. It would be mixed up with differences between special-subject groups, and there would be no way of knowing how much of the difference was due to these and how much to interviewers.

Replicated sampling, although a valuable means of investigating non-sampling errors, must not be treated as a substitute for careful fieldwork supervision and control. For one thing, numbers in the separate sub-samples tend to be small, so that detailed investigation of interviewer errors is rarely possible, only the major sources of variation being discovered; for another, replicated samples do not disclose either the systematic errors common to all interviewers, for these will appear equally in the separate sub-samples, or the compensating errors which cancel each other out over an interviewer's assignment.

A decision to be made with replicated sampling is how many replications to employ. If it is to be used as a means of studying non-sampling errors, it is usual to have only a small number of replications because of the need to allocate each sub-sample to each individual interviewer or team of interviewers. Mahalanobis (1946), for example, often used four replications. On the other hand, if it is to be used to obtain simple estimates of standard errors, more replications are desirable, because this leads to greater precision for these estimates.[1] For this purpose Deming (1960) has made wide use of ten replications.

[1] This question is discussed in greater detail on pp. 207–8.

A disadvantage of the use of many replications is that it can severely limit the amount of stratification that can be employed. Take, for instance, the case of a multi-stage sample with, say, sixty PSU's to be selected and ten replications. As each replication must contain at least one PSU from each stratum, there must be at least ten PSU's selected from each stratum. As a consequence, with the limitation of sixty PSU's in all, there can be no more than six strata. In the selection of PSU's it is usually advantageous to have more strata than this, and so this limitation is a real drawback to the use of replicated sampling with multi-stage sampling. In the case of single-stage sampling, however, the limitation is commonly unimportant. One reason is that there is often less stratification information available. But also more strata are possible: with a single-stage sample of, say, 1,500 units and ten replications, there can be as many as 150 strata, which would nearly always be more than ample.

Further discussion of replicated sampling is to be found in Chapter 15 and at the end of Chapter 8 (pp. 207–9).

6.4. Quota sampling

The types of design discussed so far have all embodied the feature of randomness, thus ensuring that every member of the population has a calculable chance of being included in the sample. A wide variety of procedures go under the name of quota sampling, but what distinguishes them all fundamentally from probability sampling is that, once the general breakdown of the sample is decided (e.g. how many men and women, how many people in each age group and in each 'social class' it is to include) and the quota assignments are allocated to interviewers, the choice of the *actual* sample units to fit into this framework is left to the interviewers. Quota sampling is therefore a method of stratified sampling in which the selection within strata is non-random. It is this non-random element that constitutes its greatest weakness.

The issue of quota versus probability sampling has been a matter of controversy for many years. Some experts hold the quota method to be so unreliable and prone to bias as to be almost worthless; others think that, although it is obviously less sound theoretically than probability sampling, it can be used safely on some subjects; still others believe that with adequate safeguards quota sampling can be made highly reliable and that the extra cost of probability sampling is not worth while. In general, statisticians have criticized the method for its theoretical weakness, while market and opinion researchers have defended it for its cheapness and administrative convenience.

Before we look at the pros and cons, the method must be described in a little detail.

The quota controls

Let us suppose that a national opinion survey is to be based on a quota sample. The first step will probably be to stratify by region, by urban/rural area and perhaps by town size, just as in a stratified random sample. Nor do the two methods necessarily part company when it comes to selecting, say, administrative districts (or constituencies) within these broad strata. Indeed it is common, although not necessary, for quota samples to employ random selection procedures at the initial stages of selection in exactly the same way as probability samples. The essential difference between probability and quota samples lies in the selection of the final sampling units, say individuals.

In quota sampling, each interviewer is given an assignment of interviews, specifying how many of them are to be with men and how many with women, how many with people in various age groups, social classes and so forth. These *quotas* are calculated from available data to arrange that, for the whole country and possibly even for each region, the sexes, age groups and social classes are represented in the sample in the right proportions. In other words, the total sample, as well as being stratified by region, urban/rural area, town size and so forth, is stratified also by sex, age and social class.

The kind of factor to be chosen as a quota control is partly determined by its usefulness as a stratification factor; if a control fails to separate the population into strata which differ in their opinions on the subject under study, it is of no value. But another consideration to be taken into account is the differences between groups of people in their probabilities of being available for interview. If working women have markedly different opinions from housewives and, as a group, are less likely to be available for interview, a quota sample which fails to use a control to ensure that both groups are properly represented in the sample would be seriously in error. If the availability for interview of the two groups were the same, the failure to include a control to separate them would result only in a loss of precision; but, if their availabilities differed, the omission would be more serious, leading to a substantial bias. Thus a second consideration in the choice of controls is that the resulting strata should, as far as possible, be homogeneous with respect to their members' availability for interview. This consideration led to the use by the National Opinion Research Center at the University of Chicago of controls forming four strata—men under thirty, men thirty and over, unemployed women and employed women (Sudman, 1966, also reproduced in Sudman, 1967, Chapter 2).

Age and sex controls are universally used as quota controls and, in

Britain at least, the social class control[1] is also widely employed. Incidentally, these three factors can rarely be used for stratifying random samples, although they can, of course, often be used for post-stratification. Neither the sex nor the age control presents much difficulty as there are statistics on which to base them and as interviewers can decide without trouble to which group a respondent belongs.

The social class control, often a vital part of quota samples, is more difficult on both counts. First, there is no reliable statistical basis for setting the quotas, since the definition of social class usually involves a combination of objective factors, such as occupation and income, and subjective factors like appearance, speech and so forth. Secondly, the definition of the control is generally vague, leaving some play to the interviewer's subjective judgement and bias. It is true, of course, that the social class grouping is often broad (often into only three or four strata) so that inaccuracies in the quotas or in the interpretation of the definitions may not cause major bias; but even so, this is an aspect of quota sampling open to criticism.

The three major controls are often supplemented by special controls (housewife/not housewife; head/non-head of household; occupation and industry; marital status) when the subject under study seems to call for them. The tendency is, however, against the use of many extra controls since they make the interviewer's task more difficult.

The assignment schemes

Once the controls and quotas have been fixed, the next step is to give each interviewer her assignment. The difference between the two common assignment schemes, respectively called 'independent' and 'interrelated' controls, is illustrated by the following hypothetical assignments:

Independent Controls

SEX	
Male	9
Female	11
Total	20

AGE	
20–29	4
30–44	6
45–64	7
65 +	3
Total	20

SOCIAL CLASS	
Highest	2
Middle	4
Lowest	14
Total	20

[1] Alternatively called income grade, economic group, social status, socio-economic status etc.

Interrelated Controls

		SOCIAL CLASS					Total
		Highest		*Middle*		*Lowest*	
	SEX	*Male*	*Female*	*Male*	*Female*	*Male*	*Female*	
AGE	20–29	1	–	–	1	1	1	4
	30–44	–	1	–	1	3	1	6
	45–64	–	–	1	1	2	3	7
	65 +	–	–	–	–	1	2	3
	Totals	1	1	1	3	7	7	20
		2		4		14		

With independent controls, only the marginal quotas for sexes, ages and social class groups are set; there is no formal attempt to relate these controls to each other, to ensure for instance that a given number of interviews in each age group are with women, a certain number with men. With interrelated controls, the numbers to be interviewed in all these sub-groups are assigned.

There are advantages in both schemes. Independent controls are simpler for the interviewer and, on the whole, less costly; they are also easier to set accurately since a statistical basis is more readily found for the marginal quotas than for the sub-groups.[1] But they are less likely to ensure sample representativeness. Thus interviewers may so select respondents that all or most of the women are elderly and the men young, and so on. True, they are instructed to avoid such 'pairing' of controls, but instructions cannot ensure that the resultant sample is equivalent to the proportional spread over the sub-groups which interrelated controls would give. Some findings on this point are given by Moser and Stuart (1953).

Whatever type of scheme is used, it is up to the interviewer, aided by instructions, to approach people she thinks will fit into her quotas, interview them if she finds they do, and otherwise politely reject

[1] It sometimes occurs with multiple stratification in probability sampling that only the marginal distributions for the stratification factors are known. In this case a technique which Yates (1960) has called 'multiple stratification without control of sub-strata' can be used. With this technique multiple stratification is employed in such a way that the *overall* proportions for each of the stratification factors are equal to those in the population, but without trying to equate the sample proportions in the individual cells. Readers are referred to Yates (1960) for a discussion.

them.[1] Unless instructed to the contrary, she may interview anywhere—at homes, in offices, factories, parks, public places or the street. Some organizations allow no street interviewing and insist that housewives are interviewed at home, working men in offices and factories. Some place-of-work interviewing is obviously desirable (unless the field-work is done in the evenings or at weekends) if important sections of the population are not to be missed.

This is one of the crucial worries with quota sampling—does it end up with representative samples of the population? For instance, unless special controls are set to ensure that different occupations are correctly represented, they may easily not be. Interviewers, being human, may tend to select people who are readily at hand (subject to instructions and controls) and thus favour certain groups. A clear-cut illustration is the following occupation distribution achieved by two comparable surveys, one based on a national quota sample, the other on a national random sample.

TABLE 6.1

Percentage distribution by occupation/industry
Quota and random samples

Occupation/industry	Men		Women	
	Quota sample	Random sample	Quota sample	Random sample
Manufacturing	6·5	24·9	4·3	7·2
Clerical	3·8	5·0	4·2	4·6
Distributive	15·7	5·9	9·0	3·0
Transport and Public Services	18·3	7·6	1·3	—
Professional and Managerial	18·1	20·0	5·4	3·2
Mining and Quarrymaking	1·4	4·6	—	—
Building and Road-making	14·3	6·3	0·2	—
Agriculture	2·4	2·8	0·3	0·8
Other Industries	15·5	8·1	10·3	5·5
Housewives	—	2·0	64·8	69·2
Retired, unoccupied, part-time	4·0	12·6	0·2	6·6
Not stated	—	0·2	—	—
Total	100·0	100·0	100·0	100·1

Source: Quota sample—British Market Research Bureau; Random sample—Government Social Survey. See Moser and Stuart (1953, p. 352).

[1] Contrast this with the task of the random sample interviewer, who is given the address and (usually) the name of every respondent, told not to take any sub-stitutes and to continue her efforts—within stated limits—until she has secured an interview with the pre-selected respondent.

This shows a large excess in the quota sample of persons employed in distribution, transport, the public services, and building and road-making, and a correspondingly small proportion of persons employed in manufacturing. Comparisons with other data showed the random sample proportions to be broadly correct.

It does not necessarily follow that this maldistribution in the quota sample would bias its results: that depends on whether the questions studied were closely related to occupation. But it does illustrate the dependence of quota sample composition on the ways and whims of interviewers. Even allowing for the controls and instructions usual in quota surveys, interviewers retain considerable freedom in deciding where, when and whom to interview.

Sampling variability

The crucial problem with quota samples, as with non-probability samples generally, is the inability to estimate their representativeness. With a non-probability sample it is impossible both to estimate sampling variability from the sample and to know about the possible biases involved.

But some progress can be made with regard to sampling variability of non-probability samples by using the ideas of replicated sampling. If the same non-probability sampling plan is applied several times, the variation between the results obtained on the different applications provides a means of assessing the variability of the sampling plan. If, for example, a quota sample of 500 interviews was required for a particular town, the total sample could be divided into, say, ten replicates of 50 interviews each, where 50 interviews represented one interviewer's assignment. If the interviewers were then given identical instructions on how to select their samples, the variation between the results obtained by the ten interviewers could be used in the manner described in Section 6.3 to provide an estimate of the variability of the total sample. The estimate so obtained measures not only the sampling error of the total sample, but it also includes interviewer variance. The sampling error is included because interviewers will differ in the samples they select for interview. The interviewer variance, a form of non-sampling error, arises from the fact that the answer recorded for a respondent might differ depending on which interviewer conducted the interview (see Chapter 15).

It is generally advantageous to include interviewer variance in measuring a sample's precision, but if it were unwanted it could be removed by modifying the design of the replicated samples (see Stuart, 1968). The design must generally also be modified for national surveys or surveys covering large areas, because it is usually not feasible to allocate widely spread interviews completely at random among the interviewers (see pp. 400–1).

While replicated sampling can be used in order to measure the precision of a non-random sample, it tells one nothing of the other major problem, selection bias. If, for example, all interviewers over-sample men from certain occupations, this bias cannot be identified by comparing the results of the various interviewers. With probability samples, the surveyor commonly uses estimators with no, or at least little, bias, and so he can concentrate his attention on the precision (sampling error) of his sample. But while the quota sampler might measure the precision of his sample by using replicated methods, he must always face the danger of an unknown, but sizeable, bias.

Stephan and McCarthy (1958, Chapter 10) discuss sampling variability of quota samples in greater detail.

The main arguments against quota sampling

(*a*) The use of random selection, as already explained, generally makes it possible to attach estimates of standard errors to the sample results. Apart from the use of replicated methods, which are generally likely to be somewhat more costly and difficult to set up, and especially so in national surveys, it is not possible to estimate sampling errors with quota sampling. This is because quota sampling does not meet the basic requirement of randomness.

It is sometimes argued that sampling errors are so small compared with all the other errors and biases that enter into surveys that it is no great disadvantage not to be able to estimate them. There is no denying the importance of other kinds of errors or the fact that, in most surveys, their precise magnitude is unknown. But the point is that, with random sampling, at least sampling error and sampling bias are under control and measurable. One does not have to worry about them. With quota sampling this security is lacking.

(*b*) Within the quota groups, interviewers may fail to secure a representative sample of respondents. They may, for instance, fill the top age group of 65 and over mainly with persons of 65 and 66, so that the very old are under-represented. This is a crucial problem of quota sampling: given that all the quotas are correctly filled—i.e. that every sampling unit is in the group to which it belongs—is the selection within groups such that a representative sample emerges? Is the spread within the groups right? Are the extremes sufficiently represented? Also, are the groups representative with respect to other variables, which were not used as quota controls? Quota samplers generally claim that instructions to, and constraints on, interviewers are sufficient to guard against the main dangers of selection bias, but this is a matter of belief rather than fact.

(c) The widely used and important social class control can be criticized on two grounds: it is based on a hazardous statistical foundation and, as generally defined, leaves a great deal to the interviewer's judgement.

(d) The method makes strict control of the fieldwork more difficult. In particular, it is not easy to check to what extent interviewers place respondents in the groups where cases are needed rather than in those to which they belong.

The main arguments for quota sampling

(a) Quota sampling is less costly. The strength of this argument is hard to assess because of the many factors involved. For example, the greater the number of controls employed the more expensive a quota sample will be, but the smaller will be the danger of selection biases; also, the wider the geographical spread of a quota sample, the costlier it will be, but the greater will be the resulting precision. From the little evidence available it seems that quota samples have greater sampling variability than probability samples (see, for example, p. 136), which also needs to be taken into account. For this kind of reason, a true cost comparison is made not in terms of cost per interview, but rather in terms of the cost of a survey for a pre-scribed level of precision. While no accurate comparisons are available, it has been suggested that, because call-backs are avoided and because there is no need to travel all over a town to track down pre-selected respondents, a quota interview costs on average only a half or a third as much as a random interview; but for most surveys it is likely that much, if not all, of this apparent saving would disappear if the proper cost comparisons were made.

(b) It is easy administratively. The labour of random sample selection is avoided, and so are the headaches of non-contacts and call-backs. Quota sampling does not of course *avoid* non-response. There are no non-contacts, in the sense of pre-selected respondents being out when the interviewer calls; but just as such persons tend to be missed in random sampling so other kinds of people (perhaps those who are most at home) tend to be missed by quota sampling. Refusals occur in both methods: an experiment by Moser and Stuart (1953) showed a refusal rate for the random samples of about 3 per cent, for the quota samples of about 8 per cent.

(c) If the fieldwork has to be done quickly, perhaps in order to reduce memory errors, quota sampling may be the only possibility.

This is the situation with the BBC Audience Research surveys, which take a national sample of 2,250 people each day and question them about the previous day's programmes (British Broadcasting Corporation, 1966). Also, by using quota sampling, the fieldwork for a national study in the United States to obtain the immediate public reaction to President John Kennedy's assassination was conducted by N.O.R.C. in about ten days (Sudman, 1966; also 1967).

(d) Quota sampling is independent of the existence of sampling frames and may be the only practicable method of sampling a population for which no suitable frame is available. If no list exists, the use of maps as a frame for area sampling usually enables a random sample of persons or households to be selected, so that generally probability sampling is possible. But a practical difficulty can arise when the survey population comprises only a small proportion of the total population, is sparsely spread over the country, and is not listed on its own; for example, this could be the case for a market research study concerned to discover the characteristics of smokers of a particular brand of cigarette. It would be possible to obtain a probability sample of these smokers by taking a much larger sample from the whole population and rejecting all those who did not smoke the brand in question, but such a procedure would probably be prohibitively expensive. Quota sampling might be the only practicable way to proceed in this case. There are, however, a variety of techniques for probability sampling of rare populations that should be considered first.

An experiment on quota sampling

The debate on the merits of quota and random sampling has gone on for a number of years, little aided by experimental evidence. When survey results obtained by the two methods could be compared, sometimes they have been remarkably close, at other times quota sampling appeared to have gone astray. To secure evidence on the subject the Division of Research Techniques at the London School of Economics undertook a research programme on quota sampling. The results have been published (Moser, 1952, and Moser and Stuart, 1953), and only some general conclusions will be mentioned here.

On two important factors, occupation and education, the quota samples were shown to be unrepresentative. These were among the factors which could (with qualifications) be checked against the 1951 Population Census figures. The occupation results largely confirm the findings shown on p. 131. The education question was that asked in the Census: 'At what age did you finally stop receiving full-time education?', and the results showed a pronounced tendency in the quota samples to under-represent those who finished education before the age of 15. It has often been suggested that quota samples obtain too educated a cross-section of the population, and the results here confirmed this view. On most of the other comparisons between the random and quota sample results, the differences were slight; there seemed little evidence of other selection biases in the quota samples.

The experiment was designed to make it possible to estimate the sampling variability of the quota samples by using replicated sampling, and the results showed that the quota sampling variance, though it varied from question to question, was generally between one and three times as great as the theoretical variance of a random sample of the same size. The authors suggested that this difference was mainly due to 'between-interviewer' variability in the selection of quota samples, i.e. that pairs of interviewers given the same assignment (in the same town and so forth) selected markedly different samples and that it was this factor, not present in random sampling, that accounted for the large difference. Some support for this view was provided in a subsequent experiment by Durbin and Stuart (1954a, p. 409). It should be pointed out that the findings reported here relate to *single-stage* sampling within large cities; and that the increase in variance of a multi-stage quota sample employing probability sampling methods in all but the final stage, over that of the equivalent multi-stage sample using probability methods throughout, would almost certainly be smaller.

It must of course be remembered that the cheapness of quota samples has to be weighed up against their higher variability. If the cost per interview was half that of random samples and the variance on average over twice as great, quota sampling would not pay—quite apart from the danger of bias in it.

That the experiment revealed relatively few major differences between the quota and random sample results does not contradict the fact that quota sampling is theoretically unsound; rather it provides one more reason for observing that, in the hands of practitioners of long experience—the quota setting and fieldwork were done by leading market and opinion research organizations—the method can give reasonably accurate overall results. Nor is this surprising. The three controls of sex, age and social class together account, as they are designed to, for a great proportion of the variation in the answers to many questions. By arranging that the sample is broadly representative on these factors, the quota sampler makes sure that the results will not be dangerously out of line.

But although skilful quota sampling can succeed in practice, it is not suitable for surveys in which it is important that the results are derived from theoretically safe methods. Only random sampling fulfils this requirement. In saying this, we are not forgetting the non-response and non-coverage problems, which some quota sampling proponents hold up as generating a theoretical weakness in random sampling on a par with the known weakness of quota sampling. This point of view is hardly supportable. In random samples, the surveyor should be able to assume that as regards about 70 to 90 per cent of the sample he is on safe theoretical ground; even as regards the remainder he is only partially in the dark since it is often possible broadly to assess the effects of non-response and non-coverage on the results. The quota sampler does not reach such comparative safety; he is—to use the words of Yates—'continually looking over his shoulder and wondering whether some extraneous factor exists which will vitiate the conclusions based on his results' (Moser and Stuart, 1953, discussion, p. 398). It is doubtful, in spite of this, whether quota sampling will ever completely disappear; there will always be the practitioner to whom the discomfort of 'continually looking over his shoulder' is compensated by the apparent saving of money.

In conclusion, mention must be made of the attempts to combine random and quota sampling. Many quota samplers, for instance, use designs in which each interviewer is assigned to a district or block and is given—in addition to the usual quotas—exact instructions on how to proceed. She may be told to call at every second house and interview everyone (or one person) in it until her quota is filled. Such a design restricts the interviewer's influence but it still does not yield a random sample. Sudman (1966, also 1967) describes the use of a prescribed travel pattern for the interviewers and, in order to distinguish this method from quota sampling lacking such detailed geographical control, calls it 'probability sampling with quotas'.

6.5. Panel and longitudinal studies

This is the most convenient point at which to discuss the panel method, in which the aim is to collect data from the same sample on more than one occasion. Problems of initial sample design are no different for panels than for single surveys, but there are special problems of maintaining sample representativeness.

The panel begins as a randomly selected sample of the survey population. Information is then sought from this sample at intervals, either by mail or by personal interview.[1] Volunteer panels are excluded from this discussion.

[1] Coombs and Freedman (1964) describe how telephone interviews were used successfully in a longitudinal fertility study in the United States.

The advantages of panels

One attraction of panels is that they offer a good way of studying trends, whether of behaviour or attitudes. If a market researcher wants to study how brand preferences change from month to month a panel enables him to do so conveniently. He could, of course, obtain this information by taking fresh samples each month, but the panel approach has several advantages.

First, there is the question of precision. A panel study nearly always measures changes with greater precision than does a series of independent samples of the same size. If a market research study yields a mean $\bar{y}_1$ for the first month and $\bar{y}_2$ for the second, the change between the months is the difference $\bar{y}_1 - \bar{y}_2$. The precision of this estimator of the change is measured by the variance (square of the standard error) of the difference, and this is given by

$$\text{Var}(\bar{y}_1 - \bar{y}_2) = \text{Var}(\bar{y}_1) + \text{Var}(\bar{y}_2) - 2\rho\sqrt{\text{Var}(\bar{y}_1) \cdot \text{Var}(\bar{y}_2)} \quad ...(6.2)$$

where ρ is the product-moment correlation between $\bar{y}_1$ and $\bar{y}_2$. With completely independent samples ρ is zero, but in a panel study, using the same sample in both months, ρ is the correlation between the individuals' responses on the two occasions. Generally responses to the same question on successive occasions will be positively correlated and, when this is so, the variance of the change will be lower for a panel study than for completely independent samples. In the above equation, the first two terms on the right-hand side represent the variance of the difference for independent samples, and the third term is the reduction (providing ρ is positive) for the correlation between the samples. In passing, it is worth noting that this equation indicates the general principle for experimental designs that when the aim is to study differences, over time or between different sub-groups of the population, greater precision is to be had if the samples can be drawn so that a positive correlation exists between them. One use of the technique of matching or blocking is to generate a positive correlation between matched pairs or groups and so get gains in precision for contrasts (see Section 9.3).

A second advantage of panels is that they can be useful for studying the effects of specifically introduced measures, such as advertisements. With one measurement before the introduction of the experimental variable and another afterwards, the design is known as the before-after design without control group. As is shown in Chapter 9, this design has severe weaknesses, and a better design is to extend the panel study to include several pre- and post-measurements, that is to make it into a time-series design (see p. 224).

Panels have another important advantage. They enable the

researcher to measure not only net changes (which independent samples could do also) but in addition to identify and study the 'changers'. The data can be conveniently set out in a *turnover table*, of which Table 6.2 contains two examples.

TABLE 6.2

Examples of a turnover table

	EXAMPLE 1				EXAMPLE 2		
	Period 2		per		Period 2		per
	Favour X	Do not	cent		Favour X	Do not	cent
Period 1		favour X	Total	Period 1		favour X	Total
Favour				Favour			
X	48	0	48	X	20	28	48
Do not favour				Do not favour			
X	6	46	52	X	34	18	52
Total	54	46	100	Total	54	46	100

In both examples, 48 per cent favoured Brand X in period 1 and 54 per cent favoured it in period 2, but there is nevertheless a marked difference between the two sets of data. In Example 1, there are very few changes, with no one ceasing to favour Brand X and just 6 per cent changing to favour Brand X in period 2. In Example 2, on the other hand, although the net change is the same—a 6 per cent increase in those favouring Brand X—there is a great deal of change, with 62 per cent of the respondents changing their answers between the two periods. By means of the turnover table, the panel method makes it possible to measure gross as well as net changes.

The turnover table relates answers to the same question at different times, but panel studies can more generally provide data for relating on an individual basis the answers to any questions asked at the same or at different times. Relationships between questions asked at the same time can be investigated from a single survey, but the relationship on an individual basis between the answers to questions asked at different times, often of great interest in social research, can only be investigated through a panel study. To illustrate the importance of this, we will cite the Population Investigation Committee's longitudinal study.[1] The study started in 1946, when information was collected on all confinements in Great Britain

[1] Many of the findings of this study are reported in Douglas and Blomfield (1958), Douglas (1964), and Douglas, Ross and Simpson (1968). A similar later national study, the National Child Development Study, was started in 1958; the first report is by Pringle and others (1966).

during the first week of March. Since that time further information has been collected at intervals on a sample of the children born in that week (excluding multiple births and illegitimate children). The information collected includes data on their families—size, changes in social status, parents' ages, etc.; on their health experience—record of accidents, major episodes of illness, doctor's examinations, hospital records, etc.; on their schooling—absences, type of schooling, tests of mental ability and achievement, G.C.E. examination results, university entrance, etc. From these data can be studied such issues as the relationship between premature births and mental ability at, say, eight years old; the relationship between mental ability at eight and eleven; and so on. A longitudinal study of this sort provides a tremendous wealth of data, and the particular advantage of the method is that it enables the inter-relationships between variables relating to different times to be investigated. Sometimes data for different times can be collected from a single survey by asking respondents to remember some past event or by referring to past records; but for many questions this procedure places undue reliance on memory and, for questions such as a respondent's attitude at a past time, it would be entirely undependable. The panel study collects data at the time of interest, and so need not rely on a respondent's ability to recall the past.

Panel studies also provide evidence on the temporal ordering of variables, an important factor in causal analysis since no effect can precede its cause. A cross-sectional study may show an association between a worker's attitude to his job and his position in the firm, but it does not indicate which came first; perhaps his favourable attitude led to promotion or promotion may have changed his attitude. A panel study recording promotions and measuring workers' attitudes at intervals would provide data for distinguishing between these two possible explanations of the association.

Administratively, panels have the advantage that the overhead costs of sample selection can be spread over many surveys and that they make for easy fieldwork planning. Further, once people have agreed to give information it is generally possible to obtain fuller and more reliable data than in a single survey.

The problems of panels

The chief problems of panels are the achievement of the initial sample, sample mortality and conditioning.

To recruit a representative panel of respondents willing to provide detailed information regularly is clearly no mean task. It is one thing to ask a housewife a few questions on one occasion; it is quite another to ask her to supply information at set intervals over an extended period. In the case of the original Attwood Consumer Panel a member of the panel had to record her purchases covering a wide range of non-durable goods in a weekly diary.[1] Initially 80 per cent of the contacts agreed to be enrolled on this panel, a satisfactory enough figure, but, by the time the first reporting period came round, 1 in 5 of these failed to co-operate. This left 64 per cent of the initial sample, and even these did not all stay the course. It is the experience of researchers that the first few weeks (or months or quarters, depending on the reporting period) always take a heavy toll of panel membership and that it then settles down. The Attwood panel lost a further 16 per cent of the total in the first six weeks, so that 48 per cent of the original sample remained. Those who refused or dropped out were replaced by households with similar demographic characteristics. What is difficult to ascertain is how typical those who refused to co-operate or who dropped out were of the remainder; they may have been less literate, busier, had bigger families, less interest in the survey and so on.[2] True, the composition of the remaining sample can be checked against known data on some factors, but this is only a partial reassurance; its representativeness with regard to the behaviour and attitudes that are the subject of the survey must remain in doubt. The respondents who drop out during the life of the panel can be compared with those remaining in terms of their earlier responses. But, even if the responses are comparable, it does not necessarily follow that the remainder of the panel is still representative; it might be that those who dropped out have changed in a different way from the rest of the panel, perhaps changing to a new brand whereas the rest do not, with the result that the new brand is under-represented in the panel's purchases. Panels of this sort are not, of course, alone in suffering from non-response, but because of their generally greater burden on respondents the problem is bigger.

For long-term longitudinal studies, like that of the Population Investigation Committee described above, the problem of panel mortality arises in a different way. In such studies the burden on respondents is generally not as great as in consumer panels, so that initial refusals and refusals to continue in the study are likely to be less serious problems. On the other hand, the difficulties of tracing respondents are far greater, especially when the interval between interviews is as long as a year or more. Some respondents will move house, and they must be traced to their new address if they are to be

[1] See Wadsworth (1952), Le Mesurier (1954), and Ehrenberg (1960) for a description of the Attwood Consumer Panel.
[2] Sobol (1959) reports the panel mortality and panel bias in a five-wave study of economic attitude formation and change, plans to buy cars and durable goods, and fulfilment of these plans, conducted by the Survey Research Center, University of Michigan.

retained in the sample. A variety of ways exist for tracing people, such as checking with the post office for a forwarding address and checking telephone directories, and all ways need to be pursued to achieve a high rate of success. One factor that can usefully be included in questionnaires for longitudinal surveys is the address of the respondent's closest relative, for if he has moved his closest relative will probably know his current whereabouts. Eckland (1968) discusses ways of tracing mobile people in the United States, and gives several examples of the high success rates (around 90 per cent and higher) that can be reached, even if the persons have to be traced over gaps of many years.

Long-term studies also suffer another kind of depletion, for some members of a panel will die, and others will leave the survey population in other ways, such as by emigration. Unlike refusals and failure to trace respondents, these losses do not cause a bias in the panel, but just reflect the natural decrease in the original population; the panel survivors are a representative sample of the surviving members of the population. On the other hand the current population may also include some persons who are not represented on the panel, such as new immigrants and births (or people reaching whatever is the minimum age for membership of the defined population). A supplementary sample of this group may be needed to make the panel representative of the full current population.

A real danger with repeat interviews from the same sample is 'panel conditioning', which is the risk that the panel members may become untypical as a result of being on the panel. This is not as fanciful as may at first appear. Members of a radio listening panel may gradually become more critical of programmes, more conscious of defects, more interested and more attentive. Those on a consumer panel may with time become more aware of different brands, of advertisements, and of different forms of presentation; they may also become increasingly conscious of their spending habits and in sheer horror tighten their belts. Members of a panel studying political opinions may try to appear consistent in the views they express on consecutive occasions. If such things happen, the panel becomes untypical—not in composition but in its characteristics—of the population it was selected to represent.

Besides affecting the panel's characteristics, conditioning may also change the accuracy of reporting. As they gain experience, panel members asked to recall events may give more accurate responses as a result of an improvement in memory. On the other hand, if they have to keep detailed records, the completeness of their recording may decrease over time through fatigue. In either case, comparisons of the results of different waves of the panel will be biased.

Panel operators are conscious of the dangers from conditioning and keep a watchful eye for signs of it. There are several possible checks, the best being the expensive one of selecting independent samples of the population at regular intervals and comparing their characteristics and results with those of the panel. Another safeguard is to give members only a limited panel life, and then to replace them with persons taken randomly from a reserve list (perhaps from within strata of family composition, social status and so on).

There is a strong case for using some form of partial replacement in panels, but it has to be rigorously applied. The method has been theoretically developed (see Yates, 1960, Kish, 1965a) and the chief objection, from the panel operator's viewpoint, is that it goes against the grain to replace panel members who are co-operative and reliable. There is a variety of rotation designs for replacing members of a panel, and some of them can be quite complex. The monthly U.S. Current Population Surveys, for instance, use a design in which households are included for eight months, but this is made up of four consecutive months followed by a gap of eight months and then another set of four consecutive months. The purpose of this '4-8-4' rotation system is to have overlaps in both monthly and yearly samples (U.S. Bureau of the Census, 1963a). In this manner, rotation designs can be fashioned to measure changes over specified intervals with greater precision than would be the case if independent samples were used, while the limited period of panel membership helps to anticipate the difficulties of panel mortality and conditioning.

6.6. Master samples

If repeated samples of the same area or population are to be taken, there are advantages in preparing some sort of master sample, from which sub-samples can be taken as and when required. This was first done on a big scale in the U.S. Master Sample of Agriculture, described by King (1945) and Jessen (1945), for which the country was divided into a large number of small areas and a master sample of 70,000 constructed, representative of every county. Sub-samples from this could be drawn to give whatever regional or national coverage was required for a survey. The main advantage of master samples is that they simplify and speed up the selection procedure.

The sample units into which a master sample is divided should be relatively permanent. There would be little point in constructing a master sample of individuals or households since, owing to deaths, births and removals, it would quickly become out-of-date; a master sample of dwellings would be of more long-term usefulness, although even here the construction of new homes would be a major cause of out-of-dateness.

F

A commonly used and valuable procedure for organizations conducting surveys repeatedly from a widely spread population is to select the primary sampling units once and then to select from within these PSU's whenever a sample is required. Thus, for example, for a national sample of Great Britain, one hundred constituencies might be selected at the first stage and then for any survey the sample would be drawn from within these constituencies. Interviewers living within each of the PSU's can be recruited, and they will not need to travel outside their own constituencies. They can be employed for several years until the sample of PSU's has to be replaced, and the cost of their training is spread over all the surveys on which they work. In addition, extra data can be collected about the constituencies in order to improve the sampling procedures adopted within them; for instance, extra stratification information could be collected about their polling districts and used in the sampling of polling districts at the second stage. Again the costs involved are spread over all the surveys taken from these PSU's. With area sampling the cost of purchasing maps and preparing materials for drawing the second and subsequent stages of the sample is often high, and so it is particularly advantageous to spread it over a number of surveys. Not all the PSU's need to be used every time and, for small surveys, the sample can be restricted to a sub-sample of the PSU's originally selected.

Successive samples taken from the same PSU's are not independent, a factor which, since it generally leads to an increase in precision for changes, can be helpful in measuring the change from one survey to the next. The correlation between the samples can be increased by selecting both samples from the same second stage or, where applicable, later stage, or even by selecting neighbouring households for successive surveys. Generally the closer together the sampled units from two surveys are, the greater the correlation will be, and hence, from equation (6.2), the more precisely will the change be measured. Panel studies constitute the limiting case of this, when the same units are used on both occasions.

With the passage of time the sample of PSU's may need changing. This arises not because all the units within the PSU's get 'used up', which in practice would not happen with PSU's as large as constituencies, but rather because changes in the population may mean that some of the PSU's would fit better in different strata, and because the measures of size used in the original probability proportional to size selection of the PSU's may become seriously inaccurate. A simple approach would be to take a completely fresh sample of PSU's, but this would probably include only a few of the earlier selections, in which so much has been invested in terms of interviewers and sample data. Techniques have therefore been developed to update the sample for measures of size and stratification and yet keep a high proportion of the original sample. These methods are discussed by Kish (1965a, Section 12.7).

NOTES ON READING

1. Most of the methods treated in this chapter are discussed in the textbooks given in the notes at the end of Chapter 5. The paper by GRAY and CORLETT (1950), based on the work of the Government Social Survey, gives a full account of the use of many of the basic designs in national surveys in this country. MOSER (1955) and, more recently, EMMETT (1964) indicate some of the changes that have taken place since that paper appeared.

2. On area sampling, the American literature gives the best treatment. It is discussed in the textbooks by KISH (1965a), HANSEN, HURWITZ and MADOW (1953, Vol. I), DEMING (1950) and DEMING (1960). There are also useful papers by KISH (1952), KEYFITZ and ROBINSON (1949) and HANSEN and HAUSER (1945). The use of area sampling in the U.S. Current Population Survey is fully described in the report by the U.S. BUREAU OF THE CENSUS (1963a).

3. A number of illustrations of replicated sampling are given in DEMING (1960). MAHALANOBIS (1946) and LAHIRI (1958) describe its use in the Indian Statistical Institute for investigation of non-sampling errors.

4. On quota sampling, readers may refer to papers by MOSER (1952), MOSER and STUART (1953), SUDMAN (1966, also in SUDMAN, 1967) and STUART (1968); and also the book by STEPHAN and MCCARTHY (1958).

5. On panels, a publication by the U.S. DEPARTMENT OF AGRICULTURE (1952) is well worth studying. So are the articles by LAZARSFELD (1948), WILSON (1954), FERBER (1953), the report by NETER and WAKSBERG (1965), the chapter in ZEISEL (1957) and the chapter by GLOCK in LAZARSFELD and ROSENBERG (1955). GOLDSTEIN (1968) discusses problems with longitudinal surveys and DOUGLAS and BLOMFIELD (1956) discuss the reliability of the Population Investigation Committee's study. Recent election enquiries using a panel study are those of BUTLER and STOKES (1969) and BLUMLER and MCQUAIL (1968). Additional references on panels and longitudinal studies are cited in the text.

CHAPTER 7

Other Aspects of Sampling

7.1. Sample size

W E H A V E now looked both at the basic ideas of sampling and at the designs that are commonly used. It remains to discuss a few other aspects of sampling of general importance—the question of sample size, the use of random sampling numbers, sampling frames, and the problem of non-response—before giving a detailed illustration of one particular sample design in the following chapter.

Anyone who advises on sample designs will know that almost invariably the first question he is asked is: 'How big a sample do I need?' He will also know how disappointed the researcher usually is when told that an accurate answer is hardly possible until he himself has provided a good deal of information relating to the survey and the population it is to cover, and until a good deal of thought has been given to the sample design itself.

Most people who are unfamiliar with sampling probably over-rate the importance of the sampling fraction, taking the view that 'as long as a large enough proportion of the population is included, all will be well'. The fallacy in this is clear as soon as one looks at any standard error formula, say (4.1) on p. 67 above. If the population is large, the finite population correction $(N-n)/N$ is close to one and the precision of the sample result is seen to depend on n, the size of the sample, not on n/N, the sampling fraction. Only if the sample represents a relatively high proportion of the population (say, 5 per cent or more) need the population size enter into the estimate of the standard error.

A large sample size, however, is not sufficient to guarantee the accuracy of the results. Although, for a given design, an increase in sample size will increase the precision of the sample results (as is made clear by any standard error formula) it will not eliminate or reduce any bias in the selection procedure. Therefore the size of the sample is not in itself enough to ensure that 'all will be well' (as the *Literary Digest* débâcle referred to on p. 79 above proved).

Returning to the researcher's opening question ('How big a sample do I need?'), if cost and other practical limitations do not enter into the picture there is no basic difficulty in determining the desired sample size. To illustrate the principle of estimating sample size, let us recall the formula for the standard error of a proportion p based on a simple random sample of size n. The purpose of the survey is to estimate the proportion π in the population with some particular attribute. The standard error of the estimator[1] is

$$\text{S.E.}(p) = \sqrt{\left(1 - \frac{n}{N}\right)\frac{\pi(1 - \pi)}{n}} \,.$$

Initially we will ignore the first factor, the finite population correction. Then

$$\text{S.E.}(p) = \sqrt{\frac{\pi(1 - \pi)}{n}} \qquad \qquad \dots(7.1)$$

and, inverting this formula, we obtain

$$n = \frac{\pi(1 - \pi)}{[\text{S.E.}(p)]^2} \qquad \qquad \dots(7.2)$$

which is an expression for n in terms of π, the population proportion and the S.E.(p). In other words, *if* some rough estimate of π can be formed and *if* one can decide how small an S.E. is desired, the required sample size can be estimated from (7.2). Having calculated this sample size, it may turn out that it represents a sizeable proportion of the population, so that the finite population correction ought to be included. If so, the adjustment to take account of the f.p.c. is simple: the final sample size is given by

$$n' = \frac{n}{1 + (n/N)} \qquad \qquad \dots(7.3)$$

where n is the solution of (7.2) and N is the population size.

Suppose we are trying to estimate the proportion of smokers in a given population, and we believe that it is about 40 per cent. If we decide that a standard error of more than 2 per cent would be undesirable, we can use formula (7.2) to solve for n. The solution is $n = 600$, which would be the required sample size if the population were large enough for the f.p.c. to be ignored. If the population size

[1] An additional multiplying factor $N/(N - 1)$ should theoretically be included in this formula, but since N is normally large the factor will be very close to 1, and so can safely be ignored.

were only 3,000 persons, the f.p.c. would not be negligible, and so the initial estimate should be reduced by using equation (7.3). In this case the final estimate of sample size to give the required degree of precision would be 500 persons.

If we were estimating a population mean, we could similarly use formula (7.4), ignoring the f.p.c.,

$$S.E.(\bar{x}) = \frac{S}{\sqrt{n}} \qquad \qquad ...(7.4)$$

where S is the standard deviation of the variable under study in the population. Inverting we then have

$$n = \frac{S^2}{[S.E.(\bar{x})]^2} \qquad \qquad ...(7.5)$$

In order to calculate n, some idea of the standard deviation in the population is required. We must also decide how big a standard error can be tolerated. If the finite population correction needs to be taken into account, equation (7.3) is again applicable. These simple formulae (7.2), (7.3) and (7.5) merely illustrate the principle involved; in practice the task of deciding on sample size is more complicated than they would suggest.

The first difficulty concerns the precision required. The researcher himself must decide how precise he wants his sample results to be, that is how large a standard error he can tolerate. Most researchers have not thought about this enough to give a confident answer; but some answer *must* be given. It requires thought as to how, and by whom, the results are to be used and how much hinges on the decisions they will determine. Since every set of survey results may be used for several different purposes, some of them unforeseeable, this is no easy task—especially as the researcher must think not only of the precision required for the overall results but also for the sub-group analyses. It is most unlikely that an estimate of the proportion of smokers in the total population is all, or even the main result, that is required. As much interest will lie in the proportions for men and women separately, for different age groups, for different regions, for different social classes, for different age-sex groups and so forth. If, say, 50 of the sample of 500 fall into a given age-sex group, the estimate of the proportion of smokers for that group will be based on $n = 50$, and will be subject to a much larger standard error than the overall estimate based on $n = 500$.

The decision on sample size will in fact be largely governed by the way the results are to be analysed, so that the researcher must at the outset consider, at least in broad terms, the breakdowns to be made in the final tabulations. He can then work out roughly what numbers are needed in *each sub-group* to give the desired precision for that sub-group, and hence what total sample size would be desirable—it may, of course, be well beyond what is practicable. But it must be clear that, without some guidance from the researcher as to the analysis and precision required, the statistician can be of little help.

This leads to the second complication. No survey is confined to one purpose: nearly always it seeks information on a number of different variables (or attributes) and a sample that is quite big enough for one variable may be inadequate for another that requires greater precision. Perhaps different clients are involved; perhaps the results for one question are to be put to particularly vital use; perhaps some of the questions are of only marginal importance. But even if the same precision *is* required for all questions, it might be achieved with a smaller sample for some than for others, since the size necessary to achieve a *given* precision depends on the variability in the population. Formula (7.2) shows that the smaller $\pi(1 - \pi)$ is, the smaller a sample is needed to achieve a given standard error; similarly formula (7.5) shows that the less variable the population, the smaller the sample necessary to represent it with a given precision.

How can this problem of the 'multi-purpose' nature of surveys be dealt with? Short of taking a sample large enough to give the desired precision for *all* the variables—which would rarely be possible—there is no perfect solution. Some order of priority for the different objectives has to be established, so that at least the principal ones are achieved with satisfactory precision.

Let us suppose these difficulties are overcome: the researcher has stated what precision he requires and has established some order of priority for the survey's various purposes. Now, in order to use formula (7.2) or (7.5) to calculate n, we need some estimate of π or S respectively. As we have seen earlier (see p. 94), for proportions in the range of 0·1 to 0·9, $\sqrt{\pi(1 - \pi)}$ varies little for different values of π; here we are concerned with the square of that quantity, $\pi(1 - \pi)$, which is somewhat more variable, but nevertheless is fairly stable. This fortunately means that if we have only an approximate idea of the value of π a reasonable guess will be adequate, for moderate errors in estimating π will have only a small effect on the calculation of sample size. The estimation of S is often somewhat more difficult, and again usually no more than a reasonable approximation is possible. Generally only a rough estimate of the required sample size can be obtained, but luckily a departure from the appropriate size means only that the intended precision is not obtained; it does not affect the validity of the survey results. A larger sample than necessary makes the results more precise than had been intended, and it is therefore perhaps safer to err in this direction.

The formulae we have been considering apply to simple random samples, but few practical designs are as straightforward as this. Suppose the sample embodies some stratification. The above formulae then no longer apply but are replaced by others, such as that on p. 89. If this formula is to be used to estimate the required sample size, one needs to estimate the variability not for the population as a whole, but *for each of the strata*. With this information, one could work out the numbers required in the individual strata and thus in the whole sample. Or again, suppose that the sample is a multi-stage one; formula (5.8) on p. 109 shows that, in order to estimate the required size for such a sample, some estimate of the variances between and within first-stage units should be made.

What this amounts to is that for normal designs the proper estimation of sample size may be quite complex, and requires a good deal of knowledge, or shrewd guesswork, regarding the population.

In practice, this complexity is sometimes by-passed by using the design effect, Deff, which is the ratio of the variance of an estimator for a particular sample design to the variance of the estimator for a simple random sample of the same size. Thus, for an arithmetic mean, we have, ignoring the f.p.c.,

$$\text{Var}(\bar{y}) = \text{Deff} \cdot \text{Var}(\bar{y}_{\text{srs}}) = \text{Deff } S^2/n$$

where $\text{Var}(\bar{y})$ is the variance of the mean for the design to be used and $\text{Var}(\bar{y}_{\text{srs}})$ that for the mean of a simple random sample of the same size. Inverting this formula and replacing $\text{Var}(\bar{y})$ by the alternative notation $[\text{S.E.}(\bar{y})]^2$ we have

$$n = \frac{\text{Deff } S^2}{[\text{S.E.}(\bar{y})]^2}.$$

The researcher can specify his desired precision, i.e. $\text{S.E.}(\bar{y})$ and, on estimating Deff and S^2, can solve as before. Information for estimating Deff can come from past surveys of the same or a similar design. If the design is a proportionate stratified multi-stage one, the stratification serves to reduce the variance, while the use of multi-stage sampling as a general rule increases it. The two effects do not, however, normally cancel each other out. Stratification often brings rather little gain while multi-stage sampling tends to increase variances considerably. The net effect is that Deff usually exceeds one.[1] This means that in order to attain his desired precision the researcher needs a larger sample than calculations based on the simple random sampling formula would suggest.

Up to now we have looked at only one side of the decision on sample size: what size would be necessary to achieve a given

[1] See pp. 200–2 for some examples of design effects in stratified multi-stage samples.

precision. In practice the sample designer's aim is either to get maximum precision at a given cost or, conversely, to attain a fixed precision at the lowest cost; so his decision on sample size is influenced as much by his estimate of costs as by standard error estimates. Of course, in many social research surveys, the desired size is unattainable in any case, because of financial, time or personnel limitations. In such a situation it is best to take the largest sample financially possible *and* to discard questions for which a much larger sample would be needed to give useful results. One must accept the limitations imposed by a shortage of resources and try to utilize the available sample to best advantage, i.e. to attain the highest precision possible by statistical ingenuity in the design.

The preceding remarks have been directed at the problem of determining the sample size for an estimate to have the desired precision. For surveys concerned with differences between means or proportions the problem is more complicated. If the aim is to measure the difference with a desired level of precision, the same approach can be applied, except that there are now two samples, a sample of n_1 yielding, say, a mean $\bar{y}_1$ and another sample of n_2 yielding a mean of $\bar{y}_2$.

In the simplest case, if the two samples are to be drawn using simple random sampling and are to be independent of each other, the standard error of the difference between the means is, ignoring the f.p.c.'s,

$$\text{S.E.}(\bar{y}_1 - \bar{y}_2) = \sqrt{\frac{S_1{}^2}{n_1} + \frac{S_2{}^2}{n_2}} \qquad \ldots(7.6)$$

If it is further assumed that $S_1{}^2 = S_2{}^2$ and that sampling costs are the same for the two populations, an appropriate allocation of resources is to choose $n_1 = n_2 = n$, say. Then, given an estimate of the common population variance and a stated desired precision, the common sample size n can be determined. On the other hand, if $S_1{}^2$ and $S_2{}^2$ vary greatly, or if sampling costs differ markedly between the populations, or both, an equal size for the two samples would not be appropriate. In this case the relative sizes can be fixed by the methods discussed on pp. 97–9, and then the actual sizes can be calculated from equation (7.6). If the samples are not to be independent, as in the case of matched samples, an extra term is needed in equation (7.6) to take into account the correlation between the means (see equation (6.2)).

If the analysis is to take the form of a test of significance of the difference between the two means, the researcher must specify a number of details of the test before the sample sizes can be determined. He must decide his null and alternative hypotheses; these might well be a null hypothesis that the population means are equal and an alternative that they are unequal. He must decide on the significance level he will use, usually either the 5 or 1 per cent levels. Then he must tell the statistician the size of difference he is interested in, and with what degree of certainty he wants his study to detect this difference; he might, for example, say that if the difference between the population means is as great as 3 units he wants to be at least 90 per cent sure that his significance test will reject the null hypothesis. In other words he must specify the *power of the test* that he requires for some particular amount of difference. In addition, of course, estimates are needed for S_1^2 and S_2^2, the relative sizes of n_1 and n_2 must be fixed, and if the samples are not independent a measure of the correlation between the means is also needed. The details of this topic are outside our scope, and the reader is referred to one of the statistical textbooks (e.g. Hays, 1963; Hodges and Lehmann, 1964).

This section may be summarized as follows. The researcher must think out what use is to be made of the results, broadly what sub-tabulations he intends to make and how much precision he requires for these as well as for the overall results. Given certain facts about the population, the statistician can then work out roughly what sample size is necessary to achieve these aims, taking account of the nature of the sample design, the costs and the money available. Then, in finally deciding on the sample size, the fact of non-response must not be lost sight of. If a sample of 2,000 is to be the aim, and it is estimated that some 20 per cent of the sample will not be 'achieved', it is advisable to start off with a sample of 2,500. This ensures adequate numbers, but is of course in no way a safeguard against the risks of non-response bias (see Section 7.4).

7.2. Random numbers

We saw in the last two chapters that there are many occasions in the sample selection when random numbers can be helpful. Their use will now be briefly illustrated.

Using an earlier example, let us suppose that a random sample of 1 in 10 is to be selected from a college population of 3,000 students stratified into six special-subject groups of which one, the 'Economics' group, numbers 350. How can tables of random numbers help us to select the 35 Economics students?

The procedure is first to number the 350 students from 1 to 350, the order being quite immaterial. Each student must have a three-digit number so that numbers less than 10 start with two zeros and numbers 10 and over but less than 100 start with one zero. The sequence of numbers is thus 001, 002, ... , 010, 011, ... , 100, 101, ... , 350. We then turn to one of the sets of random numbers, say that of

Kendall and Smith (1939). This contains 100,000 random numbers arranged in 100 separate thousands and printed in pairs and fours. The first 200 numbers are as follows:

TABLE 7.1

Extract from a table of random numbers

23 15	75 48	59 01	83 72	59 93	76 24	97 08	86 95	23 03	67 44
05 54	55 50	43 10	53 74	35 08	90 61	18 37	44 10	96 22	13 43
14 87	16 03	50 32	40 43	62 23	50 05	10 03	22 11	54 38	08 34
38 97	67 49	51 94	05 17	58 53	78 80	59 01	94 32	42 87	16 95
97 31	26 17	18 99	75 53	08 70	94 25	12 58	41 54	88 21	05 31

Source: Kendall and Smith (1939).

It does not matter from what section of the tables the numbers are picked, though in repeated sampling it is as well to avoid continually using the same section. As the population contains 350 members, the selections must consist of three-digit numbers. We start in the left-hand top corner and go systematically down sets of three-digit columns, rejecting numbers over 350 and any that come up for a second time. The first 35 numbers accepted would then represent a 1 in 10 random selection from the 350 students. With the above numbers, it would look like this:

231–055–148–126–035 and so on.

In one sense this is rather inefficient. Three-digit numbers range from 000 to 999, and if only those from 001 to 350 are used, something like two out of every three numbers in the table will be rejected. This wastes time. A more efficient procedure might be: when a number between 351 and 700 comes up, subtract 350 and accept the number corresponding to the difference; thus the number 389 would select population member 039; 575 would select 225, and so forth. Numbers over 700 would still be rejected, and the reader may wonder why, when a number over 700 is drawn, one would not deduct 700 and accept the resultant number. The reason is that the 'population' of 1,000 three-digit numbers contains only two complete sets of 350 numbers (001–350 and 351–700). The remainder (000 and 701–999) contains only 300 numbers, so if it were used the numbers 301–350 would be under-represented and thus all the 350 population members would not have equal chances of selection.

There is no basic difficulty in using random numbers, although a number of refinements are possible in practice (see Yates, 1960). What is less easy to explain is why random numbers are entitled to be called random. The trouble is that the concept of randomness is itself complex, and we must here content ourselves with a simple answer. Various devices are employed for constructing tables of random numbers. Kendall and Smith obtained theirs by a randomizing machine. Tippett got his by extracting figures from volumes of official statistics.[1] But what matters more than the source is how the tables stand up to the tests of randomness to which they are subjected —tests to check whether individual digits appear with equal frequency (allowing for sampling fluctuations), whether pairs of digits do so, and so on. The tables mentioned above have stood up to these tests and can therefore be used with confidence. Many other sets of numbers—e.g. telephone numbers—do *not* satisfy these tests of randomness (see Kendall and Smith, 1939).

The question might be asked: is anything gained by using this random number procedure? Could not the sampler himself number the 350 students at random and then pick any 35 numbers (even the first 35 on the list would do)? The argument against this procedure is that it is basically unsound to throw the onus for securing randomness on the sampler. So we take the alternative course of ordering the population in whatever is the most convenient way and using random numbers for the selection; the randomness is ensured by the arrangement of the numbers, not by that of the population.

7.3. Sampling frames

One of the decisive factors in sample design is the nature of the sampling frames available—the lists, indexes, maps or other population records from which the sample can be selected at each sampling stage. The population coverage, the stages of sampling, the stratification used, the process of selection itself—every aspect of design is influenced by the sampling frames.

The basic sampling frame problems

In discussing the qualities looked for in a sampling frame and the problems that can arise, we follow the useful classification of frame problems, and the methods of dealing with them, given by Kish (1965a, Section 2.7); and we employ the terminology of Yates (1960, Section 4.8) for the qualities required of a sampling frame. In Kish's classification there are four basic types of problem.

The first is the problem of *missing elements*, which means that elements that should be included in the population are not on the sampling frame. This problem can arise in two ways. In the first place the frame may be *inadequate*, in the sense that it does not cover the

---

[1] The Post Office uses random numbers in the draws for the Premium Savings Bond scheme, the numbers being generated by ERNIE (electronic random number generating indicator equipment). Thomson (1959) discusses ERNIE and tests some numbers generated by the machine for departures from randomness.

whole of the population to be surveyed. The property of adequacy is, of course, relative to each survey, not a general characteristic of a frame. A frame which is adequate for one purpose may be very inadequate for another. If the special subject 'Economics' in the student survey is supposed to cover Accounting students, the frame is inadequate if it excludes them, and this inadequacy will be reflected in the sample.

The second way in which the missing elements problem occurs is when the frame is *incomplete*. By this is meant that some of the population members who are supposed to be on it are in fact not on it. If some of the Economics students who are supposed to be on the list fail to register, the list is incomplete. These students have no chance of being selected, so the sample will be unrepresentative to that extent. Incompleteness can be a serious defect, especially if the people excluded tend to be of a particular type—quite a possibility if inclusion on the list is a matter of personal responsibility.[1] Incompleteness is the more serious because, generally speaking, it is not easily discovered.

One way to deal with the missing elements problem, providing the survey objectives permit, is to change the coverage of the survey from the target population to a survey population that comprises only those elements on the sampling frame (see p. 53). A second method is to cover the population not on the initial frame by using a supplementary frame, if one exists; for example, the payroll may not serve as a list of all the employees in a firm because those who have only recently joined the firm are not on it, but perhaps the personnel department can provide a list of new employees. A combination of lists, while sometimes answering the missing elements problem, can however lead to another problem, that of *duplication*, for it introduces the risk that some elements may be on more than one list. A third method of dealing with missing elements is by a linking procedure, such as the half-open interval (see footnote, p. 120). The essential requirement for this procedure is that a missing element is linked to one or more specified listings; when a listing is selected, the missing elements linked to it are given a set chance (often certainty) of selection for the sample. If, for example, there were no list of new employees, they could be incorporated onto the frame by linking them with their head of department; if the head is selected, one finds out who are the new employees in his department and includes also either all or a sample of them in the survey.

---

[1] An important practical example of incompleteness arises through dwellings which are unoccupied when the frame is constructed but occupied by the time of the survey. Often they are included in the target population, but are not found on the sampling frame.

A second basic problem of sampling frames is that of *clusters of elements*, which occurs when elements are listed not individually but in clusters. This problem arises, for instance, if a sample of individuals is required but the sampling frame is a list of addresses, there being several individuals at each address. In this case, one solution is to take all the elements in the selected clusters; but, if the clusters are large, this would generally not be a good procedure because of the large design effect that commonly goes with the complete enumeration of large clusters (see pp. 104–5). It may also be an unsuitable procedure in view of other survey considerations; for example, with attitude surveys there is the danger of 'contamination' of responses if interviews are made with more than one respondent from within a household. Another possibility is to select one of the elements at random; this means that chances of appearing in the sample are no longer equal for all members of the population (elements in large clusters having less chance), so that re-weighting is needed as an adjustment in the analysis. A third possibility is to take a sample of clusters, list all their elements, and then take a sample of elements from this list. If the list is made long enough, i.e. a sufficiently large sample of clusters is taken initially, a systematic sample of elements from the list can employ a sampling interval that ensures that each of the elements in the final sample comes from a different cluster.

Another problem with sampling frames arises from *blanks or foreign elements*: an element is given a listing but it is not a member of the survey population. One way this can occur is when the list is out-of-date and some of the people listed have died, emigrated or left the defined survey population in some other way. Another way is when the sampling frame has a wider coverage than the survey population, as for instance when the sampling frame is a list of all adults and the survey is concerned only with unemployed men. The treatment of blanks is straightforward, namely just to ignore them if they are selected for the sample; the remaining selections provide a proper sample of the rest of the list. Initially a larger sample can be drawn to allow for loss of the blanks.[1] If the blanks can be recognized immediately the sample is drawn, or if they represent only a very small proportion of the population, they are not a serious problem. The real difficulty arises when there are many blanks and it is expensive to find out which listings are in fact blanks. A very large sample from a list of all adults would be needed to give a sample of unemployed men, since a high proportion of the sampled adults would turn out to be ineligible; if it were necessary to inter-

[1] But it is wrong to substitute the next listing as a replacement for a blank since this gives that listing two chances of appearing in the sample, once in its own right and once as a proxy for the blank.

view each of the sampled adults to discover which ones were members of the survey population, the operation of forming the required sample would be expensive (see below, p. 165).

Duplicate listings constitute the fourth basic problem. Elements appearing more than once on the sampling frame have greater chances of being selected for the sample. As mentioned above, this problem can arise when the sampling frame is made up of a combination of lists which have overlapping memberships. It can also arise in other ways: for instance, the use of car registrations as a sampling frame for car owners would come up against this problem, because some car owners may register more than one car. Duplicate listings can be dealt with by re-weighting in the analysis, or by unique identification. In the latter method, one of the listings is chosen to represent the element and the others are treated as blanks. Thus a car owner might be included in the sample only if his oldest car is selected, the other cars being viewed as blanks.

In assessing a potential sampling frame, the researcher should be on the look-out for the existence of any of these basic problems, and if they are present he should take appropriate steps to deal with them. In addition there are some other practical aspects of the frame to be considered. The frame should not be merely a list of units, but should also contain other information: for one thing, the frame must contain sufficient details to ensure that each unit is identified with certainty; and for another it must contain the information required to enable the unit to be located—in the case of individuals this might well be their home addresses. And clearly this information should be *accurate*. The requirement of accuracy usually means that the frame must be *up-to-date* for information on location in particular is likely to change with time—for instance through people moving home; an up-to-date frame is also of course more likely to be complete and to contain fewer blanks.

It is also convenient, though not essential, to have the frame available in one central place, and it is helpful if it is arranged in a way suitable for sampling. If multi-stage sampling with constituencies as PSU's and polling districts as second-stage units is required, a frame that is arranged by constituencies and within them by polling districts is what is wanted; if a student sample is to be stratified by special subject, a frame arranged by special subject is a great help. It is also helpful if the units are serially numbered at the final stage, for this assists in drawing the ultimate selections, whether a random number or a systematic selection procedure is used.

The requirements for an ideal sampling frame are stringent ones and no actual frame meets them all. Most of the frames used for large-scale surveys are constructed for administrative purposes, and it would be mere coincidence if they happened to be ideal for sampling. However, the first thing a sample designer needs is to know what frames are available and how far they enable him to sample his population completely, accurately and conveniently. If no suitable frame exists, one may have to be constructed. In the United States, for example, where area sampling is facilitated by excellent maps, a field listing of units living in, say, the selected city blocks is usually necessary before the final selection can be made.[1]

We will now turn to consider the two British national sampling frames, and we will meet further examples of each of the four basic frame problems and of the solutions to them. We are fortunate in Great Britain in possessing two national lists, one of dwelling units and one of individuals, which make suitable frames for samples of the general population; these are the rating records and Register of Electors respectively.

The rating records

Local authorities throughout the country keep records of the properties in their areas. These records are kept locally and permission to use them for sampling purposes is at the discretion of Rating Officers. There is no uniform system of keeping the records, and the form in which they are kept ranges from ledgers and card indexes to computer files. The lack of a central register and the variety of the record forms are serious limitations for a national survey: if, say, 50 local authorities are chosen as PSU's, visits have to be made to each of them in order to conduct the further stages of sampling, and different sampling procedures may have to be used because of the different forms in which the records are kept.

Most local authorities' records are arranged initially in alphabetical order of streets, and within streets by street number; nowadays there is generally no division of an authority's records into smaller areas, such as wards, which, in the large authorities, might have been useful as second-stage units. Authorities vary in the frequency with which they amend their records with alterations, additions and deletions, and there is no guarantee that a set of records will be up-to-date at a particular time. Alterations and additions are made to the records on direction sheets, so causing a departure from the original alphabetical street ordering. The deletions of entries for demolished properties and of original entries for properties where the entries require alteration create the problem of blanks in the frame. For any given property, the records note the type (house, flat, cinema, shop), gross and rateable values, the name of the occupier or

[1] See also pp. 119–20. The problems of constructing a list in the field are discussed by Hansen, Hurwitz and Madow (1953) and Kish (1965a).

owner, and the address. In practice, however, the name is rarely recorded. The address is usually adequate in urban areas for interview surveys, but may not be detailed enough for postal enquiries; in rural areas, the address may contain no more than the name of the village, necessitating some searching to locate the property. A publication *Rates and Rateable Values in England and Wales* by the U.K. Ministry of Housing and Local Government and Welsh Office (1969) provides information on total number of hereditaments and total rateable value for each local authority in England and Wales, gives this information also for several categories of hereditament (domestic, industrial, shops, offices, etc.) and further divides domestic hereditaments into three strata of rateable value. This information is of great value for sample design, with uses for stratification, PPS selection, etc.

The rating records can be used as a frame for sampling dwelling units as long as care is taken to exclude non-dwelling property. For this purpose non-dwelling properties can be treated as blanks, and with some exceptions are easily identified as such from their descriptions on the records. In practice, the records are often used for selecting households rather than dwellings, which raises the frame problem of clusters of elements, since a dwelling may contain more than one household. It is instructive to examine this problem further.

A number of years ago Gray and Corlett (1950) estimated that about 94 per cent of dwellings in England and Wales contained one household, 5 per cent contained two households and about 1 per cent contained three or more.[1] Thus, although the problem of clusters of elements does sometimes arise, it is rare, and when it does occur the clusters are generally small. Suppose that one selected dwellings at random, and if there was one household in a selected dwelling included that household; if there were two or more, one of them would be selected at random. Using Gray and Corlett's estimates, the chances are that in a sample of 100 dwellings about

94 would contain 1 household, i.e. a total of 94 households

5 would contain 2 households, i.e. a total of 10 households

1 would contain 3 or more households, i.e. a total of 4 households.[2]

If the sample is to be representative of these classes of households, it should include them in the ratio 94:10:4, that is 87 per cent: 9 per

---

[1] These percentages are probably reasonable estimates of the current situation, with perhaps an increase of about a point in the percentage of one-household dwellings and a corresponding decrease in the percentage of multiple-occupied dwellings. Multiple occupation occurs more often in the conurbations, and the problem is particularly serious when using the Register of Electors to sample households in Scottish cities: the Register only distinguishes addresses, and in the Scottish tenement blocks there may be a large number of households at a single address.

[2] Assuming that the average is 4 households per dwelling (this is probably on the high side).

cent: 4 per cent. In fact our procedure results in a ratio of 94 per cent: 5 per cent: 1 per cent, so that the sample under-represents households living more than one to a dwelling. This under-representation can be corrected in the analysis by giving households selected from two-household dwellings a weight of 2, those from three-household dwellings a weight of 3, etc.

An alternative procedure is to take *all* households from selected dwellings, and this would immediately give the correct distribution of households. The sample would be larger than the number of dwellings selected (in the above case 108 households from 100 dwellings) but the increase is slight, and one could get closer to the required number of households by initially selecting a somewhat smaller number of dwellings. In a multi-stage sample of local authorities, one might select the authorities with probabilities proportional to their numbers of dwellings (N_i, which we will assume for the moment are known without error), then take a set number of dwellings at the second stage, and finally take all households per selected dwelling at the third stage. The selection equation for a sample of m PSU's is given by equation (5.11), except that the estimated sizes N_i' are replaced by the assumed correct sizes N_i. As the N_i's are assumed to be correct, this produces a sample of exactly n/m dwellings per selected local authority. But, since the number of households in these sets of n/m dwellings will vary from one authority to another, the number of households per authority is not constant. Nevertheless the sample of households is an *epsem* one, and no attempt should be made to reduce the number of households selected from authorities with many multiple-household dwellings, for this would bias the sample against such households. This is an example of local authorities being sampled with probabilities proportional to measures of size (numbers of dwellings), not to actual sizes (numbers of households): as we have seen in Section 5.5, the result is a variation in the sample size taken from different PSU's. In practice, of course, the number of dwellings per local authority used for the PPS selection might also be somewhat in error, or one might use the size of an authority's population as its measure of size, so that one would not even expect the same number of sampled dwellings for each authority.

The Register of Electors

For samples of individuals the Register of Electors generally offers the most convenient frame. The Register is compiled every October and published in the following February,[1] and, as there is no revision

[1] In practice delays often occur in some areas, and the Register for these areas may not become available until as late as mid-April or early May.

between one October and the next, not only is the new Register 4 months out-of-date when it appears, but the old one it is replacing is 16 months out-of-date. The Register of Electors aims to list all those entitled to vote in parliamentary and local elections, which effectively means British subjects aged 18 and over.[1] The exclusion of foreigners may be a serious drawback for some surveys and in some areas.

The arrangement of the Register is as follows. There is one booklet for each polling district, and the Register belonging to any one ward, constituency or administrative district can be identified. Within urban polling districts, streets are listed in alphabetical order, addresses ordered within streets up one side of the road and back down the other, and within an address the names of all those in it who are entitled to vote (and have registered) are listed, usually in alphabetical order by surname and, within surname, by first name. In most rural districts, however, the arrangement is entirely by alphabetical name order: the lack of an address order in these cases raises problems for sampling addresses. The names in a polling district are serially numbered.

A considerable convenience is that the Register is centrally available. The British Museum has a complete set; the Government Social Survey has a set for England and Wales; and a separate set for Scotland is housed in Edinburgh. Copies of all or part of the Register can be purchased.

At one time the Register was greatly distrusted as a sampling frame, being thought incomplete and out-of-date; it is widely used now because it is the only national sampling frame of individuals available, and studies of the Register, published by Gray, Corlett and Frankland (1950, reproduced in Edwards, 1956) and by Gray and Gee (1967), have been fairly reassuring as to its completeness and accuracy. A summary of Gray and Gee's findings for the 1966 Register is given in Table 7.2.[2]

The table shows the two problems that arise with the Register. First, of those entitled to be parliamentary electors, some 4 per cent

[1] The reduction from 21 to 18 in the age for voting came into effect with the Register published in February 1970. It should be noted that the studies referred to in this section apply to earlier Registers, when the age limit was 21. Actually the Register now also includes those who, though not 18 on or before 16 February when the Register comes into force, will become 18 before the following 16 February. These persons have the date at which they reach the age of 18 recorded against their name, and can vote at elections held on or after that date. The Register thus covers persons aged 17 and over. Certain groups of electors (e.g. Servicemen) are also specially marked.

[2] In 1966, the age-limits for electors were as follows: persons 21 and over at the qualifying date of 10 October 1965; together with persons whose 21st birthday fell after 10 October 1965, but on or before 16 June 1966. The latter group were entitled to vote at elections held after 1 October 1966, and were distinguishable on the Register by a mark of Y against their names.

failed to have their names included on the Register; this is in addition
to about 2 per cent of the civilian population aged 21 and over who
are ineligible to register. Variation in completeness of registration by
age was found and, in particular, it was estimated that as many as
26 per cent of the Y-voter age group were not registered at the
qualifying address; the most mobile part of the population, those
under 30, also exhibited a greater proportion, about 6 per cent, of
potential electors not registered. In fact, non-registration was found
to be highly related to mobility, with 18 per cent of those moving
between April 1965 and April 1966 being found to be not registered,
compared with only 1 per cent of those who had not moved in that
period.

TABLE 7.2

The proportion of eligible electors registered and still at the qualifying
address*

On the qualifying date Oct. 10th 1965	When the Register came into force Feb. 16th 1966	Halfway through the life of the Register August 1966	At the end of the life of the Register Feb. 15th 1967
96%	93%	89%	85%

*Excluding the Institutional population.

Source: Gray and Gee (1967, p. 13).

The second problem with the Register also relates to mobility;
persons moving during the life of a Register will not be found at their
qualifying address. About 8 per cent of those on the 1966 Register
moved in the twelve months from April 1965 to April 1966, an
average of about $\frac{2}{3}$ per cent per month. Using this rate, by the time
the Register came into force, about $4\frac{1}{2}$ months after the qualifying
date, some 3 per cent of the electors had already moved. By the end
of the Register's life, $16\frac{1}{2}$ months after registration, about 11 per cent
had moved. From the sampling viewpoint, the difficulty with movers
is how to obtain interviews with them; as their names remain on the
Register at their qualifying address, they still stand their chance of
being included in the sample. The problem is that they may be difficult to trace, and they may have moved far away from the area,
making it too expensive for interviewers to travel to their new
addresses to conduct interviews with them. It has been estimated,
however, that about 70 per cent of movers are still to be found living

near their registered addresses (Blunden, 1966), so that with diligence at least this proportion can be traced and interviewed.

Now a word about drawing a sample from the Register. To obtain a systematic sample of electors from a polling district, the sampling interval ($k = N/n$) is determined, a starting point is picked at random and then every kth name is chosen. Every individual on the Register has the same chance of being selected[1] and minor difficulties, such as eliminating Service voters by treating their entries as blanks, are easily disposed of.

If the survey aims at covering a population wider than the Register, by the inclusion for example of persons below voting age and those eligible but not registered to vote, then the problem of missing elements arises. Linking procedures can be devised to deal with this problem to some extent. For example, a non-elector can be linked with the head of the household in which he lives, and if the head is included in the sample so is the non-elector; but there may be several non-electors, in which case, if the sample is to be an *epsem* one, all of them have to be interviewed when the head is included, and this may not be a suitable procedure. Other procedures include linking non-electors to *any* elector in the household, and sampling at random one non-elector if a linked elector is selected. Neither of these gives an *epsem* sample, since in the first case the more electors there are in the household the greater is the chance of the non-electors being selected, while in the second the more non-electors there are in the household the less is the chance of selection for any one of them. Weighting is therefore needed in the analysis, and if both these procedures are used together, the weighting factor for a selected non-elector is

$$\frac{\text{the number of non-electors in the household}}{\text{the number of electors in the household}}.$$

This procedure can also be adapted to deal with the problem of movers.[2] For this purpose, an elector is defined as a person on the Register *who at the time of the survey is living at his registered address*: no attempt is made to trace movers, who are treated as non-electors. Electors are then sampled straightforwardly; whether the sampled elector still lives at his qualifying address or not, one non-elector is

[1] Apart from a small proportion of people who are wrongly on the Register twice as Parliamentary electors: Gray and Gee (1967, p. 9) give a figure of 0·6 per cent as a low estimate of this proportion. Before 1971 duplicate listings on the Register also occurred for persons who were entitled by a property-ownership qualification to vote in local government elections only at an address at which they did not reside. This qualification has, however, now been abolished.
[2] This kind of procedure is used in the National Readership Surveys conducted by the Joint Industry Committee for National Readership Surveys (JICNARS) (1968).

selected for inclusion from that address (providing there is one). In order to keep the weighting factor from getting too large, more than one non-elector can be selected from addresses with a large number of non-electors. The limitation of these linking procedures is that they provide linkages only for non-electors who live in households in which there were registered electors at the Register's qualifying date; a household containing only non-electors at the qualifying date is not represented in the Register and its occupants have no chance of appearing in the sample.

In taking a sample of addresses or households from the Register, the problem of duplicate listings occurs. If we selected every kth elector and included the address at which he was registered, the probability of an address being selected would be proportional to the number of registered electors in it, so the results would have to be re-weighted. An address with 5 registered electors would have 5 times as much chance of being selected as a single-person address and, in arriving at the final results, the former would have to be given a weight of $\frac{1}{5}$ of that given to the latter in order to adjust for these unequal probabilities. The objection to this re-weighting is that it is inefficient, and a nuisance that practitioners prefer to avoid.

An alternative is to make a preliminary selection of every kth individual (starting at a random point), noting the address and the number of electors registered at it. This latter gives the relative probability of that address's selection. Then, if we compose from this a final sample of *every* selected address containing one registered elector, every *second* address containing two electors, and so on, the result is a sample of addresses selected with equal probabilities. The same result can also be obtained by using unique identification. One elector, for simplicity the first one listed at the address, is identified with the address, and if he is selected the address is taken; the remaining electors are treated as blanks. With either of these two procedures an *epsem* sample of *addresses* is selected, and this can then be converted into an *epsem* sample of *households* in the manner described for the rating lists above.

With sufficient care, both the rating records and the Register of Electors can be used effectively for sampling purposes. Whatever their defects, these two frames certainly exercise a determining influence on British sampling practice.

They are most often used for national samples of the general population, and the question arises how useful they are for sampling special sections of the population. This will largely depend on the identifiability and size of the section. If, for example, one required a sample of British males aged 30–44 in Bristol, the Register of Electors would serve as a convenient frame, and the main decision would be to determine the appropriate sampling interval. Suppose the total population on the Register for Bristol is 400,000 and we estimate that 40,000 are males in the required age group. If the sample is to be 1,000, then the actual sampling fraction is to be $\frac{1,000}{400,000}$, but in order to allow for those on the Register who are not in the required group we would use the fraction $\frac{1,000}{400,000} \times \frac{400,000}{40,000}$, i.e. we would pick out 1 in 40, not 1 in 400.

As the first name is given on the Register, we could at the selection stage eliminate (nearly all) women who are selected, leaving us with, say, 5,000 names. The Register gives no clue to a person's age, so there is no alternative but to contact these individuals (perhaps by a mail questionnaire), find out whether they fall into the required age group, interview those who do, and reject the others.

This process is tedious and uneconomical, especially if the section to be sampled covers a small proportion of the population on the frame; but in a case like the one above, barring the construction of a new frame, there is no real alternative.[1]

Other sampling frames

Sampling frames of some kind can usually be found for special populations, and the first thing the sampler must do is find out how well they fulfil the qualities required of a frame. With care the sampler can make the best out of a bad frame, but it remains true that the quality of the sample is highly dependent on the quality of the frame.

There are, of course, some populations for which no frame can be found, and among these might be people on holiday, housewives who saw a certain film or bought a particular product last week, and people who read a given paper. (It is also worth noting that sampling frames of institutions—e.g. manufacturing establishments, offices, farms—are often difficult to come by—quite a serious obstacle to market researchers.) With such difficult populations, if none of the random sampling techniques available for dealing with rare populations is suitable, it might be necessary to resort to methods like quota sampling.

We have mainly discussed sampling from lists of names, but there are many other situations. Sometimes, for instance, it is convenient

[1] Kish (1965a, Section 11.4) and Krausz (1969) discuss a variety of techniques for sampling rare populations. An interesting example of sampling a rare population is the 21-year-olds survey carried out for the Robbins Committee on Higher Education; the technical details of the design are reported in Annex DD of *Higher Education, Appendix One* by the U.K. Committee on Higher Education (1964).

to sample dates, as was done in the enquiry into the trend of intelligence mentioned on p. 123. The main sample was an entire age group of children, and sub-samples by dates were taken from this for special purposes. One such consisted of all children born on the first three days of every month (the 36-day sample); another was of the children born on the first day of every second month (the 6-day sample).

When the population to be covered is already represented by cards or schedules, or records stored on a computer, serial-number sampling is often convenient. In a survey of university students, each of the (approximately) 20,000 students was given a serial number. Later sub-samples could easily be drawn with the aid of these. For a 10 per cent sample, for instance, a digit between 0 and 9 (inclusive) would be chosen at random and all the cards with serial numbers ending in that digit selected. A 1 per cent sample could be obtained by selecting all students whose numbers end in a randomly chosen *pair* of digits. An example of this was the 1951 Population Census, in which a 1 per cent sample of schedules was selected for early analysis. The frame was provided by the complete set of schedules, and selection was based on household serial numbers. In enumeration districts with odd reference numbers, all household schedules ending in 25 were selected; for those with even reference numbers, all ending in 76 were chosen.

7.4. Non-response

Designing a sample is a matter of technical knowledge and ingenuity, and the expert can usually design as precise a sample as the client or research worker can afford. If the sample is selected at random, the principles of sampling theory sketched in Chapter 4 apply, enabling the precision of the sample results to be estimated. But there is one weak link in this chain. The theory is based essentially on the textbook situation of 'urns and black and white balls', and, while in agricultural and industrial sampling the practical situation corresponds closely to its theoretical model, the social scientist is less fortunate. He has to sample from an urn in which some of the balls properly belonging to it happen not to be present at the time of selection, while others obstinately refuse to be taken from it. This is not quite the random sampling of the textbooks.

Non-response is a problem no investigator of human populations can escape; his survey material is not, nor ever can be, entirely under his control and he can never get information about more than a part of it. This applies as much to complete coverage surveys as to sample surveys. Fortunately a good deal of knowledge has been accumulated on how to deal with the problem, and it would be quite wrong to imply that non-response vitiates the scientific nature of sampling. With a well-designed survey it is usually possible to keep non-response down to a reasonable level and to estimate roughly what biasing effects it may have upon the results.

At the risk of explaining the obvious, we will first show explicitly why non-response cannot simply be ignored, why one should not regard the, say, 80 per cent of the sample who respond as a satisfactory final sample and leave it at that. Suppose that a random sample has been selected to cover a given population and that, for one reason or another, answers are obtained from only a part of it. If this *part* were similar, in all characteristics that matter, to the *whole* sample, there would be nothing to worry about apart from the sheer reduction in sample numbers. Experience shows, however, that the missing part does often differ materially from the rest, and certainly one should never *assume* that it will not do so.

It is helpful to think of the survey population as composed of two sub-populations or strata: respondents and non-respondents.[1] The survey succeeds in getting information about the former, not about the latter. This is, of course, an over-simplification, since whether a population unit belongs to one stratum or the other itself depends on the nature of the survey; but for purposes of illustration this simple model suffices.

Let us suppose now that the population consists of N units, of which N_1 belong to the 'response stratum', N_2 to the 'non-response stratum', and let $N_1/N = R_1$ and $N_2/N = R_2$. The purpose of the survey is to estimate μ, the mean (age, say) of the entire population. The question is, how much bias is there in using as an estimate of μ the mean of a simple random sample drawn from this population. The sample, by definition, will consist of respondents only, and we suppose that their mean age is $\bar{x}_1$; the expected value of this estimator —i.e. the average of the estimates derived from an infinite number of samples from the 'response stratum'—we can call μ_1. The unknown population mean of the non-response stratum we term μ_2. The bias due to non-response is then $\mu_1 - \mu$, and this can be written as follows:

$$\begin{aligned} \mu_1 - \mu &= \mu_1 - (R_1\mu_1 + R_2\mu_2) \\ &= \mu_1(1 - R_1) - R_2\mu_2 \\ &= R_2(\mu_1 - \mu_2) \end{aligned} \qquad \dots(7.7)$$

This result demonstrates two points about non-response, both in accordance with common sense. First, that its biasing effects will be the greater, the greater is R_2, the non-response proportion. Secondly, that the biasing effect will be the greater, the greater is the difference

[1] The formulation of the non-response problem in the next paragraph or two follows the treatment of Cochran (1963) and Kish (1965a).

between μ_1 and μ_2, i.e. that the seriousness of the non-response bias depends on the extent to which the population mean of the non-response stratum differs from that of the response stratum.

Suppose that a survey aims to find out how often, on the average, people go to the cinema each week. A simple random sample of 1,000 is selected and answers are obtained from 800. Then[1] $R_1 = \frac{4}{5}$, $R_2 = \frac{1}{5}$. The 800 respondents on the average go to the cinema once a week, so that $\bar{x} = 1$. This is an unbiased estimate of μ_1, but if we use it to estimate μ, that is if we ignore the possibility of non-response bias, we might be seriously in error. If, for instance, $\mu_2 = 2$ (one would expect non-respondents to be the more frequent cinema-goers), then the true population average is estimated by

$$R_1\bar{x}_1 + R_2\mu_2 = 1.2$$

and not 1, as estimated by $\bar{x}_1$ above. If the difference between the two strata were larger and the non-response proportion were the same, or if the non-response proportion were larger and the difference were the same, the bias would be much more marked.

At first sight it may seem from equation (7.7) that a reduction in R_2 will certainly lead to a smaller bias, but as μ_1 and μ_2 can also change if R_2 changes this is not necessarily so. Indeed, a reduction in R_2 *could* lead to a larger bias, as the following example shows. Suppose that, in the above example, the non-response stratum comprises two distinct groups, say not-at-homes and refusals, and that these two groups are of equal size, each representing one-tenth of the original sample. Further let us assume that the refusals have a mean weekly cinema attendance of only 0.1, while the mean for the not-at-homes is 3.9, the two groups combined having the same mean as before, $\mu_2 = 2$. If, in order to reduce R_2, greater efforts were made to persuade people to be interviewed, it might have the effect of turning all the refusals into respondents. If this were to happen, the new non-response proportion R_2 would be reduced to $\frac{1}{10}$, the proportion of not-at-homes, and μ_1 and μ_2 would also change. The new value for μ_2 would be simply 3.9, the mean for the not-at-homes, and that for μ_1 would be a weighted average of the mean for the original respondents and that for the original refusals, i.e.

$$\frac{\frac{4}{5} \cdot 1 + \frac{1}{10} \cdot 0.1}{\frac{4}{5} + \frac{1}{10}} = 0.9.$$

The new bias would then be

$$R_2(\mu_1 - \mu_2) = 0.1(0.9 - 3.9) = -0.3$$

[1] We continue to simplify by assuming that the non-response proportion in the sample is an exact reflection of the proportion in the population belonging to a fixed 'non-response stratum'.

which is larger than the original bias of -0.2. This increase in bias arises because the means for the two non-response groups (0.1 and 3.9) fall one on either side of the mean for the original respondents (1.0). If both means had fallen on the same side of the mean for the original respondents, there would have been a reduction in bias. While the former case could occur, in practice it is the latter that will generally apply, and hence the main method of dealing with non-response is to expend efforts on reducing the non-response rate to a minimum.

Another method of dealing with non-response is to try to get some information about the characteristics of the non-response stratum. For once one knows *something* about μ_2, one is able to assess the likely extent of non-response bias and to improve the sample estimates accordingly. Before we turn to prevention and cure, however, we must examine the different kinds of non-response and their relative importance.

Types of non-response

The first step is to clear out of the way one category which is not non-response at all, that is *units outside the population*. The sampling frame may include units that field investigation proves do not exist, such as demolished houses, non-existent addresses and people who have died. These units should be considered as blanks on the sampling frame and not as non-response; the number of blanks should be subtracted from the sample size before calculating the non-response rate. Substitutes—randomly selected—may reasonably be taken for such units in order to keep the sample up to the required size.

It is useful, then, to distinguish five sources of non-response:

(i) *Unsuitable for interview*. Every selected sample is likely to include some people too infirm, deaf or unfamiliar with the language to be interviewable. Interviewers must be instructed as to what is to pass as 'interviewable'. If a respondent claims a headache in excuse for not co-operating, this is a case for calling back at another time, not for giving him up as 'uninterviewable'.

(ii) *Movers*. Any pre-selected sample of persons or households at given addresses will include a number who have moved, either within the same or to another area. Durbin and Stuart (1954a), for instance, found that 10 per cent of their initial sample of individuals (drawn from the Register of Electors) had moved from their address. At the time of fieldwork the Register was ten months out of date. A way out of this problem has already been described on p. 163.

(iii) *Refusals*. Invariably some people refuse to co-operate, and critics of surveys often protest that they do not see why people should answer survey questions. There is indeed no formal reason. Very few enquiries (the Population Census is one) carry compulsory powers; but, as a matter of fact, few people do refuse. Most are extraordinarily willing to talk to strangers about their personal affairs, their likes and dislikes and their opinions.

(iv) *Away from home*. Every interview sample will include persons or households away from home for longer than the fieldwork period, so that ordinary re-calling is inapplicable.

(v) *Out at time of call*. Some people are out when the interviewer calls, but could be contacted by re-calling. Included in this category are people who, although in, find the time inconvenient for interview and on whom a call-back can be made at another time.

In this classification we have had in mind mainly random sample surveys in which informants are pre-selected and to be interviewed at home. Where interviewing is done in factories, colleges, offices and so forth, some of the above categories do not apply; similarly when mail questionnaires are used. In quota sampling, since there is no pre-selection, categories (ii), (iv), and (v) do not appear in the same sense. In practice, quota sample interviewers usually do have to make some home interviews, and undoubtedly not all their attempts meet with success. But these failures are not on record since the interviewer simply goes to the next house. Similarly, a quota interviewer may approach someone who turns out to be 'uninterviewable' but—unless the organization specially demands the information—this will not show in the non-response analysis.

The magnitude of non-response

How important are the various components of non-response in ordinary random sample interview surveys? The figures in Table 7.3 come from (*a*) a newspaper readership survey of the British Market Research Bureau (see Chapter 8) conducted in 1952, and (*b*) a Government Social Survey sample described by Gray and Corlett (1950). The respective sizes of the two samples were 3,600 and 8,000 adults.

The main differences between the figures derive from some special features of the B.M.R.B. survey. The interviewer, for instance, had to list all the members of a household before interviewing one of them. Of the refusals, nearly 30 per cent were due to unwillingness to give the information necessary for the listing; the remainder were refusals of the selected member to be interviewed. The overall refusal rate was thus higher than usual. In both sets of figures, units 'outside the population' and movers are excluded.

The 'out at time of calls' rate in the B.M.R.B. survey, on the other hand, was uncommonly low, because up to eight calls were made before the possibility of an interview was abandoned. In most surveys, three or four calls represent the limit of recalling. The Government Social Survey proportion of 3·9 per cent was after a minimum of three calls, and represents a more typical figure.

TABLE 7.3

Sources of non-response in two national random sample surveys

	B.M.R.B. sample	Social Survey sample
	per cent	per cent
Unsuitable for interview	1·7	1·7
Refusals	6·2	2·8
Away from home	2·4	2·0
Out at time of calls	1·6	3·9
Miscellaneous	0·4	0·5
Total	12·3	10·9

Sources: B.M.R.B. sample, Edwards (1953). Social Survey sample, Gray and Corlett (1950).

Our guess is that the above figures are below average; a more typical non-response rate is probably nearer to 20 per cent. In any case the figures refer only to straightforward interview surveys. Where anything more than answering a few questions is required, the non-response is always higher. In surveys on family expenditure, which require the household to keep accounts, a response rate of 70 per cent is considered quite good. In the official 1937-8 household expenditure survey (U.K. Ministry of Labour and National Service, 1940–41), budgets were requested at four quarterly intervals; by the end of the year only 45 per cent of the initial sample remained. In the Family Expenditure Survey, besides answering other question- naires, every member of the household aged 16 and over is asked to keep a diary record-book of his expenditures for a period of two weeks. If all members of the household co-operate, a payment of £1 is made to each of them some two to three weeks later. A response rate of 71 per cent was obtained for the 1967 Survey (Kemsley, 1969). The U.K. National Food Survey Committee (1951) tried to obtain budgets of food expenditure from the same households at four quarterly intervals but abandoned the attempt because only 35 per cent of the sample was left at the end of the year. In the National

Food Survey, besides answering other questions, housewives are asked to keep records in a log-book of their food-shopping for a period of one week. No payment is made. The response rate to the 1966 Survey was 55 per cent (U.K. National Food Survey Committee, 1968).

We may assume that, in the average interview survey, there will be no information through non-response from something like 10 to 25 per cent of the selected sample, and there is much evidence in the survey literature that non-respondents and respondents differ in important respects. Housewives with large families are more likely to be found at home than those with few or no children; daytime interviewing will fail to find many young people and working men at home; keen cinema-goers or greyhound enthusiasts are less likely to be found at home in the evenings than others. Nor is willingness to co-operate likely to be spread evenly over the whole population. In an experimental survey, Moser and Stuart (1953) found the following refusal rates:

TABLE 7.4

Refusal rates in an experimental survey—by sex, age and social class (Percentages)

Sex		Age group		Social class	
Males	6·1	20–29	4·6	Upper	12·2
Females	8·9	30–44	6·1	Middle	9·7
		45–64	11·0	Lower	6·3
		65 +	7·5		

Source: Moser and Stuart (1953).

The above figures referred to quota sampling and the overall refusal rate was high; but the differentials may not be too untypical.

The Oxford Institute of Statistics' National Savings Survey provided further findings on differential response rates. Table 7.5 shows these analysed by the rateable value of dwellings and the size of towns.

The differences in response rates between town and country are striking; so are those between the rateable value groups (similar differences have been found in the Cambridgeshire Social Accounting Survey—see Utting and Cole, 1954). The major share of this non-response was caused by direct refusals, but as the survey dealt with personal savings this was not surprising.

How should one deal with this problem—the danger of bias through non-response? Taking substitutes is no solution, because the danger arises from the possibility that non-respondents differ significantly from respondents. If substitutes are taken, all that happens is that non-respondents are replaced by respondents, so that the risk of bias remains the same. The main argument in favour of substitution is that the sample is kept up to the desired size; this may well be necessary to ensure that the numbers are adequate for the intended analysis and to keep sampling errors to their estimated magnitude (they would be inflated by a reduction in sample size). Another situation where substitutes may sometimes be useful is when the non-response rate varies between strata in a stratified sample; the problem that the strata are not then represented in the achieved sample in the planned proportions can be remedied by using substitutes.[1] Where these considerations weigh heavily, and it is felt that substitutes must be taken, they should be taken at random, e.g. from a reserve list drawn together with the initial sample. But it must be understood that this in no way helps to solve the problem of non-response bias.

TABLE 7.5

Response rates analysed by rateable value of dwelling and size of town
(Successful interviews expressed as a percentage of total possible interviews in each group)

Rateable value of dwelling	Great Britain	Size of town		
		Conurbation	Other urban	Rural
Under £10	84	73	84	90
£10 to £19	79	74	81	84
£20 to £29	68	64	69	83*
£30 to £39	63	62	63	81
£40 to £49	55	51	55	80*
£50 and over	51	46	56	57
All dwellings (weighted)	75	66	77	86

*Based on a sample of less than 50.
Source: Lydall (1955).

The first approach to this problem is to try to increase the response rate, different steps being suitable for the different types of non-response. There is little to be done about people who are *unsuitable for interview*. A particularly good interviewer may manage to

---

[1] One other point is sometimes advanced in favour of substitutes (see Gray and Corlett, 1950, p. 186). If interviewers know that in cases of non-response they will be expected to interview a substitute, they may try more determinedly to secure a response in the first place. Thus substitution acts as an incentive.

interview people who are, say, partially deaf or do not speak the language where another, less determined, would have failed; but it is not worth making an issue of this.

People who have *moved* are a rather special category. The logical procedure, if a pre-selected household has moved, is to track it down; but this is often impracticable. In the 1954 Readership Survey, conducted by the Institute of Practitioners in Advertising (1954), out of a total sample of about 17,000 individuals, 2,400 were found to have moved; of these 1,400 had moved to a known address in the area covered by the survey and were followed up.

Another way of dealing with movers is to substitute for the moved household the new one that has taken its place (see above, p. 163). With a sample of individuals, one has to select an individual from the new household by some rigorously defined procedure, such as the Kish selection table (see pp. 198–9). This method appears fairly sound since, with re-weighting, movers can be correctly represented in the final sample; it does not, however, cover movers into new housing.

Gray, Corlett and Frankland (1950, reproduced in Edwards, 1956) describe a re-weighting procedure for dealing with movers on the Register of Electors. The problem relates to persons who have moved in the, say, 'm' months between the qualifying date for the Register and the survey fieldwork. With this procedure, no attempt is made to include these movers, but instead double weight is given to persons in the sample who have moved into their new addresses in the 'm' months *before* the qualifying date. The movers-in are assumed to be representative of the movers-out, and through the double weighting they are included in the sample on their own account and also on behalf of the movers-out.

The steps a surveyor can take to minimize *refusals* are in the main matters of common sense.[1] It will always help to keep the questionnaire as brief as possible so that the burden on the respondent is at a minimum, and to aid him in giving information, perhaps with the inducement of financial rewards. But much will depend on the sponsorship and purpose of the survey itself, on the interviewers, on the questions, and on the general approach. Some people will refuse whatever the survey or the interviewer, but their number is likely to be small; certainly smaller than the group of people who, although unwilling, can be won over, i.e. whose co-operation will depend on the survey itself and on the interviewer's approach.

Durbin and Stuart (1951) in an experiment found that experienced professional interviewers had 3 to 4 per cent refusals against the inexperienced amateurs' 13 per cent; also, that with a questionnaire

[1] For a discussion of interviewing and securing co-operation see Chapter 12.

on tuberculosis, a subject of urgent public importance, the refusal rate was only about 4 per cent, but doubled for questionnaires on reading habits and on saving. The fact is that the refusal rate depends a good deal on the researcher's and the interviewer's skill; but as in most general interview surveys it is not more than 3 to 5 per cent— and even the most strenuous efforts generally fail to reduce it below the hard core of 1 or 2 per cent—it is not worth spending much thought or money on.

People who are *away from home* for the period of the fieldwork can be contacted after it is over, and this should be done if at all practicable. But generally it is not, and these non-respondents must then be written off as lost.

People who are *out at time of call* form a sizeable but not insoluble problem. Common sense must be used to make calls as productive as possible. For instance in a sample drawn, say, from the electoral register, the interviewer knows from her list the sex of nearly all the sample members, so she will not try to make her calls on men in working hours. She can also, in preparation for second or later calls, find out when people are likely to be at home or arrange appointments. Appointments may admittedly prove a two-edged weapon, in that some people may make doubly sure of being out or not answering the door when the interviewer calls; but scattered evidence shows that they do result in increased response rates. Thus Durbin and Stuart (1951) showed that, when an appointment had been made, 71 per cent of second calls resulted in interviews, as against 40 per cent when none had been made.

Sudman (1967) describes two experiments in the United States on the use of telephones to make appointments, in which it was found that through making telephone appointments the average number of calls required to complete an interview was 1·7, compared with 2·3 calls per completed case with no telephone appointment. Scott and Jackson (1960) describe the use of telephone appointments for an interview survey of the telephone service in Britain, and also show that the number of personal calls needed can be reduced thereby, without an appreciable increase in non-response. But in Britain too few persons have telephones to make this a useful procedure for most surveys of the general population, though it might have a part to play in surveys of some specialized populations.

Cartwright and Tucker (1967) carried out an experiment in making appointments by mail questionnaire, but the method failed because of the low response and high refusal rates. This latter is the danger with prior appointments; it is probably easier for the respondent to refuse to be interviewed when approached by telephone or mail enquiry than when he is face-to-face with an

G

interviewer. In one experimental study in the United States prior telephone appointments were in fact found to have a marked detrimental effect on the response rate (Brunner and Carroll, 1967).

Re-calls

However sensibly timed and arranged the first calls are, no surveyor would risk basing his results on these alone. The following figures, taken from the B.M.R.B. newspaper readership survey described in the next chapter, show one aspect of this:

TABLE 7.6

Distribution of interviews obtained at successive calls. Men and women

Number of effective interviews if a limit had been laid down of	Total		Men		Women	
	No.	per cent	No.	per cent	No.	per cent
1 call	1,243	40	367	27	876	50
2 calls	2,389	77	962	71	1,427	81
3 calls	2,880	93	1,227	90	1,653	94
4 calls	3,023	97	1,313	97	1,710	97
5 calls	3,089	99	1,348	99	1,741	99
6 calls	3,109		1,357		1,752	
7 calls	3,116		1,359		1,757	100
8 calls	3,117	100	1,360	100		

Source: Edwards (1953).

If interviewing had been confined to one call, only 40 per cent of the final sample would have been obtained and only 27 per cent of the final interviews with men. It is relevant to note that, in this survey, interviewers did not know the sex of informants in advance, so the low percentage of successful first calls on men is not surprising. Still, a sample based on first calls alone would have been entirely unrepresentative with regard to sex and many other factors.

Some re-calling is standard practice. The Government Social Survey insists on a *minimum* of four calls (i.e. three re-calls) and encourages further calls if there is hope of an interview; other organizations take three calls as their maximum. Practitioners, on the whole, do not like too much re-calling on account of its costliness. True, the *total* cost of a survey does go up as more re-calls are made, but re-calling may not raise the average cost of an interview as much as is usually supposed. At the first attempt the interviewer may achieve a sizeable number of interviews, but many respondents will be out, others will refuse and yet others will be found to be blanks. As a result, the *proportion* of calls resulting in successful interviews may well be considerably lower for the first attempt than for the second and third attempts, when appointments can often be made and calls need not be made on previous successes, refusals and blanks; after a number of attempts the proportion of successful calls will probably fall, as the remainder of the sample is reduced to the hard core of elusive respondents.[1]

Another method of dealing with the not-at-homes, suggested by Bartholomew (1961), requires only one re-call. The successes at first calls are clearly a biased sample, with the bias in favour of persons who spend a good deal of time at home. Bartholomew argues that the bias at the second call will be considerably reduced, or even eliminated, because the interviewer can either make an appointment, or, on the basis of information provided by other members of the household and neighbours, time her call so that she has a good chance of success. The successful interviews from the second call can then be weighted up to represent also the failures at second call, and these weighted interviews can be put together with the first-call successes to constitute the sample. Having gone as far as one re-call, however, it is probably worth while proceeding further, especially as some second re-calls can be made while an interviewer is in an area making first re-calls on other members of the sample.

A method for simulating an increase in the number of re-calls has been proposed by Kish and Hess (1959), particularly for use by organizations that frequently conduct surveys with similar sampling procedures. Suppose that up to three calls are made in the surveys. The non-responses for the first survey can be added to the sample for the next one: in effect they will then be receiving their fourth and, if necessary, fifth and sixth calls. The calls made on them act as 'replacements' for the additional calls that could have been, but were not, made on the non-responses of the second survey. The same process can then be applied from the second to the third survey, and so forth. The method relies on the assumption that non-respondents in one survey are similar to non-respondents in the next. It deals with both not-at-homes and refusals, but for the assumption to hold for the latter, the objectives of the two surveys involved must be similar.

Complete re-calling on a sub-sample of not-at-homes

An alternative to calling back a few times on all the initial not-at-homes is to call back persistently on a sub-sample of them. This was

[1] See Durbin (1954), Durbin and Stuart (1954a) and Kish (1965a, Section 15.5B) for a discussion of this. The paper by Durbin and Stuart reports an experiment on call-backs, the results of which broadly support the common practice of making only two re-calls.

first suggested by Hansen and Hurwitz (1946) in connection with mail surveys; the theoretical basis is beyond the scope of this discussion, but the general idea should be explained.

The method was intended primarily for situations where following up not-at-homes is more expensive than original contacting (for instance, in mail surveys where the follow-up is by personal interview). Hansen and Hurwitz provide a theoretical framework by which the optimum sub-sampling ratio for a given survey, i.e. the proportion of the non-respondents to be included in the sub-sample, with minimum variance at given cost, can be calculated. The solution involves estimating the likely not-at-home proportion, and the variability (with regard to the main question or questions under study) in the entire population and in the not-at-home stratum. If reasonable estimates of these quantities can be made, the method is certainly useful for mail surveys. Gray (1957) describes a survey in which half the non-respondents to a mail survey were followed up with interviews.

The value of the method in interview surveys is more questionable. Durbin (1954) has shown, for instance, that if the not-at-home rate is 60 per cent and the ratio of the average cost of a re-call interview to that of a first-call interview is 2:1, the relative gain in efficiency over 100 per cent re-calling on the not-at-homes is only 2·6 per cent. When the ratio is 3:1, the relative gain is 5·8 per cent. In practice, the ratios are unlikely to be as great as this, so the gains to be expected from this method in ordinary interview surveys are not large.

The Politz-Simmons method

We come next to an ingenious method of overcoming the not-at-home problem in interview surveys, which was suggested by Hartley (1946) and developed by Politz and Simmons (1949), by whose names it is generally known.

The essence of the PS method (as it will be called here) is that the members of the survey population are regarded as being grouped into strata according to the probability of their being found at home by the interviewer. Then suppose that all interviews are made in the evenings and that *only one call* is made on each sample member—all that is necessary in the PS method. The interviewer asks each respondent on how many of the previous five evenings (usually week-day evenings) he was at home at about this time.[1] Some of the

---

[1] The period covered can just as well be any other. In the experiment referred to above, by Durbin and Stuart (1954a), a complete week was taken (including Sundays). But, if the PS question covers Sundays, then interviews also should take place on Sundays, at the same rate as on other days.

population members were in every evening, so that the probability of their being found in by the interviewer was 1. Others were in no other evening apart from the one of the interview, so for them the probability was $\frac{1}{6}$. The population can thus be thought of as divided into seven strata from $P = 1$ to $P = 0$, the last comprising the few people who were not in on any of the six evenings.

Now the achieved sample will contain members from each of these strata except the last; with the interviews spread evenly over the six weekdays, one would expect to find at home about $\frac{1}{6}$ of those who are in only one evening a week, $\frac{2}{6}$ of those who are in about two evenings a week, . . . and all those who are in every evening. One would in fact obtain a sample selected with different sampling fractions from the various 'at home' strata and, in order to derive estimates from it, the results for each stratum should be weighted by the reciprocal of the sampling fraction, i.e. the reciprocal of the probability of being at home. These probabilities are unknown and must be estimated from information obtained at the interview. A qualification to the procedure is that the people with probability 0 are never found in, which may cause a slight bias. But with evening interviewing the zero proportion is so small that one need hardly worry about it.[1]

A constructed example will illustrate the working of the method:

TABLE 7.7

An example to show the working of the Politz-Simmons method

(1) Probability of being at home P	(2) Intended sample size n	(3) Achieved sample size n'	(4) Stratum means for survey variable	(5) Calculation of population mean $(4) \times (2)$	(6) Calculation of sample mean* $(4) \times (3)$	(7) Re-weighted estimates $(6) \times \dfrac{1}{P}$
1	180	180	1·0	180	180	180
$\frac{5}{6}$	180	150	1·2	216	180	216
$\frac{4}{6}$	180	120	1·4	252	168	252
$\frac{3}{6}$	180	90	1·6	288	144	288
$\frac{2}{6}$	180	60	1·8	324	108	324
$\frac{1}{6}$	180	30	2·0	360	60	360
Total	1,080	630		1,620	840	1,620

* Assuming for illustrative purposes that, within the respective strata, the sample means are equal to the population means.

[1] See the original paper by Politz and Simmons (1949) for a suggestion on how the extent of this bias can be gauged.

A sample of 1,080 is to be drawn from a population and we assume for convenience that in this population the strata of people at home one evening a week, two evenings a week and so on contain equal numbers, and that there are no people who are never at home at the relevant times. The intended sample numbers in the six strata are shown in column (2) of Table 7.7 and the achieved numbers—caused by the effect of the not-at-home proportions—in column (3).

The assumed strata means for the variable to be studied are given in column (4), and the calculations of the population mean based on the distribution in column (2) and of the sample mean based on the distribution in column (3) are shown in columns (5) and (6). We find that

$$\text{the population mean} = 1620/1080 = 1 \cdot 5$$
$$\text{the sample mean} \quad = \quad 840/\ 630 = 1 \cdot 3.$$

This downward bias in the sample mean is due to the fact that the 'low-probability' strata, which are under-represented in the sample, are the ones with the highest mean values of the variable (as might well happen in practice, e.g. if frequency of cinema-going were the subject of the survey). The PS method now involves multiplying the estimates from each stratum—i.e. the figures in column (6)—by weights which are the reciprocals of the probabilities, and then combining the figures for all strata; similarly the achieved sample sizes in column (3) are multiplied by the same weights. The results of the first of these operations are shown in column (7) and the second operation leads back to the figures shown in column (2). The re-weighted sample mean is then $1620/1080 = 1 \cdot 5$, which is equal to the population mean. We repeat that the stratum with zero probability of being at home has been ignored.

Theoretically the method is sound, and estimates of sampling errors can be made. Durbin (1954) has shown that it does not require —as is sometimes suggested—that the times of the calls and the choice of the previous occasions about which respondents are asked be chosen at random. It will generally be sufficient if the same number of calls are made on each evening of the fieldwork period, preferably by each investigator but certainly over the sample as a whole. The attraction of the method is that it enables estimates to be made on a one-call sample. Whether it is more efficient than recalling depends on the cost of re-calls and the degree of correlation between the variables studied by the survey and the probability of respondents being at home. The method is subject to relatively high sampling errors, as the weights range by a factor of 6 and, being reciprocals of the at-home probabilities, they are sample estimates and therefore themselves subject to error. The cost of re-weighting in the analysis must be taken into account, as must the fact that the interviewer has to include the extra questions necessary to estimate the at-home probabilities. Furthermore, if the stratum with zero probability is to be small, the use of the method is restricted to evening interviewing, which may be expensive and inconvenient.

There remains the question whether it is feasible to get from respondents the information on which the estimates of the probabilities have to be based. Will people tell, and accurately, on which of the previous five evenings they were at home? Practitioners have been sceptical about this, feeling that respondents might resent the intrusion into their affairs and refuse, or answer inaccurately. But in the experiment by Durbin and Stuart (1954a) only 19 out of 374 (i.e. 5 per cent) first-call respondents failed to give a complete answer to the 'times-at-home' question and only two of these refused information. Whether the replies were accurate is another matter. People may not remember when they were in or they may wilfully mislead the interviewer, perhaps fearing that the information might be useful to burglars as well as to market researchers. The low refusal rate, however, suggests that such fears are not widespread, although of course some people might find it easier to give wrong answers than to refuse altogether. How accurate their memories are is again difficult to say, but it seems likely that the answers to the PS question will be no more or less accurate than to other survey questions involving memory (see p. 331).

Adjusting for non-response bias

It follows from formula (7.7) that any success in correcting for non-response bias hinges on the possibility of gaining some knowledge, however meagre, about the non-respondents. There are several possibilities. Often the interviewer can find out something about the people she fails to interview. In the case of personal refusals, she can note the informant's sex, approximate age, perhaps broad social grouping. If she has failed to find the person, others in the house may be able to tell her something about him—his age, occupation, and the size of his family; anyway, she can see and record the type of house and its location. Interviewers should be asked to produce as much information about non-respondents as they can collect without snooping. A well-designed questionnaire will include a non-contact sheet on which this information can be recorded in a standardized form.

The composition of the achieved sample should be compared with known population data, including information available on the sampling frame, so as to give a clue to the extent and direction of non-response bias (see Lydall, 1955, for a discussion of the problems of checking survey results against external data). In a multi-phase design, the first-phase sample provides information about some of the later-phase non-respondents. Finally there are various methods of 'follow-up'. People who have refused to answer a lengthy questionnaire may yet be willing to complete a postcard asking for a few simple facts, and these may be sufficient to enable the surveyor to judge what kind of people his sample has missed.

One or more of these sources are open to most researchers, and they make possible some comparison of respondents and non-respondents. Such comparisons, however, can never prove the *absence* of bias; at best, they can reassure the researcher that the final sample is not badly out of line. He may be able to deduce that, as regards the sex ratio, age distribution, social class grouping and various other characteristics, the non-respondents are broadly similar to the respondents but, while this gives him confidence, it does not mean that the two groups are similar in respect of whatever it is the survey is studying.

As an illustration of the practical approach to the question of non-response bias, let us return to the B.M.R.B. sample, for which the non-response figures were given in Table 7.3.

There were 483 non-respondents out of a sample of 3,600.[1] Did their absence cause any marked unrepresentativeness in the sample— for instance in its sex composition?

The sex of 333 of the 483 non-respondents was known: 58 per cent of them were men and the reasonable assumption was made that the percentage was roughly the same for the other 150. The probable sex composition of the initial sample of 3,600 was then estimated, as in Table 7.8.

The achieved sample had too few men (the population proportion was 47 per cent), but this under-representation was virtually corrected by allowing for the non-response factor. A similar calculation was made for the age distribution, although on a less secure basis, and for distribution by family size. It was also done for the social class composition, to correct for the under-representation of the higher social classes.

Having found that an achieved sample is in some respects unrepresentative, is one entitled, and well advised, to adjust the results? The answer is certainly 'Yes'—but one must be quite clear what this adjustment achieves and does *not* achieve.

[1] This does not agree with the percentage of 12·3 in Table 7.3; that table excluded, while the present figures include, units 'outside the population'. Strictly they should also be excluded here, since they are not non-respondents, but in this simple illustration this has not been done; in any case their number is small and their exclusion would have no appreciable effect.

TABLE 7.8

Sex composition of B.M.R.B. sample—successful interviews and non-respondents

(1) Sex	(2) Successful interviews		(3) Non-respondents		(4) Initial sample constructed from (2) + (3)	
	No.	per cent	No.	per cent	No.	per cent
Men	1,360	43·6	280	58·0	1,640	45·6
Women	1,757	56·4	203	42·0	1,960	54·4
Total	3,117	100·0	483	100·0	3,600	100·0

Source: B.M.R.B. memorandum—see footnote on p. 188.

The aim of a sample is to estimate certain population characteristics as accurately as possible, and it would be irrational to leave a sample wrongly constituted when one has the knowledge and resources to improve it. Take the case of the sex ratio. The achieved sample contained 43·6 per cent men as against the estimated 45·6 per cent in the sample selected. (The latter figure will be used as the correct one, rather than the population figure of 47·0 per cent, so that the figures in Table 7.8 can be used for illustration. In practice, one would of course adjust by the most accurate data available.) Now suppose that, amongst the respondents, men and women differ considerably in respect of the variables under study; suppose, say, that the *Daily Tabloid* is read by 80 per cent of the men, but by only 10 per cent of the women. Without re-weighting, the estimate of readership for the two sexes combined would be

$$\frac{(43 \cdot 6 \times 80) + (56 \cdot 4 \times 10)}{100} = 40 \cdot 5 \text{ per cent.}$$

Knowing that the sample contains too few men—too few in the 'heavy readership' group—we re-weight according to the correct proportions

$$\frac{(45 \cdot 6 \times 80) + (54 \cdot 4 \times 10)}{100} = 41 \cdot 9 \text{ per cent.}$$

The difference is slight since the weights themselves—43·6 and 45·6—differ little. If the population sex ratio (47:53) were used for re-weighting, the estimate would be 42·9 per cent. What must be

2G

clearly understood is that the re-weighting ensures only that the sexes are correctly represented in the sample; it does not reduce any bias arising from unrepresentativeness *within* the strata, that is within each sex group.[1]

There is a close resemblance between this re-weighting and 'stratification after selection' (see Section 5.3), but the difference between the two is much more vital than the resemblance. In the latter method, the sample members in any stratum are a random sample of the population of that stratum. In the present context, the sample members in any stratum are a random sample only of the 'response population' in that stratum; hence the estimates based upon them are biased to the extent that respondents and non-respondents in that stratum differ from each other. This is best seen if we look at the calculation of the re-weighted result in a slightly different form. We first calculate the readership proportion for the respondents (as above), obtaining the result of 40·5 per cent. Next we calculate the readership proportion for the non-respondents assuming that here too 80 per cent of the men and 10 per cent of women are readers. The result is

$$\frac{(58\cdot0 \times 80) + (42\cdot0 \times 10)}{100} = 50\cdot6 \text{ per cent.}$$

Combining the results for the two strata, respondents and non-respondents, we obtain

$$\frac{(40\cdot5 \times 3,117) + (50\cdot6 \times 483)}{3,600} = 41\cdot9 \text{ per cent}$$

as before. This method of arriving at the result shows clearly the assumption underlying such re-weighting: that the men who are non-respondents are similar to those who are respondents, that in each group the readership proportion is 80 per cent, and similarly that in each group of women the readership proportion is 10 per cent.

An alternative, if there is no information about the composition of the non-response group, is to calculate the potential non-response bias on the most extreme assumptions possible:

(1) *Assumption that none of the non-respondents read the 'Daily Tabloid'*

$$\frac{(40\cdot5 \times 3,117) + (0 \times 483)}{3,600} = 35\cdot1 \text{ per cent.}$$

---

[1] It may even accentuate it. If the sample in the stratum that is given additional weight in the process is particularly unrepresentative of the population in that stratum, the biasing influence on the results may be increased. If the men respondents were a very unrepresentative sample of all men, while the women were a representative sample of all women, this could happen here.

(2) *Assumption that all the non-respondents read the 'Daily Tabloid'*

$$\frac{(40\cdot5 \times 3,117) + (100 \times 483)}{3,600} = 48\cdot5 \text{ per cent.}$$

These are wide limits, but then they are based on the most extreme assumptions. Many other possibilities suggest themselves: one might assume that the readership among men non-respondents is 100 per cent and among women non-respondents 0 per cent, figures which are closer to the proportions in the respondent group and more reasonable than the extreme assumptions; they would give a result of 42·8 per cent. But this is a matter of judgement and the result is worth no more than the judgement. Taking the extremes is safe, but the resultant limits are usually too wide for comfort[1]; besides, when one is dealing with a variable rather than an attribute, as here, there are often no theoretical limits in the same sense (although frequently there is a theoretical lower limit of 0). In practice, in assessing the likely influence of non-response one usually bases the calculations on a mixture of common sense and empirical evidence. The more knowledge about the non-respondents one can gain, the more realistic will the calculations be. Whatever is done, the potential influence of non-response bias has to be acknowledged, and any re-weighting done to correct for it fully described in the survey report; preferably the weighted *and* the unweighted figures should be given side by side. To many people any adjusting or weighting of results denotes something a trifle shady, and it is up to the researcher to allay such misgivings by a thorough explanation.

An interesting way of adjusting for non-response bias was used in the Family Census of the Royal Commission on Population (Glass and Grebenik, 1954). Out of a sample of approximately 1,353,000 women, 230,000 did not respond to the initial request for information, a non-response rate of 17 per cent. These were sent further letters asking them to co-operate, and 50,000 of them did so. These 50,000 were then treated as a sample of all 230,000 non-respondents and the results weighted accordingly. In actual fact, only the first 12,000 of the follow-up replies were analysed, and combined with the remainder of the sample with a weight of 230/12. While the initially achieved sample had contained considerably too few women with no or very few children, the results, after the non-response had been allowed for in this manner, corresponded well with known figures. It seems reasonable to treat the respondents to follow-up appeals as more representative of all the non-respondents than would be the full sample of all respondents. This applies to all follow-up methods,

[1] See Cochran (1963, Section 13.2).

including call-backs in interview surveys; and this is the basis of the method proposed by Bartholomew (see p. 177). If there are several follow-up waves, the results at each wave can be analysed separately, permitting any trend to be discerned. If, for instance, people who are enthusiastic about a product are more likely to respond than others, one might find the proportion expressing itself favourably on it going down with each batch of respondents to the various waves. If such a trend is discernible, it might be reasonable to assume that it would continue for the non-respondents remaining at the end.

The importance of some following-up, wherever non-response is of sizeable proportions, can hardly be exaggerated. The scale, procedure and the amount of information demanded in the follow-up are matters to be decided in the individual survey; but there are various possible economies. It is not, for instance, essential to go all out for complete information from follow-up contacts; a few key items may do. Again, it is not essential that the follow-up sample be spread over a wide geographic area; one can concentrate it in a few carefully selected areas, and use the differences between initial respondents and follow-up respondents found in *these* areas to correct the results for the entire sample.

Concluding remarks

Various types of non-response have been distinguished, and ways of reducing their magnitude and of dealing with the core of non-response that remains have been discussed. There are several methods, both of prevention and cure, which serve to reduce the seriousness of the problem, and the surveyor should at the outset lay down the procedure to be followed in dealing with it. Certainly he can never afford to ignore it. Indeed some authors (see, especially, Cochran, 1963, and Deming, 1953) have suggested that non-response bias may often be so serious as to dwarf the ordinary sampling error; in this case it might well pay to aim at a smaller sample and to spend the resources thus freed on efforts to secure a higher response rate.

NOTES ON READING

1. The subject of sample size is discussed in all the textbooks on sampling mentioned in previous chapters. For those whose algebra is adequate the chapter on sample size in COCHRAN's (1963) book is recommended.

2. On sampling frames generally, KISH (1965a) and YATES (1960) are most useful. On the Register of Electors, GRAY, CORLETT and FRANKLAND (1950), GRAY and CORLETT (1950), GRAY (1959), EMMETT (1964), BLUNDEN (1966), and GRAY and GEE (1967) should be consulted; but it should be

noted that at the time these articles were written the minimum age of voting was 21, not 18 as now. GRAY and CORLETT (1950) and BLUNDEN (1966) also discuss the rating records. A recent paper on the Register of Electors is by SHEILA GRAY (1970).

3. There is a considerable literature on non-response. Among the text-books, KISH (1965a), YATES (1960), COCHRAN (1963) and ZARKOVICH (1966) have good accounts of the subject. STEPHAN and McCARTHY'S (1958) discussion contains many examples. The main journal references have already been noted in the text.

CHAPTER 8

An Example of a National Random Sample Design

T O   C O N C L U D E the discussion of sampling, a random sample design used in a national market research survey in 1952 will be described in detail.[1] No single design can illustrate all the problems and refinements of practical sampling, since so much depends on the population to be covered, the resources available and the subject matter of the survey. However, the sample will serve as well as any to illustrate the process which links the initial decisions on design with the final allocation of names and addresses to the interviewers.[2]

The subject of the survey—the readership of newspapers and periodicals—is fairly typical of the general run of market research surveys; but in one respect this survey did differ from many others. Its prime purpose was to check the accuracy of the results achieved by a quota sample survey on the same subject, and its own reliability was therefore vital. Broadly speaking, the limits to the size and precision of this sample were time (only four weeks were allowed for the fieldwork) and the number of interviewers available, rather than financial resources. We may add that the results from this random sample showed those of the quota survey to have been substantially correct.

Population

The sample was to cover the adult civilian population aged 16 and over in Great Britain, and the question immediately arose whether

---

[1] The sample was designed and used by the British Market Research Bureau, with Mr J. Durbin and Mr C. A. Moser acting as consultants. Thanks are due to Mr T. Cauter, then Managing Director of B.M.R.B., for permission to reproduce details of this sample; and to Mr F. Edwards and Mr P. Parkinson for allowing us to draw on their memoranda on the survey. All the tables in this chapter derive from this source. The population figures used in them derive from the 1951 Census.
[2] As the survey took place in 1952, many of the numerical data are now out of date, but this is not of concern here. Our purpose is only to illustrate the *process* of drawing a national sample, and for this the sample chosen will serve well.

certain remote areas—like the Highlands of Scotland, the Southern Uplands of Scotland, Central Wales and islands other than the Isle of Wight—should be included. Interviewing in such areas is time-consuming and the cost always tends to be out of proportion to the value of the results. But, because the sample had to be beyond criticism, it was decided to include these areas.

Sample size

The sample size was fixed with regard to the time and inter-viewers available and the detail and precision required in the analysis. As we saw in Section 7.1, for a simple random sample the size required to achieve a given precision is fairly readily determined, but this simplicity disappears with the more complex samples used in large-scale surveys. The sample in this case was to be stratified by several factors and to be spread over four sampling stages. Little about the population, about the relative variability in different strata, and between and within clusters, was known in advance, and the computation of *desired* sample size was a very approximate one. It was agreed that the sample should be of the order of 3,000–4,000; the actual number finally decided on— 3,000—was determined mainly by the number of interviewers available and how many interviews could be managed in the time at the survey's disposal.

Estimating from past experience that the proportion of the selected sample yielding successful interviews (i.e. taking into account both non-response and units outside the population) would be about 84 per cent, an initial sample of 3,600 was selected. The actual proportion was 86·6 per cent (there being 3,117 successful inter-views). Details of the non-response figures relating to this survey were given in Section 7.4.

Type of design

Like most national random samples, this one was a multi-stage stratified design:

Stage	Sampling unit	Stratification
I	Administrative district	Geographical region, urban/rural, industrialization index, zoning
II	Polling district	
III	Household	
IV	Individual	

At stages I and II, selection was made with probability proportional to population size. All towns over a certain size were included in the sample so that, for these 'large town' strata, there were only three sampling stages.

Sampling frame

No existing sampling frame exactly corresponded to the population to be covered. The most suitable was the Register of Electors, which was also centrally available in London—an important advantage since time was short. The sample had to be drawn in March and April, at a time when the new (i.e. November 1951) Register was just being issued, and the old Register was 15 to 16 months out of date. The new Register was used wherever possible, namely for 60 per cent of the addresses; the remainder were taken from the old.

Sampling stage I

The choice of first-stage units lay principally between administrative districts and constituencies. Each has its advantages and disadvantages. Constituencies vary much less in population size but, as a result, some of the county constituencies representing rural populations cover wide areas; administrative districts are in general reasonably compact. The polling districts of the Register of Electors are collated into constituencies, so that the polling districts belonging to a particular constituency are readily identified; the determination of which polling districts belong to an administrative district is less straightforward. Administrative districts lend themselves to convenient stratification by the industrialization index (see below), while a useful stratification factor for constituencies is the percentage Labour vote at the last election, an index which is related to social/economic condition. In conurbations and other large urban areas there is much to be said for using constituencies as PSU's, even if administrative districts are used elsewhere.

In this survey, administrative districts were used as PSU's and, since they vary considerably in size, they were selected with probability proportional to size. The districts (1,765 of them in 1971[1]) were first stratified by geographical region, then by urban/rural district within region. For the first stratification, the Registrar-General's twelve Standard Regions were used. (In fact, the results were wanted for a different set of six regions; but these were easily derived by adding together Standard Regions.) The distribution of the population at the 1951 Census was as shown in Table 8.1.

These figures refer to the total population, whereas the sample

[1] These areas comprise 1,366 London boroughs, county boroughs, municipal boroughs, urban districts and rural districts in England and Wales and 399 large burghs, small burghs, district councils and landward areas in Scotland. There are an additional 62 county boroughs, municipal boroughs, urban districts and rural districts in Northern Ireland.

was to be the population aged 16 and over; strictly the stratification should have been based on population figures for this latter age range. Unfortunately, at the time the Population Census results by age groups were not available, but as it was known that the age group 16 and over formed a fairly uniform proportion of the total population over the different regions, the allocation of interviews was made according to the figures in Table 8.1. They were undoubtedly close enough to serve as a satisfactory basis for the stratification.

TABLE 8.1

Distribution of the population of Great Britain by region and urban/rural area. 1951

Standard Region	Urban 000's	Urban per cent	Rural 000's	Rural per cent	Total 000's	Total per cent
I Northern	2,417	4·9	723	1·5	3,140	6·4
II East and West Ridings	3,562	7·3	534	1·1	4,096	8·4
III North Midland	2,271	4·6	1,107	2·3	3,378	6·9
IV Eastern	1,945	4·0	1,151	2·4	3,096	6·4
V South-Eastern	1,779	3·6	777	1·6	2,556	5·2
VI Southern	1,721	3·5	927	1·9	2,648	5·4
VII South-Western	1,870	3·8	1,151	2·4	3,021	6·2
VIII Wales	1,812	3·7	785	1·6	2,597	5·3
IX Midlands	3,689	7·6	733	1·5	4,422	9·1
X North-Western	5,927	12·1	517	1·1	6,444	13·2
XI Greater London	8,346	17·1	—	—	8,346	17·1
XII Scotland	3,564	7·3	1,532	3·1	5,096	10·4
Total	38,903	79·5	9,937	20·5	48,840	100·0

The overall sampling fraction (based on the total population) was $\frac{3,600}{48,840,000} = 1/13,567$. It was decided to use a uniform sampling fraction throughout, on the grounds that the advantages of a variable sampling fraction would be out-weighed by the complications of weighting in the tabulation, computation and presentation. There may have been something to be said for, say, sampling the rural areas less intensively than the urban; they are more costly per interview and may be less variable on some subjects. But in this case there was no firm evidence either way, so the simpler course was followed. With a uniform sampling fraction, each stratum was

allotted a number of interviews approximately equal to
$\dfrac{\text{population in stratum}}{13{,}567}$. The resulting distribution is shown in Table
8.2.

TABLE 8.2

*Distribution of interviews over the regions
and urban/rural areas*

Region	Urban	Rural	Total
I	178	53	231
II	262	40	302
III	168	81	249
IV	143	85	228
V	131	57	188
VI	127	68	195
VII	138	85	223
VIII	134	58	192
IX	272	54	326
X	436	39	475
XI	615	—	615
XII	263	113	376
Total	2,867	733	3,600

The next question was: over how many administrative districts
should the sample be spread? The answer was determined by three
practical considerations:
  (i) The fieldwork was to be distributed over four weeks in such a
      way that in each district the interviews were spread over at
      least two 'parallel' weeks—either weeks 1 and 3, or weeks
      2 and 4 (in districts entitled to a sufficient number of inter-
      views they were to be distributed over all four weeks). In the
      intervening weeks, each interviewer covered another admin-
      istrative district.
 (ii) Approximately 40 interviewers were to be used.
(iii) It was estimated that an interviewer could do about 20 to 25
      successful interviews per week in an urban district and rather
      less in a rural district.
The combination of these factors suggested an aim of about 45
interviews per urban district and 26 per rural district. This in turn
led to the decision to use a total of 90 administrative districts, which
was the maximum the field staff could manage in the time and therefore preferable to any more clustered sample.

As is usual, it was decided to include all the 'large towns' in the sample, so that each of them was in effect a separate stratum; here 'large' was taken to mean any town with a population big enough to be entitled to about a week's interviewing. These towns are listed in Table 8.3, together with population figures and number of interviews allocated. (London was not included; it figures as a separate region— No. XI.)

TABLE 8.3

The 'large towns' by region, with population figures and number of interviews

Town	Region	Population (000's)	No. of interviews
Newcastle	I	292	22
Leeds	II	505	37
Sheffield	II	513	38
Hull	II	299	22
Bradford	II	292	22
Nottingham	III	306	23
Leicester	III	285	21
Bristol	VII	442	33
Birmingham	IX	1,112	82
Liverpool	X	790	58
Manchester	X	703	52
Glasgow	XII	1,090	80
Edinburgh	XII	467	34
Total		7,096	524

Subtracting the 'large town' allocation from the respective regions, the distribution of interviews was as shown in Table 8.4.

The number of administrative districts selected in the various sub-strata of the sample is shown in brackets in Table 8.4, and the number of interviews in any sub-stratum was divided about equally among the selected districts. Generally, there is much to be said for selecting just two districts per stratum, since it greatly simplifies the standard error calculations, but here the complicated fieldwork pattern argued against this procedure.

In addition to these regional and urban/rural stratifications, the administrative districts (other urban and rural) were stratified by the industrialization index in England and Wales, and by rateable value per head in London and Scotland. It has always seemed desirable to stratify administrative districts by some factor related to their

TABLE 8.4

Allocation of interviews to regions, 'large towns', other urban and rural districts
(*Number of administrative districts included in sample shown in brackets*)

Region	Large towns		Other urban		Rural		Total	
I	22	(1)	156	(3)	53	(2)	231	(6)
II	119	(4)	143	(3)	40	(2)	302	(9)
III	44	(2)	124	(3)	81	(3)	249	(8)
IV	—		143	(3)	85	(3)	228	(6)
V	—		131	(3)	57	(2)	188	(5)
VI	—		127	(3)	68	(2)	195	(5)
VII	33	(1)	105	(2)	85	(3)	223	(6)
VIII	—		134	(3)	58	(2)	192	(5)
IX	82	(1)	190	(4)	54	(2)	326	(7)
X	110	(2)	326	(6)	39	(2)	475	(10)
XI	—		615	(13)	—		615	(13)
XII	114	(2)	149	(4)	113	(4)	376	(10)
Total	524	(13)	2,343	(50)	733	(27)	3,600	(90)

TABLE 8.5

Extract from the list of other urban districts in Region I

Number	Name of district	Industrializa-tion index	Population (000's)	Cumulated population
1	Billingham	430	24	24
2	Melburn	164	23	47
·	·	·	·	·
·	·	·	·	·
·	·	·	·	·
·	·	·	·	·
25	Blyth	044	35	637
26	Newbiggin-by-the-Sea	043	10	647
27	Jarrow	042	29	676
·	·	·	·	·
·	·	·	·	·
·	·	·	·	·
·	·	·	·	·
72	Gosforth	001	24	2,122
73	Scabby	000	6	2,128

economic or industrial character, and it was to fill this need that the Government Social Survey first used the industrialization index. The index is the 'ratio of industrial to total rateable value in each district' and is undoubtedly useful for stratification; it is fully explained by Gray and Corlett (1950).[1]

The method of selecting administrative districts was illustrated in the same paper. To show its working, an extract from the list of other urban districts in Region I is given in Table 8.5, together with population and cumulated population figures.

Three districts were wanted from this sub-stratum, so the total population for the stratum, 2,128, was divided by 3 to give 709. A random number between 001 and 709 was drawn from a table of random numbers, and this number was 638; Newbiggin was therefore included in the sample. The other two districts were selected by adding to 638 the interval 709 and twice that interval, resulting in the choice of Tynemouth and Windermere. This procedure for selecting districts ensured that the three districts were chosen at intervals along the industrialization index scale, and thus achieved a stratification by this index.[2] In one or two regions a further stratification by geographical zoning—conurbation/non-conurbation—was used in addition.

Greater London—for which the industrialization index was not available—was divided into a North-East, a North-West and a South section, each with roughly the same population; and the districts in each of these three sections were listed in order of residential rateable value per head. The required number of districts was then selected with probability proportional to population size. In Scotland, too, rateable value per head had to be used instead of the industrialization index, but the selection procedure was broadly similar to that employed for the rest of Great Britain.

Summarizing the design so far: administrative districts were stratified by geographical region, by urban/rural district, by industrialization index (or rateable value per head) and, in a few regions, by geographical zoning. Within strata, districts were selected with probability proportional to size, a systematic random

---

[1] A useful stratification factor currently being used is the proportion of domestic property with rateable value of over £100 (£200 in London). It is used, for example, in the Family Expenditure Survey (Kemsley, 1969).
[2] In this case there are, in effect, three implicit strata, with one selection from each. A disadvantage of this procedure is that if, say, a low random number is chosen, all three selections will be near the beginning of their respective strata, i.e. in this case all will tend to be high, relative to their own strata, on the industrialization index. A way around this is to list the districts differently: put the district with the highest index first, the next highest last, and continue to alternate them so that the districts with the lowest value on the index end up in the middle. A systematic sample of the kind described then balances the selections.

196 SURVEY METHODS IN SOCIAL INVESTIGATION

method being used. 'Large towns' were placed in separate strata and treated as 'self-representing' districts (p. 116); all were included in the sample.

Sampling stage II

In deciding how to sample within each of the 90 administrative districts, the relevant considerations were:

(*a*) How much clustering was desirable for the fieldwork.

(*b*) What possibilities of stratifying the units into which administrative districts are divided—wards and polling districts—were available.

To have gone straight to a sample of households in each district would have unduly spread the fieldwork, and at least one intermediate sampling stage was advisable. Wards and/or polling districts were the possibilities. Since both vary considerably in economic and social characteristics, some form of stratification related to these characteristics was highly desirable.

Two indices for stratification were considered. One was the percentage voting, say, Labour in a ward at the last election, but this was ruled out because time was insufficient to get the necessary data. The second was the so-called J-index, which is worth describing for the idea involved although it was not in fact used for this sample and is of little value nowadays. It is due to the Government Social Survey and is explained by Gray, Corlett and Jones (1951). On the electoral register, electors liable for jury service are marked with the suffix 'J' and, since qualification for jury service is a function of the rateable value of the premises occupied by the elector (as well as of his age), it seemed reasonable that the 'percentage of registered electors with this suffix in any area might serve as an indication of the economic status of the area' (Gray and others, 1951). At that time tests of the index showed this to be the case, but since then successive revaluations have extended the liability to jury service to the majority of dwellings, so that the present-day index is not a satisfactory stratification factor. It used to be employed as a regular stratification factor by the Government Social Survey, and frequently by other organizations, but a replacement is now needed.

The index would certainly have been a good basis for stratification in this survey in 1952, but unfortunately it was not at the time available for more than a few areas. In the event, stratification of wards or polling districts was thus ruled out; even so, in view of the shortness of time and the need to concentrate the fieldwork, it was decided to use an intermediate sampling stage. A non-stratified sample of four polling districts was selected in each administrative district, the selection being made with probability proportional to electoral populations. (Where an administrative district had four or less polling districts, all were included.)

For this sampling operation, it was necessary to find out which polling districts belonged to each selected administrative district, then to search out the respective booklet of the Register of Electors (one for each polling district) and to list all the polling districts in the 90 administrative districts. As there were 4,700 polling districts involved, this was no mean task. The number of interviews to which any administrative district was entitled was divided about equally among the four polling districts (except that, in the case of administrative districts with four or fewer polling districts, the interviews were divided between the polling districts in proportion to their electoral populations). Thus any elector in the population had the same chance of inclusion in the sample. The reader can convince himself— from a selection equation similar to that given for a two-stage sample in Section 5.5—that this is in fact so. However, the sampling procedure employed did not include selected electors directly, but rather went through an intermediate stage of sampling households.

Sampling stage III

The main complication of this sample arose from the age range it had to cover. At that time the Register of Electors included electors aged 21 and over,[1] while the sample was to cover adults aged 16 and over. One possibility was to use the Register for drawing a sample of individuals aged 21 and over, and to obtain a sample of persons aged 16–20 from some other source; another was to take a sample of households from the Register, list all their members and then make a selection in the office (this would necessitate contacting the house-hold twice, once to obtain the listing and once to interview the chosen member). Neither was practicable, and the best alternative was to use the Register for drawing a sample of households and then *in the field* to use some rigorous procedure for selecting one in-dividual from each sampled household. This was the method adopted.

The required number of households in a polling district was first selected by taking every *n*th name from the Register, using a random starting point; the household to which this person belonged was the one from which an individual was to be selected. The chance of selection for any given household was thus proportional to the number of electors in it listed on the Register. The name chosen on the Register served as the 'guide' for finding the right household, and

[1] The minimum age for electors is now 18—see Section 7.3.

it and the address were recorded at the drawing stage. Thus a list of 3,600 households spread over some 320 polling districts in 90 administrative districts was obtained.

Sampling stage IV

To convert this list of households into a sample of individuals the method used was that due to Kish (1949), by which the interviewer is given simple and rigorous rules for selecting one person from a given household, the system being so devised that all individuals in a household have an equal chance of selection. Having identified the correct household with the help of the 'guide' name (this needed some care where there were several households at the address) the interviewer had to list on a 'selection questionnaire' all the persons aged 16 and over in that household. In doing so, she followed a systematic pattern, first listing the males and then the females, both in descending order of age. The *n* persons listed within the household were then given serial numbers 1, 2, ... *n*, and the interviewer made the selection by referring to two lines of figures printed on the questionnaire. The following is an example:

If total number of persons is:	1	2	3	4	5	6 or more
then interview person numbered:	1	2	2	3	4	4

This system uniquely determined the person to be interviewed. If he or she was not at home, re-calls had to be made in the usual way and no other person in the household or elsewhere was to be substituted. The interviewer's selection task was thus reasonably simple; she did not incidentally have to find out the ages of most of the household members, as only their *age order* needed to be known. For the re-weighting (see below) it was, however, necessary to record whether a person fell into the 16–20 or the 21 and over age group. The main fieldwork difficulty with the method is that the person who supplies the household listing is not usually the one to be interviewed. With skilful interviewers, however, this need not be serious, and in this survey the method worked smoothly.

So much for the practical operation of the Kish method. It is now important to see how it achieves sample representativeness. The two lines quoted are an extract from the full selection table below.

As the household addresses were brought to the office—having been taken from the Registers—they were given serial numbers from 1–60. Each selection questionnaire then had its appropriate selection lines printed on it in the office.

Inspection of the table will show that the method results in an equal chance for every person in a household for any size of household; except that there is a slight bias for five-person households and

TABLE 8.6

The Kish selection table used in the B.M.R.B. survey

Serial number of address	If total number of adults in household is					
	1	2	3	4	5	6 or more
	then select					
1–10	1	1	2	2	3	3
11–15	1	2	3	3	3	5
16–25	1	2	3	4	5	6
26–30	1	1	1	1	2	2
31–40	1	1	1	1	1	1
41–45	1	2	3	4	5	5
46–55	1	2	2	3	4	4
56–60	1	1	1	2	2	2

that in households with more than six persons, persons numbered 7 and over have no chance of being selected. For three-person households, for instance, the person listed first will be interviewed in addresses numbered 26–30, 31–40 and 56–60, that is in 20 out of 60 addresses; similarly persons listed second and third will be interviewed in a third of the cases. The same even spread over the household members applies in households with 1, 2 and 4 members. In five-person households, there will be a slight over-representation of persons listed 3 and 5. Both this bias and the bias arising through giving zero chance to persons listed 7 or over are extremely small and can be ignored in practice.

This selection method had one complicating effect, in that it necessitated re-weighting of the survey results. Since just one individual was selected from a household, whatever its size, the probability of any *individual* being chosen from a selected household was in inverse proportion to the number of persons aged 16 and over listed on the selection questionnaire.

In addition, the probability of any *household* being selected was, as we have seen, in proportion to the number of registered electors in it. For the majority of the sample, that is single-household addresses in urban and some rural districts, this number was obtained from the Register, but for households in multi-occupied addresses and in other rural districts it had to be determined otherwise. In these latter cases, the number of electors in a household cannot be found from the Register: in the case of multi-occupied addresses, the electors from a particular household cannot be identified because the several households comprising the address are not distinguishable from the

Register; in some rural districts, electors are listed solely in alphabetical order and, although their addresses are recorded, the details are often insufficient to enable the members of particular households to be identified. In both cases the number of electors in a household had to be taken to be the number of persons aged 21 and over listed on the selection questionnaire.

Taking into account both the factors given in the two preceding paragraphs, the weighting factor for an individual interview is

$$\frac{\text{Number of persons aged 16 and over in the household}}{\text{Number of registered electors in the household}}.$$

Unless the two figures in this ratio were the same, the interview results had to be re-weighted. Details of the procedure used were given by Edwards (1953).

Sampling errors

Sampling errors were not calculated at the time of the survey, partly because the calculation by the appropriate formulae would have been a forbidding task, and partly because the users of the results were satisfied with very approximate estimates of the sampling errors.

It does seem that often too little attention is paid to sampling errors in the social survey field, especially in market research. When quota sampling is used without replication, sampling errors cannot legitimately be calculated, and this is part of the price that has to be paid for using non-probability sampling. But when the sample is a random one, sampling errors can and should be calculated, and presented together with the survey estimates.

Among market researchers it is fairly common practice to estimate sampling errors (if they are dealt with at all) by means of the simple random sampling formulae. Thus the standard error of a proportion is estimated, ignoring the finite population correction, by $\sqrt{p(1-p)/n}$ (see p. 77), a formula which can be calculated on the back of an envelope, but which is inappropriate to anything but a simple random sample. When a multi-stage stratified design has been used more complicated expressions are involved, and it is impossible to say from the theory how good a guide to the correct figure the one derived from the simple formula will be.

There is, however, a body of empirical evidence on this point which suggests that, as a rough and ready rule, even for efficiently designed multi-stage stratified samples, the simple random sampling formulae generally underestimate the true standard errors. Lydall (1955), for instance, presents standard errors for seven of the items

estimated from the National Savings Survey conducted by the
Oxford Institute of Statistics, three variables and four attributes.
These standard errors are given in column (2) of Table 8.7. The next

TABLE 8.7

Estimated standard errors of selected characteristics in the total sample
(Oxford Institute of Statistics: National Savings Survey)

Description of characteristic	(1) Mean or proportion given by sample	(2) Estimated standard error of actual sample	(3) Standard error of simple random sample of same size	(4) Col (2) as per cent of Col. (3)
Mean amount per income unit	£	£	£	
Gross income	424	12·1	11·5	105
Liquid asset holdings	225	24·7	21·3	116
Total saving	+4	3·9	3·4	115
Proportion of income units who:	per cent	per cent	per cent	
own a car	8·2	0·76	0·54	141
own a television set	7·2	0·61	0·51	120
expect income to rise	26·8	1·12	0·87	129
expect to save	27·1	1·20	0·88	136

Source: Lydall (1955).

column gives the standard error for a sample of the same overall size
calculated from the simple random sampling formulae. Column (4)
expresses the former as a percentage of the latter; in other words, it
gives the square root of the design effect ($\sqrt{\text{deff}}$) in percentage terms,
deff being the ratio of the estimated sampling variance for a complex
design to that for a simple random sample of the same size. The
figures in column (4) are all seen to exceed 100 per cent.

More examples are provided by Corlett (1963), who presents a
table of $\sqrt{\text{deff}}$'s, including Lydall's results, results from Gray and
Corlett (1950), and results from two British Market Research
Bureau surveys; he observes (p. 6) that 'the majority of these ratios
lie between 1·0 and 1·5, but some are rather higher'. Kemsley (1966)
gives some results for the Ministry of Labour's 1961 Family Expenditure Survey and concludes (p. 10):

As a general rule it would appear that for the sample design used for the Family Expenditure Survey the standard error for mean expenditure is not much more than 15% above the value obtained by using the formula appropriate to single stage random sampling ... This conclusion appears to apply to most expenditure categories, but in some of the finer groups the excess may be 50% or so above the estimate from the simple formula.

In an excellent paper discussing this question, Kish (1957) presents some results for surveys conducted by the Survey Research Center at the University of Michigan and states (p. 159) that: 'For most national surveys of the SRC the actual variances are from 1 to 2 times as great as the s.r.s. variances. This means that the "effective size" of a sample of 2,000 elements is equivalent to 1,000 s.r.s. elements.' Expressed in terms of standard errors, this gives values for $\sqrt{\text{deff}}$ mostly from 1 to 1·4. Kish (1965a, Table 14.1.IV) presents further evidence which is in line with the above conclusion.

These results show, as of course follows from the theory, that the practice of estimating standard errors of complex sample designs by means of the simple random sample formulae is to be deprecated; it will generally result in a substantial understatement of sampling errors. In other words, the use of the simple formulae will usually lead to the dangerous position of attributing to the sample greater precision than it really has.

A prime reason why so much reliance is placed on the inappropriate simple random sampling formulae is the amount of computation involved in the proper standard error calculations; as an illustration of these calculations, the standard error of a proportion for the present survey is calculated below. When standard errors are required for many variables in a survey the calculations can become prohibitive, and therefore in the final part of this chapter ways for overcoming this problem are discussed.

● The calculations of standard errors for the present survey are complicated, and three simplifications will therefore be employed. The first consists of treating the sample design as one in which the PSU's were sampled *with* replacement, although in fact this was not the case; if PSU's are sampled with replacement, an estimate of the standard error is obtained from the variation *between* PSU's and the calculations of variations *within* PSU's are not needed (see p. 110). The use of this commonly employed approximation reduces the calculations considerably, but leads to an overestimate of the standard error; however, providing the sampling fraction at the first stage is small, the overestimation is unimportant, and it at least errs on the right side. Secondly, the PSU's are treated as if they were selected at random within sub-strata, rather than by the systematic procedure actually employed. Since the systematic selection gave some stratification by the industrialization index, it is the effect of this extra stratification on the precision of the sample that is not being taken into account; again this will result in an overestimate of the standard error. In fact, although extra stratification results in the gain of a certain amount of precision, ignoring it in the calculations makes the sample *appear to lose* that amount of precision, i.e. the sample will appear less precise than a sample in which the extra stratification had not been used (see, for example, Section 8.6B in Kish, 1965a, on collapsed strata, and Section 4.1C for ways of analysing systematic samples). Thirdly, the number of interviews obtained from each of the PSU's in a sub-stratum is treated as a constant although, in practice, there was a little variation in the numbers as a result of non-response and re-weighting. This results in a slight underestimation of the standard error.[1] As a result of these simplifications, only approximate values of the standard errors will be calculated for this survey, but the approximations will be close enough for our purposes.

It is generally easier to present the calculations in terms of sampling variances rather than their square roots, the standard errors, and we will therefore adopt this procedure. The approximate estimate of the component of the sampling variance from a particular stratum for a sample proportion p is then

$$\frac{\sum_{i=1}^{r} (p_i - p)^2}{r(r - 1)} \qquad \ldots(8.1)$$

where r is the number of PSU's selected from the stratum, p_i is the observed proportion in the ith PSU and $p = \frac{1}{r} \sum_{i=1}^{r} p_i$, that is the unweighted mean of the proportions in the r selected PSU's.

The large towns are included with certainty in the sample, so that they are not PSU's, but rather each town constitutes a separate stratum; in these cases the polling districts are the units for the first stage of sampling, so that they are the PSU's. In the above formula p_i therefore represents the observed proportion for the ith polling district and r is the number of polling districts selected per town (in our case 4).

In the remaining strata administrative districts are the PSU's. For these strata, p_i in formula (8.1) therefore represents the observed proportion in the ith administrative district and r is the number of administrative districts selected from the stratum, the values of r being given in Table 8.4.

The overall sampling variance is obtained by calculating a variance component for each stratum, i.e. each large town and each other stratum, and then combining these components in a weighted sum.

To illustrate, let us take the following question: 'Have you a car or cars in your family?' Some 17·1 per cent of the sample answered

---

[1] Without this simplification, the standard error of a *ratio estimate* is needed. Kish (1965a) describes the calculations needed for this standard error, and in Section 6.5A gives a detailed illustration for the case where two PSU's are selected from each stratum. In general, if there is a noticeable degree of variation in the number of interviews obtained from PSU's within a sub-stratum, the use of the formula for the standard error of a ratio estimate, rather than the approximation used here, is preferable.

'Yes', so the 'back-of-the-envelope' standard error for a simple random sample would be

$$\text{s.e.}(p) = \sqrt{\frac{p(1-p)}{n}} = \sqrt{\frac{0.171 \times 0.829}{3,117}} = 0.67 \text{ per cent.}$$

Let us now calculate it according to formula (8.1).

Large towns

Leeds will be taken as our example of a large town. Leeds had 155 polling districts, of which 4 were included in the sample ($r = 4$). First we calculate $\sum_{i=1}^{r}(p_i - p)^2$. The proportions ($p_i$) who answered 'Yes' in the four polling districts were:

$$p_1 = \frac{1}{8} = 0.125$$

$$p_2 = \frac{2}{9} = 0.222$$

$$p_3 = \frac{0}{7} = 0$$

$$p_4 = \frac{0}{8} = 0$$

p is therefore $\frac{1}{4}(0.347) = 0.087$, and

$$\sum_{i=1}^{r}(p_i - p)^2 = (0.125 - 0.087)^2 + (0.222 - 0.087)^2 + 2(0 - 0.087)^2 = 0.0349.$$

To obtain the component for Leeds, this figure must be divided by $r(r-1)$, where $r = 4$, i.e. divided by 12; the component for Leeds is thus 0·00291. This gives an estimate of the standard error of 0·054: the 'back-of-the-envelope' formula $\sqrt{p(1-p)/n}$ would have given a result of 0·051, a slight underestimate. This is due to the clustering effect not being allowed for in the simple random sampling formula.

The above calculation is repeated for all the large towns, giving the figures in Table 8.8.

In each of the large towns 4 polling districts were selected so $r(r-1) = 12$. The figures in column (3) are obtained by dividing the corresponding figures in column (2) by $r(r-1)$; they are the contributions of the various large towns to the estimate of sampling variance, and are termed var(p_j). In order to estimate the contribution for all the large towns combined, we use the formula for the estimate of the sampling variance of a proportion for a stratified sample

$$\text{var}(p_{\text{strat.}}) = \frac{\sum_{j=1}^{k} N_j^2 \, \text{var}(p_j)}{\left(\sum_{j=1}^{k} N_j\right)^2} \qquad \ldots(8.2)$$

where N_j is the population in the jth town and $k = 13$ (there being 13 towns). It may be asked why the strata variances are weighted by the population rather than the sample totals, since the two sets of figures

TABLE 8.8

Calculation of components of sampling variance for the large towns

(1) *Name of town*	(2) $\sum_{i=1}^{r}(p_i - p)^2$	(3) Col. (2) ÷ 12 var(p_j)	(4) N_j (000's)
Newcastle*	—	—	292
Leeds	0·0349	0·00291	505
Sheffield	0·0062	0·00052	513
Hull*	—	—	299
Bradford	0·0275	0·00229	292
Nottingham	0·0208	0·00173	306
Leicester	0·1773	0·01477	285
Bristol	0·0093	0·00078	442
Birmingham	0·0167	0·00139	1,112
Manchester	0·0496	0·00413	790
Liverpool	0·0133	0·00111	703
Glasgow	0·0068	0·00057	1,090
Edinburgh	0·0221	0·00184	467

* Here the terms in column (2) become zero, since all the p_i in the town were the same.

should be in proportion to each other (a uniform sampling fraction having been used) and since the sample totals, being smaller figures, would be simpler to use. The reason for preferring the population totals arises from non-response. This varied from town to town; so, although a uniform sampling fraction of the towns was *selected*, the fraction actually achieved varied somewhat. The proportion being estimated can be weighted by the population stratum totals to adjust for non-response (as described in Section 7.4) and the estimate of variance for this weighted proportion is given by equation (8.2).

The N_j are given in column (4) and it is now only necessary to square each of these, multiply the result by the corresponding figure in column (3), add these products and divide by $(\Sigma N_j)^2$, i.e. 7,096². The result of these operations is

$$\text{var}(p_{LT}) = 0·000169.$$

This is the estimated variance for large towns. The standard error, its square root, in terms of a percentage, is 1·30 per cent. If we had used the simple formula $\sqrt{p(1-p)/n}$ for the group of large towns we would have obtained a figure of 1·25 per cent. Once more the simple random sampling formula gives an underestimate.

Remaining districts

The procedure for calculating (8.1) when the PSU's are administrative districts is similar to that above, and can be illustrated for the stratum of 'other urban' districts in Region I. As Table 8.4 shows, 3 administrative districts ($r = 3$) were selected from the 73 in the stratum: Newbiggin-by-the-Sea, Tynemouth and Windermere. We first calculate $\sum_{i=1}^{r} (p_i - p)^2$. Here are the figures:

$$\begin{aligned}
\text{Newbiggin } p_1 &= 4/50 = 0 \cdot 080 \\
\text{Tynemouth } p_2 &= 8/47 = 0 \cdot 170 \\
\text{Windermere } p_3 &= 11/54 = 0 \cdot 204
\end{aligned}$$

Therefore $p = \frac{1}{3}(0 \cdot 454) = 0 \cdot 151$, and

$$\sum_{i=1}^{r} (p_i - p)^2 = (0 \cdot 080 - 0 \cdot 151)^2 + (0 \cdot 170 - 0 \cdot 151)^2 + (0 \cdot 204 - 0 \cdot 151)^2 = 0 \cdot 008211.$$

The component for this particular stratum is obtained by dividing this figure by $r(r-1)$, where $r = 3$, i.e. dividing by 6. The component is thus $0 \cdot 00137$.

We then

(i) carry out the same calculation for each of the other strata, both those containing the 'other urban' districts and those with rural districts;

(ii) combine these components in accordance with a formula of type (8.2).

The overall results for the 'other urban' and the rural strata are $\text{var}(p_{OU}) = 0 \cdot 000145$ and $\text{var}(p_R) = 0 \cdot 000669$; the standard errors, as percentages, are therefore s.e. $(p_{OU}) = 1 \cdot 20$ per cent and s.e. $(p_R) = 2 \cdot 59$ per cent.

The following table brings together these results and compares them with those obtained by the simple random sampling formula.

TABLE 8.9

Results of computation of standard errors for 'car question'

(1)	(2) *Stratum sample per- centage* $p \times 100$	(3) *Sampling variance as obtained above (in per cent²)*	(4) *Standard error in per cent terms*	(5) $\sqrt{p(1-p)/n}$ *in per cent terms*	(6) *Col (4) as per cent of Col (5):* $\sqrt{\text{deff}}$
Large towns	7·9	1·69	1·30	1·25	104
Other urban	15·6	1·45	1·20	0·82	147
Rural	27·7	6·69	2·59	1·73	150
Entire sample	17·1	0·93	0·96	0·67	143

We thus see that the approximate standard error of the estimate of 17·1 per cent (the proportion saying they own a motor car) is 0·96 per cent, so, in accordance with the discussion in Chapter 4, we can say that our confidence is approximately 95 per cent that the range $17 \cdot 1 \pm (2 \times 0 \cdot 96)$, i.e. 15·2 to 19·0 per cent, includes the population proportion. For a statement commanding greater confidence, say 99 per cent, limits at 2·6 standard errors could be taken.

The important thing to notice is that the 'back-of-the-envelope' formula would have underestimated the standard error by 43 per cent (this is of course in line with the empirical results quoted earlier). In other words the *sampling variance* as calculated above is twice as high as would be estimated by the simple random sampling formula. This is because the latter does not make allowance for the clustering effect.

It is clear that the simplicity of standard error calculations based on the simple random sampling formulae does not justify the use of such formulae with multi-stage designs, for which they may seriously underestimate the amount of sampling error. This, however, leaves the surveyor with the problem of how to estimate the standard errors, for, even with the simplifications used in our calculations, the amount of computation would have been prohibitive if standard errors had been required for every variable in the survey.

One way to deal with the problem is to use the detailed calculations to obtain standard errors for a small range of the more important results, to calculate $\sqrt{\text{deff}}$ for these cases, and for other results to adjust the simple random sampling standard error by multiplying it by an average of these $\sqrt{\text{deff}}$'s. This adjustment can of course be no more than a rough-and-ready correction since, as Table 8.7 shows, the value of $\sqrt{\text{deff}}$ depends not only on sample design but also on which variable is under study. It should, however, give a reasonable guide, and for most variables will be better than using the unadjusted simple formula. Kish (1965a, Section 14.1) discusses the details of this procedure.

Another approach is to avoid the problem as far as possible by employing a sample design for which standard errors are easily calculated. Certainly the ease of standard error computations is an important feature of a sample design, and one to which considerable attention should be paid at the planning stage.

As we have seen in Section 6.3, one main importance of replicated sampling is that it enables standard errors to be calculated extremely rapidly; if ten replications are used and if the range is used in the estimation of the standard deviation, standard errors can even be determined at sight. A disadvantage of replication with multi-stage designs is that it limits the amount of stratification that can be employed, because each replication must contain a PSU from each stratum; thus a sample with 90 PSU's and ten replications can have no more than nine strata, a severe restriction (see p. 127). It might seem that the way round this is to reduce the number of replications, but this raises another problem, that of the precision of the estimated standard error.

In general, replicated sampling provides less precise estimates of standard errors than the traditional methods, and the precision falls as the number of replications is reduced. With few replications (say, 30 or less), the sampling error in the estimate of the standard error must itself be considered. When formula (6.1), s.e.$(\bar{z}) = \sqrt{s_z^2/n}$, is used to estimate the standard error with replicated sampling, the effect of the sampling error in s.e.$(\bar{z})$ is taken into account by selecting the multiple of s.e.$(\bar{z})$ for a given confidence level from Student's 't' distribution, rather than the normal distribution as described in Chapter 4.[1] This multiple is larger than the equivalent one for the normal distribution, hence resulting in a wider confidence interval for the quantity under study. Suppose, for instance, a simple random sample

---

[1] See one of the standard statistical textbooks, for example Blalock (1960) or Hays (1963), for a discussion of the 't' distribution.

H

of 1,000 individuals were selected to estimate an arithmetic mean. Using the usual formula for simple random sampling, s.e.$(\bar{x}) = \sqrt{s^2/n}$ (ignoring the f.p.c.), the 95 per cent confidence interval is $\bar{x} \pm 1 \cdot 96$ s.e.$(\bar{x})$, the multiple $1 \cdot 96$ coming from a table of the normal distribution. If, instead, the sample were divided into ten replications, and the variations between the ten sub-sample means were used to estimate the standard error (by equation 6.1), the 95 per cent confidence interval would be $\bar{x} \pm 2 \cdot 26$ s.e.$(\bar{x})$, the multiple $2 \cdot 26$ coming from the 't' distribution with 9 degrees of freedom; if only four replications were used, the 95 per cent confidence interval would be $\bar{x} \pm 3 \cdot 18$ s.e.$(\bar{x})$, the multiple $3 \cdot 18$ coming from the 't' distribution with 3 degrees of freedom. Calculating the standard error on the basis of ten replications thus leads to a 95 per cent confidence interval which is 15 per cent wider than the interval based on the usual formula; if only four replications are used, the 95 per cent confidence interval is 62 per cent wider. This is the price that has to be paid for the ease of standard error calculations associated with replicated sampling. In addition, the use of a multiple of the range instead of s_z^2 to estimate the variation between the sub-sample results in replicated sampling leads to a further loss of precision in the estimated standard error. Corlett (1966) discusses the question of the precision of the standard error estimates, that is the standard error of the standard error, and gives a table in which the efficiency of a multiple of the range is compared to that of s_z^2 for various numbers of sub-samples.

A commonly employed sample design for which standard error calculations are somewhat simplified is the paired selection design. If an estimate of sampling error is to be obtainable, at least two selections are needed from each stratum, so that the greatest number of strata that can be made is one half of the number of selections. In multi-stage sampling, where there is often a great deal of information available for stratification, it is common to go to the limit, dividing the population into $m/2$ strata where m PSU's are to be selected, and taking two PSU's per stratum. With the paired selection design, in which exactly two selections are made from each stratum, the computations are made easier because the standard error formulae simplify; formula (8.1), for example, reduces in the case of $r = 2$ to $(p_1 - p_2)^2/4$, where p_1 is the observed proportion for one PSU and p_2 that for the other. This simplifies the calculation of the components of variance for each stratum, but there still remains the work of combining the strata results. Kish (1965a) gives details of standard error calculations for the paired selection design.

The paired selection design can, of course, be analysed more simply by treating it as a replicated sample with two replications or half-samples; one PSU per stratum can be chosen at random for one half-sample, with the remaining PSU's making up the other half-sample. The disadvantage of this approach is the very imprecise estimate of standard error obtained from only two replications. To counteract this, the operation of selecting half-samples can be repeated, and an efficient way of choosing half-samples, *balanced repeated replications*, has been devised; the variations between the set of half-samples can then be employed to estimate standard errors.[1] This technique is

---

[1] An alternative technique known as the 'jack-knife' bears some similarity to this procedure. Its application in sample surveys is discussed by Brillinger (1966).

described by McCarthy (1966, 1969) and Kish and Frankel (1968, 1970).

Finally a notable advantage of replicated methods should be mentioned, that they can provide standard errors for more complex statistics than means and proportions. Advanced statistical procedures are now being widely employed in survey analysis, but generally standard errors for the statistics they generate have not been developed for complex sample designs. As with means and proportions, the reliance on standard errors based on unrestricted sampling must be suspect; $\sqrt{\text{deff}}$ again needs to be used to modify the results. Kish and Frankel (1968) describe the use of balanced repeated replications to obtain standard errors for multiple regression coefficients, and partial and multiple correlation coefficients; they produce a body of empirical data on $\sqrt{\text{deff}}$ and show, for example, that the average $\sqrt{\text{deff}}$ for regression coefficients in the five studies they investigated was 1·06, compared with 1·17 for means. Although these data suggest that the design effects for regression coefficients are consistently lower than those for means, they are nevertheless not negligible. Replicated methods provide means of measuring standard errors for analytical statistics.

NOTES ON READING

1. A detailed discussion of the practical aspects of the sample described in this chapter is given by EDWARDS (1953).

2. The reader should read descriptions of other sample designs for comparisons. Among British surveys the following provide useful descriptions; the JOINT INDUSTRY COMMITTEE FOR NATIONAL READERSHIP SURVEYS' (JICNARS) (1968) readership surveys; U.K. NATIONAL FOOD SURVEY COMMITTEE's (1968) annual report on the National Food Survey; U.K. DEPARTMENT OF EMPLOYMENT AND PRODUCTIVITY's (1970) Family Expenditure Survey—see also the handbook of methods for this survey by KEMSLEY (1969), and KEMSLEY (1968); PEAKER (1953) describes a Ministry of Education school enquiry. In addition the reports of most social surveys contain a description of their sample design, usually in an appendix. The reports of the Government Social Survey contain descriptions of sample designs and these are recommended. For general reading *Statistical News*, the periodical publication of the U.K. CENTRAL STATISTICAL OFFICE (1968 onwards), frequently contains references to official sample surveys.

3. It will be obvious that the design described in this chapter owes much to Government Social Survey sampling, as described by GRAY and CORLETT (1950). Readers are advised to study this reference, but to note that as it was published in 1950 some of the details are now out-of-date.

4. For designs in the United States, mainly based on area sampling, the following are valuable: U.S. BUREAU OF THE CENSUS (1963a) report on the methodology of the Current Population Survey; KISH and HESS's (1965) description of the national sample of the Survey Research Center at the University of Michigan; KISH (1965a, Chapter 10) describes both the preceding designs and also gives a list of case studies; HANSEN, HURWITZ

and MADOW (1953) give in Chapter 12 five case studies; DEMING (1960) gives a number of case studies using replicated sampling. In addition the reports of many American social surveys can be consulted. HESS, RIEDEL and FITZPATRICK (1961) describe how to sample hospitals and patients. DEMING (1950, Chapter 11) describes a population sample for Greece; DALENIUS (1957) describes some Swedish samples; there are a number of reports on the large-scale Indian National Sample Survey, e.g. INDIA, CABINET SECRETARIAT (1961); HAREWOOD (1968) describes the Continuous Sample Survey of Population in Trinidad and Tobago; PLATEK, MCFAR-LANE and ROSE (1968) describe the sample design of the Continuous Social and Demographic Survey in Jamaica; SCOTT (1967) discusses samp-ling for demographic surveys in Africa; and the journal *Population Studies* has a number of articles on sample surveys in 'developing' countries. As one of 14 publications on all aspects of planning a household sample survey, using a mythical country for a case study approach, the U.S. BUREAU OF THE CENSUS (1966) has produced a unit, Unit IV, describing the details of the sample design. For a general picture, the series of pamphlets on Current Sample Surveys issued by the UNITED NATIONS STATISTICAL OFFICE (1949 onwards) should be consulted. The bibliography in YATES (1960) contains many other references.

5. For the practical sampler it is worth noting that the Government Social Survey produces a methodological series of papers written by members of its staff on all aspects of survey research. A number of these papers provide valuable information on aspects of practical sampling.

6. The subject of designing samples for the estimation of standard errors is discussed in KISH (1965a), and DEMING (1960) gives methods of repli-cated sampling. A useful paper on this subject is that by DURBIN (1967).

CHAPTER 9

Experiments and Investigations

9.1. Causality

MANY SURVEYS are designed to measure certain characteristics of the population of interest, such as the amount of tooth decay among schoolchildren, the proportion of households living in overcrowded conditions, or the attitudes of factory workers to payment by piece rates. For such descriptive surveys the general idea is relatively simple: information is collected for a sample of the population, and from this the required descriptive measures are calculated. The preceding chapters have been concerned in the main with sample designs for descriptive surveys, and methods of collecting valid data will be discussed in succeeding chapters.

Another type of survey is concerned with the possible causal connections between variables as, for instance, in the case of a study investigating the effect on tooth decay of the addition of fluoride to drinking water. The general nature of such studies is more complex than that of descriptive surveys, and will be the subject of this chapter; however, most of the practical details given in other chapters are also applicable to this kind of study.

A detailed philosophic discussion of the complex topic of causality will not be attempted here, but it will be useful to start with a few observations on its determination. Three types of evidence are relevant in assessing causality. First, if X is a *cause* of the *effect* Y, there would ordinarily be some form of association between X and Y. If drinking methylated spirits is a cause of hallucinations, one would normally expect a greater proportion of methylated spirits drinkers than of non-drinkers to experience hallucinations. Note that it is not required that *all* drinkers have hallucinations, or that *none* of the non-drinkers do. If methylated spirits drinking always led to hallucinations, it would be a *sufficient* condition for hallucinations, while it would be a *necessary* condition if hallucinations occurred only

211

after drinking methylated spirits; however, neither sufficiency nor necessity is a requirement for causality.

To make a full assessment of a causal connection, one needs to know not only of the existence but also of the *degree* of association. There is, for example, a considerable difference between the case in which 90 per cent of persons drinking methylated spirits have hallucinations and the case in which 2 per cent do; if only 1 per cent of non-drinkers have hallucinations an association exists in both cases, but the degrees of association, that is the sizes of the effect, are clearly very different. The inference of the presence of a causal connection may be valuable, but a fuller understanding of the situation requires also knowledge of the magnitude of the connection.

The second type of evidence for assessing causality concerns the *time sequence* of the variables. If Y precedes X, X cannot be a cause of Y. If the hallucinations occurred before the methylated spirits was drunk, the methylated spirits could not have caused them. In this example, the determination of time-ordering is straightforward, but this is rarely so in the real world situation. There may, for example, be a considerable latency period before the symptoms of a disease come to light: an event occurring during that period could not be eliminated as a cause of the disease on the grounds of post-dating it, for it would not be known that the true onset of the disease preceded the event.

An association between X and Y and the fact that Y did not precede X are not sufficient for inferring causality. The third kind of evidence requires that other variables can be ruled out as the explanation of the association. It might be that a 'third' variable, Z, is a cause of two effects, X and Y, and it is only for this reason that they are associated.[1] This would not make the association between X and Y any less real, and this association could still be used in the statistical prediction of X from Y or Y from X, but any causative explanation of it which omitted to take account of Z would be spurious and misleading. For example, a mental illness might increase both the likelihood of the sufferer drinking methylated spirits and of his having hallucinations, thus creating a real statistical association between the two effects.

There are several ways in which other variables may exert a disturbing influence, and these can perhaps best be seen in terms of an example. Suppose an association is observed between, say, the incomes of heads of households (I) and the extent (measured by a

---

[1] It is also possible for Z to confuse the situation when X is a cause of Y. In this case, a third variable, Z, could make the association between X and Y disappear. This shows that lack of association between two variables does not prove that they are not causally connected.

suitable index) of their Conservatism (*C*). The degree of association may be measured by a statistical index of correlation. But what does this correlation tell us? The statistician's answer is clear. It tells us to what extent two variables move together—an increase or decrease in one being associated, on average, with an increase (or decrease) in the other; it tells us nothing of cause and effect. The other two types of causal evidence also need to be examined.

The difficulty of establishing the time-sequence is clearly illustrated by this example. Which came first, the Conservative viewpoint or the high income? When, as here, one of the variables is an opinion attribute, it becomes virtually impossible to establish the time-sequence. Only if one had kept people under investigation over a long period would there be a chance of determining whether their opinions changed and of assessing how these changes were related to income rises.

But the time-sequence problem is perhaps the lesser of the complications in interpreting relationships. The main headache is to try to think of, and if possible to eliminate, the disturbing influence of other variables. The relationship between *I* and *C* might arise through the influence of, say, age (*A*) if, for instance, increasing age leads people to be both more Conservative and to have a higher earning capacity.

If we assume that *A* is the only complicating variable and that correlations have been found between *A* and *I*, and between *A* and *C*, as well as between *I* and *C*, there are several ways in which *A* might be confusing the issue. To see what they are, let us note how the three variables might be linked causally. The arrow signifies the direction of a cause-effect relation.[1]

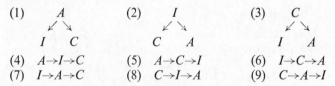

Since *A* (increasing age) can hardly be the effect of *I* or *C*, it is reasonable to exclude the schemes (2), (3), (6), (7), (8) and (9) (although with different 'third' variables, some of these schemes might have been valid). This leaves the following possible explanations:

---

[1] We exclude cases of the type $C \searrow_{I\nearrow} A$, in which the fact that *I* is also correlated with *A* in no way affects the causal relation between *C* and *I*. We also exclude cases like $A \rightarrow I \rightarrow C$ and $A \rightarrow I \leftrightarrow C$, which are more complex versions of the basic forms above.

(1) The relationship between income and Conservatism is simply due to the fact that each is an effect of a third factor, age.

(4) Growing old enables people to earn more and this leads to Conservative views.

(5) Growing old leads to Conservatism and this to higher incomes.

Schemes (4) and (5) have this in common, that the third variable A precedes the other two, so that it, rather than I or C, is the ultimate cause. More correctly A is the cause of C—in case (4)—but the causation *operates via I*, while in case (5) A is the cause of I, the causation operating via C.

In scheme (1), A confuses the issue because it is related both to I and C, between which there is no causal connection. A *explains* why I and C are correlated. The relationship between I and C is said to be spurious.

Schemes (7) and (9) typify a different situation—which, in this case, is meaningless. In (7), for example, A is the effect of I and the cause of C. It is an 'intervening' variable which helps to *interpret* how I manages to cause C. In (9), A is again an intervening variable, interpreting how C causes I.

The real-life situation is immensely more complicated than the above because, generally, not one but a large number of potential disturbing variables ought rightly to be considered. We now turn to examine how to design investigations to provide evidence of causality. As Hyman (1955, p. 81) observes, 'The explanatory survey follows the model of a laboratory experiment with the fundamental difference that it attempts to represent the design in a *natural setting*.' It will therefore be useful to look first at the design of experiments.

9.2. Validity of experiments

The preceding discussion has shown that causation involves associations or, put otherwise, contrasts. Thus for investigating whether a variable X, the *independent* or *predictor* variable, has an effect on variable Y, the *dependent* or *predictand* variable, a study designed to measure associations is needed. If the aim were, say, to see whether psychotherapy improves the mental health of neurotic patients, it would not be sufficient to subject a group of patients to psychotherapy and see how many improved. Suppose the results showed that after six months 70 per cent of the patients had improved. Before the efficacy of the treatment is established one must know how the patients might have fared in the absence of treatment; that is, a figure with which to compare the 70 per cent is needed. The association between psychotherapy and improvement or, in other words, the contrast between those who received and those who did not receive the treatment must be studied. In order to make this contrast, a comparable *control group* (C) with which to compare the *experimental group* (E) is required.

The simplest kind of design is, in the terminology of Selltiz and others (1959), the *after-only design*. The effect on Y is assessed by measuring its incidence in both E and C after the former has been exposed to the independent variable X. Thus in the above example the neurotic patients would be divided into two groups, and one group (E) would be exposed to psychotherapy but not the other (C). If it were then found, for example, that 70 per cent of the control group also improved in the period of study, the conclusion would be that the psychotherapy was ineffective.

An alternative design, the *before-after design*, uses the same individuals for E and C, measuring Y before and after the group has been exposed to X. This is obviously unsuitable for the example considered above, but may suffice for other cases. Suppose one wanted to evaluate the effectiveness of a film in changing attitudes towards drinking and driving. A before-after design might be employed here, using the change (if any) in score on an attitude inventory given before and after seeing the film to measure the film's effect. The change is a true measure of the effect, providing it is a valid assumption that without the film the attitude would not have changed during the period between the two measurements. This assumption is perhaps more reasonable here than it would be in the psychotherapy example, where one might expect many of the patients to improve in any event. However, even here it is questionable, for, unlike many physical science experiments, the subjects are not isolated from their environments, and so many other events provide possible explanations of the change in Y.

A third design that it will be useful to describe at this stage is the *before-after design with control group*. In this design both the experimental and control groups are measured before and after E is exposed to X. The effect of X is then measured by comparing the changes in Y in the two groups. As the discussion will now show, this is a better plan than the previous two designs.

In drawing conclusions of causation from such designs one must always be alert to other explanations for the change in Y, which would invalidate the conclusion that X caused the change. In comparing two designs for a particular problem, the better is the one which is less likely to lead to a false conclusion. It is impossible to design an experiment to exclude all possible sources of invalidity, so the aim should be to exclude as far as possible the more plausible rival hypotheses. Campbell gives a slogan 'Experiments *probe* theory, but do not *prove* theory' (Harris, 1963, p. 213). In designing an

2H

experiment the aim should thus be to probe theory as deeply as possible. Campbell and Stanley (1966) list twelve frequent threats to validity. They are the following:

(1) *History*. As we have seen, other events impinge on the subjects besides the experimental variable, and with some designs these may explain the change in Y. In the before-after design, for example, if reports of a serious accident caused by a drunken driver appeared in the newspapers in the time between the two measurements of Y, the newspaper reports could provide the explanation for the change of attitude. Thus the before-after design is weak against this source of invalidity. To remedy this weakness one can turn to designs with control groups. If both E and C are exposed to the newspaper reports, the reports do not explain any *differential* change in Y between the two groups. But, for the effective use of control groups to deal with history, the experimental and control groups must be treated identically (except of course for the administration of X). In medical studies, for instance, it is well known that it is sometimes the psychological effect of being treated rather than the treatment which produces the cure, and this is known as the placebo effect. Thus in studying the effect of a drug the experimenter must ensure that both E and C experience, among other things, the same psychological effect: this can be achieved by giving the members of C an inert substance which they think to be a cure. Even then there is a danger that the two groups will not be treated equally, for the doctor will not expect results from the dummy and his lack of confidence may be transmitted to the patients to whom he administers it. A way to guard against this is to keep the doctor uninformed as to which patients are in E and which in C and to make the drug and dummy indistinguishable to him also. The aim is to ensure that he does not know whether he is giving drug or dummy to a patient, and so he will be treating E and C equally. As neither patient nor doctor is aware to which group the patient belongs, this type of design is known as a double-blind trial; only the experimenter knows which patients are in which group.

(2) *Maturation*. By maturation is meant the effects of time. Suppose, for instance, that a before-after design is used to evaluate the effectiveness of a teaching programme. Students take the pre-test in the morning, attend the teaching programme during the day and are given the post-test in the late afternoon. By the time they take the post-test they may be tired, and this may of course affect the comparison. As another example, a before-after design to find out the effect on a man's reaction time of living in cold climates might take a pre-test on his arrival in the Arctic and then a post-test some five years

later. The man's speed of reaction might well have decreased because he is five years older at the time of the post-test, and this provides an alternative explanation of his slowing down. Protection against this source of invalidity is provided by the before-after design with control group, for the control group also experiences the effects of time.

(3) *Testing*. With designs involving pre- and post-tests it is possible that the experience gained through taking the pre-test may result in an increase in the post-test score. That this is not just a fanciful possibility is seen from the fact that even with intelligence tests an individual's score can be raised by practice on parallel tests (see, for example, Vernon, 1960). A testing effect is confounded with any effect of the experimental variable X in a before-after design and so this design is a poor one to use when such an effect might exist. The before-after design with control group guards against this source of invalidity also; as both E and C take the pre-test, the testing effect is common to both groups and therefore does not explain any difference in the amounts of change between them.

(4) *Instrumentation*. In a before-after design to evaluate a teaching programme on logarithms, say, two comparable tests are needed; the same test cannot be used twice over for, if it were, the testing effect might well be considerable. But if the two tests are not strictly comparable, the comparison of pre-test and post-test scores is not a fair one.

Another aspect of the instrumentation effect occurs in the grading of tests. A frequent occurrence in examination marking is a shift in the marker's standards as he proceeds, the standards becoming either progressively more lenient or more severe. If, in an after-only design, all the experimental group are marked first and then the control group afterwards, this shift in standards invalidates the comparison between the results of the two groups. Similarly if two judges are used in marking the groups, one for E and one for C, then their standards may differ and so again the comparison is invalidated. A further problem is that, if a somewhat subjective measurement is required of the marker, he may falsify the comparison through wishful thinking: in assessing neurotic patients he may, because of his belief in the treatment, say in cases of doubt that experimental patients have improved. This source of instrumentation bias can be avoided by ensuring that the judge does not know from which group a patient has come.

(5) *Statistical regression*. If individuals are chosen for the experimental group on the basis of extreme scores on Y, they will almost certainly produce on the post-test an average score closer to the overall population average. This result occurs even if any treatment

they experienced had no effect, and it is in fact merely a statistical artifact; it can arise just as a result of chance factors and measurement errors. If, say, a group of children were given a reading test and the 10 per cent with the lowest scores were then given intensive teaching, it would be expected because of the regression effect alone that the post-test averages of the 10 per cent and the other 90 per cent would be closer than their pre-test averages: comparison of the changes between pre- and post-test averages for the two groups thus does not provide a valid measure of the effect of the intensive teaching. Fuller discussion of the regression effect is given by Campbell and Stanley (1966).

(6) *Selection.* The aim in forming the experimental and control groups should be to make them as comparable as possible. If a doctor, believing in the effectiveness of his new drug, insisted on giving it to the seriously ill patients, thus not allowing such patients to appear in the control group, the comparison of E and C would be biased against the drug. An after-only study of the effectiveness of an advertising campaign for suntan lotion would be almost valueless if it measured sales per head in Bournemouth as the experimental area where the campaign was conducted and Hull as the control area. There are many differences between the two towns (climate, social class composition, etc.) and any one of them provides an alternative hypothesis for any difference observed. The essence of an experimental comparison is that the groups should be as nearly as possible the same in every respect except the independent variable. This is the particular strength of before-after designs, for changes within the same people are being studied. In the case of the after-only design, however, the problem of how to make the groups as comparable as possible is a critical one. The main techniques for this purpose, randomization, matching, and adjustment, are of such great importance that discussion of them is deferred until the next section.

(7) *Experimental mortality.* Even if a high degree of comparability in the two groups chosen for the experiment is achieved, that comparability may be weakened or lost through failure to obtain the required measurements for every member of each group. If an experimenter starts off with comparable groups in the after-only design, but loses, say, a greater proportion of the high scorers on Y from one group than the other, then the remaining members of the two groups are not comparable. In before-after designs, experimental mortality also occurs but can be dealt with. If, in a before-after design evaluating a teaching programme, some of the poorer students dropped out before the post-test, the average score on the post-test of the remaining students would for this reason be larger than the

pre-test average for all the students. Here comparability of the two groups is easily recovered by calculating the pre-test average only for those who also took the post-test.

(8) *Selection-maturation, selection-history or selection-testing interactions.* These interactions between selection and other factors arise when the effect of the other factors differs between the groups selected. Thus an interaction between selection and testing would occur in a before-after design with control group if the pre-test caused a different amount of change in Y in E compared with C.

(9) *Reactive (or interaction) effect of testing.* In before-after designs there is the danger that the pre-test may affect the responsiveness of the experimental group to the treatment. For example, a pre-test measuring knowledge about China may sensitize the subjects; as a result they may be more receptive to the information given out in a film about China, which is the treatment under study.

(10) *Interaction of selection and the experimental variable.* Suppose that a market research study of the effectiveness of an advertisement is conducted in a particular town. The restriction of the research to one test town might be adopted for the resulting convenience of the fieldwork, but there is then the danger that the effect of the advertisement is different in that town from other places: there might be an interaction between the town selected and the experimental variable. A partial answer to this problem is, of course, to carry out the study in several places of different types: if the same conclusion is reached from each place, there will be greater confidence in the findings.[1]

(11) *Reactive effect of experimental arrangements.* In order to carry out an experiment, it is often necessary to make special arrangements, and there is then the risk that these arrangements may interact with X to produce an effect, whereas without these arrangements X would have no effect or an effect of a different magnitude. It is, for example, a well-known phenomenon that subjects become involved in an experiment in which they are taking part (if they know they are doing so). The reactive effect of the experimental arrangements is often alluded to as the 'Hawthorne effect', since its importance was clearly demonstrated in the famous Hawthorne studies (Roethlisberger and Dickson, 1939). In an enquiry into the relationship between physical work conditions and productivity, the output of a group of workers was studied under various conditions. The group were treated differently from usual and knew they were the subjects of an experiment. The effect of these arrangements was found to be so strong as to hide any effects of changes in physical conditions.

[1] For a fuller discussion, see Section 9.7.

(12) *Multiple-treatment interference*. In some experiments a variety of treatments, X, is tried out on the same subjects. If X_1 is given first and X_2 afterwards, when X_2 is being studied there may remain a residual effect of X_1 which will be falsely attributed to X_2. In a comparison of the efficiency of two sleep-inducing drugs, no drug might be used the first night, drug 1 may be used for the second night and drug 2 for the third. But, in assessing the effect of drug 2, there is the danger that a residual effect of drug 1 remains or that there is an interaction between this residual and drug 2.

On inspection, it will be seen that the first eight of these sources of invalidity differ from the last four. The first eight are concerned with *internal validity*, that is they are concerned with the question of whether a true measure of the effect of X is obtained for the subjects in the experiment. The last four are concerned with the generalizability of the findings to other persons, that is with *external validity*. Often in designing studies the demands of internal and external validity compete; the stronger the design is made in internal validity, the weaker it becomes in external validity. In general, surveys are strong on external validity but weak on internal, while for experiments it is the other way round.

9.3. Controlling for the effects of extraneous variables

In experimental studies, comparison of two or more groups is a basic feature. If the groups differ on some third variable Z, this difference may explain the association between the predictor X and predictand Y. However, if the two groups can be made equivalent with regard to Z, Z cannot explain the association. In practice there are, of course, numerous extraneous variables (Z_1, Z_2, Z_3, etc.) and ideally equivalence should be obtained for all of them simultaneously. There are three ways by which extraneous variables can be controlled in order to attempt to attain equivalence.

First, there are *matching* techniques. If Z might be related to both X and Y and is therefore a potential source of invalidity, the danger of its possible biasing effect can be removed by ensuring through the method of selection that E and C are equivalent with regard to Z. Suppose the effect of a television programme on the attitude of mothers towards vaccinating their children against polio is to be examined. An experimental group E of mothers who saw the programme, and a control group C of mothers who did not, can be chosen, but then a possible explanation of an association between attitude (Y) and viewing (X) might be a third variable, say age (Z_1). If, however, E and C are chosen so that the age distributions in the two groups are the same, age does not explain the association: this technique is known as *matching* by age. But age is only one of the extraneous variables. Mother's educational level (Z_2), for example, is also likely to be associated with attitude and viewing, and matching on this variable is required as well. In practice other extraneous variables (e.g. religion, husband's income, etc.) will usually also be controlled but, for simplicity, we will restrict the discussion to just these two. There are two ways to match for a combination of extraneous variables, *precision control* and *frequency distribution control*. By precision control is usually meant pairwise matching. For each individual in one group, an individual with the same combination of categories of the extraneous variables is selected for the other group: here, for each mother in E, a mother of the same age group and educational level is selected for C. The problem with pairing is that when, say, five or six extraneous variables are being controlled, it is difficult to find matching pairs. Many of the subjects have no one with the same combination of categories in the other group and thus have to be discarded. This is an illustration of an increase in internal validity resulting in a decrease in external validity: controlling more precisely on selection bias forces a restriction of the population coverage, and thus restricts the generalizability of the conclusions. To retain generalizability either the number of matching criteria must be reduced or coarser groupings (e.g. ten-year age groups rather than five-year) must be used.

Although precision control usually means one-to-one matching, this is not essential. If the study requires the administration of an expensive experimental variable, it could be economical to pair two or more members of the control group for each member of the experimental group: the only requirement is that an equal number of members in one group is matched with each member in the other. Another occasion when many-to-one matching might be profitable is when it is difficult to find members for one of the groups; then several members of the common group could be matched with each member of the rare group (see also pp. 97–9).

Frequency distribution control attempts to gain the advantages of matching for several variables without discarding as many subjects as is necessary with precision control. With frequency distribution control the two groups are equated for each of the matching variables *separately* but not in combination. Thus the distributions of mothers' educational levels are equated for the two groups, and so are the age distributions, but there is no assurance that the combinations of educational level and age are the same in each group. It may be that the more highly educated mothers are the older mothers in one group but the younger ones in the other. Thus, although this method eliminates both age on its own and educational level on its own as being explanations of the association between attitude and viewing, it does not eliminate the effect of a combination of age and educational level. If, say, older, more educated mothers have a more favourable attitude and they are unequally divided between E and C, this would invalidate the comparison between the groups.

Matching achieves equivalence on the extraneous variables considered through control exercised in the *selection* of the groups. An alternative procedure is to make *adjustments in the analysis*. If measurements are collected on the extraneous variables for the members of each group, these measurements can be used to adjust for differences between the groups and the method is therefore often known as 'control through measurement'. There are a variety of statistical methods for this purpose, including cross-tabulation, standardization and regression; further discussion of these methods is given in Chapter 17. It is useful here to observe that the ideas of matching are similar to those of stratification, and the relationship of precision control matching to standardization is the same as that of stratification to stratification after selection (see p. 99): standardization is, in fact, matching after selection. Belson (1959b) has developed an efficient procedure, known as the stable correlate technique, for matching after selection on a combination of variables.

The problem with matching and adjustment is that even when used together they can control for only a small number of extraneous variables, but there is an unlimited number of such variables that could be considered. If an experimenter eliminates the disturbing influence of the variables Z_1, Z_2 and Z_3, a critic can always challenge his results, claiming (rightly) that he has not controlled for Z_4, Z_5 and Z_6. When it is possible, the way out of this dilemma is to use *randomization*. If subjects can be randomly assigned to E and C, then the difference between the two groups for *any* prior extraneous variable can be only a random chance fluctuation. Moreover, statistical techniques can be used to determine the probability that such random fluctuations could lead to an association between X and Y as large or larger than the one observed. Suppose mothers could be randomly assigned to E (watching the television programme) and C (not watching). Then, although somewhat more of the older mothers might by chance be allocated to E than C (say), the statistical analysis would indicate the probability of chance fluctuations like this being the cause of the observed association between X and Y. If this probability were sufficiently small, one would be highly confident that such chance fluctuations could be ruled out as the explanation of the association.

On its own, randomization will, within the limits of chance fluctuations, equalize E and C on all prior extraneous variables. However, the *sensitivity* of an experiment can be improved by using randomization together with either matching or adjustment or both. Randomization used together with matching is often known as *restricted randomization*. If some major disturbing variables can be identified, it is better not to leave to chance their equalization between *E* and *C*, but instead to use matching to control them. The more minor and unknown disturbing variables may then be treated by randomization. Thus, using precision control, mothers of the same age and educational level may be matched in pairs, and then one member of each pair randomly assigned to *E* and the other to *C*; such a design is called a *paired comparison* experiment.

Unfortunately, randomization is frequently impracticable with human populations: it is often impossible to *manipulate* the predictor variable, that is to determine which individuals are to be exposed to *X* and which are not. In the television example it might just be possible to manipulate the predictor variable by selecting a control group and asking them to do something else at the time of the programme in question (perhaps watching a different channel). To the extent that this procedure (described by Emmett, 1966, and Monk, 1963) is successful, it would ensure that a randomly selected control group did not see the programme, while, on the other hand, the randomly selected experimental group could be persuaded to watch it. But frequently with human beings randomization is impossible: for instance, people cannot be randomly assigned to be smokers and non-smokers, male and female, car-owners and non-car-owners, extrovert and introvert, etc.

Inability to randomize does not mean, however, that no attempt to establish causal connections is worth while, nor does lack of randomization make a study useless. But without randomization the conclusions must necessarily be more tentative. Instead of being able to eliminate all prior extraneous variables by randomization, the researcher must try to eliminate some of them by matching and adjustment. He cannot eliminate all of them this way, but he can eliminate the major ones. To do so he must, of course, be knowledgeable about the subject matter in order to make his choice of 'major' variables.

This brings to light the different parts played by matching and adjustment in randomized and non-randomized studies. In the former, the objective is solely to increase the sensitivity of the experiment; it is profitable to choose important extraneous variables because they will make the experiment more sensitive. If inappropriate variables are selected and important ones missed, the chance of reaching a conclusion is reduced, but any conclusion reached is still valid. With the non-randomized investigation, matching and adjustment play a far more crucial role. The exclusion of any extraneous variable creating a disturbing influence could lead to a false conclusion. In this situation painstaking research of the literature to identify the possible disturbing variables is an essential prerequisite to a good study, and careful control of variables so identified is required if any confidence is to be had in the results.

9.4. Other designs

We might now pause to consider the definition of an experiment. As Wold (1956, p. 30) observed, 'The notion of an experiment is somewhat fluid, but whether taken in a broad or a narrow sense it involves some degree of planning and control from the side of the experimenter.' We shall follow current usage and confine the use of 'experiment' to studies where the predictor variable is manipulated. If manipulation is possible, randomization can be employed in order to obtain the benefit of the considerable safeguards it provides. But, in social research, experimentation so defined is often impossible, and any causal inference must therefore be made on the basis of nonexperimental studies, which we shall call *investigations*.[1] Thus, in the designs we have already described, the after-only and before-after designs with control group are experiments if membership of the two groups is determined by a random allocation (with or without matching), while otherwise they are investigations.

Because of its great weaknesses, Campbell and Stanley (1966) call the before-after design without a control group a pre-experimental design (they also use this description for the after-only design without randomization). It has been seen above that one way to improve this design is to include a control group, preferably with random allocation to membership of experimental and control groups. Another modification, leading to a *time-series design*, is to take several observations on the predictand Y (say Y_1, Y_2, Y_3 and Y_4) at intervals prior to the introduction of the predictor X and then several observations (Y_5, Y_6, Y_7 and Y_8) at intervals afterwards. If no change occurred in the first four or the last four observations, or if there was a steady trend in each group of four, and if also there was a discontinuity between Y_4 and Y_5, the conclusion that X caused a change in Y could be made more safely than if there were only one before- and one after-measurement. In particular, the extra measurements make it less likely that maturation and testing are sources of invalidity: their effects could well explain a trend in the Y measurements, but not easily account for a discontinuity between Y_4 and Y_5.

---

[1] Various other terms, with the same or a similar meaning, have been used, for example 'quasi-experimental designs' (Campbell and Stanley, 1966), 'investigations' (Kish, 1959), 'planned surveys' (Cox, 1958), 'explanatory surveys' (Hyman, 1955), and 'observational studies' (Cochran, 1965).

The major source of invalidity for this design is history, for there is still the possibility that some event other than X, occurring between Y_4 and Y_5, caused the discontinuity. If a control group is also included in the design, and no discontinuity is found between Y_4 and Y_5 for the control group, then history is also an unlikely source of invalidity. A further advantage of taking multiple observations is to detect transient effects. In many cases, the effect of X might decay with time, and it is also possible that X has its maximum impact some time after its administration. The measurement of Y at several times after X enables the effect of X to be charted through time. A single after-measurement might show no change in Y if it occurs too soon, before X has had time to take effect, or too late, when the effect has worn off.

A common type of investigation is the *retrospective* or *ex post facto* (after the event) *study*; it is also often called an *ex post facto* experiment, but 'experiment' is avoided here because the design does not qualify as such by our definition. Such studies are of two kinds, neither of them involving actual manipulation of the experimental var:able: in the first a comparison is made of two groups, which are equated as closely as possible by matching and adjustment, but where only one group has at some past time been exposed to the predictor variable. The hypothesis of interest is tested by comparing the incidence of the predictand variable in the two groups. This research looks from the past to the present, and is usually termed a *cause-to-effect* design.

In the second kind, two groups differing in the predictand variable, but as nearly as possible equated in other respects by matching and adjustment, are compared; the researcher then looks back for possible explanations of the difference. This is the *effect-to-cause* design.

The retrospective study requires information about the past, which can be obtained either from the subject's memory or from records. In the former case there is a real danger of bias, for memory distortions are a well-known phenomenon. If it is thought that X is a cause of Y, the subject experiencing Y may well 'remember' having had X, although in fact he had not had it. The problem with records is that they were collected for some other, probably administrative, purpose, and are unlikely to contain all the details required; they may also not have been maintained with the accuracy required for such an analysis.

Thus a *prospective study*, following the subjects forward in time, has much to commend it over a retrospective study. The retrospective study, however, has the advantage of speed. In medical studies, for example, the onset of a disease may follow many years after a cause. The researcher must then wait for this period to elapse before drawing conclusions from a prospective study, while with a retrospective study the results are available as soon as the data are collected and analysed. It is also difficult to conduct a prospective study when the effect Y is a rare event. A very large group must be selected initially if a sufficient number of cases contracting Y during the study are to be obtained. This means that a large number of subjects who do not contract Y must be followed. With a retrospective study one can hunt for the Y cases and compare them with a group of non-Y cases, determining the number of non-Y cases to suit the research requirements.

9.5. Examples of investigations

To illustrate some methods and problems of investigations, let us consider the much-discussed issue of the connection between smoking and cancer of the lung. The background to the various studies on this question is the enormous increase in the incidence of the disease since the turn of the century. In England and Wales, for example, the crude death rate from it jumped from 8 per million in 1900 to 321 per million in 1952 and, when all allowance is made for changes in the age and sex composition of the population, there remains no doubt that the increase is real. Nor can improved diagnosis, which certainly accounts for *some* of the increase, explain all of it. The relatively much greater increase among men than among women, among the old than among the young, and the continuance of the overall increase in recent years, all argue against improved diagnosis being the entire explanation.

There are many environmental causes that might be responsible for the dramatic increase. Smoking[1] is certainly one, but exhaust fumes from the ever-increasing number of road vehicles, factory smoke, and increased exposure to cancer-producing substances in various occupations are among others to be considered. In order to examine these and other possible causes of the disease, various studies have been made in a number of countries. The literature on this subject is now vast, and no attempt will be made to summarize it.[2] The present discussion will be confined to the Medical Research Council studies in England and Wales by Doll and Hill (1950, 1952, 1954, 1956, 1964; also Hill, 1962). These studies are models of research design and interpretation. There is no space to go into

[1] The fact that the trends over time of smoking and of lung-cancer incidence have moved parallel has been merely suggestive—it is not in any sense evidence of a connection between them, nor has it of course been used as such by the investigators.

[2] For those wishing to follow up this subject, the following references should provide starting points: Brownlee (1965), Berkson (1963), Cutler (1955), U.S. Department of Health, Education, and Welfare: Public Health Service (1954), Royal College of Physicians (1962), Eysenck (1965) and Cornfield and others (1959).

details of methodology or results, and for these readers are urged to refer to the original papers.

The purpose of the first investigation, a retrospective effect-to-cause study, was 'to determine whether patients with carcinoma of the lung differed materially from other persons either in their smoking habits or in some way which might be related to the theory that atmospheric pollution is responsible for the development of the disease' (Doll and Hill, 1952, p. 1,271). The basis of the research was a comparison, based on interviews conducted between 1948 and 1952, of 1,465 lung-cancer patients in a number of hospitals in England and Wales, with a control group of 1,465 patients who were suffering from other diseases[1] and who were individually matched with the lung-cancer patients by sex (the great majority of both groups were men), by five-year age grouping and, in most cases, by being in the same hospital at the same time. The two samples were also closely alike in terms of social class composition.

A detailed study was made of the past smoking histories of the members of both groups and, after discussing possible biases, Doll and Hill (1952, p. 1,273) concluded that the data were 'reliable enough to indicate general trends and to substantiate material differences between groups'.

The differences did indeed prove to be very substantial. Among men, for example, only 0·5 per cent of the lung-cancer group were non-smokers ('persons who had never consistently smoked as much as one cigarette a day for as long as one year') as against 4·5 per cent in the control group. And whereas in the lung-cancer group 25 per cent had smoked (either just before their illness or, if they had previously stopped smoking, before they last gave up) more than 25 cigarettes a day, or the equivalent in pipe tobacco, the corresponding figure in the control group was only 13·4 per cent. For women similar differences were found.

The many other striking results of these researches are recorded in the original papers, but what interests us here is the design. We note that the two groups were first matched on several important extraneous variables, the choice of these being governed by common sense, knowledge of the subject matter and availability of data; and that the predictand variable, i.e the smoking habits of the patients, was studied retrospectively by questioning. These habits obviously could not be manipulated, i.e. made the subject of experiment.

As to the accuracy of people's answers, Doll and Hill used what safeguards they could to eliminate bias, and it is unlikely that incorrect answers due to bad memory were the cause of the substantial

---

[1] Patients suffering from certain diseases—e.g. cancer of the mouth—were not admitted to the control group.

association observed between smoking and lung cancer. Since they were unable to keep the interviewers collecting the data in ignorance as to whether a patient was in the experimental or control group, there was the danger of interviewer bias affecting the results; interviewers might have tended to scale up the smoking habits of the cancer patients. By taking advantage of a side-effect of the study, Doll and Hill were able to check on this danger. Some patients at the time of interview were thought to have lung cancer, but later this was found not to be the case. Comparison of the smoking habits of these patients with those with confirmed lung cancer showed marked differences; on the other hand, the smoking habits of these patients did not differ significantly from those of the control group. This check thus effectively eliminated interviewer bias as a source of invalidity. The ingenious use of these data demonstrates how the alert researcher can often search out checks on the validity of his findings.

The authors, in concluding that 'smoking is a factor and an important factor in the production of carcinoma of the lung' (Doll and Hill, 1952, p. 1,283), stressed that this did not mean that heavy smoking was a sufficient condition for lung cancer or that it was the sole cause of the observed increase in the disease. But, apart from some evidence that people living in urban areas are more prone to it than those in rural areas, tobacco smoke was the only factor for which a strong association with cancer had been demonstrated. This alone made the research findings worthy of attention.

We might now ask how the failure to conduct a controlled experiment affects the interpretation and evaluation of the results. Doll and Hill were careful to emphasize that, *taken by themselves*, the studies demonstrated only an association, not a causative connection, between smoking and lung cancer. Statistically, this observed association could just as well mean that lung cancer causes people to smoke as that smoking causes the disease; equally it is compatible with the possibility that both have a common cause. On the first point, Doll and Hill state that medical opinion refutes the idea that the disease might be the cause and smoking the effect; and they rightly stress that such 'subject-matter knowledge must be allowed to play its part in the interpretation of results'.

The second problem is more troublesome. Since it was not possible to decide the membership of the two groups at random, and since the groups of patients being compared could only be matched on a few factors, one cannot be certain that the groups did not differ with regard to some crucial uncontrolled factor, *this* factor being responsible for the observed association.

To reduce this uncertainty, Doll and Hill compared the two groups on several relevant variables—occupational exposure, social class, place of residence, residence near gasworks, exposure to different kinds of heating, previous respiratory disease—and on none of these factors were there significant differences between the two groups. It was therefore reasonable to dismiss them as possible causes.

But of course this kind of 'control through measurement' could not conceivably be done with all the variables that might be affecting the issue. Let us suppose, for instance, that the observed association between lung cancer and smoking was due, not to a direct causal relationship, but to an uncontrolled variable, say extroversion[1]; i.e. that extroverted people tend both to smoke more and also to be more liable to develop lung cancer than others. Smoking and cancer would still—correctly—be shown to be statistically associated although they are not causally related.

Now if data on extroversion had been collected for each respondent one could determine whether this third variable did or did not 'explain' the association. Without such data, on the other hand, with the above kind of design one cannot (on statistical grounds) rule out the possibility that the association between smoking and lung cancer was due to this common factor, extroversion. As the allocation of sample members to each group depended on whether they did or did not have lung cancer and as their smoking habits were taken as given, it is feasible that the heavy-smoking (and lung cancer) group might have recruited itself largely from the extroverted sections of the population, and *vice versa*. As we have seen, when the membership of the experimental and control groups is, so to speak, determined by nature, one can never be *certain* that an observed statistical association between two variables is not due to one of these uncontrolled (and perhaps even unsuspected) variables.

These early studies by Doll and Hill were retrospective studies, but as Hill observed, 'if the forward approach can be employed, it is, I believe, almost always the right way to go to work; in any observational inquiry its possibility should invariably be considered' (Hill, 1962, p. 378). They therefore continued their investigations with a prospective study. In October 1951 questionnaires were sent to all members of the medical profession in the United Kingdom to discover their current smoking habits and smoking history, and over 40,000 replies were received. Doll and Hill then collected, with the assistance of the Registrars-General in the United Kingdom, the General Medical Council and the British Medical Association, details of the deaths of doctors dying in the succeeding 53 months.[2]

[1] Eysenck (1965) found cigarette smoking to be positively associated with extroversion, non-smokers and pipe smokers being less extroverted than cigarette smokers.
[2] In a longer term follow-up Doll and Hill (1964) have confirmed the findings of the preliminary analyses.

From their analyses they were able to show an association between smoking and deaths from lung cancer. In addition they were able to measure the relative risks of death from lung cancer among different groups. For example they demonstrated that higher risks existed for heavy smokers than for light smokers, and for cigarette smokers than for pipe smokers. It is rarely feasible for a retrospective study to provide such measures, and this is thus another advantage of the prospective approach. Note, however, the large population that had to be studied and the length of time needed before a sufficient number of cases of lung cancer deaths were obtained for the statistical analysis. This was the price that had to be paid for the advantages of the prospective study.

9.6. Factorial designs

In the preceding sections we have discussed designs comprising only two groups, an experimental and a control group. Often, however, studies are more complex than this. There are several reasons why this should be so.

For one thing, until now the predictor variable has been described as an all-or-none quantity, the experimental group being exposed to X and the control group being unexposed; but one may want to go further and investigate the effects of different amounts of X. The purpose of a study of the effect of alcohol on the ability of subjects to solve problems might be to find out how ability varies according to different amounts of alcohol consumed. For such a study, a control group and several experimental groups drinking, say, one whisky, two whiskies, etc. would be needed. By comparing the various groups, the way in which ability varies with amount of alcohol consumed could be charted. As before, the groups need to be made comparable, using techniques such as matching, adjustment and randomization. The extension of pairwise matching is known as *blocking*: instead of choosing two individuals alike on a number of extraneous variables, several such individuals are chosen, one for the control group and one for each of the experimental groups.

Another case where more than two groups are needed is when more than one control group is to be used. One might, for example, want to discover not only whether a drug is effective in treating a disease but also how it compares with the existing form of treatment. There might then be three groups, an experimental group given the new drug, a control group given a dummy and another control group given the currently used treatment.

A third reason for using several groups is for investigating the effects of more than one predictor variable. To this point we have been concerned with distinguishing between an experimental and a control group by their difference in one factor only, but there is much to be gained by studying several groups and deliberately varying more than one factor. To illustrate the advantages, we will take as an example an experiment by Marquis (1969) investigating the effects of two interveiwing techniques on the reporting of chronic sickness conditions in household interviews. The two techniques we will consider were, first, lengthening the questions asking about chronic conditions by adding superfluous phrases to them and, secondly, using 'reinforcement' to encourage the respondent (for instance by having the interviewer say 'We need to know that' after the respondent has reported something). Each of these factors was taken at two *levels*—a short or a long question, with reinforcement or without reinforcement—and all combinations, 2×2 or 2^2, were used:

(1) No reinforcement, short questions
(2) Reinforcement, short questions
(3) No reinforcement, long questions
(4) Reinforcement, long questions.

Such a design, using all possible combinations, is known as a *complete factorial experiment*. The object of this experiment was to compare these four procedures in terms of the degree of agreement between the responses given in interviews in which they were employed and information obtained from the respondents' physicians. For this purpose blocks of four women (the study being confined to white females aged 18–60 living in Detroit) were formed by matching on geographical area, and some control on age group and 'sickness' group was also employed. Then, within each block, the women were randomly allocated between the four procedures. Interviews were conducted with the women using the appropriate procedure and their reports of chronic conditions were compared with those provided by their physicians.

The effect of each factor in the experiment could now be measured in two ways—the effect of reinforcement by comparing the mean level of agreement in groups (1) and (2) or groups (3) and (4), and that of question length by comparing groups (1) with (3) or (2) with (4)—and it is in fact this feature of being able to measure an effect in different ways that is the special strength of factorial experiments. If the same answer is obtained whichever way is used (within the bounds of sampling error), the gain of the design is that it enables the findings to be generalized more widely; had this been so here, it would have meant, for instance, that the effect of longer questions is the same whether reinforcement is present or not. Without the factorial experiment, the findings on the effect of longer questions would relate either to a situation in which reinforcement is used or to one in which it is not used, but not to both.

When the various ways of measuring an effect yield different answers there is said to be an *interaction* between the factors involved, for the size of the effect of one factor depends on the level of another factor (see pp. 455-6 for a fuller discussion of interaction effects). There was in fact an interaction effect in the present example, for while lengthening the questions improved the degree of agreement with physicians' reports when no reinforcement was used—i.e. in the comparison of (1) with (3)—this was not so when reinforcement was used—the comparison of (2) with (4). Both longer questions and reinforcement improved the degree of agreement, but when the two were used together their effects appeared to partially cancel out. It is only through factorial experiments that interaction effects like this can be detected.

Factorial designs can readily be extended to more than two factors and to factors at more than two levels. A discussion of such designs is beyond the scope of this treatment, but the interested reader is referred to the excellent simple account by Cox (1958). We will conclude the section with a brief description of the factorial design employed by Himmelweit and others (1958) in a study of the effects of television on children. Their main comparison groups were children viewing television and those not doing so. However, they took four other factors into account:

1. Two age groups (10-11 and 13-14 years)
2. Boys and girls
3. Three levels of intelligence within each age group
4. A twofold social class division.

Their design thus had 48 treatment combinations: 2 (viewing or not) × 2 (age groups) × 2 (sexes) × 3 (I.Q. levels) × 2 (social classes). Since the analysis of a factorial design is simple when there is an equal number of observations for each treatment combination, they aimed at 40 children for each treatment combination, so that a total sample of 1,920 children was required. In the event, this equality was not achieved, with the result that the analysis became more complex. In addition to the use of a factorial design, pairwise matching of viewers and non-viewers was employed. The four factors (age, sex, I.Q. and social class) were more stringently controlled by this means than would have been the case if only the factorial design matching had been used. Furthermore, as far as possible, matching was also done within classrooms so that geographical factors, the influence of teachers, the school, and other children were controlled. By employing a factorial design, results of wider applicability were obtained than would have been the case had the study been restricted to, say, middle-class boys aged 10–11 of average intelligence.

Another example of a factorial design in social research is provided by Keyfitz (1953). For an example of a complex design used for an experiment in survey methodology, see Durbin and Stuart (1951).

9.7. Sample designs for experiments and investigations

Various sources of invalidity were described in Section 9.2, and the purpose of this section is to take up one of these sources for further discussion. To repeat, there are two aspects to validity: there is *internal validity*, which deals with the question of whether a true measure of the effect of the experimental variable is obtained for the subjects of the experiment; and there is *external validity*, which relates to the generalizability of the findings to some wider population. The particular source of invalidity to be treated here, the interaction of selection with the experimental variable, is a threat to external validity.

In a sense the attainment of internal validity is more crucial than that of external validity, for without the former the study is valueless; if the latter is missing, at least the results hold for the subjects under study. Still, external validity is of great importance and it should be given due consideration in designing a study; here we are concerned with the question of how to select the subjects in order to be able to generalize the results.

Often too little attention is paid to this question in experiments and investigations. For convenience researchers may collect a sample of volunteers or choose their sample purposively. If a university psychologist advertises for student volunteers, with or without a payment for their services, his sample cannot be assumed to be representative of the student body, let alone the general population. Equally, a test town chosen for a market research study for reasons of convenience cannot be held to be representative of the whole country. If the effect of the experimental variable were the same for everyone in the population, it would not matter how the selections were made and the samples in these two examples would be adequate. In the same way if, in a descriptive survey, all the population had the same value for the variable under study, it would not matter how the sample were selected and non-probability procedures could be employed without risk. But in descriptive surveys it cannot be assumed that there are no differences in the population for the variable; similarly, in experiments and investigations, it should not be assumed that the effects of experimental variables are constant over all parts of the population and independent of variations between those parts.[1] And, if the assumption of a constant effect for the experimental variable cannot be made with a great deal of confidence, there is a clear case for careful sampling.

This idea can perhaps best be explained in terms of a concrete, but hypothetical, example. The effect of an educational film is to be examined by means of an experiment in which a randomly chosen experimental group of schoolchildren aged between eleven and thirteen are shown the film and in which there is a control group who are not shown the film. We will pass over aspects of the general design and concentrate on the selection of the two groups of children. A simple approach would be to gain the co-operation of a neighbouring school and carry out the experiment on one of the classes, dividing the class into experimental and control groups at random, probably after some matching. This design would be administratively easy, but would suffer badly in terms of external validity: if the class comprised children of above-average intelligence, would the results also hold for children of lesser intelligence? If this was a class of eleven-year-olds, would the results also hold for thirteen-year-olds? These questions could be dealt with by extending the survey to cover children of different levels of intelligence and of different ages, but other questions would arise, such as: do the results hold for urban and rural schools, for schools in the north and in the south, in both large and small schools? To answer these questions, the study must be extended to include children in a variety of schools.

Rather than proceed in this way, a better approach would be to start off with a definition of the population to which the findings should apply, and then arrange to draw the sample for the experimental and control groups from that population. In choosing the sample, the methods already outlined for descriptive surveys, such as stratification and multi-stage sampling, can be applied. If the population is defined as all children in the stated age groups in schools in Great Britain, one might start by selecting a stratified PPS sample of schools at the first stage, stratifying by geographical region, urban/rural etc. Then a number of classes could be randomly chosen from within the selected schools, after first stratifying the classes by, say, stream, age group etc. If a particular sub-population, such as children in Scotland, forms a domain of study, or if a comparison, such as that between children in urban and rural schools, is of special interest, stratified sampling with a variable sampling fraction (see

---

[1] The argument for a constant effect is a common one, although, as argued here, a fallacious one. It can also be expressed in terms of analytical statistics: for example, that in measuring the difference between the mean scores of experimental and control groups or that in measuring a regression coefficient, it does not matter how the sample is selected. See also McGinnis (1958) and Kish (1959) on this topic.

Section 5.3) can usefully be employed. Finally, within each class, the children could be matched together in pairs, by sex, ability etc., and then one member of each pair could be chosen at random for the experimental group, the other member going into the control group. With this design, the children are equated in terms of the characteristics used for matching within the classes, and additional matching comes from the fact that both members of a matched pair are in the same class in the same school.

The advantage of this approach is that all types of children are represented by the sample. If some groups of children react differently to the film, the findings will show this to be the case. Moreover, the experimental and the control group each constitute a probability sample of the population, which means that estimates of population averages and the standard errors of these estimates can be calculated. From the experimental sample an estimate of the average score of the population as if they had all seen the film can be made; for the control sample the estimated average score applies to the situation where none of the population had seen the film. The difference between these average scores measures the average effect of the film *for this particular population*, and is of some interest. But generally, when the effect of an experimental variable differs between sub-groups of the population, the average effect is of lesser concern than a detailed study of the effects in the various sub-groups. The average effect is an average of the sub-group effects and therefore depends on the relative sizes of the sub-groups in this population: with the same sub-group effects a population with a different distribution of members among the sub-groups would show a different average effect. A full understanding of the effect of the experimental variable is to be found by a sub-group analysis; the average effect calculated on the basis of the distribution over the sub-groups of the population under study is nevertheless a meaningful and often a useful summary figure. Probability sampling procedures like the one described enable this average effect and its standard error to be calculated.

The purpose of this example is merely to show how probability sampling can be applied in experimental studies. In practice there will be difficulties, such as, possibly, a high rate of refusal to co-operate. Also, of course, the concern with representation has led to a far more expensive enquiry than the simple one-class study from which we started.

In situations where randomization is impossible, there are more difficulties. Suppose, for instance, that a study is to be conducted to investigate the effect of smoking on a variable X. To secure representation, two random samples could be selected, one from the population of smokers and the other from that of non-smokers; but then a straightforward comparison of the average amount of X in the two samples would not take account of the effects of extraneous variables; for example, more of the smokers are men and this might invalidate the comparison. To deal with this and other extraneous variables, matching can be employed. But matching forces the distribution of the matched variables to be the same in each of the two samples and, since this is not the case in the populations, a loss of representation in at least one of the samples must result; standardization, which is matching in the analysis, faces the same problem. If a representative sample of smokers were drawn first and then a sample of non-smokers matched to it, the difference between the average scores of the two samples would measure the average effect of smoking *on the population of smokers*. If the non-smokers were selected first, and the smokers matched to them, the difference in average scores would measure, so to speak, the average effect of non-smoking *on the population of non-smokers*. In general, the magnitudes of these two average effects will differ and care is needed in their interpretation. Again, as with experimental studies, a clearer understanding is reached by an analysis of the various effects in the separate sub-groups. Sometimes the effect of the experimental variable will be constant, or nearly so, for all sub-groups, and this would mean that a simple overall analysis could be made, and any sample would do. But this cannot be relied on, so a more detailed analysis should be carried out to investigate possible interaction effects between the experimental variable and other characteristics of the sample; and, especially important, the samples should be chosen carefully so that the findings can be validly generalized. Like descriptive surveys, experiments and investigations also need proper sampling procedures.

NOTES ON READING

1. A useful reference on the subject of this chapter is the chapter by CAMPBELL and STANLEY in GAGE (1963), which has been reprinted separately, CAMPBELL and STANLEY (1966). A similar treatment is provided in the chapter by CAMPBELL in HARRIS (1963). Among the textbooks, the treatments in SELLTIZ and others (1959), RILEY (1963), MADGE (1953) and KERLINGER (1964) are particularly worth consulting, as are the chapters by FRENCH and by FESTINGER in FESTINGER and KATZ (1953). Another useful reference is KAPLAN (1964), and BEVERIDGE (1953) has written a stimulating book on the methods of scientific investigation generally. Early books on experimental sociology are those of CHAPIN (1947) and GREENWOOD (1945).

2. Valuable articles on various aspects of the problems discussed in this chapter are those of KISH (1959), COCHRAN (1965), STOUFFER (1950)—also reprinted in STOUFFER (1962)—and EHRENBERG in MARKET RESEARCH SOCIETY (1963a).

3. The stable correlate technique is described by BELSON (1959b) and various applications of the technique are described in BELSON (1967a) in relation to television research. An interesting paper on the design of investigations in television research is that of EMMETT (1966).

4. The book by HILL (1962) contains many examples of good medical investigations. The book by WITTS (1964) is also recommended for a discussion of medical studies.

5. On orthodox experiments the book by COX (1958) provides a particularly lucid account of the underlying ideas. The chapter by ROSS and SMITH in BLALOCK and BLALOCK (1968) is also valuable. Among the statistical texts on experimental design, those by COCHRAN and COX (1957), DAVIES (1956) and FISHER (1960) are especially recommended.

CHAPTER 10

Methods of Collecting the Information I—Documents and Observation

10.1. Introduction

IN THE last few chapters we have been concerned with the coverage of surveys and particularly with methods of sampling. The collection of the information, to which we now turn, brings us up against difficulties much more serious, in one sense, than those of sampling. The selection of samples rests on well-developed theories and the surveyor can, broadly speaking, make the sample as precise as resources permit. Methods of collecting the information are not so developed and systematized. There is a wealth of experience and a formidable literature describing them, but few would claim that this amounts to a coherent set of principles or a theoretical framework. Every survey expert has his own ideas, but however well grounded in past experience these are, they have neither the certainty nor the objectivity that goes with his choice of sample design. Perhaps matters like interviewing and questionnaire design can never achieve a theoretical basis in the sense that sampling has one, but research on methods of data collection must be given priority if the development of this aspect of surveys is to catch up with that of sampling and analytical techniques.

Methods of obtaining data about a group of people can be classified in many ways. For our purpose, the following grouping is convenient:

(*a*) Documentary sources
(*b*) Observation
(*c*) Mail questionnaire
(*d*) Interviewing

In the United States telephone interviewing is also of some importance, especially in radio research. In Britain and many other countries, however, too few households have telephones to make the method useful in surveys of the general population, though it might be applicable to specific populations, such as telephone subscribers, doctors, lawyers or firms; for instance Horton (1963) describes a pilot survey by telephone of telephone subscribers in the Birmingham area. Sudman (1967) and Coombs and Freedman (1964) describe the use of telephone interviewing in surveys in the United States, and Hochstim (1967) compares the findings from three strategies of data collection, one of which was mainly by telephone interviewing, the others being mainly by personal interviewing and mainly by mail questionnaire. Telephone interviewing will not be discussed further here.

While the above grouping is a useful classification for our discussion, it should not be thought to imply that the methods cannot be combined. Indeed a combination of methods is often appropriate to make use of their different strengths. Gray (1957) describes how a mail questionnaire survey was supplemented by interviewing to increase the response rate. As part of another mail survey, Gray and Parr (1959) collected a sample of cigarette stubs for observational measurement. In interview surveys, direct observational methods are often valuable, for the interviewer can obtain the information for herself, rather than rely on the possibly inaccurate replies given by respondents. Thus, for example, in a survey of the postal services, to find out the effects of moving letter-boxes from the front doors of houses to a box at the garden gate, interviewers measured the dimensions of the present box and paced out the distance from it to the gate, as well as interviewing people for their reactions to such a change (Scott, 1959); in a survey of motorcycle riders on the use of crash helmets, the interviewer noted whether the driver and passenger were wearing helmets when stopped for interview (Scott, 1961b); and in a survey of the blind by Gray and Todd (1967), information about opinions, attitudes and mobility of the blind was obtained by straightforward interviewing, with the interviewers also measuring reading performance at Braille and Moon by timing the reading of a short passage and asking a few questions to establish that the passage had been understood.

Not only can more than one method be used in any one survey, but also some problems can be usefully investigated through separate surveys involving different approaches. In a study to estimate the audience for advertising on the outside of London buses, for instance, Day and Dunn (1969) employed both an interview survey of adults and an observational survey in which cameras mounted on a bus took photographs at set times along a series of bus routes.

As we shall see, each method has its limitations, and in many instances a combination of methods has much to commend it. In this chapter the limitations and advantages of documentary sources and

I

observation are discussed; mail questionnaires and interviewing will be dealt with in Chapters 11 and 12.

10.2. The use of documentary sources

The value of documentary sources in the *planning* of surveys was discussed in Chapter 2. The reader was warned not to 'hurry into the field' without first consulting the necessary book and journal literature, past and present investigations of relevance, official reports and statistics, records of institutions and so forth.

In this chapter the interest is in documents in a more restricted sense, and we will now discuss how different types of documents can supplement data obtained by observation, mail questionnaire and interviewing.

(*a*) *Sources giving information about the survey population.* It is usually possible to answer some of the questions a survey is intended to cover from available data. For example, in planning a social survey of a town's population, one *could* omit questions on, say, marital status or occupation, in so far as the figures are available from the Population Census or other official sources. This must not be misinterpreted. In practice one almost certainly would *not* omit these questions because (i) the answers would provide a check on the accuracy of the survey and (ii) the answers to other questions in the survey are probably to be related to those on marital status and occupation, and this can be done only if all these pieces of information are ascertained for each individual in the survey.

In a survey on the structure of National Health Service practices, some information about the population of practitioners operating it could be obtained from the British Medical Association, the Department of Health and Social Security, Local Executive Councils and Regional Hospital Boards. It could form a statistical background against which to judge the significance of the survey results. An enquiry concerned with the leisure activities of a town's population may usefully begin by getting statistical data about the use made of the local libraries, attendances at cinemas and football matches, membership of clubs and societies and so forth. A good example of such use of statistical material appears in the book on *The Communication of Ideas* by Cauter and Downham (1954).

In short, a mass of information about the populations studied by social surveys is available in historical documents, statistical reports, records of institutions and other sources; it is up to the surveyor to derive what help he can from it. He must, however, first consider carefully its suitability for his purposes. Does it, for example, have the same population coverage as his survey? Are the same definitions employed? How accurate is the information from this other source?

Is it sufficiently up-to-date? Frequently the answers to such questions will lead the surveyor to discard the information completely or at least to treat the findings as no more than rough guides. In particular, the accuracy of routine records is often found on investigation to be too questionable to make them useful for a surveyor's purposes.

(b) *Sources giving information about individual 'units of enquiry'*. It is much more difficult to supplement the information about individual survey units from documentary sources.[1] Not that there is any lack of information; the difficulty is in gaining access to it if it was collected for quite another purpose. Government departments possess a mass of information relating to individuals (census schedules, employment records, insurance cards, health records, income tax returns, family budget records and so on) but this has generally been collected with at least the implied assurance that it would not be used for purposes other than that for which it was requested, so it is not generally available to the outside researcher.

Nor is it only Government departments that possess data relating to individuals or groups. Institutions like hospitals and prisons, adoption societies, professional institutes and business firms all have in their files information which a surveyor might on occasion like to use; but, save in special circumstances, he can hardly expect to gain access to it.

In addition, much material collected in the form of case records by, for instance, probation officers, psychiatric social workers and almoners is of interest to the sociologist and psychologist; nor can one doubt that it deserves more widespread dissemination and systematic analysis than the original social worker can give it. But such material has the limitation for the research worker that it can only represent a highly specialized population—the cases that happen to come before social workers. Even when this limitation does not apply, as for example in the case of general practitioners' records, there are other major obstacles to the use of existing case records. Records written without thought for subsequent classification and analysis are unlikely to lend themselves to these purposes. For one thing the data are often incomplete; while, for instance, a doctor may fail to record certain information for particular patients because it was unimportant in their cases, for statistical classification complete information is essential. Also, the terms used in the records are likely to be vague, while classification requires precise definitions. For this reason the records are, and must be treated as, subjective statements; the comparison and aggregation of the findings of different workers is, to say the least, difficult.

[1] We say 'supplement' since we are not concerned with researches which are entirely documentary.

The problem of individuality and subjectivity of a case record is the most fundamental. The value of case records to the researcher is diminished by the extent to which they are reflections of the recorder as well as of the case being studied. This will be discussed later in relation to interviewing, for the great objection to the informal interview is that the results 'contain too much of the interviewer', so that it is difficult to compare and to aggregate.

It is relevant here to recall an aspect of a classic survey by Booth (1889–1902) at the end of the last century. Booth wanted information about the living conditions of a large number of families and obtained the bulk of it through the school attendance officers. These officers—like social workers—obtained in the course of their work a wealth of information about living conditions and kept detailed records in their notebooks. Booth recognized the danger of individual biases in these reports, even of the possibility that the mere choice of words and expressions might colour the impression they gave; to overcome these drawbacks he interviewed the school attendance officers, making their notes the basis for the discussion of each individual family. To use the words of Beatrice Webb, he 'would extract from the school attendance officer, bit by bit, the extensive and intimate information with regard to each family, the memory of these willing witnesses amplifying and illustrating the precisely recorded facts in their notebooks.' She goes on to suggest that 'what was of greater significance . . . than any of the facts revealed was the way in which this method of wholesale interviewing and automatic recording blocked the working of personal bias.' (Webb, 1926, p. 230). Although the social worker's case records and these notebooks are in many respects dissimilar, the principle of using the records as a documentary basis for interviews is a sound one. In a survey of problem families, for instance, case record material thus treated could be a valuable supplement to data obtained by direct study. This procedure requires, of course, detailed and accurate knowledge by the social worker of each individual case and, if some knowledge is lacking, it would be inappropriate; mostly it could not be safely used, for example, with a general practitioner who, caring for perhaps 2,500 persons, could not be expected—even with the aid of his records—to remember the precise details of an illness which occurred some time ago. Where it cannot be safely employed, it would almost certainly be preferable to undertake a prospective study. With a prospective study, the recorders—social workers, general practitioners and so on—can be taught to apply standardized definitions and be asked to keep records in a systematic way, probably on a specially designed recording form. This capitalizes on their skills as recording agents and the unique nature of their relationship with the subjects of the study. But it means that the researcher must wait for the data to be collected, which may take a long time; with existing records there is no such delay.

(c) *Personal documents.* So far we have considered documents which could provide the surveyor with information originally collected for another purpose, so that their contents, reliability and representativeness have been beyond his control. What about those personal documents which come directly from the informants, such as diaries, letters, autobiographies and essays? The term 'personal document' is sometimes used in a wider sense to include interview and questionnaire data, but this is clearly not appropriate in our context.

Like case records, personal documents provide a richness and detail not achieved by the more standardized methods of social surveys. They can give insight into personal characteristics, experiences and beliefs that formal interviewing can rarely, perhaps never, attain, and as they are unsolicited the possibility of any investigator bias colouring their contents is eliminated. It is only fair to add, however, that this does not mean they are free from bias; necessarily they were produced for *some* purpose and related to this there might be bias, caused by such factors as a desire for prestige or a desire to justify some action. One is therefore generally more ready to trust the truthfulness and completeness of a diary than of a letter, of a private document than of one intended for publication, certainly of one that has been written spontaneously rather than at request. While the motives for producing personal documents should be considered and care should be exercised in their interpretation, at their best they can give a personal and authentic picture of how people see themselves and their environment. But the use of personal documents in social surveys has many difficulties.

There is, first of all, the question of how to get them. When they are produced spontaneously they may be highly revealing, but this fortuitous source of data has little relevance to the methods and approach dealt with in this book. As soon as one tries to *solicit* personal documents from someone being interviewed, problems appear. This is not to say that essays and diaries[1] can never be secured. Isaacs and others (1941), for instance, in the Cambridge Evacuation Survey, obtained from child evacuees essays describing their experiences in Cambridge and their attitudes to it; and Lambert (1968) had children in boarding schools keep for two or three days a diary in which they recorded privately and frankly what happened to them and what they thought and felt throughout the day. Other examples within the framework of social surveys could also be given.

[1] We are excluding here the kinds of recording diaries used often in household expenditure and health surveys. These are discussed in Chapter 13.

But what is always hard is to get a representative collection of documents; some people are more able and ready to write letters, diaries, essays and so forth than others, and if one wants to reduce such bias through selection one must select the sample first and then request the documents. Even then not everybody will produce them. In any case, the step of *asking* people for personal documents is a crucial one. The more the investigator comes into the picture, the more danger there is of personal distortion by the respondent. The children in the Cambridge Evacuation Survey were asked to write on a given subject, in a particular context of time and place and by an investigator known to them; the essays had to be studied in this light. The presence of the researcher at the scene, of someone *for whom* the document is written, in fact takes us one stage nearer the formal interview—the next stage being informal interviewing, in which the researcher, not the informant, does the writing. By and large, personal documents are at their most valuable when unsolicited, and this means that they are less helpful in collecting data about a population than in gaining insight into particular individuals. But, even in the typical social survey, they can be illuminating in the exploratory stages as a means of orientation and a source of hypotheses.

10.3. Observation

Observation can fairly be called the classic method of scientific enquiry. The accumulated knowledge of biologists, physicists, astronomers and other natural scientists is built upon centuries of systematic observation, much of it of phenomena in their natural surroundings rather than in the laboratory. On the face of it, the relatively infrequent use of observational methods by social scientists is surprising, especially when one reflects that they are literally surrounded by their subject matter, that they have only to open their eyes and observe their fellow men and women, and the institutions and societies they have created, in action. Looked upon as a means of general orientation, observation certainly plays as much a part in the social as in any of the sciences. A social scientist can hardly avoid being influenced in his choice of research problem, his ideas and his theories, by what he observes around him. Observation as a *systematic* method of collecting data, however, is quite another matter. For it is not sufficient that the subject matter is there to be observed. The method must be suitable for investigating the problem in which the social scientist is interested; it must be appropriate to the populations and samples he wishes to study; and it should be reasonably reliable and objective.

One point of terminology must be mentioned. In the strict sense, observation implies the use of the eyes rather than of the ears and the voice: *The Concise Oxford Dictionary* defines it as 'accurate watching and noting of phenomena as they occur in nature with regard to cause and effect or mutual relations'. In social science, the term is often used in a much wider sense. The participant observer, for example, shares in the life and activities of the community, observing —in the strict sense—what is going on around him but supplementing this by conversations, interviews and studies of records. The distinguishing feature of observation in the extended sense is that the information required is obtained directly, rather than through the reports of others; in the case of behaviour one finds out what the individual does, rather than what he says he does. In what follows, both the strict and the extended sense of the term will be used as the context requires, and we do not think that any confusion will result.

In considering observation as a method of enquiry, its value must be assessed in relation to that of the alternative method of collecting information, that is asking people about their actions and beliefs and about the behaviour of others. Direct observation can have a number of advantages over asking for information from informants. In the first place, if the informants are unable to provide the information or can give only very inexact answers, questioning must be ruled out and observation is the only way to proceed. This can arise when technical information is needed; few housewives, for example, would know whether their car battery is charged by alternator or d.c. generator, but this could quickly be determined by looking under the car bonnet. It would be equally inappropriate to ask people about the level of their blood pressure or the degree of their shortsightedness or loss of hearing; direct observation would again be needed. Studies of young children may also have to rely on observation because of the children's inability to comprehend and answer any but the simplest questions; inability to express themselves on certain issues can similarly be a restriction on interviewing methods for other sections of the population.

In the case of the survey of postal services referred to earlier (p. 239) respondents would probably have given answers to a question asking for the distance from their letter-box to the front gate, but the results would almost certainly have been unreliable; often observation is a much more dependable way of collecting data in the form of measurements of distances and times. Another reason why information gathered by questioning may be unreliable is because of its dependence on the informant's memory; on some topics fallibility of memory can cause reported data to be seriously distorted, in a way which observation of events as they occur would avoid.

For predicting future behaviour, answers to questions are notoriously weak; but then observation of present behaviour is hardly a less precarious guide. Sometimes, however, observational methods can be useful in this area. If future conditions can be simulated on a sample basis, the behaviour of the sample may provide a good indicator of future behaviour. Thus Scott (1959) describes how, in the survey of postal services, in order to discover how many people would co-operate if address postal codes were introduced, a General Post Office leaflet was sent to a sample of households asking them to put a code on all items posted in the following four weeks. To measure their co-operation they were sent during the four-week period a mail questionnaire on television and radio from an apparently independent source. The returns were examined to see if they contained the address code. A similar approach was used by Wilkins (1949) in a survey to predict the demand for campaign medals after the Second World War. The efficacy of such procedures depends on how well the future can be simulated and on the assumption that timing is relatively unimportant, i.e. that people's behaviour now in a set situation is the same as it will be in the same situation in the future.

Even if informants can answer questions accurately, it does not follow that they will be willing to do so, or that they will give the true answers. The subject of response errors is taken up in Chapter 15, and it is sufficient to observe here that an informant may give a false reply because he misunderstands the question or because, consciously or subconsciously, he distorts his answer; the latter can occur for a variety of reasons, such as the desire for prestige or the desire by the informant to give the answer he thinks is expected of him. These dangers do not exist with direct observation. But, like interviewing, observation is open to the danger that the fieldworker will introduce a bias—the observer by the way in which he or she perceives the information, and the interviewer by the way in which she interprets and records the information reported by the informant.

Observer and interviewer bias can, however, usually be kept under control by careful training of the fieldworkers. Observer training in an enquiry into *The Effects of a Local Road Safety Campaign on the Behaviour of Road Users* conducted by the Government Social Survey in a provincial town in 1951 is described by Moss (1953, p. 488):

> It was necessary as a preliminary to train investigators to observe accurately and this was done by having them watch road safety films and make recordings of actual behaviour in the films. Those who were unable to give accurate recordings of the activities on the roads in the films were not put into the field for this study. The selected investigators were given a series of observations to make with a sample of sites in the chosen town; the investigators at each particular site observing only one particular form of behaviour during a particular

selected time in the day. Observations were repeated on a sufficient scale to take account of random variation in road behaviour. Twenty-six different kinds of behaviour were observed in this controlled way before and after the publicity campaign. The conclusion from the survey was that the campaign in this particular town had had no measurable effect on actual road behaviour.

This enquiry is also of interest in other respects. It shows how, rather than find out by question-and-answer methods whether the campaign had increased people's *knowledge* of road safety, the enquiry studied by observation whether the campaign had had any marked effect on their road *behaviour*. It also demonstrates an application of observational methods in an experimental setting, a before-after design, and illustrates the importance of proper time and location sampling in the study of behaviour that might vary over these dimensions.

But, though observation as a method has some important merits, there are also limitations. There are for instance circumstances in which observation offers little help. A researcher interested in events or activities that belong to the past will have to rely on documents or more probably on what people tell him, although he knows that the latter information will be subject to memory errors. In addition, observation is rarely the most appropriate method for studying opinions and attitudes. There are situations where the link between opinion and behaviour is close enough for observation of the latter to afford a good clue to the former—Campbell, Kruskal and Wallace (1966), for example, used the seating patterns of Negroes and whites in a classroom to form an index of attitude—but generally direct questioning is necessary. Also difficulties are often encountered in obtaining a representative sample for the observation of behaviour. If the characteristics of a population are to be inferred from those of a sample, the sample should ideally be randomly selected. With interview and questionnaire methods this is readily ensured; but it is not always so with observation of behaviour. To instruct investigators to observe people of all types, men and women, of different ages, social classes and so on, does not make the sample a random one; it does not even ensure that the resultant group is representative.

Unrepresentativeness in another sense may also arise with 'overheards'. These provide the researcher with a valuable, but uncontrollable, source of data, rather like unsolicited documents, in interpreting which it is always necessary to remember that some people are more self-expressive than others. 'Overheards' may give an unrepresentative picture of the attitudes of a group rather as an M.P.'s mail gives an unrepresentative picture of the views of his constituents.

In some parts of the field covered by social surveys, the time

21

needed for observation is another serious drawback. This limitation is brought out if we consider something like a family budget or nutrition survey, where detailed information, extending over time, is required from each family. An observer could live with a family and study its expenditure pattern but, if this is possible at all, it can be done only on a very small scale; record keeping and interviewing, although providing less accurate data, are more appropriate methods in such cases. For similar reasons, data on *frequency* of behaviour are hard to obtain by observation. One can easily ask a person how often he goes to church (though he might distort his answer), but it would be difficult to observe the frequency of his attendance.

One way by which direct recording of frequency of behaviour can be realized is by replacing the human observer by a piece of apparatus that does the recording for him. An example is provided by the SET meter, a device which, when attached to a television set, records on paper-tape the channel to which the set is tuned and the times at which it is switched on or over to another channel. The tape is subsequently read on a computer. From the SET meter, Audits of Great Britain Ltd (AGB) obtains minute-by-minute measurement of audiences on all channels. This, combined with individuals' viewing data from diaries completed by the households equipped with SET meters, is the method used by the Joint Industry Committee for Television Advertising Research (JICTAR) to measure television audiences.[1]

Other forms of hardware, particularly tape recorders and cameras, are also useful for direct observation of behaviour; we have referred earlier (p. 239) to the use of a camera in the London Transport study determining the audience for advertising on the outside of London buses. Such equipment enables much more detailed information to be collected at the time of observation than would be possible by an observer working alone and, since the information is recorded, it can be analysed in depth at some later time. The existence of a permanent record also means that several investigators can reproduce the analyses, thus permitting an examination of the possibility that the initial investigator has allowed a biased viewpoint to affect his interpretation.

The replacement of the observer by a piece of apparatus can have another advantage. The presence of an observer may influence the behaviour he is observing, an effect which can be avoided if the observer is replaced by an unnoticed piece of recording apparatus. Besides tape recorders and cameras, two-way mirrors are sometimes used to avoid the effect of observer interference. There are often,

[1] Other forms of meter used in television audience measurement are the Audiometer (U.S.A.) and the Tammeter (Republic of Ireland).

however, serious ethical problems to be faced if apparatus is used in this way. Has a researcher the right to collect information on individuals without their knowledge and consent? This issue frequently has to be faced with observational methods, but is perhaps particularly acute when hidden hardware is used and a permanent record is secured.

Participant observation

In the preceding discussion we have concentrated on the use of observational methods for obtaining particular sets of information since this is generally the kind of application suitable for the quantitative approach discussed in this book. We must also refer, however, to another application of observation, of considerable importance as a method of social enquiry, and often known as *participant observation*.

With this method the observer joins in the daily life of the group or organization he is studying. He watches what happens to the members of the community and how they behave and he also engages in conversations with them to find out their reactions to, and interpretations of, the events that have occurred. He studies the life of the community *as a whole*, the relationship between its members and its activities and institutions—the type of study typical of social anthropology. The community may be as small as a family or as large as a city. It may be a 'closed' community, like a family or a tribe, or an 'open' one, such as a factory, a town or a village. An important difference between the two is that in the 'open' community an observer can sometimes remain unnoticed, while in the 'closed' this is impossible.

The observer's task is to place himself in the best position for getting a complete and unbiased picture of the life of the community, and this at once raises the question: what is the best role for the observer to adopt in the community?

There is no general answer to this, for so much depends on the nature and size of the community, on what the observer wishes to observe and on his own personality and skill. Sometimes the question will answer itself. If the community is very small or 'closed'—say a family—the researcher may live with it and share in its activities, but he cannot become a full member of it; he must remain to a certain extent an outsider.

With a bigger and less naturally restricted community, the extent of participation is largely a matter of choice. If the observer can become so accepted as part of the community that its members are unaware of being observed, he will naturally get a more authentic, because less self-conscious, picture of its behaviour. Particularly with small communities, there is the risk that the introduction of another person, especially since that person has the special role of observer, will alter the processes the observer is there to study. The danger of such a *control effect* is reduced if the observer is unknown to the community. He may, for instance, be able to take a job and work in the community without disclosing his true purpose: Robb (1954), as part of a study of anti-semitism in the East End of London, worked for some time as a bartender in a public house in the area; and Sullivan and others (1958) describe how a research officer 'enlisted' as a basic trainee in the U.S. Air Force to be a covert observer in a study to investigate the motivations and attitudes of personnel in training.

When complete integration is impossible, this is not necessarily a handicap; there is much to be said for being a partial outsider able to ask questions a member of the community would not ordinarily ask (or expect a frank answer to if he did). The observer has what Whyte (in Jahoda and others, 1951) calls 'stranger-value'.

Much will depend of course on how he introduces himself to the community and how good a relationship he builds up with its members. He must be able to explain what he is trying to do in a way that is acceptable to the key people, and show genuine interest in what is going on.

A risk with participant observation is that the role adopted by the observer will restrict his understanding of the situation. This is what Riley (1963) calls the *biased-viewpoint effect*. In playing a clearly defined role in the community, the observer's understanding of the situation is thereby restricted. He will have access only to sources of information associated with that role; by being friendly to some members of the community, he will be cutting himself off from others. Miller (1952) notes a case in which the observer established such good relations with one section of the community under study—the workers' leaders—that they prejudiced his relations with the rank-and-file and he was forced to abandon parts of his intended field of enquiry for fear of antagonizing the leader group. The ideal of being able to enter into the life of a community at several different levels, so as to get a complete picture, is rarely attained by a single observer.[1] Moreover, if the observer's role involves him too closely in the community, his vision, so to speak, may be impaired; what is novel and noteworthy initially may, after a period of intensive contact with the community, be passed over as commonplace. This is a point in favour of recruiting observers from outside the community, for

[1] In a study of Banbury, described by Stacey (1960), three observers, male and female, and of upper, middle and working class origins were able to overcome this problem to a considerable extent, since each observer participated in a different sector of the town's life.

at least at the start of the research they will see things in a fresh light.

It hardly needs emphasizing how much the success of the participant observer's approach depends on his skill and personality. If these command the respect and friendship of the community, and if they are combined with an ability to interpret and describe what he sees, the method enables him to present a picture more vivid, complete and authentic than is possible with other procedures. But any defects in his approach and ability can easily arouse suspicion and so undermine his position and its possibilities. Participant observation is a highly individual technique.

A classic example of its use in studying an advanced community is the famous pair of surveys of Middletown by Robert and Helen Lynd (1929, 1937). The authors lived in a mid-Western American city for a considerable period, observed the community at work and play, participated in many of its activities, talked with all types of people, and studied all kinds of documents—newspapers, historical papers, records of institutions and so on. The result was a well-rounded picture of a community seen as a whole, which stands as a model of empirical sociology. It was such a successful utilization of observational methods that we should note some of its features.

First, the observers were skilled sociologists with years of practice and thought behind them; and were fully aware of the risks of getting a biased and unrepresentative picture. Such awareness may not in itself ensure that these risks will be avoided, but it is a necessary step towards that goal. They possessed a maturity and skill in observation, understanding and reporting that could not be expected in an average team of fieldworkers, even if specially trained.

Secondly, since Middletown was a large city, there were none of the problems met with in using participant observation in small communities. There was no likelihood that the observers would be constantly noticed and that the behaviour of the community would become self-conscious and untypical.

Thirdly, to collect their material, the Lynds made a prolonged stay in the community. This was not a quick, superficial enquiry.

Lastly, the material obtained by observation was supported where necessary by other methods, which gave the observers an unusual insight into past events, into the 'why' as well as the 'how' of particular actions, into the working of institutions and the like.

In this country, participant observation was the main method used in a study of Banbury in the period 1948–51, but it was also supplemented by other methods including a sample survey (Stacey, 1960). There have also been a number of small-scale studies using participant observation as one tool among several. An example is a study of a

Welsh village by Rees (1951). The Tavistock Institute of Human Relations has frequently used participant observer methods in its researches on human relations in industry,[1] and some of the earlier Mass Observation researches used the technique (see, for instance, its study of pub-going and drinking habits—Mass Observation, 1943).

Participant observation is commonly used in an exploratory way, at least in the initial stages. Becker (1958) distinguishes three stages in the fieldwork, the first being the selection and definition of problems, concepts and indices. The participant observer's early observations help to develop his ideas on these subjects and he then proceeds, for the second stage, to check which of the numerous preliminary ideas are worth pursuing. This is done by collecting further data to check on the frequency and distribution of phenomena in the community. The third stage of fieldwork consists of attempting to incorporate the individual findings into a model of the social system under study. After the fieldwork, there is a further stage in which the final systematic analysis, checking the models and re-building them if necessary, is conducted. An important feature of the procedure is its sequential nature, the observer beginning with speculations suggested by observation and developing his ideas until he can try to build a general model.

It is clear that, if the technique is to be successful, participant observers must have special abilities. A community survey, like that of Middletown, very obviously requires the skill and understanding of the sociologist or anthropologist. But even with less ambitious projects the observer needs considerable skill and discernment for all the stages of the research; clearly his job is generally more difficult than that of the survey interviewer.

Efficiency in observation and recording may be attainable through training,[2] but objectivity is more elusive. The social investigator, unlike his natural science colleague, has to observe something of which he himself is a part. The situations or activities to be observed are so familiar that it is hard for him to view them with the sort of detachment a biologist achieves in observing the behaviour of animals. Even the social anthropologist studying a primitive society fundamentally different from his own is at an advantage, compared to the investigator studying his fellow men in his own environment.

The problem of objectivity has several facets, first among them being that of *selection*. In any complex situation, the observer can hardly be expected to observe and note everything relevant to his

[1] See its journal, *Human Relations*.
[2] See the chapter by Heyns and Zander in Festinger and Katz (1953) for a discussion of different types of schedules for recording observations.

subject, and his selection of the aspects of behaviour and environment which he notes may follow certain channels. Because what he is
studying is so familiar, he may fail to note the obvious; extreme
forms of behaviour, deviations from the normal, 'exotic data', may
catch his eye most easily and, unless he takes care to give the normal
its due place, the overall picture may be false. We all tend to note
the unusual more readily than the normal.

On the other hand, the observer's *preconceptions* of how people
normally behave may also colour his picture; not, we trust, of what
he sees but of what he thinks he sees. In other words, instead of
recording what he actually observes, he may fit this into the stereo-
types to which he is accustomed. Such a tendency may counteract
that suggested in the previous paragraph.

This brings us to the difficulty of distinguishing between *observation* and *inference*, vividly brought out by the remarks of Bertrand
Russell (1927)[1]:

> You say 'What can you see on the horizon?' One man says, 'I see a
> ship.' Another says, 'I see a steamer with two funnels.' A third says,
> 'I see a Cunarder going from Southampton to New York.' How much
> of what these three people say is to count as perception? They may all
> three be perfectly right in what they say, and yet we should not concede
> that a man can 'perceive' that the ship is going from Southampton to
> New York. This, we should say, is inference. But it is by no means easy
> to draw the line; some things which are, in an important sense, in-
> ferential, must be admitted to be perceptions. The man who says 'I see
> a ship' is using inference. Apart from experience, he only sees a queerly
> shaped dark dot on a blue background. Experience has taught him that
> that sort of dot 'means' a ship.

Three observers seeing the same thing describe it differently,
failing to make the subtle distinction between observation and inference. It is difficult enough when the object of observation is
inanimate, like a ship; how much more so when the observer is
studying his fellow men and women. Striving for observation un-
tinged with inference and interpretation is perhaps striving for the
impossible, but at least researchers should be conscious of the
problem.

We have suggested that observers are so much part of their subject
matter that they may fail to see it objectively; that their vision may
be distorted by what they are used to seeing or what they expect to
see; and that they may find it hard to present a report in which
observation is satisfactorily distinguished from inference and interpretation.

Participant observation is, as we have seen, a somewhat individual

---

[1] Quoted by Madge (1953, p. 122) who discusses this point in detail.

method. One cannot expect it to yield a completely faithful and objective picture, nor suppose that several observers studying the same situation would bring back identical pictures.[1] The same difficulties do not of course arise in observing physical environment (always a valuable supplement to interview data) or in carrying out simple counts.[2]

Concluding remarks

The range of application of observational methods in social surveys is limited but, when they can be employed, they have a notable advantage. If information is obtained by questioning informants there is always the possibility that their reports will be inaccurate; they may not know the precise facts or, for one reason or another, they may distort their answers. In many areas this is a very real danger and one that can sometimes be avoided by the use of direct observation. Although it will usually be impossible to obtain all the data needed from a social survey by observational methods, there are many occasions when some of the data can be collected by observation and the remainder by interviewing. On other occasions both methods can be applied to give information on the same subject, the comparison of the results serving as a checking procedure. With ingenuity greater use could probably be profitably made of observational methods in social surveys.

Participant observation has the merit of providing a means of studying a whole system with its many inter-relationships in great detail, but it also has serious drawbacks, as we have seen. A dual approach can also be of help here with a large-scale social survey supplementing the participant observation; an extensive survey can provide a framework against which to assess the results of the intensive observation.

Finally, it must be emphasized that this discussion has been largely confined to the observational method in the context of social surveys, and that we have not attempted to cover controlled laboratory observation or observation in the study of intra-group behaviour (e.g. committees, management-worker meetings).

[1] An example of notable differences between the views of two participant observers is demonstrated by a comparison of the reports on the Mexican village of Tepoztlan by Redfield and by Lewis. Although the many changes occurring in the gap of seventeen years between the two studies could explain the divergent views, it seems likely that the explanation lies rather in the differences in temperament and cultural orientation—differences in the 'personal equation'—between the two observers. Paddock (1961) discusses this issue, and some comments based on Paddock's article are given in Sjoberg and Nett (1968).
[2] For a discussion of the 'moving observer' method in counting the number of people in a street (or shop) see Section 3.16 in Yates (1960); and Section 10.15 for a discussion of road traffic censuses.

NOTES ON READING

1. There is not much literature on the use of documentary sources. On personal documents, the reader should study the well-known volumes by ALLPORT (1942) and by GOTTSCHALK, KLUCKHOHN and ANGELL (1945). The former deals with their use in psychology, the latter with their use in history, anthropology and sociology. The chapter by ANGELL and FREEDMAN in FESTINGER and KATZ (1953) and the chapter in DUVERGER (1964) are good summaries of all different kinds of documents. The reader is also referred to the references on content analysis given at the end of Chapter 16.

2. Among the textbooks, MADGE (1953), FESTINGER and KATZ (1953), SELLTIZ and others (1959), SJOBERG and NETT (1968) and the chapter by WEICK in LINDZEY and ARONSON (1968, Vol. 2) are the most useful on the subject matter of this chapter. In addition, the book by WEBB and others (1966) is concerned solely with observational methods.

3. The earlier edition of SELLTIZ and others by JAHODA and others (1951) contains a particularly illuminating discussion of participant observation by WHYTE. The second edition of WHYTE's (1955) *Street Corner Society* contains an interesting appendix on the research methods employed. The chapter in STACEY (1969a) refers to a number of studies using participant observation. Unit 2 in RILEY (1963) gives a good discussion of the method. Some discussion of the relative advantages of intensive and extensive research in sociocultural anthropology is contained in the chapter by BENNETT and THAISS in GLOCK (1967). The chapter by DALTON in HAMMOND (1964) contains a discussion of the relative advantages and disadvantages of participant observation. Useful articles on participant observation are those by KLUCKHOHN (1940) and BECKER (1958). The book on participant observation edited by MCCALL and SIMMONS (1969) comprises a useful collection of papers on the subject.

4. An interesting critique of the early methods of Mass Observation was that of FIRTH (1939).

CHAPTER 11

Methods of Collecting the Information
II—Mail Questionnaires

11.1. The role of direct questioning

THE TWO sources of information dealt with in Chapter 10—documents and observation—are suitable for certain survey situations. But if one wants to find out what a person thinks about capital punishment or how much he knows about capital gains tax, how often he went to the cinema last week or why he reads the *Daily Tabloid*, how he spent last month's salary, when he was married and whether he intends to vote Labour or Conservative at the next election, one must ask him and rely on what he says. One knows full well that he may be giving distorted answers, may have misunderstood the questions or, with matters relating to the past, that his memory may be playing him false, but there is no alternative; it is one of the surveyor's most difficult tasks to try to detect such errors.

We shall here consider the problems connected with mail questionnaires.[1] The personal interview method will be dealt with in Chapter 12.

Mail questionnaires used to be widely condemned because of the difficulty of securing an adequate response. Although the high response rates achieved in some recent mail surveys significantly reduce the force of this argument, this difficulty remains a serious consideration. It should not, however, blind one to the merits of the method. On occasions when a high response rate can be secured, the gains from using a mail questionnaire can be substantial. And even when a mail questionnaire may not achieve as high a response rate as interviewing, its merits may be strong enough to weigh the balance in its favour, particularly if an estimate can be made of the effect of

[1] In this chapter, as indeed in most of the book, we are concerned primarily with surveys of individuals and households. Mail questionnaires are the almost universal method with economic and industrial surveys of firms, but such surveys are not covered by our present discussion.

the non-response. The problem can, like many others in survey methodology, be reduced to simple economics. Mail questionnaires are cheaper to send out than interviewers, but is the saving in cost sufficient to justify the acceptance of a lower response rate? Let us look at the points for and against mail questionnaires and, in particular, at the non-response problem.

11.2. The advantages of mail questionnaires

Without doubt, the mail questionnaire is generally cheaper than other methods. In the startling words of Selltiz and others (1959): 'Questionnaires can be sent through the mail; interviewers cannot.' Little is known (or, at any rate, published) about interviewing costs in this country; but it is clear that the cost of using mail questionnaires, in which postal charges take the place of interviewers' salaries and expenses, is often only a small fraction of that of a field survey, certainly if the latter is based on a random sample. Sometimes the population to be covered may be so widely and thinly spread, and the funds available so limited, that the mail questionnaire is the only feasible approach. This was the position in surveys of senior psychiatrists in England and Wales and in New York State described by Cooper and Brown (1967). The response rate in England and Wales was in fact 92 per cent and, although not quite as good, that in New York State was still as high as 79 per cent; on this score at least, the researchers had no need to regret their forced choice of method. But even if limited resources alone do not dictate the choice of the mail questionnaire, its economy and potential efficiency must always be considered. Of course it is not *necessarily* a cheap method; the response to a mail survey may be so low that the cost per completed questionnaire is higher than with an interview sample.

While the advantage of being able to have a widely spread sample with a mail questionnaire is of especial value for rare and scattered populations, it also applies more generally. As we have seen in Section 5.4, the clustering of the sample in cluster or multi-stage designs will generally result in less precision for a given sample size; this clustering is necessary in interview surveys in order to avoid excessive travel costs for the interviewers, but mailing costs remain the same however scattered the sample. Multi-stage sampling may be used with mail surveys to make the selection of the sample manageable, but the degree of clustering need not be nearly as high as that required for interview surveys.

At first sight it might seem that a mail questionnaire is a particularly quick method of conducting a survey. It certainly takes little time to send out the questionnaires, and the bulk of the returns will probably be received within two weeks. But time must be allowed for late returns and responses to follow-up attempts. As a result a period of a month or more is probably needed from the date of the initial mailing to the commencement of the final analysis.

The mail questionnaire of course avoids the problems associated with the use of interviewers; there are several sources of interviewer errors, which may seriously undermine the reliability and validity of survey results, and it is reassuring not to have to worry about them.

Mail questionnaires also have something to commend them when information concerning several members of a household is required. The housewife might be hard put to it to give accurate figures of the earnings of individual members of the household, their average weekly expenditure on meals out or even their exact ages (e.g. where lodgers are included) and in such situations a mail questionnaire, allowing some 'intra-household consultation', may lead to more accurate information than a doorstep interview.

The same holds with questions demanding a considered rather than an immediate answer. In particular, if the answer requires—or would be more accurate as a result of—consultation of documents, a questionnaire filled in by the respondent in his own time is preferable. Examples are questions like: 'When was this house built?' and 'How much ground rent do you pay?' (and, of course, the sort of questions asked of firms, shops, etc.).

Some people may answer certain questions—perhaps those of a personal or embarrassing nature—more willingly and accurately when not face to face with an interviewer who is a complete stranger. Whether the mail answers give a more truthful picture is another matter, although the slight evidence available does suggest that respondents make critical comments and report the less socially acceptable responses somewhat more readily on a mail questionnaire.

An interesting study providing supporting evidence for some of these conjectures was reported by the U.S. National Center for Health Statistics (1965b).[1] This is one of the few studies investigating the *validity* of survey responses, that is comparing the replies given in the survey with known facts. In this study a sample was selected from Detroit hospital records of residents of the Detroit area who had been in hospital during the year preceding the study (excluding those whose only hospital stay was for a normal delivery). Three procedures of collecting the required information were compared. The first, Procedure A, was the standard interview schedule and procedure of the Health Interview survey; the second, Procedure B, used a revised interview schedule and was followed by a mail form in which in-

[1] The study was directed by Cannell and Fowler, who also reported some of the findings in Cannell and Fowler (1963).

formation about hospital stays overlooked in the interview was to be recorded by the respondent; and the third, Procedure C, eliminated questions about hospitalization from the interview and instead the information was to be recorded on a self-completed form which was given to the respondent at the end of the interview. In each case information was collected for every member of the sampled family.

In terms of the completeness of reporting of hospital episodes Procedure B turned out to be the best; in that procedure, 9 per cent of known hospital episodes went unreported, compared with 17 per cent for Procedure A and 16 per cent for Procedure C. Three of the other conclusions relevant to our discussion are worth quoting:

> Respondents reported their own episodes considerably better than they reported the episodes of others in Procedure A. This tendency was reduced in Procedure C and eliminated in Procedure B.
>
> Procedure C proved to be significantly better than Procedure A in obtaining correct reports of the number of days involved in hospital episodes.
>
> For all three procedures the degree of social threat or embarrassment of the diagnosis leading to hospitalization was negatively related to the rate of reporting. (U.S. National Center for Health Statistics, 1965b, p. 2.)

In assessing the significance of the second of these findings, the nature of the information should be borne in mind. The question was one for which more thought might be needed to recall the information accurately than could be given in an interview, for which it might be useful to check records or diaries, and for which family consultation might be valuable, especially for episodes relating to members of the family other than the respondent. Moreover, the number of days in hospital is a definite and clearcut piece of information. Where judgement is needed to assess what constitutes a full answer, interviewing is likely to be preferable. Scott (1961a), for example, describes how, in a sample of people sent a mail questionnaire and subsequently also interviewed, a substantially larger proportion of the responses to the mail questionnaire than those to the interviewer were unclassifiable with respect to occupational class; Hochstim (1967) also found a greater proportion of occupation descriptions uncodable with a mail questionnaire than with personal or telephone interviewing. Interviewers can be trained to collect sufficient details for complex questions such as occupation, where without probing an inadequate response might often be given.

A final point in favour of mail questionnaires is that the problem of non-contacts, in the strict sense of respondents not being at home when the interviewer calls, is avoided.

11.3. The limitations of mail questionnaires

Apart from the vital question of non-response (dealt with separately in Section 11.4), there are six main disadvantages to the mail questionnaire method.

First, the method can be considered only when the questions are sufficiently simple and straightforward to be understood with the help of the printed instructions and definitions. What is sufficiently simple and straightforward naturally depends on the population being surveyed, and the language employed needs to be chosen with the survey population clearly in mind. Of course no mail questionnaire can elicit replies from people who are completely illiterate (unless someone else completes the questionnaire for them), but other less educated people should not be eliminated by the use of an unnecessarily complicated questionnaire. Ambiguity, vagueness, technical expressions and so forth must be avoided even more sedulously than when the questionnaire is filled in by an interviewer.[1] A mail questionnaire is most suited to surveys whose purpose is clear enough to be explained in a few paragraphs of print; in which the scheme of questions is not over-elaborate (not too many questions depending on answers to previous ones—e.g.: 'If "No" to section (i) of Q.3(b), answer Q.6 but not Q.7'); and in which the questions require straightforward and brief answers. It is unsuitable where the objective and purpose of the survey take a good deal of explaining, where the respondent is being asked difficult questions or where it is desirable to probe deeply or get the respondent talking.

Secondly, the answers to a mail questionnaire have to be accepted as final, unless re-checking or collection of the questionnaires by interviewers can be afforded. There is no opportunity to probe beyond the given answer, to clarify an ambiguous one, to overcome unwillingness to answer a particular question or to appraise the validity of *what* a respondent said in the light of *how* he said it. In short, the mail questionnaire is essentially an inflexible method.

Thirdly, the mail questionnaire is inappropriate where spontaneous answers are wanted; where it is important that the views of one person only are obtained, uninfluenced by discussion with others; and where questions testing a person's knowledge are to be included.

Fourthly, when the respondent fills in the questionnaire he can see all the questions before answering any one of them, and the different answers cannot therefore be treated as independent. In an interview, an early question might be: 'Can you name any detergents currently

---

[1] This is sometimes referred to as a recording schedule to distinguish it from a questionnaire filled in by the respondent. See Chapter 13.

on the market?' and a later one: 'Do you ever use WISK, DREFT ...?' In a mail survey, the previous question would be pointless.

Fifthly, with a mail questionnaire the surveyor cannot be sure that the right person completes the questionnaire. Although he clearly states on the questionnaire that it is a particular person's response he wants, this will not be sufficient to ensure that he gets it. He can ask the respondent to put his name on the questionnaire in order to check that the right person has completed it, but this of course conflicts with a desire for anonymity, and serves only to detect unwanted answers; it does not produce the answers from the selected respondent. Scott (1961a) reports that in one mail survey where persons were asked not to pass the questionnaire on to someone else (but where the name of the selected person was given only on the delivery envelope), a check on the signatures to the returned questionnaires showed that about 10 per cent of them had certainly been passed on, probably in most cases to the selected person's spouse (usually from husband to wife). He suggests two situations in which the questionnaire may often be completed by someone else. The first is when the selected person thinks it does not matter who responds, and this would seem to include opinion surveys. The second is when the questionnaire contains (after an initial filter question) a long series of questions which do not apply to some members of the sample; these members may falsely conclude that the questionnaires were not intended for them and may then pass them to persons to whom the questions do apply.

Sixthly, with a mail questionnaire there is no opportunity to supplement the respondent's answers by observational data. An interviewer can describe the respondent's house and neighbourhood, his appearance and manner, his attitude to the survey and the way he reacted to different questions; all this is valuable background material.

It may be noted that some of the disadvantages of the mail questionnaire can be overcome by combining it with interviewing. Thus questionnaires can be sent by mail and collected by interviewers, who can clear up difficulties, check answers and ensure completeness. Conversely, questionnaires can be delivered in person and returned by mail, the visit being used to explain the purpose and methods of the survey and to elicit co-operation. Personal delivery can also help to deal with the problem of inadequate addresses, for an interviewer can spend more time than a postman could afford in locating such an address. In the case of the U.K. Census of Population, the enumerators both deliver and collect the Census schedules, which are completed by the householders. At the time of delivery, they tell the householders what is expected and give any help they can; when collecting the schedules, they check for omissions and obvious errors and, if they find any, they ask the householder to make the necessary corrections.

11.4. Non-response in mail surveys

The main problem with mail surveys is that of getting an adequate response rate. Non-response in general has been discussed in Chapter 7; its especial importance in mail surveys arises from the fact that the response rates reported for many mail surveys have been very much lower than those for interview surveys. It is not of course the loss in sample numbers that is serious, but the likelihood that the non-respondents differ significantly from the respondents, so that estimates based on the latter are biased.

Mail surveys with a response of as low as 10 per cent are not un-known, while rates of over 90 per cent have been reported on a number of occasions. It used to be thought that if the sample was of the general population, rather than of a special group, strenuous efforts would be needed to bring the response rate above about 30 or 40 per cent; but in 1957 Gray reported a response rate of 93 per cent for a Government Social Survey mail enquiry of the general adult population, and since that time a number of other mail surveys of the general population have achieved response rates in the high eighties and the nineties. In an excellent paper on mail surveys on which we rely extensively, Scott (1961a), besides reviewing the literature, reports on five mail surveys carried out by the Government Social Survey, in all of which the response rates were in the region of 90 per cent. In view of these recent findings, we must ask the two related general questions: what factors affect the response rate to a mail survey; and what steps can be taken to increase response? As we shall see, there are many factors to be taken into account.

Over three of the influences on the response rate in a survey the surveyor has limited control—its sponsorship, its population and its subject matter. In one of the surveys described by Scott, an enquiry about radio and television, the identical questionnaire and letters were sent out to comparable samples ostensibly from three different organizations, the Central Office of Information, the London School of Economics and the British Market Research Bureau. After four weeks the response rate of 93 per cent for the government-sponsored questionnaires was significantly greater than the rates of 89 per cent and 90 per cent for those sponsored by the university college and the commercial organization. The gain was small but real, and indicates that the question of sponsorship is of some importance. If a survey lacks a sponsor it would be wise to attempt to secure the sponsorship of a body connected in some favourable way with the population under study. In the survey of psychiatrists in England and Wales mentioned earlier (p. 257), for instance, the researchers were fortunate that the Council of the Royal Medico-Psychological Association agreed that the questionnaire should be sent out under their auspices.

There is little a surveyor can do about his particular population, except to consider how suitable a mail survey is for it. Some evidence on this question can come from the analyses of the non-respondents to other mail surveys. It has, for example, often been found that the less educated, those in the lower occupational categories and those uninterested in the subject of the survey have higher than average rates of non-response. Scott reports that, for the radio and television survey, persons with below average letter writing activity and, among women, married women and women in households with above average numbers of children had higher non-response rates. If the surveyor finds that the characteristics of his population are such that, whatever he does to encourage response, he can expect only a low response rate, he may need to alter his procedure, perhaps by interviewing a sub-sample of the non-respondents to his mail questionnaire, or even by rejecting the mail approach entirely and relying solely on interviewing.

The subject matter of the survey of course to a large extent dictates the length of the questionnaire, for the surveyor must ask all the questions he needs for his analyses. Although it seems obvious that there must be a limit to the length of the questionnaire if a satisfactory response rate is to be achieved, the available evidence gives little support for this view. In Scott's radio and television survey an experiment was conducted on this point. One third of the sample received one short questionnaire, another third a second short questionnaire, and the remaining third a long questionnaire which consisted of the two short ones put together. The response rate for the mean of the short questionnaires was 90·5 per cent, which did not differ significantly from the 89·6 per cent for the long questionnaire. However, in assessing this finding it should be observed that even the long questionnaire was very short by most standards; the questionnaire extended to only two sides of foolscap paper and would take merely a few minutes to complete.[1]

A difficulty with assessing the effect of the length of the questionnaire is that any difference in response rate might be the effect of the additional questions on the long questionnaire rather than the extra length itself; this point was covered in the above experiment by the technique of putting two short questionnaires together to make the long one. Cartwright and Ward (1968) conducted a study of the part

[1] A copy of the long version is reproduced on p. 306–7 below.

played by general practitioners in family planning, in which half the sample of general practitioners received a one-page questionnaire and the other half a three-page one. The shorter questionnaire had a significantly higher response rate (90 per cent) than that of the longer (73 per cent); but, although this suggests that the length of the questionnaire affected the response rate, there is the alternative explanation that the nature of the additional questions—on abortion, sterilization, views on help to unmarried people and doctor's religion—was responsible for the greater non-response to the longer questionnaire.

Although the surveyor must include on the questionnaire all the questions to which he needs answers, he still has a certain degree of flexibility in his choice of questions, for he is not *restricted* to the essential ones. If the basic questionnaire is likely to lack appeal for his population, he can add interesting 'throw-away' questions to act as an incentive to completion. Space left for comments can also be an incentive, for it allows respondents to write what they want rather than simply answer the surveyor's questions.

On the other hand, the inclusion of a single awkward question might result in a high rate of non-response, a fact which emphasizes the need for especially careful pilot work with mail surveys. Pilot studies are also particularly important for mail surveys, as compared with interview surveys, because there in no one present to clear up for the respondent any ambiguities in the final questionnaire. Besides checking on the clarity of the instructions and explanations, pilot studies can also be used to investigate on an experimental basis different approaches to gaining the co-operation of respondents; various types of covering letters, different formats for the questionnaire, and other forms of inducement to respond can be tried out.

A covering letter needs to be sent out with the questionnaire to take the place of the interview opening, and as such it must try to overcome any prejudice the respondent may have against surveys. It should make clear why and by whom the survey is being undertaken, how the addressee has come to be selected for questioning and why he should take the trouble—for such it is—to reply. This last point is crucial. Surveyors are all too ready to *expect* people to answer their questions without being told what it is hoped to gain from the survey.

The surveyor must decide what tone to adopt in the covering letter. If the survey is genuinely expected to lead to changes beneficial to the respondents, the mention of this will be an inducement. But this is rarely the case. With most surveys the changes (if any) expected as their consequence are too distant and indirect to constitute a 'selling point'. Should one then appeal to the respondent's sense of duty or spirit of helpfulness? Should one plead or persuade?

Be authoritarian or excessively polite? No clear and general answer to these questions has emerged from research to date. Perhaps the best approach is to explain in simple terms why the survey is being undertaken, and why and by whom it is considered important. In the case of a research survey, one may begin by saying that: 'We (The Research Institute) want to find out . . .', or: 'This information is needed by a professor writing a book' or: 'We hope that this information will lead to public recognition of . . . problem . . . and to action . . .' Research on the method of salutation suggests that it does not matter whether the letter begins with a personal greeting like 'Dear Mr Smith' or an impersonal one like 'Dear Sir' or 'Dear Householder'; the impersonal approach is obviously a lot easier since it can be printed uniformly on all questionnaires, rather than needing to be added afterwards. One factor that has been found to increase response is a hand-written note on the covering letter urging reply. Scott also found that printing the covering letter on the same sheet as the questionnaire produced a slightly higher response than when it was put on a separate sheet (95·8 per cent compared with 93·6 per cent).

A natural courtesy and a common-sense step to increase response is to enclose a stamped addressed or business reply envelope. The latter has the advantage that it is generally administratively more convenient, but the former has been found to produce a higher response rate (for the radio and television survey, Scott reports 89·2 per cent for the franked return label compared with 93·3 per cent for the stamped envelope). The respondent may feel that the stamp represents money which he cannot easily throw away, yet it would be dishonest for him to steam it off and anyway it would not be worth the trouble; his way out of the quandary is to complete the questionnaire and send it back. On the other hand he can discard the franked label without feeling he is throwing away money. In the United States the use of special delivery or air-mail for the outgoing mailing has also been reported to increase response rates; as yet there are no findings reported on the use of first-class mail in Britain.

Sometimes a payment or gift can be offered as an incentive for the completed questionnaire; but, if the payment is more than nominal, this may offset a main advantage of the method—its cheapness. In commercial surveys concerned with product testing people may agree to fill in questionnaires simply because they like receiving free samples. In the United States a sum of 25 cents has been found to yield a substantial increase in response, whereas larger amounts bring in little more. It has also been found that a payment enclosed with the questionnaire is more productive than one promised for a response.

Other possible factors affecting the response rate, such as the assurance of anonymity and confidentiality, the day of the week, the time of the year, and the colour of the stationery, have been suggested; there is, however, no evidence that they have an appreciable effect.

There remains the most important method of raising the response rate—the use of follow-ups. This is a method which can boost the response rate to a considerable extent. The Government Social Survey has generally employed two follow-ups. The first consists of a short reminder letter sent about one week after the initial mailing to persons who at that time have not replied; the second, consisting of a short letter together with the original letter, another copy of the questionnaire and another return envelope, is sent about a week after the reminder letter to those who have still not replied. Scott describes how in one enquiry the pilot survey yielded a response rate of 74·8 per cent with no reminders, while in the main survey using the above procedure the rate was 95·6 per cent. The two reminders thus brought in about a further 20 per cent of replies. He also describes an experiment in another enquiry in which the first reminder was dropped for about half the sample while it was retained for the other half; both halves received the second reminder. The response rate for the half with only the second reminder was 85·9 per cent, compared with 93·2 per cent for the half with both reminders. The inclusion of the first reminder thus increased the response rate by about 7 per cent. It might be that if another copy of the questionnaire were sent out with the first reminder its effect would be even greater. As a rough guide, it seems that sometimes something like the same proportion of persons sent questionnaires respond to each mailing; thus, if 60 per cent reply to the first mailing, one might expect around 60 per cent of the 40 per cent of initial non-responders (i.e. a further 24 per cent of the initial mailing) to reply to the first follow-up, and so on.

The use of follow-ups is clearly an important feature of mail surveys, but it has its limitations. First, there is the question of anonymity. If the surveyor is to send follow-ups only to non-respondents he needs to be able to identify the respondents, and this is commonly done by a serial number on the questionnaire. But this means that the questionnaire is not anonymous, and so the surveyor cannot claim to be providing this safeguard. All he can do is to promise respondents that replies will be treated as confidential. There are some ingenious ways out of this difficulty (see Scott, 1961a) but the evidence available suggests that lack of anonymity is generally not a serious obstacle.

Another limitation of follow-ups is that the quality of the returns may decline with successive mailings. This effect was found in the hospitalization study reported by the U.S. National Center for

Health Statistics (1965b) referred to earlier, and also in another American study by Sirken and Brown (1962). A likely explanation is that persons who do not respond to the first mailing are less keen to be helpful and hence, if they are later persuaded to complete the questionnaire, they put less effort into it.

A number of variations of the follow-up procedure are possible. One can, for example, send the reminders to only a sub-sample of the initial non-responders. The sub-sample results can then be weighted up to represent the whole stratum of non-respondents. However, since there is little variation in costs from one mailing to the next, this procedure is unlikely to be an economic proposition (see p. 178). Another possibility is to make the assumption that the respondents to a second mailing are a random sample of all the non-respondents to the first mailing and weight them up accordingly; this obviates the need for further mailing but its validity rests on the basic assumption. It is likely that the non-respondents are closer in their characteristics to those who respond to the follow-up effort than to those who do so to the initial mailing, but the assumption that they are the *same* is dubious. A third possibility is to send a shorter version of the questionnaire, even one asking for only a few key items, to the non-respondents after the initial, or some later, mailing. The replies may indicate how different the non-respondents are from the rest. A more sophisticated method is to send one (short) questionnaire to one set of non-respondents, a different one to a second set, and so forth. In this way, data covering the entire range of the original questionnaire might be collected.

Yet another approach is to use a different survey procedure at one of the follow-ups, either for all the non-respondents at that stage, or for a sample of them. Direct interviewing and telephone interviewing have been used for this purpose. In view of the generally much greater costs of direct interviewing than mail questionnaires, the use of sub-sampling for follow-up interviews is often sensible; the method of Hansen and Hurwitz (1946)—see pp. 178-9—develops a theoretical basis for the optimum sub-sampling rate. With a combination of methods there is, however, the over-riding problem: can answers to questions collected in different ways be regarded as comparable? Hochstim's (1967) results are fairly reassuring on this point, although he did find that more women claimed at a personal interview than at a telephone interview or on a mail questionnaire that they never drink alcoholic beverages!

This discussion has been concerned with the methods of reducing the amount of non-response in mail surveys. Non-response is a problem because of the likelihood—repeatedly confirmed in practice —that people who do not return questionnaires differ from those who do. It has been shown a number of times that mail questionnaires addressed to the general population tend to result in an upward bias in social class composition and educational level; this is only what one would expect. It has also been shown frequently that response is correlated with interest in the subject of the survey. Filling in a questionnaire takes time and trouble and people are obviously more likely to afford both if they are interested in its contents.

For such reasons, it is clear that in mail surveys every effort must be made to secure a high response rate. If the response rate is not high enough to eliminate the possibility of serious bias, care must be taken to judge the extent of the unrepresentativeness and to take account of it in making the final estimates.

It may seem easy to check on the unrepresentativeness of a sample: all one need do is to include in the questionnaire one or two questions for which the results can later be checked with population figures, e.g. on the geographical spread of the sample, its age and sex break-downs, the distributions of household composition and occupation. It is true that obvious unrepresentativeness can thus be revealed, but such checks can never *prove* the representativeness of the sample. Even if the sample were judged satisfactory by all the above criteria, it might still be unrepresentative on others, including the one that matters most—the subject of the study. On this no check of repre-sentativeness is possible, for otherwise there would be no need for the survey.

Thus the only safe way to deal with non-response is to reduce it to a level sufficiently low as to ensure that it cannot cause a serious bias. A poor response rate must constitute a dangerous failing, and if it does not rise above, say, 20 or 30 per cent the failing is so critical as to make the survey results of little, if any, value. Yet the literature contains many reports of mail surveys with response rates no higher than this, and for this reason mail questionnaires had fallen into disrepute; it was thought that only with special populations and in special circumstances would the response rate be high enough to justify their use. Recently, however, using a variety of methods to secure co-operation, a number of mail surveys of the general popu-lation have achieved high response rates, rates as good as, or even better than, those achieved in interview surveys.

It seems likely that this recent experience will lead to a greater use of mail questionnaires, and to a raising of standards as to what constitutes an acceptable response rate with their use. It suggests that, provided they are carefully planned and executed and due regard is paid to the question of the response rate, surveys of the general population on simple subjects can often profitably be conducted by mail questionnaire.

Finally, we might remark on a particular application of mail questionnaires—as an economic way of locating rare populations. A large first-phase sample of the general population can be sent a mail questionnaire which simply asks whether or not they are members of the rare population of interest. Those replying in the affirmative can then form the second-phase sample and can be interviewed for the main survey; the remainder can be discarded. This two-phase procedure represents a relatively inexpensive way of eliminating persons who are not members of the rare population. Its application by Cartwright (1964) to obtain a sample of persons who had recently been in hospital has already been described (p. 123). With this use of mail questionnaires, as with any other, efforts must be made to secure a high response rate; but the questionnaire asks so little of the respondent that this should not be difficult.

NOTES ON READING

1. The article by SCOTT (1961a), on which we have relied heavily, is a major contribution to the subject of this chapter. It includes an extensive bibliography.

2. Although not including the recent work, GOODE and HATT (1952), PARTEN (1950) and MARK (1958) give good accounts of the practical aspects of mail questionnaire surveys.

3. On the comparison of mail questionnaires with interviewing, the references given in the text are useful—U.S. NATIONAL CENTER FOR HEALTH STATISTICS (1965b), CANNELL and FOWLER (1963), and HOCHSTIM (1967). Reports of other comparisons are given in HYMAN and others (1954, Chapter 4).

4. SUDMAN (1967, Chapter 4) describes the results of an experiment in which interviewers left a self-administered questionnaire at selected households, with three different methods of collection being compared. KEMSLEY and NICHOLSON (1960) describe an experiment on using postal methods with the Family Expenditure Survey record books.

5. The journal *Public Opinion Quarterly* contains numerous articles on mail questionnaires.

6. The articles by GRAY (1957) and CARTWRIGHT and WARD (1968) have been referred to in the text. In addition the report of the U.K. ROYAL COMMISSION ON DOCTORS' AND DENTISTS' REMUNERATION (1960) is worth consulting for its description of mail enquiries on professional earnings: the technical aspects are described by KEMSLEY in Appendix A. They are also described in an article by KEMSLEY (1962).

CHAPTER 12

Methods of Collecting the Information
III—Interviewing

12.1. Types of interviewing

THE METHOD of collecting data most usual in social surveys is personal interviewing. Although observation and mail questionnaires could probably be employed more frequently than at present, interviewing is without doubt generally the most appropriate procedure, even though it introduces various sources of error and bias. These errors are the subject of Chapter 15, and the present chapter discusses the interviewer's task, the selection and training of interviewers, and various points of organization. It also deals with informal interviewing.

Many situations merit the description 'interview', but we can in the present context confine ourselves to that in which the interviewer is neither trying to help the informant nor to educate him, neither to gauge his suitability for a job nor to get his expert opinion: the situation where she[1] is simply seeking information from, and probably about, him and where he is likely to be one of many from whom similar information is sought. This does not mean that the discussion is confined to the typical 'doorstep interview' which comes immediately to mind.[2] Formal interviewing, in which set questions are asked and the answers are recorded in a standardized form, is certainly the norm in large-scale surveys, but we must also consider the less formal variants, in which the interviewer is at liberty to vary the sequence of questions, to explain their meaning, to add additional ones and even to change the wording. Less formal still, she may not have a set questionnaire at all but only a number of key points around which to build the interview.

In practice, the choice is not between the completely formal and

---

[1] Since most interviewers are women, they will be referred to throughout as of the female sex.
[2] The term 'doorstep interview' is in fact inappropriate, since many organizations train their interviewers to ask to enter the respondent's home and to conduct their interviews indoors.

the completely informal approach, but between many possible degrees of informality. Social surveyors tend to keep to the formal end of the scale, and so we will examine this first. Before doing so, however, we will discuss the nature of the survey interview in more general terms.

12.2. The nature of the survey interview

A survey interview is a conversation between interviewer and respondent with the purpose of eliciting certain information from the respondent. This might appear a straightforward matter, with the respondent just giving straight answers to the questions asked of him. The attainment of a successful interview is, however, much more complex than this suggests.

Cannell and Kahn (Lindzey and Aronson, 1968, Vol. 2) distinguish three broad concepts as necessary conditions for a successful interview. First there is the *accessibility* of the required information to the respondent. If the respondent does not have the information he cannot answer the question. This may arise because, although he once knew it, he has now forgotten it; because he has repressed information which involves some emotional stress to him; or because he cannot answer in the manner required—he may not think of things in the way the question has been framed and so may be unable to answer it in the specified terms of reference.

The second condition is that of *cognition*, or understanding by the respondent of what is required of him. In entering on an interview the respondent is adopting a particular role, and he needs to know what is expected of him in that role. He must, for example, establish means of deciding what is relevant information to give, how completely he should answer, and in what terms of reference he should express his answers. It is part of the interviewer's job to teach the respondent his role, both in her initial explanation of the survey and of what is being asked of the respondent and in the way she treats the answers he gives, in particular by probing for further details when his answer is incomplete or off the point.

The third requirement for a successful interview is *motivation* on the part of the respondent to answer the questions accurately. This includes his initial decision to co-operate and his subsequent decisions to continue with the interview. But, more than that, it also includes his motivation to give *accurate* answers, for a seriously distorted answer is no better than no answer at all. It is also a part of the interviewer's job to try to reduce the effect of factors tending to decrease the level of motivation and to build up the effect of those tending to increase it. Among the former are the desire to get on with other activities, embarrassment at ignorance, dislike of the

K

interview content, fear of the consequences and suspicions about the interviewer, while the latter may include curiosity, loneliness, politeness, a feeling of duty, a keenness to help the sponsor of the enquiry and a liking for the interviewer.

This last-mentioned factor is a reminder that the interview is a social process involving two individuals, the interviewer and respondent. The outcome of the interview must be seen in this light, and must take into account the *interaction* of interviewer and respondent. During the course of the interview the respondent is sizing up the interviewer, and his inferences about her can influence the way he answers questions. Also, the interviewer is being influenced by the respondent, so that the total process is a complex one. This operation begins as soon as the two meet and it continues throughout the interview. Before a word is spoken, they have each observed the outward appearance of the other, and may have been affected by it; indeed if a respondent particularly likes or dislikes the interviewer's looks this may weigh the balance in his decision of whether to be interviewed. From then on, the behaviour of the interviewer—the way she asks the questions, anything else she says, her facial expressions, her movements and so on—are perceived as clues by the respondent that may influence his motivation. In the same way, the respondent's answers to questions and his other behaviour serve as clues to the interviewer and may affect her subsequent behaviour.

What is clear from this viewpoint is that interviewers cannot be regarded as merely a means of extracting and recording information. They can—and research has confirmed that this does happen—affect the recorded answers (see Chapter 15). In the case of attitudinal questions, particularly when the respondent may not have thought through his position before the interview, the danger of interviewer bias is perhaps obvious; but it has been found to apply also with factual questions.

One way to increase the accuracy of the interview data is by careful interviewer training. The interviewer can be trained to avoid stating her own views, to ask probe questions phrased in an impartial way, to appear to have a permissive attitude so that the respondent feels free to express any view, and generally to deport herself in a way that is least likely to influence the respondent's answers. Training can also improve the quality of her recording of answers, and can teach her when she needs to get further details.

We will take up the question of selection and training of interviewers in Section 12.4, but the first step is to look at the various tasks the interviewer performs; asking questions is only part of her job.

12.3. The interviewer's task

The core of the interviewer's task is to locate (or select) her sample members, to obtain interviews with them and to ask the questions and record the answers as instructed. Although the amount of time the interviewer spends on different aspects of her work depends on such factors as the length of the questionnaire and the nature of the sample, Sudman (1965; also 1967) found a surprising uniformity for three American organizations in the proportion of time their interviewers spent actually interviewing: only about one-third of the time was spent on interviewing, the other two-thirds being divided between travel time and locating respondents (about 40 per cent of total time), editing the interviews and other clerical work (about 15 per cent) and studying materials and administrative matters (about 10 per cent).

Finding the sample members

In considering characteristics desirable in interviewers, one easily overlooks how much of their working time is spent in simply finding the respondents. An applicant may express a strong 'interest in people' and be enthusiastic about interviewing; but if she is going to hate walking or driving around a town, or cannot read maps, she will be a liability to her employer and will probably soon give up the work.

How difficult or responsible a task the finding of respondents is depends on the sampling method. In quota sampling, as shown in Section 6.4, interviewers themselves make the selection and their freedom of choice, though limited by the quotas, may be considerable; with random sampling they have, of course, no freedom of choice. With random sampling from lists, interviewers are given the names of persons to be interviewed. Often the names and addresses are inserted on the questionnaires themselves or on record sheets, together with any other information about the respondent—such as sex—deducible from the sampling frame.

With random samples from maps, that is area sampling, the interviewer's first task is likely to be concerned with sampling, either listing dwellings or segmenting within selected blocks (see Section 6.1). In either case the work has to be done with great care, for it is easy to miss dwellings in a casual listing. A sample of dwellings is then chosen by a random procedure, and the interviewer must conduct her interviews in these dwellings. For a sample of individuals, the interviewer lists all the individuals in a selected dwelling and selects one or more of them by an objective scheme over which she has no control, such as the Kish selection procedure described in Chapter 8.[1]

The sample allocated to any one interviewer may be spread widely over a town or district, and interviewers are generally left to arrange their own itinerary. With random samples they interview only selected individuals or households, and this necessitates call-backs, perhaps several of them, on people whom they do not find in; it also makes some evening work unavoidable if the sample is one of the general population. Interviewers are usually required to record the results—e.g. questionnaire completed, refusal, non-contact—of the first call and of the call-backs and are instructed how to deal with various kinds of non-response. Call-backs are perhaps the most frustrating part of an interviewer's work.

Obtaining an interview

Having located the respondent, the interviewer has to obtain an interview. The aim of her introductory procedures must be to increase the respondent's motivation to co-operate. How should she go about this? She will usually begin by stating the organization she represents (though in commercial surveys the sponsor's name can often not be disclosed) and perhaps showing an authorization card. In many cases, this, together with a brief statement of why the survey is being done, is enough to secure co-operation. Most people are only too ready to talk about themselves and to air their views, and common politeness, mixed with curiosity, does the rest.

The form of the interview opening is nevertheless crucial to win those who are less willing to co-operate. The time may be inconvenient, the subject of the survey may be one they are not prepared to talk about, or they may be antagonistic towards surveys in general. Then it is that the interviewer's, and also the researcher's, attitude counts. Both should recognize that the call *is* an encroachment upon people's time, although one which many do not resent. The request for information needs justification. There is no need for excessive diffidence or apologies; but it should be the interviewer's duty to explain precisely why, and for whom, the survey is being done, what is expected to emerge from it, to whom the results will be of interest and so on. This can be done, and indeed is best done, briefly. Cannell and Kahn (Lindzey and Aronson, 1968, Vol. 2, p. 578) for example report the following short introduction used in connection with surveys of consumer finances:

Interviewer: 'I'm from the Survey Research Center of The University

---

[1] This procedure applies generally when individuals are to be selected at random in the field from within selected dwellings. For example, it was used in the sample described in Chapter 8.

of Michigan. We're doing a survey at this time, as we have for a number of years now, on how people feel things are going financially these days. The study is done throughout the country, and the results are used by government and industry.

The addresses at which we interview were chosen entirely by chance, and the interview will take only about a half hour. All information is entirely confidential, of course.'

There are many satisfactory ways of framing this introduction and any further remarks needed to reassure a respondent, but a few general principles can be applied. First and foremost, the 'sales talk' should be entirely honest. There is no excuse for implying that the survey will lead, directly or indirectly, to concrete benefits or indeed to any action, when such is not expected; nor should its urgency or importance be overstated. Many surveys are done simply because someone wants some information, and most people will co-operate with an interviewer who asks for it pleasantly and unpretentiously, even if at heart they think the survey futile. Indeed perhaps the respondent's view of the survey matters less than the interviewer's. Dorothy Cole's (1956) findings suggest that the interviewer's interest in the survey, and her conviction of its value, can materially affect the response rate.

When the survey answers are to be treated as confidential or anonymous, this should be made clear to the respondent. It is often worth explaining, in simple terms, how the sample was selected, and that lack of co-operation would make it less representative. The interviewer should remove any suspicion that she is out to ask test questions (e.g. to find out how much the respondent knows) or to educate. Since door-to-door salesmen sometimes claim to be conducting interviews, the interviewer may need to reassure the respondent that she is not trying to sell or advertise anything. Some interviewers are no doubt better than others at establishing what the psychologists call 'rapport' and some may even be too good at it— the National Opinion Research Center studies reported by Hyman and others (1954) found slightly less satisfactory results from the highly extroverted and sociable interviewers who are 'fascinated by people'!

Asking the questions

In most large-scale surveys, the aim is to attain uniformity in the asking of questions and recording of answers. In consequence the training of interviewers is oriented towards efficiency in following instructions. They are expected to ask *all* the applicable questions; to ask them in the order given and with no more elucidation and probing than is explicitly allowed; and to make no unauthorized variations in the wording. If complete uniformity could be achieved and interviewers acted like machines, answers could be regarded as independent of the way the questions were asked.

But interviewers are not machines. Their voices, manner, pronunciations and inflections differ as much as their looks, and no amount of instruction will bring about complete uniformity in technique. Every interviewer will be tempted on occasion to add a word of explanation or make a change in the wording and sequence of the questions, but the researcher can minimize the temptation by intelligent design. If questions are phrased in everyday language, interviewers will be less inclined to re-phrase them. If interviewers are allowed to probe on some questions, the danger of unauthorized probing becomes less. If the order of the questions is such that, with occasional linking phrases, the interview flows logically and conversationally, there will be less temptation to omit questions or change their sequence.

The importance of interviewing uniformity itself varies with the type of question. Opinion questions are more 'sensitive' than factual ones to variations in wording, phrasing or emphasis by the interviewer. Questions such as 'How many children have you?' are less vulnerable in this respect than 'Do you believe the Government is doing a good job?' or even 'Do you like Rownbury's milk chocolate?' In questions of the latter type, exact wording is of utmost importance. If an interviewer inserted the word 'really' before 'like' in the last question, she would immediately alter its tone and affect the way it was answered. She should be warned of this and told to keep to the prescribed wording and not to give any lead by explanations.

An interview, however, consists of more than just asking and answering a set of questions from a schedule, and the other aspects of the interview are much harder to standardize. An important part of the interviewer's task is to assess the adequacy of the responses and, where necessary, to probe for further details; indeed this part of her task is a strong argument in favour of interviewing over self-completed questionnaires. Yet, by its nature, it involves a lack of control by the researcher, for the interviewer must decide on the spot what means to use to persuade the respondent to amplify his response.

Kahn and Cannell (1957, pp. 217–8) distinguish five principal symptoms of inadequate response. These are: *partial response*, in which the respondent gives a relevant but incomplete answer; *non-response*, when the respondent remains silent or refuses to answer the question; *irrelevant response*, in which the respondent does not answer the question asked; *inaccurate response*, when the question is answered by a reply which is biased or distorted; and the *verbalized response problem*, when the respondent explains why he cannot answer the question, perhaps because he fails to understand it, because he lacks the information necessary for answering it, or because he thinks it is irrelevant or inappropriate. These five types of inadequate response can be considered as symptoms which give clues to the underlying cause of failure to get a satisfactory response; and, as such, they should be taken into account by the interviewer in deciding how to proceed.

There are a number of techniques for dealing with an inadequate response. The big danger is that, in forming a supplementary question on the spur of the moment, the interviewer may phrase it in a biased way, perhaps giving an indication of her own position. The surveyor has been able to spend a lot of time in arriving at his questions and has, or should have, conducted pilot studies to test them out, but all this effort is wasted if biased supplementary questions are used to complete a response. It is in fact asking too much of the interviewer to expect her to develop neutral supplementary questions on sensitive subjects during the interview. On the other hand, no single supplementary question will be suitable for all situations. The answer is to train interviewers in a set of standard techniques for probing inadequate responses.

One simple way of eliciting further information is for the interviewer to allow a brief expectant pause to develop, thus indicating that something more is required; but the pause must not be allowed to become a long one or it may have a negative effect. Expectant glances can also be useful, though they can similarly be overdone. Another kind of probe is to give the respondent encouragement by expressions such as 'Uh-huh', 'That's interesting' or 'I see'. When the interviewer needs to ask a supplementary question it must be a neutral one, such as 'How do you mean?', 'Can you tell me more about that?' or 'Can you explain a little more fully what you mean by that?' Sometimes merely repeating the original question suffices. Repeating part of the respondent's answer in a questioning manner can also be useful; but an attempt to summarize the respondent's answer for him is dangerous because he may tend to accept the summary, whether it truly reflects his position or not.

In the Government Social Survey's *A Handbook for Interviewers* (Atkinson, 1967) three types of questions are distinguished: factual, opinion and knowledge (an example of the last type, taken from the *Handbook*, is: 'Do you think that during a year more people die in road accidents or from lung cancer?'). The Survey interviewers are allowed to rely on their own discretion for probing on factual questions, though of course they should employ neutral wordings for their supplementary questions. They are required to obtain a precise answer (exact income, for example) if they can, but, if they cannot, they should record as good an answer as they can get and mark it 'e' to identify it as only an estimate. With opinion and knowledge questions, the Survey interviewers are allowed less freedom in probing. They are permitted to use only the Survey's stock phrases and they must not invent their own probes. The *Handbook* distinguishes two types of probe: clarifying and exploratory probes. The aim of the former is to clarify the respondent's answer, which may have been ambiguous or inexplicit; probes like 'How do you mean?' and 'In what way?' can be used as clarifying probes. The latter are used to try to tap other aspects of the respondent's opinion, if there are any; 'Is there anything else?' or 'Are there any other reasons?' can be used for this purpose.

The distinction between the kind of probing allowed for factual questions on the one hand and opinion and knowledge questions on the other is understandable. With factual questions, the surveyor wants the set answer, and his concern is to get it as accurately as possible. A 'Don't know' answer is a failure but one which must be accepted on some occasions; over-probing is a danger to be avoided for, if the respondent does not know a fact, too great a pressure may force him to make a guess at it and may seriously lower his motivation to co-operate further. Tighter control is needed over probing with opinion questions because of the ease with which slight wording variations can affect the respondent's opinions. On no account must the interviewer give an indication of her own views; for thus respondents of an argumentative disposition might be led to take the opposite view, while others might give the replies they think the interviewer would favour. In either case the answers would misrepresent the respondent's true opinions. With knowledge questions also, there is a danger that explanations may influence answers by 'educating' the respondent and leading him to give a substantive answer where 'Don't know' would have been more accurate. Respondents should be made to feel that a 'Don't know' answer to a knowledge question is not only in order but that many people give it; otherwise they may hesitate to admit ignorance.

Probing is one of the most challenging aspects of an interviewer's work, and requires a good deal of skill. To learn to probe effectively and without bias requires careful training, combined perhaps with a certain innate ability. The importance of probing should not be underrated: by intelligent and neutral probing the interviewer can make the respondent feel at ease about the information he is revealing, can ensure complete and meaningful data and can make the interview flow interestingly. Skill in probing is a major determinant of good interviewing.

On some questions, interviewers are instructed to 'prompt', i.e. to make the respondent aware of the possible answers. For instance, with question 69(*b*) on the Gallup Poll questionnaire reproduced on pp. 332-9, 'If you had to say which social class you belong to, what would you say?', the interviewer was instructed to read out all five alternatives—upper, upper-middle, middle, lower-middle and working. The same idea is involved in the 'aided recall' method. Thus a BBC Audience Research interviewer investigating which programmes a person listened to on the previous day may help a respondent having difficulty in remembering by showing him a 'log' listing the previous day's programmes.

A form of prompting which is increasingly popular is to show the respondent a card listing the possible answers, so that he simply has to indicate which one applies.[1] This method was used, for example, in a survey (see questionnaire on pp. 312-4) when the following question was asked: 'Where are you living? Would you show me on this card which applies to you?' The card read

At home	1
As a lodger or a boarder with a family	2
In a hotel/hostel/boarding house/hospital/institution	3
Elsewhere	4

Further details were asked only from those answering 4. The technique is sometimes used for questions such as income, where the respondent may be reluctant to tell the interviewer the amount involved: with a card, his disclosure of income is less obvious since he tells the interviewer only the code number. It is also useful when the respondent is being asked to rank a series of statements.

Visual aids are also much used. In the National Readership Surveys of the Joint Industry Committee for National Readership Surveys (1968) respondents are asked about their reading of all kinds of newspapers and periodicals and, to help them to remember, they are shown reproductions of mastheads of all the publications.

Recording the answers

In most interview surveys the interviewers themselves have to record the answers. The exceptions are those in which questionnaires are left and collected by interviewers but filled in by the respondent, and the rare cases in which a secret ballot is used (see Cantril, 1944).[2] The former includes surveys in which the respondents are requested to keep diary records, as in the Family Expenditure and the National Food Surveys.

[1] Care has to be taken in interviewing illiterate respondents and those with poor eyesight! It is a good rule in any case to read out, as well as show, such card lists.
[2] In the less formal methods of interviewing, tape recorders may be particularly useful for recording what the respondent has to say.

The recording of answers would seem a simple enough task, and one that interviewers might be expected to perform with accuracy. That they sometimes make substantial errors is due to several factors. First of all, their job is a fairly tiring one. With random sampling, the interviewer may have travelled and walked a good way before getting to the respondent. Once there, she has to go through what is often a lengthy, complex, and always somewhat repetitive operation. She might well be forgiven, then, if she is harassed or bad-tempered—especially if the respondent is unhelpful. Secondly, the interviewer often has to code answers according to complicated instructions. Thirdly, she is rarely able to confine her entire attention to one task: while recording the answer to one question, she is perhaps preparing to ask, or actually asking, the next. At the same time, she has to be on the alert for vague and qualified answers, for 'red herrings' and for signs that the question has been misunderstood.

In discussing the recording of answers, the distinction between open and pre-coded questions,[1] treated fully in Chapter 13, must be mentioned. Examples—taken from the questionnaire[2] on pp. 312–4—will show the difference:

An open question

'What kinds of things would you like to spend more time on in your leisure hours?'

A pre-coded question

'When did you last go to the pictures?'

Within last 7 days......	1
8–14 days ago	2
15–28 days ago.........	3
More than 28 days ago	4
I never go	5
Don't know	6

With pre-coded questions the interviewer's task is to decide on the appropriate code and ring it; errors may arise through faulty judgement and carelessly ringing the wrong code. Many pre-coded questions, of course, hardly require judgement. The question 'Are you married?' admits of a 'Yes' or 'No' answer and there is no problem of judgement so long as the interviewer knows the definitions —e.g. how to code a divorced person. The question on cinema-going similarly provides little room for the exercise of judgement. The risks of more difficult pre-coded questions are discussed in Chapter 13.

---

[1] Alternative terms for 'open' are 'free-answer', 'free-response' or 'write-in'; 'closed' or 'check-answer' are sometimes used in place of 'pre-coded'.
[2] This comes from the experiment on quota sampling by Moser and Stuart (1953) mentioned in Section 6.4. It will be used for illustration in this and ensuing chapters.

Open questions present a more difficult recording task. Should the interviewer record everything that the respondent says, only remarks that she considers relevant, or should she paraphrase the respondent's answer? The danger with the last two procedures is clear, that the interviewer will introduce a bias by her choice of what to record, and in most cases the verbatim report is probably the best solution. The Government Social Survey interviewers are instructed to record open responses verbatim, word-for-word, in the first person, exactly as the respondent gives his answer, and to record the answer at the time of interview. This is by no means an easy task (especially with a garrulous respondent), but skill at it can be substantially improved through practice.

One possible solution to the recording problem for open and intensive interviews is the use of tape recorders to record everything the respondent says.[1] The interviewer is then free to concentrate on the interview, and moreover the surveyor has a record of how the interview was conducted. But there is the risk that the use of tape recorders will lower the response rate and the accuracy of reporting, especially for surveys on sensitive subjects. There is also the expense of coding the information from the recording. Belson (1967b) reports an experiment on the use of tape recorders for recording answers to a newspaper readership questionnaire, in which he found that the accuracy of response was reduced for the upper social grouping but increased for the lower groupings, the net effect being no loss in accuracy for the sample as a whole. A good deal more research is needed before the value of tape recorders for large-scale surveys can be fully evaluated, but they can certainly play a useful part in pilot work and in interviewer assessment and training.

At the close of the interview, the interviewer must edit the questionnaire to check that she has asked all the questions and recorded all the answers, that she has ringed the right codes and that there is no inconsistency between answers. If she has used her own abbreviations in recording open responses, these must be eliminated so that the coder will be able to understand what she has written. She must ensure that everything is legible. She should also record in a thumbnail sketch her impressions of, and observational notes on, the interview. It may be useful at the analysis stage to know in what kind of environment the respondent lives and what type of person he is; to know his attitude to the survey and the interviewer's assessment of the validity of his answers. The more the interviewer adds by way of comments to the bare skeleton of a completed questionnaire, the better it is.[2]

[1] Bucher and others (1956) discuss tape-recorded interviews in social research.
[2] See Sheatsley (1947-48) for a discussion of interviewer report forms.

12.4. Selection and training

The description of an interviewer's task suggests a number of desirable personal characteristics. She should make a pleasant impression at first meeting and possess tact and some social sense; she should be accurate, reliable and honest and able to stand up to what is often tiring work; and obviously she should be available for the sort of routine and hours demanded in surveys. What more does one require of her? Need she be particularly intelligent and educated? Does it matter what kind of social background she comes from? Is the age—and, for that matter, the sex—of the interviewer relevant?

Such questions are not easy to answer. Survey experts have their own views on the relative importance of various characteristics, but little systematic evidence has been published in this country. Logically the desirable characteristics should be those that are found to be associated with good interviewing ability. But what is 'good' interviewing? Is it to be measured in terms of the truthfulness of the answers the interviewer brings home? If so, we must resign ourselves to being able to measure interviewing quality on only a small fraction of survey questions. Or is it to be gauged by the proportion of refusals, of 'Don't know' answers, of incomplete answers, of recording errors and so forth? If so, it would have to be admitted that we were measuring only part of the whole. There is a real difficulty in measuring 'good' interviewing and in deciding what interviewer characteristics are desirable.

Added to this, the importance of any one characteristic naturally varies from survey to survey. Sometimes an expert knowledge of the survey subject is an advantage, sometimes it is unnecessary. Evident racial characteristics are undesirable in certain surveys, but irrelevant in others. Often one tries to avoid using interviewers with strong opinions and prejudices on the subject of the survey since they may influence answers. All in all, it is impossible to lay down any specification to suit all surveys. The trend is to select interviewers according to their performance on certain clearly defined tasks, rather than on personal characteristics.

Selection

There is, however, a considerable range of practices regarding the selection of interviewers, only some of it explained by differences in the work of the organizations. Various practices used in commercial organizations are described by the Market Research Society's working party on interviewing methods (Market Research Society, 1968).

One type of procedure is that used by The Gallup Poll. Everyone applying is sent a detailed application form and leaflet explaining what the work involves. To test their reactions to the interviewing situation, they also receive questionnaires for four (unpaid) trial interviews, to be made with people who are strangers to them. Only 10–20 per cent proceed with their application beyond this point. Some of these applicants are rejected as unsuitable, for example those with insufficient time available, door-to-door salesmen or students. Of those completing the trial interviews satisfactorily, about 80 per cent are accepted. They are paid by the hour for work done.

New interviewers receive a detailed *Interviewer's Manual* on interviewing procedure. A probationary period operates in the initial stages, while the interviewer gains experience and learns to maintain a satisfactory standard of work. Each survey is accompanied by a job specification. Where technical knowledge connected with the survey topic is needed, and in area studies where detailed local organization is involved, the survey may be preceded by a technical or planning meeting.

From January, 1970, the computer has played a major role in sample design, selection of interviewers to work on individual surveys and quality control. First of all a master sample of 300 constituencies throughout England, Scotland and Wales[1] has been selected and some 600 part-time interviewers are concentrated in these constituencies. Secondly, each interviewer receives an experience and quality-of-work coding, which is continuously updated. These codings, together with their name, address and other relevant details are stored in the computer. Selection of interviewers for any particular survey is then made by computer to ensure (*a*) accurate distribution of sampling points and (*b*) optimum selection of interviewers in relation to the nature, size and timetable of the particular job in hand.

On each survey a large number of interviewers is used, each doing only a few interviews—rarely more than 15 and often less. There are specific technical reasons for these small assignments. The Gallup Poll finds that by using a large number of interviewers, each doing only a few interviews on any given survey,

(*a*) sampling is improved owing to the wide scatter of a large number of sampling points on any given survey

(*b*) high success rates are obtained in random samples; the interviewer has more time and energy for any necessary recalls, particularly as the work is local

---

[1] Resident interviewers in Northern Ireland and Eire also work on behalf of Gallup, but as most surveys are concentrated in Great Britain, these interviewers form a separate group.

(c) the risks of interviewer bias, interviewer fatigue and low morale are minimized

(d) large-scale surveys can be carried out quickly.

The BBC Audience Research Department (British Broadcasting Corporation, 1966) also has a large staff of interviewers—about 750 of them—spread over the country. For them, too, interviewing is a spare-time job, consisting of occasional assignments of about three weeks a time; about 150 of them are actively engaged at any moment. They are recruited and supervised by the full-time members of the Audience Research staff.

The British Market Research Bureau has a field staff of about 500 interviewers, plus field administration and supervisory staff. Two separate field forces are maintained. On the one hand, there are the general research interviewers, all of whom are women, employed on a part-time basis, and located throughout the country. They are trained in formal interviewing methods and are controlled from one of four regional offices. On the other hand, there is a force of about fifty specialist interviewers trained in informal interviewing, motivational research and industrial interviewing. Because of the nature of their work they are based mainly in London, but a limited number are located in the Midlands and the North. Where desirable, male interviewers are employed for industrial interviewing.

The Government Social Survey employs a general field force of 300 or more part-time interviewers, spread all over the country, trained and supervised centrally by the Field Branch in London. Its selection procedure is probably the most rigorous in this country and is worth describing. Before being interviewed applicants are scrutinized on the basis of their written applications. (Some applicants may live in an area where no interviewers are needed.) In the late 1960's the Survey received over 3,000 applications a year, but some 80 per cent dropped out almost immediately; about two-thirds of the applicants withdrew their applications when made aware through the literature sent to them of the conditions of service, hours of work, availability required and so forth. The remainder were given a lengthy interview designed to find out what kind of people they were, what they expected the work to be like, their availability, and so on. It also served to give them a clear picture of the nature of the work. A clerical test, designed to test accuracy in recording, summarizing, checking and classifying data and in carrying out the kind of elementary arithmetic which features on many questionnaires, was taken by almost all those who attended this interview. A further 15 per cent of the original applicants failed to pass this stage, about 6 per cent withdrawing of their own volition. The remaining 5 per cent of the original applicants passed on to training and all but a few of them completed it.

This is a complex scheme, which the *ad hoc* survey team, let alone the solitary researcher, cannot hope to adopt. Its underlying principle is, however, worth following: it is to give applicants every opportunity to withdraw if they begin to get dubious about their suitability or enthusiasm for the work. Thus many potential misfits are kept out of the field from the beginning and the researcher's time and money are not wasted on training people who will not stay the course. Even so, interviewer turnover remains a major problem; in recent experience, the Government Social Survey has a turnover of almost a quarter in a year, in spite of its efforts in selection and training.

A noteworthy feature of the scheme is the emphasis on testing performance on routine tasks. It is no good engaging people who will send in slipshod or illegible work, who cannot do simple arithmetic or follow instructions. However good she might be at other aspects of the work, a person who cannot record accurately and fully will not make a good interviewer. Clerical tests, dummy interviews with the field personnel and observed interviews in the field are among the most useful tools in the selection process. The value of intelligence and aptitude tests of various kinds remains under debate and offers considerable scope for research.

Amidst all this uncertainty, the researcher can at least seek comfort in the knowledge that there is no such being as an ideal interviewer. Many personal qualities may be desirable, but few of them are so vital that an applicant could be rejected solely for not possessing them. The following are amongst the least controversial:

(*a*) *Honesty*. There can be no dispute about this: interviewers must be honest and scrupulous. Cheating, in the sense of complete or partial fabrication of a questionnaire response, is fairly easily detected; unscrupulousness in following instructions is not. Honesty and integrity are not characteristics that can be easily assessed at the selection stage, but interviewers who are later found deficient on these scores can and should be quickly dismissed. The Market Research Society keeps a 'Black List' of fraudulent interviewers to protect companies with members in the Society from employing an interviewer dismissed by another company for serious cheating (Market Research Society, 1968).

(*b*) *Interest*. Interest in the work is highly desirable. Errors and poor-quality work are much more likely if the interviewer is bored and regards the work as valueless. The quality of most interviewers' work deteriorates after a time—an important consideration to remember when they are being engaged for a lengthy period. For this reason, some experts believe in occasional assignments rather than full-time work.

(c) *Accuracy.* Interviewers should be accurate in their recording of answers, in the way they follow instructions, apply definitions and carry out their administrative duties. Everyone makes mistakes sometimes; what one tries to avoid is the person who tends to make them habitually.

(d) *Adaptability.* If the interviewer is likely to be employed on a variety of surveys, including different types of questions, subjects and respondents, she should be a person who easily adapts herself to varying circumstances; who happily carries out a survey on living conditions in the slums one week and one on cigar preferences the next. In engaging interviewers for a single survey this is not so relevant, although even here interviews with many different *types* of people will probably be required. Persons with strong prejudices against certain groups of the population which they might be required to interview are obviously unsuitable.

(e) *Personality and temperament.* The danger of 'over-rapport' between interviewer and respondent has already been noted, and there is something to be said for an interviewer who, while friendly and interested, does not get too emotionally involved with the respondent and his problems. Interviewing on most surveys is a fairly straightforward job, not one calling for exceptional industry, charm or tact. What one asks is that the interviewer's personality should be neither over-aggressive nor over-sociable. Pleasantness and a business-like manner is the ideal combination.

(f) *Intelligence and education.* Ordinary survey interviewing does not call for very special intelligence. Persons of the highest intelligence and education will be the most easily bored by its repetitiveness and the least happy to follow instructions allowing little room for discretion. What is needed is sufficient intelligence to understand and follow complicated instructions and to be adaptable, within given limits, to each respondent and situation.

The Market Research Society's (1968) working party on interviewing methods gives a number of criteria which are involved in deciding an applicant's suitability as an interviewer, some of which have already been mentioned. Other factors usually of primary importance are: age, persons outside the age range of 25 to 45 being likely to be eliminated; sex, women generally being preferred for a variety of reasons including their availability, especially for evening and weekend work; personal appearance, being neither untidy nor oversmart; middle-class, with the ability to approach people of both higher and lower social standards; and clear speech, with a regional accent being acceptable and even possibly an advantage.

Occasionally it may be desirable to use specialist interviewers. A good example of this was the Survey on Maternity conducted by the Joint Committee of the Royal College of Obstetricians and Gynaecologists and the Population Investigation Committee (1948), in which the interviewing was done by Health Visitors. Their work gave them a close professional interest in the survey and a natural access to the respondents, circumstances at least partly responsible for the survey's remarkable success.

In small-scale social research studies, where the interviewing is done by perhaps a handful of investigators, it is the rule, rather than the exception, for these to be sociologists, anthropologists, social workers and the like, rather than professional interviewers. For the formal interviewing used in most large-scale surveys, although the interviewer must know enough about the subject to be able to answer the questions the more curious of her respondents will ask, she does not require the knowledge or skill of the specialist.

Training

On the training of interviewers there is as much diversity of opinion and practice as on the selection. Some organizations give virtually none, relying on a quick dismissal of those whose performance fails to come up to scratch; others take the utmost trouble in training their new staff.

The Market Research Society's (1968) working party distinguishes three main methods of training. There is, first of all, the formal training course, usually lasting for three to five days. Such courses may be made up of three components: lectures, practice of mock interviews in the office, and interviews in the field. An alternative training method is by on-the-job instruction, with the trainee going to interviews with a supervisor, perhaps watching the supervisor perform the first few interviews and then taking over herself. A third procedure is to rely completely on written instructions. This is clearly a cheap and easy method, but it is unlikely to be adequate except for the most routine type of survey.

In the Government Social Survey's training programme, recruits are first sent *A Handbook for Interviewers* (Atkinson, 1967) to study and are then asked to attend a three-day initial office training class during which they listen to lectures and take part in discussions and mock interviews. Those passing this stage enter next on their first field training, in which they have their initial taste of fieldwork, accompanied by a training officer. After giving a demonstration interview, the officer observes the first few interviews done by the trainee. At the end of this basic training, interviewers commence their probationary service, during which some further field supervision will probably be given. To complete their probation, interviewers are given a test comprising a written paper on the survey principles given in the *Handbook* and some tape-recorded interviews. Interviewers not achieving a satisfactory level of work at this stage are dismissed. Further field supervision is then given at irregular intervals to interviewers accepted on the Survey's interviewing panel, and there is also the opportunity to attend further formal training courses. In addition, interviewers are required to attend briefing meetings for each of the surveys on which they work.

The main ingredients of any sound training scheme are here: a training manual, talks and discussion in the office, observation of expert interviewers at work, trial interviews, continuing training. The manual itself is comprehensive, including a description of the Survey's work, of the methods used in all stages of its surveys and of how the interviewer's job should be done. It also gives standard definitions used in its questionnaires.

To illustrate another training scheme, we quote Utting and Cole (1954, p. 308), writing on the social accounting enquiry of the Department of Applied Economics at Cambridge:

> All our interviewers have been recruited by local advertisement, and although mostly women they have varied backgrounds. They all receive an initial 15 to 20 hours' training which covers the general objects of the survey, survey methods and interviewing technique. This is followed by practice interviews in the field which are discussed afterwards. In the last course of training we made considerable use of recorded interviews . . .

To summarize, a researcher wishing to train a team of interviewers might proceed as follows. New interviewers should be given some insight into the general work of the organization and told why the survey is being done, by whom and how the results are to be used, and how the rest of the survey (apart from interviewing) is going to be handled. The importance of the interviewer's role should be explained to her so that she is made to feel, as is indeed the case, that the value of the survey depends on the accuracy and completeness of the information she and her colleagues collect.

Then could follow some instruction on interviewing methods. A manual or, more modestly, a sheet of general instructions would serve as the basis of talks by selected members of the research team. Films and recordings showing how interviews should and should not be handled are valuable; and experienced interviewers can give demonstration interviews, which are afterwards discussed. If time permits, the new interviewers might try their hand at interviewing each other in the presence of experienced investigators (in turn acting the role of respondent and interviewer); if these dummy interviews can be recorded for subsequent re-playing, all the better. Next, the interviewers can be given their first taste of fieldwork on pre-testing the questionnaire and instructions; they should also be asked to edit and code some of the test questionnaires, so as to experience how problems can arise.[1]

A scheme of this sort, though allowing for talks and discussions, emphasizes *learning by experience*, and one concrete study of the value of experience is worth quoting. Durbin and Stuart (1951) conducted an experiment to compare the success of experienced professional and inexperienced student interviewers in *obtaining* interviews. Three groups of interviewers took part in the experiment: professionals from the Government Social Survey and the then British Institute of Public Opinion (Gallup Poll) and students from the London School of Economics. Some results are given in Table 12.1.

TABLE 12.1

Results of attempted interviews. Experienced and inexperienced interviewers

	Social Survey per cent	B.I.P.O. per cent	L.S.E. per cent
Success	83·7*	81·3*	69·6*
Refusal	3·8*	3·2*	13·5*
Non-contact	5·0	6·7	5·8
Gone away	5·4*	7·5*	10·1*
Other	2·2	1·2	1·0
Total	100·1	99·9	100·0
Sample size	(504)	(504)	(504)

* Significant at the 1 per cent level.

Source: Durbin and Stuart (1951, p. 173).

By 'success' was meant that the questionnaire was wholly or partially completed (regardless of the number of calls). The striking difference in the success rates between the experienced and inexperienced interviewers was maintained through the three districts sampled (Bermondsey, Tottenham and Wandsworth) and was

[1] Not everyone would agree with the wisdom of this last step; there is a risk that interviewers will gain not only an insight into their errors, but an insight into how to hide them on future surveys.

independent of which questionnaire was used (Tuberculosis, Reading or Saving) and of the age and sex of the respondents. It is worth noting that the two professional organizations hardly differed in their response rates, which suggests that the additional training to which the G.S.S. interviewers were subjected (as against the B.I.P.O. group) did not affect the response rates to any extent.

The authors suggested in their conclusions that 'though the enquiry has demonstrated the inferiority of the students in obtaining interviews when compared with professional interviewers it tells us nothing of the causes of the differences and whether they can easily be remedied. Is it simply a matter of inexperience, or are the differences due in part at least to deeper causes such as students' youthfulness or the personality characteristics of people who go to universities?' (Durbin and Stuart, 1951, p. 184). Although most practitioners would probably now agree on the unsuitability of students as interviewers, the general question of the effect of training on success at interviewing is one that remains largely open to investigation.

One would also like to know to what extent training and experience improve the *quality* of interviewing, but this is difficult to assess. Certain aspects, however, can be checked. The Bureau of the Census has reported an experiment[1] in which two groups of interviewers were given the full (1950 Census) training course of 16 hours, while two other groups were given a five-hour course plus a two-hour review session after two days' interviewing. The questionnaires were then analyzed regarding 'the proportion of entries which were blank or not acceptable'—'not acceptable' meaning that occupation was too vague to be coded, that there was an entry in the labour force block for persons 13 years or under (for whom no entries were required) and so on. Table 12.2 shows the results of the analysis. The report on the experiment felt it reasonable

to conclude that exposure to the complete training did improve the quality of the enumeration. On the other hand, the gains for some items were not particularly startling and for other items even the complete training does not show too encouraging a picture. Since the complete training course meant a training expenditure by the Bureau more than three times the training expenditure for the short course, the question of whether the training technique used gave the Bureau the most for its money is still an open one. The abbreviated training course was prepared in considerable haste and did not by any means represent the best utilisation of the 5 hours allocated to it. It is possible that a course of this length might have been just as effective as the complete training with a better distribution of the points of emphasis. (Survey Research Center, University of Michigan, 1951.)

---

[1] In the report by the Survey Research Center, University of Michigan (1951) on a conference held in 1951.

TABLE 12.2

Percentage of total entries required which were not reported or not acceptable

	Long course per cent	Short course per cent
Occupation—not acceptable	3·5	7·2
omitted	1·9	1·8
Industry—not acceptable	7·5	16·8
omitted	2·0	2·5
Worker classification—not acceptable	2·4	2·8
omitted	3·3	4·0
Sample line information omitted	18·4	31·0
Migration	1·5	2·7
Labour force, incorrect patterns	2·0	4·2
Household composition incorrect	0·2	0·4

Source: Survey Research Center, University of Michigan (1951, p. 62).

These conclusions stress the vital point that both selection and training cost money and that the operative point to the researcher is the extent to which this expenditure is repaid in terms of increased efficiency. Some money is worth spending, but how much? The answer depends on the relation of this outlay to interviewer turnover, on the one hand, and to the quality of interviewing, on the other. Our knowledge on all this remains scanty and what there is, at least in Britain, is largely unpublished. Each survey expert takes his stand on the basis of experience and resources. The social researcher, with no permanent organization and fund of experience behind him, must be guided by such considerations as have been mentioned in this section, by common sense, and by whatever experimentation he can afford in preparing his enquiry.

12.5. Some practical points

This section brings together a few practical aspects of interviewing, which arise whatever the nature of the survey and however modest the scale of the organization.

Interviewer instructions

An important part of any interview survey are the fieldwork instructions and briefing. What ground they cover depends on the training the interviewers have already had, but they generally indicate how the respondents were, or are to be, selected and how they are to be found (e.g. 'the names and addresses of your respondents are given in columns 1 and 2 of the record sheet; no sub-stitutes may be taken'), how many re-calls are to be made, how to deal with various types of non-response, how to open the interview, ask the questions and record the answers. The instructions should draw the interviewers' attention to any non-standard questions, should explain any documents issued for the survey, and should deal with the administrative routine, such as the length of the fieldwork period, whom to contact in the case of problems, and what to do with the completed questionnaires.

Most important perhaps are the questionnaire instructions. These may be printed on the questionnaire or issued as a separate document; in either case, they should state whether any deviation from the printed order and wording of questions is permissible, and what probing is to be allowed. They must further give the definitions needed for the interpretation of questions and tell the interviewer what to do in the case of vague or doubtful answers. Thus question 6 in the questionnaire on p. 312 asked 'Roughly, how long does it take you to get to work? (Record as stated)' and interviewers were instructed 'If the informant says that "it varies", find out what is most usual for him or her and record this.' However complete and clear the instructions, they should always be supplemented by one or more briefing meetings. Personal briefing and discussion of doubtful points, perhaps also with some trial interviews, can do more than any number of pages of instructions to impress upon interviewers the operational details of their task.

Field supervision

Some supervision of interviewers is essential, both to detect bad work and to keep fieldworkers up to the mark. With a small mobile field staff, one or two centrally located supervisors may take care of all supervision; with a large field staff spread throughout the country, a localized organization is more usual, each region being in the charge of a supervisor. In either case, the supervisor is the main link between field staff and head office. She may do the briefing locally, having first been briefed herself at the office; she may have to direct the sample selection if this is done from local lists; and she will have to decide which interviewers are to participate and to give them their sample assignments. Queries and difficulties are referred to her, and she is expected to keep in touch with interviewers during the field-work period and to receive their completed questionnaires. Checks on individual interviewers are usually carried out by her. There is no need to emphasize, then, how important the supervisor's task is in a survey organization. For the researcher engaged on an *ad hoc* survey, personal supervision on this scale is usually out of the question, but some attempt to see that interviewers are doing their work efficiently, scrupulously and pleasantly should be made.

Fieldwork checks[1]

As has been said before, interviewers are human beings and therefore liable to make mistakes. However sound the selection procedure, not all who get on to the field staff will prove satisfactory, while some of those who start well will deteriorate. It is therefore advisable to keep the quality of the fieldwork constantly under review and to investigate any case where an interviewer appears to be doing unsatisfactory work.

The main objects of fieldwork checks are to test (a) whether an interviewer in fact made all the interviews claimed; (b) whether her response rate is satisfactory; (c) whether she is asking the questions, and interpreting and recording the answers, in accordance with instructions.

The first check can be made by sending postcards to all or a sample of the respondents, asking them whether they were interviewed. (It is becoming standard practice in quota sampling to obtain names and addresses, so that such checks are not confined to random sampling.) The main problem with postcard checks is that they are subject to non-response. In a survey described by Durbin and Stuart (1954a), 70 per cent of the check cards were returned. No case was found of an interviewer having dishonestly recorded an interview, but no information was available, of course, regarding the remaining 30 per cent. Might people who had in fact not been interviewed be less likely to return the cards?

An experiment conducted by the UNESCO Institute for Social Sciences in Cologne is relevant here.[2] This was based on a sample of 3,500 interviews; in order to check on these, check cards were sent to approximately 1,070 reported contacts, asking a few questions and requesting the person to put a cross if no interview had taken place. Of these cards, 396 (37 per cent) were returned, and 10 were marked with a cross. The question now was whether people who had been interviewed were more or less likely to have returned a card. In either case, the proportion 10/396 would give a false impression.

To check on this, similar cards were sent to 100 people randomly selected from the same population, but who had definitely *not* been interviewed. Only 9 were returned, all marked with crosses. The experimenters then reasoned that the bias could be measured by the

[1] A fuller discussion of interviewer errors and biases, and the checks used to detect them, will be found in Chapter 15.
[2] The following details were communicated by Dr. E. Reigrotzki, of this Institute, and are quoted with his permission.

ratio of percentage replies from the 'interviewees' and the 'non-interviewees', i.e. 37/9: 'the rate of interviews reported as having been made but yielding a negative check is thus, if we accept the estimate of the bias, in the neighbourhood of

$$\left(\frac{10}{396} \times 100 \times \frac{37}{9}\right) \text{ per cent} = 10 \text{ per cent.'}$$

The experiment was felt to have been too small to be conclusive (taking account of the sampling error, one would get very wide limits around this estimate) but it did point to the existence of a bias. In any case the idea is ingenious and it provides a way of correcting the non-response bias for the check cards.

Coming to the second type of check, the response rate[1] an interviewer achieves in successive assignments is worth studying. If she is consistently less successful than her colleagues, or shows signs of deteriorating, it may be time to dismiss or 'rest' her for a while. A different guide to efficiency is provided by response rates on individual questions. If an interviewer is consistently getting more refusals than the average on difficult questions it is time to review her work. The same applies if she is getting an excessive number of 'Don't know' replies, or is reporting too many ambiguous or incomplete answers. As Steinkamp (1964) has shown, such factors are not necessarily related at all closely to the response rate, which cannot therefore be used as a complete index of interviewer effectiveness; each of these factors needs to be taken into account. In short, the researcher can lay down certain operational standards (possibly on the basis of *average* performance) and check on the work of any 'sub-standard' interviewers.

The most difficult of all points to check is whether an interviewer is asking the questions in the right way, and correctly interpreting and recording the answers. Some inaccuracies in coding and recording may be spotted by a scrutiny of the completed questionnaires, but many types of error will not; one can rarely tell from the questionnaires whether the interviewer deviated from the printed wording or sequence, whether she used unpermitted probes, whether she probed too little or too much and whether she recorded the answer incorrectly.

There are broadly six ways of checking upon the quality of interviewing, other than by scrutinizing the completed questionnaires. One is to use high-grade interviewers or supervisors to re-interview some of the respondents and to compare the two sets of results, the

---

[1] By which we mean the proportion of an interviewer's assigned interviews from which she gets completed questionnaires. A different issue is 'number of interviews a day'. This is also worth keeping a check on, though the effect of size of town, region, travel facilities must be borne in mind.

presumption being that the high-grade interviewers are more likely to be correct. In spite of the obvious snags of re-interviewing, such quality checks can be useful (see Chapter 15). A second way is to have supervisors observing interviewers at work. This is useful when an interviewer is thought to be falling below the required standards, but one can never be sure that interviewers conduct all their interviews as they do those under observation. The same qualification applies to the third method, which is to have interviewers conduct test interviews in the office. The most that can be hoped for is that such interviews will disclose any persistent bad interviewing habits the interviewers have got into. The fourth way is to record the interviews mechanically. This can be a good check if the interviewers are left unaware that it is being done; but if they themselves work the recording apparatus, their performance can again not be regarded as typical of everyday work. Fifthly, if the survey is designed on the basis of replicated samples (see Section 6.3) major differences between interviewers, though not consistent biases, can be discerned. Finally, the quality of the interviewer's work can be gauged to the extent that answers to survey questions can be checked against other data.

Working conditions

Selection and training are one side of interviewer efficiency, morale is another. Payments to interviewers, working conditions, hours of work, assignments, contact with the research team—all of these are related to morale and thus to efficiency. Interviewers spend a large part of their working time away from their colleagues and so, as well as the formal contacts, informal ones like parties, social visits and newsletters can be valuable in making them aware that they are part of a team doing an important job.

Payment should be good enough to attract the right sort of people and to keep them satisfied. Payment is usually on a time basis, since piece rates may easily lead to slipshod work; differential rates can be paid according to seniority or ability and bonus payments can be made for more difficult assignments or for work of high quality. In general pay rates for interviewing are low, and one cannot wonder that labour turnover is a major problem in professional organizations.

Interviewers should be given reasonable assignments. If they are full-time workers they cannot be expected to do much at weekends and in the evenings; but part-timers are likely to do most of their work at these times. Frequent long journeys for dispersed interviews are discouraging, as are interviews in difficult localities. If an interviewer has been long in the field, a spell in the office or a complete rest from surveys is often beneficial; time spent in the organization's coding section can provide a particularly useful break from interviewing because it also acts as further training, the interviewer learning the problems coders face in dealing with poorly completed questionnaires. An interviewer's interest is bound to flag after a time and the surveyor may be able to help by varying the types of assignments and by offering encouragement in any way he can.

Finally, it is worth making the obvious remark that researchers cannot expect interviewers to do a decent job if they produce over-lengthy or ill-designed questionnaires and ask questions which most people find unintelligible, uninteresting or futile.

12.6. Informal interviewing[1]

So far we have been concerned with formal interviewing, in which the questions that are asked, their sequence and wording, are worked out *beforehand* and one aims to have the interviews conducted in a uniform way.[2]

The case for formal interviewing is simple. Only if all respondents are asked exactly the same questions in the same order can one be sure that all the answers relate to the same thing and are strictly comparable. Then, and then only, is one justified in combining the results into statistical aggregates.

The intention is understandable enough. The surveyor wants to feel sure that if the respondent is questioned by interviewer B rather than interviewer A (or interviewer A on another occasion), the questions asked would be the same and the same answers would be obtained. But the standardization of formal interviewing is un-fortunately not sufficient to ensure that the questions have the same *meanings* for all respondents; some questions may even not be understood by certain types of respondent. Different groups of people, in different social classes, regions of the country, town rather than country, use different vocabularies and have differing language usage, and may therefore not place the same interpretation on the meaning of a standard question asked in a standard way. With informal techniques the interviewer can tailor the wording of questions to each particular respondent and can ask the questions in an order that is appropriate for him. Through interviewing skills and study of

---

[1] There are many other terms in use to distinguish between what are called here 'formal' and 'informal' interviewing: 'structured' and 'unstructured'; 'mass' and 'formative'; 'inflexible' and 'flexible'; 'standardized' and 'qualitative'; 'controlled' and 'uncontrolled'; 'extensive' and 'intensive'.

[2] It is sometimes suggested that the 'open' question is the first step towards in-formal interviewing. This is not in accord with the present use of the term, at any rate. In formal survey interviews, both 'open' and pre-coded questions are sup-posed to be *asked* in a specified form; they differ only in the form in which the answer is recorded. But the interviewer has no freedom to alter the course of the interview, which is the essence of what we are calling informal interviewing.

the respondent, the interviewer tries in this way to equate the meaning of questions for all respondents.

For questions that are not too complex or sensitive, and for surveys of populations that are fairly homogeneous, respondents will generally interpret standardized questions in more or less the same way, and should respond similarly to the ordering of questions. In such cases the benefits of standardization argue for formal interviewing as the appropriate method. On the other hand, where the survey subject is highly complex or emotional, it may be that the greater flexibility of the informal approach succeeds better than set questions in getting to the heart of the respondent's opinion.

This is not intended to imply that there is no flexibility at all in formal interviewing; the interviewer can always adapt her opening remarks to the situation confronting her, and explain, probe, and adjust the speed of the interview within the defined limits. But these limits are fairly rigid. Probing, for instance, is sometimes allowed only on some questions and only according to instructions. And, except with factual questions, interviewers are hardly ever allowed to change the wording or order of questions or to ask additional ones.

This is where the contrast with informal interviewing is most striking, for here the conduct of the interview is largely in the hands of interviewer and respondent. Just how extensive their respective influence is varies with the type of interview.

These types can be visualized along a scale of increasing formality. At one end there is the completely *non-directive* interview[1] which has more affinity to the psychoanalyst's approach than to the usual survey interview. The informant is encouraged to talk about the subject under investigation (usually himself) and the course of the interview is mainly guided by him. There are no set questions, and usually no pre-determined framework for recording answers. The interviewer confines himself to elucidating doubtful points, to re-phrasing the respondent's answers and to probing generally. It is an approach especially to be recommended when complex attitudes are involved and when one's knowledge of them is still in a vague and unstructured form. Suppose we wished to study how a group of parents felt about the effects of 'comics' on their children. In the early stages of the research, at any rate, one would probably treat the subject, not in terms of set questions, but by an informal approach which will show what points are worth attacking in the later and more structured stages.

[1] Other terms are 'depth' or 'non-guided' interview. One of the classic examples of this form occurred in the famous Hawthorne experiments, reported by Roethlisberger and Dickson (1939).

Then we have the kind of *conversational* or *casual* interviewing used by Mayhew (1861–62), and revived by Zweig in his various studies. In the introduction to his best known book Zweig (1948, p. 1) says 'I dropped the idea of a questionnaire, or formal verbal questions put forward in the course of research; instead I had casual talks with working-class men on an absolutely equal footing and in friendly intercourse. These were not formal interviews but an exchange of views on life, labour and poverty.' There is no doubt that, in Zweig's hands, this highly individual method was successful.

Moving towards more formal methods, we come to the situation in which the interviewer, whilst allowing the respondent a good deal of freedom, aims to cover a given set of topics in a more or less systematic way. This is best termed the *guided* or *focused* interview. Again there is no set questionnaire and most of the questions are open ones, designed to encourage the respondent to talk freely around each topic. A good example is given in a paper by Marriott (1953), which describes a survey among industrial workers aimed to study what factors made for satisfaction and what for discontent among them. The individual interview was guided around eight topics that previous study had found to be crucial in the context: operation of the actual task performed; hours of work; shift system; amount of wages; payment system; firms and higher management and their policies; supervision; and workmates. A few simple factual questions introduced each subject, and were followed by the open questions that formed the core of the discussion for every topic; finally, respondents were asked to assess their own contentedness as regards each topic.

Such interviewing gets away from the inflexibility of formal methods, yet gives the interview a set form and ensures that all the relevant topics are discussed. The respondents are all asked for certain information, yet they have plenty of opportunity to develop their views at length. Interviewers, on their side, are free to choose when and how to put their questions and how much to explore and probe, all the time keeping within the framework imposed by the topics to be covered. The focused or guided interview is thus more formal than the non-directive interview; there are numerous examples of its application in the literature.

Informal interviewing raises various issues, some on the debit, others on the credit side, and these will repay looking at.

Interviewer skill

Informal interviewing clearly calls for greater skill than the formal survey interview. More than a careful following of instructions is involved. The conduct of the interview calls for intelligence, understanding and tact, and for a deeper knowledge of its subject matter than is required in formal interviewing. In the latter, the skilful part of the process is, as far as possible, taken out of the field and into the office. The less formal the method, the more skill is required in the field; and informal methods at their best demand the abilities, not of professional interviewers briefed by the sociologist, but of the sociologist himself. They do not, therefore, lend themselves well to the large-scale surveys that are the main subject of this book.

Interviewer bias

Informal interviewing gives much greater scope to the personal influence and bias of the interviewer than the formal approach. The investigator at least partly determines what form the interview takes, the questions that are asked and the details that are recorded.[1] There is, in the report of an informal interview, 'more of the interviewer' than on the standard survey questionnaire, which is another way of saying that the process is often not so reliable.

Depth

The chief recommendation for informal methods is that they can 'dig deeper' and get a richer understanding than the formal interview. The importance of this 'digging' depends on the questions that are being asked. If a survey is designed to collect simple facts about individuals, such as their age, their marital status, the size of their family, their purchases and so forth, there is no need to look beyond the formal approach. But when it sets out to study more complex things, particularly attitudes, formal interviewing may limit the investigation to too superficial a level to be appropriate. A method that is suitable for ascertaining a person's age is not necessarily the best for discovering the structure of his attitudes to homosexuality.

Survey experts have long recognized that simple poll-type questions are inadequate when complex attitudes are involved, and have made increasing use of 'attitude batteries' and scaling devices. A large number of questions relating to the subject matter are asked, and the answers combined, by more or less sophisticated means, to give a wider picture of an attitude than could be obtained by a few simple questions. But the essential limitation of the formal interview, its inflexibility in the face of different situations and respondents, is still there. This becomes clear if we consider a hypothetical survey on attitudes to homosexuality. Most people have views on this subject. Some people feel strongly about it, others are little moved by it; some are too inhibited to talk about it, others only too glad to do so;

---

[1] Unless the full interview is tape recorded. Tape recording is particularly useful for informal interviews.

the views of some are straightforward and rational, those of others complex and highly emotional. Although a set of well-framed standardized questions can try to chart the major dimensions of the attitude, one cannot hope that they will get to the core of the attitude for each respondent. The extent to which they do will vary from person to person. With informal interviewing, if skilfully done, the interviewer should be able to cut through any embarrassment and emotional inhibitions surrounding the subject and to 'dig as deep' as may be necessary to get to the heart of each person's attitude. The structure of this attitude, all the qualifications surrounding it, its causes, implications and intensity, should emerge, resulting in a fuller and more rounded picture than is attainable by formal methods.[1]

It does not of course follow that the fuller description is *necessarily* the more valid one. As was suggested by the National Opinion Research Center studies reported by Hyman and others (1954), some people may not have hidden depths, in which case a snap answer to a snap question may be more valid than a complicated answer arrived at by lengthy discussion! The discussion may influence the respondent in the answer he gives, and may lead him to rationalize. Also, because in the informal interview the interviewer's personality and views tend to come more into the open, the respondent may be led to present a biased picture of his own views. A very interesting problem for research—and a difficult one to tackle—is the comparison of the validity and reliability of answers resulting from formal and informal interviewing techniques.

Analysis

A basic objection to informal methods is the difficulty of summarizing and quantifying the material. There are essentially three facets to this. One is that, as interviewers are free to determine the run of the interview, different *items* of information may be obtained from different respondents, so that it is hard to compare and aggregate the results.

Secondly, even if interviewers have asked for the same items, differences in wording and so forth may make the answers not truly comparable. Thirdly, the results of descriptive, non-quantified interviews do not easily lend themselves to statistical analysis as answers to straight questions do. If quantification is desired, coding must precede it, and this is relatively hard with descriptive interview

---

[1] Rose (1945) even suggests that, in order to draw out the respondent's real attitude to a subject, the interviewer may find it useful to use biased words and leading questions, to express an attitude of her own (real or assumed), to give the respondent—whose expressed attitude may be based on misinformation—any necessary information.

material.[1] The material obtained from depth, non-directive or casual interviews has to be used quite differently from that obtained in formal surveys. The point of the informal approach is to obtain a more complete picture of, say, a person's attitude than a formal interview would. If this gain is not to be sacrificed, the analysis must retain a fair amount of detail and not merely be compressed into a series of statistical tables.

Conclusions

It can be seen that the choice between formal and informal methods depends on the character of the survey problem and the use to be made of the results. The formal approach achieves greater uniformity, and this is a weighty factor when comparability between interviews is important and when the interest is in the characteristics of the aggregate more than in those of the individual. In any case the method is quite adequate for the simple type of questions involved in many administrative surveys and market research.

Its use becomes questionable when complex phenomena are under study: formal questioning may then be too superficial and crude for the task. For this reason alone, informal techniques will continue to be used in much sociological research. They do, however, require a great deal more skill in the interviewer and more alertness to the danger of personal bias than formal methods: they are also relatively slow and expensive.

Informal techniques will remain invaluable at the pilot stage of even formal surveys, to provide guidance on what are the important questions and how they should be asked. Where feasible, they may sometimes also be usefully employed together with formal surveys in researching complex problems: in some situations the use of a combination of methods, each method having its own strengths and weaknesses, can provide a more powerful research strategy than the reliance on any one method used alone.

NOTES ON READING

1. Perhaps the best way to get the 'feel' of an interviewer's job is to read one of the manuals issued by professional bodies for their field staff. The Government Social Survey's *A Handbook for Interviewers* by ATKINSON (1967) is the most detailed in Great Britain. The paper by FOTHERGILL and WILLCOCK (1955), which is also included in EDWARDS (1956), has a good discussion of interviewing problems, in the context of the Social Survey's work. The report of the working party on interviewing methods of the

---

[1] See pp. 437–8 for some references on the coding of non-quantified material.

MARKET RESEARCH SOCIETY (1968) reviews the variety of interviewing practices used in commercial organizations.

The *Interviewers' Manual* of the SURVEY RESEARCH CENTER, UNIVERSITY OF MICHIGAN (1969) includes instructions for area sampling as well as general interviewing instructions.

Among the textbooks, GOODE and HATT (1952) and PARTEN (1950) discuss the interviewer's job in particular detail.

2. The books by KAHN and CANNELL (1957), RICHARDSON, DOHREN-WEND and KLEIN (1965) and the report on the National Opinion Research Center studies by HYMAN and others (1954) are well worth studying. The chapters by CANNELL and KAHN in FESTINGER and KATZ (1953) and in LINDZEY and ARONSON (1968, Vol. 2) and the chapter in SELLTIZ and others (1959) are recommended; as is also the article by KAHN and CANNELL (1968). The SURVEY RESEARCH CENTER, UNIVERSITY OF MICHIGAN (1951) sponsored a conference on *Field Methods in Sample Interview Surveys*. The report summarizes the proceedings, which ranged over the whole field of selection, training, instruction, supervision and so forth. It is a concise and very much to-the-point discussion of outstanding problems.

3. SUDMAN (1967) contains three chapters on time allocation, costs, and quality of interviewers. STEINKAMP (1964) discusses methods of measuring the effectiveness of interviewers. CANNELL, FOWLER and MARQUIS (1968) report on a study investigating the effects of psychological and behavioural variables of both interviewer and respondent on reporting.

4. The classical article on non-directive interviewing is that by ROGERS (1945); on focused interviewing the best reference is the book by MERTON, FISKE and KENDALL (1956). Other interesting papers on informal techniques are those by LAZARSFELD (1944), which is reprinted in KATZ and others (1954), and by ROSE (1945). MADGE (1953) has a good summary of all these methods.

5. Numerous articles on interviewing are spread through the pages of the *Public Opinion Quarterly*.

CHAPTER 13

Questionnaires

13.1. General principles of design

I N THE last two chapters the principal ways of collecting survey data, mail questionnaires and personal interviews, have been discussed. We now turn to the instrument on which both approaches depend, the *questionnaire* or *recording schedule*.

As briefly noted above, these two terms are sometimes used to distinguish between the situation in which the respondent himself fills in the answers and that in which an interviewer asks the questions and records the answers.[1] To the survey designer the distinction is important, for in one case he is producing a document to be used and, he hopes, understood by the respondent unaided, while in the other the users will be persons especially trained to handle such documents. The questionnaire used in the Government Social Survey's radio and television enquiry, which was referred to in Chapter 11, is a good example of the former type and is reproduced on pp. 305–7.[2] In this enquiry an experiment was carried out on the wording of the covering letter; half the sample were sent a relatively impersonal letter and the other half a relatively personal one. There was no significant difference in the response rate for the two halves of the sample. In both cases the letter is brief, but covers the essential points: the letter heading indicates the sponsorship of the enquiry, and the contents inform the respondents of the subject of the enquiry and of the fact that they represent a cross-section of the population and tell them clearly what they are asked to do. The questionnaire itself is carefully and clearly laid out, with bold type

[1] The discussion throughout this chapter is confined to formal interviewing. The type of schedule used in some kinds of informal interviewing is best called an interview guide.
[2] Three illustrative questionnaires or schedules are reproduced in this book: the radio and television enquiry questionnaire and its covering letters; a Gallup Poll questionnaire (reset, see p. xv); and the questionnaire used in the quota sampling experiment by Moser and Stuart (1953) mentioned earlier.

and capitals being widely used to emphasize particular words and instructions.[1] What is more, the questions themselves are simple and it looks as if a genuine effort was made to keep them to a minimum.

The requirements for a recording schedule are in some respects different from this. Since it is handled by interviewers, it can be a fairly formal document, in which efficiency of field handling rather than attractiveness is the operative consideration in design. It can be in a highly codified form, with instructions and definitions printed on the schedule.

In designing either a questionnaire or, more particularly, a recording schedule, the convenience of the office staff as well as that of interviewer and respondent should be considered. Layout and printing should be such that editing and coding can proceed smoothly. As it is sometimes desirable to prepare punched cards straight from the questionnaire or schedule it should be designed with this in mind; code numbers should stand out clearly so that punch operators can spot them quickly. But of course it is the interviewer, rather than the office worker, who has to cope with the schedule under the most difficult circumstances, so it is her convenience that must be given top priority.

One of the skills in designing either type of document is to make clear which questions are to be answered by whom. Sometimes whole sections concern only a sub-class of respondents, in which case this should be quite plain to whoever is recording the answers. The schedule on p. 312 is a good example: here questions 4 to 7, for instance, were to be asked 'only of informants with jobs'. If, when a particular answer is given, the next question or series of questions is to be skipped over, a useful device is to use an arrow on the questionnaire to link that answer to the next applicable question.

Frequently 'a question' consists of a main question and one or more 'dependent' or sub-questions. In the schedule just cited, question 3(a) is asked of all, question 3(b) only of those who answer 'Has job' to the former. In the Gallup Poll schedule[2] on pp. 332–9, question 63(a) asks each respondent whether he or anyone else in his household runs a car; question 63(b) asks those answering 'Yes' to 63(a) for details of the car, including whether it is a replacement or a first car; and question 63(c) asks those answering 63(b) by saying that the car is a replacement for details of the previous car. Sub-questions

---

[1] An experiment on the effect of the length of questionnaire on the response rate was also part of this enquiry (see p. 263). The questionnaire reproduced here is the long version.

[2] The numbering of questions in the Gallup Poll questionnaire is to assist with the analysis; the question number is the first column number of the punched card on which the information is to be recorded. Early columns of the card are used for other information, so the questions start at 13.

½ 1

THE CENTRAL OFFICE OF INFORMATION

JUBILEE HOUSE,
1, QUAY STREET,
DEANSGATE,
MANCHESTER, 3

Dear Sir or Madam,

Radio and Television Enquiry

This is a survey to find out a few important facts about people's likes and dislikes in radio and television.

We are writing to a cross-section of people throughout the country and asking them to give us their opinions. In order to be sure that all points of view are taken into account we are anxious to get a reply from every person we write to.

The questions are on a sheet enclosed with this letter. Would you please fill in your answers and post the sheet back to us, using the enclosed reply-paid envelope.

Please note that it is *your own* view that we want. Do not ask anyone else to fill in the form instead of you, or we will not have a true cross-section of opinions.

We are just as anxious to have the answers of those who do *not* listen to the radio or view television, as of those who do.

We should be most grateful for your help.

Yours faithfully,

Scott

Please send your reply to : Mr. C. Scott
Central Office of Information
1, Quay Street
MANCHESTER, 3

½ 2

THE CENTRAL OFFICE OF INFORMATION

YORK STREET,
BAKER STREET,
LONDON, W.1

Dear Sir or Madam,

Your Opinions of Radio and Television

May I ask for your help in a survey we are making ? We are trying to find out a few important facts about people's likes and dislikes in radio and television.

I am sending this letter to you and to a cross-section of people throughout the country, and asking you to give us your opinions. To make sure that we hear all points of view, we are anxious to get a reply from each person we write to. I hope you will be willing to co-operate.

You will find the questions on a sheet enclosed with this letter. Would you be kind enough to fill in your answers and post the sheet back to us, using the enclosed reply-paid envelope ?

We would like to have *your own* views. Please do not ask anyone else to reply instead of you, or we will not have a true cross-section of opinions.

If you *don't* listen to the radio or view television, we are still just as anxious to have your answers.

I hope that you will agree to help.

Yours faithfully,

Scott

Please send your reply to : Mr. C. Scott
Central Office of Information
York Street
LONDON, W.1

Radio and Television survey. Covering letter.
Impersonal version.

Radio and Television survey. Covering letter.
Personal version.

9

RADIO AND TELEVISION ENQUIRY

In the questions on this page, we are asking about the programmes you have listened to ON SOUND RADIO (not TV).

It does not matter whether you listened at home or somewhere else.

1. **Have you** listened to BBC SOUND RADIO (not TV) in the last **7 days** ? ....

2. **Here are** some different types of programme on BBC sound radio.

Please put a TICK (√) against any which you think should be broadcast MORE	Light music ....
	News ....
Put a CROSS against any which you think should be broadcast LESS	Religious services ....
	Full length plays ....
Put O against any which you think are broadcast about the right amount at present	Variety ....

Would you make sure that you have put EITHER a tick, OR a cross, OR a nought in EACH ONE of the five spaces above

3. During the **last 4 weeks** have you listened to any of the radio stations below ?

Radio Luxembourg	....
Radio Eirann (Athlone)	....
American Forces Network (AFN)	....
BBC Oversea Short-wave	....
Other short-wave, not BBC	....
European stations on medium and long waves	....

Put a tick (√) against any you have listened to in the LAST 4 WEEKS

IF YOU HAVE LISTENED TO NONE OF THESE, WRITE "NONE" HERE......................

Please turn over

Radio and Television survey. Questionnaire. 'Long' version. FRONT
A sticker was attached to the top of the page saying: 'Please answer all questions you ca
even if you have no radio or TV.'

4. Do you watch TELEVISION regularly . ...

Have you seen BBC television in the last 7 days ? (Write YES or NO) : ....

Have you seen ITV in the last 7 days ? (Write YES or NO) : ....

Is there any particular KIND of
programme which you specially like ? ....

(Please state which kind)

5. Here are some different types of TV programme.

Please put a TICK (√) against any which
you think should appear MORE on TV

Put a CROSS against any which
you think should appear LESS.

Put O against any which you think appear
about the right amount on TV at present

Travel programmes ....

News ....

Westerns and crime ....

Plays ....

Variety ....

Would you make sure that you have put EITHER a tick,
OR a cross, OR a nought in EACH ONE of the five spaces above_____

6. It has been found that people of different ages and in different jobs have different interests in radio and TV.
To help us study this, we are asking you to give your age and describe your job below.

Please show your age by putting a tick against one of the groups below.

AGE	20 to 29	30 to 39	40 to 49	50 to 59	60 or over

Please describe the work you do below. The more detail you can give, the better.

If you are a MARRIED WOMAN, please describe your husband's work only.
If retired, or not working at present, describe last job.

PLEASE
GIVE
FULL
DETAILS
OF JOB
HERE
....

If Civil
Service or
H.M. Forces,
please state
grade or rank.

If an engineer,
say exactly
what kind.

Is the above job paid weekly or monthly ? ....
(If self-employed, please say so and state how many people you employ.)

7. In case you have any comments you would like to make about radio or TV, would you write them below ?

Name : Mr/Mrs/Miss .... Date ....
If a widow, please say so

can become complicated and clear layout and printing are essential.

Having made the distinction between questionnaires and recording schedules, we will not labour it unduly. Where the distinction is of particular relevance, it will be used; otherwise, the more convenient term 'questionnaire' will be used for both types of document.

It has been said that 'no survey can be better than its question-naire', a cliché which well expresses the truth that, no matter how efficient the sample design or sophisticated the analysis, ambiguous questions will produce non-comparable answers, leading questions biased answers and vague questions vague answers. Discussion on the questionnaire must begin at the start of the planning stages and will not end until the pilot surveys are completed. It is fair to say that question design is the survey director's most persistent headache, particularly since it is still so largely a matter of art rather than science.

There are admittedly a number of general principles guiding question design and some pitfalls to beware of (it needs no theorist for instance to point out that if uninfluenced answers are required it would be foolish to put a question in the form 'You don't think . . ., do you?'). Yet for virtually every conceivable question there are several possible, and theoretically acceptable, forms; in choosing between them, knowledge of the survey population and subject matter, common sense, past experience and pilot work are at present the surveyor's main tools.

The value of these tools is not questioned, but clearly surveys would be greatly strengthened if there were a more scientific basis to question design; if the choice between the alternative forms of a question could more often be based on theoretical principles or on firm empirical evidence. By the latter is meant more than the surveyor's recollection that a particular question form was unsuccessful on a particular occasion; an alternative form might after all have been equally unsuccessful. If, on the other hand, different forms of questions were tried out experimentally or in pilot surveys, the comparison of their success—however judged—would be a solid basis for choice. The difficulties in all this are obvious, which is why surveyors continue to rely heavily on common sense and hunches. It is easy enough to compare several question forms experimentally, but such comparisons always relate to a particular question, time, and group of respondents; it is exceedingly hard to derive com-parisons of *general* relevance. Apart from which, even if two question forms produce different results, it is often hard and sometimes im-possible to judge which result—if either—is correct.

The first step in designing a questionnaire is to define the problem to be tackled by the survey and hence to decide on what questions to ask. The temptation is always to cover too much, to ask everything that might turn out to be interesting. This must be resisted. Lengthy, rambling questionnaires are as demoralizing for the interviewer as for the respondent, and the questionnaire should be no longer than is absolutely necessary for the purpose. Certain questions will, so to speak, include themselves, but a problem of choice inevitably arises with marginal ones. Let us consider a hypothetical survey to ascertain what daily newspapers different kinds of people read. A number of newspaper questions, together with those asking for necessary personal data, automatically suggest themselves. Then, as the discussion of the planning of the survey warms up, many extensions of interest occur to those taking part. Would it be useful to include reading of periodicals and books? Would the main results be more meaningful if they could be viewed against the background of the respondents' leisure habits as a whole? Would it be wise to find out something about how much money and time different people have available for newspaper buying and reading? Should one ask a question or two about the use of libraries? Should one go beyond the facts of reading and ask people's opinions on individual newspapers?

And so it goes on, with the questionnaire growing from a short list of questions to a document many pages long. Enquiries in the professional survey field, where the questionnaire is tailored to a client's precise requirements, usually avoid this process; but in social research, where a survey is often aimed to study a certain *field*, rather than to collect specific information, it is exceedingly common. Nor is there any simple way of deciding what limit to put on the range of a questionnaire. The extra cost (in time and money) of adding further questions can be estimated from trial interviews, but these are not the only variables. Length of questionnaire must be presumed to affect the morale of both interviewer and respondent, and probably also refusal rates and the quality of the data; these are unknown quantities unless special efforts are made in the pilot survey to estimate them. The difficulty again is to develop any general principles. Perhaps the only certainty is that the shorter the questionnaire the better the interviewer and respondent will like it, which is about as useful as saying that the bigger the sample the more precise will be the results. Both statements are unexceptionable, but neither suffices as a guide for action. An enormous sample may be desirable but financially out of reach; a short questionnaire may suit the respondent but not the purpose of the enquiry (nor does it *necessarily* suit the interviewer; too short a questionnaire gives little chance to create 'rapport' and secure full co-operation).

It is obvious that the survey planner must rigorously examine every question, and exclude any that are not strictly relevant to the survey's objectives. In this, the pilot survey is his most helpful tool. Here all the marginal questions can be tested out and dummy tabulations made from the results. Questions likely to prove of small importance in the final analysis can be spotted, as can those which turn out to be not worth asking unless a host of others is also included.

In settling the scope of a questionnaire, one other criterion should be applied, namely that the questions should be practicable. This merits emphasis, even though no amount of textbook admonition can take the place of common sense. It is no good asking a person's opinion about something he does not understand; about events too long ago for him to remember accurately; about matters which, although they concern him, he is unlikely to have accurate information on or that are so personal or emotional that valid answers cannot be expected by formal direct questioning.

13.2. Question content

In considering any question, then, it is wise to ask oneself whether respondents are likely to possess the knowledge, or have access to the information, necessary for giving a correct answer. It is unsafe to *assume* that respondents will voluntarily admit ignorance. On the contrary it has often been shown that they will give some kind of answer to most questions, even if they are ill-informed and know it. Similarly, they will express opinions on matters they have given little thought to or which they barely understand.

Let us look at it from the viewpoint of the respondent. He finds himself confronted by an interviewer, who is a total stranger to him, asking his opinion on some matter and thereby implying, albeit subtly, that he has an opinion to offer. Why should he belittle himself by saying that he has never considered the issue, that he does not know what the question means or that he has no opinion to give? There is little reason for him to do so unless he is directly asked about the extent of his knowledge—in which case he is quite likely to admit ignorance, and may indeed welcome the opportunity in the hope of avoiding further questions.

Such difficulties do not apply only to opinion questions. In asking a respondent for factual information, one needs also to be sure that he is in a good position to give it. There is no difficulty in asking women about their husbands' incomes, or in obtaining answers from most of them, but such answers may have little accuracy. Again, to what extent is one entitled to expect accurate answers to the many survey questions involving memory? Naturally, this must depend on the nature of the questions, but a number of research studies have demonstrated that fallibility of memory can be an important source of error.

To summarize, the surveyor should aim to ask questions only from those likely to be able to answer them accurately; to ask about past events only if he can reasonably expect people to remember them accurately (perhaps with the help of recall methods); and to ask their opinions only if he can be reasonably sure that they understand what is involved and are able to give meaningful answers. It is always well to remember that most survey questions are addressed to a variety of people very differently qualified to answer them.

So much for taking account of the *ability* of people to give accurate answers. Quite as important is their *willingness* to do so. Except in the rare surveys where people are compelled to give information, there is no formal reason why they should answer survey questions. That they generally do so is due in part to general helpfulness, in part to their liking to talk about themselves and their views and in part to the innocuous nature of the questions themselves.

But willingness is no guarantee that the answers will be accurate. If information is sought on a personal subject about which people are reluctant to talk, the surveyor must adapt his interviewing approach accordingly and be prepared to go to some lengths in checking on the accuracy of the replies.[1]

Any subject which is surrounded by strong social conventions, on which some types of behaviour and opinions are more 'respectable' than others, demands from the surveyor sufficient subtlety of approach to overcome his respondents' temptation to mislead, to understate, to exaggerate. Even the ordinary factual questions on a schedule are exposed to the influence of prestige feelings: witness the case of the woman who impressively described her husband as 'a man who knows about dust'—correctly enough, for he was a dustman; or, to quote from Payne (1951, p. 185), the man who described himself as a 'bank director'—again correctly, since it was his job to 'direct' the bank customers to the proper official or window! More seriously, people might tend to understate their age and their alcohol consumption; and to exaggerate their education, their reading, their church-going, and so forth.

Factual questions

Most survey questions are concerned with either facts or opinions. There are also questions dealing with motivation ('Why did you go to

[1] See the reports of the surveys on sex behaviour by Kinsey and others (1948, 1953) for an interesting illustration of accuracy checks. It is also worth looking at the papers by Cochran and others (1953, 1954), which contain an evaluation of Kinsey's methodology. The book by Hyman (1955) contains, in Chapter 4, a thorough discussion of accuracy checks.

Serial Number of

Informant...

---

1 (a) I am from the Survey Research Unit, and we are trying to find out a few things about what people do in their spare time. Would you mind telling me, are there any things which you would like to spend more time on?

Yes	1
No	2
Don't know	3

(b) **If YES (1) to Q.1:** What, for instance? **(Record fully)**

....

....

....

For office use

Y	X	0	1
2	3	4	5
6	7	8	9

ASK QUESTION 2 OF ALL WOMEN IN-FORMANTS. FOR MEN GO ON TO QUES-TION 3.

2 Are you a housewife—that is, the person who is mainly responsible for domestic duties in your household?

Yes	1
No	2
Not applicable	3

ASK ALL.

3 (a) I know that your job makes a lot of difference to the amount of spare time you get, so would you mind telling me whether you have a paid job?

Has job	1
Has no job	2

If "Has Job" to Q.3 (a):

3 (b) What is your job? **(Obtain fullest possible description of occupation and industry.)**

Occupation ....

....

Industry ....

....

ASK Q.4–7 ONLY OF INFORMANTS WITH JOBS. FOR THOSE WITHOUT JOBS GO ON TO Q.8.

4 Is your job full-time or part-time? **(part-time means less than 30 hours per week)**

Full-time	....
Part-time	....
Not applicable	

5 On how many days a week are you at y job? **(Record as stated)**

....

....

....

Not applicable ...

For office u

Y	X	0
2	3	4
6	7	8

6 Roughly, how long does it take you to ge work? I only mean going to work, coming home. **(Record as stated)**

....

....

Not applicable ...

For office u

Y	X	0
2	3	4
6	7	8

7 (a) How do you generally get to work? **(R** all mentioned)

On foot	....
Bicycle	....
Motor cycle	....
Car	....
Public transport (bus, tram, train, etc.)	...
Not applicable	....

(b) **If PUBLIC TRANSPORT (5) to Q.7** How much per week altogether do spend on fares to and from work? **(Rec as stated)**

....

....

Not applicable ...

For office u

Y	X	0
2	3	4
6	7	8

Q.8 ONWARDS OF ALL INFORMANTS

Will you tell me, when did you last go to the pictures?

Within last 7 days	1
8-14 days ago	2
15-28 days ago	3
More than 28 days ago	4
I never go	5
Don't know	6

If within last 7 days (1) to Q.8: How many times have you been in the last seven days? (Ring number stated)

Don't know			Y
Not applicable			X
1	2	3	4
5	6	7	8

During this last football season did you go in for any football pools?

Yes (alone)	1
Yes (shared)	2
No	3
Don't know	4

Do you smoke?

Yes	1
No	2

If YES: How many cigarettes did you smoke yesterday? (Record as stated) (Number SMOKED is asked for, irrespective of when or by whom they were bought)

....

....

....

Not applicable 9

For office use

Y	X	0	1
2	3	4	5
6	7	8	

Do you hold a ticket in your own name for the public library?

Yes	1
No	2
Don't know	3

Did you read any daily morning newspapers yesterday? Which ones? (If interview is on Monday, ask of previous Saturday)

RING EVERY PAPER MENTIONED

None	Y
Don't know	X
Daily Mirror	0
Daily Graphic (Sketch)	1
Daily Express	2
Daily Mail	3
Daily Herald	4
News Chronicle	5
Daily Telegraph	6
Manchester Guardian	7
The Times	8
Daily Worker	9
Birmingham Gazette	91
Birmingham Post	92
Western Daily Press and Bristol Mirror	93
Scotsman	94
Glasgow Herald	95
Others (list below)	96

....

....

13 Did you read any Sunday newspapers last Sunday? Which ones?

RING EVERY PAPER MENTIONED

None	Y
Don't know	95
News of the World	X
The People	0
Sunday Express	1
Sunday Graphic	2
Sunday Pictorial	3
Sunday Chronicle	4
Sunday Dispatch	5
Reynold's News	6
Empire News	7
The Observer	8
Sunday Times	9
Birmingham Sunday Mercury	91
Sunday Mail	92
Sunday Post	93
Others (list below)	94

....

....

14 Now I would like to ask you a few details about yourself and your household. Are you married?

("Divorced and married but living apart" should be coded "3")

Married	1
Single	2
Widowed and other	3

15 Where are you living? Would you show me on this card which applies to you? (Please call by number)

At home	1
As a lodger or boarder with a family	2
In a hotel/hostel/boarding house/ hospital/institution	3
Elsewhere (give details below)	4

....

....

16 (a) If AT HOME: What kind of house is it? Would you show me on this card which applies to you? (Please call by number)

Whole detached house	5
Whole semi-detached house	6
Whole terrace house	7
Self-contained flat	8
Other (give details below)	9
Not applicable	Y

....

....

(b) **If whole house (5, 6, 7) to Q.16(a):** Do you rent your house, or is it your own?

Rented	1
Own	2
Other (give details below)	3
Not applicable	4

....

....

....

17 Now will you tell me who are the people living in your household?
Fill in first line for informant, whose age should be obtained. Other ages are only required if under 21.

Relationship to Informant	Sex		Age
1. ......INFORMANT	M	F	......
2.	M	F	......
3.	M	F	......
4.	M	F	......
5.	M	F	......
6.	M	F	......
7.	M	F	......
8.	M	F	......
9.	M	F	......
10.	M	F	......
11.	M	F	......
12.	M	F	......

No. in Household aged:

0–4	...	...	...	....
5–15	...	...	...	....
16–20	...	...	...	....
21 and over	...	...		....
TOTAL	...	...		

18 Have any of you a motor car?

Yes 1
No 2
Don't know 3

19 Do you have a television set yet?

Yes 1
No 2

20 (a) Have you a telephone?

Yes 1
No 2

(b) **If YES:** Is it in the directory under your (family) name?

Yes ....
No ....
Don't know .
Not applicable

21 At what age did you finally stop rece[iving] full-time education?

11 or under ....
12 ....
13 ....
14 ....
15 ....
16 ....
17 ....
18 ....
19 ....
20 or over ....
Don't know ....
Not yet finished ....

22 Now, one final question. Do you [mind] telling me from this card which income g[roup] **your own** income last week fell into?

(a) **If informant is working, add:** I mean, [before] deducting income tax and National [In]surance, but including overtime [and] bonuses.

(b) **If informant is not working, add:** I m[ean] income of your own.
(Housewives' housekeeping money should be included)

G

None ....
Up to £3 ....
Over £3, up to £5 ....
Over £5, up to £7 10s. ....
Over £7 10s. up to £10 ....
Over £10, up to £20 ....
Over £20 ....
Don't know ....
Refused ....

Name of Informant ....

....

Address of Informant ....

....

....

Interviewer's No. ..../ ..../ ..../ ...

RING DATE OF INTERVIEW

	Sun.	Mon.	Tues.	Wed.	Thur.	Fri.
APRIL	—	28	29	30	—	—
MAY	—	—	—	—	1	2
	4	5	6	7	8	9
	11	12	13	14	15	16
	18	19	20	21	22	23
	25	26	27	28	29	30
JUNE	1	2	3	4	5	6

the cinema last night?'), and knowledge questions ('What do the initials N.A.T.O. stand for?'), but the main points of methodology will emerge if we consider factual and opinion questions.

One major difference between them is the amount of latitude generally given to the interviewer to probe, explain, vary the wording and so on. With factual questions (whether the facts relate to the respondent, to people he knows or to events) interviewers—for instance in the Government Social Survey—are allowed to take any reasonable steps to ensure that respondents have correctly interpreted the questions and that they, the interviewers, have correctly understood the answers.[1] With opinion questions, such latitude would be too risky and so is not permitted. It is well recognized that changes in wording, sequence and even emphasis may materially affect the answers.

Leaving aside public opinion polls, the majority of questions asked in surveys are probably concerned with facts. In saying this the word 'fact' is being used in a wide sense. We would call the question 'How much did you spend on beer last week?' factual, although the answers given by many would be a mixture of fact, wishful thinking, vague recollection, and a desire to give the answer the interviewer is believed to be looking for. But that is irrelevant here. The adjective 'factual' refers to the type of information the question seeks, not to the accuracy with which it is given; so to describe a question as 'factual' does *not* imply that the answers given are necessarily accurate.

Many examples of factual questions are contained in the questionnaire on pp. 312–14, for instance those on the respondent's method of travelling to work, the composition of his family, occupation, income; on his living conditions, possessions and leisure pursuits.

Some of these are so-called 'classification' questions, asked chiefly to provide information by which the main groups of respondents can be distinguished in the analysis. Questions 14 (marital status) and 17 (household composition), amongst others, are of this type. Classification questions require careful definitions, and these may be given in separate instructions or, in the case of a permanent organization, the Interviewers' Manual. The Government Social Survey's *A Handbook for Interviewers* by Atkinson (1967), for instance, contains a chapter on 'Classification standard definitions', in which definitions of twelve commonly collected items of background information are laid down.

Classification questions are usually left to the end of the interview so as to avoid crowding the opening minutes with personal questions. An important exception occurs in quota sampling. At the beginning

[1] This is not a general rule. Some organizations allow no more latitude for factual questions than for others, believing that the facts hinge so much on precise definition that this would be too risky.

of an interviewer's assignment, virtually every person approached fits into the sample, but towards the end it becomes increasingly difficult to find people to fit the quota group. Many who are approached have to be rejected, and it would be wasteful (and a temptation to mis-classify) to go right through the interview only to find at the end that the informant does not belong to the required age group or social class. Accordingly, the classification questions relevant to quotas are usually asked at the beginning.

Wherever the questions are placed, they need a special introduction. After all, a respondent who agrees to answer questions about his leisure pursuits or to give his opinions about television may legitimately wonder why he should supply details about his family, his age, his education, his occupation and even his income. In the questionnaire on p. 313, question 14, which opens this group, acknowledges that the content of the questions is shifting and leaves it at that.

With regard to classification questions Government Social Survey interviewers are told:

> Explain purpose of classification questions in simple words to the informant. Tell him of our need to relate given views or facts on the subject matter of the survey to the kinds of people who have been interviewed. Names do not help us on this, we do not use names in our report. It is sensible for us to take into account the ages, sizes of family and like factors which describe to us the person who has been interviewed. (Atkinson, 1967, p. 139).

Classification questions also of course need an introduction in mail questionnaires. An example of such an introduction is given by the first two sentences of question 6 in the radio and television enquiry questionnaire reproduced on p. 307.

The chief difficulties with factual questions are to ensure that interviewers understand, and manage to convey to the respondents, precisely what facts are wanted. Some of the definitions may be tricky but, in most cases, the chances of either interviewer or respondent misunderstanding the question, not understanding it at all, or the latter being influenced in his answer by the words chosen are much slighter than with opinion questions.

Opinion questions

With these the problems are much more fundamental. Though we would not venture into the psychologist's territory and discuss concepts of opinion and attitude in any detail, some attempt must be made to analyse why the study of opinions is basically so much more troublesome than that of facts. Why would one be more confident with a question asking a respondent whether he owns a wrist-watch than with one asking whether he is in favour of capital punishment? There are several related reasons:

(*a*) A respondent either does or does not possess a watch, and one may reasonably assume that he knows whether he does or not. All the surveyor has to do is to make clear to the respondent what he wants to know, and to be sure he understands the respondent's answer. It may be that the respondent wishes not to give the correct answer, but at least he knows what it is. With the opinion question it is not so simple. The respondent's attitude to capital punishment may be largely latent, and he may never have given the matter any conscious thought until he was confronted by the question. The first problem with opinion questions thus arises from the uncertainty whether the respondent, in any meaningful sense, 'knows' the correct answers. To say whether he possesses a watch or not needs no 'thinking' on the respondent's part; to give a genuine opinion on capital punishment may require thought and 'self-analysis'.

(*b*) A person's opinion on virtually any issue is many-sided. On capital punishment there are moral, medical, legal and other aspects; it is possible to be against it on moral grounds, in favour on legal ones. A person may be against it in all but certain circumstances, or against it whatever the situation. He may be in favour of abolishing it experimentally, or as an irrevocable step whatever the consequences. In short, there probably is *no one correct answer* to the survey question as there is to that on watch ownership. The answer the respondent actually gives will depend on the aspect of the issue that is uppermost in his mind—quite possibly because the wording of the question, or the context created by previous ones, has put it there.

(*c*) Closely related to this is the problem of intensity. On any given subject some people feel strongly, some are indifferent, some have settled and consistent views, others are highly changeable in their attitude. In any attempt to get more than snap answers, the problem of assessing the intensity of opinion and attitude must be faced.

(*d*) Finally, it must be repeated that answers to opinion questions are more sensitive to changes in wording, emphasis, sequence and so on than are those to factual questions. The pages of the *Public Opinion Quarterly* and other journals are full of evidence on this point, and the reader can also refer to Cantril (1944) and Mosteller and others (1949) for examples. This established sensitivity of opinion questions does not imply instability of opinion among respondents. Rather it is a reflection of the point made in (*b*) above. Opinion is many-sided, and questions asked in different ways will seem to 'get at' different aspects of the opinion: if they result in different answers, it is largely because respondents are in effect answering different questions.

There is a secondary difficulty here. With factual questions, it is often feasible to compare the merits of different forms of the same question by checking the answers against known data. With opinion questions this is impossible, although checks on validity can and should be made; where, for instance, opinions are closely related to measurable behaviour, a check on behaviour can be used to test the validity of an expressed opinion (see Chapter 14).

In the face of these problems, two quite distinct approaches are used in opinion and attitude enquiries. One, the most common in opinion polls, attempts simply to estimate what proportion of the survey population say they agree with a given opinion statement; the second goes further by including a number of opinion statements, and assessing the respondents' answers to the set of questions as a whole. In the terminology of the survey literature, this is the distinction between asking for opinions and measuring attitudes.

The Gallup Poll questionnaire (pp. 332-9) has many examples of opinion questions; for instance questions 18 to 28 ask for opinions on many issues concerned with Britain joining the Common Market. Question 30(b), asking how the respondent thinks the Financial Times Index of ordinary share prices will have changed in six months' time, is another example. To this question the respondents can reply 'Higher', 'Lower', 'Same' or 'Don't know', but no attempt is made to measure the strength of their opinions or to ascertain what had led them to their answers; and the only indication of the extent to which they have thought about the issue comes from their answers to question 30(a). In this type of case the pollster simply wants a snap answer to a snap question to enable him to count the number who react in a given way to that particular stimulus.

The second approach attempts to *measure* the respondent's attitude, which typically means combining the answers to a set of opinion questions into some sort of score. This is the method of attitude scaling, discussed in Chapter 14.

13.3. Question wording

The literature on the wording of questions is bewildering. Numerous papers have appeared showing the relative advantages of various specific questions, the danger of using a certain word or phrase, the sensitivity of answers to changes in wording and presentation; but it is exceedingly difficult to build out of them any general principles. We shall confine ourselves to some aspects of wording which are of general importance in social research surveys.

(a) *Questions that are insufficiently specific.* A common error is to ask a general question when an answer on a specific issue is wanted.

If one is interested specifically in a canteen's meal prices and the quality of its service, the question 'Are you satisfied or dissatisfied with your canteen?' is unsatisfactory, since it fails to provide the respondent with the necessary frames of reference. As there are two distinct frames of reference of interest here, two questions are needed, perhaps 'Are you satisfied or dissatisfied with the prices of meals in your canteen?' and 'Are you satisfied or dissatisfied with the service in your canteen?' Although these two questions now cover the topics required in a seemingly straightforward way, they still need to be pre-tested to check on their suitability for the particular situation. It may, for instance, be the case that the canteen serves special meals once a week at a higher cost and that, although generally satisfied with the canteen's prices, a respondent objects to the cost of the special meals; or he may be dissatisfied only with one particular aspect of the service. In cases like these he would have difficulty answering the questions. Such problems are brought to light by pre-testing and pilot work, the importance of which for question wording cannot be overrated.

In the above example the general question was faulted because it failed to specify the required frames of reference; but there are occasions when no required frame of reference is wanted, and then a general question may be appropriate. However, even in this case, if the surveyor is to understand the answers properly he still needs to know the frames of reference chosen by the respondents; often this extra information can be discovered by asking the supplementary probe question 'Why?' after the general question.

Another way to make questions more specific is to frame them in terms of the respondent's personal experience rather than in general terms. An example comes from the penultimate chapter of Payne's (1951) book, in which he applied the principles outlined in his previous chapters to the question: 'Which do you prefer—dichotomous or open questions?' In this form the question has obvious defects; so it does in the other thirty-nine forms that Payne discusses, and dismisses, in turn. Only the forty-first attempt finds his favour: 'Which questions did you like best—those stating two answers to decide between, those stating more than two answers, or those leaving the answers for you to state?'

This is essentially a different question from the first: respondents are now asked to state a preference between question types in the context of immediate experience rather than to give a general opinion. All the answers will now refer to specific, well-defined issues.

(b) *Simple language.* In choosing the language for a questionnaire the population being studied should be kept in mind. The aim in question wording is to communicate with respondents as nearly as possible in their own language. A survey of the members of a particular profession, for instance, can usefully employ the profession's common technical terms; not only are such terms part of the informants' common language, but they also normally have a single precise meaning, unlike everyday terms, which particularly to professionals are often vague and ambiguous.

Technical terms and jargon are, however, obviously to be avoided in surveys of the general population. The hypothetical question quoted above included the word 'dichotomous', and such a word would not of course be used in practice. The use of the common word 'open' would equally have to be avoided, for its use in this technical sense is quite unfamiliar to the lay public. And obviously we would not ask a respondent whether his household is run on matriarchal lines, what he thinks about bilateral trading, amortization of the National Debt, and fiscal policy.

Much less easy to recognize and reject are words which, though everyday usage to the university-trained survey expert, are far from common in ordinary conversation. Words like hypothetical, irrespective, aggravate, deprecate, and hundreds more are in this category.

Question designers try to put themselves in the position of their typical, or rather their least educated, respondents, but they are not always the best judges of the simplicity and clarity of their own questions. The reactions of typical respondents—not only of their professional colleagues—should be sought (informally and in pretests) to ensure that the questions are comprehensible. Payne (1951) names a large number of words which analysis of American magazines has *shown* to be in common usage by writers; this does not necessarily mean that they are suitable for survey questions, but at least they are known to be much used. Gowers (1954) mentions many words which can often be replaced by simpler alternatives. The following are a few from his list:

Acquaint	Inform or tell
Assist	Help
Consider	Think
Initiate	Begin; start
Major	Important; chief; main; principal
Purchase	Buy
Require	Want; need
Reside	Live
State	Say
Sufficient	Enough
Terminate	End

With surveys of the general population, the first principles in wording are that questions should use the simplest words that will convey the exact meaning, and that the phrasing also should be as simple and informal as possible. It is more natural to ask: 'Do you think ...?' than: 'Is it your opinion ...?'; 'What is your attitude to ...?' than: 'What is your attitude with regard to ...?' In fact the more questions sound like ordinary conversation the smoother the interview will be. Of course, this should not be overdone. Bad grammar may be more common than good, but one would not advocate its deliberate use in survey questions. Nor are slang expressions advisable; as with technical jargon, not everyone uses the same expressions. It is not indeed enough to know that a word or phrase is commonly used; one must equally be sure that it is used in the same sense by all groups of respondents. Even words like 'dinner' and 'tea' have different meanings in different parts of the country. A simple case is the word 'book', which in some parts of the population is taken to include magazines. Hence the phrasing of the following question in a readership survey by Stuart (1952): 'During the past week roughly how many hours would you say you had spent reading *books*—I mean books not magazines or papers?'

Clarity can be still further ensured by remembering that a simple question is more readily understood than a long complex one. Payne (1951) has suggested that the more complex a question is, the more 'sensitive' to wording will it tend to be.

An instance of a question which is too complex for comfort occurred in the enquiry into Family Limitation conducted for the Royal Commission on Population and reported by Lewis-Faning (1949): 'Has it happened to you that over a long period of time, when you neither practised abstinence, nor used birth control, you did not conceive? YES/NO.' This question is vague (what is 'a long period?'), too formal ('Has it happened to you ...?') and complex, because of its length and double negative.

There is a temptation to ask complex questions when the subject matter is inherently complicated, involving a variety of different facets. This, for example, would be the case in a housing survey in which one wanted to discover how many households comprised three-generation families, that is grandparents, parents and children. Once the term 'three-generation family' has been precisely defined (how about widowed grandparents, unmarried mothers, divorced or separated parents?), one might with ingenuity design a single question to obtain the information, but many respondents would certainly fail to understand it. Rather than rely on a single complex question, a series of simple questions should be asked, the number of such questions depending on the degree of simplicity required.

Household composition is generally a complex subject and one for which several descriptive indices are required; the information is usually best obtained by using a 'household box' on the questionnaire in which the household members are listed together with their relevant characteristics, e.g. age, sex, marital status, working status and educational level (see question 17 on p. 314 for a simple example, and the Household Schedule of the Family Expenditure Survey— Kemsley, 1969—for a more detailed one). From these basic data the surveyor can determine for himself all the indices he requires for his analysis.

Another example of a complex subject is income, which is extremely difficult to determine accurately. Among the many aspects to be considered are: income before or after tax; income from subsidiary employment; state benefits; deduction for superannuation, etc.; expenses; and income from investments. The reader is referred to the Income Schedule of the Family Expenditure Survey to see the number of questions needed to measure income accurately (Kemsley, 1969).

Complex questions are typically long and complexity is certainly to be avoided; but this does not mean that the shortest questions are necessarily the best. There is some evidence indicating that the longer the interviewer speaks, the more the respondent will say in reply. An experiment on increasing the length of some questions in a health questionnaire is reported by Marquis (1969). The longer questions were formed from the short ones by adding superfluous remarks; in going through a list of symptoms, for example, the short version of one question was: 'Bad sore throats?' and the longer one was: 'Now a question about bad sore throats. We're looking for information about these. Have you had bad sore throats?' In checking on chronic conditions reported in answer to such questions with information obtained from the respondents' physicians, the replies to the longer versions were found to agree more closely with the physicians' reports, thus suggesting that they had greater validity.[1]

(c) *Ambiguity.* Ambiguous questions are to be avoided at all costs. If an ambiguous word creeps in, different people will understand the question differently and will in effect be answering different questions. The following example is taken from a university research survey:

---

[1] This experiment was a factorial one and is described in Section 9.6. As noted there, another part of the experiment examined the effect of interviewer 're-inforcement', by which the interviewer encouraged the respondent reporting a chronic condition or symptom with a remark such as 'That's the kind of information we need'. Reinforcement was also found to reduce the mismatches with the physicians' reports; but, strangely, the combination of longer questions and reinforcement did not lower the mismatch rate, the effects of the two techniques apparently partially cancelling each other out.

'Is your work made more difficult because you are expecting a baby?'
The question was asked of all women in the survey, irrespective of
whether they were expecting a baby or not. What, then, did a 'No'
answer mean? Depending on the respondent, it might have meant
'No, I'm not expecting a baby' or 'No, my work is not made more
difficult by the fact that I'm expecting a baby'.

Ambiguity also arises with double barrelled questions, such as the
following question on public transport: 'Do you like travelling on
trains and buses?' Respondents liking one and disliking the other
would be in a dilemma in answering this question. Clearly it needs
to be divided into two questions, each concerned with a single idea,
in this case with a single mode of transport.

(*d*) *Vague words*. Vague questions encourage vague answers. If
people are asked whether they go to the cinema regularly or occasionally, the meaning of their answers will be vague. (This common
choice of alternatives is strictly illogical; the word 'occasional' refers
to frequency, the word 'regular' does not. However, this may be a
case where logic can give way to common usage.) The meaning can
easily be made more precise, as in the following question from the
1968 National Readership Survey: 'How often these days do you go
to the cinema? Would it be nearer to—twice a week or more often;
once a week; once a fortnight; once a month; three or four times a
year; less often; or do you never go these days?'

Vague words and phrases like 'kind of', 'fairly', 'generally',
'often', 'many', 'much the same', 'on the whole' should be avoided,
unless one is only seeking vague answers. If one asks 'What kind of
house do you have?' without specifying a frame of reference, some
people will answer that it is semi-detached, others that it is suburban,
others that it is very pleasant, and so on.

A similar type of vagueness occurs in 'Why' questions. In answering the question: 'Why did you go to the cinema last night?' some
respondents will say that they wanted to see that particular film,
some that they did not want to stay at home, others that 'the wife
suggested it', or that they hadn't been since last week. The word 'Why'
in this question—as the phrase 'kind of' in the previous one—can
mean so many different things that its use would produce a useless
mixture of answers.[1] Lazarsfeld (1935) discusses the problems of the
'Why' question.

(*e*) *Leading questions*. A leading question is one which, by its content,
structure or wording, leads the respondent in the direction of a
certain answer. The question form: 'You don't think ... do you?'

[1] There are exceptions to even this statement. The surveyor might want to see
what type of reason each respondent produces when asked this question, what
factors are uppermost in his mind.

as obviously leads to a negative answer as the form: 'Should not something be done about . . .?' leads to a positive one.

Equally, a question which suggests only some of the possible answers may lead in their direction. Take the question: 'Do you read any weekly newspapers, such as the *New Statesman* or *Punch*?' Respondents, especially if they are not sure of their correct or complete reply, may seek refuge in the answers named; either all or none of the alternatives should be stated.

There are numerous words that have been shown on occasion to have a 'leading' influence in survey questions (see Payne, 1951, and Cantril, 1944). The word 'involved' in a question like: 'Do you think that the Government should get involved in . . .?' may have a sufficiently sinister ring to lead people in the negative direction. Similarly, the wording: 'Do you agree that the Government is right in staying out of . . .?' invites a 'Yes' answer. The 'leading' nature of these examples is obvious, but more subtle leads can often creep unnoticed into survey questions.

In addition to 'leading words', there is the risk that the general context of a question, the content of those preceding it and the tone of the whole questionnaire or interview can lead the respondent in a given direction. An interesting argument related to this was provoked by an article by Kornhauser (1946–47) entitled 'Are Polls Fair to Organised Labor?'

An example nearer home was the 1954 ballot on attitudes to the (Football) Pool Betting Bill.[1] As a result of a debate in Parliament, the Pools Promoters' Association conducted a ballot among their clients. A statement by the Association arguing against the Bill was circulated with the football pool coupons in a certain week and each client was asked to vote for one of the following alternatives by placing a cross against it:

(1) 'I agree with what you say in the statement which you sent me and I am against the Bill.'

(2) 'In spite of what you say in the statement which you sent me I support the Bill.'

As many as 75 per cent of the votes were cast for (1), 7 per cent for (2), and 18 per cent of the clients did not vote. At the same time the Gallup Poll asked a sample of the population: 'At present football pool promoters do not have to publish accounts. A Bill is being introduced to make it compulsory for them to show each week where the money goes. Do you think that this is a good or bad thing?' Of the sample, 63 per cent said it was a good thing, 15 per cent that it was a bad thing, and 22 per cent expressed no opinion. Of those in the sample who filled in coupons, 66 per cent said it was a good thing.

[1] Reported in *The Times*, 8th March, 1954.

That the two surveys produced such contradictory results must in part be attributed to the fact that the Pools Promoters' questions were printed on the weekly football coupon and were in no way secret or anonymous; for this reason alone, it is difficult to accept the results at face value. But this point apart, the differences between the two surveys in the context and wording of the questions could account for some of the differences in results. The alternatives proffered by the Pools Promoters were preceded by a detailed and somewhat complicated statement on football pool finance, which stressed how the cost of complying with the Bill's requirements would affect the amount of money available for dividends. Finally, the phrase 'in spite of' in the second alternative suggests that this would be a rather irrational view. The Gallup question was set in a more neutral context, but here the phrase 'to show each week where the money goes' might be thought to carry a slight implication that this is a clear and obvious duty for a Pools Promoter.

There were, in this instance, several complicating features, and the difference in results cannot with certainty be attributed to the question forms. Yet the example is instructive in that it shows how differently the same issue can be presented. Some issues are so clear and well-understood that such differences would hardly affect results. But when an issue is complex and many-sided, when its implications are not widely or easily understood, then one must expect answers to be sensitive to the way it is presented.

(*f*) *Presuming questions.* Questions should not, generally speaking, presume anything about the respondent. They should not imply that he necessarily possesses any knowledge or an opinion on the survey subject, or that he engages in the activity about which he is being asked. Questions like: 'How many cigarettes a day do you smoke?' or 'How did you vote in the last General Election?' are best asked only after a 'filter' question has revealed that the respondent does smoke cigarettes and did vote in the last election.

On occasion, however, one might deliberately depart from this procedure. Kinsey and others (1948) did not first ask respondents *whether* they had engaged in certain sexual practices, but went straight into questions about frequency and detail. Respondents were thus spared the embarrassment of admitting the experiences directly and were made to feel that these represented perfectly usual behaviour: thus they found themselves able to talk freely and give detailed answers. The case for such an approach is obvious, but one cannot ignore the possibility that it may discourage 'I never do' answers and thus cause an upward bias in the results.

(*g*) *Hypothetical questions.* Questions of the 'Would you like to live in a flat?' type are of very limited value. Most people would like to try anything once, and an affirmative answer would have little value as a prediction of behaviour. It is another matter if one has first made sure that the person has experience of both flat and house dwelling. Equally, answers to the 'What would you do if . . .?' kind of question, although perhaps a good reflection of wishful thinking or of what people feel to be right and proper, are unsafe pointers to future behaviour.

Yet prediction of future behaviour on the basis of survey questions plays, and must be expected to play, a central role in survey applications. Market researchers would like—and try—to predict how people will react to a proposed change in the price of a product, to an alteration to its quality or packaging; how many people are likely to buy cars, radios or television sets in a given period, and so on.[1] They may rely on straight questions (a Gallup Poll question in 1950 was: 'Supposing the price of (a certain newspaper) went up from 1d. to 1½d. would you change over to another paper where the price hadn't gone up?') but the answers are recognized to be imperfect guides to future behaviour. People are not good at predicting their behaviour in a hypothetical situation and the prediction has somehow to be taken out of their hands and made by the researcher himself— naturally on the basis of the information he has obtained.

Another kind of hypothetical question is 'Would you like a more frequent bus service?' or 'Would you like an increase in wages?' Such questions are unlikely to be of any value because the respondent is being asked if he would like something for nothing. It is hard to see how he could possibly say 'No'. If he did, it could only be because he has taken into account some hidden factors of his own, or because he has failed to understand the question.

(h) *Personalized questions.* It is often necessary to decide whether a question should be asked in a personalized form or not. This is well illustrated by the following questions which appeared, one after the other, in a schedule dealing with health matters (see David, 1952): 'Do you think it is a good idea to have everyone's chest regularly checked by X-ray?' and 'Have you ever had yours checked?' Some 96 per cent of the respondents answered 'Yes' to the first question, but only 54 per cent to the second. As the author suggested, the opinion given in answer to the first question 'is more a pious hope for some vague corporate decision than a considered aim involving personal action'.

---

[1] There is a sizeable literature on obtaining consumer buying intentions from surveys. Three recent articles on this subject in the *Journal of the American Statistical Association* are those of Mueller (1963), Friend and Adams (1964), and Juster (1966).

(*i*) *Embarrassing questions*. Subjects which people do not like to discuss in public present a problem to the questionnaire designer. Respondents are often embarrassed to discuss private matters, to give low-prestige answers, and to admit to socially unacceptable behaviour and attitudes. If, for instance, questions on sexual behaviour, frequency of taking a bath, cheating in examinations or attitudes to Communism were asked in the usual way, many respondents would probably refuse to reply and others would distort their answers.[1] There are several ways of attempting to deal with this problem.

One method of reducing the threatening nature of a question is to express it in the third person; instead of asking the respondent for his views, he is asked about the views of others. An example from market research of an indirect question of this sort is given by Smith (1954): 'Some women who use this cleanser find a lot of faults with it. I wonder if you can guess what they are objecting to'.[2] The purpose of this wording was to make the housewives feel free to criticize the product. The aim of such questions is to obtain the respondent's own views, but he may of course answer the question asked, and give what he believes to be the views of others. For this reason it is often advisable to follow the indirect question by a direct one asking the respondent whether he holds the views he has described.

There are several other indirect methods which can be useful in dealing with embarrassing topics. The respondent can for instance be shown a drawing of two persons in a certain setting, with 'balloons' containing speech coming from their mouths, as in comic strips and cartoons. One person's balloon is left empty and the respondent is asked to put himself in the position of that person and to fill in the missing words. Another method is that of sentence completion; the respondent is given the start of a sentence and is asked to complete it, usually under time pressure to ensure spontaneity. Oppenheim (1966) describes the use of the following two examples of sentence completion in a study among psychiatric nurses in a mental hospital:

'I wish that doctors . . .'
'Patients who are incontinent . . .'

The different ways in which a group of student nurses and a group of nurses with twelve or more years of experience completed these

---

[1] Perhaps this risk can be overstated. On sexual behaviour, for example, the studies of Kinsey and others (1948, 1953), Schofield (1965a, 1965b), and others have been impressive.
[2] Quoted by Selltiz and others (1959).

sentences showed the difference of attitude and approach of the two groups. For a discussion of other projective techniques the reader is referred to the chapters on this subject in Oppenheim (1966) and Selltiz and others (1959).

Belson (1968a) describes a study of a randomly derived sample of London teenage boys on the sensitive subject of stealing. A variety of procedures were employed in this study to make it easier for the boys to admit that they had stolen things. On arrival at the interviewing centre a boy chose a false name and, in order to preserve his anonymity, he was introduced under his false name to the interviewer, who knew him only by that name. After an extended initial phase, the interview proceeded to the card-sorting technique by which the information on stealing was to be obtained. The interviewer and the boy sat on either side of a table, with a screen in between so that they could not see each other. Through a slot in the screen the interviewer passed to the boy a card on which one type of stealing (e.g. 'I have stolen cigarettes') was recorded. The boy was asked to put the card in a box labelled 'Yes' if he had ever done what was recorded on it, and in a box labelled 'Never' if not. This was repeated for 44 kinds of theft. At the end of this sorting stage, the interviewer went through a procedure which tried to reduce the force of a boy's resistances, and to strengthen his feeling of willingness, to admitting thefts. Then the boy was asked to re-sort all the cards he had put in the 'Never' box. Finally he was asked for further details on each type of theft he had admitted. This detailed procedure elicited reports of many types of theft from many boys with, for example, 69 per cent of boys admitting 'I have stolen something from a shop' and 58 per cent 'I have stolen money' at least once in their lives.

Finally we should mention an ingenious recent development known as the randomized response technique. This was proposed by Warner (1965) and has been further developed by Abul-Ela and others (1967) and Greenberg and others (1969b). The basic idea of the technique is that the respondent chooses to answer one of two (or more, but we will restrict the discussion to two) statements, one of which is the sensitive statement under study. The choice is made by means of a random device provided by the surveyor, who therefore knows the probability of selection for each statement. The respondent employs the random device to choose one of the statements, and then answers 'Yes' or 'No' to the selected statement, without disclosing to the interviewer which statement he is answering. By this means the respondent maintains his privacy and this, it is hoped, leads him to give a truthful answer.

To see how the procedure works, let us look at the equation relating the proportion of respondents answering 'Yes' to whichever statement they have chosen, λ, to the proportion answering 'Yes' to the sensitive statement, π_1, and the proportion answering 'Yes' to the other statement, π_2. The equation is

$$\lambda = P\pi_1 + (1-P)\pi_2 \qquad\qquad ...(13.1)$$

where P is the probability that the sensitive statement is chosen by the random device, and hence $(1-P)$ is the probability that the other statement is chosen. The surveyor observes the value of λ for the sample and determines P by the way he forms the random device, but there still remain two unknowns (π_1 and π_2) in the equation so that it cannot be solved as it stands; another equation is needed. Warner obtained the additional equation by choosing two related statements of the form 'I have A' and 'I do not have A' where A is the sensitive factor; the additional equation is then $\pi_1 + \pi_2 = 1$, since one, and only one, of the statements must be true. Greenberg and others (1969b) extended the theory to unrelated questions, for which two situations can be distinguished: the first is where the proportion answering 'Yes' to the other statement, π_2, is known or can be estimated from external sources; the second is when π_2 needs to be estimated from the survey. The solution in the first case is straightforward, the known value of π_2 being substituted in (13.1); the second can be solved by dividing the survey into two samples, employing different random devices giving different values of P for the two samples.

Greenberg and others (1969a) describe an application of the randomized response technique in a survey of women aged 18–44 in North Carolina, designed to estimate abortion rates and the use of oral contraceptives. The two statements for the abortion enquiry were:

'1. I was pregnant at some time during the past 12 months and had an abortion which terminated the pregnancy.
2. I was born in the month of April.'

In this case the proportion answering 'Yes' to the second statement could be estimated from external data, from the distribution of months of births for live births in North Carolina between 1924 and 1950; the estimate so obtained was $\pi_2 = 0.0826$. The random device by which the respondent chose which question to answer was a box containing 35 red and 15 blue balls. She tipped the box to allow one of the balls to appear in a window; if a red ball appeared she answered the abortion question; if a blue ball, the other question. The probability of a respondent answering the abortion question was thus $P = 35/50 = 0.7$, and of the other question $(1-P) = 15/50 = 0.3$. The values of π_2, P and $(1-P)$ can be substituted in equation (13.1) to give

$$\lambda = 0.7\pi_1 + (0.3 \times 0.0826)$$

from which, knowing λ from the sample, π_1 is easily calculated. In this case the value of π_1 was 0·0342, or 3·42 per cent of women having an abortion in the last year.

A price to be paid for the randomized response technique is that the sampling error of the estimate of π_1 is increased through the use of the random device. The approach is a sophisticated one and it may prove difficult to convince respondents that it is not a trick; Greenberg and others (1969a) report, however, that most of their respondents said they were satisfied that it was legitimate and did protect their privacy. There is also the danger that respondents may cheat by answering the inoffensive statement when they have selected the sensitive one. They may argue that, if the interviewer really cannot tell which statement they are responding to, their cheating cannot be detected; on the other hand, if the interviewer can tell, they do not want to respond to the sensitive statement. More research is needed on the applications of the technique before its usefulness can be firmly established.

(*j*) *Questions on periodical behaviour.* An interesting choice arises in studying the frequency of periodical behaviour. The main choice of questions can be illustrated with reference to cinema-going:

   (i) 'How often have you been to the cinema during the last fortnight (or any other period chosen)?'
   (ii) 'How often do you go to the cinema on the average?'
   (iii) 'When did you last go to the cinema?'

The first question covers a number of different possibilities corresponding to the period chosen, and answers will depend on the type of activity and on the extent to which one is willing to rely on the respondent's memory (see (*k*) below). In any case, the three question types might produce different results, and there is little evidence on which to choose between them. At first sight, (i) seems to be most specific, but many people's answers might simply be an estimate of their average cinema-going rather than the actual figure; i.e. if they normally go twice a fortnight, they may give this as an answer, although they went only once in the last fortnight. As a case in point, Belson (1964a) reports that an intensive interview follow-up enquiry of respondents to the National Readership Survey suggested that people frequently answered in terms of what publications they *usually* looked at, rather than what they had *actually* looked at, which was what was required. Of course the two answers will often be the same, and it is only when a difference arises that an answer in the wrong terms produces error.

Many survey questions involve this type of choice, e.g. questions on newspaper reading, radio listening, television watching, and consumer purchases. It is a matter deserving further research.

(k) *Questions involving memory.* Most factual questions to some extent involve the respondent in recalling information. His degree of success in doing this accurately is thus a basic determinant of the quality of his response. With certain questions, such as 'Are you married, single or widowed?', there is no such problem, but with a large range of survey questions recalling information does present a problem, the severity of which depends on what is to be recalled. Two factors of primary importance in memory are the length of time since the event took place and the event's importance to the respondent; events the respondent considers insignificant are likely to be forgotten almost immediately and even the recollection of significant events decreases as time elapses. Moreover, for events not forgotten in their entirety, memory acts selectively, retaining some aspects and losing others, thus producing distorted images. For questions dealing with the past, serious attention must therefore be given to the respondents' abilities to recall the required information accurately, and to ways by which they can be helped to do so.

As an example of a memory problem, let us see how we might collect reasonably accurate information from housewives on when their present washing machines were purchased, a type of information often difficult to recollect. One approach would be to try to avoid reliance on memory by asking the housewives to consult records if they have them, perhaps a cheque-book stub for the date the payment cheque was made out, a hire-purchase agreement, a receipt, or a guarantee certificate. Failing this, a housewife might be helped in placing the event by questions designed to provide a contextual framework, such as 'Was it before or after your holidays?', 'Was it before or after Christmas?', or 'Was it before or after the children returned to school?' In the stress of the interview situation, the respondent may be unable to recall the information without such assistance.

Another memory problem arises with questions asking respondents to provide a list, as would be the case for instance if they were asked which television programmes they had viewed yesterday, or which newspapers they had read or looked at in the preceding seven days; without help many respondents would be unable to give a complete list. A sensible way to aid recall in this case is to provide the respondent with a list of all television programmes transmitted yesterday (or a list of all newspapers), from which he can pick out the ones he had seen (or read, or looked at). In the National Readership Surveys, for example, respondents are asked about their readership of each

This form is the property of:

© SOCIAL SURVEYS (GALLUP POLL) LIMITED 1969
211 Regent Street, London, W.1.

THE GALLUP POLL
CQ 658 November 1969

Private and Confidential

| 11/12 | Interviewer's No. | Contact No. |

Ask the questions exactly as they are worded. DO NOT READ OUT THE ANSWERS unless indicated.

13 Thinking back over the last 7 days have you discussed with members of your family or friends, or thought about, any of these things? (Show CARD X and mark all mentioned.)

1	2	3	4	5	6	7	8	9
10	20	30	40	50	60	70	80	90
100	200	300	400					None of these
								–V

16a) If there were a General Election tomorrow, which party would you support?

1 Conservative
2 Labour
3 Liberal
4 Nationalist*
5 Other
–6 Don't know

b) *If don't know:* Which would you be most inclined to vote for?

7 Conservative
8 Labour
9 Liberal
0 Nationalist*
X Other
–V Don't know

*Welsh or Scottish

ASK ALL

17 Were you able to go and vote in the General Election in March, 1966 or were you prevented?

–1 No, did not vote

Yes, voted for:

2 Conservative
3 Labour
4 Liberal
5 Other

Ask all who voted: For which candidate did you vote?

20 How important would you say these difficulties are in the way of Britain joining the Common Market:

	Very Impor- tant	Impor- tant	Not very Impor- tant	Not at all Impor- tant	Don't know
a) The difficulties facing our agriculture if the Government subsidies have to be withdrawn?	1	2	3	4	R
b) The difficulties for the Commonwealth if Britain has to end the preference which she now gives to Commonwealth goods?	5	6	7	8	R
c) The difficulty of getting the Common Market to meet the problems of the other European countries now with Britain in the European Free Trade Area?	9	0	X	V	R

21 What do you think would be the advantages to Britain of joining the Common Market? Any other advantages or arguments *for* joining the Common Market? (Write in fully below and ring all appropriate codes)

18 Now that British membership of the Common Market or European Community is again in the news, here are some issues which will have to be settled between Britain and the members of the Common Market.

Taking each one separately, do you think it would be a good thing or a bad thing for Britain to agree to: (Read out and mark for each. For every other contact begin at (h) and work upwards.)

	Good	Bad	Don't know
a) Gradual removal of all trade barriers between members	1	2	3
b) The removal eventually of all subsidies and other protection to industries, like agriculture	4	5	6
c) Unemployment policies and social services to be brought more into line with each other	7	8	9
d) Inviting workers here from other member countries, to take up jobs which cannot be filled by our own labour	0	X	V
e) Adopting the principle of "equal pay for equal work" as between men and women	1	2	3
f) Pooling our resources to develop atomic energy for peaceful uses	4	5	6
g) Supporting a common tariff for customs barrier against all countries not in the Common Market	7	8	9
h) To have as the goal achieving closer political relationships	0	X	V

1 Keep down the cost of living, cheaper goods
2 British industries/agriculture will benefit/expand
3 Full employment will be maintained
4 Better wages/working conditions
5 Social/medical/educational services will improve
6 Good (in the long run) for the Commonwealth
7 Fewer travel restrictions in ECM countries
8 Wider range of goods in the shops
9 Closer *political* links with European countries
0 Closer *military* links with European countries
X Other advantages
V No advantages at all
R Don't know

22 And what would be the disadvantages of joining the Common Market? Any other disadvantages or arguments *against* joining the Common Market? (Write in fully below and ring all appropriate codes)

1 Cost of living, prices will go up
2 British industries/agriculture will suffer
3 Employment in Britain will be affected, labour imported from Europe
4 Cut in wages/working conditions
5 Increased competition for British industry
6 Social/medical/educational services will suffer
7 Commonwealth will be affected
8 Loss of political identity/sovereignty
9 Too close *political* links with European countries
0 Too close *military* links with European countries
X Other disadvantages
V No disadvantages at all
R Don't know

23 What do you think would be the effects on the general standard of living and economic well-being of people in this country—to raise the standard of living, lower it, or leave things as they are?

1 Raise
2 Lower
3 Leave
4 Don't know

24 What effect do you think joining the Common Market would have on the prices we pay in Britain for:

	Rise a lot	Rise a little	Stay same	Go down a little	Go down a lot	Don't know
a) Food?	1	2	3	4	5	—6
b) Other goods?	7	8	9	0	X	—V

25a) If Britain joined the Common Market, do you think she would become more favourably inclined, would she have to take a back seat to some other country, or do you see the Common Market as a group in which all countries are equal?

1 Britain the leader
2 All equal
Britain take back seat to:
3 France
4 Germany
5 Italy
X Other (write in)

_____

V Don't know

b) *If back seat:* To which country?

26a) Would you say you are becoming more favourably inclined towards the Common Market or less

1 More favourably inclined
2 Less favourably inclined
3 Same
4 Don't know

(Question 29 is not reproduced here : see over page.)

30a) Have you any stocks and shares quoted on the Stock Exchange or any unit trusts? (Mark all mentioned)

1 Stocks and Shares
2 Unit trusts
3 No, neither

b) In six months time, do you think that the Financial Times Index of ordinary share values will be higher than it is now, lower than it is now, or about the same as it is now?

4 Higher
5 Lower
6 Same
7 Don't know

c) In six months time, do you think that the yields from unit trusts will be higher than they are now, lower, or about the same as they are now?

8 Higher
9 Lower
0 Same
X Don't know

b) If Britain has to join with other countries in order that she may hold her place in the world, would you rather see her join with America, or with Europe?

5 With America
6 With Europe
7 Don't know

27a) As far as you, yourself and your family are concerned, do you think it will be a good thing or a bad thing if Britain joins the Common Market, or won't it make any difference to you one way or the other?

1 Good thing
2 Bad thing
3 No difference
4 Don't know

b) Do you approve or disapprove of the Government applying for membership of the Common Market?

5 Approve
6 Disapprove
7 Don't know

28 About how many years do you think it will be before Britain becomes a member of the Common Market, or will she never be invited to join it?

About _____ years

X Join but don't know when
V Never join
R Don't know if join or not

(Questions 31, 32 and 33 are not reproduced here: see over page.)

M

The third page of the questionnaire contained questions 39 to 56, all of which were confidential questions for private clients, and these questions are therefore not re-produced here. Questions 29, 31, 32 and 33 on the second page of the questionnaire were also of this type, and are similarly not reproduced. The full questionnaire thus contained twenty-two more questions than are shown here.

	Cine-camera	Camera	Cigarette lighter	Electric shaver	Watch
	1	2	3	4	5

57 Which of these things are you at all likely to buy during the next 12 months for your own use or as a present for somebody else?
Expect to buy

	Cine-camera	Camera	Cigarette lighter	Electric shaver	Watch
Expect to buy	1	2	3	4	5

For each mentioned

58 Will you buy it outright or by weekly or monthly payments?

	Cine-camera	Camera	Cigarette lighter	Electric shaver	Watch
Buy it outright	1	2	3	4	5
Weekly/monthly (H.P.)	6	7	8	9	0

59 About how much do you expect to pay in all for it?

Cine-camera	Camera	Cigarette lighter	Electric shaver	Watch
1 £15 or under	1 £2 or under	1 10s or under	1 £5 or under	1 £2 or under
2 £16–£20	2 £3–£5	2 11s–15s	2 £6	2 £3 or £4
3 £21–£25	3 £6–£10	3 16s–20s	3 £7	3 £5 or £6
4 £26–£30	4 £11–£15	4 21s–25s	4 £8	4 £7 or £8
5 £31–£35	5 £16–£20	5 26s–30s	5 £9	5 £9 or £10
6 £36–£40	6 £21–£30	6 31s–35s	6 £10	6 £11–£15
7 £41–£50	7 £31–£40	7 36s–40s	7 £11	7 £16–£20
8 £51–£60	8 £41–£50	8 41s–60s	8 £12	8 £21–£30
9 £61 or more	9 £51 or more	9 61s or more	9 £13 or more	9 £31 or more
–V	–V	–V	–V	–V

60 In which month are you most likely to get it?
Code month, write in year

Cine-camera	Camera	Cigarette lighter	Electric shaver	Watch
1 Jan 7 Jul	1 Jan 7 Jul	1 Jan 7 Jul	1 Jan 7 Jul	1 Jan 7 Jul
2 Feb 8 Aug	2 Feb 8 Aug	2 Feb 8 Aug	2 Feb 8 Aug	2 Feb 8 Aug
3 Mar 9 Sep	3 Mar 9 Sep	3 Mar 9 Sep	3 Mar 9 Sep	3 Mar 9 Sep
4 Apr 0 Oct	4 Apr 0 Oct	4 Apr 0 Oct	4 Apr 0 Oct	4 Apr 0 Oct
5 May X Nov	5 May X Nov	5 May X Nov	5 May X Nov	5 May X Nov
6 June V Dec	6 June V Dec	6 June V Dec	6 June V Dec	6 June V Dec
–R 196 . .	–R 196 . .	–R 196 . .	–R 196 . .	–R 196 . .

61 Do you, or your family, own your home or do you rent it? *If rent:* From whom are you renting?

Ask Q.62 before Q.61.

1 Own; buying mortgage
2 Rent from council
3 Rent from private landlord
4 Employers; with job
5 Lodging with family
–6 Hostel etc.

62 How old were you when you finished your full-time education?

4 14 or under
5 15
6 16 or over
X University

68a) What is your occupation?
or
b) What was your occupation?
or
c) *If married woman not working:* What is/was your husband's occupation? *(Write in and code)*

Occupation:

Non-manual:
8 Professional
9 Director; propr; manager
0 Shop; personal service
X Office; students, etc.

Manual: Mark both type AND grade

Type	Grade
1 Factory	5 Skilled
2 Transport	6 Semi-skilled
3 Building	–7 Unskilled

household run a car?
1 Yes, one car
2 Yes, two or more

b) *If Yes (ask about largest car if two or more cars owned)*
What make? _____
And what model? _____ 19 ___
In what year was it first registered? 19 ___
Was it bought new or secondhand?
3 New
4 Secondhand
–R

Is this your first car or was it a replacement for another car?
7 First car *(To Q.63d)*
8 Replacement
–R

c) *If replacement*
What was the make of the car replaced? _____
And what model? _____
In what year was your previous car first registered? 19 ___
Was your previous car bought new or secondhand?
9 New
0 Secondhand
–R

63d) Do you have a TV set?
–X Yes, TV set
V No TV set

64a) How many people are there in your household, including yourself and any children? _____ Total

b) How many are aged 21 or over? _____ Adults 21

c) *If any under 21:* That means there are (is).....under 21 in this household. How old are they (is he/she)?
9 16-20 years
0 11-15 years
X 5-10 years
V 0-4 years

Record number in EACH age group; check that the number of adults plus children agrees with TOTAL

ASK ALL:
67a) Are you, yourself, employed?
1 Full-time
2 Part-time
3 Self-employed } *To Q.67b*
4 Student
5 Unemployed
6 Rt'd; pension } *To Q.68b or c*
7 Not working

b) Are you paid monthly or weekly?
8 Monthly
9 Weekly
–X Other method

---

b) If you had to say which social class you belong to, what would you say? *(Read out all five alternatives)*
7 Upper
8 Upper-middle
9 Middle
0 Lower-middle
X Working
–V

70 Can you tell me your date of birth please?
(Write in and code)
Date of birth:
0 16 or 17
1 18-20
2 21-24
3 25-29
4 30-34
5 35-44
6 45-49
7 50-54
8 55-64
9 65 and over
–X

c) Socio-economic group:

Non-manual	Manual
7 A	0 C2
8 B	X D
9 C1	V E

71a) Sex:
1 Man
2 Woman—housewife
3 Woman—Not housewife
–C

b) Marital status:
4 Married
5 Single
6 Widowed, divorced

75a) May I please have your name, initials and address:
(Please PRINT full details)
Mr./Mrs./Miss
Address
Town _____ County _____

b) Are you on the telephone?
0 Yes
–V No phone

c) May I have the number please? Telephone No *(Write in)*
196 ___

76a) *Place of interview:*
9 Home
X Street –V Elsewhere
Date

76b) *Day of interview:*
1 Sun 3 Tues 5 Thur 7 Sat
2 Mon 4 Wed 6 Fri

I hereby attest that this is a true record of an interview made strictly in accordance with your requirements, with a person who is a stranger to me and that this form was completed at the time of the interview.
Signed: _____

publication from a complete list of every publication with which the surveys are concerned. With the interviewer they go through booklets containing the title blocks of the publications, and are asked about each one in turn. The use of the title blocks in these recall-aid booklets is an example of another useful device, visual aids, to assist recall.

With questions like the readership one, there are two types of memory error. The first is the 'recall loss', occurring when the respondent fails to report an activity in the recall period because he has forgotten about it, and this loss is likely to be more serious the longer the period. The second occurs when he reports an activity in the recall period when it actually took place outside that period; the tendency to report as occurring in the current period events which in fact occurred earlier has been termed the 'telescoping effect'. A greater telescoping effect for shorter recall periods has been suggested as part of the explanation for the commonly found effect of relatively greater reporting rates for short recall periods.

In panel studies, 'bounded' recalls can be used to deal with the telescoping effect. At the second and subsequent interviews, the respondent can be told of the activities he had reported previously and, if he reports an activity again, the interviewer can verify with him that he is not giving a duplicate report of the earlier activity. Neter and Waksberg (1965) used bounded and unbounded recalls to investigate the telescoping effect, in an experiment in which house-owners were interviewed about the number and size of jobs undertaken for alteration and repair of houses. They found that, for the number of jobs of 100 U.S. dollars or more, with a one-month recall period the reporting at the unbounded recall was about 55 per cent higher than that at the bounded recall; with a three-month recall period, the unbounded recall rate was about 26 per cent higher. Both findings indicate substantial telescoping effects.

With serious memory errors having been demonstrated in many studies, it is natural to look for a procedure which does not rely heavily on an informant's ability to recall information. One obvious possibility is to persuade informants to keep diaries of the events of interest, as is done in the Family Expenditure and National Food Surveys. Diaries, however, have their own limitations. First, the amount of work asked of the respondent is much greater with the diary method, and this may make it difficult to gain the co-operation of the selected sample—the refusal rate may be high. Secondly, the diary method is likely to be more expensive, for interviewers will probably need to contact informants at least twice. One visit is needed to gain the informant's co-operation and to explain the recording procedure, and another is needed to collect the completed diaries. During the recording period other visits may be made to ensure that the instructions have been understood, to check that the data are being correctly recorded, and to maintain morale. The last visit serves not only for the collection of the diary, but also as an opportunity for the interviewer to edit the diary with the respondent; were it not for this editing, the last visit could perhaps be dispensed with, for the diaries could be returned by post.

Even with careful editing, however, the standard of informants' recording cannot be expected to reach that achieved by well-trained interviewers. Surveys of the general population contain people from a wide range of educational levels and with varying amounts of form-completing experience; it can be anticipated that some of them will fail to understand from one interview exactly what they are to do. In addition, others may lack the motivation to complete the diaries as accurately as is required. One particular way in which informants may deviate from instructions is by failing to record the events while they are fresh in their memories; the main strength of the diary approach is the avoidance of reliance on memory, but, if the informant does not keep the diary up-to-date, at least part of that strength is lost. Another source of error is that, although instructed not to change their habits as the result of their recording, some informants will do so; in consumer expenditure surveys, for instance, housewives keeping log-books of their purchases may become more aware of their shopping habits, and this may for example persuade them of the advantages of buying larger items and of shopping in supermarkets. This is the panel conditioning effect which was discussed in Section 6.5.

These limitations of the diary method must be balanced against the memory errors involved in the recall method. The choice between the methods depends on the subject matter of the survey and, in particular, on the ability of respondents to recall accurately the necessary details of the information required. In situations where, even with assistance from the interviewer, informants are unable to recollect details accurately, the recall method is inappropriate and the diary method may be the only possible approach.

13.4. Open and pre-coded questions

The relative merits of open and pre-coded questions have been the subject of a good deal of research and debate. In an open question the respondent is given freedom to decide the aspect, form, detail and length of his answer, and it is the interviewer's job to record as much of it as she can. In the case of pre-coded questions, either the respondent is given a limited number of answers from which to choose or the question is asked as an open question and the interviewer allocates the answer to the appropriate code category.[1] Examples of the two types of question (in addition to those given on p. 280 above) are contained in the questionnaires reproduced on other pages:

(i) *Open questions*
   S.R.U. schedule, p. 312.

   Q.1(*b*) is a typical open question, not only in its form and content, but also in that it opens the interview. It is often desirable to start the interview with an open question to get the respondent talking and to make him feel at ease.

   Radio and television enquiry questionnaire, p. 307.

   The part of Q.6 on the respondent's (or her husband's) work.

(ii) *Pre-coded questions, respondent given limited choice*
   S.R.U. schedule.

   With most of the questions here only a few answers are *possible*. Q.2 asked women whether or not they are housewives; Q.10(*a*) asked respondents whether or not they smoked.

   Gallup Poll schedule, pp. 332–9.

   Many of the questions here are opinion questions in which respondents are given the choice between 'Good' and 'Bad', 'Very important', 'Important', 'Not very important' and 'Not at all important' (together with 'Don't know'). This type of question is common in opinion research.

(iii) *Pre-coded questions, interviewer codes*
   S.R.U. schedule.

   Q.8(*a*) here asks 'When did you last go to the pictures ...?' The respondent answered in his own terms and the interviewer coded accordingly.

The essential difference thus lies in the stage at which the information is coded, whether in the office, by the respondent or by the interviewer. If the researcher wants a very detailed answer, or wishes to find out what aspects of an issue are uppermost in the respondent's mind, (i) is to be preferred. Even if it has to be summarized subsequently, all the detail is there, not merely a number representing the nearest code answer. Any summarizing or coding can be carried out uniformly in the office, uninfluenced by the circumstances of the interview or the reaction of the respondent to the interviewer. But, of course, open questions have their problems. The detail obtained is

---

[1] Often several answers may be coded, e.g. in a question asking which newspapers the respondent reads.

partly a reflection of the respondent's loquacity, so that different
amounts (as well as different items) of information will be available
for different people. A second difficulty lies in the task of compressing
a written, qualitative answer into code categories. Again, although
the remoteness of the office from the interview situation ensures some
gain in coding objectivity, it also has drawbacks. Just as questions
can sound different if asked by different people, so the meaning of an
answer is communicated partly by the way it is given, and this will
not be reflected in the written record. Finally, there is the difficulty
of getting a verbatim report of what is said. All interviewers probably
exercise some selection in recording answers and, to the extent that
this happens, bias may creep in.

Pre-coded questions may offer two or more alternative answers
(referred to respectively as dichotomous and multiple-choice—or
'cafeteria'—questions) and their advantages are evident. To combine
the recording and coding of answers in one operation simplifies the
whole procedure; and, in a very real sense, the interviewer is the
person best placed to arrive at an accurate coding, since she hears the
answers in full and thus has more data to work on than the office
coder. On the other hand, once she has ringed a code there is little
hope of detecting errors of recording or judgement. Also, she is
working under pressure and may be unable to give sufficient time and
attention to the needs of a complex coding operation.

If the range of answers to a question is limited and well established,
pre-coding is generally to be preferred. Most factual questions—with
regular exceptions like questions on occupation—belong to this
category. If, however, one cannot reasonably determine in advance
what the main categories will be, it is best to begin with open questions,
progressing to pre-coded ones as the range and distribution of
answers become clear. This is why open questions play such a
valuable role in pilot surveys.

The alternatives offered in pre-coded questions must above all be
exhaustive and mutually exclusive. (The code 'Other, specify . . .' is
usually added for rare or unthought-of answers.) In questions of type
(ii) all the possible answers must be given. The following question
occurred in an opinion survey: 'What happens to the copy of the . . .
(newspaper); for instance, does anyone take it to work?'

Stays in house	1
Regularly taken to work, left there	2
Occasionally taken to work, left there	3
Taken to work, brought home	4

It is likely that the form of the question disfavoured the first code
answer. If any of the answers are to be suggested, *all* should be. A

2 M

respondent who has never considered the subject of the question carefully may seize upon any lead given by the mention of a possible answer.

A risk with pre-coded questions is that answers may be forced into a category to which they do not properly belong. Take the hypothetical question: 'Do you think the present Government is doing a good or bad job?' Many people will have clear views and will unhesitatingly say 'Good' or 'Bad'. But what of those who are inclined to say 'Good, but . . .' or 'Bad, except that . . .'? The coding demands a decision one way or the other and may result in qualified responses being forced into categories to which they do not genuinely belong. To try to avoid this, survey designers leave space for qualifications or allow in the codes for finer shades of opinion. Up to a point, a greater number of codes has the added advantage that more information is collected. But there is a limit: if too many codes are used, respondents will be unable to make a rational choice between several of the alternatives and, faced with so many codes, they may have difficulty in making a choice at all.

Besides fixing the number of codes to be used, with opinion questions the survey designer has also to decide whether or not to code for a neutral position, in other words he must decide whether he wants to force respondents to come down on one side or other of the fence. If he does provide a neutral code, he may well find that many people take up that option. The following question was included in a schedule on saving habits: 'During the coming year do you think things will get much better or worse for people in your position or do you think there is not likely to be much change?' The last phrase offered a neutral escape, and 44 per cent of the respondents chose it. These answers may of course express genuine opinions, but there is clearly a risk in suggesting a non-committal answer to the respondent.

Pre-coded questions of type (ii) are generally easier than questions of types (i) and (iii) for the respondent to answer, for he has the list of choices specified for him. In some cases the alternatives can indicate to him the question's frame of reference. They can also tell him how precise an answer is required: he may, for example, not know the exact distance involved in his journey to work but he may know that it certainly lies in one of the specified groups. On the other hand, giving the respondent a list of alternatives can also have disadvantages. If, for instance, a question is asked on an issue which the respondent has not previously considered, he has little incentive to work out his views when a choice of answers is given to him, for all he need do is simply choose one of the offered alternatives; without specified alternatives he would have to formulate his ideas, and this would encourage him to reach a considered view. Or, if the respondent is uninformed on the topic of a question, the choice of any one of the offered alternatives is sufficient to hide his ignorance; if part of the purpose of the question is to find out how many respondents are uninformed, alternatives should not be offered. Again, if the respondent fails to understand, or misunderstands, a pre-coded question he can still give an apparently appropriate answer. To keep a check on this, Schuman (1966) has suggested that interviewers follow up a randomly selected set of pre-coded questions with probes like 'I see—why do you say that?' From the responses to these probes the surveyor can then see if his pre-coded question has been understood, if the question and the alternative answers have a common interpretation among respondents, and if this interpretation coincides with his own. This proposal brings into the full survey a type of procedure that has been found valuable in pre-tests and pilot studies.

When answers are to be prompted (see Chapter 12) with a list of alternatives, it may be preferable to show them to the respondent on a card rather than read them out. In either case the answers may be affected by the order in which the alternatives are presented. It has been shown that alternatives stated at the beginning or end of the list are apt to be favoured (see, for instance, Mosteller and others, 1949, p. 170). Another effect that has often been observed is that, with opinion statements requiring answers like 'Yes' or 'No' or 'True' or 'False', respondents more frequently give affirmative answers to the statements than negative answers to their opposites; this effect is known as the 'acquiescence response set'. One reason why a set of attitude statements usually contains some positively and some negatively worded statements is to counteract this effect.

Several writers have proposed ways of combining open and precoded questions. The principle is generally to ask a series of questions, beginning with open types and going over to pre-coded ones as the subject matter becomes more clearly structured, enabling more specific questions to be asked. The so-called *Quintamensional Plan of Question Design* of Gallup (1947) is of this kind.[1] It suggests that, for many issues, a series of five types of question is useful:

Q.1. Designed to find out whether the informant is aware of the issue at all, whether he has thought about it.

Q.2. Designed to get his general feelings on the issue. Invariably of the free-answer variety.

Q.3. Designed to get answers on specific parts of the issue. This is done by pre-coded questions.

[1] See also Lazarsfeld (1944).

Q.4. Designed to find out reasons for the informant's views.
Q.5. Designed to find out how strongly they are held.

13.5. Question order

In putting the individual questions together to form the questionnaire, the order of questions needs to be planned. The order may
affect the refusal rate and there is plenty of evidence that it may also
influence the answers obtained (e.g. Mosteller and others, 1949,
Cantril, 1944, Whitfield, 1950), especially so when one is concerned
with opinions that are unstable or marginal.[1]

At the start of the interview the respondent is unsure of himself and
so the opening questions should be ones to put him at ease and build
up rapport between him and the interviewer. They should be interesting questions which he will have no difficulty in answering, and they
should not be on sensitive topics, for otherwise he may refuse to
continue with the interview. The questions should then proceed in a
logical manner, moving from topic to topic in a way that indicates
to the respondent the relationship between the questions; where an
obvious break in subject matter occurs it is usually advisable to give
a sentence or two explaining the break and the relevance of the new
set of questions. Since questions on highly sensitive topics may lead
to the respondent refusing to continue with the interview, they may
be best left until last; then, if a refusal is met, relatively little information is lost.

When determining the order of questions within a topic (and also,
for that matter, between topics) the conditioning effect of earlier
questions should be considered. It is no good asking: 'Can you name
any washing powder?' if a previous question has mentioned 'Tide' or
'Dreft'; in other words knowledge questions must not be preceded by
others giving relevant information. Even though interest may centre
on specific issues, it can be a good idea to start with broad questions
about the subject and then to narrow down to the specific issues, using
what is known as a *funnel sequence* of questions (Kahn and Cannell,
1957). Thus a general open question on the achievements of the
present Government may be the beginning of a sequence leading
to specific questions on the Government's actions in the field of
labour relations; a mention of labour relations in reply to the first
question suggests that the respondent attaches some importance to
the subject. On the other hand, if one is interested in the broader
question and one thinks the respondents do not hold considered
opinions about it, an inverted funnel sequence may be useful. In this
case, the early questions ask about the range of issues involved and,

[1] It has indeed been suggested that one way of gauging the intensity of opinion
is by the sensitiveness of answers to changes in question order and wording.

in answering them, the respondent is led towards forming a considered opinion on the broader question.

A fairly common situation is one in which the respondent is taken through a list of items by the interviewer, who asks the same initial question about each item in turn. If the respondent answers this question in a certain way the interviewer asks supplementary questions; otherwise she proceeds to the next item. Respondents soon learn in this situation that they can complete the interview more rapidly by avoiding the replies leading to supplementary questions, and this may tempt some to falsify their replies. This risk is easily avoided, however, by asking the supplementary questions only after answers to the initial question have been obtained for all the items on the list.

Another problem with long lists of items is that of respondent fatigue; towards the end of a list of, say, 90 items (about the number of publications in the National Readership Surveys) the respondent can be expected to experience fatigue, which may result in him failing to recall the later items and hence answering the questions about them negatively. In the National Readership Surveys, for instance, it has been found that the readership level for the group of weeklies when they appeared last in the presentation order (after the groups of dailies, Sundays and monthlies) was only about three-quarters of that when they appeared first (Belson, 1964a); fatigue probably provides at least a partial explanation of this finding. In these surveys, to avoid bias arising from the order of presentation, the order of the four groups is varied by a rotation scheme throughout the sample; in addition, for one half of the sample the publications within a group are presented in one order and in the other half in the reverse order. This procedure may mean that somewhat better comparisons can be made between the readership levels of different publications, because they have on average about the same presentation position (although account must also be taken of the variation in the 'rotation effect' for the different publications), but it does not make the absolute readership levels for all publications more accurate.

13.6. Concluding remarks

We have not attempted to deal comprehensively with the subject of question wording. The points selected for discussion have been those thought to be of most interest to the student or researcher embarking on a survey. To the problem of questionnaire design in general there is no easy solution. Even if one follows all the accepted principles, there usually remains a choice of several question forms, each of which seems satisfactory. Every surveyor tries to phrase his questions in simple, everyday language, to avoid vagueness and ambiguity and to use neutral wording. His difficulty lies in judging whether, with any particular question, he has succeeded in these aims. He may appreciate perfectly that leading questions are to be avoided, but how can he know for sure which words will be 'leading' with the particular question, survey and population that confront him, perhaps for the first time?

The answer to this question lies in detailed pre-tests and pilot studies: more than anything else, they are the essence of a good questionnaire. However experienced the questionnaire designer, any attempt to shortcut these preparatory stages will seriously jeopardize the quality of the questionnaire; past experience is a considerable asset, but in a fresh survey there are always new aspects which may perhaps not be immediately recognized, but which exist and must be investigated through pre-tests and pilot studies.

The interviewing technique for pre-tests tends to resemble the informal interviewing described in Section 12.6 rather than the formal interviewing of the final survey. At the outset, the interview may be of the form of a guided or focused interview, the interviewer merely raising a few topics and encouraging the respondent to talk about them. This can be valuable in charting the important aspects of the topic, in order to ensure that they are all considered for the questionnaire. Then, even when draft questions have been devised, the aim of the pre-test is not to get standard comparable answers but rather to discover what the respondent understands by the questions, and in the case of prompt questions by the answer-codes, and whether he is able and willing to provide the answers. To understand a respondent's interpretation of a question, the interviewer may need to probe deeply into the meaning of the words to him. Tape recorders can be especially valuable for pre-tests to record the detailed answers and they can also give the questionnaire designer a feel for how smoothly an interview went. The surveyor may test out sensitive questions on groups for which he already has the facts; providing the groups are unaware that he knows the answers, a comparison of the question responses with the known facts provides a check on the truthfulness of reporting. The final pilot survey, being a dress rehearsal for the main survey, is likely to use fairly formal interviewing, but even here the surveyor is as much—if not more—interested in the interviewers' comments on the way the interviews went as in the answers given by the respondents.

Question designing remains a matter of common sense and experience and of avoiding known pitfalls. It is not as yet, if indeed it ever can be, a matter of applying theoretical rules. Alternative versions of questions must be rigorously tested in pre-tests and the pilot survey, for in the absence of hard and fast rules, tests of practicability must play a crucial role in questionnaire construction.

NOTES ON READING

1. One of the most readable discussions of questionnaire design will be found in the book by PAYNE (1951) referred to in the text. Other valuable sources are: the appendix by KORNHAUSER and SHEATSLEY in SELLTIZ and others (1959); OPPENHEIM (1966); the chapter by CANNELL and KAHN in FESTINGER and KATZ (1953); KAHN and CANNELL (1957); the chapter by CANNELL and KAHN in LINDZEY and ARONSON (1968, Vol. 2); and RICHARDSON and others (1965).

2. On opinion questions CANTRIL (1944), MOSTELLER and others (1949), MCNEMAR (1946), and OPPENHEIM (1966) are worth consulting. GALLUP (1948) himself has published an account of Gallup Poll methods and aims. The journal literature on questionnaire design in general, and opinion questions in particular, is enormous; much of it is concentrated in the *Public Opinion Quarterly*. BELSON (1964b) reviews some of the findings. BELSON and DUNCAN (1962) report on a comparison of check-list and open-response questioning systems with respect to readership reporting. BELSON (1968b) presents some interesting results from a research project on respondents' understandings of survey questions.

3. ZARKOVICH (1966) discusses memory errors and recall periods. The report by NETER and WAKSBERG (1965), describing the results of an experimental study on response errors in the collection of expenditure data, is well worth consulting on these subjects. Another useful report is that by MOONEY (1962), which reports on experiments involving memory errors and recall periods in health surveys; diaries are also discussed. LOGAN and BROOKE (1957) discuss the memory factor in relation to the British Survey of Sickness, a survey which was discontinued in 1952. GRAY (1955) also discusses memory problems in surveys. TURNER (1961) discusses the marked differences in the reports of the purchase of one commodity between the first and second weeks' diaries of the Family Expenditure Survey; the diary used in the Family Expenditure Survey is described by KEMSLEY (1969). MOSER (1950) describes and discusses the use of a diary for recording the work and leisure activities of a sample of housewives.

CHAPTER 14

Scaling Methods

14.1. Introduction

ON VIRTUALLY every subject ever tackled by a survey one could make a list of relevant questions far longer than any reasonable questionnaire could include—not merely because wording variations enable one to ring numerous changes on a single question, but because there are generally so many aspects of the subject that could be explored. Suppose one wished to know the attitudes of a group of workers towards their management. At once a number of possible questions suggest themselves: 'Do you think the management is making a good or a bad job of things?'; 'How well qualified do you think the managers are for their task?'; 'In what ways do you think the relationship between management and workers could be improved?'; 'What do you think of the management's part in improving working conditions?'

All these questions—a small sample from the vast number one could formulate—have a bearing on the 'favourableness to management' attitude, but they all approach different aspects of it. In a straightforward opinion survey one might include, say, ten or twenty questions, tapping different aspects of the subject, and simply count the number of respondents giving various answers. One may argue that such an approach is superficial, but then its aim is modest and unsophisticated. No pretence is made—or should be made—that it *measures* attitudes in the strict sense; it merely *counts* how many people choose to express certain views. To go further than this, to try to combine the answers a respondent gives to the various questions into a measurement of the extremity and intensity of his overall attitude, requires a different analytical approach; and this is where scaling devices find their place. If we may assume that—for the population under study—there is such a thing as 'attitude towards management', then we may proceed, by one of several techniques, to find out where along a scale ranging from extreme favourableness to extreme unfavourableness a particular attitude lies. This may properly be called attitude measurement.

As we have seen in the case of the management example, an attitude can be approached from many different angles, and this explains why a series of questions is needed to measure it; it is a more general concept than can be accurately determined from the answer to a single specific question.[1] Although a belief on a specific issue tends to suggest an attitude, a particular individual's belief on that issue may be heavily weighted by an idiosyncratic component which makes his belief untypical of his more general position; a worker may reasonably believe, for example, that the managers are well qualified for the task, and yet he may still have a generally unfavourable attitude to management. A single belief is a poor indicator of a person's more general attitude and so, to measure the latter more accurately, a sample of beliefs covering a range of aspects of the attitude needs to be obtained and the set of answers combined into some form of average. The purpose of averaging over a set of beliefs is to reduce the effects of idiosyncracies of particular respondents in respect of particular aspects of the attitude; the set of statements for ascertaining beliefs must be chosen with this in mind. The choice is a kind of sampling problem: from the universe of content, that is all the possible statements that could be made about the object of the attitude, a 'representative sample' is required for putting to the respondents. If the sample covers—or is heavily weighted towards—only one aspect of the attitude, the idiosyncracies of that aspect will not be averaged out; or, in other words, the measurements will refer to that aspect only and not to the full universe of content. Although this sampling analogy is useful it must not be pushed too far; with attitudes there is the obvious limitation that the universe of content from which the sample of statements is drawn cannot be determined.

Scaling methods come into play essentially when one wishes to utilize simultaneously a number of observations on each respondent. Individually the pieces may be of no more interest than the single pieces of a jigsaw puzzle; what really matters is the total picture. The difficulties of the scaling process can be separated into three parts: the first is to decide what are the appropriate pieces, ensuring that they are logically related and all refer to the same attitude dimension, which between them they span adequately; the second is to fit the pieces together into a meaningful whole; and the third is to test the properties, particularly the reliability and validity, of the

[1] The approach here follows that of Likert scaling and the common factor model (Section 14.7), rather than that of Thurstone or Guttman scaling (Sections 14.6 and 14.8).

scale thus constructed. An incidental advantage of basing survey interpretations on the combined answers to many questions is that the risk of bias through wording is thereby reduced.

Before turning to methods of constructing attitude scales, we will first discuss in the next two sections some important general considerations in scaling.

14.2. Types of scales

The basis of attitude measurement is that there are underlying dimensions along which individual attitudes can be ranged. By employing one of the various attitude scaling procedures a person can be assigned a numerical score to indicate his position on a dimension of interest. A natural question to ask about such scores is: what meaning can be attached to them? As a preparatory stage for answering the question we will discuss in this section the various measurement levels for a dimension or continuum, and these will be mentioned here in increasing order of 'measurement sophistication'.[1]

The crudest is often called a *nominal* scale, which classifies individuals into two or more groups, the members of which differ with respect to the characteristic being scaled, without there being any implication of gradation or distance between the groups. It is a way of classification rather than an arrangement along a continuum, and the question of dimensionality does not arise. If desired, one could assign numbers to the various groups as a labelling device, but it would not matter which number was assigned to which group, and no meaningful calculations could be performed using these numbers.

The next major step is to the *ordinal* type of scale, which ranks individuals along the continuum of the characteristic being scaled, but again carries no implication of distance between scale positions—the step from position 1 to position 2 may be greater, smaller or the same as from position 4 to position 5. This kind of scale arises, for instance, with the rank order of contestants in a beauty contest and with the form position of schoolchildren. Conventionally in these cases the integers 1, 2, 3, ... are assigned to indicate relative positions, but any set of numbers maintaining the order could equally be used.

Next, one may distinguish what is generally called the *interval* (or cardinal) type of scale, which has equal units of measurement, thus making it possible to interpret not only the order of scale scores but also the distances between them. The position of the zero point in such a scale is a matter of convenience so that one may add or subtract a constant to all the scale values without affecting the form

---

[1] This classification follows that of Stevens (1946). For a detailed discussion of the theory of data, see Coombs (1964).

of the scale; hence one cannot rightly multiply or divide the values. In other words, one can say that two persons with scale positions 1 and 2 are as far apart as two persons with scale positions 4 and 5 but not that a person with score 10 feels 'twice as strongly' as one with a score 5. Temperatures measured in Centigrade or Fahrenheit provide examples of interval scales: one can, for instance meaningfully talk of a 10 °C rise in temperature but not of 10 °C as being ten times as hot as 1 °C.

The highest level of measurement is a *ratio* scale, which has the properties of an interval scale together with a fixed origin or zero point; weights, lengths and times are obvious examples. With a ratio scale one can compare both differences in scores and the relative magnitude of scores: for instance the difference between five and ten minutes is the same as that between ten and fifteen minutes, and ten minutes is twice as long as five minutes. However, most attitude scaling is not so ambitious, attempting nothing higher than the interval level of measurement.

14.3. Reliability and validity

Whatever approach to attitude scaling one cares to adopt, there always remains the question (which ideally should be answered before a scale is put to research use) as to what extent the scale is reliable and valid.

A scale or test is *reliable* to the extent that repeat measurements made by it under constant conditions will give the same result (assuming no change in the basic characteristic—e.g. attitude—being measured). Ideally one would wish to gauge reliability by repeating the scale (or test) on the same people using the same methods. The practical difficulty of the *test-retest method* is however self-evident; and even if persons were to submit themselves to repeat questioning, a comparison of the two sets of results would hardly serve as an exact test of reliability, since they could not be regarded as independent. At the retest, respondents may remember their first answers and give consistent retest answers, an action which would make the test appear more reliable than is truly the case. Alternatively, the first questioning may make them think more about the survey subject, they may make less effort the second time to give accurate answers, or events occurring between the two tests may cause them to change their views on the subject. In any of these circumstances, the test and retest scores are not exactly comparable, so the difference between the two is a mixture of unreliability and change in the characteristic itself; the effect of this is that an underestimate of reliability is obtained. The longer the interval between test and retest, the less is the risk of the memory effect but the greater is the risk of intervening events causing respondents to change their views; the problem is to choose an interval long enough to deal adequately with the first risk and yet short enough to deal adequately with the second. In assessing the correlation between test and retest scores it is often difficult to decide the balance between the memory effect and the effect of changes in views, that is to decide whether the correlation is an inflated or deflated estimate of a test's reliability.

A different possibility is the *alternate forms method*, in which two supposedly equivalent versions of the scale are given to the same individuals and the results correlated. Here there is the difficulty that differences between the two sets of answers will be a mixture of unreliability and differences between the items used, and there is no way of separating the effects. However, there is less danger of the first questioning affecting answers on a subsequent occasion; indeed, the two scales can even be administered at the same time, thus eliminating the risk of respondents genuinely changing their views between tests. To draw attention to the nature of the difference between the test-retest method and the alternate forms method when the tests are administered at the same time, correlation coefficients obtained from the former method may be called measures of *stability* because they relate to constancy over time, while those obtained from the latter are measures of the *equivalence* of the two forms. The use of alternate forms at different times clearly involves both stability and equivalence.

The most widely used way of measuring reliability is by the approach loosely known as the *split-half method*. The set of items in the test is divided into two matched halves and the scores for the two halves are correlated, as in the alternate forms method. The correlation so obtained relates to a test of half the full length and it therefore needs to be corrected to give the *stepped-up* reliability of the whole test. The test could alternatively be divided into more parts—thirds, quarters, etc.—or even into individual items, providing all the items are comparable. The stepped-up reliability for a test divided into n equivalent parts is given by the generalized Spearman-Brown formula:

$$r_w = \frac{nr_p}{1 + (n-1)r_p} \qquad \ldots(14.1)$$

where r_w is the stepped-up reliability and r_p is the correlation between any two parts. This formula can be derived as a special case of the more recently developed coefficient alpha which is now widely used as a measure of reliability; discussion of alpha is beyond our scope and the reader is referred to Lord and Novick (1968) for a general discussion and to McKennell (1970) for a discussion of its use with cluster or factor analysis in attitude measurement. Like the alternate forms method, the split-half method does not investigate stability; it measures only the internal consistency of the test.

The implications of formula (14.1) are worth considering. If two equivalent items could be used in a scale, but only one is in fact used, the correlation between the items is a measure of reliability for the one item. Say that correlation is 0·5. If both items were used, we could use formula (14.1) to calculate that together they would have a reliability of 0·67. If further items all intercorrelated 0·5 were added to the scale, the reliability would increase. Thus, given a desired level of reliability, the number of items needed to achieve that level can be determined; for instance, if r_w were set at 0·9, nine items intercorrelating 0·5 would be needed. This demonstrates a main justification for including a number of items in a scale, that the reliability can thereby be increased to a satisfactory level. With attitude measurement the set of items rarely intercorrelate highly, and, in order to attain an adequate level of reliability, several items need to be put together to form a scale.

The formula shows that the number of items needed to reach a given reliability level depends on the homogeneity of the items, that is on the intercorrelations between them; for instance only four items intercorrelating 0·7 are needed to make $r_w = 0·9$, compared with nine intercorrelating 0·5, and 21 intercorrelating only 0·3. Since it is important to keep a survey questionnaire as short as possible, it would seem that the approach should be to use as homogeneous a set of items as possible. However, homogeneity is often attained only by restricting the breadth of the scale, and a surveyor wanting to measure a broad attitude may either have to use a large number of items or have to make do with a low level of reliability.

Reasonable reliability is one attribute needed in a scale, *validity* is another. By validity is meant the success of the scale in measuring what it sets out to measure, so that differences between individuals' scores can be taken as representing true differences in the characteristic under study. It is clear that to the extent that a scale is unreliable it also lacks validity. But a reliable scale is not necessarily valid, for it could be measuring something other than what it was designed to measure. While it is easy to explain what is meant by validity, to measure it in practice is exceedingly hard. Four main approaches are commonly distinguished.

The problem may be treated superficially by claiming that, since the common thread of, say, attitude to management runs through all the scale items, the resultant scale has 'face validity' for that attitude. A more systematic approach is involved in investigating what is known as *content validity*. Not only should the items contain the common thread of the attitude under study, but between them they should also cover the full range of the attitude, and cover it in a balanced way; this relates to the problem referred to earlier as that of obtaining a representative sample of items from the universe of content. The assessment of content validity is essentially a matter of judgement; the judgement may be made by the surveyor or, better, by a team of judges engaged for the purpose.

In situations where a scale is developed as an indicator of some observable criterion, the scale's validity can be investigated by seeing how good an indicator it is. If, for example, a questionnaire is designed to identify psychiatrically disturbed persons, the questionnaire's validity might be determined by comparing its diagnoses with those made by a psychiatrist on the basis of clinical interviews. This approach leads to two categories of validity, *predictive validity* and *concurrent validity*, which are essentially the same except that the former relates to future performance on the criterion whereas the latter relates to performance at approximately the same time that the scale is administered. Predictive validity is thus concerned with how well the scale can forecast a future criterion and concurrent validity with how well it can describe a present one.

The difficulty of applying rigorous and objective tests of validity in attitude measurement arises from the fact that such measurement is invariably indirect—in the sense that the attitude is *inferred* from the verbal responses. An attitude is an abstraction and in consequence it is generally impossible to assess its validity directly. An approach for this situation is that of *construct validity*; on the basis of theoretical considerations, the researcher postulates the types and degrees of association between the scale and other variables and he then examines these associations to see whether they confirm his expectations. The essence of construct validity is its dependence on theory, and the examination of the observed associations is as much a test of the theory as of the scale's validity. If, for instance, one were concerned with a scale measuring degree of 'religiousness', although one could not conceivably test validity directly, one might judge the success of the scale in discriminating between church-goers and others. It is hardly necessary to point out the weakness of this sort of check, which begs the question as to how far attitudes and actual behaviour are related. The most one can say is that its results would give an increased (or decreased) confidence in the scale. Another example would be the tests of a social class scale by correlating its scores with occupation, education, car ownership and other criteria. Although these tests again cannot provide a complete answer, the existence of good correlations acts as supporting evidence. But it is not only good correlations that serve to test validity; if the theory predicts zero or low correlations between the scale and other measures, the conformity of these correlations to expectation equally provides a test. Also, when a new scale is developed it will probably be intended to be distinctive from existing scales; then, if the correlation between the new and an existing scale is very high, they are too similar and discrimination between them is missing. Discriminant validity can thus be another type of construct validity (see Campbell and Fiske, 1959).

In conclusion it should be noted that the reliability and validity of a scale—unlike those of a foot-rule—are always specific to a particular population, time and purpose, not invariant characteristics. In any given study the researcher has to decide what degree of unreliability and invalidity he will regard as acceptable.

14.4. General procedures in attitude scaling

In succeeding sections we will discuss various specific attitude scaling techniques, but before doing so it may be useful to review the basic stages involved. Although these stages are common to Thurstone, Likert and Guttman scaling, the actual procedures employed differ between the techniques; as is seen in Section 14.9, the semantic differential employs adjective pairs rather than attitude statements, but the general approach is similar.

The first stage is to assemble a set of statements (items) from which those employed in the final scale will be selected. In the choice of items for this item pool, the principles of wording discussed in the previous chapter are of course generally applicable: excessively complex items, ambiguous items, items involving double negatives, vague items, etc., should be avoided. But, more basically, each item should be chosen to differentiate between those with favourable and those with unfavourable attitudes on the subject under study. For this reason items to which all, or nearly all, respondents respond in the same way are unsatisfactory. Although factual items can sometimes be useful as indirect measures of attitude, they are perhaps generally best avoided, for there is always the possibility that some respondents will answer according to their knowledge rather than their beliefs. Between them, as we have seen, the items must range over all the various aspects of the attitude, and informal interviewing is a useful method of ensuring that no important aspect is missed. Statements made in unstructured interviews can be a valuable source of items for the item pool, and they have the considerable advantage that they are expressed in the everyday words and terms of respondents, rather than having been contrived by the researcher. For instance, in the case of the Likert scale reproduced on p. 363, which

was designed to measure general practitioners' attitudes to emotionally disturbed patients, the original item pool was formed by taking
verbatim statements from a series of unstructured, sometimes tape-
recorded, interviews with general practitioners. Other fruitful sources
of items are newspaper reports, magazine articles and essays on the
subject commissioned by the researcher.

Having assembled the item pool, the next stage is to choose from
it the items to be used in the final scale. With Likert, Guttman and
semantic differential scales, this choice can be made on the basis of an
exploratory study in which a group of individuals are asked to respond
to all the items, while with Thurstone scales it is made on the basis of
the assessments of a group of judges. In either case, the data can first
be analysed to pick out unsuitable items, that is items which do not
'hang together' with the general pool, and these can be discarded;
unsuitable items will include both those with wording faults, such as
ambiguity, and those not relating to the same attitude dimension as
the general pool. After removing the unsuitable items, a selection is
made from the remaining items in the pool to form the final scale. In
making this selection, care should be taken to see that the universe of
content is adequately covered and that the items fully span the
attitude dimension; the selection of items to meet the latter
requirement can be based on information from the exploratory
study.

Once the scale is formed, checks can be made on its reliability and
validity and, if these prove satisfactory, the scale can then be
administered in the full survey.

14.5. Rating scales[1]

In brief, the idea of using scaling methods is that, instead of
learning whether or not a respondent is favourably inclined on an
issue (as judged by his answers to specific questions), one gets a
measure, and a reasonably reliable one, of his actual position on the
attitude continuum: instead of being satisfied with differences in
kind, one attempts to measure differences in degree. Before discussing
scaling methods proper we must refer to some modifications of the
Yes/No type of answer choice, which can be regarded as rough
approximations to them.

The simplest way of 'measuring' the strength of a person's attitude
is to ask him to rate that strength himself. This can be done in a
number of ways. The easiest perhaps is to present him with a number
of attitude statements of varying intensity—e.g. 'I feel very strongly

[1] This discussion is confined to rating and self-rating scales as part of the ordinary
questionnaire approach. Applications such as the rating of occupational prestige
by a panel of judges are not discussed.

that Britain's entry into the Common Market is a good thing'; 'I am not sure whether Britain's entry into the Common Market is a good thing or not'; etc.—and to ask him which statement comes closest to his own attitude. Or one may give him a single statement but offer a number of possible answers, say ranging from 'strongly against' to 'strongly in favour'.

Yet another way is to present the hypothetical range of attitudes, from extreme favourableness to extreme unfavourableness, graphically or pictorially. The 'scale' may take the form of a straight line or of a picture of a thermometer, with regular divisions marked on it and the extremes indicated, so that the respondent can be asked to place his own attitude. The Gallup Institutes have often used the scalometer method (designed by the Netherlands Institute of Public Opinion) in which the respondent is shown a diagram of ten squares placed one above the other. The top five are white and are marked with a plus sign, the bottom five are black and are marked with a minus sign. The respondent is asked to indicate his attitude position by pointing to the square which he considers most appropriate, taking the ten blocks to range from extreme favourableness to extreme unfavourableness.

A decision to be made with rating scales is the number of scale points to use: if the scale is divided too finely the respondents will be unable to place themselves, and if too coarsely the scale will not differentiate adequately between them. Often five to seven categories are employed, but sometimes the number is greater. The choice between an odd or even number depends on whether or not respondents are to be forced to decide the direction of their attitude; with an odd number there is a middle category representing a neutral position, but with an even number there is no middle category, so that respondents are forced to decide to which side of neutral they belong. Another factor to take into account in fixing the number of categories is that respondents generally avoid the two extreme positions, thus effectively reducing the number they choose between.

The avoidance of extremes is a common occurrence with rating scales, and has been termed the error of central tendency. Other errors are those of leniency and severity, the former occurring with respondents who dislike being critical and the latter with those who set high standards. When an object (say a particular commodity in a market research survey) is being rated on several scales by each respondent, there is also the danger of a halo effect, which means that respondents classify the object on each scale according to their general impression, rather than according to the scale's meaning: if, for instance, a respondent generally likes the commodity he will score it favourably on all the scales. The halo effect of course causes a bias in the ratings, and it also introduces a spurious correlation between the various scales.

On the credit side, self-rating methods have the merits that they are simple to operate in the field, demand little effort from respondent or interviewer and, in the case of the pictorial variants, avoid dangers of verbal bias. Moreover, they are certainly more sensitive and informative than a straight Yes/No choice of answers. A rating scale is, however, a single item and as such is likely to be highly unreliable. And one must also recognize that self-rating methods are entirely subjective, the assessment of attitude position being left to the respondent. This may not matter so much with straightforward survey topics, but it makes one reluctant to rely on them with complex and emotion-laden subjects on which the respondent may not be able to assess his own attitude objectively.

Nor is it necessarily an improvement to substitute someone else's subjective judgement for the respondent's, e.g. to leave the assessment of attitude to the interviewer. It is true that the manner and tone of an answer often afford vital clues as to how strongly a person feels, so that the interviewer is certainly better placed than any other outside judge to measure attitude. But, even so, this is too subjective an approach to be a good substitute for scaling methods proper.

14.6. Thurstone scales

One of the best-known approaches to attitude scaling is Thurstone's method of 'equal-appearing intervals', which attempts to form an interval scale of measurement.

The first step in the procedure is to collect for the item pool a large number of items, consisting of statements on the survey subject (say attitude to management) ranging from one extreme of favourableness to the other. These are reduced, by cutting out obviously ambiguous items, duplicates and so forth, to somewhere near a hundred, each of which is written on a card. A large group of 'judges'—perhaps fifty or so—are then asked to independently assess the items. Each judge is given the task of sorting the items into a set number of piles according to his assessment of their degrees of favourableness on the attitude in question, and he is asked to form the piles so that they appear to him to be about equally spaced along the attitude continuum. The number of piles is often eleven, but seven and nine are also used, and the middle pile is sometimes labelled 'neutral'. It is worth emphasizing that the judges are asked to make objective evaluations of the positions of the items on the attitude continuum and not to express their own views. Judges whose sortings indicate that they have failed to perform the task adequately —perhaps through a misunderstanding of instructions or just carelessness—can be eliminated. Then, scoring the piles from 1 to 11 (or 7 or 9), for each item a median value is calculated—the value such that half the remaining judges give the item a lower position and half a higher—and also the interquartile range, which measures the scatter of judgements (the extent to which various judges place the item at different parts of the scale). The list of items is now reduced by (a) discarding those with a high scatter, for they are clearly in some sense ambiguous or irrelevant; and (b) selecting from the remainder some twenty or so which cover the entire range of attitudes (as judged by the medians) and which appear to be about equally spaced (again, as judged by the medians) along the scale. At the final selection stage it may be possible to choose a second set of items in the same way so that the alternate forms method can be used to measure the scale's reliability; or, alternatively, the scale may be formed as two halves so that the split-half method can be used.

The items so selected are then embodied in a questionnaire, in random order, and each respondent is asked to endorse all the items with which he agrees. The average (mean or median) of the median values of all the items he endorses is his scale score. From the respondent's viewpoint the procedure is very simple, requiring no scoring or judging of distances, but merely a checking of items he agrees with; the judgement of distances is part of the construction process.

Thurstone scales are sometimes termed *differential* scales, in the sense that, given a sound and reliable scale, the individual will agree only with items around his scale position, disagreeing with those more extreme on either side—as distinct from *cumulative* scales, in which he would ideally be expected to agree with all items less extreme than his position, and disagree with all those which are more extreme.

A frequent criticism of the method has been that the characteristics and attitudes of the people who judge the items in the item pool may be very different from those of the respondents whose attitudes are to be scaled, and that the former may affect the scale values. In fact, empirical evidence on this point is conflicting, but there are some fairly reassuring indications of the independence of the scale values from the judges' own attitudes.

Another criticism of Thurstone scaling is its laboriousness. The judges' task requires careful application and a certain level of skill, and it may not be easy for the researcher to gain the co-operation of a large number of persons able and willing to do the work. A point in favour of the other scaling methods we shall discuss is that they do not need the services of judges.

14.7. Likert scales

In Likert scaling the respondent is not asked to decide just whether he agrees or disagrees with an item, but rather to choose between several response categories, indicating various strengths of agreement and disagreement. The categories are assigned scores and the respondent's attitude is measured by his total score, which is the sum of the scores of the categories he has endorsed for each of the items. Reflecting these main characteristics of Likert scaling, the scales are also known as *summated* and *summated rating* scales.

Five categories are normally employed for each item, although three and seven have sometimes been used. The usual descriptions for the five categories are 'strongly approve' (strongly agree), 'approve' (agree), 'undecided', 'disapprove' (disagree) and 'strongly disapprove' (strongly disagree). Although more complex scoring has been attempted, assigning scores of 1, 2, 3, 4 and 5 or 5, 4, 3, 2 and 1 has generally been found to be adequate. The choice between the two orderings of scores for an item depends on whether 'strongly approve' indicates a favourable or an unfavourable attitude. Some items on the scale will be expressed positively, so that the answer 'strongly approve' indicates a favourable attitude, and others negatively, 'strongly approve' then indicating an unfavourable attitude; thus, to make the total score meaningful, positive items must be scored in one order and negative ones in the reverse order.

In forming the item pool, three considerations should be borne in mind. First, since the aim of an item is to spread the respondents over the response categories, no purpose is served by extreme items to which nearly everyone in the population under study will respond in the same way. Secondly, it has been found that neutral items do not work well in Likert scales. Thirdly, it is advisable to have a roughly equal number of positively and negatively worded items in the scale. Variation between positive and negative items forces the respondent to consider each item carefully, rather than to respond automatically to them all in the same way. It also acts to minimize the effect of a response set towards either agreement or disagreement with whatever statement is made. In the Likert scale reproduced on p. 363 from Shepherd and others (1966, p. 197), items 2, 6 and 7 were positively worded and items 3, 4, 5, 9 and 10 negatively worded. The scale, which was designed to measure the attitudes of general practitioners in relation to emotionally disturbed patients, was part of a self-completion questionnaire, and for this scale the practitioners were asked to put a tick in the appropriate column for each item. Items 1 and 8 were discarded from the scale because all the practitioners responded to them in the same way, but this fact was nevertheless of interest in itself. As the items comprising a Likert scale are themselves rating scales they can often usefully be analysed individually.

	Strongly Agree	Agree	Uncertain	Disagree	Strongly Disagree	COMMENTS
1. The treatment of emotional problems is a major part of a general practitioner's work.						
2. Personally, I feel competent to treat most of the emotionally disturbed patients I see.						
3. Neurotic patients impose a greater strain upon the general practitioner than do other types of patient.						
4. Neurotic patients, by and large, tend to be ungrateful for the trouble taken with their treatment.						
5. Under present conditions, it is not practicable for a general practitioner to engage in psychotherapy.						
6. The training of general practitioners to deal with neurotic illness is one of the most urgent needs in medicine.						
7. I should like to undergo further training myself in the management of neurotic disorders.						
8. Until the advent of more effective methods of treatment, there is little to be done for psychiatric patients.						
9. The distress shown by many neurotic patients is due more to lack of control than to real suffering.						
10. Neurotic patients often behave as if their illness absolved them from responsibility.						

Once a large item pool has been compiled, it is administered to a sample of people reasonably representative of those whose attitudes are to be scored. Unlike the judges in Thurstone scaling, these people are asked only to respond to each item by choosing the category representing their own opinion. The item analysis for eliminating poor items involves examining the consistency of their responses to the various items. One way of investigating this internal consistency is to correlate the scores of individuals on each of the items with their total score (or total score less the score on the item involved); items failing to correlate highly with the total score are rejected. Another way is to eliminate those items that fail to discriminate between people with high and low total scores, say the top and bottom 25 per cent of the sample. From the remaining items with high correlations, or good discriminatory power, a selection is made for the scale. The number of items needed depends on their homogeneity and the desired level of reliability; twenty or so are often used, although, as in the scale on p. 363, the number may be smaller than that. Probably because they collect more information per item, Likert scales seem to have higher reliability than Thurstone scales of the same length, or, expressed in another way, they require fewer items than Thurstone scales to reach a given level of reliability. When the items have been selected, it only remains, apart from testing reliability and validity, to ask the actual respondents to indicate their attitudes by checking one of the categories of approval or disapproval for each item. The total score is derived as above, and we note that scores are allocated according to intensity of opinion, not according to the content of the item.

As will be seen in the next section, a major concern in Guttman scaling is with the property of *reproducibility*, which is the ability to reproduce an individual's answers to each item from a knowledge of his total score. Perfect reproducibility would exist with a Likert scale if the correlations between each of the item scores and the total score were perfect, i.e. plus one, but in practice the correlations fall well short of this value. Likert scales are therefore poor on reproducibility. (Thurstone scales also lack reproducibility, but generally to a lesser extent than Likert scales.) The model involved in Likert scaling differs from that in Guttman scaling, and the total score on a Likert scale can be, and often is, made up in many different ways.

A Likert scale is clearly not an interval scale, and no conclusions can be drawn about the meaning of distances between scale positions. But then there are doubts as to whether Thurstone scaling, which attempts to attain interval measurement, produces a true interval scale; the Likert scale appears to be a reasonable ordinal scale, and it is somewhat simpler to construct and is likely to be more reliable than a Thurstone scale.

An important variant of the Likert scaling procedure described above involves the use of factor analysis. This statistical technique is too complex to be described here, but its use with Likert-type items deserves some comment. The general idea behind factor analysis is that the score on any scale item can be thought of as consisting of a number of components, which represent the contributions of underlying factors to the item; an individual's factor scores are weighted according to the relative importance of the various factors in the item and combined together with an error component to form his item score. In practice, however, the item scores are observed and the factor scores unobserved, so factor analysis tries to work backwards to estimate factor scores from a knowledge of item scores. It is useful in factor analysis to distinguish between three types of factor: a *general* factor is one that contributes to all the items on the scale; a *group* factor contributes to more than one, but not to all, items; and a *specific* factor contributes to just one item. Factors contributing to more than one item, that is group and general factors, are termed *common* factors.

If a battery of items comprises items containing one general factor and specific factors only, or if in addition there are group factors which each contribute to only a small proportion of the items, an individual's total score over all the items will tend to consist predominantly of his general factor score; and, since the items have been chosen to measure the attitude under study, the general factor should measure that attitude. This is the basis of the Likert scaling procedure described above. In choosing items for such a scale, the aim is to cover the universe of content in order to measure the general factor, but to avoid including too many items on any particular aspect of the attitude, for this would generate an important group factor. If there is only one general factor and no group factor, and if the battery contains a reasonably large number of items, then the simple total of an individual's item scores—as described above—will generally provide an adequate, although not the most efficient, measure of his attitude.

When more than one common factor is involved in a battery of items, factor analysis may be used to examine the complex interrelationships between the items. The starting point is the *correlation matrix*, which is just a systematic grid layout of the correlations between all possible pairs of items; from this matrix, factor analysis attempts through one of several possible techniques of 'factor extraction' and of 'factor rotation' to identify the underlying common factors. Calculating all the correlations and performing the factor analysis are laborious operations if done by hand, but, providing the item battery is not too large, they can be done fairly easily by computer. The output of the analysis includes for each item on each factor a *factor loading*, which represents the importance of the particular factor in the item concerned. The researcher can try to interpret and label each factor by contrasting the items on which it has positive, near zero, and negative loadings. If a factor appears to cover an attitude dimension he wants to measure, he can then proceed to obtain estimates of the individual's scores on that factor; for example, a simple way to do this is to form a sub-scale of the items with high loadings on the factor and to calculate for each individual his total score for this sub-scale. Individuals' factor scores can be estimated for as many factors as are of interest, so that several dimensions of attitude can be measured from one battery of items.

Factor analysis is widely used with Likert and semantic differential items (see Section 14.9) as an exploratory device and, as such, it plays a particularly important role at the pilot stage. A large number of items relating to a wide range of aspects in the attitude area under study can be included on the pilot questionnaire, and factor analysis can then be used to explore the underlying structure of this area. The researcher attempts to identify the resulting factors and chooses from them the ones that he wants to pursue in the main study. He can then select items from the initial pool to form sub-scales for each of the factors in which he is interested. Thus, rather than assume a single attitude dimension, the researcher examines from empirical evidence the dimensionality of the attitude area and keeps as many of these dimensions as he wishes for the main survey.[1]

Examples of the use of factor analysis in attitude scaling are provided by Eysenck (1954) and Schofield (1965a). McKennell (1966) describes some uses of factor analysis in social surveys. References on factor analysis are given at the end of the chapter.

14.8. Guttman scales

Apart from the use of factor analysis, we are confining our discussion of attitude scaling to methods based on the assumption that the various attitude statements in the scale all belong to the same dimension.[2] With the Thurstone method, the only—and clearly not very powerful—evidence comes from the relative agreement of

---

[1] The use of factor analysis to explore the structure of attitudes is described by McKennell (1970), who also discusses the use of cluster analysis as a simpler technique in place of factor analysis for this purpose.

[2] See Torgerson (1958) and Coombs (1964) for discussions of multidimensional scaling. Some more recent developments are included in papers by Kruskal (1964a, 1964b) and in a number of papers by Guttman and Lingoes—for instance the paper by Lingoes (1968), which includes references to earlier papers.

those who judged the scale position of the individual items. In the ordinary Likert method the correlations between item scores and total score provide some evidence, but perfect correlations are needed for complete unidimensionality, and the actual correlations usually fall well short of this. With Guttman scaling, however, the attainment of a high degree of unidimensionality is a major concern.

The construction of a Guttman scale starts out by defining the total attitude (the universe of content) being scaled. A 'sample' of items representing this universe is selected for possible inclusion in the scale, these items are administered to a sample of persons, and then—this being the central feature of the method—the responses are subjected to what is called scalogram analysis to test the 'scaleability' of the items. This is meant in the technical sense that the questions should belong to the same attitude dimension, and it is important to emphasize that the criterion of unidimensionality lies, not in the views of outside judges, but in the pattern in which the respondents' answers arrange themselves. Since Guttman scales are of the cumulative type (see p. 361), the requirement of the *perfect* scale is that every respondent endorses all the items less extreme than the most extreme one with which he agrees. To illustrate this point we will take the commonly used illustrative example of a test of arithmetical ability. The following five problems are ordered in terms of difficulty:

(1) $3 + 4 =$
(2) $29 + 37 =$
(3) $47 + 59 - 17 =$
(4) $(33 \times 17) - 15 =$
(5) $(46 \times 15) \div (26 - 19 + 3) =$

We might reasonably expect that anyone who obtains a correct answer to problem (5) will also get problems (1) to (4) right, anyone who gets (4) right will get problems (1) to (3) right, etc. Thus we might anticipate only six patterns of answers (assuming no one makes a slip), which may be set out as follows (with a ' + ' indicating the correct answer and a ' − ' not the correct answer):

| | Problem | | | | |
(1)	(2)	(3)	(4)	(5)	Score
+	+	+	+	+	5
+	+	+	+	−	4
+	+	+	−	−	3
+	+	−	−	−	2
+	−	−	−	−	1
−	−	−	−	−	0

N

A diagram in which the individuals' responses are laid out as above is called a scalogram. If a set of n attitude items is perfectly scaleable in the above sense, the scalogram contains only $(n+1)$ response patterns, which are known as *scale types*, and one can infer from an individual's total score precisely which items he agreed and disagreed with. As we have already seen, this is fundamentally different from the Thurstone and Likert techniques, with both of which a final score of a given magnitude can result from quite different patterns of response, so that it is impossible to tell from the score what the individual answers were. With the Guttman technique, the perfect scale implies that a person who answers a given question favourably will have a higher total score than a person who answers it unfavourably. In this situation the *number of items* endorsed by a respondent, giving a complete picture as to *which* items he agreed and disagreed with, serves as his score. That this score is not a measure on an interval scale is easily demonstrated by comparing the above scale with one in which the first four problems are the same but problem (5) is replaced by another involving logarithms and square roots: as the distances between scores 0, 1, 2, 3 and 4 are the same for both scales but the distances between 4 and 5 differ, it is clear that at least one of the scales is not an interval one. There is, of course, no reason to suppose that either of them is, from which we see that Guttman scaling provides only ordinal measurement.

So far we have been assuming a perfect scale which, as only one misplaced answer would destroy it, is of course a rarely found phenomenon. The existence of *errors*, together with the fact that the ordering of the items is unknown in practical situations, make the scaling procedure more complicated than has been suggested so far. Two operations are needed to deal with these complications: first, the item responses must be analysed to discover the ordering of the items, in other words to find out which response patterns constitute scale types; and secondly an index is needed to measure the extent to which the scale approximates to a perfect scale.

The first of these operations involves arranging the items and respondents in the scalogram in such a way that the resultant pattern is as close as possible to that of a perfect scale. From the initial haphazard ordering of respondents and items, a useful first step is to rearrange the items into an order of popularity of endorsement (the most popular on the left) and the respondents according to the number of items they endorse (the respondent endorsing the most items at the top). If there were no errors this one step would produce the perfect scale, that is a solid block of pluses in the upper left-hand part of the scalogram and minuses elsewhere, but with errors it gives only a first approximation to the best fit. The approximation may be taken as adequate as it is, but if not, further rearrangements are carried out. If there are, say, 100 respondents and many items, these rearrangements become tedious and time-consuming if done by hand. There are available, however, punched-card methods using unit record equipment, and computer methods; also Guttman has designed a piece of apparatus known as a scalogram board on which the rearrangements can be easily made (see Chapter 4 by Suchman in Stouffer and others, 1950, for a description of the board and its use).

The final solution to the rearrangements is the one that is closest to the perfect scale, that is the one for which the errors are minimized. For the purpose of defining an error an individual's scale score is taken as that of the scale type which his response pattern most closely resembles, and Guttman has then defined an error as the false prediction of an individual's item response on the basis of this scale score. In the above scale of arithmetic ability a response pattern of $(+ + - + +)$ is closest to the scale type $(+ + + + +)$ and is given a scale score of 5; there is one error of reproducibility, for with a score of 5 item (3) is wrongly predicted to have been answered correctly. A response pattern of $(- - + + +)$ is also closest to $(+ + + + +)$ and hence has two errors. A pattern of $(+ + - + -)$ is equally close to two scale types $(+ + - - -)$ and $(+ + + + -)$, with scale scores of 2 and 4 respectively; it does not matter which is used for determining the number of errors, for two equally close scale types must both give the same answer, in this case one error. The problem raised by this last example is what score to give this pattern in the analysis; a commonly used general solution is to assign to each individual a score equal to the number of items he endorses.

Having arranged the scalogram so that it resembles the perfect scale as closely as possible, the next operation is to measure how successfully this has been achieved. Guttman's overall index for this purpose is the *coefficient of reproducibility*, which is defined as

$$\text{Rep} = 1 - \frac{\text{total number of errors}}{\text{total number of responses}}$$

where the total number of responses equals the number of items in the scale multiplied by the number of respondents. Another way of expressing Rep is to say that it is the proportion of responses that can be correctly predicted from the individuals' total scores. A coefficient of reproducibility can also be calculated for each item individually as the proportion of responses on that item that are correctly predicted; Rep is the simple average of these item coefficients.

Although Rep has an intuitive appeal, on closer examination it is found to have some unfortunate properties, which can make its obvious interpretation misleading. One undesirable feature is its dependence on the popularities of the items in the scale. The reproducibility of any item cannot be less than the larger of the proportion responding positively and the proportion responding negatively to it; for instance an item with which 90 per cent of respondents agree or 10 per cent agree (i.e. 90 per cent disagree) has a minimum reproducibility of 0·90. And, since the overall coefficient is the average of the item coefficients, it therefore clearly also depends on the item popularities. In addition it depends on the number of items being scaled. With a small number of items the value of Rep can be expected to be high even if the items are completely independent of each other; for example, four independent items with popularities of 20, 40, 60, and 80 per cent have an expected Rep of just over 0·90, and even nine independent items with popularities of 10, 20, 30, 40, 50, 60, 70, 80, and 90 per cent have an expected Rep of 0·83 (Torgerson, 1958, p. 323).

It is plain from these characteristics of Rep that it cannot stand alone as the measure of scalability; the conventional minimum level of a Rep of 0·90 for a set of items to form a scale has to be made conditional on an adequate number of items and their popularities. Common standards are that at least ten dichotomous items are required and that their popularities should range between 20 and 80 per cent endorsement. In addition it is usually specified that the pattern of errors should be haphazard, because the existence of a frequently reported non-scale pattern would indicate the presence of a further dimension.

The troubles with Rep as an index of scalability are that it is not meaningfully assessed against a benchmark of 0, and the number of items and their popularities have to be taken into account. To deal with these points the observed Rep can be compared with the expected value of Rep for a set of the same number of *independent* items with the same popularities—E(Rep). A suitable index for such a comparison is

$$\frac{\text{Rep} - \text{E(Rep)}}{1 - \text{E(Rep)}}.$$

Thus a set of items yielding a Rep of 0·95, but having an E(Rep) of 0·90, produces an index of 0·5. Such an index avoids suggesting the near attainment of a perfect scale when this is not the case, and therefore seems preferable to Rep. This approach is used in the index of consistency proposed by Green (1956), and other similar indices have been suggested.

Several significance tests for Rep have been developed,[1] but significance in scalability is only a minimum requirement. The tests examine whether a coefficient is significantly better than that for an equivalent set of independent items, but this is a far cry from seeing whether the responses have only small departures from a perfect scale. In terms of the index suggested above, a significance test examines whether the index differs significantly from 0, whereas the question that really needs to be answered is whether it is sufficiently close to 1.

The significance tests also apply only when the set of items is taken in full, whereas in practice this is often not the case. Part of the item analysis in Guttman scaling frequently consists of examining the item coefficients of reproducibility individually, and discarding items with low coefficients. This, of course, means that the overall Rep for the remaining items is larger than that for the full set, and the significance test is not applicable to such a 'purified' scale.

Returning to the construction of the scale, let us assume that, possibly after the rejection of one or two items, the responses of a pilot sample have proved to scale adequately. All the remaining items may now be left in the scale to be used in the full survey, or a selection may be chosen from them. An important factor in making a selection is the popularities of the items. Two items with the same popularities only duplicate each other and produce but one scale type; the addition to a scale of an item with the same popularity as one already included will thus, apart from errors, add nothing to the differentiation between respondents. The set of items chosen should try to cover the range of popularities; for instance, with a four-item scale, it might be appropriate to choose items with popularities close to 20, 40, 60 and 80 per cent, for these would separate respondents into five roughly equal-sized groups. Although we have discussed Guttman scaling in terms of dichotomous items, multi-category items can also be employed, and they have the useful feature that they can be split at different points to form dichotomous items with different popularities. A Likert-type item with five response categories can, for instance, be split into two parts in four ways—'strongly approve' versus the rest, 'strongly approve' and 'approve' versus the rest, etc.; the choice of split can be made according to the popularity required. Once the items have been chosen, it remains only to incorporate them in the survey questionnaire, probably in random order, and to administer them to the final sample.

One criticism of Guttman scaling is its analytical complexity.

[1] See the articles by Green (1956), Goodman (1959), Sagi (1959), Schuessler (1961), and Jobling and Snell (1961). Chilton (1969) reviews and compares the tests proposed by the first four of these authors.

Another is that there is no guarantee that the items will scale and that items that do scale generally cover a narrow universe of content. Even if the initial item set is fairly broad in content, the item analysis may well lead to the rejection of items in a way that leaves a scale of homogeneous items. The wider the range of the item set, the less realistic it is to treat it as virtually unidimensional. Guttman scales are therefore perhaps more appropriate for scaling ordered behaviour (e.g. degree of intimacy in sexual relations—see Schofield, 1965a, and Podell and Perkins, 1957) than less structured and broader based attitudes.

The difficulty in attaining Guttman scales is caused by the strict deterministic nature of the underlying model, namely that a person who responds positively (negatively) to one item *must* respond positively (negatively) to a series of others. As a result, departures from scale types have to be treated as aberrations or errors. An alternative way of accounting for departures is to relax the model from a deterministic to a probabilistic one. This leads to the latent structure models and the method of analysing them, *latent structure analysis*, due to Lazarsfeld and his colleagues.

Latent structure analysis deals in terms of the associations between the responses to the set of items, and the basic idea is that these associations can be accounted for by the latent variable underlying them. The task of the analysis is to infer back to the latent variable from the response patterns to the set of items, to determine the parameters of the latent structure model employed and, on the basis of their response patterns, to classify individuals on the latent variable. The reader may observe the resemblance of latent structure analysis to factor analysis, both techniques seeking latent variables from the associations between observed variables; in the case of the former technique the observed variables are qualitative, and the latent variable may be either qualitative or quantitative depending on the model employed, while for the latter both observed and latent variables are quantitative. To date there have been few practical applications of latent structure analysis in attitude measurement. Further details of the method are too intricate to be explained here and readers interested in them must turn to the references cited at the end of the chapter.

Before leaving this section, another technique with which Guttman's name is associated (and Suchman's among others) is worth mentioning. This technique—applicable to any attitude scale—involves an ancillary device, by which the respondent is not only asked to say whether he agrees with a given statement but also how strong his agreement—or disagreement—is, this *intensity* usually being classified into five categories. We thus get for each respondent not only a content score from the regular scaling process but also an intensity score; and these two may be plotted against each other on a graph. The result is often, though not always, an approximately U-shaped curve, the more extreme views in either direction being held with greatest intensity. Guttman suggests taking the content score at the lowest point reached by this curve as the dividing line between favourable and unfavourable responses. It is claimed that this lowest point, and therefore the percentage estimated to feel favourably on the issue, will not be affected by the form or wording of the individual items; and that this method therefore provides an objective way of dividing respondents into 'Pros' and 'Cons'. The argument is developed at length by Suchman and Guttman (1947) and by Suchman in Stouffer and others (1950, Chapter 7). Some doubts on it have been expressed by Peak in Festinger and Katz (1953).

14.9. Semantic differential

The semantic differential technique was developed by Osgood and his colleagues for their measurement studies in semantics and is fully described by Osgood and others (1957). To examine the meaning of a certain concept (e.g. father, Churchill, United Nations, Socialism) groups of subjects were asked to complete a series of graphical rating scales on the concept. Seven-point scales were employed— although obviously other numbers of points could also be used— with the ends of a scale being described by adjectives which were polar opposites. Examples of these scales, using polar adjectives taken from Osgood and others (1957), are:

```
  good ____: ____: ____: ____: ____: ____: ____ bad
  kind ____: ____: ____: ____: ____: ____: ____ cruel
  true ____: ____: ____: ____: ____: ____: ____ false
strong ____: ____: ____: ____: ____: ____: ____ weak
  hard ____: ____: ____: ____: ____: ____: ____ soft
severe ____: ____: ____: ____: ____: ____: ____ lenient
active ____: ____: ____: ____: ____: ____: ____ passive
   hot ____: ____: ____: ____: ____: ____: ____ cold
  fast ____: ____: ____: ____: ____: ____: ____ slow
  sane ____: ____: ____: ____: ____: ____: ____ insane
```

Subjects were asked to go through a set of scales for a particular concept and to place a check-mark in one of the spaces on each scale to indicate their rating of the concept's position with respect to the adjectives involved. The positions were then assigned scores 1 to 7.

Osgood and his co-workers applied this technique to a range of concepts and a wide variety of adjective pairs; and they investigated the correlations between the scores given to a set concept on different bipolar scales by conducting a series of factor analyses. Three main factors recurred in these analyses: the first, the factor which was usually dominant, had high loadings on polar adjectives such as good-bad, positive-negative, true-false and beautiful-ugly, and was labelled *evaluation*; the second, with high loadings on polar adjectives like hard-soft, strong-weak, and heavy-light, was called *potency*; and the third, with high loadings on polar adjectives like active-passive, fast-slow and hot-cold, was called *activity*. Other factors also occurred.

Osgood and others (1957, Chapter 5) suggest that attitude can be identified with evaluation, and that an attitude scale can therefore be formed from a series of bipolar rating scales measuring the evaluative factor. For this purpose, suitable adjective pairs are those which have been found to consistently load highly on evaluation and minimally on other factors (e.g. good-bad, optimistic-pessimistic, positive-negative), and which are applicable to the subject under study. To form an attitude scale, then, all that needs to be done is to decide the description of the issue to be evaluated and to choose suitable adjective pairs for it. For presentation to respondents, the position of the poles should be varied between scales to counteract the biasing effect of response sets; thus, for instance, one scale might run from 'good' to 'bad' from left to right (or, with a vertical scale, from top to bottom), while another might run from 'dishonest' to 'honest'. A respondent's total score (using consistent scoring of scales with, say, low scores at the unfavourable end and high scores at the favourable one) is the measure of his attitude. Thus the semantic differential, like a Likert scale, is a summated rating scale; however, while with Likert scaling there is a range of statements but typically only one standard form of response (strongly agree, agree, etc.), with the semantic differential there is a range of areas of response but only one issue to evaluate. Osgood and others have found high correlations between semantic differential and Thurstone scale scores for three concepts—the Church, capital punishment, and the Negro—and between semantic differential and Guttman scale scores on the subject of farmers' attitudes towards crop rotation. These correlations provide supportive evidence for the use of the evaluative factor of the semantic differential as an attitude scaling technique.

There is, however, no need to restrict attention to the evaluative factor and generally the semantic differential is used more broadly. A common application is to provide profiles of objects, such as for example those of various competitive brands of a good in a market research enquiry, and in this case the adjective pairs are chosen because they represent aspects of interest to the researcher. In comparing the images of different car models one might for instance employ 'overpowered-underpowered', 'constricted-spacious', 'comfortable-uncomfortable', 'safe-dangerous', 'expensive-cheap' and 'ordinary-individualistic' to measure characteristics of particular concern; but a number of more indirect scales such as 'youthful-mature', 'colourful-colourless' and 'masculine-feminine' might also be included to tap less obvious aspects of the models' images. The data obtained from administering these scales to a set of respondents can be analysed simply by calculating mean scores for each car on each scale and putting these means on a graph to give comparative profiles of the various cars, or a more detailed analysis can be made using factor or cluster analysis to investigate and measure the different dimensions involved. In this more specific kind of application of the semantic differential, factor analysis has been found to identify factors which depend on the subject matter of the study; and these factors are thus not identical with the three factors that recurred in the more general investigations of Osgood and his colleagues.

An illustration of the broader use of the semantic differential is given by McKennell and Bynner (1969). The aim of the survey was to investigate among schoolboys aged 11 to 15 the images of four concepts: 'the kind of boys who smoke cigarettes', 'the kind of boys who do not smoke cigarettes', 'the kind of person you are' and 'the kind of person you would like to be'. For each concept the same set of three-point bi-polar scales was used. For the pilot survey 50 scales were employed and factor analysis was performed on the results to identify the major dimensions. Using the findings from this analysis, the 50 scales were reduced to 19 for the main survey; examples from the final set of scales are 'Good at school work-Not good at school work', 'Neat and clean-Scruffy', 'Tough-Gentle' and 'Interested in girls-Not interested in girls'. A factor analysis of the responses to the 19 scales in the main survey yielded three main factors, which were labelled 'Educational Success', 'Toughness' and 'Precocity'. Using these three factors, the images of the four concepts were then compared for different groups of boys (smokers, triers and non-smokers), and among the findings were for instance the facts that each group sees the smoker as less successful educationally, tougher and more precocious. The study, as well as illustrating the use of the semantic differential, also demonstrates the general approach of including many scales at the pilot stage, of applying factor analysis to the pilot survey results to explore the structure of the attitudes, and of selecting on the basis of this analysis a smaller set of scales for the main survey. This exploratory approach has the considerable benefit that the survey yields for each individual not just a single attitude

2N

measure but a set of measures reflecting more fully the structure of his attitude.

14.10. Concluding remarks

Attitude is a complex concept involving many different facets and it has been the subject of much study in social psychology; there is now a vast literature on it. In this chapter we have not tried to discuss the concept as such, but have kept to the everyday imprecise meaning of the term. We have confined ourselves to outlining some scaling techniques for measuring direction and extremity of attitudes and, among these, to techniques which have proved appropriate for use in large-scale surveys; even so we have necessarily given no more than a simplified introduction. The interested reader is referred to the readings at the end of the chapter as sources for further study of these techniques and others that have not been mentioned here.

In conclusion we should note that attitude scales have been developed for many subjects, and that a researcher may be able to employ an existing scale in his enquiry. But before adopting an existing scale, he must of course ensure that it is applicable to his population, and this may necessitate some pilot work; if he can use an established scale, he not only saves on the construction of the scale and on the testing of its reliability and validity, but also has the results of other studies with which to compare his own results. Several collections of scales have been published, for example by Robinson and Shaver (1969), Shaw and Wright (1967) and Miller (1964).

NOTES ON READING

1. Good introductory texts on attitude measurement are those of OPPEN-HEIM (1966) and EDWARDS (1957); a more advanced book is that of TORGERSON (1958). Useful collections of articles on attitudes are those of FISHBEIN (1967), JAHODA and WARREN (1966) and SUMMERS (1970). Good single-chapter summaries of scaling methods are: SCOTT in LINDZEY and ARONSON (1968, Vol. 2); GREEN in LINDZEY (1954, Vol. 1); UPSHAW in BLALOCK and BLALOCK (1968); the chapter in SELLTIZ and others (1959); the introductory chapters in SHAW and WRIGHT (1967); and the chapter in GOODE and HATT (1952). A popular introduction to attitude measurement is given by EYSENCK (1953). The MARKET RESEARCH SOCIETY (1960) has published a collection of papers on attitude scaling.

2. Mnch of the work on reliability and validity derives from mental test theory; see for example LORD and NOVICK (1968) and GUILFORD (1954). A good discussion of these topics is given by SELLTIZ and others (1959) and by KERLINGER (1964). The paper by CAMPBELL and FISKE (1959) is worth consulting.

3. For the scaling methods outlined in this chapter, the serious student should consult the original papers by THURSTONE and CHAVE (1929), LIKERT (1932), the volume by STOUFFER and others (1950) for Guttman scaling, and OSGOOD and others (1957) for the semantic differential, as well as the references in note 1 above. KERLINGER (1964) also contains a chapter on the semantic differential. BOGARDUS (1925, 1933) developed an early cumulative scale, a social distance scale. STOUFFER and others (1952, reproduced in STOUFFER, 1962) have developed a method for improving cumulative scales, the H-scale. SMITH (1958, 1960) has written two papers discussing Guttman scaling. EDWARDS and KENNEY (1946) report the results of a comparison of the Thurstone and Likert scaling techniques.

4. There are a number of textbooks on factor analysis. A good one is that of HARMAN (1967): also recommended are those of THURSTONE (1947), CATTELL (1952), HORST (1965), LAWLEY and MAXWELL (1963) and—at a simpler level—FRUCHTER (1954) and BAGGALEY (1964). Useful introductions are provided by the last chapter of GUILFORD (1954) and by Chapter 36 in KERLINGER (1964).

5. For a discussion of latent structure analysis the reader is referred to LAZARSFELD and HENRY (1968). Among earlier treatments of the technique by LAZARSFELD are his chapters 10 and 11 in STOUFFER and others (1950); LAZARSFELD (1954); and his chapter in KOCH (1959, Vol. 3).

CHAPTER 15

Response Errors

15.1. Response bias and response variance

WE HAVE at many points in the previous four chapters referred to errors that may occur in the collection of survey data. This chapter discusses response errors systematically and with particular reference to interviewing, though many of the points apply equally to mail questionnaires. The rather different types of error to which observational techniques are subject were discussed in Chapter 10.

What is meant by response errors? Let us assume that for each individual covered by the survey there is an individual true value (ITV).[1] This value is quite independent of the survey, of the way the question is asked and by whom. If we ask the respondent how old he is, there is one unique correct answer; if we ask him how much he spent on chocolate last week there is again a unique correct answer. It is true that many questions are not so simple and—for instance with opinion questions—it would often be difficult to define the ITV. However, this difficulty is beside the point here.

We assume then that there is for each individual an ITV; it is this that the researcher is trying to ascertain. In only some cases will he succeed and the number of 'successes' in a survey will depend on the nature of the question, the way it is put and by whom, and how much precaution has been taken to minimize the chance of error. In any case, the difference between an ITV and the value recorded on the schedule[2] is the *individual response error* (IRE). Unlike sampling errors, response errors do not apply only to *sample* surveys; they can arise whatever the coverage of the population.

If the respondent says truthfully that he is 27 years old but the interviewer out of carelessness writes 25, then this is a response error.

[1] We here follow the useful terminology of Hansen, Hurwitz and Madow (1953).
[2] Errors of processing and analysis are left out of the present discussion, although most of it applies equally to them. 'Measurement errors' would be an appropriate term for the aggregate of these and response errors.

378

If the interviewer somehow makes her own political leanings felt and the respondent is thereby led to misrepresent his own views, this is again a response error. If the respondent went to the 'pub' three times last week but tells the interviewer he went once—either because his memory is at fault or because he does not want to admit more frequent visits—we again have a response error.

Let us pursue these three examples a little further:

(a) If an interviewer through carelessness misrecords an answer, a response error results. Such errors are unlikely to be highly systematic. On one occasion the interviewer may under-record the age, on another she may over-record. The chances are that, for each interviewer and over the entire sample, there will be about as many errors in one direction as in the other and that the net error in the average age, say, will be small.

(b) By contrast, in the second example, typical of what is usually meant by the term 'interviewer bias', the interviewer may, by the way she asks the questions or interprets the answers, or through the effect of her personality upon the respondent, influence the answers that are given. One strongly pro-Labour interviewer may systematically 'err' in that direction, while her colleague with the opposite views may produce a systematic error in the other. For a particular interviewer such errors will not cancel out with each other but accumulate. Her results will thus be *biased*, in the sense that if she were to interview an infinite number of samples from this population, the average (expected value) of her results would differ from the true population average. The difference would constitute her net bias.

This does not mean that there will necessarily be a bias for the sample as a whole. If the net biases of the individual interviewers go equally in opposite directions, averaging to zero, there will not be any overall net bias. Hence the suggestion, sometimes made, that an interviewing staff should be made up of two equal groups of interviewers, biased in opposite directions. In practice such cancellation of interviewer effects is probably rare. Interviewers tend to come from a relatively narrow population stratum in terms of social class, age and education, and it is more likely that their biases, if any, will be in the same direction. Even if bias could be dealt with in this way, there would still remain variability between the results of different interviewers caused by their individual net biases, and this would lower the precision of the sample estimate.

(c) Finally, there is the 'pub-going' example. If, for reasons best known to themselves, most people are reluctant to admit to a strong addiction to this habit, a systematic error will be produced. There is no likelihood of errors cancelling out.

We observe then that some response errors may be self-compensating for each interviewer, while others may be systematic but offset each other over the sample as a whole, while others still leave an overall net bias. Even this is a simplified picture, for errors that cancel out over the sample as a whole may not do so over any particular section of it. Instead of the systematic error in case (c) we may suppose—somewhat fancifully—that old people are concerned about appearing respectable and understate their frequency of 'pub-going', while young ones, if anything, exaggerate theirs. The effect might be that for the sample as a whole there would be little net bias, but that, for each age group separately, the results would be distinctly biased in one direction or the other. Or, in the interviewer bias example, if an interviewer conducted all the interviews for one region, the results for that region would be subject to her possibly sizeable individual interviewer bias, even though the overall net interviewer bias for the whole sample might be negligible. Since the bulk of survey analysis deals with sub-groups and not with the sample in its entirety, it is never sufficient to know that there is no net bias for the whole sample.

To develop the ideas of response errors more fully and to explain the meaning of response variance, a new theoretical notion is required. This is to treat a survey as being conceptually repeatable over a large number of trials, each of which employs the same survey procedure under the same essential conditions. The trials are thought of as relating to the same instant of time, and no trial in any way influences the responses at any other trial. The point of this conception is to generate a model in which an individual can give different responses at different trials, though of course it is also possible for him to give the same response throughout. An actual survey is then considered as the realization of one trial from the set of trials, and involves collecting the responses of the selected sample of individuals for that particular trial. Response variance is concerned with the variation in the survey results on repeated trials.

To clarify the distinction between response bias and variance, let us take the example of a complete census for measuring the average age of a population. On the conceptually repeatable trials of the census an individual could state his age differently, and the variation between his answers would be his individual response variance. The average of his various answers may or may not be his true age; the difference between this average and his true age is in fact his individual response bias. The averages of the individual response variances and biases over the whole population are the *response variance* and *response bias* respectively. Since some individual response biases may be positive and others negative, it is possible that they cancel out over the population to give no overall response bias. This cannot happen, however, in the case of response variance since variances are necessarily non-negative quantities.

The distinction between response bias and response variance, indeed between bias and variance generally, is important for several reasons. In the first place, the effect of bias remains constant for any sample size whereas the effect of variance decreases as the sample size increases, although not necessarily proportionately. Secondly, bias and variance have different effects on different statistics; while, for instance, with an arithmetic mean based on a large sample, bias is likely to be of greater concern, with the difference between two means the biases may often reasonably be expected to cancel out, making the variance the more serious problem. Thirdly, with suitable sample designs, variances can be measured from the sample itself, while biases can be assessed only by reference to data from some external source. These points are made clear from the models described in the rest of this section.

● For a more detailed examination of response bias and response variance we will employ a simple model for response errors.[1] In this model the observed value of the variable for the ith individual on the tth trial is written as

$$y_{it} = \mu_i' + d_{it}$$

where μ_i' is the average of the y_{it} over all trials and d_{it} is the response deviation of the observed value on the tth trial from this average value. The individual response bias β_i for this person is then taken as the difference between the average of his y_{it}'s over all trials, μ_i', and his individual true value, μ_i (say). Now suppose that the purpose of the survey is to estimate the population mean of the individual true values $\Sigma \mu_i / N$; the average of the observed values over all possible trials and all possible samples (assuming an *epsem* selection) is $\Sigma \mu_i' / N$. The difference between these two quantities is termed the *response bias*. The response bias is thus the average of the individual response biases ($\beta = \Sigma \beta_i / N$) which, as we have seen, may or may not cancel out. It is worth pointing out that the difference between the mean of the observed values for a complete enumeration and the true mean is not the response bias but just an estimate of it; a complete enumeration represents only one trial, and response bias is defined as the average of the trial estimates of response bias over the set of such trials.

In the model it is the variability resulting from the term d_{it} which gives rise to the response variance. The special case of a complete enumeration is again worth noting, for when all the individuals are included in the survey there is no sampling variance. There remains response variance, however, because the enumeration is itself a sample of one trial from the set of trials.

---

[1] This model applies equally to all measurement errors. To a large extent this treatment follows that of Cochran (1963) in his analysis of a measurement error model; also that of Hansen, Hurwitz, and Bershad (1961).

As a special case of this model, let us assume that there is no response bias ($\beta = 0$) and that the d_{it}'s are uncorrelated within the trial. This latter assumption means, for instance, that there is no consistent tendency for errors to be positive in one trial and negative in another. Then, if the trial is a simple random sample of size n from a population of size N and one response is obtained from each selected individual, the variance of the sample mean is

$$\text{Var}(\bar{y}_t) = \left(1 - \frac{n}{N}\right) \frac{S_{\mu'}^2}{n} + \frac{\sigma_d^2}{n} \qquad \ldots (15.1)^1$$

where $S_{\mu'}^2$ is the variance of the μ_i', and σ_d^2 is the average variance of the response deviations d_{it}. The first term in this formula is the *sampling variance* and the second term the *response variance*; in the case of a complete enumeration $n = N$ and the sampling variance is zero, but the response variance remains as σ_d^2/N. If there were no response errors, the equivalent formula to (15.1) would be $(1 - f)S_\mu^2/n$ where $f = n/N$: this is the same as the sampling variance in (15.1) except that S_μ^2 replaces $S_{\mu'}^2$, that is the variance of the individual true values (μ_i's) replaces the variance of the μ_i''s which are the sums of the individual true values and individual response biases ($\mu_i' = \mu_i + \beta_i$). It often happens that $S_{\mu'}^2$ is greater than S_μ^2 and this, together with the additional contribution σ_d^2/n in (15.1), frequently means that the response errors in this model lead to an increase in total variance, that is a decrease in the sample's precision. Remarkably, however, this is not so when the estimate is a proportion; then the variance of the proportion based on the observed responses is less than or at most equal to that based on the true responses (Hansen and others, 1961). But in any case the response errors should be taken into account in assessing the survey findings and fortunately, for the model described, this is easily done: if the finite population correction is negligible, the usual variance estimator for a simple random sample s^2/n (see Chapter 4) in fact conveniently covers both sampling and response errors of the types described. Indeed, when the f.p.c. is negligible, it also holds for complex designs, such as stratified and multi-stage samples, that the appropriate variance estimator covers both sampling and response variance, providing the d_{it} are uncorrelated.

Let us now take another special case, resulting from the use of replicated sampling (see Section 6.3). Although the approach can be applied for other sources of error also (e.g. coders), we will assume for simplicity of exposition that interviewers are the only source to be investigated. We will also continue to assume that there is no response bias. Suppose that a simple random sample of size n is made up of k independent simple random samples of size m (with $n = mk$), that k interviewers are chosen at random from a large population of interviewers, and that each selected interviewer conducts all the interviews for one particular sub-sample. The individual interviewer bias for any one sub-sample will then produce a tendency for the errors d_{it} to go consistently in one direction within that sub-sample (trial), that is the d_{it}'s will be correlated within sub-samples. In order to return to a

---

[1] For a proof of this formula, see Cochran (1963, pp. 377–8).

model with uncorrelated residual errors, the individual interviewer bias will be identified as a separate component. The new model is then

$$y_{ijt} = \mu_i' + \alpha_j + d_{ijt}$$

where the additional subscript j denotes the jth interviewer, μ_i' the average of the y_{ijt} over all interviewers and all trials, α_j the individual interviewer bias of interviewer j (the average of the α_j over the population of interviewers being zero), and d_{ijt} the deviation of y_{ijt} from $(\mu_i' + \alpha_j)$ on trial t. We will now assume the d_{ijt} to be uncorrelated. The variance of the mean for the full sample is then, ignoring the f.p.c.,

$$\text{Var}(\bar{y}_t) = \frac{S_{\mu'}^2}{n} + \frac{\sigma_d^2}{n} + \frac{\sigma_\alpha^2}{k} \qquad \dots(15.2)$$

where σ_α^2 is the variance of the individual interviewer biases α_j, and can be called the *interviewer variance*. To see the effect of the correlation between the observed values within the same sub-sample this formula may be expressed as:

$$\text{Var}(\bar{y}_t) = \frac{\sigma_y^2}{n} [1 + (m-1)\rho] \qquad \dots(15.3)$$

where $\sigma_y^2 = S_{\mu'}^2 + \sigma_d^2 + \sigma_\alpha^2$ is the variance of the observed values and $\rho = \sigma_\alpha^2/\sigma_y^2$ is the intra-class correlation of the observed values within sub-samples (see Section 5.4 for a discussion of intra-class correlation). This intra-class correlation is the variation between sub-samples (excluding random variation) as a proportion of the total variation in the observations. Since, apart from the effects of random chance, the only difference between sub-samples is that different interviewers conduct the interviews, ρ measures the proportion of the total variance accounted for by interviewer variance. In formula (15.2) the first term again represents the sampling variance, and the second two terms the response variance; if σ_α^2 were zero (i.e. $\rho = 0$), formulae (15.2) and (15.3) would, apart from the neglected f.p.c., simplify to formula (15.1). Besides making formulae (15.2) and (15.3) more complex, the presence of the intra-class correlation means that the simple random sample variance estimator s^2/n no longer covers the response errors; its use will produce an underestimate of the total variance if ρ is non-zero, as it typically is. However, with replicated sampling of the type described, an alternative variance estimator (the square of the standard error in formula (6.1) on p. 124) can be used to cover both sampling and response variance.

Finally we will consider the effect of the response bias β. A variance is unaltered by a constant bias so that, when a bias is present, the variance is inadequate to stand alone as a complete index of a sample estimator's precision. As we have seen in Section 4.3, the mean square error is an appropriate way to combine variance and bias. This is given by

$$\text{MSE} = \text{Var}(\bar{y}_t) + \beta^2 \qquad \dots(15.4)$$

Variance estimators attempt to measure only the first component in the MSE and not to cover the constant bias.

Two important points are indicated by the above results. First, response bias is not reflected in the variability within a survey, and so can be assessed only by comparing the survey results with results obtained from another source; high quality re-interviewing and existing accurate records are two such sources (see Section 15.4 below). Variable response errors in which the d_{it} are uncorrelated are, however, automatically covered by the usual variance estimators, and correlated variable errors like interviewer variance can be covered by the use of replicated sampling.

Secondly, the effect of a response bias is not reduced by increasing the sample size. The variance term in equation (15.4) decreases as n increases, but not the bias term. As a result the latter becomes a proportionately more important component of the mean square error as the sample size increases. The effect of the bias can be reduced only by improving the method of measurement. On the other hand, equation (15.1) shows that when the variable errors d_{it} are uncorrelated, the response variance, like the sampling variance, decreases as n increases. The situation portrayed by equation (15.2) is more complex; the first two terms decrease as n increases but not the third, which depends on the number of interviewers, k. If the interviewer variance is sizeable and if there is only a small number of interviewers, each conducting a large number of interviews, the third term may dominate the variance; a way to reduce its effect (to which we will return later) is of course to increase the number of interviewers.

A further important contrast between response bias and response variance, indeed bias and variance generally, is their differing effects on different statistics. In estimating the mean of a large sample, bias is likely to be the major concern because variable errors will probably have only a small effect. On the other hand, in estimating the difference between the means obtained by the same survey procedure on two separate occasions, the variable errors are likely to be more important; the biases for the two means are probably almost the same, and so will tend to cancel out from the difference. It is also worth noting that if two variables are subject to random measurement errors, their means will be unbiased, but the correlation between them will be attenuated (see, for example, McNemar, 1969); regression coefficients are also attenuated if both variables are subject to random measurement errors (see, for example, Johnston, 1963).[1]

The difference between bias and variable errors can be obscured by the other commonly made distinction between sampling and non-sampling errors. As regards *source*, the distinction between sampling and non-sampling (response, processing, etc.) errors is the appropriate one; as regards *estimation*, it becomes confused and the really important distinction is between variance (sampling and non-sampling), which can be estimated from the sample itself, and bias (sampling and non-sampling), which cannot.

---

[1] Other useful references on the effect of measurement errors on the relationship between variables are Blalock (1964), Cochran (1968a), and the chapters by Siegel and Hodge in Blalock and Blalock (1968) and by Koch and Horvitz in Johnson and Smith (1969).

15.2. Sources of response errors

To make the discussion more concrete, we shall now enumerate the various kinds of response errors. In this a clear distinction is needed between the sources from which such errors arise and the way in which they operate. An individual response error may be *due* to the interviewer possessing a strong opinion of her own; it may *result* in an error because of the way in which she asks the questions or interprets the answers. Equally, of course, her strong opinion may not result in an error at all. The distinction between sources and means is of practical importance. In order to decide on preventive action the surveyor needs to know what interviewer characteristics, if any, lead to substantial response errors and at what points in an interview there is scope for the introduction of errors. In this section we shall discuss sources of error; how they operate will be treated in the next.

In a sense it is unrealistic to discuss the various sources of error as separate entities. To say that the respondent's unwillingness to give a correct answer is a potential source of error clearly must not be taken to imply that this unwillingness is independent of the interviewer or of the way she asks the questions. An interview is an interaction between two people who may affect each other in various ways, and this should be borne in mind throughout the discussion of errors.

Characteristics of interviewers

Until the N.O.R.C. studies[1], the only interviewer effects which had received any attention were those arising from the personal characteristics of interviewers and from their opinions. Practitioners were concerned that the personal characteristics of an interviewer, her sex, age, education and social type, might influence the answers she obtained, either because of the impression she made on the respondent, the way she asked the questions, or perhaps because respondents might give answers more willingly—and differently— to different types of interviewer. A number of studies have indeed shown differences in results obtained by different interviewers to be related to their background characteristics. Wilkins (1949, pp. 22–3), for instance, in his enquiry into the demand for campaign medals after the Second World War, found that 'the ex-Service men gave replies to elderly women interviewers which showed a greater desire

---

[1] The N.O.R.C. studies, the work of Hyman and his colleagues (1954), represent a very valuable contribution to the subject of interview errors. They include case-studies of the interview situation, seen from the angle of respondent and interviewer; a review of the literature on interviewer effects to that time; an analysis of the various components of interviewer errors; and, most important, many experimental studies of their operation.

for medals than the replies they gave to young women'.[1] In addition to background characteristics, it is possible that some types of temperament and personality are more prone to lead to error than others.

Opinions of interviewers

The predominant interest of early research workers in this field was in the biasing influence of interviewers' opinions. Would such opinions, if strongly held, communicate themselves to the respondents and influence their answers? If the interviewers' opinions were evident from the way they asked the questions, then some respondents would undoubtedly tend to agree—or disagree—with them, depending on their temperament. Or, if their opinions influenced the way interviewers interpreted—and coded—doubtful answers or paraphrased the replies to open questions, bias would result. Although several studies have found interviewers' opinions to be related to the responses they have obtained, the N.O.R.C. report on the whole showed interviewers' ideology to be a less important source of error than had commonly been supposed.

Most studies on this topic have been concerned with opinions on political and social issues. One is led to wonder to what extent response errors may arise, say, in market research through an interviewer's partiality for her employer's products.[2]

Interviewer expectations

One of the most interesting findings from the N.O.R.C. studies was that interviewer effects often arose not so much from the interviewers' social and personal characteristics or ideology as from their expectations of the respondent's views and behaviour. This may not surprise the psychologist, but survey experts had not, prior to the N.O.R.C. work, concerned themselves with such expectational biases. To make clear what is involved, we will follow the N.O.R.C. distinction between three types of expectational errors:

(a) The first are *attitude-structure expectations*. Answers to questions early in the interview give the interviewer an indication of the respondent's attitudes. If she—perhaps unconsciously—expects people to be consistent in their attitudes, she may interpret answers later in the interview in the light of these expectations. This is particularly likely—and was found to operate—where interviewers had to code vague or marginal answers. Smith and Hyman (1950) report an experiment on this point. Two recorded interviews, each containing the same series of questions, were played to a group of

---

[1] See Hyman and others (1954) for a number of other examples.
[2] See the discussion of the 'sympathy effect' in Yule and Kendall (1950, p. 550).

interviewers. In the one interview the respondent answered all the questions preceding the test question as if she held isolationist views, in the other the respondent answered them as if an internationalist. The test question was the same on both interviews and so was the answer to it, a lukewarm and somewhat ambiguous one. The interviewers listening to the record were asked to code this answer. Some 75 per cent of them allocated it to the isolationist code for the first interview, but only 20 per cent did so for the second.

(b) Secondly, and more important for factual enquiries, are *role expectations*. The interviewer gains early in the interview an impression of the kind of person she is interviewing—how old, what social type, what occupation and income, personality and so on. If she is later confronted with doubtful, ambiguous or marginal answers, she may interpret them in the light of the answers she expects from this type of person. The N.O.R.C. studies produced evidence of this effect. In the extreme case, and especially when an interview is proving difficult, an interviewer may omit to ask certain questions altogether in the belief that she will be able to fill in the answers herself with fair accuracy. This applies equally to attitude-structure expectations. To the extent that expectations of types (a) and (b) operate in normal survey conditions, the effect would be to produce a more uniform set of responses than actually exist.

(c) Finally there are *probability expectations*. An interviewer may expect a certain distribution of opinions or characteristics among her respondents; for instance, she may think, rightly or wrongly, that about half of the total sample should be Labour supporters. If, as she works through her assignment, she has noticeably less than this proportion she may begin to interpret doubtful answers in the Labour direction (or, in the extreme case, distort them purposively). This seems the least plausible type of expectational error and we note that the N.O.R.C. findings on it were largely negative.

Errors arising from respondents

The respondent may give an answer other than the correct one because he lacks the knowledge to give the latter, because his memory plays him false, because he misunderstands the question or because, consciously or unconsciously, he does not wish to give the correct answer. Although such errors are appropriately laid at the door of the respondent rather than the interviewer, the root cause is essentially the reaction of one to the other. A respondent may overstate his frequency of church-going in order to appear respectable in the eyes of the interviewer; he may give a false picture of his political opinion because the interviewer has put his back up; he may state what he feels would be the interviewer's opinion because he wants to get the interview over. This sort of thing is an ever-present risk; as in everyday life, what people say and how they say it varies with circumstances and according to the person they are talking to.

15.3. Operation of response errors

How do these potential sources of response errors translate themselves into actual errors? In the case of errors due to the respondent's unwillingness or inability to give the correct answers, this question does not arise. But in what way do the personal characteristics, views or expectations of interviewers result in errors? They may, in the first place, operate directly. A respondent may be put off by the very sight of an interviewer; he may react badly to her personality and manner, be put off by someone of her age or social type or be influenced by what he feels to be her standpoint on the subject of the survey.

But there are also many indirect causes of response errors. In spite of the standardization of the modern survey interview, there still remains some scope for the interviewer's individual judgement and discretion and hence for errors arising from her characteristics, opinions and expectations. In addition there is scope, as in every job, for errors due to forgetfulness, inefficiency, fatigue and so forth. Let us run through the main possibilities.

Asking the questions

Interviewers are usually instructed to keep to the wording and order on the schedule and to ask questions in a stated manner. To what extent uniformity can be achieved is difficult to say, but there is clearly scope for interviewer effects to operate. Such effects may be accidental, in the sense that an interviewer alters the wording of a question by mistake, or they may be related to her characteristics, views or expectations. In the former case, the errors would probably cancel out; in the latter they would tend to produce a net interviewer bias.

The likelihood of interviewers disobeying instructions is dependent on the questionnaire itself. If the questions are long and rambling, or if they are expressed in unsuitable language, the interviewer will have a strong incentive to simplify them and put them in everyday terms. If the questionnaire does not proceed smoothly and logically from one topic to another, the interviewer will be tempted to alter the question order. Clearly a major method of achieving uniformity in the asking of questions is to provide the interviewer with a workable questionnaire.

Probing

In spite of instructions, interviewers may differ in the extent to which they probe in order to arrive at what they consider to be an accurate response. One interviewer might accept a 'Don't know' answer, where another might try to find out whether it was genuine. One interviewer may accept a vague or ambiguous answer where another would, by further probing, try to ascertain exactly what was meant. Differential probing, both in extent and the way in which it is done, undoubtedly gives scope for the operation of response errors.

Recording the answer

Carelessness in recording is another potential source of error.[1] Interviewers may omit to record answers, or may record them incorrectly or ambiguously. With open questions, some will be more successful than others in getting down the complete response. If they in effect paraphrase the reply, there is again scope for the operation of interviewer effects, for instance those arising from attitude expectations. If a respondent gives a long rambling answer, the interviewer may, perhaps unconsciously, select for recording that part of it which tallies best with the other answers.

Coding

Interviewers are often required to code answers on the spot. If the coding instructions are not fully understood or if the answer is thought ambiguous or is marginal between two codes, the interviewer's judgement on the matter may cause a response error.

Cheating

An altogether different cause of response error is conscious distortion or cheating. It has been much discussed in the literature (see Notes on Reading).

Some experts regard cheating as a serious, others as a negligible, problem; some look on it as a matter of inherent dishonesty, others as a function of interviewer morale connected with rates of pay, working hours, difficulty of questionnaires and general attitude to the job.

It is, of course, almost impossible to obtain accurate information on the extent of cheating in a survey, but survey experts appear to be fairly confident that falsification of entire questionnaires, at any rate, is rare. If employed on piece-rates, fieldworkers would indeed stand to gain by filling in the forms themselves, but the chance of detection is considerable, particularly when a system of checking on a sample of the interviews is in operation. The known existence of this is a valuable safeguard.

Much less amenable to checks, and probably much more common

[1] See Booker and David (1952) for some findings on accuracy and completeness in recording answers.

than complete falsification, is partial cheating on isolated questions. The interviewer may—particularly in a difficult interview—leave the questionnaire incomplete and fill in some or all of the remaining questions in accordance with her experience. With quota sampling the interviewer may falsify the respondent's age or social class in order to place him in one of the quotas she needs to fill.[1]

No view can be expressed here as to the extent of interviewer cheating in everyday surveys. Most survey organizations have their methods for detecting it but the details are, understandably, not made public.

Relationship to the conditions of the survey

We have so far covered components of response error arising from interviewer, respondent, and the interaction of the two. It will be clear to the reader that these errors are closely dependent on the other conditions of the survey. The chief factors will merely be summarized here; most are discussed more fully elsewhere in the book.

(*a*) *The length of the questionnaire.* The nature and magnitude of response errors in a survey depend partly on the length of the questionnaire. Respondent and interviewer both tend to become less attentive and accurate after a certain time.

(*b*) *The order of questions.* Earlier questions on the schedule may set the tone of the interview and a general frame of reference for later questions, or they may provide the respondent with information of use in answering later questions. The order of the questions can thus affect the answers obtained.

(*c*) *Question structure.* With questions involving a number of sub-questions (i.e. 'If answer to Q.3 is Yes, . . .'), the interviewer may be tempted to avoid complications by filling in the answer *not* requiring further sub-questions, particularly if there is room for doubt; if he finds out how to do so, the respondent also may avoid answering in a way which leads to supplementary questions. The seriousness of response errors may vary according to whether open or pre-coded questions are asked; and, in the latter case, with the number and order of the alternative answers presented to the respondent.

(*d*) *Question content.* Questions involving prestige, social gain, personal circumstances and so on may lead respondents, consciously or otherwise, to give inaccurate answers. Questions involving memory have their own considerable risks of error.

---

[1] The possibilities for cheating in quota sampling (dishonest completing of quotas) are discussed by Moser (1951).

(e) *Question wording.* The use of leading words, of technical or uncommon terms, of ambiguous or vague words and phrases may lead to error. Such errors may operate differentially with different interviewers.

(f) *Interviewer instructions.* The training given to the interviewers on the subject of the particular survey, as well as their general training, will help to determine the accuracy of the information they collect. Their ability to perform their task in the required manner depends on the clarity of the instructions they receive and the success of the briefing sessions.

(g) *Designated respondent.* The accuracy of information may depend on the person from whom it is collected. In household surveys it is sometimes specified that the information must come from the head of household, sometimes from his wife, sometimes from the head or his wife, and sometimes from any adult member of the household. The wider the latitude allowed the interviewer in choice of respondent, the fewer calls she will need to make and the greater her success rate will probably be, but these assets may have to be balanced against a greater amount of response error. Some information about households is generally the province of a particular household member (e.g. shopping for the housewife, income for the head) and serious response errors may occur if the information is obtained from someone else.[1]

A related problem is when one member of the household is asked to provide information for other members, rather than each of them being interviewed individually. A number of studies have found, for instance, that respondents report a greater level of illness for themselves than for others in the household (see for example Cartwright, 1957, and Mooney, 1962); this indicates the existence of response errors.

(h) *Place of interview.* The physical location (and possibly time) of the interview may have an influence upon response errors, as also may the presence of a third person. Schofield (1965a) in his survey on the sexual behaviour of young people, for example, stressed that an interview in a teenager's home should be conducted in strict privacy, and arranged for the interview to be conducted in a nearby office hired for the research if the teenager preferred.

(i) *Interest in the survey.* The accuracy as well as the willingness of

[1] See Neter and Waksberg (1965) for an experiment on respondent designation effects in connection with the number and the size of jobs for repair or alteration of houses. They found no systematic difference between the four respondent designation procedures: head of household; wife; head and wife together; and any knowledgeable adult.

response probably depends partly on the respondent's interest in the subject matter of the survey. The interviewer's accuracy also is affected by her own interest.

(*j*) *Sponsorship.* The sponsorship of the enquiry may affect response errors. The respondent may try, for instance, to give prestigious answers to an enquiry sponsored by a university or by government, whereas he may not do so to one sponsored by a commercial firm.

15.4. Detection of response errors

The potential sources of response error are thus plentiful, and so are the points in the interview at which they can operate. What does this mean in terms of the average survey? Do the potential errors become actual errors; and, if so, how big are they and to what extent do they cancel out? Answers to these questions have to be tentative. There is a substantial amount of *general* experience on the adequacy of different survey procedures, and there are numerous findings on errors introduced in specific situations. But each survey is in some respect novel, and what is lacking is a satisfactory methodology of measuring the size of response errors in the individual survey.

The simplest approach, on paper, is to check the accuracy of survey responses against data from other sources, and certainly no such checks should ever be left untried. One may try to check individual answers, thus arriving at an assessment of *gross errors* (total response error) irrespective of whether they subsequently cancel out, or one may look only at the *net error* remaining after any cancellation has taken place. A justification for the latter procedure is that it is the net errors that create a bias in survey results in the form of totals, averages and percentages; on the other hand, measures of association are affected by self-cancelling gross errors. In any event, from the methodological point of view the researcher's concern should certainly be with gross errors. Any hope of eliminating or reducing errors rests on knowing where and why they occur, which one cannot do by looking only at the final results. The study of gross errors is never easy and often—as with opinion questions— virtually impossible.

Gross errors

It goes almost without saying that the first step is to check the completed schedules. But editing (discussed in the next chapter), even at its most thorough, can detect only the more obvious mistakes and inconsistencies. Fothergill and Willcock (1955; reproduced in Edwards, 1956) report a Government Social Survey experiment in which 56 interviewers interviewed dummy informants under observation. All errors of procedure were noted and it was subsequently found that only 12 per cent of these could be detected from the completed questionnaires. The main categories among the 'invisible' errors were insufficient probing, altering the scope of the question through wording changes or biased probing, and wrong classification of answers.

The detection of procedural errors—failure to ask all the questions, to use all the appropriate prompts, to probe to the right extent, to record accurately and completely—is an important part of maintaining or raising the quality of fieldwork, irrespective of whether, in a particular case, they produce errors in the results (a failure to prompt correctly does not *necessarily* produce the wrong answer). In the present section we shall concern ourselves with 'effective' errors only.

(a) *Record checks.* We come then to the individual validity checks—designed to ascertain how close the answer recorded on the schedule is to the individual true value. Sometimes it can be checked against records or documents of some kind. Birth records can be used to check on the accuracy of age reporting, employers' records on wages, bank records for the size of savings accounts, doctors' records for illnesses, etc. But one's first reaction is that the opportunity for such checks is very limited. Yet Eckler and Pritzker (1951) report the use of the following record checks in connection with the 1950 U.S. Population Census:

(i) Birth certificates on file in our State Offices of Vital Statistics—to check age reporting.
(ii) Records of military service on file in our Veterans Administration —to check reporting on veteran status.
(iii) Tax returns on file in our Bureau of Internal Revenue offices— to check income reporting.
(iv) Reports by employers on file in our Social Security Administration—to check reporting on wages and salary income and reporting on industry.
(v) Naturalization and alien records on file in our Immigration and Naturalization Service—to check reporting on citizenship status.
(vi) Returns from the 1920 Census—to check age and birthplace reporting for persons who were thirty years old or over in 1950. This check is being made to supplement the birth-certificate check because it is known that our birth certificate records for many States are decidedly incomplete for 1920 and earlier years.

Besides indicating the scope for record checks, this programme also brings out two of their limitations.[1] In the first place, with the procedures employed, check data were located for only about 50 to 80 per cent of the check samples; and secondly, since no further fieldwork was conducted, it was not possible to reconcile differences

[1] See U.S. Bureau of the Census (1963b).

between the census returns and the check data. As a result the 1950 record checks proved inconclusive to a considerable extent; in the Evaluation and Research Program of the 1960 Census, content record checks were made only on occupation, industry and income.

Thus record checks, apart from being confined to a limited class of survey data, have their difficulties. The records may themselves be inaccurate, they may be incomplete—in which case one has to judge whether the people for whom records are not found are typical of the rest—and matching and finding of records for survey individuals is often troublesome and expensive. Errors may occur in matching an individual's survey and record data and, if no attempt is made to reconcile differences, such mismatches may indicate response errors where none exist.[1] In addition, many potential records will not be accessible to non-official agencies. There are problems, certainly, but if response errors are to be taken seriously these problems should at least be tackled.

(b) *Consistency checks.* Record checks are useful if one has reason to believe that the records are more accurate than the survey answers. Many checks used in surveys merely ascertain whether two sources produce the same or different answers, with little cause for believing one to be more accurate than the other. An interesting example was the technique of Kinsey and others (1948) of asking both husband and wife questions relating to their sexual life within marriage, and then comparing the answers. This was useful but, like all consistency checks, negative. If the two answers agree, the surveyor is entitled to feel increased confidence. If they do not, and he has no reason to believe one to be more accurate than the other, he merely has a measure of variation. Still, this is useful knowledge since he can then go on to investigate reasons for the difference and try to find out which answer is right.

A common type of consistency check is to ask for the same information in two or more ways. As a crude example, one could ask the respondent, perhaps early in the interview, when he was born and casually ask him, at a later stage, how old he is. This is again a one-directional check and, even if the two answers agree, there is no proof that they are correct. To realize this, one has only to think of a woman consistently under-stating her age. It is indeed hard to invent consistency checks so disguised that the respondent who is determined to give a false answer will be caught out. The interviewer must be warned of the existence and purpose of consistency checks, for otherwise she might also try to make the answers consistent. If the

---

[1] See Neter, Maynes, and Ramanathan (1965) for two models of matching errors and their implications.

questions are asked on separate occasions one reduces the chance
that the respondent will remember the answer he gave the first time,
but then such checks only have point with factual data unlikely to
change with time.

(c) *Re-interviewing*. In a sense, the most natural way of checking on
the accuracy of a measurement is to repeat it. True, if the two
measurements are made in the same way, a difference in results is
only an indication of response variance and does not tell one anything about the individual response bias. But if the second measurement can be made by a more trustworthy instrument than the first,
one is in a good position to gauge the accuracy of the earlier measurement.

These principles apply in the present context. If an interviewer—
either the original one or one similar in 'quality'—is sent to re-
interview a respondent the difference in answers gives an indication
of variability.[1] In order to check more fully on the accuracy of the
initial answer, the second interviewer has to be of a higher 'quality'.

There have been a number of re-interview experiments. Among the
earliest were those reported by Mosteller in the well-known book by
Cantril (1944). A group of respondents were visited by interviewers
and classified by economic status into four groups, the main criterion
being income. After three weeks the same interviewers revisited them,
and on a second classification 77 per cent retained their original
grouping. In a parallel experiment, but with different interviewers
doing the second interview, only 54 per cent of the cases retained
their former classification. Mosteller reports similar findings on other
variables.

Such researches give an indication of response variance, of how
much variation is found in repeated measurement. To get at the
accuracy of the measurement the quality of the second interview
needs to be raised above that of the first, and ideally it should result
in no response errors.

This is the basis of the re-interview checks—known as quality
checks or Post-Enumeration Surveys—which have in recent years
become a regular feature of census-taking in the United States. The
scale of these censuses—whether of Population, Housing, Agriculture or Manufacture and Business—is so enormous that it is

[1] Strictly speaking, if the same interviewer is used on both occasions we get a
measure of what is generally called *reliability*. If different interviewers are used—
a more practicable proposition—we get a measure of *variability*.

One assumption must be noted, that the two measurements are independent of
each other. With an opinion question, the first interview may affect the respondent's thinking and thus influence the second answer; or, with any question, the
respondent may remember his earlier answer and make his later one consistent
with it. These effects would undermine the value of the re-interview check.

impossible to attain the quality feasible with smaller enquiries. In Britain the first post-enumeration survey for the Census of Population was held after the 1961 Census and is described by the U.K. General Register Office (1968). The survey was designed to check both on the coverage of the Census and on the quality of response; in view of the former purpose, area sampling was employed. For the latter purpose interviews were conducted in a sample of about 7,300 households in the period of one to three weeks after the Census. Being a pioneering effort in this country, the survey was not completely successful in its aims but it did nevertheless draw attention to some weaknesses in the Census. A contributory factor in the survey's failure was the fact that its interviewers were insufficiently trained. They were recruited from among the Census enumerators and, although drawn from among the better of these, they were not as skilled as fully trained professional interviewers. It also proved possible to give them only very limited instruction. As a result they failed to obtain adequate answers to some of the survey questions, which meant that some comparisons between Census and post-enumeration survey data could not be made and others were not completely satisfactory.

The U.S. quality checks have been intensive studies of small samples[1] (relative to the size of the census) and every effort has been made in them to attain the highest level of accuracy possible. In the Content Evaluation Study for Population Characteristics (CES) for the 1960 Census, for instance, the U.S. Bureau of the Census (1964c, p. 6) reported the following four differences between the census and CES procedures, all designed to make the CES data as accurate as possible:

1. Superior interviewers were selected and they were given more intensive training than was possible for the census interviewers.
2. The CES interviewers were paid hourly rates instead of the piece rates used in the census.
3. Information on CES characteristics for an adult was obtained from the person himself by direct interview. In the census, information for all members of a household was obtained either from a self-enumeration form or from any responsible member of the household who was home when the interviewer called.
4. The CES interviewers conducted an intensive interview. The interviewers probed much more deeply than did the regular census

[1] The re-enumerative studies of content error (response error) for the 1960 U.S. Censuses of Population and Housing involved intensive interviews at about 5,000 households (U.S. Bureau of the Census, 1964c). Another check was made on content error by matching the Census returns with the individual schedules of the Current Population Survey (U.S. Bureau of the Census, 1964d). Other evaluative studies of the Census were conducted to investigate coverage errors—both under- and over-enumeration—and response variance; references are given in the Notes on Reading. We should note that these quality checks are used largely for analytical purposes, not as a means of adjusting the original results.

questionnaire in order to get as accurate information as possible on the characteristics being studied.

For these reasons the CES data were more trustworthy than those of the census, although they were of course not completely accurate. It must be admitted that, however much trouble is taken, even quality checks will contain errors. But they are probably as close as one can get to accuracy in real life, so one must be satisfied with them. One practical question is: should the interviewer on the second occasion know what answers were given on the first? There are strong arguments in favour of her knowing. One of the values of the quality check is that it tracks down reasons for a difference between first and second answer, and so enables one to make sure that the second is the correct one. The interviewer must therefore know what the original answer was. The only danger is the possible tendency to confirm, rather than contradict, the original answer. Marks, Mauldin and Nisselson (1953) report some evidence to this effect. However, such a tendency should be responsive to careful training and instructions and, if it can be satisfactorily remedied, it would seem preferable on every count for the second interviewer to be aware of the original answers. In the post-enumeration survey for the 1961 Census in Britain, interviewers were in fact provided with the returns made on the Census schedules. In the U.S. Content Evaluation Study three different procedures were employed. In one sample, the CES interviewers did not know the census responses for the sampled persons but, when discrepancies between the census and CES responses occurred and it seemed that more information could be collected in an additional interview, the case was referred to interviewers for reconciliation. In the second sample the interviewer conducted the CES interview without referring to the census data, but then went through the census data and reconciled any differences on the spot. In the third sample the census data were not made available to the interviewer and no attempt was made at reconciliation.

Another practical question with a quality check is when to take it. Since the purpose is to check on the typical quality of responses in the main survey, such checks are usually taken afterwards, for this ensures that the answers in the main survey have not been influenced by those in the quality check. A quality check should come soon afterwards, for the longer the interval between it and the main survey, the more changes will actually occur in the respondents' characteristics; for changeable characteristics, the respondent must try to recollect his state at the time of the main survey and, if this was some time before, memory errors may seriously jeopardize the accuracy of the check data. Also, as time passes, people will move from their addresses at the time of the main survey, and may not be available for interview in the quality check; some may prove impossible to trace and others may have moved to areas to which it is too expensive to send interviewers. On the other hand, there are practical difficulties in organizing an immediate quality check. It may be, for instance, that the supervisors of main survey interviewers are to conduct the check interviews. If so, the quality check cannot be started until they have finished supervising the main survey and have received any additional training necessary. It may also be advisable to defer choosing the quality check sample until the main survey has been completed, in order to avoid the risk of the main survey interviewers learning which individuals have been selected for the check; if they knew the members of the quality check sample they might make more strenuous efforts to gain accurate data from them.

Quality checks can rarely establish with certainty the *correctness* of the original results, but they can and often do prove that the earlier result was wrong. If the first and second answers disagree, and the interviewer finds out that the original question had been misunderstood, an error has been established. There are many such ways of locating errors in the original returns, but not even a quality check can help in the case of consistent errors, such as a woman consistently under-stating her age. Although more intensive interviewing may uncover some of these errors, nothing short of a birth certificate or a psychoanalyst would bring all of them to light.

To the extent that a quality check can be considered free of error, the comparison of the original and the quality check responses yields valuable information on *gross* errors. While knowledge of the net error may be sufficient to indicate the accuracy of survey data for some purposes, information on gross errors also sheds light on the ways in which errors have arisen, and can thus help in suggesting likely remedies for controlling and reducing them in the future. It seems to us that quality checks constitute a development of great importance for large-scale enquiries, and that they should become standard practice for censuses and major (especially continuous) surveys. In other surveys we also feel that quality checks are worth attempting even if they consist only of supervisors re-interviewing a small sample of respondents.[1] They keep the field staff up to scratch and are more likely than any other means to disclose sources of response error.

Net errors

The difficulty in studying gross errors is that there is generally

---

[1] Kish and Lansing (1954) report a study in which the accuracy of the original answers (on house values) was checked by sending along professional appraisers of house values.

no accurate and readily available source of data with which to compare the survey responses (if there were, there would be no need to ask the survey question in the first place). As a result, a purely methodological enquiry is needed, either to collect data from a difficult source or to conduct re-interviews of high quality. Net errors are easier to detect than gross errors, and it is therefore easy enough to understand why most research workers have concerned themselves only with the net errors remaining in the final results, that is the errors which have failed to cancel out over the sample as a whole. But even accuracy checks for aggregates are not at all plentiful. Demographic variables like sex, age, household composition and so forth can generally be checked. But, for most of the questions which appear on survey questionnaires, external data suitable for checks are fairly hard to come by (and are not always more accurate than the survey results).

Comparison of the results with data (on the same subject and population) secured in other surveys may strengthen, or weaken, confidence in their accuracy, but there are generally too many differences between the surveys to make this a firm check.

Many of the earlier studies of net errors were based on quota samples. Differences between the survey results and the check figures could then be due to a mixture of selection and response errors, with no hope of separating them. Mosteller and others (1949) found this a handicap in trying to unravel why the forecasts of the 1948 U.S. Presidential Election went wrong. This illustrates a general 'weakness' of checks upon net errors. Discrepancies between survey results and the check figures may be due to response errors, to bias in selection, or to non-response, and are most likely to be due to a combination of all these factors. Checks on gross errors are not confused in this way.

Another limitation of checks on net errors is that they are frequently available only for the overall results, so that the sub-group figures—which may be quite as important—are impossible to validate. Lack of bias in the overall results does not guarantee the same for the sub-group results, for the latter may have individual biases which compensate each other in the sample as a whole. The problem is even more acute when the sub-group classification is itself open to response errors. In relating age and income, for instance, both variables may be subject to response errors; the income distribution for any one age group then contains response errors due to wrong incomes being recorded and also due to age misstatements, some respondents being wrongly included in the age group and others wrongly excluded from it. Although the two variables individually may show no bias, the results for a particular sub-group, the results

o

for the comparison between sub-groups, and any measure of association between the variables may still be biased. Despite these limitations, checks on the overall net error are worth making, for they do to some extent serve as tests for biases in the sample results.

Interviewer variance

One aspect of response errors that has always attracted attention is the fact that interviewers, working on equivalent samples and under similar conditions, tend to obtain different results. There are two reasons why this problem has received so much attention. One is that studies to estimate interviewer variance are easy to design. The other, and more important, is that the very difficulty of testing the validity of survey results leads surveyors to concentrate on their reliability. As Henry (1954) put it:

> You are probably familiar with the story of the mother who watched her son's infantry regiment marching along the street and exclaimed: 'Look, my John is the only one in step!' It is always possible, I suppose, in our sort of work that the one investigator who differs from all the others *may* be the only one really in step, but as we have no criteria by which to judge this, all we can do is to insist that, right or wrong, he falls into line with the others.

Consistency, that is low interviewer variance, becomes the aim, resulting in the ever-increasing standardization of interview procedures. By suitable selection and training, by strict instructions and by rigid control of the interview, the risks of substantial interviewer variance are reduced.

It may be unwise to put too many eggs into this basket of consistency and not to make efforts with the—admittedly much more difficult—problem of validity. It is true, of course, that substantial interviewer variance inflates the total variance and hence lowers precision, but at least it can, with suitable designs and formulae, be estimated from the sample itself; bias cannot.

The estimation of interviewer variance in essence requires the method of replicated or interpenetrating sampling (see Section 6.3 and also pp. 382–3 above) which Mahalanobis (1946) first used for this purpose. The main difficulty with a straightforward application of replicated sampling to this problem is the requirement that the interviewers' workloads comprise completely comparable samples. This means that, in a multi-stage design, each interviewer must conduct interviews in all the primary sampling units and so, if the PSU's are widely scattered, will have to engage in a great deal of travel; a considerable economy with non-replicated designs is that each interviewer usually interviews in one, or at most a few, of the PSU's. For this reason interviewers are seldom, if ever, assigned full replications to interview in national surveys or other surveys covering large areas; interviewer variance can, however, still be investigated in such surveys by using some form of restricted replication. A pairwise replication scheme is commonly used for this purpose. To illustrate this, suppose that a multi-stage design is stratified so that two PSU's are selected per stratum (the paired selection design), and that at least part of the stratification is geographical. Then, instead of one interviewer working in one PSU, the two interviewers chosen to work within a particular stratum can each conduct their interviews in both the stratum's PSU's according to a replicated sampling procedure. Comparison of the results achieved by the two interviewers then leads to a measure of interviewer variance for the stratum, and this can be combined with similar measures for other strata to form an overall index of interviewer variance (see, for example, U.S. Bureau of the Census, 1968a).

There have been numerous studies of interviewer variance using some form of replicated sampling. Two of them are reported by Kish (1962) who also summarizes the results of some earlier studies.[1] As we have seen above (p. 383), the amount of interviewer variance can be indicated by the intra-class correlation coefficient ρ, measuring the proportion of the total variance in the observations accounted for by the interviewer variance. Kish found that for his attitudinal questions the range of ρ's was mostly 0 to 0·07 for the first study of 46 variables and 0 to 0·05 for the second of 48 variables; these ranges are fairly comparable with that of 0 to 0·08 for the attitude questions in the study by Gray (1956). Gray's data yielded also a range of 0 to 0·02 for eight 'factual' items; and the 1950 U.S. Census data (Hanson and Marks, 1958) gave ranges of 0 to 0·005 for 31 'age and sex' items, 0 to 0·02 for 19 'simple' items, 0·005 to 0·05 for 35 'difficult' items, and 0·01 to 0·07 for eleven 'not answered' entries.

At first sight these intra-class correlations seem small, but they can nevertheless considerably decrease the precision of the sample estimates. As formula (15.3) shows, ρ appears in the variance of a sample mean as part of the multiplier $[1 + (m - 1)\rho]$; if m—the number of interviews per interviewer—is large, even a small value of ρ can lead to a sizeable multiplier. If, say, m were 31 and ρ were 0·033, the multiplier would be 2, i.e. a doubling of the variance; to neglect such an effect is to seriously underestimate the true variance of the sample estimate.

Although even a small interviewer variance may have a serious

---

[1] Among other studies are those of Stock and Hochstim (1951), Gales and Kendall (1957), Gray (1956), Durbin and Stuart (1954a), Hanson and Marks (1958), Hansen and others (1961), Eckler and Hurwitz (1958), Kemsley (1960), Kemsley (1965) and U.S. Bureau of the Census (1968a).

effect on a sample's precision, interviewer variance should not be the only concern. It should be made clear, for instance, that a small interviewer variance is not necessarily inconsistent with substantial gross errors. An interviewer can make substantial gross errors without causing any net error; and, even if she does have a net error, other interviewers may produce net errors in the same direction, in which case interviewer variance may still be small. Let us look at these two arguments more closely.

If an interviewer makes a great many errors which are due to misunderstanding or carelessness rather than to biasing influences like strong views or expectations—and the N.O.R.C. studies show evidence that this tends to be the case—these errors may cancel out on average for each interviewer, leaving little in the way of individual interviewer biases; this means that interviewer variance, the variation in the individual interviewer biases, will be small.[1] Interviewer variance becomes larger the more individual interviewers make systematic rather than compensating errors.

Now suppose that the errors made by an individual interviewer *are* non-compensating and thus result in a net error for that interviewer. If all the other interviewers have net errors in the same direction, gross errors will be substantial and there will be a net error for the sample as a whole; but interviewer variance will probably still be small. Take a case where all the interviewers unconsciously exert a pro-Conservative influence. This will cause many gross errors because it tends to make people express, say, more Right-wing views than they really hold. There will be a net (pro-Conservative) error for each interviewer and a net error over the whole sample, the survey overestimating the pro-Conservative tendencies in the population. But this effect is not reflected in the interviewer variance—indeed any part of the variance—because of the consistency of the net errors; rather it represents a response bias. Thus low interviewer variance is consistent with substantial gross errors. In practice, net errors are unlikely to be as uniform as in this example and, to the extent that interviewer variance is present, it will inflate the total variance.

Although there have been a number of studies of interviewer variance, the subject is far from closed. More evidence is needed from everyday surveys and for a wide range of questions. Interviewer variance is not something to be described once and for all by a few basic parameters but rather, as Kish (1962, p. 115) observes:

It is more likely that interviewer errors differ greatly for various characteristics, populations, designs and resources (this last including

---

[1] These cancelling errors contribute to σ_d^2 in formula (15.2), not to the interviewer variance σ_a^2.

questionnaires, the nature and training of interviewers, etc.). Therefore knowledge about this source of variation, as about sampling variation, can be accumulated only from a great deal of empirical work spread over the length and breadth of survey work.

One would also like to know how the cancellation of errors comes about and the extent to which it occurs. Does a small interviewer variance arise because individual interviewers have little net bias associated with them or because their net biases all tend in the same direction? This requires studies of interviewer variance in conjunction with gross error checks on sub-group and overall results. Finally, more needs to be known about the root causes of interviewer variability. Does it arise mainly in the asking of questions, interpreting of answers or their recording?

15.5. Control and measurement of response errors

In the early sections of this chapter were listed the potential sources of response error and the ways in which interviews gave scope for their operation. The evidence on the actual operation of errors comes from many isolated researches and is often contradictory. At one time or another most types of error have been found to exist and not to exist. Still, perplexing though it often is, there is enough evidence to suggest that response errors ought to engage the surveyor's serious attention. Indeed Hansen and others (1953, Vol. II, p. 280) remarked that 'The paucity of dependable data on response errors is unquestionably the greatest present obstacle to sound survey design'. Although there have been several good studies of response error since that was written, the remark still holds true today. Leaving aside experimental researches in this field, the question is, how can we control and reduce response errors?

One approach was dealt with in the preceding section. However much is done to prevent errors, their influence on results should be assessed, wherever possible, by validity checks on individual answers, sub-group results and overall results.

But what should be done to keep response errors down to the minimum? In considering this, we should recall the distinction between response variance and response bias. The former can, with suitable designs and formulae, be estimated from the sample results themselves and can be included as part of the total variance; the latter cannot. Response variance causes concern because it inflates total variance; response bias because its magnitude is often unknown. If the surveyor had a genuine choice, he might concentrate mainly on controlling the bias-producing errors, since his ignorance of the extent of bias is a most serious weakness. This control can be achieved only by improving the survey methods. On the other hand, the contribution of a source of response variance can be reduced by increasing the number of source units employed in the survey. As formula (15.2) shows, the contribution of interviewer variance to the total variance of the sample mean is σ_α^2/k, and is therefore reduced by increasing the number of interviewers, k; this applies also to other sources of measurement variance, e.g. coder variance (see below).

Some potential sources of error one associates essentially with bias. A leading question is to be avoided precisely because it will cause response error in a constant direction; the same applies to the use of a prestige name in a question and to other aspects of wording. For the same reason one might avoid employing interviewers with very strong views on the survey subject, which might cause systematic error. In short, many of the principles current in survey planning amount to an attempt to reduce response bias.

The most sensible course for the surveyor is to treat response errors as a serious problem and to take all steps, empirical and analytical, to keep them under control. We now come to specific possibilities.

Selection, training and supervision of interviewers

The selection, training and supervision of interviewers is closely bound up with response errors. If we knew what kinds of people made 'error-free' interviewers, we could select accordingly. But survey life is not as simple as that. In the first place, there is probably no such thing as a good interviewer-type; some people are better for some surveys than for others, with some respondents than with others. Secondly, interviewing involves a number of different skills and a person who is satisfactory on one score may be hopeless on another. An accurate recorder is not necessarily a good interviewer. We need more knowledge, on the lines of the N.O.R.C. findings, about the relationship between different interviewing skills, and what characteristics make for good interviewing. However, this subject has already been discussed in Chapter 12 and all we need stress is that response variance and bias must be to some degree responsive to careful selection, training and supervision of the field staff.

Control of interview

We saw in Section 15.3 that there were various danger-spots in the interview at which scope for response errors was greatest. If field coding gives rise to substantial errors, perhaps office coding is preferable. If the recording of verbatim answers gives rise to many errors, it might be wise to forego their advantages and to use pre-coded questions. If differential probing is a source of trouble, perhaps probing should be more strictly controlled. It is easy to understand why the modern surveyor hankers after standardized methods. The more formal and standardized the technique, and the stricter the instructions, the less room there will be for the play of the interviewer's judgement. Portable tape recorders are used occasionally, and through them errors made in the asking of questions and recording of answers can be detected.[1]

Increasing the number of interviewers

One way of reducing interviewer variance is to select, train and supervise the field staff so as to achieve maximum uniformity; an alternative way is to decrease its effect by increasing the number of interviewers. Since the contribution of interviewer variance to the variance of a sample mean is a function of the number of interviewers, the greater this number the smaller—*other things being equal*—the contribution will be. But other things are not generally equal. Using more interviewers may mean accepting a lower grade or spending less money on their training and supervision. Then the variation in the population of interviewers might itself increase, and offset the gain from increased numbers. If all potential interviewers were of the same quality then—on the model implied in formulae (15.2) and (15.3)—it would be an advantage to have more rather than less of them. Indeed, ignoring hiring and training costs it would be best to have as many interviewers as respondents, each interviewing one randomly assigned respondent. If hiring and training costs are taken into account, the optimum number of interviews per interviewer depends on the intra-class correlation, measuring the interviewer variance as a proportion of total variance, and on the relative costs of hiring and training to the cost per interview. Kish (1962) shows for instance that if the relative costs are $18:1$ and $\rho = 0.02$ the optimum interviewer workload is 30 interviews.

It is worth remarking that even if there is a sufficient number of interviewers to make the effect of interviewer variance small for the sample as a whole, this does not necessarily also apply for the subgroups. If only a few interviewers conduct all the interviews for a particular sub-group (as is clearly likely to be the case when the sub-group is a geographical region), then interviewer variance may have a sizeable effect on the sub-group results. There was strong evidence in the 1950 U.S. Census that interviewer variance did indeed have a considerable effect on the statistics for small areas, and it was to reduce the effect of interviewers that self-enumeration was

---

[1] There is also on the market—but not, as far as we know, in operational use—a machine that asks the questions previously recorded on it in the office! Interviewer variability is thus largely eliminated, but with what effects on validity one does not know. The aim of using this kind of machine may be understandable, but there is something distasteful and bizarre about some of these mechanical survey developments.

introduced on a large scale in the 1960 Census (U.S. Bureau of the Census, 1968a).

The basis of the above discussion is the model of interviewer variance outlined in Section 15.1. As formula (15.3) shows, for a fixed sample size the variance decreases as the number of interviews per interviewer (m) decreases, i.e. as the number of interviewers increases. In fact if there are as many interviewers as respondents (i.e. $m = 1$), the multiplier $[1 + (m - 1)\rho]$ is unity, leaving the variance as σ_y^2/n. The variance of the observed values σ_y^2 includes a component for the interviewer variance, but when each interviewer conducts only one interview there is no intra-class correlation factor. In this special case, the model reduces to the first model we discussed, the one with uncorrelated errors, and this means that, if the f.p.c. is ignored, the appropriate variance estimator covers response variance, including interviewer variance, as well as sampling variance. The danger with increasing the number of interviewers is of course that σ_α^2 in formula (15.2) may increase, and hence ρ may increase, if their average quality is lowered.

Matching of interviewers to respondents

We have seen that response errors may occur through the interaction of interviewer and respondent. A working-class man, who perhaps had left school at 14, may resent being asked questions about his education by an obviously educated, well-spoken interviewer, but might be prepared to give the information to a person of his own type. On paper at least, some matching of respondents and interviewers seems attractive. But, apart from common-sense cases such as not sending Jewish-looking persons to conduct interviews on anti-semitism, two points argue against matching. First, one is in practice limited to the interviewers who are available, and this rules out matching on any scale. Secondly, and much more important, one would need to know much more than is known at present about the operation of such interaction errors before one could confidently embark on any matching. For all one knows, the working-class man may be more, not less, willing to talk about education to a person of quite a different type than to someone like himself. There is, for instance, some evidence that interviewers who establish a high degree of rapport with their respondents tend to obtain more biased answers (e.g. Weiss, 1968–69). Without secure evidence, there is no case for interviewer–respondent matching.

Analytical methods

Finally, we must refer briefly to the analytical approach to response errors. It has to be admitted that none of the above ways of detecting gross and net errors, or for controlling them, is very powerful; all encounter snags in application. So, whether or not they succeed in reducing errors, one must try in the analysis to estimate what response error remains. As we have seen, with a suitable sample design, response variance can be studied by setting up a theoretical model according to which the response variance arising from different components, notably interviewers, can be estimated. Such models are useful in helping to clarify how response errors may affect the estimates one makes from a survey, both those of the population values and of total variances; and they are helpful in trying to determine the best sample design. Reinforced with cost data, they should make it possible to decide in advance what is the optimum number of interviewers to be used, how much it is worth spending on training and supervision, and so forth. The theory involved in all this is beyond our present scope, but references for further reading are given below.

Among the analytical methods we should perhaps refer again to consistency checks. Some such checks may be simple, like asking for the same information twice in different ways on the questionnaire, others can be more intricate. When collecting data on frequency of a particular behaviour, such as being ill or buying a particular good, a check can be made on the comparability of the information provided for different reference periods; for example, without an external explanation, a much higher report of illness during the last month than in the last month but one before interview indicates the presence of response errors, probably memory and telescoping errors.[1] Many other checks depend on special features of the subject matter and therefore no general methods can be given. A simple demographic example is the check that the number of married men is about equal to that of married women. Another is the study of the last digit in respondents' reports of their exact ages, in which it is commonly found that certain digits (particularly 0) are preferred; response errors would be indicated, for example, if far more people gave their age as 40 than those giving their age as 39 or 41.[2] The researcher should be alert to the possibility of such checks for his particular subject matter and employ any he can. Hopefully the results will give him greater confidence in his data but otherwise they will at least warn him of the presence of response errors.

We have in this chapter, as indeed throughout the book, concentrated on general methods and principles rather than practical

---

[1] See Logan and Brooke (1957) for a comparison of illness reporting in the month before interview and the month before that. Kemsley (1961) and Turner (1961) compare the expenditures reported in diary records in different weeks of the diary.

[2] See, for example, Myers (1954) for an index of digit preference.

20

details. Even given that response errors are important and may undermine survey accuracy, there must be a limit to what it is worth spending on their reduction. Money may be as difficult to obtain as accuracy, and in practice the surveyor, like anyone else, has to cut his cloth according to his purse. At any rate, we hope to have made clear that sampling errors are not everything. It is always worth asking whether some of the resources needed for keeping them down (e.g. by increasing sample size) might not be better spent in reducing response errors.

NOTES ON READING

1. The importance of the N.O.R.C. studies has been emphasized at several points and readers are referred to the volume by HYMAN and others (1954) for details. The following papers are worth consulting; several of them arose from the N.O.R.C. programme: CAHALAN and others (1947), CRUTCHFIELD and GORDON (1947), FELDMAN, HYMAN and HART (1951–52), FISHER (1950), GUEST (1947), GUEST and NUCKOLS (1950), HART (1948), HYMAN (1950), KATZ (1942), PARRY and CROSSLEY (1950), SHAPIRO and EBERHART (1947), SMITH and HYMAN (1950), SHEATSLEY (1949), STEMBER (1951–52), STEMBER and HYMAN (1949, 1949–50), JAEGER and PENNOCK (1961), EL-BADRY (1961), EVANS (1958), GOLDBERG (1958) and HANSON and MARKS (1958).

2. There have been a number of studies of response errors in health reporting: see, for example, MOONEY (1962), U.S. NATIONAL CENTER FOR HEALTH STATISTICS (1961, 1965a, 1965b) and FISHER (1962). There have also been a number of response error studies for financial data (incomes, expenditures and stock holdings) including NETER and WAKSBERG (1964, 1965), DAVID (1962), FERBER (1965), BORUS (1966), MAYNES (1968), FERBER and others (1969), and SIRKEN and others (1958). An area of particular concern relates to anticipated consumer purchases: see, for instance, JUSTER (1966), and NETER'S chapter in JOHNSON and SMITH (1969).

3. Among the literature on cheating, readers might find useful CRESPI (1945–46, 1946), DURANT (1946), and BLANKENSHIP and others (1947).

4. A well-known paper on errors is that by DEMING (1944). MOSER (1951) discusses the literature on interviewer bias up to about 1950. The book by CANTRIL (1944) contains some of the earliest findings in this field. The chapter in KAHN and CANNELL (1957) and CANNELL and KAHN'S chapter in LINDZEY and ARONSON (1968, Vol. 2) are worth consulting. KISH (1962) is a good reference on interviewer variance. Other papers on the topic were noted in Section 15.4.

5. There have been a number of papers on the U.S. Census checks. Particularly useful are ECKLER (1953), ECKLER and PRITZKER (1951), HANSEN (1952), HAUSER (1950), MARKS and MAULDIN (1950), MARKS, MAULDIN and NISSELSON (1953), ECKLER and HURWITZ (1958), HANSEN, HURWITZ and BERSHAD (1961), and BAILAR (1968). For reports on the Evaluation and Research Program of the U.S. Censuses of Population and

Housing 1960, see U.S. BUREAU OF THE CENSUS (1963b, 1964a, 1964b, 1964c, 1964d, 1965, 1968a). The post-enumeration survey and other quality checks on the 1961 Census of Population in Great Britain are described by the U.K. GENERAL REGISTER OFFICE (1968).

6. For a theoretical treatment the books by COCHRAN (1963), HANSEN, HURWITZ and MADOW (1953), SUKHATME and SUKHATME (1970), MURTHY (1967) and RAJ (1968) are worth consulting, as are the papers by HANSEN, HURWITZ and BERSHAD (1961), FELLEGI (1964) and COCHRAN (1968a). The book by ZARKOVICH (1966), devoted to the subject of the quality of statistical data, covers both theoretical and practical aspects of the subject. The chapter in KISH (1965a) is a useful one.

7. The study by BELSON (1962) gives interesting data on the mechanics of response errors in the National Readership Surveys; and the study by KISH and LANSING (1954), reporting on response errors in the U.S. Survey of Consumer Finances, is also particularly illuminating.

CHAPTER 16

Processing of the Data

16.1. Editing

WITH THE field part of the survey completed the processing of the matetial and the highly skilled task of analysing it begins. First, the questionaires have to be checked; secondly, the mass of detail has to be reduced to manageable proportions so that the wood can be seen for the trees; thirdly, the material has to be summarized in tabular form or otherwise analysed so as to bring out its salient features; finally, the results have to be interpreted and presented in a report.

A characteristic feature of these final stages of a survey is the continual interplay between the research worker in charge, the coders and the staff responsible for the production of tabulations and other statistical analyses (in small-scale research surveys, they may all of course be one and the same person). Yet it is an obvious convenience to consider the operations separately, since they each have their specific purposes and problems. In this chapter editing, coding and tabulating will be discussed, leaving the analysis and interpretation to Chapter 17.

The three operations now to be studied differ basically from each other. Editing is a routine task—though one which requires scrupulous care. Some types of coding are similarly reducible to repetitive operations, but others allow a crucial role to judgement and skill. Tabulation in very small surveys may perhaps be done by hand and, if so, requires care, accuracy and patience rather than technical skill; if the work is done using an electronic computer or unit record equipment, some acquaintance with the mode of analysis is needed. The planning of tabulation, as distinct from its actual execution, of course requires a good deal of skill in any case.

At the various stages in a survey, from the collection of information from the respondents through to the production of the results for the survey report, errors can creep in. In processing the data the aim must be to keep these errors to a minimum.

Editing of the survey schedules is intended to detect and as far as possible eliminate errors in the completed questionnaires. It is certainly one of the least exciting parts of a survey; the work tends to be slow, repetitive and dull and gives cause for none of the enthusiasm associated with the initial planning, while also lacking the interest involved in collecting the data and the ingenuity required to analyse them.

Yet anyone who has ever glanced through completed questionnaires returned from the field will be aware of the absolute necessity for careful editing. Even the best interviewers are liable to make errors, omit to ask questions or to record answers and, when the field staff is inexperienced, editing assumes a crucial importance. The interviewers should themselves edit their own questionnaires immediately they have completed each interview, but this does not obviate the need for office editing. Before the questionnaires can be regarded as ready for coding, tabulation and analysis, they should be checked in the office for completeness, accuracy and uniformity.

(a) *Completeness.* The first point to check is that there is an answer to every question. If the interviewer has forgotten to ask a question or to record the answer, it may be possible to deduce from other data on the questionnaire what the answer should have been and thus to fill the gap at the editing stage.

At other times the interviewer may be able to fill in the gap from memory. If she has omitted to record what type of house the respondent lived in, she may be able to recollect it later. At the worst, but only if the information is vital, one may return to the respondent for the missing information, most economically by a postal enquiry.

An omission is especially trying when neither the context of the question, nor answers to other questions, enable one to decide whether (i) the respondent refused to give an answer, (ii) the interviewer forgot to ask the question or record the answer, or (iii) the question was not applicable to the respondent. Non-applicability can most easily be deduced from other data, but it is usually difficult to choose between the other explanations of an omission.

In most organizations, interviewers are instructed to record an answer for every question (there always being a 'not applicable' category) and good interviewers should not often be guilty of errors on this score. If many questions are unanswered (more likely because the respondent was unwilling than because the interviewer was inefficient) the whole questionnaire may have to be abandoned. But this is done only as a last resort. If the information that is on the questionnaire can be regarded as accurate, it is inefficient to throw it away even though it may cover only a small part of what was asked for.

Checking the completeness of the answers recorded for open questions is virtually impossible. Apart from seeing that the answer is legible enough for the coder (this applies to all types of answers, of course) and that it makes sense—i.e. that the interviewer has written down enough to make the meaning of the answer clear— there is little one can do; unless, of course, the interview has been tape-recorded or respondents have been re-interviewed.

(b) *Accuracy.* It is not enough to check that all questions are answered; one must try to check whether the answers are accurate. In the first place, inconsistencies should be looked for. Let us take the cigarette-smoking questions in the schedule on p. 313. If code (2) —'Doesn't smoke cigarettes'—has been ringed in answer to Q. 10(a) and the answer 'about 10' recorded for Q. 10(b), clearly something is wrong. Here one could unhesitatingly alter the former code to (1), but often the matter is not so easily settled. If a questionnaire tells us that a clerk aged 35 is earning £80 per week, we may suspect that there is an error somewhere. His age may have been understated or his income overstated, or the interviewer may have failed to record that he is a Town Clerk. Every effort should be made to resolve *clear* inconsistencies, but care should be taken to make corrections only where there has quite obviously been an error; apparent inconsistencies *may* be genuine, and to iron them out would result in a false picture.

Inaccuracy may be due to carelessness or to a conscious attempt to give misleading answers, and it may arise from either respondent or interviewer. In the stress and strain of an interview, the interviewer may easily ring the wrong code or so place the ring that it is not clear which of two codes is intended. Answers needing arithmetic, even of the simplest kind, often cause trouble. If the interviewer is asked to summarize a household composition table (such as for Q. 17 on p. 314), she may give an inaccurate total; if she has to convert from one unit to another (say days into hours), she may similarly slip up. Thus it is generally better to have arithmetic done in the office rather than by the interviewer. Where answers have to be written (e.g. 'five days') rather than codes ringed, mistakes can also occur. Some, though by no means all, of these errors can be caught by careful editing.

(c) *Uniformity.* The editing stage gives an opportunity for checking that interviewers have interpreted questions and instructions uniformly. In a survey of the use of laundry facilities conducted by a student group, one question asked how much per week the housewife spent on laundry. This was asked only of those who sent laundry out. It was discovered at the editing stage that some interviewers had mistakenly ringed the answer 'under 1s. 6d.' (the lowest category), instead of 'not applicable', for housewives who did not send their laundry out.

In another survey, the instructions for the income question omitted to specify whether interviewers were to take account of Family Allowances in deciding upon the appropriate answer code. Some did, others didn't. Since a woman with more than one child was entitled to Family Allowances, errors could sometimes be corrected during the editing. In brief, the editing staff should keep a keen look-out for any lack of uniformity in the way data have been collected or the replies recorded.

If the analysis is to be carried out on a computer—and also if it is to be conducted on unit record equipment—the initial office editing will almost certainly be supplemented by a more detailed, rigorous and dependable computer editing just before the start of the analysis (see pp. 434–5).[1] In this case the initial editing is of lesser importance and, if there is good reason to believe that there are very few errors in the questionnaires, it may even be dispensed with entirely. On the other hand, if there could be a number of errors (as one might anticipate when inexperienced fieldworkers are used), an initial editing will still be worth while, because errors found early in the processing are easier to correct than those detected later.

A related question is whether all, or only a sample, of the questionnaires should go through the initial editing. No general rule can be laid down since the decision must depend on the balancing of the various error risks. There is no point in spending the bulk of one's resources on a complete edit if the errors thus corrected are relatively minor and if it means ignoring other important sources of error. But a sample check can only correct errors found in the selected questionnaires and so is more useful as a measure of the quality of the data than as an error-correcting procedure. If the questionnaires are unlikely to contain many errors, a useful combination is to take an initial sample quality check followed by a complete computer or unit record edit later on.

There remains the question whether in the initial editing a questionnaire should be edited as a whole or whether one section, even one question, should be edited at a time for all questionnaires. It is probably easier to avoid mistakes if one can concentrate on one or two questions at a time. On the other hand, editing a whole

---

[1] Evans (1958) notes how, at the U.S. Bureau of Labor Statistics, statistical clerks edited a file of data and detected 323 errors, and yet a subsequent mechanical screening uncovered 199 additional errors.

questionnaire facilitates viewing the individual case *as a whole*, noting the relationship between answers to the different questions and detecting inconsistencies. It also facilitates the judging of an interviewer's ability, and (a practical point) enables one to get on with the editing as the questionnaires come in, instead of having to wait until the fieldwork is complete.

Finally we should draw attention to the value of an efficient record system for locating the questionnaires. Particularly with large-scale surveys, different questionnaires may have reached different stages of the processing operation: some may be being edited, others coded, others may be with the punch operators and yet others may be with the interviewers, either because the interviews have yet to be conducted or because the questionnaires were found to lack certain answers and were therefore returned to the interviewers for completion. In this kind of situation the only way the researcher can hope to keep track of all the questionnaires is by setting up a routine and easily updated record system.

16.2. Coding

Let us now suppose that the data have been through the initial editing and are ready to be prepared for analysis. In most surveys, certainly whenever results are to be put in quantitative form, the intermediate stage is the coding of the answers. Sometimes this and the initial editing are joined in a single operation.

The purpose of coding in surveys is to classify the answers to a question into meaningful categories, so as to bring out their essential pattern. Before discussing this operation a rather specialized application of coding techniques should be mentioned. This is *content analysis*,[1] which is typically a systematic analysis and description of the content of communication media. Newspapers may be analysed to study the changing attention given to a certain political issue over several years; the content of different papers (or books) in a country may be studied to bring out their differing attitudes to an issue or their different propaganda techniques and so forth. The reader interested in this field is recommended to consult the references at the end of this chapter; we will here confine ourselves to the use of coding in summarizing survey answers.

The process involves two distinct steps. The first is to decide on the categories to be used, the second to allocate individual answers to them. Following Government Social Survey practice, the set of

---

[1] One could legitimately use the terms 'coding' and 'content analysis' interchangeably, since both refer to the same process. In practice, the former term is generally used for research data, the latter for material existing in the normal course of events, like newspapers, books, etc.

categories will be referred to as the coding frame. The set of coding frames covering all the information to be abstracted from the questionnaires is commonly known as the code book.

The coding frame

Mostly a coding frame relates to a single question, and in cases where there are only a few possible answers to the question the preparation of the frame raises no problems. The question: 'Have you smoked any cigarettes today?' admits only of the answers 'Yes' and 'No', together with 'Don't remember', 'Refuse to answer', 'Not applicable', so that the frame decides itself. Most of the questions in the schedule on pp. 312–4 are of this kind and could be given in pre-coded form for just this reason—that the set of possible answers could easily be decided upon ahead of the fieldwork. Where the frame does not determine itself automatically, it is a matter of deciding how detailed a grouping to allow for in the coding, which in turn will depend on how the answers are expected to be distributed and what analysis is being planned. As an example take Q. 16(a) from the schedule on p. 313:

> If (respondent lived) at home
> What kind of house is it? . . .
>
> | Whole detached house | 5 |
> | Whole semi-detached house | 6 |
> | Whole terrace house | 7 |
> | Self-contained flat | 8 |
> | Other (give details) | 9 |
> | Not applicable | Y |

It was believed that these represented the main alternative answers[1] and that it was useful to keep them distinct. Codes 5, 6 and 7 might have been combined to constitute a 'Whole house' code, but the difference between the three types was here of interest. One cannot lay down any hard-and-fast rules for this kind of decision. By and large, it is advisable to retain more rather than less detail in the coding since it is easier to amalgamate groups in later analyses (particularly if a computer is used) than to split one group into several when they have been coded alike. On the other hand, a very detailed coding is extravagant as regards punched cards or other computer input media and makes the analysis unwieldy, and at the same time increases the difficulty of allocating answers accurately. The whole point of coding is to summarize the data, and it is as unhelpful to retain too many categories as it is misleading to use too few.

[1] Pre-coding for 'type of house' questions actually causes a number of minor problems—e.g. how to allow for flats over shops, caravans, etc.

Establishing a coding frame is, however, not generally as easy a task as the remarks so far suggest. Some coding frames will relate not to single questions but to a combination of questions or even the whole questionnaire. These frames, which are useful for tapping areas on which no direct questions have been asked but for which information is provided by the respondents' answers to some of the open questions on the questionnaire, can be very difficult to construct. But then one need think only of the general run of open questions to realize how hard it may be to set up, ahead of the actual interviews, a list of categories which will be exhaustive, mutually exclusive and suitable for the purposes of the survey.

Answers to a question like: 'In what way are you affected by rising prices?' (see p. 425 below) may cover all sorts of points: about the cost of living in general as well as particular goods, about consequent changes in purchasing habits and leisure pursuits, about tax effects, about resultant changes in employment or wage claims, about effects on political attitudes and so forth. Any single answer may cover several of these aspects so that the researcher has to decide in terms of which factors (or dimensions, to use the technical word) the coding is to be done. He might wish to concentrate on the dimension of *general cost of living*, and to code according to how severely people feel themselves to be affected, or he might be chiefly interested in the individual price changes mentioned and categorize these; or he might take a number of dimensions, coding according to each in turn; he might even code all items mentioned. The point is that the coding frame has to be designed in accordance with the aim of the research, which will partly determine the dimensions chosen for coding and the number of categories distinguished for each. But, in addition, the frame must also be influenced by the types of answer actually given. Respondents may, for one reason or another, not answer in the terms and at the level expected by the researcher, and this must be allowed to influence the coding frame. In other words, the frame must suit the respondents' chosen terms of reference as well as the purposes of the survey. The researcher may begin by setting up the code categories according to his own ideas and aims, but he must be prepared to modify them in the light of an analysis of a sample of replies.

This is indeed the usual procedure. A representative sample of completed schedules is examined and the answers to the particular question noted. (The Government Social Survey generally examines some 10 per cent of the schedules for this purpose.) Gradually a pattern emerges and on this the final coding frame is based. Groups containing very few cases can be combined into a 'Miscellaneous' category—care being taken not to lose anything which may be of substantive interest later on. A category with very few cases may be interesting just for this reason: if, in a survey of families waiting to be rehoused, hardly any of the respondents mentioned a desire for central heating in their new accommodation, this negative finding could be of considerable interest but would have been lost if the few cases had been thrown into a residual group. This minor point emphasizes that the construction of the coding frames is not a task to be delegated to routine clerks; it has to be done by somebody fully in touch with the purposes of the survey and of the way the results are to be used. Before a frame is finalized, every opportunity should be given to coders to test it further on samples of replies, so as to examine their coding differences and eliminate ambiguous or troublesome codes. This not only results in a better frame but also serves as good training for the coders. If insufficient trouble is taken at this preparatory stage, the final coding will be repeatedly held up because answers do not seem to fit properly in any code or, just as bad, could reasonably be assigned to more than one category. Furthermore, the more doubtful decisions there are to be taken, the greater the variability between coders will be.

Many of the coding frames will need to be developed to cater specifically for the purposes of the survey in hand, but even so account should be taken of existing frames; if a researcher can reasonably make his frame consistent with a frame used in another survey, he has the benefit of being able to compare his results with those of the other survey. Comparability of definitions is of obvious importance in social research, and towards this end the British Sociological Association and the Social Science Research Council have published a book entitled *Comparability in Social Research*, edited by Stacey (1969b), examining the definitions of some basic variables—education, family and household, income and occupations; a further eight variables are under investigation by a working party of the British Sociological Association.

Nearly all surveys of individuals collect certain personal background data and the coding frames for most of these pose no serious problems. Age, sex and marital status are relatively easy to treat, though the question of whether to code exact ages or age groups, and if the latter what groups to use, has to be decided. An important background variable, but a difficult one to code, is social status. It has been found to be influential in a wide range of analyses but its definition and determination are complicated.[1] Since a man's job is perhaps the most important determinant of his social position, most

---

[1] See also p. 464. The Market Research Society set up a working party to study social class definition for market research and has published an interim report on the subject (Market Research Society, 1963b).

social status scales are based on occupation. In Britain, the Registrar-General (U.K. General Register Office, 1966) has produced a five-point social class classification for use in Censuses, and this detailed coding frame is widely used by other researchers; it has the notable advantage that the Census reports provide the researcher with a wealth of comparative data. The Registrar-General also uses a sixteenfold classification of socio-economic groups. Another British social status scale is the Hall-Jones Scale of Occupational Prestige for Males (see Hall and Jones, 1950, and Glass, 1954, and Oppenheim, 1966, also provides a listing of occupations and their scale positions). In the United States, the U.S. Bureau of the Census has its occupational codes, and Duncan has constructed a socio-economic index for occupations (see Chapters 6 and 7 of Reiss, 1961).

In discussing the general principles of constructing coding frames no reference has yet been made to the mode of analysis to be employed, but this also dictates certain characteristics in the form of the coding frame. If the analysis is to be conducted on unit record equipment, the coded data must first be transferred to punched cards. With computer analysis, punched cards are usually—but not always—the primary means of input for survey data. Thus the features of a punched card have an influence on the nature of a coding frame.

An example of an ordinary punched card is reproduced on p. 420. It has 80 columns, and each column has ten marked punching positions, 0, 1, 2, . . . 9, together with two more unmarked positions above the 0. These two positions are variously known as X, Y; X, V; 10, 11; $-$, $+$; L, U; etc. for the lower and upper positions respectively. To record a code in a particular column, a hole is punched in that column of the card in the code position required. The principle involved in using punched cards to record survey data is easily illustrated. Let us take Q. 7(a) from p. 312. This has six possible answers, represented by codes 1–6. In the layout of the card, one column, say column 15, is allocated to this question and each card (representing one respondent) is punched on column 15 according to the code ringed. Similarly, two or more columns can be used to punch codes which cannot be condensed to one column; for example, if exact age were to be coded in, say, columns 6 and 7, column 6 would contain the tens and column 7 the units so that a respondent aged 35 would have a 3 punched in column 6 and a 5 in column 7 of his card. On the other hand, if ages were grouped into bracket codes they could be recorded on a single column, e.g. under 20 code 1, 20–29 code 2, 30–39 code 3, . . . 80 and over code 8.

One point to remember when designing the card layout is that some of the columns, usually at the beginning of the card, have to be reserved for an identification code, so that the questionnaire to which the card relates can be determined. If there are, say, 2,500 questionnaires, the first four columns could be used for an identification number, numbering the questionnaires from 0001 to 2500. If all the information from one questionnaire cannot be recorded on one card, more than one can be used; each card must then contain its questionnaire's identification number and, in addition, another column—the same one for all cards—has to be used to distinguish between the several cards relating to the one questionnaire.

Apart from columns needed for identification purposes, the rest of the card is free to use for recording the questionnaire responses. As has been described, each column has twelve possible codes—there could even be thirteen if the lack of a punch in any position in a column were allowed, but blank columns are best avoided since they can lead to errors in coding and punching. The two upper codes X and Y present no problems with unit record equipment, but they may not be acceptable for all forms of computer analysis. Although many computer tabulation programs recognize all twelve or thirteen codes, this is often untrue of programs for other statistical analyses, which may not distinguish between X, Y, 0 and a blank column (treating them all as 0). Unless the analyses are to be confined to cross-tabulations, it is therefore safer to restrict the codes to the ten positions 0–9.[1] This 0–9 coding also has the advantage that it can be used with other computer input media (e.g. paper or magnetic tape) as well as punched cards.

Besides unacceptable codes, another common problem is multiple punched columns. Some questions allow the respondent to give several answers, and the simple way to code such data is to punch all the answers on one column. Questions 7(a), 12 and 13 on pages 312 and 313 all permit several answers. For example a respondent might have read yesterday the *Daily Mirror*, the *Daily Mail* and the *Daily Telegraph*, so that the codes 0, 3 and 6 would all apply. This form of multiple coding is simple and uses little space on the punched card, but it has serious disadvantages. Although it can be analysed with unit record equipment, it makes the task of finding out the frequencies of occurrence of various combinations of codes extremely tedious. It is a relatively straightforward matter to discover how many respondents read, say, the *Daily Mirror*, but it is less easy to find out how many read a combination of papers such as the *Mirror*, the *Mail* and the *Telegraph*. With computer analysis there is in

---

[1] Unacceptable coding is however not disastrous. If a researcher finds his coding is unacceptable for a program he wants to use, he should be able to employ another program, a recoding program, to recode his data in the computer into an acceptable form.

An IBM punched card

The above card is a life-size reproduction of a standard punched card. There are 80 columns, the numbers of which can be seen running across the bottom of the card. The ten punching positions 0–9 are marked for each column and the wide space at the top of the card contains the two other positions.

For illustrative purposes this card has been punched 0 in column 1, 1 in column 2, ..., 9 in column 10. Column 11 is punched in the uppermost position (here called +) and column 12 in the lower of the two unmarked positions (here called −). Columns 13, 14 and 15 are examples of multi-punched columns, column 13 being punched 1 and 4, column 14, 1, 3 and 4, and column 15, +, 4, 5 and 9. Across the top of the card are typed the punches that have been made in each column; this typing was done by the keypunch as the card was being punched and is known as *interpreting* the card. The optional facility to interpret cards is a useful one since it makes them much easier to read (except in the case of multi-punches, which are over-typed). The notch taken out of the right-hand side of the card shows that it has been verified (see p. 431).

addition the danger that the computer programs to be used will not accept multi-punched columns; even for tabulations a special program may be needed. For these reasons multi-punched columns are better avoided (although if they are used a recoding program will probably be available to unscramble the multi-punches within the computer).

There are two ways of circumventing multi-punching. One is to put each category of response on a separate column, coding, say, 1 if the category applies, 0 if not. For example, if the respondent read the *Daily Mirror* column 30, say, would be coded 1, if not, 0; if he read the *Daily Mail* column 31 would be coded 1, if not, 0; etc. This procedure has the disadvantages that it uses up a large number of columns, and that to interrelate the answers requires a many-way table cross-tabulating all these columns together. For many purposes a more economical way to proceed is to use a geometric code. To illustrate this type of coding, we will simplify the example to just five papers—*Mirror, Express, Mail, Telegraph* and *Times*. The coding would be as follows:

Mirror	01
Express	02
Mail	04
Telegraph	08
Times	16

Then the code for a particular respondent is the sum of the codes of the newspapers he has read: if, for example, he read the *Mirror*, *Mail* and *Times* his code would be $01 + 04 + 16 = 21$. In this way, the information on readership of the five papers has been reduced to two columns, and any score uniquely identifies the exact combination of newspapers read.

Multi-punched columns also arise when the researcher decides to record the responses to more than one coding frame in one column. For example, the sex of a respondent requires only two codes, say male as 0, female as 1, leaving the other codes in the column unused. In order to save space the researcher may then decide to use codes 2–9 for another dimension, perhaps age. This procedure suffers the disadvantages of multi-punching—in particular one would almost certainly want to relate age and sex—and so should be avoided. Where two dimensions are generally to be used jointly for the analysis, it may be beneficial to have them together on one column, but the column should be single-punched. Thus, for example, age and sex could be combined as: male, under 30—0; male, 30 to 49—1; male, 50 to 64—2; male, 65 and over—3; female, under 30—4; etc.

The intention of the preceding remarks has been to indicate that the coding frames to be employed should not be designed without reference.to the means of analysis. Early advice on the suitability of the proposed coding frames for the mode of analysis to be used can help to avoid time-consuming and expensive problems later on.

Coding the answers

So much for the construction of the coding frames. The actual allocation of answers to individual categories can, as we saw earlier, be done by the respondent—as with questions offering a specific choice of answer; by the interviewer—as with questions answered freely but coded in the field; or by the office coder. The first two cases involve pre-coded questions and all the interviewer (or, in a mail questionnaire, the respondent) has to do is to ring, tick or underline the appropriate code or codes.

The third type of coding is used where an open question has been asked and the answer recorded as nearly verbatim as possible. It has now to be coded in the office. The coder may be required simply to note whether the answer contains a reference to a particular item (e.g. to the cost of living in general) or he may have to allocate the answer to one of several categories, according to the strength of the reference or according to the various points made. Sometimes the coding is based on the answer to only this question; at others, the coder may have to look at the answers to several questions before coding this one. Coding instructions should be specific on such points.

One issue to be decided is whether the codes are to be recorded on the questionnaire or whether a transfer sheet is to be used. If a large proportion of the questions are pre-coded the use of a transfer sheet means that the coders spend much of their time wastefully copying codes onto transfer sheets, and may of course make a few errors in doing so. In such cases it may be preferable to record the coding of open questions on the questionnaire, having printed on it ready for use either a set of code numbers (e.g. Q. 1(*b*) on p. 312) or more commonly an empty box in which the code number is to be written. The disadvantage of this method is that the punch operator then has to punch the cards straight from the questionnaires, and this is a more difficult task, and hence more prone to error, than punching from well-designed transfer sheets. In addition the design of the questionnaire is more complex for, besides all the other points to be borne in mind in its construction, its layout must be made to fit the needs of the punch operator. For these reasons, if the questionnaire is a complex one involving many open questions, it is likely to be better to use transfer sheets.

It is clear that the quality of the coding will depend on how well the initial editing has been done, on the soundness of the coding frames and on the skill and care of the coders. If the frames are not well constructed, the coders will continually come up against answers which either do not fit anywhere or might fit into several categories. But even if they are carefully designed, such problems will sometimes still arise. Careful training of the coders, including some trial coding of interviews picked out for their variety of responses, can help to reduce these problems. A detailed check on the coding of the first batch of questionnaires can detect mistakes made by coders and can act as a further form of training. In addition check-coding of a sample of questionnaires throughout the coding operation measures the reliability of the coding, provides a means of assessing individual coders, and acts as an incentive to the coders to maintain their concentration. With particularly difficult coding frames it may be advisable to leave the coding to one or two coders who receive specialized training in the subject matter; for example, this might well apply to social class coding.

However, despite all the care taken in the construction of the code book and training of coders, problems can and often do still arise in the production coding. Coders will probably require clarification of some of the codes, and extra codes may even have to be added to the coding frames. In the case of this latter eventuality, great care is needed to ensure that all coders are made aware of, and fully understand, the changes, and that coding in questionnaires already processed is corrected, where necessary, to take account of the changes. Changing codes during production is an error-prone operation, and should not be undertaken unless essential. The researcher himself is the only person who can sensibly make a decision on whether it is essential, and decide how to deal with similar problems, and he therefore needs to keep in close touch with the coding process. Otherwise the coders will be forced to use their own discretion, may make wrong decisions, and may well reach different decisions one from another.

An experiment on coding variability

Even assuming the maximum help from the coding frame and the interviewer, coding is rarely a matter of automatically applying given rules. For all but the simplest questions, there will be doubtful answers on which the coder has to exercise judgement. In these cases there is inevitably scope for personal bias and for differences between coders (as well as errors due to carelessness). The variability of coding—that is the extent to which different coders would arrive at different codings—is a factor of importance in surveys, just as is the variability between interviewers, and it is worth referring to an experiment on the subject by Durbin and Stuart (1954b).[1]

Four professional coders and four students took part, each having to carry out ten different coding operations; these ranged from purely mechanical tasks to the coding of answers to open questions. The same 400 completed schedules were used throughout and each coding operation was completed before the next was begun. Thus, when the first coder had completed operation 1, the second carried out this operation, then the third, and so on, until the operation had been done by all eight coders; then followed operation 2 etc. Furthermore, having completed a particular operation for all the schedules, each coder had to code the first 50 of them again (his earlier codings not being available to him).

Note that each coder dealt with only one question at a time, coding it for all the schedules. This is one method, but there is the alternative of coding an entire schedule before proceeding to the next. As with editing, this has the advantage that each schedule is treated as a unit, so that inconsistencies are more easily noticed. However, the system used in the experiment enabled the coder to concentrate on one question at a time and so saved him from errors he might have committed if he had had to bear in mind a large number of points.

We give first a few particulars of the coding operations, since they illustrate well the range of the coder's task in surveys.

Operation 1

Coders had to classify each respondent according to his marital status and age; there was one code number for each of 12 combinations.

Operation 2

Coders had to classify each household according to its composition; the requisite data were given in the usual type of household composition table. This coding took account of the relationship to the respondent of the various household members and their ages. Nine categories were distinguished.

Operation 3

Coders had to work out each household's income by adding together the incomes of the household members (these incomes were themselves given on the schedule in code form).

Operation 4

Coders were given a table showing minimum household income in relation to size of household. Each of the 400 households had to be

[1] We wish to thank the authors and the editor of the *Journal of Marketing* for allowing us to draw so extensively on this paper.

coded according to whether its income fell below the minimum for its size or not, or whether there was insufficient information.

All the above were routine operations, on which coders might make mistakes, but on which there was no scope for judgement. This was not so with the other six operations (5a, 5b, 6a, 6b, 7a, 7b). These were based on three open questions, the answers to each of which had to be coded in two distinct ways. We shall use one of the questions as an example: 'In what way are you affected by rising prices?' The following codes were to be used (Durbin and Stuart, 1954b, p. 58):

A. 'Cost of living' rising; general rise in all prices; 'in every way' lower standard of living.
B. General *household* expenses higher; difficult to make housekeeping money go round.
C. Had to cut down spending on pleasures, luxuries, non-essentials in general.
C_1. Had to cut down spending on drink, tobacco.
C_2. Had to cut down spending on entertainments, sports.
C_3. Had to cut down spending on non-essentials.
D. Specific item mentioned whose price has risen.
D_1. Food prices risen.
D_2. Clothes prices risen.
D_3. Other specific price rises.
E. Saves less; had to spend savings.
F. Increased taxation.
G. Had to take a job, or extra part-time work, to make ends meet.
H. Wages or income not rising to keep pace with prices.
I. Other answers (give details on separate sheet).
J. Recorded answer illegible.

Operation 5a
Here coders were to code every item mentioned in the reply. Thus, if the reply was 'Clothes going up, food going up, everything going up', then they should have coded: D_2, D_1, A.

Operation 5b
Here coders were to use the single code appropriate to the most important part of the reply. In the example, the code would have been A.

Both systems (a) and (b) are common in surveys. There were two other open questions, each of which was tackled in both these ways, making a total of 10 operations.

The results were presented in two quite different ways. One was simply to compare the overall frequencies produced by the different coders, e.g. what proportion of the 400 schedules were (on a particular question) given code 1, 2, . . ., and so on. This analysis shows the extent of *net* differences between coders. The second type of analysis was to look at each reply (to a question) and note how the different coders coded it. This leads to a measure of *gross* discrepancies between coders. Since some of these will cancel out, the first analysis gives little idea of the real extent of coding differences. Admittedly, for many purposes, it is the first kind of analysis which shows to what extent the survey results would be thrown out by using the different coders, but one could never *rely* on the cancellation of discrepancies. What is important from the point of view of assessing the reliability of the coding or of deciding on the amount of supervision and checking is the extent of gross discrepancies. We confine ourselves to this analysis here, only adding the remark that, for the coding of the open questions, even the *net* differences were sometimes substantial.

The most telling analysis was that showing, for each operation, on what percentage of the schedules there were a maximum of 8, 7, 6, . . . agreements on a code. Two coders were regarded as agreeing when

> their codings of a particular question are identical in all respects. Thus in operations 5a, 6a and 7a, which involve multiple coding of each reply, two coders were regarded as agreeing only if each gives the same set of codes for the reply. Thus there is a greater scope for disagreement on the (*a*) codings than on the (*b*) codings of operations 5, 6 and 7. (Durbin and Stuart, 1954b, p. 62.)

The results are shown in Table 16.1 below.

TABLE 16.1

Percentage of replies in which 8, 7, 6, etc., coders agreed

Coding Operation	Maximum number of agreements							
	8	7	6	5	4	3	2	Total
1	84	15	*	*	—	—	—	100
2	91	8	1	—	—	—	—	100
3	88	8	2	1	1	—	—	100
4	91	8	—	*	1	—	—	100
5a	33	13	9	12	12	13	8	100
5b	38	12	14	13	14	7	2	100
6a	30	16	15	12	13	10	4	100
6b	44	15	13	11	12	4	—	100
7a	46	8	13	10	11	10	2	100
7b	66	11	6	9	6	1	—	100

— denotes zero; * denotes less than 0·5 per cent.
Source: Durbin and Stuart (1954b, p. 62).

On the routine operations 1–4, there was a good deal of agreement; on the others, however, and especially in the multiple codings of open-question answers, considerable discrepancies were found. As the authors say:

Even at stage (b), where coders were simply asked to code the most important element in each reply, complete agreement was only obtained on the average in about half of the 400 replies. Furthermore, the disagreements were not due to the oddities of one or two coders, as may be seen from the slow falling away of the frequencies as we move across the table to the right. (Durbin and Stuart, 1954b, p. 63.)

One other interesting analysis was that comparing each coder's re-coding of the first 50 schedules with his original coding. Table 16.2 shows the number of discrepancies (out of a possible 50) made by each coder on each operation:

TABLE 16.2

Discrepancies in re-coding 50 replies

Coding Operation	Students				Professionals			
	I	II	III	IV	V	VI	VII	VIII
1	2	1	3	1	—	3	—	—
2	—	—	7	2	—	2	2	—
3	3	8	1	1	2	1	1	—
4	2	5	2	1	1	1	1	1
5a	18	8	15	18	13	14	11	4
5b	10	6	12	23	8	11	12	6
6a	14	16	16	16	7	16	16	8
6b	5	12	13	10	7	12	12	7
7a	12	9	12	10	5	7	11	5
7b	5	6	11	4	1	4	3	5

Source: Durbin and Stuart (1954b, p. 65).

The number of discrepancies for operations 5–7 were considerable even for the professionals. The paper suggests, with substantiating evidence, that the discrepancies were due not to a 'learning effect' brought about by coding the intervening 350 schedules, but to a 'substantial inherent variability "within" coders'. In other words, their *reliability* appeared to be low.

In summary, the experiment revealed substantial discrepancies between coders, and for the same coder at different times. It was admittedly only a small-scale enquiry, but its results suggest that the subject merits serious research. Although the discrepancies in operations 5-7 were far more serious, the results of operations 1-4 also showed a certain amount of unreliability. One implication that might be drawn from this is that, to avoid errors, coding operations should be kept as simple as possible; complex codings can then be derived from the simple codings by the computer, for example by performing the necessary calculations (adding incomes) and by working out combination codes (household classification or age with marital status). Providing the coders perform the simple tasks well, the computer will produce reliable complex codings.

16.3. Tabulation[1]

In the majority of surveys, the data, once edited and coded, are put together in some kinds of tables and may also undergo some other forms of statistical analysis. There is nothing statistically sophisticated about tabulation. It amounts to no more, basically, than a counting of the number of cases falling into each of several classes. The editing and coding have sought to ensure that the information on the individual schedule is accurate and categorized in suitable form. It now remains to 'add all the schedules together', to count how many of them have answer (X) for question A and how many answer (Y).

The process can be done manually. Hand tabulation is exceedingly simple, involving no technical knowledge or skill; and it need not, even for cross-analyses, be particularly laborious. If one wants an analysis showing the distribution of income by occupation, all that is required is a table skeleton showing one of the variables horizontally and the other vertically; tally marks are made in this as one goes through the schedules. If a number of tables have to be constructed, it may be inconvenient to go through the schedules afresh each time, and an alternative is to first transfer the relevant schedule data on to sheets from which counts can more easily be made.

Although hand tabulation can in principle be used in any survey, in practice, because of its tedious nature, slowness and liability to error, it is mainly restricted to simple situations. If the number of survey cases is small, say of the order of 100-200 or less, there may be little point in tabulating by machine since this necessitates putting the data on to punched cards and a certain amount of extra trouble. For small surveys most of the tables to be constructed will be simple ones, involving only one or two variables at a time, and then hand tabulation is quick and straightforward. But for survey analyses requiring complicated cross-tabulations, involving more than two

---

[1] This section discusses general principles, not how to make tables or to operate unit record equipment or computers. For references on these matters, see the Notes on Reading.

variables, or even requiring just a large number of two-way tabulations, hand tabulation will be slow and unwieldy.

The flexibility of machine tabulation is one of its greatest advantages. Once the data have been put on punched cards the construction of tables is speedy and straightforward. When one is not certain what tabulations are going to be wanted, machine tabulation is preferable, for then the loss of time and work is not too great if some of them are not used. On the other hand, this convenience also spells one of the minor dangers of machine tabulation. It is all too tempting to run off any number of tabulations, worrying little as to whether they will really be needed. This is the 'let us run off the tables and see what we can get out of them' attitude, reasonable up to a point, but a waste of resources if it gets out of hand. Many a research worker would have to admit to the possession of tables which have barely been looked at. But, this minor danger apart, the flexibility of machine tabulation is a formidable advantage. However carefully the tabulation plans have been worked out, the surveyor is bound to think of new analyses as he goes along. He may have done tabulations of, say, the answers to the question 'Do you smoke?' by the respondents' income and the respondents' sex, but not according to their sex *and* income, i.e. a three-way tabulation. With the answers on punched cards the latter table is easily prepared, and at low extra cost. With hand tabulation, such 'afterthoughts' can take a good deal of time.

A very practical, but nevertheless important, factor in deciding between hand and machine tabulation is whether there is unit record equipment or a computer with programs for tabulation readily available. If there is a facility with easy access, the terms of use are also important. While machine analysis is generally quicker than hand tabulation it can be expensive, and for a fairly small survey it could easily take up a substantial proportion of the total budget. Hand tabulation can be done directly under the researcher's eye, if he does not indeed do it himself. This has a certain advantage, if only because it brings to his notice the peculiarities of individual cases. Machine analysis, more likely than not, involves giving instructions to an operator; it *certainly* requires expert advice. And one early piece of advice to be obtained is a fairly good estimate of the likely cost of the required set of tabulations.

For any survey which involves large numbers or for which many cross-tabulations are required, machine analysis is almost invariably the right way to proceed. For a survey organization equipped with a computer or unit record equipment, the question of hand versus machine tabulation hardly arises. But with small *ad hoc* social research surveys, the choice is often a real one, and some of the factors on which it should be based have been outlined above.

In concluding this discussion, we should mention a method which aims to get some of the best of both worlds. This is based on a type of card (e.g. the Cope Chat card) in which answers are punched along the edges. Thus, the edge positions numbered 1–6 might be assigned to the answers 1 . . . 6 for Q. 7(a) on p. 312, and the relevant code for a respondent (there being one card per respondent) is punched by a ticket-punch, so that the hole at that position is opened up. This is done for all the cards. If a needle is then put through the stack of cards at, say, hole position number 3, all the cards in which this hole has been opened to the edge can be made to fall out. They are then counted by hand.[1] The punching is fairly laborious but the method as a whole is quicker than ordinary hand tabulation. A useful feature is that the body of the card can be used for written material, so that the card represents a readable record of the data.

Punching the cards

Unit record equipment performs the analyses on punched cards, and punched cards are also the usual primary input media for computer analysis. Thus if either of these means is to be used the next task after the coding is to transfer the coded data to punched cards, and this is normally done by a *keypunch*, a machine that is rather like a typewriter.[2] Punching is a routine task which can be performed at high speed and with considerable accuracy by skilled punch operators. To maintain speed and avoid errors, however, the operator should be enabled to read off the code to be punched for each column without having to search for it in the body of the questionnaire or to check its accuracy; this is a point to be borne in mind when the layout of the questionnaire is being planned. Besides punching a hole for the code, some keypunches also 'interpret' the card, that is they type at the top of each column of the card the code that has been punched in that column—see the example on p. 420; the typed

---

[1] For a description of a mechanical device for counting, see a note in *Applied Statistics*, **1**, 2, 1952, p. 139.
[2] Occasionally the method of mark sensing is used, obviating the need for punching. In its earlier forms, interviewers were given ordinary punched cards on which they recorded the code answers, using special graphite pencils. The cards were then fed into a machine which read the marks and punched holes accordingly. Alternatively a special recording card (bigger and more convenient than a punched card) can be used and fed into a machine, which then punches holes on to an ordinary punched card. Another development allows mark sensing to be used with an ordinary-sized schedule which is then micro-filmed; the micro-film is mechanically translated into punched tape and the tabulation done straight from the tape. See Yates (1960, Chapter 10) for a discussion of mark sensing, and Sudman (1967, Chapter 10) for a report of an experiment in the use of optical scanners for survey data. A recent development is optical character recognition, for reading handwritten capital letters or typing into a computer.

codes make it much easier to read what has been punched. It is especially valuable to have the columns containing the questionnaire identification numbers interpreted, because from them any particular card can be readily picked out.

Skilled punch operators can work with considerable accuracy, but nevertheless they will make a few errors. The error rate for experienced operators is likely to be of the order of 2 in 100 punches, but with inexperienced operators it can be considerably higher. One way to detect errors is to use a *verifier*. This machine is similar to a key-punch, with the operator typing in the codes, but the input card is the card already punched by the keypunch and the verifier does not actually punch holes. If the code typed on the verifier agrees with the hole already punched, the punch is accepted; if not, a light comes on and the machine locks. The verifier operator then decides if it is her mistake and, if so, corrects it; if not, the card is in error and must be repunched. To show that a card has been verified, the verifier makes a mark on it, often in the form of a notch in the right-hand edge. Verification will not eliminate all errors for it is, of course, possible for both operators to punch the same erroneous code, but the chances of this happening are generally slight. It can, however, easily occur when the codes are not written clearly and both operators interpret a code in the same (wrong) way. Careful hand-writing in coding is therefore important.

Unit record equipment

If it has been decided to analyse the survey data by machine, there is the choice between using an electronic computer and using unit record equipment. If a computer is available, there are great advantages in its use and, as a result, in the last decade computers have to a considerable extent replaced the earlier equipment for survey analysis. Although computers are nowadays widely available, not every researcher has access to one. Some researchers may still use unit record equipment, and for that reason we will give a brief description of some of the more important of these machines.

Once punched and verified, the cards can go on to the unit record machines, and what is done then depends on the analysis required. A good deal can be achieved on the *sorter*, a machine which 'looks' at one column at a time and distributes the cards into stacks according to the hole punched in that column. With a code occupying two columns, by sorting first on the one column and then on the other, the cards can be grouped into 144 cells. A *counter-sorter* at the same time counts the cards falling into each answer-group and shows the total in the counter above it. Such a machine can do most of the tabulations required in censuses and surveys and is reasonably

P

convenient even for the many cross-tabulations that are generally required. Thus an income/occupation tabulation could be done by first sorting into income groups and then sorting the cards in each group by occupation. (There are elaborate types of counter-sorters which can deal with several columns simultaneously.)

With any sizeable punched-card installation there will also be some kind of *tabulator*. These machines can add the numbers punched in a given column (or set of columns) on all the cards, arrive at any totals required and print both the numbers and the totals. They can also be used to carry out complicated cross-tabulations. The use of the tabulator requires specialist skills or, at any rate, familiarity with the machine. Given this, the operator can carry out on the machines all the tabulations ever required in social surveys and some of the statistical calculations as well. Sorter and tabulator are thus the basis of any punched-card installation; other more specialized machines, such as the reproducing punch, interpreter, collator and multiplier, are valuable for special tasks. An extremely useful machine, an electronic statistical machine, is able to combine the functions of many of the machines already mentioned; specialist skill is needed for its operation, but its flexibility makes it a valuable tool for survey analysis—it can for example efficiently carry out a cross-tabulation and print the results, and so can take the place of both sorter and tabulator. The subject of unit record equipment is complex and for details the reader must be referred to the literature recommended at the end of the chapter.

Computers

The development of electronic computers has led to tremendous advances in survey analysis. Not only has it resulted in great ease in tabulation but, more importantly, it has led to the use and development of high-powered multivariate statistical procedures. Before the advent of computers, the enormous amount of computation required for multivariate statistical analyses in large-scale surveys limited the use of these methods drastically. Multivariate methods were employed by only a few survey researchers, and even they had to restrict the extent of their analyses severely. Others relied almost entirely on cross-tabulations. Nowadays, although tabulations still play an important part in survey analysis, other techniques are increasingly being used.

It is far outside our scope to give a general introduction to computers; instead we will confine ourselves to a few remarks on their uses for survey analysis. At the outset it should be made clear that, in order to use a computer for routine analyses, the researcher does not in fact need to know a great deal about the computer. Most computer installations have large libraries of computer programs and the researcher only has to discover how to use the programs of interest to him. For this purpose he does not need to know about computer languages such as FORTRAN, ALGOL and COBOL, or how to write programs. All the information he requires should be clearly given in the documentation of the programs he plans to use. Of course, if he wants to conduct an analysis for which no program has been written for his computer, one will have to be developed, and this will require the skills of a computer programmer. Sometimes a program written for another computer can be adapted for the machine to be used by the researcher, and when this is so it is generally much easier than starting completely afresh; however, it still needs specialist skills. Adaptation and development of programs can be lengthy tasks and the researcher therefore needs to find out at an early date whether programs exist for his analyses on the computer he plans to use; if they do not, the work of adaptation or development should be started as soon as possible. As there now exists a wide range of programs for survey and statistical analysis, it is almost certain that for any routine analysis a program will already have been written.

If this is the case, the researcher should study the manual describing its facilities, and should make sure that it is adequate for his purposes. He should particularly note the form in which the data should be coded for input to the program and should ensure that his coding is consistent with the program's requirements. Most library programs are general-purpose programs and the researcher must then work out how to get the program to meet his particular needs. This is normally done by specifying his requirements on a series of *control cards*, punched cards containing program instructions written in the particular format required by the program. Thus, for example, a general tabulation program might allow the researcher to tabulate any set of columns (perhaps up to a maximum of five) against one another, to percentage tables across the rows or down the columns or both, to calculate arithmetic means and standard deviations, to group codes together, etc. Within this general framework the researcher must specify through the control cards what he wants. If he needs a table of 'Do you smoke?' by 'Age', in five-year age groups say, with the exact ages being recorded on the punched cards, he must give the necessary instructions for the construction of the table through control cards produced according to the specifications in the program manual. Of course, he would probably want a substantial number of tables and this would mean a whole set of control cards.

The existence of a program for a particular analysis does not guarantee that it will meet the researcher's needs. The program may not provide all the facilities that he requires, and it may have other limitations which make it unsuitable for him. With a tabulation program, for example, the following are the sorts of questions to be investigated: Will it deal with several cards per case? Is there a limit to the number of cases that it can analyse? How will it treat multi-punches? How will it treat the two upper codes, X and Y? Will it group codes, e.g. form age groups from codings of exact ages? How complex a cross-tabulation can it produce? If the survey sample has been selected with unequal probabilities, weighting is needed in the analysis: will the program enable weighting to be employed? Will it allow certain groups, such as the 'not applicable' and 'no answer' groups, to be removed before percentages are calculated? What types, if any, of statistics will it produce— arithmetic means, standard deviations, correlation coefficients (and, if so, which ones)? Can new variables be derived by taking functions (e.g. additions, subtractions, etc.) of existing codes and, if so, what functions can be employed? These are only some of the questions to be asked about a tabulation program. For many surveys, a lot of these questions will be irrelevant or unimportant, but there may be other requirements. Some of a program's limitations may be met by employing the right coding, for example by avoiding X and Y codes and multi-punches. Others may perhaps be dealt with by alternative means. For instance, if there is no weighting facility, cards requiring weights of, say, two could be duplicated and thus be put twice into the analyses. But in some cases there will be no easy way out of a problem and the researcher will need to look for another program.

As well as a tabulation program and programs for various types of statistical analyses, there are two other programs which often prove useful in survey analysis. One of these is an editing program.[1] As we have seen, errors can occur at the various stages of manipulation of the questionnaire responses. Using the computer to edit the data is particularly valuable because it provides a thorough check on the data in its final form, at the end of all the human manipulation processes. There are four common simple forms of computer edit. First, a check can be made that all codes fall within their correct ranges; for example, if sex is coded male as 1, female as 2, a card punched, say, 5 in that column would obviously be in error. Secondly, the internal consistency between codes can be checked; a respondent coded as a non-smoker in one column should not in another be coded as smoking between 10 and 15 cigarettes a day. Thirdly, improbable combinations of codes can be picked out

---

[1] W. J. Stuart (1966) discusses the experience of the U.S. Bureau of Labor Statistics in computer editing of its manpower surveys.

for detailed checking; it is unlikely that a man aged 20 has retired from work, and this would merit investigation. Fourthly, arithmetic checks can be made; for instance, if a total is coded as well as its constituent parts, a check can be made that the total is the sum of the parts. More sophisticated checks, such as looking for outliers with ratio or regression techniques, can also be used. Some of the errors found by a computer edit would have shown up anyway in the analysis, but even for them the edit is worth while. Errors shown up by the analysis mean that the initial results have to be corrected, and it is far easier to use a computer edit to 'clean' the data initially than to make corrections during the analysis.

Another useful type of program for survey analysis is a recoding program. One use for it is to recode information originally coded in a form unsuitable for a program needed for the analysis, such as by recoding X's and Y's and unscrambling multi-punched columns. It can also be used to group exact codes into bracket codes, for example exact ages into age groups, and can be used more generally to form combination codes. (Some forms of these types of recoding are available as part of some tabulation programs.) The latter facility has many applications: it may permit unweighted or weighted total scores to be formed from individual item scores, the identification of respondents who answer any one of a set of questions in a particular way, the identification of respondents who answer question A in one specified way and question B in another, etc. A flexible recoding program allows a great deal of data manipulation to be carried out by the computer.

In conclusion, we should mention that punched cards are not the only input media for computers, though for survey analysis they are the most common form of primary input. Paper tape is an alternative form of primary input but is rather unsuitable for survey work. The big disadvantage with punched cards is the relatively slow speed with which they can be read into the computer. There are therefore often considerable savings to be had from transferring the data on the first computer run from the punched cards to a different form of data storage, generally either magnetic tape or disc.[1] Survey analysis typically develops in stages, with early results suggesting later analyses, so that usually a number of computer runs are needed before the work is completed. If all the runs after the first use tape or disc input, both of which can be read into the computer very much faster than cards, substantial savings in time and hence cost will accrue.

[1] Punched cards may indeed be replaced as the major form of primary input when the new development of keyboard punching directly on to magnetic tape becomes established.

In this brief section it has been possible to give only a few words of general advice about the use of computers for survey analysis; for fuller discussions the reader is referred to the references at the end of the chapter. The introduction of computers means that survey researchers can now very easily use library programs to carry out advanced multivariate statistical techniques, a notable advance which however carries with it certain dangers. For one thing, with a computer the researcher can so easily conduct a whole variety of analyses that he may try all of them 'to see what turns up', a wasteful procedure if carried to extremes without a rational framework. For another, he can conduct a high-powered analysis using an existing computer program without understanding the technique at all. As a result, there is a clear danger of misapplication of complex statistical procedures by statistically unsophisticated researchers. The fact that the computer can be used to perform the calculations increases rather than reduces the need for expert advice on the use of all forms of statistical analyses.

Sampling in the analysis

This is the most convenient point for referring to the possibility of basing the analysis on only a sample of the results.[1] If, for example, results are needed quickly, a sample of the schedules can be processed and analysed first to produce preliminary results. The 1951 Census of Population in Great Britain is an important example of this.

But quite apart from the pressure of time, it is sometimes sufficient, for the precision required, to analyse only a sample of the responses. It might seem that, in such a case, the information should have been *collected* only from a sample of the required size in the first place, but there are sometimes obstacles to this. One cannot always decide in advance how much accuracy is going to be required for each question; and, even if this can be decided, it may be difficult to predict how big a sample will need to be analysed to produce that accuracy. Only when some of the data are available can this be seen and one may then still achieve some economy by analysing only a sample of returns. Apart from all this, a sample analysis can give very useful guidance for planning the final analysis and is often sufficient when the researcher decides on special studies of the survey material long after the main analyses are over.

Computations

This is not the place to discuss methods of computation, but the importance of computational checks may usefully be stressed. When a computer is used many of the computations, especially the more

[1] For a fuller discussion see Zarkovich (1965, Chapter 6).

difficult ones, will be done by it, but a few may still be done by hand on desk calculating machines. When unit record equipment is used, only a few calculations can be performed from the punched cards and most will have to be done by hand. The tasks of the operators of desk calculators will range from simple percentaging to computations involving a complicated series of steps. The calculation of standard errors, for instance, typically involves a long series of operations and, while nothing complicated is involved in any single step, the chain as a whole is complex. A good deal then depends on the analyst's skill in laying out the computations and instructions.

However, human computors inevitably make mistakes (unlike the electronic computer, which is virtually error-free) and it is wise to check their work, the more so since errors made towards the end of the analysis are likely to have particularly serious effects. An odd recording or punching error made in the early stages is quite likely to cancel out with others and be swamped in the final results; but an error made in the analysis will tend to affect aggregates, not just individual observations, and this is much more serious. All in all, every precaution to check the computations must be taken. Whether this is done by making computors do each job twice or by having it repeated by others (clearly a better check) is a matter of preference and resources. The best check of all is to use two different methods of arriving at a result. The analysis, too, can usefully be designed so as to give cross checks. If a large number of computors and operations have to be checked, quality control techniques are applicable.

NOTES ON READING

1. Detailed practical instructions on some of the processes described in the chapter are given by PARTEN (1950) and in a paper by BOYAJY, BARRY, KUENSTLER and PATON (1949).

2. The literature on coding—apart from the general textbooks—is small, but a few useful references can be mentioned. HARRIS (1955; also in EDWARDS, 1956) describes the work of the Government Social Survey coding section, and DOWNHAM (1955; also in EDWARDS, 1956) discusses coding problems in the light of commercial experience. The coding manual of the Survey Research Center, University of Michigan, edited by MUEHL (1961) is worth consulting. FASTEAU and others (1964) describe the techniques for controlling the quality of coding for the 1960 U.S. Censuses. COALE and STEPHAN (1962) describe how they located some punching errors in the punched cards for the 1950 U.S. Census of Population.

3. Qualitative coding is discussed by GOODE and HATT (1952), by SELLTIZ and others (1959) and by CARTWRIGHT in FESTINGER and KATZ (1953). All these deal with content analysis and the last gives an excellent account of applications. Other references on content analysis are LASSWELL,

LEITES and associates (1949), BERELSON and LAZARSFELD (1948), NORTH and others (1963), a chapter by HOLSTI in LINDZEY and ARONSON (1968, Vol. 2) and HOLSTI (1969). A computer program for content analysis, the General Inquirer, is described by STONE and others (1966). SUDMAN (1967) discusses in Chapter 9 the use of computers to code free-response answers in survey research.

4. On tabulation, both the references in (1) are useful. MARK (1958) gives a simple treatment of hand tabulation in Chapter 13. YATES (1960), in Chapter 5, gives a thorough account of unit record machine methods, punched card layout and so on, and in Chapter 11 discusses electronic computers for survey analysis. JANDA (1965) is a useful book on data processing, with chapters on punched cards, unit record machines, and computers, and a description of the NUCROS tabulation program.

5. Chapter 5 of JANDA (1965) discusses electronic computers. Other useful introductions are HULL (1966) and GREEN (1963). BORKO (1962) and VELDMAN (1967) are also useful for social science applications. A clear description of the commonly used computer language FORTRAN IV is given by MCCRACKEN (1965).

6. Much of the literature on checking and verification in the processing stages derives from the U.S. Bureau of the Census. Readers are referred to HANSEN, HURWITZ and MADOW (1953, Vol. I, Chapter 12); HANSEN (1952); VOIGHT and KRIESBERG (1952); DEMING, TEPPING and GEOFFREY (1942); and DEMING and GEOFFREY (1941). PRITZKER, OGUS and HANSEN (1966) and FREUND and HARTLEY (1967) discuss automatic data editing, including imputing values where a figure is obviously in error. The paper by STUART (1966) has been referred to in the text. ZARKOVICH (1966, Chapter 12) discusses quality checking of processing.

CHAPTER 17

Analysis, Interpretation and Presentation

17.1. Introduction

WE HAVE now reached the concluding stages of the survey. The data obtained from or about respondents have been edited and coded and the first steps of summarization, usually a matter of constructing basic tables, have been taken. What follows is in many ways the most skilled task of all, the analysis and interpretation of the results. Certainly it is a task calling for the researcher's own judgement and skill, not one to be delegated to assistants. The routine of analysis may not be difficult, but properly to guide it and the accompanying interpretation requires a familiarity with the background of the survey and with all its stages, such as only the survey director himself is likely to possess.

These final stages of a survey are the least easy to discuss in general terms. The range of statistical methods applicable in survey analysis is too great to attempt to summarize here. That subject is the province of statistical textbooks,[1] and no systematic treatment will be attempted in this chapter. Instead we will confine ourselves to discussing the general approach to survey analysis.

To begin with, let us distinguish four different aspects of this approach:

(1) Analysis of survey material does not necessarily have to be statistical. To the extent that interest centres on the individual case rather than on the characteristics of the aggregate, non-quantitative methods of analysis and evaluation may be preferred; and, even in surveys concerned chiefly with aggregates, non-quantitative methods can play an important part. However, here the discussion will be confined to quantitative methods since, in large-scale surveys at least, they are the most important part of analysis.

(2) Part of what is called analysis is a matter of working out

[1] See some suggestions at the end of Chapter 4.

statistical distributions, constructing diagrams and calculating simple measures like averages, measures of dispersion, percentages, correlation coefficients and so forth. In a sense, analysis is too sophisticated a word for this activity: statistical description would be a better term, since all one is doing is describing the features of the survey aggregate.

(3) Statistical description in this sense is, however, only one part of survey analysis. Inference—in the widest meaning of the word —is the other. One kind of inference is brought into play whenever the survey data are based upon a sample of the population about which conclusions are to be drawn. The researcher then has the problem of estimating the population characteristics from those of the sample and also of estimating sampling errors.

(4) Problems of inference also arise in a different context. It is one thing to work out a measure of correlation between two variables covered in a survey, it is quite another to seek an explanation by analytical methods of how this demonstrated relationship comes about. The use of complicated statistical techniques in surveys often stems from the desire to establish and interpret multivariate relationships.

17.2. Statistical description

The ordinary methods of describing survey data are quite straightforward. The schedule reproduced on pp. 312–4, for instance, consists of 29 questions (including the sub-questions) and was answered by about 5,000 people. Each completed schedule can thus be looked upon as a series of 29 observations denoting the traits of that particular respondent: whether or not he has a paid job; whether he gets to work on foot, by bicycle, motor-car . . .; whether he lives at home, as a lodger . . .; and so forth. Survey analysis begins typically by taking these traits one, two or possibly three at a time, and showing how the respondents are distributed on them. One might start by constructing a *frequency distribution* of the answers for each question (i.e. a table stating how frequently each answer is given). It might show, for instance, that 1,250 of the respondents get to work on foot, 500 on a bicycle, 50 by motor-cycle, 500 by car and 2,700 by public transport. The next step might be to convert these into proportions (e.g. $1,250/5,000 = 0.25$) or percentages (e.g. $1,250 \times 100/5,000 = 25$ per cent) and this will virtually exhaust the information to be squeezed out of the answers to this question, at any rate if it is treated in isolation.

If the answers take a numerical form (in technical language, if one is dealing with a *variable* rather than an *attribute* question), one can go further. Q.8(b), on the same schedule, asked respondents, who said they had been to the pictures in the last seven days, how often they had gone during this period. The 'Don't know' category apart, the answers would be in numerical form. Again the first step would be to tabulate how many people said 'once', 'twice' and so forth, in fact to make a frequency distribution. The frequencies could then be converted to proportions or percentages as above, but one might also want some measure of *average*, of what is typical of this sample of respondents. Several kinds of average are available and the researcher must decide which is most suitable to his purpose. Once an average has been calculated, the question arises how representative a figure it is—that is, how closely the answers are bunched around it. Are most of them very close to it or is there a wide range of variation? This calls for one of the several *measures of dispersion*, and the choice between them again demands judgement.

These are the most elementary tools of statistical description, and a glance through a selection of survey reports will show that analysis often does not go much beyond distributions, percentages, averages and measure of dispersion, supplemented by suitable diagrams.

This does not of course mean that such analysis proceeds necessarily by taking one variable or question at a time. Quite the contrary; usually it will involve cross-classifications and consequently a study of relationships. The researcher wants to know whether the people who vote Labour are also those, on the whole, who think that the National Health Service is a good thing; whether those who go to the cinema a great deal spend less time watching television than those who go rarely; whether there is evidence of an association between a person's education and the newspapers he reads; whether the proportion of households owning a car increases with household size. In short, he is interested in whether the possession of one attribute is related to the possession of another, or several other, attributes.

In its most elementary form the study of relationships may go no further than 'breaking down' the sample by attribute x before analysing by attribute y. The report of the Oxford Institute of Statistics Savings Survey states that: 'Almost all the items were cross-tabulated with at least four of the classification attributes, such as region, size of town, age, sex and occupation of head, number of persons in the income unit and gross income group' (Lydall, 1955, p. 230). In market research it is standard practice to cross-classify responses to almost every question by age, sex and social class of respondents. Breakdowns of this type are an invariable part of survey analysis and one barely thinks of them as studies of relationships.

Within such basic breakdowns there may be further cross-classification of variables, and measures like percentages, averages, etc. can be computed as means of comparison. But, over and above these, one often wishes to have a measure of the *degree and direction* of the relationship between two (or more) variables. For this purpose again, several types of measure are available, and the survey analyst intending to use one of the several coefficients must be familiar with its characteristics and sure of its suitability. Their computational simplicity easily misleads; and anyone who blindly applies the text-book formulae without understanding their limitations or the assumptions underlying them can quickly fall into error.

Although it is measures of statistical description like those mentioned above that predominate in survey reports, they far from exhaust the possibilities of analysis. Anyone who has glanced at the volumes on *The American Soldier* by Stouffer and others (1949), *Social Mobility in Britain* edited by Glass (1954), *Prediction Methods in Relation to Borstal Training* by Mannheim and Wilkins (1955), *The Analysis of Family Budgets* by Prais and Houthakker (1955), *Income and Welfare in the United States* by Morgan and others (1962), *Productive Americans* by Morgan and others (1966), or *The American Occupational Structure* by Blau and Duncan (1967), to name only a few examples, will not need to be convinced that statistical techniques more intricate than percentages, averages and the like play their part in survey analysis. Moreover, by using a computer it is now quite practicable to employ sophisticated multivariate statistical procedures in analysing survey data. We will return to some further remarks on the subject of multivariate analysis after discussing two other aspects of survey analysis—the making of inferences from sample to population and the interpretation of re-lationships.

17.3. Population estimates and sampling errors

To the extent that the survey data are based on a sample of the population about which conclusions are to be drawn, one has to decide (*a*) how to make estimates from sample to population and (*b*) how to estimate the sampling errors. Both tasks are often a good deal more complicated than the introductory presentation of Chapters 4, 5 and 6 might suggest.

In the first place, the theory was discussed only in relation to averages and proportions for the total sample. When comparisons are to be made between different sections of the population which cut across the strata of the sample design, estimation and sampling error procedures become complicated (see Yates, 1960, Chapter 9, and Kish, 1965a, Chapter 4, for discussions of this class of problems). The procedures are also far more complicated for other statistics, such as correlation coefficients, regression coefficients and index numbers.

In addition, the explanations were generally simplified by the assumption that *epsem* sampling, that is sampling in which every element has the same probability of appearing in the sample, was used. For *epsem* samples, the straightforward proportions and averages calculated from the sample provide estimates of the population values, but when the sample is not *epsem* the sample values have to be weighted in the analysis to correct for the unequal selection probabilities. The sample estimates and their sampling errors are also more complex when supplementary data external to the survey are used to improve the estimation procedure (e.g. by stratification after selection, or ratio or regression estimation). The estimation of sampling errors can equally be very intricate when a complex design is used, i.e. when there are several sampling stages, phases, stratifications and varying probabilities of selection. The reader is referred to the books by Kish (1965a) and Yates (1960) for a thorough technical presentation. Suffice it here to stress three points. First, that with random samples such errors can generally be estimated from the sample itself. Secondly, that their estimation can be simplified if the sample is designed with this object in mind; in particular, their estimation is simple for replicated samples and for the paired selection design (see Section 6.3). Thirdly, that every report of a random sample survey should give an indication of the sampling errors affecting the results.

Two more points about population inferences can usefully be referred to here: the generality claimed for the findings and the interpretation of significance test results. There is never any justification for claiming more generality for survey findings than is their due. Often the population coverage actually achieved differs from that initially intended: the sampling frame may have turned out to be incomplete or substantial population segments may have been lost through non-response. Whatever the reason, the resultant loss in coverage, as far as it is known to the researcher, must be acknowledged, and the conclusions generalized only to the population actually covered.

Similarly, when a survey has for reasons of convenience or lack of resources been confined to, say, one town, the researcher must resist the temptation of generalizing to the whole country—even if the town appears to be fairly typical on various relevant factors. The localization of a research project is often highly desirable, but the researcher must be prepared to accept the consequent limitation in his final conclusions.

Sometimes the research approach altogether excludes the possibility of statistical sampling. This was so with Zweig (1948), who conducted several hundred interviews in public houses, parks and the like where he could hardly have used random selection. One could not deny that he managed to cover a wide range of workers, yet no strict rules of statistical generalisation were applicable. All one can ask in such a case is that the investigator should be aware of any major lack of representativeness in his collection of cases, and that his claims of generality should err on the side of caution.

Many survey analyses entail the comparison of results for different parts of the sample—e.g. the proportion of men who smoke with the proportion of women who smoke—and, as both results are based on samples, the comparison must take account of the sampling error affecting each of them. One might carry out a statistical significance test of the difference between the proportions to see how likely it is that the observed difference is due to sampling errors alone.

The mechanism of significance tests was explained in Section 4.5, and our purpose here is to comment on the interpretation of their results. To say that a difference (whether between two sample statistics or between one such statistic and a parameter fixed by hypothesis) is not statistically significant—at a given significance level—is just saying that it can be accounted for by sampling errors alone; in terms of the example, this means that the difference between the proportions of the two sexes who smoke is no larger than might reasonably occur as a result of chance sampling fluctuations alone. A statement about statistical significance is therefore a statement about sampling errors and, since sampling errors are a function of sample size, such a statement is a function of the sample sizes involved. The larger the samples (and therefore, other things being equal, the smaller the sampling errors), the greater the chance that a difference of a given size will be found statistically significant.

This is one reason why the results of significance tests should be interpreted with caution and understanding. When a test produces a negative result—not statistically significant—this does *not* necessarily mean that the effect does not exist in the population, i.e. that between the populations of men and women from which the samples were selected there is no difference in the proportions of people smoking. It means only that these particular samples have failed to demonstrate a difference. This is a comment on the so-called 'power' of the significance test for showing up the observed difference as significant, and the power relates directly to the sizes of the samples. It is vital to the interpretation of significance tests to know what this power is, but this is complicated because, besides depending on the sample sizes, it depends also on the amount of difference between the two population values—for given sample sizes a statistical test is more likely to produce a significant result if the true proportions of men and women who smoke differ substantially than if they differ only slightly. In an experiment on sampling methods Moser and Stuart

(1953) found that most of the significance tests carried out on the differences between the results obtained from various types of sample gave negative results. Yet, ignoring sampling errors, many of these non-significant differences were large enough to be important to survey practitioners. The question was then asked: 'How large must the difference (between methods) have been in order to have a reasonable chance of detection by the experiment?' 'Reasonable chance' was taken to be 50 per cent, with a 2 per cent significance level, and this 50 per cent can be considered to be a minimum requirement for the power of a test. Even so the calculations showed that the differences would have had to be much larger than those observed to have had a 'reasonable chance' of detection, which means that the experiment was insufficiently sensitive for this particular task.

This example demonstrates that, if a test has a negative result, the researcher ought not to conclude that the effect has no importance or reality. But, conversely, he must also exercise caution in interpreting significant findings. An effect that has been shown to be statistically significant may yet be so small in magnitude that it is of no substantive interest. In other words, statistical significance and substantive (e.g. sociological, political, medical, economic) significance are not the same thing. In practice the two are often confused: effects are written off as unimportant simply because they have not 'come up' significant, or are given great prominence because they have. In order to keep a clear distinction between statistical and substantive significance, the former adjective should always accompany statements based on significance test results.

In addition to these general comments on significance tests, there are some other points to be made which relate particularly to their use in survey analysis. To illustrate the basic idea, consider an experiment designed to test whether two groups differ in their mean scores. Let us suppose that there is in fact no difference in the population means, and also that, for simplicity, the standard error of the difference for the experiment is known. Further suppose that the experiment is conducted independently a large number of times and that a significance test is carried out each time. Then, if a 5 per cent significance level is being used, 1 in 20 of the tests can be expected to turn up statistically significant differences by chance alone. From this it can be seen that a researcher who conducts an experiment, say, eight times, and who chooses the largest difference to test, invalidates the ordinary significance test. By studying the data and picking out the largest difference he is capitalizing on chance, for, if any of the differences are significant, the one he chooses will be. In this example, the true significance level is in fact 33·7 per cent, not the nominal 5 per cent. The essential mistake here lies in searching through the data for a difference likely to show significance. In survey research similar mistakes can arise in different ways, but with the same result of invalidating significance tests.

Selvin and Stuart (1966) in fact describe three common ways, which they call 'snooping', 'fishing' and 'hunting', in which significance tests can be misapplied in survey analysis. To illustrate the meaning of 'snooping', let us take an example of a researcher who wants to compare the proportions of households in six geographical regions owning their own homes. He may find that an overall significance test shows the proportions to be significantly different, but he will then want to find out for which pairs of regions the differences are significant and for which pairs they are not. Testing all fifteen possible differences is a simple example of snooping, which is defined generally by Selvin and Stuart as 'the process of testing from the data all of a *predesignated* (though possibly infinite) set of hypotheses'. With a large number of tests involved it is incorrect to carry out the separate tests in the ordinary way because this capitalizes on chance. However, valid statistical procedures known as multiple comparisons tests have been developed for this situation. Snooping is in no sense wrong; it is necessary only to ensure that the right method of testing is employed. 'Fishing' is defined as 'the process of using the data to choose which of a number of candidate variables to include in an explanatory model'. A common procedure in survey analysis is to try to explain, often by multiple regression analysis, the variation in a particular variable (the dependent variable) by the variation in a set of independent variables. If some independent variables are discarded from the analysis because they are found to make no useful contribution to the explanation, the model involving just the remaining variables cannot be tested on the same data. Retaining only the important explanatory variables means keeping the variables which are most likely to show significance, and this invalidates the significance test. Again, fishing is not wrong in itself, but it is invalid to develop a model and test it on the same data. The model must be developed on one set of data and tested on another. Frequently the researcher has no clear-cut prior hypotheses for some of the issues investigated in his survey, but instead wants to generate his hypotheses from the data. He will then dredge the data for information in the area of interest, and it is this operation that Selvin and Stuart have termed 'hunting'. As surveys generally serve many purposes and are commonly at least partly exploratory, a full set of clearly defined hypotheses is seldom specified before survey data are collected, and the temptation to hunt is therefore great. There is of course nothing wrong in using data in an exploratory way for generating hypotheses, indeed quite the contrary; the mistake that may be made lies in attempting to test an hypothesis on the same data that generated it. Hypotheses generated by one set of data have to be tested for significance on another set.

A final warning about significance tests relates to the application of the tests described in statistical textbooks to survey data. Significance tests deal with sampling errors and, as we have seen, sampling errors depend on the method of sampling employed. An assumption behind the tests given in the ordinary statistical textbooks is that unrestricted sampling is used. This is almost never the case in survey sampling, although it may sometimes be a reasonable approximation. In tests of differences between two means or between two proportions, a valid significance test can be made for a complex sample by ensuring that the correct formula for the standard error of the difference is used, but for many other cases there is no such straightforward solution. In particular, the usual chi-square test and F-test in the analysis of variance depend on unrestricted sampling, and should therefore not be applied uncritically to survey data. If, as is commonly the case, the design effect of the complex sample (see pp. 200–2) exceeds one, these tests could identify differences as significant when the correct analysis would show them to be nonsignificant: the researcher would in fact be working with a larger significance level than he intends.

The purpose of these comments is to warn against too sweeping an interpretation of significance test results. Perhaps an even more general warning is not out of place. There is noticeable in the social science literature—possibly in other fields too—an altogether excessive emphasis on significance tests, to the detriment of the estimation of the magnitude of effects. When all is said and done, what is usually of importance is the magnitude of effects (e.g. the size of the difference between proportions in the population) rather than a test of whether the difference is statistically significant or not. Concentration on the latter question sometimes leads researchers to close their report when the tests have been made, not progressing to the generally more important task of estimation.

17.4. Interpreting relationships

The study of relationships between two or more variables is straightforward so long as one is content merely to state the extent and direction of the association. But as soon as one tries to investigate its meaning, to make cause-effect inferences, difficulties arise. As was seen in Chapter 9, the likely 'third' variables need to be eliminated as possible explanations of an association before a causal connection can be assumed with any degree of confidence. One approach towards this end, discussed in Section 9.3, is to control for 'third' variables by matching or randomization in the selection of the sample. An alternative is to eliminate their potentially disturbing effects by adjustments in the analysis, and that is the concern of this section.

Let us take a hypothetical example, similar to one used in Chapter 9, to illustrate the ideas involved. A survey is carried out to see whether a television programme about polio vaccination encourages mothers to have their children vaccinated. A random sample of 1,800 mothers who prior to the programme had not had their child vaccinated is selected, and then interviewed four weeks after the programme. (For simplicity we assume that no matching has been done in the sample selection.) The following data are obtained from the interviews:

	Mothers		
	Viewing	*Not viewing*	
Children	*programme*	*programme*	*Total*
	(X)	$(\bar{X})$	
Vaccinated (Y)	400	280	680
Not vaccinated $(\bar{Y})$	400	720	1,120
Total	800	1,000	1,800

Since 50 per cent ($400 \times 100/800$) of mothers viewing the programme have now had their children vaccinated while only 28 per cent ($280 \times 100/1,000$) of the non-viewers have done so, we see that there is indeed an association between viewing and vaccination.

The question is whether this association can be explained by a disturbing variable, or 'test factor'. A method of controlling for a test factor in the analysis is by *elaboration*[1], by which is meant splitting the sample into sub-groups according to the categories of the factor and examining the associations within each sub-group. Let us take social class (middle v. working class) as being one such test factor. Its introduction into the analysis might then lead to the following breakdown of the original table:

EXAMPLE 1

	X	$\bar{X}$			X	$\bar{X}$			X	$\bar{X}$
					Middle class (T)				*Working class* $(\bar{T})$	
Y	400	280		Y	360	120		Y	40	160
$\bar{Y}$	400	720	$=$	$\bar{Y}$	240	80	$+$	$\bar{Y}$	160	640
	800	1,000			600	200			200	800

[1] For a fuller discussion of elaboration, see Hyman (1955), Rosenberg (1968) and the papers by Lazarsfeld—for example Lazarsfeld (1958) and Lazarsfeld and Rosenberg (1955, pp. 115–125).

In this case social class does account for the association between vaccination (Y) and viewing (X), for there is no difference between viewers and non-viewers with regard to vaccination within either the middle class or working class sub-groups. The associations within sub-groups are known as *partial associations*, and here they are seen to be non-existent: in the middle class 60 per cent $(360 \times 100/600)$ of mothers who viewed the programme (X) and 60 per cent $(120 \times 100/200)$ of those who did not $(\overline{X})$ had their children vaccinated; and in the working class 20 per cent $(40 \times 100/200)$ of the viewers and 20 per cent $(160 \times 100/800)$ of the non-viewers did so. The overall association between viewing and vaccination is in fact completely explained by the so-called *marginal associations* of social class with viewing and social class with vaccination. Such an outcome of elaboration is known as *elaboration by marginals*.

On the other hand the elaboration could have led to an extremely different result, for instance:

EXAMPLE II

	X	$\overline{X}$			(T)				$(\overline{T})$	
					X	$\overline{X}$			X	$\overline{X}$
Y	400	280	$=$	Y	100	70	$+$	Y	300	210
$\overline{Y}$	400	720		$\overline{Y}$	100	180		$\overline{Y}$	300	540
	800	1,000			200	250			600	750

Here the partial associations are the same as the association in the full table; in the overall sample and in the middle class and working class sub-groups individually 50 per cent of the viewers compared with 28 per cent of the non-viewers had their children vaccinated. These data thus provide an example of a case in which the marginal associations of the test factor social class with viewing and with vaccination do not account for any part of the overall association. The overall association is completely explained by the partial associations, and this outcome is therefore known as *elaboration by partials*.

In Example II the two partial associations are the same, both being equal to the overall association, but this need not be so; indeed, with elaboration by partials, it is often of interest to compare the relative sizes of the partial associations. In particular, it may even be the case that there is no partial association in one sub-group (T) but a large one in the other $(\overline{T})$; had this occurred in Example II it would have meant that the television programme affected only the middle class mothers watching it. The examination of partial associations with elaboration brings this kind of situation to light and can thus be important in clarifying the nature of the overall association.

In general, for a fuller understanding of elaboration, another feature of the variables must be considered—the time ordering. We will assume that X precedes Y, and the question then is, when does the test factor T occur in relation to X and Y? There are two possibilities: T can precede X, or it can come between X and Y. The two extreme outcomes that we have discussed above, elaboration by marginals and elaboration by partials, can now be analysed for each of these cases. There are then four possibilities: elaboration by marginals with T antecedent (type MA); elaboration by marginals with T intervening (MI); elaboration by partials with T antecedent (PA); and elaboration by partials with T intervening (PI).

In type MA there are no partial associations between X and Y after controlling for T, so there is no direct causal link between X and Y. Since T precedes X, the relationship between the variables can be diagrammed as

The XY association in this case, being accounted for by the antecedent T, is said to be *spurious*. Example I is in fact an illustration of a spurious association, for it is elaboration by marginals with the test factor, social class, antecedent. In interpreting associations one needs to be particularly on the lookout for this kind of explanation.

In type MI, T intervenes between X and Y and so the relationship can be diagrammed as

$$X \rightarrow T \rightarrow Y,$$

there again being no direct arrow from X to Y as the partial associations are non-existent. In this case X is a cause of Y (assuming there is no other antecedent test factor to explain the association), but one which operates via T. The introduction of T into the analysis thus *interprets* the association. Comparison of types MA and MI shows the importance of the time ordering: in the former case elaboration by marginals means no causal connection, while in the latter the connection remains, the elaboration merely interpreting it.

As has been seen above, the concern in elaboration by partials is likely to be with the relative magnitudes of the partial associations. In type PA, when there is no partial association in the sub-group $\overline{T}$, T is said to be a *condition*; if T is present beforehand, X is a cause of Y, but if T is absent there is no causal connection. For instance, depressing the light switch (X) causes the light to go on (Y), a condition (T) for this being that the power is connected. In type PI, with no partial association in the sub-group $\overline{T}$, T is said to be a *contingency*; if T happens at some time between X and Y, X will be a cause of Y, but if T does not happen there will be no causal connection. Here an example is putting fertilizer on a lawn (X) makes the grass grow (Y), if it rains (T) soon after the fertilizer has been administered—the contingency (assuming that if it does not rain the fertilizer has no effect).

In the preceding discussion we have attempted to present some of the basic logic of survey analysis for interpreting relationships. In the remainder of this section the ideas of elaboration are examined in more detail, the problems of controlling for several test factors simultaneously and of controlling for non-dichotomous test factors are considered, and some other techniques for controlling for test factors are outlined.

● Clearly the two examples we have given, of elaboration by marginals and elaboration by partials, do not exhaust the possible outcomes of elaboration, but only illustrate two extremes. The general scheme can be more readily understood by means of an equation showing how the overall association can be decomposed. For this some symbols are needed. Let p_x be the proportion of the sample with X (in our example, the proportion of mothers viewing), p_Y be the proportion with Y (the proportion of children vaccinated), p_T be the proportion with T (the proportion in the middle class), $p_{\overline{T}}$ the proportion with $\overline{T}$ (the proportion in the working class) and p_{XY} be the proportion with both X and Y (the proportion who both watched the programme and had their children vaccinated). For both our examples, $p_x=800/1,800$, $p_Y=680/1,800$ and $p_{XY}=400/1,800$; $p_T=800/1,800$ and $p_{\overline{T}}=1,000/1,800$ for Example I; and $p_T=450/1,800$ and $p_{\overline{T}}=1,350/1,800$ for Example II. If there were no association between X and Y, the proportion of the X group having Y should equal the proportion of the total sample having Y; from this equality it is easy to derive algebraically that p_{XY} should equal the product of p_X and p_Y, or equivalently that $p_{XY}-p_Xp_Y$ should equal zero. The quantity $[XY]=p_{XY}-p_Xp_Y$, which is known as the *cross-product*, can in fact be used as a measure of association. As $[XY]$ relates to the full sample, it has the same value for both of the examples, namely

$$[XY]=\frac{400}{1,800}-\frac{800}{1,800}\cdot\frac{680}{1,800}=0\cdot054.$$

Since $[XY]$ is in this case non-zero, there is some degree of association in the full sample.

The general outcome of elaboration can now be seen by decomposing the $[XY]$ association according to the following formula:[1]

$$[XY]=p_T[XY|T]+p_{\overline{T}}[XY|\overline{T}]+\frac{[XT]\cdot[YT]}{p_T\cdot p_{\overline{T}}}$$

[1] This equation is a special case of the breakdown of total covariance into its components: see, for example, Alker (1965). Fennessey (1968) and Schuessler in Borgatta (1969) discuss the relationship of elaboration to other forms of statistical analysis serving a similar purpose.

where $[XY|T]$ and $[XY|\bar{T}]$ are the partial associations, that is the cross-products in the T and $\bar{T}$ sub-groups respectively. $[XT]$ and $[YT]$, the cross-products of X and Y with the test factor T, are the marginal associations.

For Example I, in the middle class the cross-product is

$$[XY|T] = \frac{360}{800} - \frac{600}{800} \cdot \frac{480}{800} = 0$$

and in the working class it is

$$[XY|\bar{T}] = \frac{40}{1,000} - \frac{200}{1,000} \cdot \frac{200}{1,000} = 0,$$

so that both the partial associations are zero. The marginal associations are calculated from the following tables (derived from the figures in Example I):

	X	$\bar{X}$	Total		Y	$\bar{Y}$	Total
T	600	200	800	T	480	320	800
$\bar{T}$	200	800	1,000	$\bar{T}$	200	800	1,000
Total	800	1,000	1,800	Total	680	1,120	1,800

Thus

$$[XT] = \frac{600}{1,800} - \frac{800}{1,800} \cdot \frac{800}{1,800} = 0 \cdot 1358$$

$$[YT] = \frac{480}{1,800} - \frac{680}{1,800} \cdot \frac{800}{1,800} = 0 \cdot 0988$$

$$p_T = \frac{800}{1,800} = 0 \cdot 4444 \text{ and } p_{\bar{T}} = \frac{1,000}{1,800} = 0 \cdot 5556.$$

From these results the overall cross-product can be decomposed by the elaboration equation into:

$$[XY] = 0 + 0 + \frac{0 \cdot 1358 \times 0 \cdot 0988}{0 \cdot 4444 \times 0 \cdot 5556} = 0 \cdot 054.$$

This example, where both partial associations are zero, illustrates the special case of elaboration by marginals. The elaboration equation simplifies in such cases to

$$[XY] = \frac{[XT] \cdot [YT]}{p_T \cdot p_{\bar{T}}}.$$

Example II is another special case, the case where the marginal associations are zero, so that the general equation reduces to elaboration by partials:

$$[XY] = p_T[XY|T] + p_{\bar{T}}[XY|\bar{T}].$$

In Example II both $[XT]$ and $[YT]$ are zero but, since they appear as a product, only one of them needs to be zero to give elaboration by partials. As we have already seen, with elaboration by partials interest often centres on the comparison of the partial associations, $[XY|T]$

and $[XY|\bar{T}]$. The fact that $[XY|T]=[XY|\bar{T}]$ is a special feature of the data in Example II; it is not generally so.

In passing, it is worth noting from the elaboration equation how spurious associations can be avoided by the choice of sample design. If the samples are chosen with regard to an antecedent test factor T in such a way that $[XT]=0$, elaboration of $[XY]$ by T is necessarily elaboration by partials, so that the $[XY]$ association cannot be spurious with respect to T. Matching experimental (X) and control $(\bar{X})$ groups on T makes $[XT]=0$—in our example this would be matching the samples of viewers and non-viewers on social class. Random allocation to experimental and control groups also makes $[XT]$ zero, but only within random chance fluctuations; however it covers all antecedent test factors. In our example, it would involve randomly choosing one sample of mothers to be the experimental group watching the programme and another sample to be the control group not watching it. These ideas have already been discussed in Chapter 9.

So far we have taken all the variables to be dichotomous and have assumed that there is only one test factor of interest. While the ideas of elaboration can be readily extended to other forms of data, serious difficulties may arise in practice.

If, for example, T has more than two categories, all that need be done is to divide the sample into the various categories of T and assess the XY association within each category. This procedure also enables control for several test factors to be exerted simultaneously. For instance, the two test factors sex and social class (classified into upper, middle and working class) can be combined into a new single test factor with the following six categories: (1) male upper class, (2) female upper class, (3) male middle class, (4) female middle class, (5) male working class and (6) female working class. Dividing the sample into these six sub-groups and studying the partial associations within the sub-groups is a means of controlling for both the original test factors at the same time. This method can be extended to include more test factors, but the number of sub-groups rises rapidly as additional factors are introduced; as a consequence the numbers of cases within the sub-groups quickly become too small to provide stable estimates of the partial associations. With four test factors, the first having, say, two categories, the second three and the other two four each, and with the requirement of an average of 40 cases per sub-group, the total sample size needed would be $40 \times 2 \times 3 \times 4 \times 4 =$ 3,840 cases. The introduction of another test factor with, say, three categories would treble this figure. In practice the sample size is rarely large enough to permit control to be exerted simultaneously in this manner for more than four or five test factors. One way by which extra factors can be introduced is to use fewer categories for each one, for example by combining upper and middle social classes into one category. By this means, using five dichotomous factors and one factor with three categories, the sample of 3,840 cases could in fact be split on six factors simultaneously and still have an average of 40 cases per cell. However, the use of fewer and hence coarser categories means that the effects of the factors are not completely eliminated; in particular, collapsing a factor with many categories into a dichotomy is unlikely to result in an adequate degree of control.

On some occasions, when the researcher finds his sub-groups are too small to yield stable estimates, he may be willing to make an assumption about the form of the sub-group associations. He may, for instance, be willing to assume that the difference between the proportions of the experimental (X) and control $(\bar{X})$ groups having the attribute (Y) is the same in all sub-groups. If so, he can then combine the unstable sub-group estimates of the constant difference into a stable weighted average for the sample as a whole, in such a way that control over the various test factors is maintained. Standardization is a method of doing this, and is discussed in relation to survey analysis by Rosenberg (1962) and Kalton (1968).

We have been considering elaboration when the test factor T has more than two categories, and we will now note what happens when X and Y are not dichotomous variables.[1] In general, all that is needed is to employ an alternative to the cross-product for assessing the association. When both X and Y are continuous variables, the product-moment correlation coefficient may provide a suitable measure of association and, if T is a categorized variable, the statistical technique of analysis of covariance may be appropriate for the analysis. If X is categorized and Y continuous, the differences in the mean values of Y for the various classes of X can be used as an indication of association and, if T is categorized, the analysis of variance may be the appropriate analytic technique.

If the test factor T is continuous, it can be categorized by grouping scores into classes, but this grouping results in a lack of complete control for T in the analysis. The fewer classes employed the less will be the control. Cochran (1968b) has shown that if Y and T increase together, and T is dichotomized at a suitable point, only about 64 per cent of the biasing effect of T is removed. If T is formed into three well-chosen classes the figure becomes 79 per cent; if four, 86 per cent; if five, 90 per cent; and if six, 92 per cent. These results show that a continuous variable with an important disturbing effect needs to be grouped into several classes if it is to be effectively controlled.

But if T is continuous it need not be categorized. When Y is also continuous, T's effect can be removed by regression analysis, a technique widely used in survey analysis. While an adequate treatment of the technique is not possible here, a few comments are in order. In general, multiple regression is concerned with the situation where the variation in a dependent variable, y, is to be explained by the variation in a number of independent variables, $x_1, x_2, \ldots, x_p$. We will take the case with two independent variables, where y is an individual's attitude score, x_1 is his age, and x_2 is his income. As is shown in statistical textbooks, regression analysis would produce the equation

$$y = \bar{y} + b_1(x_1 - \bar{x}_1) + b_2(x_2 - \bar{x}_2) \qquad \ldots(17.1)$$

where $\bar{y}$, $\bar{x}_1$ and $\bar{x}_2$ are the sample arithmetic means for the three variables, and b_1 and b_2 are also quantities calculated from the sample data and are known as regression coefficients. For illustration let us say that the analysis gave $b_1 = 0.2$, $b_2 = 0.005$, $\bar{y} = 50$ points, $\bar{x}_1 = 30$ years and $\bar{x}_2 = £1,000$, so that the equation is

$$y = 50 + 0.2(x_1 - 30) + 0.005(x_2 - 1,000).$$

---

[1] A variety of statistical techniques will be mentioned in the next few pages. The reader is recommended to consult a statistical textbook for a discussion of these techniques; some references are given at the end of the chapter.

If an individual's age, say 40, and income, £1,200, were known, his attitude score could be predicted from the equation as $50 + 0.2(40-30) + 0.005(1,200-1,000) = 53$ points. On the other hand, if nothing was known of this individual, his attitude score would be predicted as $\bar{y} = 50$. By taking account of his age and income and the knowledge that older and richer people have higher attitude scores, a better estimate of his attitude score—one likely to be closer to his true score—has been produced by using the regression equation.

If the purpose of the analysis is to investigate whether the correlation between attitude score (y) and age (x_1) can be explained by the test factor income (x_2), this can be done by seeing whether the regression coefficient b_1 in the above regression equation is zero. As in this case $b_1 = 0.2$, income appears not to provide a full explanation of the correlation, but sampling errors also need to be considered: it may be that the population value of b_1 is 0 and that the discrepancy of the observed value of 0.2 from 0 is merely the result of sampling error. A significance test can be conducted to find out the likelihood of this possibility.

An advantage of multiple regression analysis is that a large number of independent variables can be treated simultaneously. By the use of a model like (17.1), many more variables can be analysed together than is possible with cross-tabulation analysis, where the sample is soon segmented into sub-groups which are too small for study. But this gain is bought at the price of the assumptions made in the regression model. One of these is the assumption of *linearity*. The equation states that, for each year of age, there is a predicted increase of 0.2 in attitude score (with no change in income). This assumption would be invalid if, for example, attitude scores were highest among the middle-aged, i.e. if middle-aged people scored higher than both older or younger people. While equation (17.1) assumes a straight-line relationship between attitude score and age, and between attitude score and income, it is possible to adapt the model to allow for non-linear relationships. However, this adaptation must be an active step taken by the researcher rather than being an automatic feature of the technique.

Secondly, the model assumes that the effects of age and income are *additive*. The individual's score was estimated as the average 50, plus 2 because he was ten years above the average age, plus 1 because his income was £200 above average. The model used does not allow for an *interaction effect* as would occur, for example, if the income effect were stronger among older people. Here too it may be possible to adapt the model to take account of non-additivity, but this is not a routine part of the technique.

In order to explain the concept of interaction more simply, let us consider an example with categorized data.[1] The dependent variable is, say, annual income, and the two independent variables are age, classed as 'old' and 'young', and sex. The mean incomes in the four cells of the table might be:

	Men	Women	All
Young	£900	£500	£700
Old	£1,500	£1,100	£1,300
All	£1,200	£800	£1,000

[1] See Cox (1958, Section 6.5) for a fuller discussion of the interpretation of interaction.

Here it is assumed that the number of persons is the same in each of the four cells. The *main effects* are the differences from the overall mean of the means for the classes of the independent variables. For sex, the main effect is £1,200 – £1,000 = + £200 for men and £800 – £1,000 = – £200 for women; for age the main effect is £700 – £1,000 = – £300 for the young and £1,300 – £1,000 = + £300 for the old. In this example the cell values are found simply by adding the main effects of the two independent variables to the overall mean; for example, the mean income of young men is £1,000 + £200 – £300 = £900. Since the interaction effect is the difference between the actual cell mean and the figure derived by this additive procedure, it can be seen that in this case there is no interaction.

To show an interaction, let us change the example to, say:

	Men	Women	All
Young	£700	£300	£500
Old	£2,100	£900	£1,500
All	£1,400	£600	£1,000

Now the main effects are: men + £400, women – £400; and young people – £500, old people + £500. Using the additive effects of the independent variables, the figure for young men is £1,000 + £400 – £500 = £900. The actual figure is £700, so that the interaction effect is –£200. The presence of interaction means that the effect of one of the independent variables is not the same for every class of the other independent variable. In the table the effect of being male among young people is £700 – £500 = £200, and among old people is £2,100 – £1,500 = £600. The main effect for men, which is the average of these two figures, is not sufficient to give a true description of this situation. When there is no interaction a main effect is a useful figure—in the first example a concise and valid description of the situation is to say that men earn £200 above the average—but if there is sizeable interaction a main effect can be virtually meaningless.

In this example we have described a *first-order interaction*, which is all that is possible if there are only two independent variables. However, if there are more variables, many different interaction effects can occur. With, say, four independent variables (*A, B, C* and *D*) there could be, in addition to the four main effects, six first-order interactions, which are the pairwise effects of the variables (*AB, AC, AD, BC, BD, CD*), four second-order interactions, which are all the three-way effects (*ABC, ABD, ACD, BCD*), and one third-order interaction (*ABCD*).

Let us return to regression analysis. It has been introduced as a technique for handling continuous variables on interval scales, but it can also be applied to categorized independent variables by turning them into what are known as *dummy variables*. The simplest case arises when the independent variable comprises only two categories, such as male or female, yes or no. Then one category can be scored $x = 1$, the other $x = 0$, and the dummy variable x can be entered into the regression analysis. With more than two categories, several dummy variables are needed; in fact $(r - 1)$ dummy variables are needed for

r categories. Marital status, for instance, might be classified into single, married, widowed and divorced. These four categories can be represented by three dummy variables, for example: $x_1 = 1$ if the person is single and 0 otherwise; $x_2 = 1$ if married and 0 otherwise; and $x_3 = 1$ if widowed and 0 otherwise. There are then four acceptable patterns of scores for these three variables, one pattern for each of the categories of marital status, as follows:

	x_1	x_2	x_3
Single	1	0	0
Married	0	1	0
Widowed	0	0	1
Divorced	0	0	0

The nominal variable marital status can by means of these three dummy variables be employed in regression analyses.

Besides making possible the inclusion of independent variables measured on nominal or ordinal scales in a regression analysis, dummy variables also provide one way of dealing with problems of non-linearity and non-additivity. If, although measured on an interval scale, an independent variable is thought not to be linearly related to the dependent variable, it can be grouped into a number of categories and these categories can then be turned into dummy variables for the analysis. For example, age might be classified as under 25, 25–44, 45–64 and 65 and over, and these age groups might then be represented by three dummy variables in the regression model; by this means the assumption of a linear relationship between age and the dependent variable is avoided. If the effects of some categorized independent variables are thought to be non-additive, they can be formed into one composite variable and then turned into dummy variables. In terms of our earlier example, instead of using two dummy variables—$x_1 = 1$ for men and 0 for women and $x_2 = 1$ for young people and 0 for old—a composite variable with four classes—young men, young women, old men, old women—can be formed and turned into three dummy variables, which will then take into account the interaction effect. The advantages of the dummy variable approach have led to the development by Andrews, Morgan and Sonquist (1969) of a computer program, called Multiple Classification Analysis (M.C.A.), which treats all the independent variables as dummy variables. However, while dummy variables routinely avoid the problems of non-linearity, they do not cater for interaction effects in a general way; particular interactions are measured only by adding specific extra terms to the regression model. Sonquist and Morgan (1970) have developed another program, called the Automatic Interaction Detector (A.I.D.), which is designed to investigate interactions. As interaction effects are common in social research, this approach has much to commend it.

It may be inferred from the above discussion that the choice between elaboration, analysis of variance, analysis of covariance, and regression analysis, depends on the measurement levels of the variables involved. Elaboration is applicable when all the variables are categorized. Each of the other three techniques treats the dependent variable as being on an interval scale. They differ with regard to the measurement levels of the independent variables: in analysis of variance, the independent variables are all on nominal scales; in analysis of covariance some are on nominal scales, others are on interval scales; and in regression analysis all are on interval scales. Another technique, which has not been mentioned so far, is discriminant analysis, where the dependent variable is on a nominal scale and the independent variables are on interval scales. While this scheme may provide a useful codification, ·it should not be taken to mean that completely different techniques are employed according to the measurement levels of the variables. For one thing, as we have seen, dummy variables can be used to turn a variable on a nominal scale into a series of variables on interval scales; a variable on an interval scale can also clearly be grouped into categories and hence treated as a nominal variable. More basically, all the techniques are special cases of the *general linear model*, which is the unifying framework relating them one to another. This will not be developed further here, but instead the reader is referred to the article by Fennessey (1968).

17.5. Causal models

● The previous section was concerned with methods for investigating the possible causal connection between two variables, but a better understanding of causal mechanisms may come from a causal model in which the connections between several variables are studied simultaneously. Then, instead of a single dependent variable, there can be several of them, and a dependent variable in one relationship may be an independent one in another.

Here only a brief introduction to the construction of causal models will be given, and the discussion will be confined to situations where a definite causal ordering of the variables can be assumed.[1] The variables in the model will be labelled $X_1, X_2, \ldots X_k$ according to their causal ordering, so that a variable X_i can depend on preceding variables (i.e. $X_1, X_2, \ldots X_{i-1}$), but not on succeeding ones ($X_{i+1}, X_{i+2}, \ldots X_k$). When there is a definite time ordering of the variables this will be the causal ordering, for no effect can precede its cause. Without an identifiable time ordering the causal ordering must be determined otherwise.

If linear additive effects—as in the multiple regression equation described in the previous section—are assumed, a simple set of equations can be built up showing how each variable depends on preceding variables. If every variable depends directly on all preceding variables the equations may be written as

$$X_2 = p_{21}X_1 + R_2$$
$$X_3 = p_{31}X_1 + p_{32}X_2 + R_3$$
$$X_4 = p_{41}X_1 + p_{42}X_2 + p_{43}X_3 + R_4$$
$$\cdots\cdots\cdots\cdots\cdots\cdots\cdots\cdots\cdots\cdots\cdots\cdots\cdots$$
$$X_k = p_{k1}X_1 + p_{k2}X_2 + \ldots + p_{k,k-1}X_{k-1} + R_k$$

---

[1] The assumption here of a causal ordering rules out a causal looping from a variable back to itself. Thus both direct feedback loops of the form $X_i \leftrightarrow X_j$ and indirect loops like $X_i \to X_j$ are excluded. Although not treated here, some

$$X_k$$

forms of causal looping can be included in causal models, and Duncan and others (1968) present a sociological example of instantaneous reciprocal causation.

where the variables X_1, X_2, ... X_k are measured in standardized form.[1] Each equation expresses the dependent variable as the linear additive effects of all the preceding variables together with a residual term R, which may be thought of as the effect of variables not included in the model. If the residuals are assumed uncorrelated with the independent variables in their equations, the coefficients of the X's are known as *path coefficients*, and they measure the importance of the direct effect of the independent variables on the dependent variables; thus p_{ij} measures the direct effect of X_j on X_i. A set of equations like that above, in which the equations can be ordered so that a variable X_i appears only as an independent variable in equations later than the one in which it is the dependent variable, is known as a *recursive system*.

It is not necessary to analyse the whole of the causal system given by the above equations. Some of the earlier equations can be left out of the model, in which case the correlations between the early variables are not analysed. For example, the first two equations, in which X_2 and X_3 are the dependent variables, could be dropped, leaving equations only for the variables X_4, X_5, ... X_k. In this case the variables X_1, X_2 and X_3 whose correlations are unanalysed (i.e. the variables which do not appear as dependent variables in the set of equations) are said to be *exogenous variables*; variables appearing as dependent variables are known as *endogenous variables*.

There are too many unknown quantities to permit the system of equations to be solved as it stands, and therefore some assumptions need to be made. It is generally assumed that the residual term R is uncorrelated with any of the independent variables in its equation, for otherwise the coefficients p_{ij} would be difficult to interpret. On the basis of some social theory it may sometimes also be assumed that certain of the path coefficients are zero; if p_{ij} is put equal to zero, this means assuming that in the model X_i is not directly dependent on X_j.[2] In a complete recursive system, where none of the p_{ij} are assumed to be zero, lack of correlation between the residual terms and the independent variables implies that the residuals are uncorrelated with each other, but this does not follow for an incomplete system. Thus for the latter system lack of correlation in the residual terms can in fact comprise a further type of assumption.

With a complete recursive system the assumptions that the residual terms are uncorrelated with the independent variables in their equations are sufficient to enable the equations to be solved for the path coefficients. Furthermore, in this simple case, the path coefficients can be obtained by a series of regression analyses, taking each equation in turn; they are in fact standardized regression coefficients which are commonly known as beta coefficients.[3] Duncan (1966) used this

---

[1] A variable is transformed to standardized form by subtracting the mean from each observation and dividing by the standard deviation, i.e. $(x_i - \bar{x})/s$. Variables in standardized form have means of zero and standard deviations of one. The use of standardized variables is the reason that there are no constant terms in the equations.
[2] Here we are referring only to the case when X_i is later in the causal ordering than X_j. The assumed causal ordering has itself meant that all path coefficients from later variables to earlier ones are zero; however, the present discussion is not referring to these coefficients.
[3] See Blalock (1960, pp. 343–346) for a discussion of beta coefficients.

approach in an illustrative analysis of data from Turner's study of the determinants of aspirations (Turner, 1964). Two of the five variables in the analysis, a background index (X_1) and school socio-economic rating (X_2), were taken as exogenous, and the other three variables, an ambition index (X_3), intelligence quotient (X_4), and class values index (X_5), were treated as endogenous. The causal ordering of the exogenous variables need not be determined since the correlation between them is unanalysed; after these variables, the causal ordering of the other three was taken to be ambition, intelligence quotient, and finally class values. In the model each endogenous variable was allowed to depend on all the prior endogenous and on both exogenous variables. The regression analyses yielded the following three equations:

$$X_3 = 0 \cdot 27 X_1 + 0 \cdot 23 X_2 + 0 \cdot 90 R_3$$
$$X_4 = 0 \cdot 11 X_1 + 0 \cdot 12 X_2 + 0 \cdot 37 X_3 + 0 \cdot 87 R_4$$
$$X_5 = 0 \cdot 06 X_1 + 0 \cdot 15 X_2 + 0 \cdot 19 X_3 + 0 \cdot 12 X_4 + 0 \cdot 92 R_5.$$

Here, unlike the earlier representation, the residuals have been expressed in standardized form, so that they also have path coefficients. A useful way to present these findings is by means of a causal diagram, and Duncan's diagram is reproduced in Figure 17.1. The convention in the diagrammatic representation is to write the path coefficients on one-way straight-line arrows and the unanalysed correlations between exogenous variables on two-way curved arrows.

The reason for calling the coefficients 'path coefficients' is clear from another feature of the analysis. The correlation between two variables in the system can be decomposed into components associated with the various paths connecting the variables. The basic theorem of path analysis is that the correlation between an earlier variable X_j and a later variable X_i is given by

$$r_{ij} = \sum_q p_{iq} r_{jq} \qquad \qquad \text{...(17.2)}$$

where the summation extends over all the variables X_q that lead directly to X_i. Successive application of this formula produces a fuller decomposition of the correlation r_{ij}. To illustrate the theorem we will decompose the correlation of $0 \cdot 28$ between the class values index (X_5) and school socio-economic rating (X_2). Application of the formula yields

$$r_{52} = p_{51} r_{21} + p_{52} r_{22} + p_{53} r_{23} + p_{54} r_{24} \qquad \qquad \text{...(17.3)}$$

where the correlation of a variable with itself (here r_{22}) is necessarily 1. Re-application of the formula can be used to decompose both r_{23} (i.e. r_{32}) and r_{24} (i.e. r_{42}). Thus

$$r_{32} = p_{31} r_{21} + p_{32}$$

and
$$r_{42} = p_{41} r_{21} + p_{42} + p_{43} r_{32}$$
$$= p_{41} r_{21} + p_{42} + p_{43} p_{31} r_{21} + p_{43} p_{32}$$

Substituting for these correlations back in equation (17.3) gives

$$r_{52} = p_{52} + p_{51} r_{21} + p_{53} p_{31} r_{21} + p_{53} p_{32}$$
$$+ p_{54} p_{41} r_{21} + p_{54} p_{42} + p_{54} p_{43} p_{31} r_{21} + p_{54} p_{43} p_{32}$$

Substituting the numerical values of the path coefficients and correlations gives

$$r_{52} = 0.28 = 0.15 + 0.03 + 0.02 + 0.04 + 0.01 + 0.01 + 0.01 + 0.01$$

The reported data are not detailed enough to enable an exact decomposition of the correlation to be computed, but these calculations indicate the procedure. It is instructive to trace on the diagram the various paths and their contributions. The direct effect of X_2 on X_5 is given by $p_{52} = 0.15$ and the remaining $0.28 - 0.15 = 0.13$ is contributed by the various indirect effects. Of this 0.13, 0.03 comes from the correlation of X_2 with X_1 and the direct path of X_1 to X_5; 0.02 from the correlation of X_2 with X_1 and the paths from X_1 to X_3 and X_3 to X_5; 0.04 from the paths from X_2 to X_3 and X_3 to X_5; etc.

Of course, causal models do not prove causal connections. In building the model certain crucial assumptions have been required and it may well be that these assumptions are invalid. In the above example,

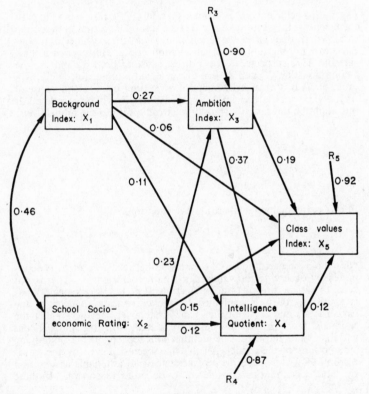

FIGURE 17.1

Duncan's causal model from Turner's data, with path coefficients estimated for the male sample.
(*Reproduced from Duncan, 1966.*)

besides the assumptions of the causal ordering, each of the residual terms R has been assumed to be uncorrelated with all the independent variables in its equation. The validity of the model hinges on the validity of these assumptions.

To develop this a little further, let us take another example where the possible causal connection between two variables X_2 and X_3 is to be examined, with the direction of causation—if there is one—being from X_2 to X_3. If no other variables are considered and if R_3 is assumed to be uncorrelated with X_2, the model is simply:

and the single causal equation is

$$X_3 = p_{32}X_2 + R_3.$$

The path coefficient p_{32} is from equation (17.2) just r_{32}. If a path coefficient is non-zero there is a direct causal connection between the variables, so that, *under the assumptions made*, the existence of a non-zero correlation establishes a causal connection.[1] However, if a third variable X_1 is suspected to be a direct cause of both X_2 and X_3, the assumption that X_2 and R_3 are uncorrelated is untenable. If X_1 is a cause of X_3 it is necessarily included in R_3, and if it is also a cause of X_2 it will be correlated with X_2; hence X_2 and R_3 will be correlated. If this might be the case, X_1 should be introduced into the model, thus:

For this extended model there are two equations:

$$X_2 = p_{21}X_1 + R_2$$
$$X_3 = p_{31}X_1 + p_{32}X_2 + R_3'.$$

Now the existence of a causal connection between X_2 and X_3 is determined by observing the value of the path coefficient p_{32}. If it is not zero, there is a direct causal connection. If $p_{32} = 0$, the correlation r_{32} is spurious, for it is explained by the correlation of each of the variables X_2 and X_3 with the prior variable X_1. But here again the residuals are assumed to be uncorrelated with the independent variables, and the causal deductions still depend on the underlying assumptions of the model. All that has been achieved by the introduction of X_1 has been the replacement of an untenable assumption by other assumptions considered to be more reasonable. If these

---

[1] For simplicity, the question of sampling error is ignored in this discussion. In practice, empirical data will almost certainly not generate a path coefficient or correlation coefficient of exactly zero; a significance test can be applied to see whether sampling errors can reasonably explain the difference between the observed value and zero.

assumptions are still dubious, further variables can be brought into the model, but ultimately any model must be based on some assumptions and any causal deductions will depend on their validity.

In the complete recursive system, the number of assumptions involved in assuming the residuals to be uncorrelated with the independent variables in their equations is the minimum number required for the solution of the equations. The number of equations generated by the assumptions is equal to the number of unknown path coefficients, and this means that the equations can be solved to yield a single solution for each coefficient. However, the researcher may be willing to make more assumptions than are strictly necessary and there will then be more equations than unknowns. This procedure has the advantage that it furnishes a test of the causal model. If the model holds, the set of equations should be mutually consistent; if they are inconsistent, the model needs to be modified, for not all the assumptions are valid.

As an illustration, consider the following simple causal chain:

$$X_1 \xrightarrow{\quad} X_2 \xrightarrow{\quad} X_3 \xrightarrow{\quad} X_4$$

with $R_2 \searrow$, $R_3 \searrow$, $R_4 \searrow$ above X_2, X_3, X_4.

The set of equations for this model is then:

$$X_2 = p_{21}X_1 + R_2$$
$$X_3 = p_{32}X_2 + R_3$$
$$X_4 = p_{43}X_3 + R_4$$

Suppose that it is assumed that the residual terms are uncorrelated with the independent variables in their equations (three assumptions) and that they are uncorrelated with each other (three more assumptions). These assumptions yield six equations, but as there are only three unknown path coefficients there are then three more equations than unknowns. As compared with the complete recursive system, the extra assumptions are $p_{31} = 0$, $p_{41} = 0$ and $p_{42} = 0$. Given some numerical data, the model can be tested by seeing whether the calculations yield zero values for these coefficients (within the bounds of sampling error). As an alternative to path coefficients, partial correlation coefficients can be used in this case, as in the treatment of Blalock (1964). The equation $p_{31} = 0$ is equivalent to $r_{13 \cdot 2} = 0$; $p_{41} = 0$ is equivalent to $r_{14 \cdot 23} = 0$; and $p_{42} = 0$ is equivalent to $r_{24 \cdot 13} = 0$. In fact, in this simple model it can be shown that $r_{14} = r_{12}r_{23}r_{34}$. Of course, if the numerical data show the set of equations to be inconsistent, this does not necessarily mean that p_{31}, p_{41} and p_{42} are not zero; an alternative explanation is, for instance, that the assumptions of lack of correlation among the residuals are wrong. If the model stands up to the tests, confidence in it is strengthened; if it does not, all that is indicated is the need to make some change in the assumptions on which it depends.

The purpose of these few remarks about causal models has been to indicate their uses and limitations. Their great value is that they provide a framework for dealing with the causal connections between several variables simultaneously. They must, of course, depend on assumptions, and there is always the danger that these assumptions are false, but the formal representation of causal connections in a

Q

model has the virtue of forcing the assumptions to be made explicit. Attention can then be focused on the assumptions to assess the reasonableness of the model. Suggestions for further reading on causal models are given at the end of the chapter.

17.6. Index construction

The previous sections have described how several variables usually have to be taken into account in causal analyses. Another situation where a number of variables (questions) covered by a survey are considered in conjunction is when several of the observations for each individual are combined into some kind of index or scale value, as in attitude scaling, or when an individual is allocated to one of several groups on the basis of a number of his characteristics. A preliminary analysis to form such indices or classifications may well precede the causal analysis, as was in fact the case for the example quoted in the previous section.

Let us imagine that we wish to combine several of the observations obtained for each survey unit into some kind of score. A simple illustration of this occurred in *The Communication of Ideas* by Cauter and Downham (1954). Here the authors sought an index to measure a person's participation in ten 'communication activities'— e.g. church-going, cinema-going, radio-listening, reading and so on. They decided on a system for scoring the frequency of a person's participation in any one activity and for combining these scores into a participation index.

The problems of constructing such indices are essentially similar to those encountered in attitude scaling (see Chapter 14). First, one has to decide what are the appropriate indicators of whatever it is one is trying to measure. What, for instance, are the appropriate indicators of a person's social class—occupation, income, whether or not he possesses a car, level of education? Common sense will suggest many possible indicators, and from these a limited number will have to be chosen. The choice can be governed by statistical techniques, resulting in a combination which is in some stated sense the 'best' index of social class. This does not necessarily measure what the sociologist means by the term, but that may be, and is often claimed to be, strictly immeasurable. All one can do is to decide on a combination of measurable indicators that can be regarded as a reasonable approximation.[1] When this is done, the relevant data (each person's occupation, income and so forth) are collected and the various items combined into an index or scale value. In this combination it is the relative weights attached to each of the items that is

[1] See Downham (1954) and Wilkins (1952) for some discussion of indices of 'social class'. Gales (1957) discusses the use of discriminant analysis for allocating sample members to social class categories.

crucial, and methods for determining them range from arbitrary choices to sophisticated multivariate statistical techniques.

In some cases one might be able to employ the techniques of multiple regression or discriminant analysis, which were referred to in Section 17.4. Suppose, for instance, that a researcher wants to combine a number of questionnaire responses into a numerical index of psychiatric state for use in a large-scale survey. The index might be developed in the following way. For each individual in a small sample a psychiatrist's rating could be obtained, as well as the individual's questionnaire responses. The best weighting of the responses for predicting the psychiatrist's rating could be determined from a multiple regression analysis, and then this weighting could be used in the formation of the required index. If the psychiatrist had classified individuals, instead of giving them numerical scores, discriminant analysis could have been used in place of regression. In order to make use of either of these techniques it is necessary to have available an external criterion—or, in statistical terms, a dependent variable—which in this case is the psychiatrist's rating. However, although available for the small sample, the external criterion will of course not be readily available in a general way for, if it were, there would be no need for the index. The index formed from the questionnaire responses is after all only an estimate of the psychiatrist's rating, and so the latter would presumably be preferred for use in the large-scale survey if that were practicable.

Without access to an external criterion a different approach must be used. Instead of weighting the indicators to obtain a 'best' predictive measure, the weighting has to be done according to the way in which the indicators are related among themselves. The range of analytic techniques for this purpose includes component analysis, factor analysis, latent structure analysis and Guttman scalogram analysis. Especially when an index is formed according to the internal correlations between the items rather than via an external criterion, careful attention has to be paid to the question of its validity (see Section 14.3).

The important and obvious feature common to these procedures is that they utilize simultaneously a number of the characteristics of each survey unit, thus getting away from the 'one trait at a time' type of analysis. In looking through completed schedules one is sometimes struck by the distinct *pattern* of answers. The people who read certain papers also tend to go to the cinema a good deal, to smoke a good deal, to be of a certain age, education, sex and so on. One then feels that it would be illuminating to treat the schedule not as a series of traits but as a unit, to typify a certain kind of person. Such a pattern cannot easily be brought out by tabulation alone, for even these few questions would demand a six-way table. There are two possible solutions to this problem. One is to follow the 'case study approach'. This is often—fallaciously—talked of as if it were a special way of collecting information, but its distinguishing characteristics are simply that each respondent (group or institution, etc.) is looked upon as a unit and that the analysis aims to retain this unitary nature of the individual case and to emphasize the relationship between its various attributes. Generally this is achieved by 'writing-up' the material in mainly non-quantified form.

The other solution, leading in the opposite direction, is to try to express the pattern by summarizing a number of the observations into a scale value or index, the obvious advantage being that such an index reflects simultaneously several of the respondent's characteristics. Yet there is some risk in this. In the example of the preceding paragraph, although there would be little technical difficulty in combining the six variables into some sort of index, the result would be sociologically meaningless. An index or scale must start from a concise conception of what it is one is trying to measure, and the most crucial step in its construction is the choice of the relevant indicators.

One further point on the use of refined methods of analysis may be made. It sometimes seems that, where previously percentages or averages represented the height of statistical sophistication, the reader of a survey report must now be prepared to grapple with the complex techniques of multivariate statistical analysis. In their place refined techniques are invaluable, but their glamour—a glamour which percentages and averages altogether lack—may tempt the researcher to use them too readily. The use of refined methods of analysis on crude data—as those of surveys often are—is to be deprecated when it is used to give the results a quite misleading appearance of precision. Researchers must also avoid the danger of paying more attention to the mathematical requirements of a scaling or other analytical device than to making sure that the end-product means what it is supposed to mean. Refined analytical methods can be an invaluable part of the survey process, but their application needs much care.

Concluding remarks on analysis

'Interpretation' of survey results is often no more than common-sense reading of simple tables and explanation of simple descriptive measures. Where sample data are involved, this interpretation is set in the context of sampling errors, and where complicated relationships are concerned it may be quite intricate. But, whatever the nature of the data, the task of interpretation falls squarely on to the shoulders of the researcher himself. Some research workers take the view that it is their job merely to present their results in logical and convenient form, leaving it to the readers to draw their own conclusions. For an enquiry like a population census this may be the only practicable course, but for the general run of surveys it seems entirely mistaken. Most readers of a research report, fellow-scientists or laymen, lack the time and perhaps the will-power to go through the tables and pick out the crucial results. But, even if they had both, it would be wrong to leave the interpretation entirely to them. There is after all more to a piece of research than can be seen from the tables, and the researcher in interpreting his results is inevitably—and rightly—influenced by all that has gone before, by his acquaintance with the raw material behind the figures, and by his own judgement. While every reader is entitled to draw his own conclusions, the writer of the survey report should not shirk the duty of giving his own.

Nor need he view his task too narrowly. The researcher who cautiously confines his conclusions to those strictly justified by the data may be safe from criticism, but he is not making his own full potential contribution. There is surely room in every research report for the research worker's own ideas and speculations, even if he cannot offer chapter and verse to substantiate them. In the course of his work he must inevitably develop theories and hunches, and, so long as he makes clear that they are no more than this, it is a pity to omit publishing them with the results. As Cochran and his colleagues (1953, p. 707) write in a methodological review of the first Kinsey report:

> We are convinced that unsubstantiated assertions are not, in themselves, inappropriate in a scientific study. In any complex field, where many questions remain unresolved, the accumulated insight of an experienced worker frequently merits recording when no documentation can be given. However, the author who values his reputation for objectivity will take pains to warn the reader, frequently and repetitiously, whenever an unsubstantiated conclusion is being represented and will choose his words with the greatest care.

17.7. Presentation

The final step of a survey is to present its results, details of its methodology, any necessary background information and the conclusions drawn from the results, in some kind of report, the form of which will depend on the type of reader for which it is intended. A report written as a private document for the department or firm that sponsored the survey will emphasize different things, perhaps give less space to methodology, than one written by a social scientist and intended to interest fellow-experts. Both will be more formal and technical than a report issued for the general public.

The researcher must keep constantly in view the kind of readers he is writing for, the extent of their knowledge, the type of problem and question that is likely to be of interest to them and the kind of language to which they are accustomed. Whatever the likely audience, he will do well to try to avoid the jargon and style that has become common in social science writing. Other sciences suffer from the same danger, but at least their technical jargon is often in Latin or Greek—truly an advantage, for then the reader is at least never in doubt whether he is, or is not, managing to understand. With social science writing it is otherwise, for although the words used are in the main everyday ones, they are used in complicated contexts and often with specialized meanings. As a result there is sometimes confusion and often an appearance of pretentiousness and pomposity.

Typical of this is a sentence taken from an unnamed sociological work and quoted by Goode and Hatt (1952, p. 366). 'These concepts can hold only for ranges of variation of circumstances not too large to invalidate the assumption that for practical purposes the particular constant relations between the values of analytical elements which these type concepts in the concrete case represent, will not be so unreal as to exceed an acceptable margin of error.' It may be that some social scientists can understand this passage without difficulty; more probably most of them would find it unintelligible or confusing. What is more important, anyone unaccustomed to the social sciences and venturing to read in this field would soon be discouraged by such a passage. To the report writer, clarity of exposition must be the first objective, taking priority over all else, including elegance of expression and style.

An allied duty, which he must keep constantly in view, is to translate technicalities into language that will be understood by the reader primarily interested in the substantive (e.g. sociological, economic, medical) results of the survey. The report writer has no right to confront the reader with numerous standard errors, significance test results, correlation matrices, regression equations, factor loadings and the like without telling him what these results mean in terms of the subject matter of the survey. Whether these technicalities are put in the text or in an appendix is a matter of taste; what is crucial is that—except, of course, if the object of the research was primarily to study these techniques—they are entirely subsidiary to the presentation and interpretation of the results in sociological, economic, or medical terms.

As regards the contents of survey reports, we cannot do better than quote the relevant sections from the *Recommendations for the Preparation of Sample Survey Reports* (*Provisional Issue*) issued by the United Nations Statistical Office (1964).[1] This document contains the recommendations of an international group of sampling experts, which was convened in 1963 to revise an earlier set of recommendations issued by the United Nations Statistical Office (1950). Three types of report—a preliminary report, a general report and a technical report—are distinguished, and the recommendations for the nature and content of these reports are reproduced below.

The United Nations Recommendations

PRELIMINARY REPORT

A preliminary report is often required to make available data of current interest as rapidly as possible; such results may relate to selected important characters sometimes based on a sub-sample of the full sample. It should contain a brief statement concerning the survey methods and the limitations of the data. As a very minimum, information should be given concerning the size of the sample, the method of selecting the sample and discrepancies observed between external and internal data. Fuller details can be given in the general and technical reports on the survey.

GENERAL REPORT

This should contain a general description of the survey for the use of those who are primarily interested in the results rather than in the technical statistical aspects of the sample design, execution and analysis. The general description should include information on the following points:

1. *Statement of purposes of the survey:* A general indication should be given of the purposes of the survey and 'margin of error' which would be permissible for the purposes of the survey, and the ways in which it is expected that the results will be utilized. In this connexion it is useful to distinguish the following types of surveys:

(i) *Integrated survey:* In an integrated survey, data on several subjects (or items, or topics) are collected for the same set of sampling units for studying the relationship among items belonging to different subject fields. Such surveys are of special importance in studies on levels of living. Integrated surveys of consumption and productive enterprises are also of special importance in developing countries where the related activities are frequently undertaken in an integrated manner in the household.

(ii) *Multi-subject survey:* When in a single survey operation several subjects, not necessarily very closely related, are simultaneously investigated for the sake of economy and convenience, the investigation

---

[1] Our thanks are due to the Statistical Office of the United Nations for permission to quote these extracts. The full document contains seven sections: Section I is a brief introduction; Sections II to IV, which are reproduced here, deal with the contents of three types of report—preliminary, general and technical; Section V gives a brief description of common types of sampling and gives definitions for some technical terms; Section VI briefly describes methods of sample selection; and Section VII defines and explains terms used in statistical analysis.

may be called a multi-subject survey. The data on different subjects need not necessarily be obtained for the same set of sampling units, or even for the same type of units (e.g., households, fields, schools, etc.).

(iii) *Continuing surveys:* The most usual example of these surveys occurs where a permanent sampling staff conducts a series of repetitive surveys which frequently include questions on the same topics in order to provide continuous series deemed of special importance to a country. Questions on the continued topics can frequently be supplemented by questions on other topics, depending upon the needs of the country.

(iv) *Ad hoc survey:* This is a survey without any plan for repetition.

(v) *Multi-purpose survey:* This term is sometimes used in connexion with sampling organizations which conduct surveys in various fields of interest to several departments or parties, keeping in view their diverse purposes. This permits economies in the technical and other resources and their more effective use, particularly in developing countries.

(vi) *Specialized or special-purpose survey:* This may be defined as an investigation focussing on a single set of objectives which, because of their nature or complexity, requires specialized knowledge or the use of special equipment by a technical staff with training in the subject field of enquiry.

2. *Description of the coverage:* An exact description should be given of the geographic region or branch of the economy or social group or other categories of constituent parts of a population covered by the survey. In a survey of a human population, for example, it is necessary to specify whether such categories as hotel residents, institutions (e.g., boarding houses, sanatoria), persons without fixed abode, military personnel, were included and to indicate the order of magnitude of the categories omitted. The reporter should guard against any possible misapprehension regarding the coverage of the survey.

3. *Collection of information:* The nature of the information collected should be reported in considerable detail, including a statement of items of information collected but not reported upon. The inclusion of copies of the questionnaire or other schedules, and relevant parts of the instructions used in the survey (including special rules for coding and classifying) is of great value, and such documents should therefore be reproduced in the report if possible.

The information may be collected by direct investigation, or by mail or telephone. Direct investigation may involve objective methods of observation or measurement. The method of collection should be reported, together with the nature of steps taken to ensure that the information is as complete as possible (e.g., methods of dealing with non-response). The extent and causes of non-response, etc. should be stated.

It is of importance to describe the type and number of investigators, e.g., whether whole or part-time, permanent or temporary, with particulars of their training and qualifications.

4. *Repetition:* It is important to state whether the survey is an isolated one or is one of a series of similar surveys. Where the survey is repeti-

tive and some of the sampling units reappear in the successive stages, this should be stated.

5. *Numerical results:* A general indication should be given of the methods followed in the derivation of the numerical results. Particulars should be given of methods of weighting and of any supplementary information utilized, for example to obtain ratio estimates. Any special methods of allowing for non-response should be described.

6. *Date and duration:* There are two periods of time which are important for any survey: (i) the period to which data refer, or *reference period*, (ii) *period of collection*, that is, the period taken for the field work.

In order to minimize memory lapses, the *length* of the reference period is sometimes fixed but not the end points, as in 'preceding week' questions (the collection period being comparatively long). In such cases, the reference period may be called *moving* in contrast with a *fixed* reference period when the end points are fixed. The reference period, if properly selected, enhances the use and value of the information collected in the survey. Sometimes different reference periods are used for different topics in the same survey. This is done with a view to eliciting more accurate information from the respondents, as in a family budget survey, where questions on food items may be asked for the preceding week or month, but information on clothing or furniture or some durable goods may be asked for the whole year. In health surveys, different reference periods are used for different items, e.g., illness during the preceding two weeks, hospitalization during the year. When the field work is conducted on a continuous and successive basis, the parts of the survey which are operationally separate are called *rounds*.

7. *Accuracy:* A general indication of the accuracy attained should be given and a distinction should be made between sampling errors and non-sampling errors.

8. *Cost:* An indication should be given of the cost of the survey, under such headings as preliminary work, field investigations, analysis, etc. Resources used in the conduct of the survey but not included in the costs should be stated.

9. *Assessment:* The extent to which the purposes of the survey were fulfilled should be assessed.

10. *Responsibility:* The names of the organizations sponsoring and conducting the survey should be stated.

11. *References:* References should be given to any available reports or papers relating to the survey.

TECHNICAL REPORT

Technical reports should be issued for surveys of particular importance and those using new techniques and procedures of special interest. In addition to covering such fundamental points as the purposes of the survey, conditions to be fulfilled and resources available for the survey, the report should deal in detail with technical statistical aspects of the sampling design, execution and analysis; the operational and other special aspects should also be fully covered.

1. *Specification of the frame:* A detailed account of the specification of the frame should be given; this should define the geographic areas and categories of material included and the date and source of the frame. If the frame has been emended or constructed *ab initio* the method of emendation or construction should be described. Particulars should be given of any known or suspected deficiencies.

2. *Design of the survey:* The sampling design should be carefully specified, including details such as types of sampling unit, sampling fractions, particulars of stratification, etc. The procedure used in selecting sampling units should be described and if it is not by random selection the reporter should indicate the evidence on which he relies for adopting an alternative procedure.

3. *Personnel and equipment:* It is desirable to give an account of the organization of the personnel employed in collecting, processing and tabulating the primary data, together with information regarding their previous training and experience. Arrangements for training, inspection and supervision of the staff should be explained; as also should methods of checking the accuracy of the primary data at the point of collection. A brief mention of the equipment used is frequently of value to readers of the report.

4. *Statistical analysis and computational procedure:* The statistical methods followed in the compilation of the final summary tables from the primary data should be described. If any more elaborate processes of estimation than simple totals and means have been used, the methods followed should be explained, the relevant formulae being reproduced where necessary.

It frequently happens that quantities of which estimates are required do not correspond exactly to those observed; in a crop-cutting survey, for example, the yields of the sample plots give estimates of the amount of grain, etc., in the standing crop, whereas the final yields will be affected by losses at various stages, such as harvesting, storing, transport, marketing, etc. In such cases adjustments may have to be made, the amount of which is estimated by subsidiary observations, or otherwise. An account should be given of the nature of these adjustments and the ways in which they were derived.

The steps taken to ensure the elimination of gross errors from the primary data (by scrutiny, sample checks, etc.) and to ensure the accuracy of the subsequent calculations should be indicated in detail. Mention should be made of the methods of processing the data (punched cards, hand tabulation, etc.) including methods used for the control of errors.

In recent years electronic computers have been applied to the making of estimates from sample surveys. In addition, they have been programmed to tasks of editing with consequent improvement of consistency of the primary data and possibly of its accuracy. Their use goes beyond the mere speeding up of existing methods and lowering cost. They have made possible some forms of estimation (e.g., the fitting of constants in analysis of variance with unequal numbers in the sub-classes) on a scale which would have been impracticable with hand methods. In some instances regression on previous surveys of a series with overlapping samples can substantially improve the precision of estimates. The use of these computers makes possible changes in the allocation of resources between the collection of the data and the processing.

The amount of tabular matter included in the report, and the extent to which the results are discussed, will depend on the purposes of the report. If a critical statistical analysis of the results embodied in the final summary tables has been made, it is important that the methods followed should be fully described. Numerical examples are often of assistance in making the procedure clear. Mention should be made of further tabulations which have been prepared but are not included in the report, and also of critical statistical analyses which failed to yield results of interest and which are therefore not considered to be worth reporting in detail.

The inclusion of additional numerical information which is not of immediate relevance to the report but which will enable subsequent workers to carry out critical statistical analyses which appear to them to be of interest should be carefully considered. If, for example, in addition to the class means of each main classification of the data, the sub-class numbers (but not the means) of the various two-way classifications are reported, a study of the effects of each of the main classifications freed from the effects of all other classifications can be made (provided the effects are additive) without further reference to the original information.

5. *Accuracy of the survey:*

(i) *Precision as indicated by the random sampling errors deducible from the survey:* Standard deviations of sampling units should be given in addition to such standard errors (of means, totals, etc.) as are of interest. The process of deducing these estimates of error should be made entirely clear. This process will depend intimately on the design of the sample survey. An analysis of the variances of the sampling units into such components as appears to be of interest for the planning of future surveys, is also of great value.

(ii) *Degree of agreement observed between independent investigators covering the same material:* Such comparison will be possible only when interpenetrating samples have been used, or when checks have been imposed on part of the survey. It is only by these means that the survey can provide an objective test of possible personal equations (differential bias among the investigators). Any such comparisons or checks should be fully reported.

(iii) *Other non-sampling errors:* The existence and possible effects of non-sampling errors on the accuracy of the results, and of incompleteness in the recorded information (e.g., non-response, lack of records, whether covering the whole of the survey or particular areas or categories of the material), should be fully discussed. Any special checks instituted to control and determine the magnitude of these errors should be described, and the results reported.

Another source of error is that due to incorrect determinations of the adjustments (referred to in Section VII-4) arising from observation of quantities which do not correspond exactly to the quantities of which estimates are required.

6. *Accuracy, completeness and adequacy of the frame:* The accuracy of the frame can and should be checked and corrected automatically in the course of the enquiry, and such checks afford useful guidance for

the future. Its completeness and adequacy cannot be judged by internal evidence alone. Thus, complete omission of a geographic region or the complete or partial omission of any particular class of the material intended to be covered cannot be discovered by the enquiry itself and auxiliary investigations have often to be made. These should be put on record, indicating the extent of inaccuracy which may be ascribable to such defects.

7. *Comparisons with other sources of information:* Every reasonable effort should be made to provide comparisons with other independent sources of information. Such comparisons should be reported along with the other results, and the significant differences should be discussed. The object of this is not to throw light on the sampling error, since a well designed survey provides adequate internal estimates of such errors, but rather to gain knowledge of biases, and other non-random errors.

Disagreement between results of a sample survey and other independent sources may of course sometimes be due, in whole or in part, to differences in concepts and definitions or to errors in the information from other sources.

8. *Costing analysis:* The sampling method can often supply the required information with greater speed and at lower cost than a complete enumeration. For this reason, information on the costs involved in sample surveys are of particular value for the development of sample surveys within a country and are also of help to other countries.

It is therefore recommended that fairly detailed information should be given on costs of sample surveys. Costing information should be given under such headings as planning (showing separately the cost of pilot studies), field work, supervision, processing, analysis and overhead costs. In addition, labour costs in man-weeks of different grades of staff and also time required for interviewing, travel and transport costs should be given. The collection of such information is often worthwhile, since it may suggest methods of economizing in the planning of future surveys. Moreover, the preparation of an efficient design involves a knowledge of the various components of costs as well as of the components of variance. It should be emphasized that the concept of cost in this respect should be regarded broadly in the sense of economic cost and should therefore take account of indirect costs which may not have been charged administratively to the survey. Wherever possible, the costing data should distinguish the time and resources devoted to the various operations involved in the survey.

9. *Efficiency:* The results of a survey often provide information which enables investigations to be made on the efficiency of the sampling designs, in relation to other sampling designs which might have been used in the survey. The results of any such investigations should be reported. To be fully relevant the relative costs of the different sampling methods must be taken into account when assessing the relative efficiency of different designs and intensities of sampling.

Such an investigation can be extended to consideration of the relation between the cost of carrying out surveys of different levels of accuracy and the losses resulting from errors in the estimates provided. This provides a basis for determining whether the survey was fully adequate for its purpose, or whether future surveys should be planned to give results of higher or lower accuracy.

10. *Observations of technicians:* The critical observations of technicians in regard to the survey, or any part of it, should be given. These observations will help others to improve their operations.

Concluding remarks on presentation

This is the provisional issue of the revised U.N. recommendations, and it remains only to emphasize one or two points. Special attention should be given to the first sentence of paragraph 1 under the General Report. The researcher himself may have been interested in the subject of the survey for so long that nothing seems to him more natural than to have undertaken the enquiry; but for the reader it is otherwise. He may genuinely wonder why anyone should want the information the survey has provided or why the subject should have been approached as it was. It is up to the surveyor fully to explain his purpose and approach.

The detail and form in which the results are presented vary with each survey, and the report writer inexperienced in these matters should acquaint himself with the principles of presenting statistical information: how to arrange tables, what symbols to use, how much accuracy to give in the figures, what diagrams to employ for different purposes, and so on. Enlarging on paragraph 5 under the General Report and paragraph 4 under the Technical Report, we would emphasize that non-quantified material has a useful place in every social survey report. To many readers, statistical tables are dull and difficult to comprehend, and a certain amount of verbatim quotation of answers, as well as verbal summary of the tables, enlivens the report and makes it easier to digest.

The presentation of sampling errors sometimes causes awkwardness. To accompany each figure by its corresponding standard error satisfies the most rigorous requirements but hardly makes for easy reading. On the other hand, simply to give details of sample size (and standard deviations, where variables are concerned) and leave it to the reader to estimate any sampling errors he may be interested in— probably by using the simple random sampling formulae together with his own evaluation of the likely value of the design effect for the complex sample employed—is to shirk one's duty and to impose an undeserved burden on the reader. There are some useful compromises.[1] If the figures in the report are all proportions, one can print a simple two-way table, in which the columns represent, say, different values of the sample proportion and the rows different sample sizes. In the

[1] See Kish (1965a, Section 14.1) for a discussion of the presentation of sampling errors.

body of the table, approximate values of the standard error, or a multiple of it (for instance a multiple of 2 for a 95 per cent confidence interval), can then be given. A similar approach can be used for the standard errors of the difference between two proportions that relate to different sub-groups of the sample; however in this case a three-fold table is needed since there are the two sub-group sizes as well as the average proportion to take into account. Ideally, standard error figures should be quoted for two or three confidence levels, so that the reader can take his choice. Guidance on interpretation should also be given.

A more fundamental point arises in regard to the presentation of inconclusive or negative results, which workers tend to be reluctant to publish. It is as important to make known negative results as positive ones. However sure a researcher feels that his hypothesis is right, if the research results point clearly against it he must say so. If the results are inconclusive, not pointing decisively in one direction or the other, it may be useful to future workers to be told so, since often there is some lesson to be learned regarding the scale or design of the research. We do not suggest that it should be made a rule to publish the results of every piece of research, but inconclusiveness does not seem to us *necessarily* an argument against publication. As Durbin and Stuart (1954a, p. 427) put it, in replying to a discussion on their paper on 'Callbacks and clustering in sample surveys':

We are also against the suggestion that one should always wait until one feels able to deliver some kind of 'judgement' before publishing one's results. It is possible that the belief that such an obligation exists might account for the small proportion of the survey experience gained in this country which has been made available to the public. If any statement of principles is called for, we would say simply that a worker has a right to publish his findings and his inferences from them without assuming any judicial capacity.

But, of course, one of the researcher's main duties must always be to point out any limitations of his results. That he should state the sampling errors is obvious, and has been emphasized repeatedly. But this is not all. As paragraphs 5–10 under the Technical Report in the U.N. recommendations well bring out, there are many other relevant questions: how complete was the coverage, how far did the achieved sample differ from that intended initially, how efficient was the design, what evidence was there of the size of response errors, and so forth. Nor is it enough to evaluate the methods of the survey in general terms. The results on each individual question must be qualified in terms of what is known about errors caused by its wording, definitions, interpretation and so forth. As social researchers become more conscious of the accuracy or otherwise of their observations, so research reports will give increasing space to reporting errors. This will be all to the good.

Research workers writing for fellow scientists are generally careful to emphasize limitations; indeed they sometimes fall over backwards to argue that what they have been doing is worthless. But particularly when writing for a general audience, the temptation to soft-pedal limitations is strong; the writer feels that the significance of technical shortcomings will not be appreciated, and shortage of space further encourages him to skip them. There is little need to stress how serious such omissions can be. One need only think of the harmful effects that can follow if the results of researches into, say, preventive measures for tuberculosis or polio are carelessly translated into popular literature. The original report may have paid due attention to the limitations attending the results, but these limitations are soon lost in its translation for the general reader. This sort of risk makes the hesitation to publish inconclusive results understandable.

As an illustration of how, in the heat of the moment, survey reports can deviate from desirable standards, we quote one of the conclusions offered in the authoritative U.S. Social Science Research Council study of the 1948 Election forecasts:

> In interpreting the results of the pre-election polls and presenting them to the public, the pollsters went far beyond the bounds of sound reporting of the results of pre-election polls. They attempted the spectacular feat of predicting the winner without qualification. The presentation of the results gave the impression of certainty as to the outcome. The final releases carried very little indication of the limitations of polling and the tendency in past election forecasts to underestimate the Democratic vote. Statements of conditions under which different outcomes of the election might occur were dropped almost completely before the end of the campaign.
>
> The polls also failed to provide the public with sufficient information about the methods of poll operation to permit assessment of the degree of confidence that could be placed in the predictions. The number of cases used, the type of sampling employed, the corrections introduced, the way returns from individuals who did not know how they would vote were tabulated, were not discussed adequately. It is recognised that there is pressure from newspaper editors and readers to omit qualifications and 'technicalities', but pollsters and social scientists have an important responsibility for educating readers of poll results to evaluate them and understand their limitations. (Mosteller and others, 1949, p. 302.)

One final point. The survey report should aim to give leads to future researchers. It should explain the relationship of this research to previous work on the subject and suggest what part of the field would benefit from a further attack, perhaps on a bigger scale or from a different angle. This would help to avoid an appearance of finality in these conclusions when, in the researcher's more informed opinion, they are only speculative. At the same time it would lessen the risk of fruitless duplication.

NOTES ON READING

1. Most of the books recommended at the end of Chapter 1 deal with the subject matter of the present chapter. Chapters 11 and 12 in SELLTIZ and others (1959) are worth consulting, and PARTEN (1950) goes into much of the practical detail that we have omitted.

2. There have been a number of papers dealing with significance tests in survey research. SELVIN (1957) wrote a paper on the subject and subsequent papers were those of McGINNIS (1958) and KISH (1959). A detailed discussion is given by GALTUNG (1967) in Section 4.4 of Part II. The paper by SELVIN and STUART (1966) has been referred to in the text.

3. Among the treatments of cross-tabulation and elaboration, those of ROSENBERG (1968), ZEISEL (1957), HYMAN (1955), LAZARSFELD in LAZARSFELD and ROSENBERG (1955), KENDALL and LAZARSFELD in MERTON and LAZARSFELD (1950) and LAZARSFELD (1958) are recommended. Linkages between elaboration and other forms of statistical analysis are provided by FENNESSEY (1968) and SCHUESSLER in BORGATTA (1969).

4. FOTHERGILL and WILKINS (1955) have presetned a paper on analysis and interpretation. MORGAN and SONQUIST (1963) discuss some problems in survey analysis. References to the M.C.A. and A.I.D. programs have been given in the text; the former was widely used in the analyses for *Income and Welfare in the United States* by MORGAN and others (1962) and the latter for *Productive Americans* by MORGAN and others (1966). ROSS and BANG (1966) describe the use of the A.I.D. program in a study of the adoption of family planning in Koyang. Both M.C.A. and A.I.D. are further discussed by SONQUIST (1970). A general discussion of analytic problems is given by HIRSCHI and SELVIN (1967).

5. Some of the simpler statistical techniques referred to in this chapter are discussed in introductory texts, such as those given at the end of Chapter 4. For other techniques reference must be made to books at an intermediate or higher level. BLALOCK (1960) provides a simple account and SNEDECOR and COCHRAN (1967) give a good practical treatment. There are several books on psychological statistics which are useful for analyses of variance and covariance and regression, for instance HAYS (1963) and McNEMAR (1969). COHEN (1968) discusses multiple regression as a general analytic technique and DRAPER and SMITH (1966) is a valuable reference on this technique. On multivariate analysis COOLEY and LOHNES (1962), KENDALL (1957), SEAL (1964) and MORRISON (1967) are recommended. References for factor analysis and latent structure analysis have been given at the end of Chapter 14.

6. There is now a considerable literature on causal models in social research. Articles by SIMON (1954, also reproduced in SIMON, 1957) and by WOLD (1956) are worth consulting. As well as many papers, BLALOCK (1964, 1969) has written two books on the subject, and the book edited by

BLALOCK and BLALOCK (1968) contains chapters on causal analysis by BLALOCK, SIEGEL and HODGE, and BOUDON. The volume edited by BORGATTA (1969) contains papers on path analysis by LAND, HEISE, and DUNCAN. DUNCAN (1966) provides a valuable introduction to path analysis with some sociological examples, and other useful references are DUNCAN and others (1968) and BLAU and DUNCAN (1967). Path coefficients were developed by WRIGHT for use in genetics, and there are several references in this area, e.g. WRIGHT (1934, 1960) and his chapter in KEMPTHORNE and others (1954), LI (1955, 1956, 1968) and TURNER and STEVENS (1959). The serious student should also consult the econometric literature.

The problem of detecting causal priorities in panel study data has been discussed by PELZ and ANDREWS (1964), YEE and GAGE (1968), ROZELLE and CAMPBELL (1969) and DUNCAN (1969).

7. On presentation, we need hardly add further references to the report of the UNITED NATIONS STATISTICAL OFFICE (1964), from which we quoted at length. All the books on survey methods of course discuss the subject. The MARKET RESEARCH SOCIETY (1954b) in Britain has published a short statement on survey reporting standards. An amusing book on the pitfalls of statistical presentation is that by HUFF (1954), and an excellent small volume on psychological aspects of presenting technical information is by KAPP (1948).

CHAPTER 18

Concluding Remarks

I T H A S been our aim throughout this book to give due prominence both to the strengths and the limitations of the social survey approach. One should not pretend that all the techniques used in the survey process have attained an equally advanced stage of efficiency, and it may be appropriate to close with a discussion of the developments we may look to in the future.

In this it is helpful to recall the three phases into which survey methods conveniently divide: deciding on the population units to be studied; collecting from or about them whatever information is required; and subjecting this information to various stages of processing, analysis and interpretation. Perhaps still the most striking feature of current survey methods is the lag—in terms of our knowledge and the efficiency attained—of the middle phase behind the other two, and particularly the first.

This is probably contrary to the view of the position held by the average researcher who is not wholly familiar with survey techniques. To him the main worry, certainly the one to which he most often gives expression, is sampling. He does not find it easy to accept that a public opinion survey to cover the entire country may, given sound sampling designs and techniques, confidently be based on 2,000 or 3,000 interviews. To the practitioner, it is fair to say, sampling has ceased to be the major problem. By this we do not mean that the subject has been so well developed that there remains no room for progress, or that sample design in practice causes no difficulties. The sample designer is often handicapped by lack of knowledge about the population and about costs involved in the various survey stages; uncertainty about the uses to be made of the survey results often makes it difficult to decide on the precision required; lack of a suitable sampling frame can create serious problems; and situations where one is sampling for relatively rare events cause headaches. Moreover, even well-designed samples can go wrong in the field (as in the 1961 Population Census). There are also a number of theoretical difficulties in the estimation of sampling errors yet to be overcome and, as noted in the chapters on sampling, a certain amount of complication in sample design is caused by the 'multi-purpose' character of most surveys.

Thus it would be misleading to suggest that the sample designer's task is necessarily easy or a matter of automatically applying set principles. But in spite of the technical problems that remain un-solved the difficulties are no longer fundamental, and the developed body of sampling theory is sufficient to enable the designer broadly to tailor his samples to the client's specifications and cost limits. Future developments should be mainly in refinements rather than on general principles or approach.

These remarks relate to the design of samples, and we are conscious of the major problem that still remains on the practical side: non-response. This problem is brought into special prominence with random sampling, and it is right that survey experts should be giving it increasing attention. Nevertheless it is not true, as enthusiasts for quota sampling sometimes suggest, that non-response entirely undermines the soundness of random sampling, and that one might as well use non-random techniques. We suggested in Chapter 7 that in most surveys there are ways of reducing the magnitude of non-response to fairly reasonable proportions and of broadly assessing what bias may be introduced by the non-response that remains. As long as there is *any* non-response, the margin of uncertainty sur-rounding the survey results must be wider than one would choose, but with careful planning, analysis and interpretation it need by no means undermine the value of the results. It would be well, however, if practitioners made a practice of thinking of non-response bias and sampling error in conjunction, rather than separately. It is wasteful to make strenuous efforts to ensure that the sampling error does not exceed one per cent if the non-response bias is ten times as large. There is indeed evidence that non-response bias often swamps the sampling error, in which case it may pay to cut down on overall sample size, thus tolerating a larger sampling error, and to spend more money on increasing response.

Turning now to the middle phase of surveys—the collection of the data—it seems to us that here we are faced by problems different in kind, not in degree, from those attending sample design and achieve-ment. Our knowledge of data collection is, by comparison, primitive. The choice of a particular method or of a question form is based mainly on experience, opinion, and common sense, and although these are essential ingredients of any decision they are not comparable to the theoretical basis of sample design.

The surveyor's most satisfactory guide in the data-collecting phases of a survey is direct experimentation. This can take the form of special experiments separate from the survey, or be incorporated into pre-tests and pilot surveys. Even the main survey can be designed on an experimental plan so that the answers obtained, say, to different forms of a question, can be compared. This is nothing more than the classical 'split-ballot' method, but with modern methods of experimental design it is an easy matter to arrange for a number of different question forms and other variations in data-collecting methods to be compared simultaneously. It is to be hoped that survey practitioners will increasingly try to base their choice of these methods, of questions, of interviewer selection and training and so forth, on experimental test; and to re-examine those parts of their methodology that are at present based largely on common sense and hunches.

There remains another, and in a way more serious, aspect of the non-sampling phases of surveys, namely the role of measurement errors, and particularly response errors.[1] We tried to show in Chapter 15 how different types of response errors may operate in surveys, and suggested that the possibility of such errors cancelling out was not very helpful to the survey designer, since it is equally possible that they will leave a net bias. Because of the difficulty of checking validity, bias is very hard to detect, whatever its cause; and the surveyor is therefore well advised to make some effort to check on gross errors (see Chapter 15). Post-enumeration surveys (as developed in the United States) should become standard practice.

There is incongruity in the present position. One part of the survey process (the sampling) is tackled by a tool of high precision that makes accurate estimates of errors possible, while in the other parts errors of generally unknown proportions subsist. This incongruity has a double implication. It means, first of all, that the survey designer is only partly able to plan towards his goal of getting the maximum precision for a given outlay of money, since the errors (and even costs) associated with the various non-sampling phases cannot be satisfactorily estimated in advance. And secondly, so long as these errors cannot be properly estimated from the results of the survey, the practitioner is in a position to give his client an estimate of the sampling error only, not of the total of *all* kinds of error. This is a weakness, and there is here a fertile field of research for students of survey methodology. It is of the greatest importance for all engaged in surveys. The operation of memory errors, the kinds of errors introduced in informal as against formal interviewing, the effects of length of questionnaire on errors, the errors associated

[1] See footnote on p. 378.

with different kinds of question, the influence of interviewer selection, training and supervision, the errors introduced in coding and tabulation—these are but a few of the many fields in which, despite the work already done (notably at the U.S. Bureau of the Census) there remains scope for research. Some of this can be done by special experiments, but every single survey gives opportunity for some study of measurement errors. We therefore repeat our hope that, in the planning of the major censuses and surveys in Great Britain, the departments concerned will do what they can to study such errors.

In the final phase of surveys—processing, analysis and interpretation—methodology is advancing in a number of ways. The use of computers is the major factor in the improvement of processing, whereas in analysis and interpretation further developments are looked for, especially in the field of multivariate relationships. In particular the interpretation of such relationships and the construction of causal models—as outlined in Chapter 17—are complex problems requiring continued theoretical and empirical research.

This discussion of methods has focused so much on the aspects that need strengthening that we must record the other side of the picture and point out how markedly survey methodology has advanced in recent years. Most striking has been the raising of standards in sampling, and in processing and analysis, but in one way or another it characterizes all survey activity. Far more surveys have resulted in published reports, and the standard of reporting, both of methods and results, has been much raised. In many universities, courses on survey methods are now given and research on techniques (as well as theory) carried out. Commercial users of survey methods, realizing that they have few secrets from each other, are increasingly willing to do joint research, to discuss methods in public, and to publish. As a result, those who commission surveys will demand increasingly high standards, and this can have nothing but a good effect on market research and all engaged in it.

The *value* of social surveys has also been established beyond all question and in widely different fields. We are not thinking primarily of the handful of surveys that have attracted attention because they are known to have saved their sponsors large sums of money; money-saving is not the most important criterion of usefulness. But it would be easy to quote, from many diverse fields, surveys that have provided their official, commercial or academic sponsors with knowledge interesting in itself or valuable as a basis for policy decisions. Whether, in the latter cases, use was always, or even often, made of the survey results is of course another question.

The use made of the results of different types of surveys, and their influence on decisions, would indeed be a fascinating subject for study. It might begin with the poverty surveys at the turn of the last century, which certainly caused a stir and probably helped to pave the way for the welfare legislation passed in succeeding years. Nearer our own day, one would like to know what influence the numerous town-planning surveys have had on the actual form of planning. The impression is that in the early days the influence was slight, but that in recent years social, demographic and economic surveys have been more directly and constructively integrated with planning. Certainly there is hardly a field in which social surveys *ought* to play a greater part than urban planning. Again, what use has been made of the many fact-finding surveys carried out for government departments since 1945? No sensible person necessarily looks for immediate and dramatic changes of plan being made in the light of survey results, or the delaying of all decisions until such results are available; indeed, such devotion to surveys would be misguided. But it would be encouraging to know that the survey reports were seriously considered by the appropriate departments, as one essential basis for their decision-making. Or, in the field of market research, one would like to know what use is made of survey results once they reach the client. Not even the greatest enthusiast for market research surveys would wish the client's policy to be based entirely on survey results; but one would hope that these results, together with an intelligent appraisal of their implications, are considered by those who shape policy—again as merely one part of the total picture.

One's general impression is that, in government administration, commerce, broadcasting, public opinion research and the social sciences, surveys are now playing a role of solid usefulness, but that there remains room for further extensions in all these fields. In the official sphere, for instance, sample surveys are not yet used as much as in the United States. Not all the government departments are equally willing to avail themselves of surveys, although the situation has changed enormously over the last few years. As we showed in Chapter 1, surveys are now done for a great range of departments and cover almost every conceivable subject. Just how much they influence decision-making is hard to say, but there is plenty of circumstantial evidence indicating their policy importance. What is noteworthy in addition is the role surveys have come to play in the deliberations of Royal Commissions and other government committees: the reports associated with the names of Crowther, Wolfenden, Robbins, Buchanan, Maud, Plowden, Beeching, Fulton, to name only a few, all used survey results as part of their supporting evidence. No one would want official committees to be in the straitjacket of survey findings; but they can gain immeasurably from such findings, as these committees, among many, have shown.

That social surveys have come to play such an important part in government is due largely to the Government Social Survey, which has demonstrated time and again the value of surveys and has established a high standard of methodology. Now that it has combined with the General Register Office into the Office of Population Censuses and Surveys, there should also be better links between surveys and censuses. There is also the new system of continuous 'multi-purpose' household surveys, which gives government a flexible and far-reaching regular survey capacity which it had previously lacked.

In market research, the bulk of present work is devoted to mass-produced consumer goods, such as chocolate, soap, detergents, drinks, and the like; and to the readership of newspapers and to advertisement policy generally. As regards methods, market researchers—to whom, it is fair to add, much of the early stimulus to survey developments is due—are sometimes reluctant to venture outside the range of the straightforward, and there is scope for more use of experimental designs, of more advanced analytical techniques for prediction surveys and so on. But, by and large, professional standards are high, and there is certainly increasing interest in development work.

There is a considerable interest in what has come to be known as 'motivation research'. Increasingly market researchers—and other users of surveys—aim to look beyond a mere description of behaviour towards a study of the motives underlying it. Since the respondents themselves may not be fully aware of their motives, or willing to formulate them, this means indirect questioning (e.g. projective tests) such as is common in personality research: and it also means psychological skill in interpreting the replies. In America this type of work has been going on for some years, and its use in Britain is also developing fast. It is good to see academic researchers interesting themselves increasingly in this kind of work.

The value of radio and television research surveys was stressed earlier in the book, and so was the interest of public opinion polls. Here we would only add our lack of sympathy for those who continue to see in opinion polls a positive danger to democracy. Surveys, like everything else, can be used dishonestly and irresponsibly. An unscrupulous businessman, as much as an unscrupulous politician, may use them to his own ends, in which case they may be most harmful. But one would hardly be justified in arguing that it was the survey that is at fault. Used properly, and in accordance with present-day standards, public opinion polls can be valuable in telling the politician, as well as the general public, what people are thinking about current issues. It is up to the politician to pay what attention he likes to the results; he can ignore them or otherwise, but certainly they deserve more attention than the balance of opinions contained in his mail.

The case of election forecasts is more difficult. The *raison d'être* of these forecasts lies partly in the light they throw on the efficiency of survey methods and partly (*mainly*, as far as the general public is concerned) in showing how the election campaign is progressing. Recent elections have left no doubt that politicians and party officials, as well as the statistician and the man in the street, watch the forecasts with close interest. However, one cannot deny that forecasts *may* have an influence upon voting behaviour—adherents of the leading party may become apathetic about voting, supporters of their opponents may make a special effort to vote, some people may switch loyalties in order to be on the winning side (the so-called 'band-waggon' effect), others may do the opposite in order to prevent excessive majorities. For all we know, these influences will cancel out, but it would be dishonest to deny that they may not. It is a subject requiring serious thought and more research, however difficult this may be.

So much for the role of surveys in the official sphere, in market research, and in the study of public opinion. Least easy to summarize is their usefulness in the field of academic social and economic research. Where the purpose is straightforward fact-collecting, no doubts about usefulness need arise and many—perhaps most—of the social research surveys mentioned in this book are fact-collecting enquiries, just as much as are the bulk of Government Social Survey or market research enquiries. Nor is the preoccupation of social scientists with descriptive, fact-finding enquiry anything to be ashamed of. As Professor Sprott (1949, p. 36) has put it:

> Sociology is still to a large extent in the classifying, ordering, and descriptive stage, because we are still not sure what is relevant and what is not. The result is that a great deal of sociologising is more like a kind of random botanizing, a collecting of data, i.e. statistics, personal case histories and the like, uncontrolled by the purpose of verification. This is inevitable, and certainly provides material on which the theorist can build, but at the same time it must be admitted that, while unbased and unverified hypotheses are empty, a mere collection of data is blind.

Our illustrative list of examples in Chapter 1 showed how surveys have figured in major social science researches in a wide range of fields. This is in spite of serious hurdles. The academic researcher, unlike his colleagues in the commercial and official spheres, has to operate without a survey organization at his ready service; and the existing organizations will often be too expensive for him or may be unwilling to take on what are often very small-scale projects. One can therefore welcome wholeheartedly the decision of the Social

Science Research Council (itself responsible through its grants for many survey projects) to set up a Survey Unit, which will in various ways help academic social scientists with their surveys.

There is no denying, as Professor Sprott implies, that social researchers have on occasion been led into blind and scrappy fact-collecting of no benefit to anyone. A fourth leader from *The Times*[1] expresses the futility of fact-collecting at its worst, and we quote from it the first and last paragraphs:

It has been ascertained—and not a moment too soon—that out of 1,200 Somersetshire children between the ages of three and fourteen only two-thirds were present when their shoes were bought. This pregnant intelligence comes as a reminder that almost all over the world, almost all the time, research is going on into the habits and opinions of *homo sapiens*. Sometimes the results prove, or anyhow indicate, that in the political field the Independent Democratic Unionists are losing ground slightly to the Democratic Union of Independents; sometimes they show that 93 per cent of housewives between the ages of 40 and 50 would rather not swim the Channel than not own a television set; while from others it is possible, though not particularly rewarding, to trace a statistical connexion between porridge-eating and goldfish-owning. It is rather sad how seldom we are able to take very much interest in the results of these meticulous inquiries. There are, on the other hand, various foibles and idio-syncracies which do seem to offer profitable fields for research but which nobody ever looks into. Much, for instance, might be learnt about our national character if a survey were to be made of our prac-tice in the matter of touching wood to ward off ill luck . . .

There are, of course—corresponding roughly to the staunch, im-pervious minority of don't knowers at the bottom of the public opinion polls—a certain number of people who never say 'touch wood'. Research would probably disclose that a high proportion of them also walk under ladders. Captains of their fate, they have no use for antiquated superstitions and make a point of writing their name against number thirteen when the list for a sweepstake on the Derby goes up in their club. It would be important to establish what pro-portion of this proportion used to say 'touch wood' when they were children but have since given it up: why they gave it up: and what (while we are about it) were their mothers' maiden names. But these and other matters into which the research team would have to delve pale into insignificance before the vital, the transcendent, the sixty-four dollar question: Are people who say 'touch wood' less unlucky than those who do not? It is to be feared that the difficulties of evolving a statistical yardstick with which to measure bad luck (and particularly bad luck which people have not had) might well prove too much for the research-team. Its devoted members—for in the unending battle for cer-tainty there are bound to be casualties—might even have to be pulled out of the line and transferred, after a rest and refit, to comparatively light duties, such as computing the number of umbrellas lost in Mon-mouthshire during 1953.

[1] *The Times*, 3rd August, 1955. Reproduced by permission of the Editor.

Of course, the moral that not all facts are worth collecting applies as much to market, opinion and government researchers as to social scientists, and is relevant to any empirical research, whether it uses survey methods or not. What is undeniable, though, is that the development of large-scale sampling methods has made fact-collecting along methodologically sound lines an easy and attractive way of doing research. It has accordingly stimulated a number of relatively useless, as well as many valuable, survey projects. The sometimes excessive enthusiasm for surveys may still be excused by the relative youth of social research, and it is reasonable to expect that, with the years, surveys will be used with increasing discrimination; also, that social researchers will become more discerning in the *type* of survey approach they apply to a given problem. As we have said earlier, not every empirical research project requires the formal apparatus of the large-scale survey. Sometimes it is more profitable to study intensively a handful of available cases rather than a representative sample; to use conversational rather than formal interviewing; not to aim at a set of statistics about a group so much as at a full description of each individual. There are many shades of survey approach and the researcher's art is to know which to use for his particular problem.

If survey methods have on occasion been used without sufficient discernment, it is still true that on balance they make a very considerable contribution in advancing the social scientist's knowledge. Many outstanding researches in his field would have been impossible without modern survey methods; many others could not have been done so satisfactorily. It is proper to temper one's impatience with some surveys with an appreciation of the value of a great many others.

Bibliography

ABEL-SMITH, E. and GALES, K. E. (1964). *British doctors at home and abroad.* (Occasional Papers on Social Administration, no. 8.) Codicote Press, Welwyn.

ABEL-SMITH, B. and TOWNSEND, P. B. (1965). *The poor and the poorest: a new analysis of the Ministry of Labour's family expenditure surveys of 1953-54 and 1960.* (Occasional Papers on Social Administration, no. 17.) Bell, London.

ABRAMS, M. A. (1951). *Social surveys and social action.* Heinemann, London.

ABUL-ELA, A.-L. A., GREENBERG, B. G. and HORVITZ, D. G. (1967). A multi-proportions randomized response model. *Journal of the American Statistical Association,* 62, 990–1008.

ALKER, H. R. (1965). *Mathematics and politics.* Macmillan, New York; Collier-Macmillan, London.

ALLPORT, G. W. (1942). *The use of personal documents in psychological science; prepared for the Committee on Appraisal of Research.* U.S. Social Science Research Council (Bulletin, no. 49), New York.

ANDREWS, F. M., MORGAN, J. N. and SONQUIST, J. A. (1969). *Multiple classification analysis: a report on a computer program for multiple regression using categorical predictors.* Survey Research Center, Institute for Social Research, University of Michigan, Ann Arbor, Michigan.

ATKINSON, J. (1967). *A handbook for interviewers: a manual for Government Social Survey interviewing staff, describing practice and procedures on structured interviewing.* (Government Social Survey, no. M136.) H.M.S.O., London.

BACKETT, E. M., HEADY, J. A. and EVANS, J. C. G. (1954). Studies of a general practice (II). The doctor's job in an urban area. *British Medical Journal,* 1954 (I), 109–115.

BACKETT, E. M., SHAW, L. A. and EVANS, J. C. G. (1953). Studies of a general practice (I). Patients' needs and doctors' services: a description of method. *Proceedings of the Royal Society of Medicine,* 46, 707–712.

BACKSTROM, C. H. and HURSH, G. D. (1963). *Survey research.* Northwestern University Press, Evanston, Ill.

BAGGALEY, A. P. (1964). *Intermediate correlation methods.* Wiley, New York.

BAILAR, B. A. (1968). Recent research on reinterview procedures. *Journal of the American Statistical Association*, 63, 41–63.

BAKKE, E. W. (1933). *The unemployed man: a social study*. Nisbet, London.

BANTON, M. P. (1959). *White and coloured: the behaviour of British people towards coloured immigrants*. Cape, London.

BARR, H. (1966). *Probation research: a survey of group work in the probation service (a Home Office Research Unit report)*. (Studies in the Causes of Delinquency and the Treatment of Offenders, no. 9.) Home Office, London.

BARR, H. and O'LEARY, E. (1966). *Probation research, national study of probation: trends and regional comparisons on probation, England and Wales: a Home Office Research Unit report*. (Studies in the Causes of Delinquency and the Treatment of Offenders, no. 8.) Home Office, London.

BARTHOLOMEW, D. J. (1961). A method of allowing for 'not-at-home' bias in sample surveys. *Applied Statistics*, 10, 52–59.

BECKER, H. S. (1958). Problems of inference and proof in participant observation. *American Sociological Review*, 23, 652–660.

BELL, C. R. (1968). *Middle class families: social and geographical mobility*. Routledge and Kegan Paul, London.

BELSON, W. A. (1959a). *Television and the family*. British Broadcasting Corporation, London.

BELSON, W. A. (1959b). Matching and prediction on the principle of biological classification. *Applied Statistics*, 8, 65–75.

BELSON, W. A. (1962). *Studies in readership: a report of an enquiry*. Business Publications, London.

BELSON, W. A. (1964a). Readership in Britain. *Business Review* (Australia), 6, 416–420.

BELSON, W. A. (1964b). Research on question design. *Business Review* (Australia), 7, 14–19.

BELSON, W. A. (1967a). *The impact of television: methods and findings in program research*. Crosby Lockwood, London.

BELSON, W. A. (1967b). Tape recording: its effect on accuracy of response in survey interviews. *Journal of Marketing Research*, 4, 253–260.

BELSON, W. A. (1968a). The extent of stealing by London boys and some of its origins. *Advancement of Science*, 25, 171–184.

BELSON, W. A. (1968b). Respondent understanding of survey questions. *Polls (International Review on Public Opinion)*, 3(4), 1–13.

BELSON, W. A. and DUNCAN, J. A. (1962). A comparison of the check-list and the open response questioning systems. *Applied Statistics*, 11, 120–132.

BELSON, W. A., MILLERSON, G. L. and DIDCOTT, P. J. (1968). *The development of a procedure for eliciting information from boys about the nature and extent of their stealing*. Survey Research Centre (Duplicated Report, no. 7), London School of Economics, London.

BENJAMIN, B. (1970). *The population census*. (Social Science Research Council. Reviews of Current Research, no. 7.) Heinemann, London.

BENNEY, M., GRAY, A. P. and PEAR, R. H. (1956). *How people vote: a study of electoral behaviour in Greenwich*. Routledge and Kegan Paul, London; Grove Press, New York.

BERELSON, B. R. and LAZARSFELD, P. F. (1948). *The analysis of communication content . . . preliminary draft* (mimeographed). Universitetets Studentkontor, Oslo.

BERKSON, J. (1963). Smoking and lung cancer. *American Statistician*, **17**(4), 15–22.

BEVERIDGE, W. I. B. (2nd ed. 1953). *The art of scientific investigation.* Heinemann, London.

BIRCH, A. H. and CAMPBELL, P. (1950). Voting behaviour in a Lancashire constituency. *British Journal of Sociology*, **1**, 197–208.

BLACKSTONE, T. A. V., GALES, K. E., HADLEY, R. D. and LEWIS, R. W. (1970). *Students in conflict: L.S.E. in 1967.* (L.S.E. Research Monographs, no. 5.) Weidenfeld and Nicolson, London.

BLALOCK, H. M., Jr. (1960). *Social statistics.* McGraw-Hill, New York.

BLALOCK, H. M., Jr. (1964). *Causal inferences in nonexperimental research.* University of North Carolina Press, Chapel Hill.

BLALOCK, H. M., Jr. (1969). *Theory construction from verbal to mathematical formulations.* Prentice-Hall, Englewood Cliffs, N. J.

BLALOCK, H. M., Jr. and BLALOCK, A. B., eds. (1968). *Methodology in social research.* McGraw-Hill, New York.

BLANKENSHIP, A. B. and others (1947). Survey on problems of interviewer cheating. *International Journal of Opinion and Attitude Research*, **1**(3), 93–106.

BLAU, P. M. and DUNCAN, O. D. (1967). *The American occupational structure.* Wiley, New York.

BLUMLER, J. G. and McQUAIL, D. (1968). *Television in politics: its uses and influence.* Faber, London.

BLUNDEN, R. M. (1966). Sampling frames. *Commentary (Journal of the Market Research Society)*, **8**, 101–112.

BOGARDUS, E. S. (1925). Measuring social distances. *Journal of Applied Sociology*, **9**, 299–308.

BOGARDUS, E. S. (1933). A social-distance scale. *Sociological and Social Research*, **17**, 265–271.

BONHAM, J. (1954). *The middle class vote.* Faber, London.

BOOKER, H. S. and DAVID, S. T. (1952). Differences in results obtained by experienced and inexperienced interviewers. *Journal of the Royal Statistical Society*, *A*, **115**, 232–257.

BOOTH, C., ed. (1889–1902). *Labour and life of the people of London.* 17 volumes. Macmillan, London.

BORGATTA, E. F., ed. (1969). *Sociological methodology 1969.* Jossey-Bass Inc., San Francisco.

BORKO, H., ed. (1962). *Computer applications in the behavioral sciences.* Prentice-Hall, Englewood Cliffs, N. J.

BORUS, M. E. (1966). Response error in survey reports of earnings information. *Journal of the American Statistical Association*, **61**, 729–738.

BOTT, E. (1957). *Family and social network: roles, norms, and external relationships in ordinary urban families.* Tavistock Publications, London.

BOURNVILLE VILLAGE TRUST (1941). *When we build again: a study based on research into conditions of living and working in Birmingham.* Allen and Unwin, London.

BOWLEY, A. L. and BURNETT-HURST, A. R. (1915). *Livelihood and poverty: a study in the economic conditions of working-class households in Northampton, Warrington, Stanley and Reading.* Bell, London.

BOWLEY, A. L. and HOGG, M. H. (1925). *Has poverty diminished?: a sequel to 'Livelihood and poverty'.* King, London.

BOYAJY, J. S., BARRY, J. W., KUENSTLER, W. P. and PATON, M. R. (1949). Tabulation planning and tabulation techniques. *Journal of Marketing*, **13**, 330–355.

BRENNAN, T. (1948). *Midland city: Wolverhampton social and industrial survey*. Dobson, London.

BRENNAN, T., COONEY, E. W. and POLLINS, H. (1954). *Social change in South-West Wales*. Watts, London.

BRILLINGER, D. R. (1966). The application of the jackknife to the analysis of sample surveys. *Commentary* (*Journal of the Market Research Society*), **8**, 74–80.

BRITISH BROADCASTING CORPORATION (2nd ed. 1966). *BBC audience research in the United Kingdom. Methods and services, 1966*. British Broadcasting Corporation, London.

BRITISH MEDICAL ASSOCIATION (1953). A field survey of general practice, 1951–2 (by S. J. Hadfield). The practitioner and the hospital service (by H. Ogilvie). General practice and the hospital (by J. G. M. Hamilton). General practice to-day and to-morrow. The G.P., the consultant, and the hospital. Some points in the postal inquiry. Midwifery in general practice. Some changes in general practice since 1948. *British Medical Journal*, **1953** (II), 683–714, 717–722.

BRITISH TRAVEL ASSOCIATION (1969). *Patterns in British holidaymaking 1951–1968*. British Travel Association, London.

BROOKES, B. C. and DICK, W. F. L. (2nd ed. 1969). *Introduction to statistical method*. Heinemann, London.

BROWNLEE, K. A. (1965). A review of 'Smoking and Health'. *Journal of the American Statistical Association*, **60**, 722–739.

BRUNNER, G. A. and CARROLL, S. J. (1967). The effect of prior telephone appointments on completion rates and response content. *Public Opinion Quarterly*, **31**, 652–654.

BUCHER, R., FRITZ, C. E. and QUARANTELLI, E. L. (1956). Tape recorded interviews in social research. *American Sociological Review*, **21**, 359–364.

BURT, C. (4th ed. 1944). *The young delinquent. (The sub-normal school-child. Vol. 1.)* University of London Press, Bickley, Kent.

BURT, C. (1950). The trend of national intelligence (review article). *British Journal of Sociology*, **1**, 154–168.

BUTLER, D. H. E. (1952). *The British General Election of 1951*. Macmillan, London.

BUTLER, D. H. E. (1955a). Voting behaviour and its study in Britain. *British Journal of Sociology*, **6**, 93–103.

BUTLER, D. H. E. (1955b). *The British General Election of 1955*. Macmillan, London.

BUTLER, D. H. E. and KING, A. (1965). *The British General Election of 1964*. Macmillan, London.

BUTLER, D. H. E. and KING, A. (1966). *The British General Election of 1966*. Macmillan, London.

BUTLER, D. H. E. and ROSE, R. (1960). *The British General Election of 1959*. Macmillan, London.

BUTLER, D. H. E. and STOKES, D. E. (1969). *Political change in Britain: forces shaping electoral choice*. Macmillan, London.

BUTLER, N. R. and ALBERMAN, E. D. (1968). *Perinatal problems: the second report of the 1958 British Perinatal Mortality Survey*. Livingstone, London.

BUTLER, N. R. and BONHAM, D. G. (1963). *Perinatal mortality: the first report of the 1958 British Perinatal Mortality Survey.* Livingstone, Edinburgh.

CAHALAN, D., TAMULONIS, V. and VERNER, H. W. (1947). Interviewer bias involved in certain types of opinion survey questions. *International Journal of Opinion and Attitude Research,* 1(1), 63–77.

CAMPBELL, D. T. and FISKE, D. W. (1959). Convergent and discriminant validation by the multitrait-multimethod matrix. *Psychological Bulletin,* 56, 81–105.

CAMPBELL, D. T., KRUSKAL, W. H. and WALLACE, W. P. (1966). Seating aggregation as an index of attitude. *Sociometry,* 29, 1–15.

CAMPBELL, D. T. and STANLEY, J. C. (1966). *Experimental and quasi-experimental designs for research.* Rand McNally, Chicago.

CANNELL, C. F. and FOWLER, F. J. (1963). Comparison of a self-enumerative procedure and a personal interview: a validity study. *Public Opinion Quarterly,* 27, 250–264.

CANNELL, C. F., FOWLER, F. J. and MARQUIS, K. H. (1968). *The influence of interviewer and respondent psychological and behavioral variables on the reporting in household interviews: a methodological study of the relationship of the behaviors, attitudes, perceptions, and information levels of the respondent and the interviewer to the levels of reporting health information in household interviews.* (U.S. Department of Health, Education, and Welfare. National Center for Health Statistics. Vital and Health Statistics, Series 2, no. 26.) U.S. Government Printing Office, Washington, D.C.

CANTRIL, H., ed. (1944). *Gauging public opinion.* Princeton University Press, Princeton.

CARR-SAUNDERS, A. M., MANNHEIM, H. and RHODES, E. C. (1942). *Young offenders: an enquiry into juvenile delinquency.* Cambridge University Press, Cambridge.

CARTWRIGHT, A. (1957). The effect of obtaining information from different informants on a family morbidity inquiry. *Applied Statistics,* 6, 18–25.

CARTWRIGHT, A. (1964). *Human relations and hospital care.* Routledge and Kegan Paul, London.

CARTWRIGHT, A. (1967). *Patients and their doctors: a study of general practice.* (Institute of Community Studies Report, no. 16.) Routledge and Kegan Paul, London.

CARTWRIGHT, A. (1970). *Parents and the family planning services.* Routledge and Kegan Paul, London.

CARTWRIGHT, A. and TUCKER, W. (1967). An attempt to reduce the number of calls on an interview inquiry. *Public Opinion Quarterly,* 31, 299–302.

CARTWRIGHT, A. and WARD, A. W. M. (1968). Variations in general practitioners' response to postal questionnaires. *British Journal of Preventive and Social Medicine,* 22, 199–205.

CATTELL, R. B. (1952). *Factor analysis. An introduction and manual for the psychologist and social scientist.* Harper, New York.

CAUTER, T. and DOWNHAM, J. S. (1954). *The communication of ideas: a study of contemporary influences on urban life.* Chatto and Windus, London.

CENTRAL ADVISORY COUNCIL FOR EDUCATION (ENGLAND) (1954). *Early leaving: a report.* H.M.S.O., London.

CENTRAL ADVISORY COUNCIL FOR EDUCATION (ENGLAND) (1959–1960). *15 to 18: a report. Vol. 1. The report. Vol. 2. Research and surveys.* H.M.S.O., London.

CENTRAL ADVISORY COUNCIL FOR EDUCATION (ENGLAND) (1967). *Children and their primary schools.* 2 vols. H.M.S.O., London.

CENTRE FOR URBAN STUDIES (1964). *Land use planning and the social sciences: a selected bibliography: literature on town and country planning and related social studies in Great Britain, 1930–1963.* Centre for Urban Studies, London.

CHAPIN, F. S. (1947). *Experimental designs in sociological research.* Harper, New York.

CHILTON, R. J. (1969). A review and comparison of simple statistical tests for scalogram analysis. *American Sociological Review,* **34,** 238–245.

COALE, A. J. and STEPHAN, F. F. (1962). The case of the Indians and the teen-age widows. *Journal of the American Statistical Association,* **57,** 338–347.

COCHRAN, W. G. (2nd ed. 1963). *Sampling techniques.* Wiley, New York.

COCHRAN, W. G. (1965). The planning of observational studies of human populations. *Journal of the Royal Statistical Society, A,* **128,** 234–265.

COCHRAN, W. G. (1968a). Errors of measurement in statistics. *Technometrics,* **10,** 637–666.

COCHRAN, W. G. (1968b). The effectiveness of adjustment by sub-classification in removing bias in observational studies. *Biometrics,* **24,** 295–313.

COCHRAN, W. G. and COX, G. M. (2nd ed. 1957). *Experimental designs.* Wiley, New York.

COCHRAN, W. G., MOSTELLER, F. and TUKEY, J. W. (1953). Statistical problems of the Kinsey Report. *Journal of the American Statistical Association,* **48,** 673–716.

COCHRAN, W. G., MOSTELLER, F. and TUKEY, J. W. (1954). Principles of sampling. I. Samples and their analysis. II. Systematic errors. *Journal of the American Statistical Association,* **49,** 13–35.

COHEN, J. (1968). Multiple regression as a general data-analytic system. *Psychological Bulletin,* **70,** 426–443.

COLE, D. E. (1956). Field work in sample surveys of household income and expenditure. *Applied Statistics,* **5,** 49–61.

COLE, D. E. and UTTING, J. E. G. (1962). *The economic circumstances of old people.* (Occasional Papers on Social Administration, no. 4.) Codicote Press, Welwyn.

COOLEY, W. W. and LOHNES, P. R. (1962). *Multivariate procedures for the behavioral sciences.* Wiley, New York.

COOMBS, C. H. (1964). *A theory of data.* Wiley, New York.

COOMBS, L. and FREEDMAN, R. (1964). Use of telephone interviews in a longitudinal fertility study. *Public Opinion Quarterly,* **28,** 112–117.

COOPER, B. and BROWN, A. C. (1967). Psychiatric practice in Great Britain and America: a comparative study. *British Journal of Psychiatry,* **113,** 625–636.

CORLETT, T. (1963). Rapid methods of estimating standard errors of stratified multi-stage samples: a preliminary investigation. *The Statistician,* **13,** 5–16.

CORLETT, T. (1966). The standard error of the standard error. *Commentary (Journal of the Market Research Society),* **8,** 81–91.

CORNFIELD, J., HAENSZEL, W., HAMMOND, E. C., LILIENFELD, A. M., SHIMKIN, M. B. and WYNDER, E. L. (1959). Smoking and lung cancer: recent evidence and a discussion of some questions. *Journal of the National Cancer Institute*, **22**, 173–203.

COX, D. R. (1958). *Planning of experiments*. Wiley, New York.

CRESPI, L. P. (1945–46). The cheater problem in polling. *Public Opinion Quarterly*, **9**, 431–445.

CRESPI, L. P. (1946). Further observations on the 'cheater' problem. *Public Opinion Quarterly*, **10**, 646–649.

CRUTCHFIELD, R. S. and GORDON, D. A. (1947). Variations in respondents' interpretations of an opinion-poll question. *International Journal of Opinion and Attitude Research*, **1**(3), 1–12.

CULLINGWORTH, J. B. (1965). *English housing trends: A report on the Rowntree Trust Housing Study*. (Social Administration Research Trust. Occasional Papers in Social Administration, no. 13.) Bell, London.

CUTLER, S. J. (1955). A review of the statistical evidence on the association between smoking and lung cancer. *Journal of the American Statistical Association*, **50**, 267–282.

DALENIUS, T. (1957). *Sampling in Sweden: contributions to the methods and theories of sample survey practice*. Almqvist and Wiksell, Stockholm.

DANIEL, W. W. (1968). *Racial discrimination in England: based on the P.E.P. report*. Penguin (Specials, S257) Books, Harmondsworth, Middlesex.

DAVID, M. H. (1962). The validity of income reported by a sample of families who received welfare assistance during 1959. *Journal of the American Statistical Association*, **57**, 680–685.

DAVID, S. T. (1952). Public opinion concerning tuberculosis. *Tubercle* (*Journal of the British Tuberculosis Association*), **33**, 78–90.

DAVIES, M. (1967). *The use of the Jesness inventory on a sample of British probationers*. (Studies in the Causes of Delinquency and the Treatment of Offenders, no. 12.) Home Office, London.

DAVIES, O. L., ed. (2nd ed. 1956). *The design and analysis of industrial experiments*. Oliver and Boyd, Edinburgh.

DAY, D. J. and DUNN, J. E. (1969). Estimating the audience for advertising on the outside of London buses. *Applied Statistics*, **18**, 209–220.

DEMING, W. E. (1944). On errors in surveys. *American Sociological Review*, **9**, 359–369.

DEMING, W. E. (1950). *Some theory of sampling*. Wiley, New York; Chapman, London; Dover, New York.

DEMING, W. E. (1953). On a probability mechanism to attain an economic balance between the resultant error of response and the bias of non-response. *Journal of the American Statistical Association*, **48**, 743–772.

DEMING, W. E. (1960). *Sample design in business research*. Wiley, New York.

DEMING, W. E. and GEOFFREY, L. (1941). On sample inspection in the processing of census returns. *Journal of the American Statistical Association*, **36**, 351–360.

DEMING, W. E., TEPPING, B. J. and GEOFFREY, L. (1942). Errors in card punching. *Journal of the American Statistical Association*, **37**, 525–536.

DE REUCK, A. V. S. and PORTER, R., eds. (1968). *The mentally abnormal offender: a Ciba Foundation Symposium*. Churchill, London.

R

DOBY, J. T., ed. (2nd ed. 1967). *An introduction to social research.* Appleton-Century-Crofts, New York.

DOLL, R. and HILL, A. BRADFORD (1950). Smoking and carcinoma of the lung. Preliminary report. *British Medical Journal,* **1950**(II), 739–748.

DOLL, R. and HILL, A. BRADFORD (1952). A study of the aetiology of carcinoma of the lung. *British Medical Journal,* **1952**(II), 1271–1286.

DOLL, R. and HILL, A. BRADFORD (1954). The mortality of doctors in relation to their smoking habits: a preliminary report. *British Medical Journal,* **1954**(I), 1451–1455.

DOLL, R. and HILL, A. BRADFORD (1956). Lung cancer and other causes of death in relation to smoking: a second report on the mortality of British doctors. *British Medical Journal,* **1956**(II), 1071–1081.

DOLL, R. and HILL, A. BRADFORD (1964). Mortality in relation to smoking: ten years' observations of British doctors. *British Medical Journal,* **1964**(I), 1399–1410, 1460–1467.

DONNISON, D. V., COCKBURN, C. and CORLETT, T. (1961). *Housing since the Rent Act: An interim report from the Rowntree Trust Housing Study.* (Occasional Papers on Social Administration, no. 3.) Codicote Press, Welwyn.

DOUGLAS, J. W. B. (1964). *The home and the school: a study of ability and attainment in the primary school.* MacGibbon and Kee, London.

DOUGLAS, J. W. B. and BLOMFIELD, J. M. (1956). The reliability of longitudinal surveys. *Milbank Memorial Fund Quarterly,* **34**, 227–252.

DOUGLAS, J. W. B. and BLOMFIELD, J. M. (1958). *Children under five: The results of a national survey made by a Joint Committee of the Institute of Child Health (University of London), the Society of Medical Officers of Health and the Population Investigation Committee.* Allen and Unwin, London.

DOUGLAS, J. W. B., ROSS, J. M. and SIMPSON, H. R. (1968). *All our future: a longitudinal study of secondary education.* Davies, London.

DOWNHAM, J. S. (1954). Social class in sample surveys. *Incorporated Statistician,* **5**, 17–38.

DOWNHAM, J. S. (1955). The function of coding. *Incorporated Statistician,* **5** (Supplement), 73–81.

DRAPER, N. R. and SMITH, H. (1966). *Applied regression analysis.* Wiley, New York.

DUNCAN, O. D. (1966). Path analysis: sociological examples. *American Journal of Sociology,* **72**, 1–16.

DUNCAN, O. D. (1969). Some linear models for two-wave, two-variable panel analysis. *Psychological Bulletin,* **72**, 177–182.

DUNCAN, O. D., HALLER, A. O. and PORTES, A. (1968). Peer influences on aspirations: a reinterpretation. *American Journal of Sociology,* **74**, 119–137.

DUPEUX, G. (1954–55). Electoral behaviour. A trend report and bibliography. *Current Sociology (UNESCO),* **3**(4), 279–344.

DURANT, H. (1946). The 'cheater' problem. *Public Opinion Quarterly,* **10**, 288–291.

DURANT, H. (1954). The Gallup Poll and some of its problems. *Incorporated Statistician,* **5**, 101–112.

DURANT, R. (1939). *Watling: A survey of social life on a new housing estate.* King, London.

DURBIN, J. (1954). Non-response and call-backs in surveys. *Bulletin of the International Statistical Institute,* **34**(2), 72–86.

DURBIN, J. (1967). Design of multi-stage surveys for the estimation of sampling errors. *Applied Statistics*, **16**, 152–164.
DURBIN, J. and STUART, A. (1951). Differences in response rates of experienced and inexperienced interviewers. *Journal of the Royal Statistical Society, A*, **114**, 163–205.
DURBIN, J. and STUART, A. (1954a). Callbacks and clustering in sample surveys: an experimental study. *Journal of the Royal Statistical Society, A*, **117**, 387–428.
DURBIN, J. and STUART, A. (1954b). An experimental comparison between coders. *Journal of Marketing*, **19**, 54–66.
DUVERGER, M. (1964). *Introduction to the social sciences with special reference to their methods*. (Translated by M. Anderson.) Allen and Unwin, London.
ECKLAND, B. K. (1968). Retrieving mobile cases in longitudinal surveys. *Public Opinion Quarterly*, **32**, 51–64.
ECKLER, A. R. (1953). Extent and character of errors in the 1950 Census. *American Statistician*, **7**(5), 15–21.
ECKLER, A. R. and HURWITZ, W. N. (1958). Response variance and biases in censuses and surveys. *Bulletin of the International Statistical Institute*, **36**(2), 12–35.
ECKLER, A. R. and PRITZKER, L. (1951). Measuring the accuracy of enumerative surveys. *Bulletin of the International Statistical Institute*, **33**(4), 7–24.
EDWARDS, A. L. (1957). *Techniques of attitude scale construction*. Appleton-Century-Crofts, New York.
EDWARDS, A. L. and KENNEY, K. C. (1946). A comparison of the Thurstone and Likert techniques of attitude scale construction. *Journal of Applied Psychology*, **30**, 72–83.
EDWARDS, F. (1953). Aspects of random sampling for a commercial survey. *Incorporated Statistician*, **4**, 9–26.
EDWARDS, F., ed. (1956). *Readings in market research: a selection of papers by British authors*. The British Market Research Bureau, London.
EHRENBERG, A. S. C. (1960). A study of some potential biases in the operation of a consumer panel. *Applied Statistics*, **9**, 20–27.
EL-BADRY, M. A. (1961). Failure of enumerators to make entries of zero: errors in recording childless cases in population censuses. *Journal of the American Statistical Association*, **56**, 909–924.
EMMETT, B. P. (1964). Reflections on the state of population sampling in the United Kingdom. *Applied Statistics*, **13**, 146–157.
EMMETT, B. P. (1966). The design of investigations into the effects of radio and television programmes and other mass communications. *Journal of the Royal Statistical Society, A*, **129**, 26–59.
ERRITT, M. J. and NICHOLSON, J. L. (1958). The 1955 Savings Survey. *Bulletin of the Oxford University Institute of Statistics*, **20**, 113–152.
EVANS, W. D. (1958). The control of non-sampling errors in social and economic surveys. *Bulletin of the International Statistical Institute*, **36**(2), 36–43.
EYSENCK, H. J. (1953). *Uses and abuses of psychology*. Penguin Books, Harmondsworth, Middlesex.
EYSENCK, H. J. (1954). *The psychology of politics*. Routledge and Kegan Paul, London.
EYSENCK, H. J. (1965). *Smoking, health and personality*. Weidenfeld and Nicolson, London; Four Square, London.

498   SURVEY METHODS IN SOCIAL INVESTIGATION

FASTEAU, H. H., INGRAM, J. J. and MINTON, G. (1964). Control of quality of coding in the 1960 Censuses. *Journal of the American Statistical Association*, **59**, 120–132.

FELDMAN, J. J., HYMAN, H. and HART, C. W. (1951–52). A field study of interviewer effects on the quality of survey data. *Public Opinion Quarterly*, **15**, 734–761.

FELLEGI, I. P. (1964). Response variance and its estimation. *Journal of the American Statistical Association*, **59**, 1016–1041.

FENNESSEY, J. (1968). The general linear model: a new perspective on some familiar topics. *American Journal of Sociology*, **74**, 1–27.

FERBER, R. (1953). Observations on a consumer panel operation. *Journal of Marketing*, **17**, 246–259.

FERBER, R. (1965). The reliability of consumer surveys of financial holdings: time deposits. *Journal of the American Statistical Association*, **60**, 148–163.

FERBER, R., FORSYTHE, J., GUTHRIE, H. W. and MAYNES, E. S. (1969). Validation of consumer financial characteristics: common stock. *Journal of the American Statistical Association*, **64**, 415–432.

FERGUSON, T. (1952). *The young delinquent in his social setting: a Glasgow study*. Oxford University Press, London.

FESTINGER, L. and KATZ, D., eds. (1953). *Research methods in the behavioral sciences*. Holt, Rinehart and Winston, New York; Staples Press, London.

FINNEY, D. J. (1956). The statistician and the planning of field experiments. *Journal of the Royal Statistical Society*, *A*, **119**, 1–27.

FIRTH, R. (1939). An anthropologist's view of Mass Observation. *Sociological Review*, **31**, 166–193.

FISHBEIN, M., ed. (1967). *Readings in attitude theory and measurement*. Wiley, New York.

FISHER, G. (1962). A discriminant analysis of reporting errors in health interviews. *Applied Statistics*, **11**, 148–163.

FISHER, H. (1950). Interviewer bias in the recording operation. *International Journal of Opinion and Attitude Research*, **4**, 391–411.

FISHER, R. A. (7th ed. 1960). *The design of experiments*. Oliver and Boyd, Edinburgh.

FISHER, R. A. and YATES, F. (6th ed. 1963). *Statistical tables for biological, agricultural and medical research*. Oliver and Boyd, Edinburgh.

FLANDERS, A., POMERANZ, R. and WOODWARD, J. (1968). *Experiment in industrial democracy: a study of the John Lewis Partnership*. Faber, London.

FOLKARD, S. and others (1966). *Probation research: a preliminary report. Part 1. General outline of research. Part 2. Study of Middlesex probation area (SOMPA)*. (Studies in the Causes of Delinquency and the Treatment of Offenders, no. 7.) Home Office, London.

FORCESE, D. P. and RICHER, S., eds. (1970). *Stages of social research: contemporary perspectives*. Prentice-Hall, Englewood Cliffs, N.J.

FORD, P. (1934). *Work and wealth in a modern port: an economic survey of Southampton*. Allen and Unwin, London.

FOTHERGILL, J. E. and WILKINS, L. T. (1955). Analysis and interpretation. *Incorporated Statistician*, **5** (Supplement), 93–117.

FOTHERGILL, J. E. and WILLCOCK, H. D. (1955). Interviewers and interviewing. *Incorporated Statistician*, **5** (Supplement), 37–56.

FRANKENBERG, R. (1966). *Communities in Britain: social life in town and country.* Penguin Books, Harmondsworth, Middlesex.

FREUND, R. J. and HARTLEY, H. O. (1967). A procedure for automatic data editing. *Journal of the American Statistical Association,* **62**, 341–352.

FRIEND, I. and ADAMS, F. G. (1964). The predictive ability of consumer attitudes, stock prices, and non-attitudinal variables. *Journal of the American Statistical Association,* **59**, 987–1005.

FRUCHTER, B. (1954). *Introduction to factor analysis.* Van Nostrand, Princeton, N.J.

GAGE, N. L., ed. (1963). *Handbook of research on teaching.* Rand McNally, Chicago.

GALES, K. E. (1957). Discriminant functions and socio-economic class. *Applied Statistics,* **6**, 123–132.

GALES, K. E. and KENDALL, M. G. (1957). An inquiry concerning interviewer variability. *Journal of the Royal Statistical Society, A,* **120**, 121–147.

GALLUP, G. H. (1947). The quintamensional plan of question design. *Public Opinion Quarterly,* **11**, 385–393.

GALLUP, G. H. (2nd ed. 1948). *A guide to public opinion polls.* Princeton University Press, Princeton.

GALTUNG, J. (1967). *Theory and methods of social research.* (International Peace Research Institute, Oslo. Basic Social Science Monographs, no. 1.) Universitetsforlaget, Oslo; Allen and Unwin, London; Columbia University Press, New York.

GAVRON, H. (1966). *The captive wife: conflicts of housebound mothers.* Routledge and Kegan Paul, London; (1968) Penguin (Pelican) Books, Harmondsworth, Middlesex.

GIBBENS, T. C. N. (1963). *Psychiatric studies of Borstal lads.* (Institute of Psychiatry. Maudsley Monograph, no. 11.) Oxford University Press, London.

GLASS, D. V., ed. (1954). *Social mobility in Britain.* Routledge and Kegan Paul, London.

GLASS, D. V. and GREBENIK, E. (1954). *The trend and pattern of fertility in Great Britain: a report on the family census of 1946.* (Royal Commission on Population. Papers. Vol. VI.) H.M.S.O., London.

GLASS, R., ed. (1948). *The social background of a plan: a study of Middlesbrough.* Routledge and Kegan Paul, London.

GLASS, R. (1960). *Newcomers: the West Indians in London.* (Centre for Urban Studies Report, no. 1.) Centre for Urban Studies and Allen and Unwin, London.

GLASS, R. and GLASS, D. V. (1950). Social survey. *Chambers's encyclopaedia* (Newnes, London), **12**, 667–670.

GLASS, R. and others (1964). *London: aspects of change.* (Centre for Urban Studies Report, no. 3.) MacGibbon and Kee, London.

GLASS, R. and WESTERGAARD, J. H. (1965). *London's housing needs: statements of evidence to the Committee on Housing in Greater London.* (Centre for Urban Studies Report, no. 5.) Centre for Urban Studies, London.

GLOCK, C. Y., ed. (1967). *Survey research in the social sciences.* Russell Sage Foundation, New York.

GOLDBERG, S. A. (1958). Non-sampling error in household surveys. A general review of some Canadian work. *Bulletin of the International Statistical Institute,* **36**(2), 44–59.

GOLDSTEIN, H. (1968). Longitudinal studies and the measurement of change. *The Statistician*, **18**, 93–117.
GOLDTHORPE, J. H., LOCKWOOD, D., BECHHOFER, F. and PLATT, J. (1968a). *The affluent worker: Industrial attitudes and behaviour.* (Cambridge Studies in Sociology, no. 1.) University Press, Cambridge.
GOLDTHORPE, J. H., LOCKWOOD, D., BECHHOFER, F. and PLATT, J. (1968b). *The affluent worker: Political attitudes and behaviour.* (Cambridge Studies in Sociology, no. 2.) University Press, Cambridge.
GOODE, W. J. and HATT, P. K. (1952). *Methods in social research.* McGraw-Hill, New York.
GOODMAN, L. A. (1959). Simple statistical methods for scalogram analysis. *Psychometrika*, **24**, 29–43.
GOODMAN, N. and PRICE, J. (1967). *Studies of female offenders.* (Studies in the Causes of Delinquency and the Treatment of Offenders, no. 11.) Home Office, London.
GOTTSCHALK, L., KLUCKHOHN, C. and ANGELL, R. (1945). *The use of personal documents in history, anthropology and sociology.* U.S. Social Science Research Council (Bulletin, no. 35), New York.
GOWERS, E. A. (1954). *The complete plain words.* H.M.S.O., London; Penguin (Pelican) Books, Harmondsworth, Middlesex.
GRAY, P. G. (1955). The memory factor in social surveys. *Journal of the American Statistical Association*, **50**, 344–363.
GRAY, P. G. (1956). Examples of interviewer variability taken from two sample surveys. *Applied Statistics*, **5**, 73–85.
GRAY, P. G. (1957). A sample survey with both a postal and an interview stage. *Applied Statistics*, **6**, 139–153.
GRAY, P. G. (1959). *More about the electoral register.* Government Social Survey (no. M105), London.
GRAY, P. G. and CORLETT, T. (1950). Sampling for the Social Survey. *Journal of the Royal Statistical Society, A*, **113**, 150–206.
GRAY, P. G., CORLETT, T. and FRANKLAND, P. (1950). *The register of electors as a sampling frame.* Government Social Survey (no. M59), London. Also in EDWARDS, F., ed. (1956), *which see.*
GRAY, P. G., CORLETT, T. and JONES, P. (1951). *The proportion of jurors as an index of the economic status of a district.* Government Social Survey (no. M60), London. Also in EDWARDS, F., ed. (1956), *which see.*
GRAY, P. G. and GEE, F. A. (1967). *Electoral registration for parliamentary elections; an enquiry made for the Home Office.* (Government Social Survey, SS391.) H.M.S.O., London.
GRAY, P. G. and PARR, E. A. (1959). The length of cigarette stubs. *Applied Statistics*, **8**, 92–103.
GRAY, P. G. and TODD, J. E. (1967). *Mobility and reading habits of the blind; an enquiry made for the Ministry of Health, covering the registered blind of England and Wales in 1965.* (Government Social Survey, SS386.) H.M.S.O., London.
GRAY, S. (1970). *The electoral register: practical information for use when drawing samples, both for interview and postal surveys.* Government Social Survey (no. M151), London.
GREATER LONDON COUNCIL (1969). *Movement in London: transport research studies and their context.* Greater London Council (Publications, no. 251), London.
GREEN, B. F. (1956). A method of scalogram analysis using summary statistics. *Psychometrika*, **21**, 79–89.

GREEN, B. F. (1963). *Digital computers in research: an introduction for behavioral and social scientists.* McGraw-Hill, New York.

GREENBERG, B. G., ABERNATHY, J. R. and HORVITZ, D. G. (1969a). A method for estimating the incidence of abortion in an open population. Paper read at the 37th Session of the International Statistical Institute, London, 1969.

GREENBERG, B. G., ABUL-ELA, A.-L. A., SIMMONS, W. R. and HORVITZ, D. G. (1969b). The unrelated question randomized response model: theoretical framework. *Journal of the American Statistical Association,* 64, 520–539.

GREENWOOD, E. (1945). *Experimental sociology: a study in method.* King's Crown Press, New York.

GREY, E. (1969). *Workloads in children's departments.* (Home Office Research Studies, no. 1.) H.M.S.O., London.

GRUNDY, F. and TITMUSS, R. M. (1945). *Report on Luton.* Gibbs, Bamforth, Luton.

GUEST, L. (1947). A study of interviewer competence. *International Journal of Opinion and Attitude Research,* 1(4), 17–30.

GUEST, L. and NUCKOLS, R. (1950). A laboratory experiment in recording in public opinion interviewing. *International Journal of Opinion and Attitude Research,* 4, 336–352.

GUILFORD, J. P. (2nd ed. 1954). *Psychometric methods.* McGraw-Hill, New York.

HALL, J. and JONES, D. C. (1950). Social grading of occupations. *British Journal of Sociology,* 1, 31–55.

HALSEY, A. H. and CREWE, I. M. (1969). *The Civil Service. Evidence submitted to the Committee under the chairmanship of Lord Fulton 1966–1968. Vol. 3. Surveys and investigations. (1) Social survey of the Civil Service.* (Command Paper, 3638.) H.M.S.O., London.

HALSEY, A. H., FLOUD, J. and ANDERSON, C. A., eds. (1961). *Education, economy, and society: a reader in the sociology of education.* Free Press of Glencoe, New York.

HALSEY, A. H. and TROW, M. A. (1971). *British academics.* Faber, London.

HAMMOND, P. E., ed. (1964). *Sociologists at work: essays on the craft of social research.* Basic Books, New York.

HANSEN, M. H. (1952). Statistical standards and the census. *American Statistician,* 6(1), 7–10.

HANSEN, M. H. and HAUSER, P. M. (1945). Area sampling—some principles of sampling design. *Public Opinion Quarterly,* 9, 183–193.

HANSEN, M. H. and HURWITZ, W. N. (1946). The problem of non-response in sample surveys. *Journal of the American Statistical Association,* 41, 517–529.

HANSEN, M. H., HURWITZ, W. N. and BERSHAD, M. A. (1961). Measurement errors in censuses and surveys. *Bulletin of the International Statistical Institute,* 38(2), 359–374.

HANSEN, M. H., HURWITZ, W. N. and MADOW, W. G. (1953). *Sample survey methods and theory. Vol. I. Methods and applications. Vol. II. Theory.* Wiley, New York; Chapman and Hall, London.

HANSON, R. H. and MARKS, E. S. (1958). Influence of the interviewer on the accuracy of survey results. *Journal of the American Statistical Association,* 53, 635–655.

HAREWOOD, J. (1968). *Continuous Sample Survey of Population. General report. Rounds 1–8.* Central Statistical Office, Trinidad and

Tobago (Continuous Sample Survey of Population, Publication no. 11), Port of Spain.

HARGREAVES, D. H. (1967). *Social relations in a secondary school*. Routledge and Kegan Paul, London.

HARMAN, H. H. (2nd ed. 1967). *Modern factor analysis*. University of Chicago Press, Chicago.

HARRIS, A. I. (1955). The work of a coding section. *Incorporated Statistician*, **5** (Supplement), 82–92.

HARRIS, A. I. (1968). *Social welfare for the elderly: a study in thirteen local authority areas in England, Wales and Scotland; an enquiry carried out on behalf of the National Corporation for the Care of Old People and the Scottish Home and Health Department. Vol. I. Comparison of areas and summary. Vol II. Area reports.* (Government Social Survey, SS366.) H.M.S.O., London.

HARRIS, C. W., ed. (1963). *Problems in measuring change: proceedings of a conference sponsored by the Committee on Personality Development in Youth of the Social Science Research Council, 1962.* University of Wisconsin Press, Madison, Milwaukee.

HART, C. W. (1948). Bias in interviewing in studies of opinions, attitudes, and consumer wants. *Proceedings of the American Philosophical Society*, **92**, 399–404.

HARTLEY, H. O. (1946) [Commenting on paper by YATES, F. (1946), which see.] *Journal of the Royal Statistical Society*, *A*, **109**, 37–38.

HAUSER, P. M. (1950). Some aspects of methodological research in the 1950 Census. *Public Opinion Quarterly*, **14**, 5–13.

HAYS, W. L. (1963). *Statistics for Psychologists*. Holt, Rinehart and Winston, New York.

HENRY, H. (1954). The importance of controlling investigators. Paper read to conference of the European Society of Opinion and Market Research.

HESS, I., RIEDEL, D. C. and FITZPATRICK, T. B. (1961). *Probability sampling of hospitals and patients.* (Bureau of Hospital Administration. Research series, no. 1.) University of Michigan, Ann Arbor, Michigan.

HILL, A. BRADFORD (1951). The doctor's day and pay. Some sampling inquiries into the pre-war status. *Journal of the Royal Statistical Society*, *A*, **114**, 1–36.

HILL, A. BRADFORD (1962). *Statistical methods in clinical and preventive medicine*. Livingstone, Edinburgh.

HILL, A. BRADFORD (8th ed. 1966). *Principles of medical statistics*. Lancet, London.

HILTON, J. (1924). Enquiry by sample: an experiment and its results. *Journal of the Royal Statistical Society*, **87**, 544–570.

HIMMELWEIT, H. T., OPPENHEIM, A. N. and VINCE, P. (1958). *Television and the child: an empirical study of the effect of television on the young*. Oxford University Press, London.

HIRSCHI, T. and SELVIN, H. C. (1967). *Delinquency research: an appraisal of analytic methods*. Free Press, New York; Collier-Macmillan, London.

HOCHSTIM, J. R. (1967). A critical comparison of three strategies of collecting data from households. *Journal of the American Statistical Association*, **62**, 976–989.

HODGES, J. L. and LEHMANN, E. L. (1964). *Basic concepts of probability and statistics*. Holden-Day, San Francisco.

HOLE, V. and ALLEN, P. G. (1962). Dwellings for old people. *Architects' Journal*, **135**, 1017–1026.

HOLE, V. and ALLEN, P. G. (1964). Rehousing old people. *Architects' Journal*, **139**, 75–82.

HOLSTI, O. R. (1969). *Content analysis for the social sciences and humanities*. Addison-Wesley, Reading, Mass.

HORST, P. (1965). *Factor analysis of data matrices*. Holt, Rinehart and Winston, New York.

HORTON, M. (1963). *A survey by telephone*. Government Social Survey, (no. M106), London.

HOUSE, J. W. and KNIGHT, E. M. (1965). *Migrants of North-East England, 1951–1961: character, age and sex*. (University of Newcastle-upon-Tyne. Department of Geography. Papers on Migration and Mobility in Northern England, no. 2.) The University, Newcastle.

HUFF, D. (1954). *How to lie with statistics*. Gollancz, London.

HULL, T. E. (1966). *Introduction to computing*. Prentice-Hall, Englewood Cliffs, N.J.

HUNT, A. (1968). *A survey of women's employment. Vol. 1. A survey carried out on behalf of the Ministry of Labour by the Government Social Survey in 1965. Vol. 2. Tables*. (Government Social Survey, SS379.) H.M.S.O., London.

HYMAN, H. H. (1950). Problems in the collection of opinion-research data. *American Journal of Sociology*, **55**, 362–370.

HYMAN, H. H. (1955). *Survey design and analysis: principles, cases and procedures*. Free Press, Glencoe, Ill.

HYMAN, H. H. and others (1954). *Interviewing in social research*. University of Chicago Press, Chicago.

INDIA, CABINET SECRETARIAT (1961). *The National Sample Survey, Number 49: Report on Morbidity*. The Cabinet Secretariat, Government of India, Delhi.

INSTITUTE OF PRACTITIONERS IN ADVERTISING (1954). *The National Readership Survey—1954 edition*. I.P.A., London.

ISAACS, S. and others (1941). *The Cambridge evacuation survey: a wartime study in social welfare and education*. Methuen, London.

JACKSON, B. and MARSDEN, D. (1962). *Education and the working class: some general themes raised by a study of 88 working-class children in a northern industrial city*. (Institute of Community Studies Report, no. 6.) Routledge and Kegan Paul, London; (rev. ed. 1966) Penguin (Pelican) Books, Harmondsworth, Middlesex.

JAEGER, C. M. and PENNOCK, J. L. (1961). An analysis of consistency of response in household surveys. *Journal of the American Statistical Association*, **56**, 320–327.

JAHODA, M., DEUTSCH, M. and COOK, S. W., eds. (1951). *Research methods in social relations, with especial reference to prejudice. Vol. I: Basic processes. Vol. II: Selected techniques*. Dryden Press, New York. [*See* SELLTIZ, C., JAHODA, M., DEUTSCH, M. and COOK, S. W. (1959) for revised edition.]

JAHODA, M. and WARREN, N. eds. (1966). *Attitudes: selected readings*. Penguin Books, Harmondsworth, Middlesex.

JANDA, K. F. (1965). *Data processing: applications to political research*. Northwestern University Press, Evanston, Ill.

JESSEN, R. J. (1945). The master sample of agriculture. II. Design. *Journal of the American Statistical Association*, **40**, 46–56.

JOBLING, D. and SNELL, E. J. (1961). Use of the coefficient of reproducibility in attitude scaling. *Incorporated Statistician*, 11, 110–118.
JOHNSON, N. L. and SMITH, H., Jr., eds. (1969). *New developments in survey sampling. A symposium on the foundations of survey sampling held at the University of North Carolina, Chapel Hill, North Carolina.* Wiley (Interscience), New York.
JOHNSTON, J. (1963). *Econometric methods.* McGraw-Hill, New York.
JOINT COMMITTEE OF THE ROYAL COLLEGE OF OBSTETRICIANS AND GYNAECOLOGISTS AND THE POPULATION INVESTIGATION COMMITTEE (1948). *Maternity in Great Britain: a survey of social and economic aspects of pregnancy and childbirth.* Geoffrey Cumberlege (Oxford University Press), London.
JOINT INDUSTRY COMMITTEE FOR NATIONAL READERSHIP SURVEYS (JICNARS) (1968). *Fieldwork period February-December 1968 National Readership Survey. Volume 3: Analysis by sex, age, social grade, etc. Readership profiles. Readership among special groups.* JICNARS, London.
JONES, D. C., ed. (1934). *The social survey of Merseyside.* 3 vols. University Press of Liverpool, Hodder and Stoughton, London.
JONES, D. C. (1948). *Social surveys.* Hutchinson (University Library, no. 28), London.
JONES, W. R. (1969). *A report on the 1960 national attainment survey: a survey of education attainment in Wales.* D. Brown and Sons Ltd., Cowbridge, Glamorgan.
JUSTER, F. T. (1966). Consumer buying intentions and purchase probability: an experiment in survey design. *Journal of the American Statistical Association*, 61, 658–696.
KAHN, R. L. and CANNELL, C. F. (1957). *The dynamics of interviewing; theory, technique, and cases.* Wiley, New York.
KAHN, R. L. and CANNELL, C. F. (1968). Interviewing: I. Social research. *International Encyclopaedia of the Social Sciences* (Macmillan and Free Press, New York), 8, 149–161.
KALTON, G. (1966). *Introduction to statistical ideas for social scientists.* Chapman and Hall, London; Barnes and Noble, New York.
KALTON, G. (1968). Standardization: a technique to control for extraneous variables. *Applied Statistics*, 17, 118–136.
KAPLAN, A. B. (1964). *The conduct of inquiry: methodology for behavioral science.* Chandler, San Francisco.
KAPP, R. O. (1948). *The presentation of technical information.* Constable, London.
KATZ, D. (1942). Do interviewers bias poll results? *Public Opinion Quarterly*, 6, 248–268.
KATZ, D., CARTWRIGHT, D. P., ELDERSVELD, S. and LEE, A. M., eds. (1954). *Public opinion and propaganda: a book of readings.* Holt, New York.
KAY, D. W. K., BEAMISH, P. and ROTH, M. (1964). Old age mental disorders in Newcastle upon Tyne. Part I: A study of prevalence. Part II: A study of possible social and medical causes. *British Journal of Psychiatry*, 110, 146–158, 668–682.
KELSALL, R. K. (1955). *Higher civil servants in Britain from 1870 to the present day.* Routledge and Kegan Paul, London.
KELSALL, R. K. (1963). *Women and teaching: report on an independent Nuffield survey following-up a large national sample of women who*

entered teaching in England and Wales at various dates pre-war and post-war. (Ministry of Education.) H.M.S.O., London.

KEMPTHORNE, O., BANCROFT, T.A., GOWEN, J. W. and LUSH, J. L. eds. (1954). *Statistics and mathematics in biology.* Iowa State College Press, Ames, Iowa; (reprinted 1964) Hafner, New York.

KEMSLEY, W. F. F. (1960). Interviewer variability and a budget survey. *Applied Statistics,* **9,** 122–128.

KEMSLEY, W. F. F. (1961). The Household Expenditure enquiry of the Ministry of Labour. Variability in the 1953–54 enquiry. *Applied Statistics,* **10,** 117–135.

KEMSLEY, W. F. F. (1962). Some technical aspects of a postal survey into professional earnings. *Applied Statistics,* **11,** 93–105.

KEMSLEY, W. F. F. (1965). Interviewer variability in expenditure surveys. *Journal of the Royal Statistical Society, A,* **128,** 118–139.

KEMSLEY, W. F. F. (1966). Sampling errors in the Family Expenditure Survey. *Applied Statistics,* **15,** 1–14.

KEMSLEY, W. F. F. (1968). Redesigning the Family Expenditure Survey. *Statistical News,* no. 1, 1.10–1.13.

KEMSLEY, W. F. F. (1969). *Family Expenditure Survey. Handbook on the sample, fieldwork and coding procedures.* (Government Social Survey, SS800.1.) H.M.S.O., London.

KEMSLEY, W. F. F. and NICHOLSON, J. L. (1960). Some experiments in methods of conducting family expenditure surveys. *Journal of the Royal Statistical Society, A,* **123,** 307–328.

KENDALL, M. G., ed. (1952–57). *The sources and nature of the statistics of the United Kingdom.* 2 vols. Oliver and Boyd, Edinburgh.

KENDALL, M. G. (1957). *A course in multivariate analysis.* Griffin (Statistical Monographs and Courses, no. 2), London; Hafner, New York.

KENDALL, M. G. and BUCKLAND, W. R. (2nd ed. 1960, with combined glossary in English, French, German, Italian, Spanish). *A dictionary of statistical terms.* Oliver and Boyd, Edinburgh.

KENDALL, M. G. and SMITH, B. BABINGTON (1939). *Tables of random sampling numbers.* (University College London. Department of Statistics. Tracts for Computers, no. 24.) Cambridge University Press, Cambridge.

KENDALL, M. G. and STUART, A. *The advanced theory of statistics.* [Three volume edition.]
(3rd ed. 1969). *Vol. 1. Distribution theory.*
(2nd ed. 1967). *Vol. 2. Inference and relationship.*
(2nd ed. 1968). *Vol. 3. Design and analysis, and time-series.*
Griffin, London; Hafner, New York.

KERLINGER, F. N. (1964). *Foundations of behavioral research: educational and psychological inquiry.* Holt, Rinehart and Winston, New York.

KEYFITZ, N. (1953). A factorial arrangement of comparisons of family size. *American Journal of Sociology,* **58,** 470–480.

KEYFITZ, N. and ROBINSON, H. L. (1949). The Canadian sample for labour force and other population data. *Population Studies,* **2,** 427–443.

KING, A. J. (1945). The master sample of agriculture. I. Development and use. *Journal of the American Statistical Association,* **40,** 38–45.

KINSEY, A. C., POMEROY, W. B. and MARTIN, C. E. (1948). *Sexual behavior in the human male.* Saunders, Philadelphia.

KINSEY, A. C., POMEROY, W. B. and MARTIN, C. E. (1953). *Sexual behavior in the human female.* Saunders, Philadelphia.

KISH, L. (1949). A procedure for objective respondent selection within the household. *Journal of the American Statistical Association*, **44**, 380–387.

KISH, L. (1952). A two-stage sample of a city. *American Sociological Review*, **17**, 761–769.

KISH, L. (1957). Confidence intervals for clustered samples. *American Sociological Review*, **22**, 154–165.

KISH, L. (1959). Some statistical problems in research design. *American Sociological Review*, **24**, 328–338.

KISH, L. (1961). Efficient allocation of a multi-purpose sample. *Econometrica*, **29**, 363–385.

KISH, L. (1962). Studies of interviewer variance for attitudinal variables. *Journal of the American Statistical Association*, **57**, 92–115.

KISH, L. (1965a). *Survey sampling*. Wiley, New York.

KISH, L. (1965b). Sampling organizations and groups of unequal sizes. *American Sociological Review*, **30**, 564–572.

KISH, L. and FRANKEL, M. R. (1968). Balanced repeated replications for analytical statistics. *Proceedings of the Social Statistics Section, American Statistical Association*, **1968**, 2–10.

KISH, L. and FRANKEL, M. R. (1970). Balanced repeated replications for analytical statistics. *Journal of the American Statistical Association*, **65**, 1071–1094.

KISH, L. and HESS, I. (1959). A 'replacement' procedure for reducing the bias of nonresponse. *American Statistician*, **13**(4), 17–19.

KISH, L. and HESS, I. (1965). *The Survey Research Center's national sample of dwellings*. Institute for Social Research, University of Michigan, Ann Arbor, Michigan.

KISH, L. and LANSING, J. B. (1954). Response errors in estimating the value of homes. *Journal of the American Statistical Association*, **49**, 520–538.

KLUCKHOHN, F. R. (1940). The participant-observer technique in small communities. *American Journal of Sociology*, **46**, 331–343.

KOCH, S., ed. (1959). *Psychology: a study of a science. (Study I. Conceptual and systematic.) Volume 3. Formulations of the person and the social context.* McGraw-Hill, New York.

KOKAN, A. R. and KHAN, S. (1967). Optimum allocation in multivariate surveys: an analytical solution. *Journal of the Royal Statistical Society, B*, **29**, 115–125.

KORNHAUSER, A. (1946–47). Are public opinion polls fair to organized labor? *Public Opinion Quarterly*, **10**, 484–500.

KRAUSZ, E. (1969). Locating minority populations: a research problem. *Race*, **10**, 361–368.

KRUSKAL, J. B. (1964a). Multidimensional scaling by optimizing goodness of fit to a nonmetric hypothesis. *Psychometrika*, **29**, 1–27.

KRUSKAL, J. B. (1964b). Nonmetric multidimensional scaling: a numerical method. *Psychometrika*, **29**, 115–129.

KUPER, L., ed. (1953). *Living in towns: selected research papers in urban sociology.* Cresset Press, London.

LAHIRI, D. B. (1951). A method of sample selection providing unbiased ratio estimates. *Bulletin of the International Statistical Institute*, **33**(2), 133–140.

LAHIRI, D. B. (1958). Observations on the use of interpenetrating samples in India. *Bulletin of the International Statistical Institute*, **36**(3), 144–152.

LAMBERT, R. with MILLHAM, S. (1968). *The hothouse society: an exploration of boarding-school life through the boys' and girls' own writings.* Weidenfeld and Nicolson, London.

LAND, H. (1969). *Large families in London (a study of 86 families).* (Social Administration Research Trust. Occasional Papers in Social Administration, no. 32.) Bell, London.

LASSWELL, H. D., LEITES, N. and associates (1949). *Language of politics: studies in quantitative semantics.* Stewart, New York.

LAWLEY, D. N. and MAXWELL, A. E. (1963). *Factor analysis as a statistical method.* Butterworths, London.

LAZARSFELD, P. F. (1935). The art of asking why. *National Marketing Review*, 1, 26–38.

LAZARSFELD, P. F. (1944). The controversy over detailed interviews—an offer for negotiation. *Public Opinion Quarterly*, 8, 38–60.

LAZARSFELD, P. F. (1948). The use of panels in social research. *Proceedings of the American Philosophical Society*, 92, 405–410.

LAZARSFELD, P. F., ed. (1954). *Mathematical thinking in the social sciences.* Free Press, Glencoe, Ill.

LAZARSFELD, P. F. (1958). Evidence and inference in social research. *Daedalus*, 87, 99–130.

LAZARSFELD, P. F. and HENRY, N. W. (1968). *Latent structure analysis.* Houghton Mifflin, Boston.

LAZARSFELD, P. F. and ROSENBERG, M., eds. (1955). *The language of social research: a reader in the methodology of social research.* Free Press, New York; Collier-Macmillan, London.

LE MESURIER, T. H. F. T. (1954). Problems in maintaining and continuing basis. *ESOMAR Journal* (European Society for Opinion Surveys and Market Research), no. 1, 73–80.

LEWIS-FANING, E. (1949). *Report on an enquiry into family limitation and its influence on human fertility during the past fifty years.* (Royal Commission on Population. Papers. Vol. I.) H.M.S.O., London.

LI, C. C. (1955). *Population genetics.* University of Chicago Press, Chicago.

LI, C. C. (1956). The concept of path coefficient and its impact on population genetics. *Biometrics*, 12, 190–210.

LI, C. C. (1968). Fisher, Wright, and path coefficients. *Biometrics*, 24, 471–483.

LIEPMANN, K. K. (1944). *The journey to work: its significance for industrial and community life.* Kegan Paul, London.

LIKERT, R. (1932). *A technique for the measurement of attitudes.* (Archives of Psychology, no. 140.) Columbia University Press, New York.

LINDZEY, G., ed. (1954). *Handbook of social psychology.* Addison-Wesley, Cambridge, Mass.

LINDZEY, G. and ARONSON, E., eds. (2nd ed. 1968). *The handbook of social psychology. Vol. 2. Research Methods.* Addison-Wesley, Reading, Mass.

LINGOES, J. C. (1968). The multivariate analysis of qualitative data. *Multivariate Behavioral Research*, 3, 61–94.

LITTLE, K. L. (1948). *Negroes in Britain: a study of racial relations in English society.* Kegan Paul, London.

LIVERPOOL UNIVERSITY, SOCIAL SCIENCE DEPARTMENT (Social Research Series) (1954). *The dock worker: an analysis of conditions of employment in the port of Manchester.* University Press of Liverpool, Liverpool.

LOCK, C. M. and others (1947). *The County Borough of Middlesbrough: survey and plan*. Middlesbrough Corporation, Middlesbrough.

LOGAN, W. P. D. (1960). *Morbidity statistics from general practice. Volume II (Occupation)*. (General Register Office. Studies on Medical and Population Subjects, no. 14.) H.M.S.O., London.

LOGAN, W. P. D. and BROOKE, E. M. (1957). *The Survey of Sickness 1943 to 1952*. (General Register Office. Studies on Medical and Population Subjects, no. 12.) H.M.S.O., London.

LOGAN, W. P. D. and CUSHION, A. A. (1958). *Morbidity statistics from general practice. Volume I (General)*. (General Register Office. Studies on Medical and Population Subjects, no. 14.) H.M.S.O. London.

LONDON BOROUGH OF CAMDEN (1968, republished 1969). *Housing in Camden. Vol. 2. Report on the housing rents study by the Centre for Urban Studies*. Borough of Camden, London.

LORD, F. M. and NOVICK, M. R. (1968). *Statistical theories of mental test scores*. Addison-Wesley, Reading, Mass.

LUPTON, T. (1963). *On the shop floor: two studies of workshop organization and output*. (International Series of Monographs on Social and Behavioural Sciences, Vol. 2.) Pergamon Press, Oxford.

LYDALL, H. F. (1955). *British incomes and savings*. (University of Oxford. Institute of Statistics. Monograph no. 5.) Blackwell, Oxford.

LYND, R. S. and LYND, H. M. (1929). *Middletown: a study in contemporary American culture*. Constable, London; Harcourt, Brace, New York.

LYND, R. S. and LYND, H. M. (1937). *Middletown in transition: a study in cultural conflicts*. Constable, London; Harcourt, Brace, New York.

McCALL, G. J. and SIMMONS, J. L., eds. (1969). *Issues in participant observation. A text and reader*. Addison-Wesley, Reading, Mass.

McCARTHY, P. J. (1957). *Introduction to statistical reasoning*. McGraw-Hill, New York.

McCARTHY, P. J. (1966). *Replication: an approach to the analysis of data from complex surveys: development and evaluation of a replication technique for estimating variance*. (U.S. Department of Health, Education, and Welfare. National Center for Health Statistics. Vital and Health Statistics, Series 2, no. 14.) U.S. Government Printing Office, Washington, D.C.

McCARTHY, P. J. (1969). Pseudo-replication: half samples. *Review of the International Statistical Institute*, **37**, 239–264.

McCRACKEN, D. D. (1965). *A guide to Fortran IV programming*. Wiley, New York.

McGINNIS, R. (1958). Randomization and inference in sociological research. *American Sociological Review*, **23**, 408–414.

McKENNELL, A. C. (1966). *Some uses of factor analysis in social survey work*. Government Social Survey (no. M125), London.

McKENNELL, A. C. (1970). Attitude measurement: use of coefficient alpha with cluster or factor analysis. *Sociology*, **4**, 227-245.

McKENNELL, A. C. and BYNNER, J. M. (1969). Self images and smoking behaviour among school boys. *British Journal of Educational Psychology*, **39**, 27–39.

McKENZIE, R. T. and SILVER, A. (1968). *Angels in marble: working class Conservatives in urban England*. Heinemann, London.

McNEMAR, Q. (1946). Opinion-attitude methodology. *Psychological Bulletin*, **43**, 289–374.

McNEMAR, Q. (4th ed. 1969). *Psychological statistics*. Wiley, New York.

MADGE, J. H. (1953). *The tools of social science.* Longmans, London.
MAHALANOBIS, P. C. (1946). Recent experiments in statistical sampling in the Indian Statistical Institute. *Journal of the Royal Statistical Society,* **109**, 326–378.
MANN, P. H. (1968). *Methods of sociological enquiry.* Blackwell, Oxford.
MANNHEIM, H. and WILKINS, L. T. (1955). *Prediction methods in relation to Borstal training.* (Home Office. Studies in the Causes of Delinquency and the Treatment of Offenders, no. 1.) H.M.S.O., London.
MANNHEIMER, D. and HYMAN, H. (1949). Interviewer performance in area sampling. *Public Opinion Quarterly,* **13**, 83–92.
MARK, M. L. (1958). *Statistics in the making: a primer in statistical survey method.* (Bureau of Business Research Publication, no. 92.) Bureau of Business Research, College of Commerce and Administration, The Ohio State University, Columbus, Ohio.
MARKET RESEARCH SOCIETY (1954a). *Readership surveys: a comparative survey.* (Market Research Society. Publication, no. 1.) Market Research Society, London.
MARKET RESEARCH SOCIETY (1954b). *Standards in market research.* Market Research Society, London.
MARKET RESEARCH SOCIETY (1960). *Attitude scaling.* (Market Research Society. Publication, no. 4.) Market Research Society and Oakwood Press, London.
MARKET RESEARCH SOCIETY (1963a). *New developments in research.* (Market Research Society. Publication, no. 8.) Market Research Society and Oakwood Press, London.
MARKET RESEARCH SOCIETY (1963b). *Social class definition in market research: objectives and practice.* (Working Party on Social Class Definition. First report.) Market Research Society, London.
MARKET RESEARCH SOCIETY (1968). *Fieldwork methods in general use.* (Working party on Interviewing Methods. First report.) Market Research Society, London.
MARKS, E. S. and MAULDIN, W. P. (1950). Response errors in census research. *Journal of the American Statistical Association,* **45**, 424–438.
MARKS, E. S., MAULDIN, W. P. and NISSELSON, H. (1953). The Post-Enumeration Survey of the 1950 Census: a case history in survey design. *Journal of the American Statistical Association,* **48**, 220–243.
MARQUIS, K. H. (1969). *An experimental study of the effects of reinforcement, question length, and reinterviews on reporting selected chronic conditions in household interviews.* Survey Research Center, Institute for Social Research, University of Michigan, Ann Arbor, Michigan.
MARRIOTT, R. (1953). Some problems in attitude survey methodology. *Occupational Psychology,* **27**, 117–127.
MARSDEN, D. (1969). *Mothers alone: poverty and the fatherless family.* Allen Lane The Penguin Press, London.
MARTIN, J. P. (1962). *Offenders as employees: an enquiry by the Cambridge Institute of Criminology.* (Cambridge University. Institute of Criminology. Studies in Criminology, Vol. 16.) Macmillan, London.
MARTIN, J. P. and WILSON, G. G. (1969). *The police: a study in manpower; the evolution of the service in England and Wales, 1829–1965.* (Cambridge University. Institute of Criminology. Studies in Criminology, Vol. 24.) Heinemann, London.
MASSEY, P. (1942). The expenditure of 1,360 British middle-class households in 1938–39. *Journal of the Royal Statistical Society,* **105**, 159–196.

MASS OBSERVATION (1943). *The pub and the people: a worktown study.* Gollancz, London.

MAYHEW, H. (1861–62). *London labour and the London poor; a cyclopædia of the condition and earnings of those that will work, those that cannot work, and those that will not work.* 4 volumes. Griffin, Bohn, London.

MAYNES, E. S. (1968). Minimizing response errors in financial data: the possibilities. *Journal of the American Statistical Association,* 63, 214–227.

MELHUISH, R. M. (1954). The use and operation of the Nielson Indices. *ESOMAR Journal* (European Society for Opinion Surveys and Market Research), no. 1, 64–71.

MERSEYSIDE AREA LAND-USE TRANSPORTATION STUDY (1969). *Report to the steering committee.* Merseyside Area Land-Use Transportation Study Steering Committee, Liverpool.

MERTON, R. K., FISKE, M. and KENDALL, P. L. (1956). *The focused interview: a manual of problems and procedures.* Free Press, Glencoe, Ill.

MERTON, R. K. and LAZARSFELD, P. F., eds. (1950). *Continuities in social research: studies in the scope and method of 'The American Soldier'.* Free Press, Glencoe, Ill.

MILLER, D. C. (1964). *Handbook of research design and social measurement.* McKay, New York.

MILLER, F. J. W., COURT, S. D. M., WALTON, W. S. and KNOX, E. G. (1960). *Growing up in Newcastle upon Tyne: a continuing study of health and illness in young children within their families.* Oxford University Press, London.

MILLER, S. M. (1952). The participant observer and 'over-rapport'. *American Sociological Review,* 17, 97–99.

MILLER, S. M. (1960). Comparative social mobility: a trend report and bibliography. *Current Sociology* (UNESCO), 9(1), 1–89.

MILNE, R. S. and MACKENZIE, H. C. (1954). *Straight fight: a study of voting behaviour in the constituency of Bristol North-East at the General Election of 1951.* Hansard Society, London.

MONK, D. M. (1963). Some aspects of advertising research. *The Statistician,* 13, 117–126.

MOONEY, H. W. (1962). *Methodology in two California health surveys— San Jose (1952) and Statewide (1954-55).* (U.S. Department of Health, Education, and Welfare. Public Health Monograph, no. 70.) U.S. Government Printing Office, Washington, D.C.

MORGAN, J. N., DAVID, M. H., COHEN, W. J. and BRAZER, H. E. (1962). *Income and welfare in the United States.* McGraw-Hill, New York.

MORGAN, J. N., SIRAGELDIN, I. A. and BAERWALDT, N. (1966). *Productive Americans: a study of how individuals contribute to economic progress.* Survey Research Center (Monograph, no. 43), Institute for Social Research, University of Michigan, Ann Arbor, Michigan.

MORGAN, J. N. and SONQUIST, J. A. (1963). Problems in the analysis of survey data, and a proposal. *Journal of the American Statistical Association,* 58, 415–434.

MORRIS, J. N. and CRAWFORD, M. D. (1958). Coronary heart disease and physical activity of work: evidence of a national necropsy survey. *British Medical Journal,* 1958(II), 1485–1496.

MORRIS, J. N., HEADY, J. A., RAFFLE, P. A. B., ROBERTS, C. G. and PARKS, J. W. (1953). Coronary heart-disease and physical activity of work. I. Coronary heart-disease in different occupations. II. Statement and testing of provisional hypothesis. *Lancet*, **265**(2), 1053–1057, 1111–1120.

MORRIS, P. J. (1965). *Prisoners and their families*. Allen and Unwin, London.

MORRIS, P. J. (1969). *Put away: a sociological study of institutions for the mentally retarded*. Routledge and Kegan Paul, London.

MORRISON, D. F. (1967). *Multivariate statistical methods*. McGraw-Hill, New York.

MORTON-WILLIAMS, R., FINCH, S. and POLL, C. (1966). *Undergraduates' attitudes to school teaching as a career. A survey carried out among English and Welsh university students in November, 1963 for the Department of Education and Science*. (Government Social Survey, SS354.) H.M.S.O., London.

MOSER, C. A. (1949). The use of sampling in Great Britain. *Journal of the American Statistical Association*, **44**, 231–259.

MOSER, C. A. (1950). Social research: the diary method. *Social Service*, **24**(2), 80–84.

MOSER, C. A. (1951). Interview bias. *Review of the International Statistical Institute*, **19**, 28–40.

MOSER, C. A. (1952). Quota sampling. *Journal of the Royal Statistical Society, A*, **115**, 411–423.

MOSER, C. A. (1955). Recent developments in the sampling of human populations in Great Britain. *Journal of the American Statistical Association*, **50**, 1195–1214.

MOSER, C. A. and STUART, A. (1953). An experimental study of quota sampling. *Journal of the Royal Statistical Society, A*, **116**, 349–405.

MOSS, L. (1953). Sample surveys and the administrative process. *International Social Science Bulletin*, **5**, 482–494.

MOSTELLER, F., HYMAN, H., MCCARTHY, P. J., MARKS, E. S. and TRUMAN, D. B. (1949). *The pre-election polls of 1948: report to the Committee on Analysis of Pre-election Polls and Forecasts*. U.S. Social Science Research Council (Bulletin, no. 60), New York.

MUEHL, D., ed. (1961). *A manual for coders: content analysis at the Survey Research Center, 1961*. Survey Research Center, Institute for Social Research, University of Michigan, Ann Arbor, Michigan.

MUELLER, E. (1963). Ten years of consumer attitude surveys: their forecasting record. *Journal of the American Statistical Association*, **58**, 899–917.

MURTHY, M. N. (1967). *Sampling theory and methods*. Statistical Publishing Society, Calcutta.

MYERS, R. J. (1954). Accuracy of age reporting in the 1950 United States Census. *Journal of the American Statistical Association*, **49**, 826–831.

NATIONAL INSTITUTE OF ECONOMIC AND SOCIAL RESEARCH (1956). *Register of research in the social sciences and directory of research institutions. Number 13, 1956/7*. Aslib, London.

NETER, J., MAYNES, E. S. and RAMANATHAN, R. (1965). The effect of mismatching on the measurement of response errors. *Journal of the American Statistical Association*, **60**, 1005–1027.

NETER, J. and WAKSBERG, J. (1964). A study of response errors in expenditures data from household interviews. *Journal of the American Statistical Association*, **59**, 18–55.

NETER, J. and WAKSBERG, J. (1965). *Response errors in collection of expenditures. data by household interviews: an experimental study.* (U.S. Department of Commerce. Bureau of the Census, Technical Paper, no. 11.) U.S. Government Printing Office, Washington, D.C.

NEWSON, J. and NEWSON, E. (1963). *Infant care in an urban community.* Allen and Unwin, London.

NEWSON, J. and NEWSON, E. (1965). *Patterns of infant care in an urban community.* Penguin (Pelican) Books, Harmondsworth, Middlesex.

NEWSON, J. and NEWSON, E. (1968). *Four years old in an urban community.* Allen and Unwin, London.

NICHOLLS, D. C. and YOUNG, A. (1968). *Recreation and tourism in the Loch Lomond area: a report to the County Council of Dunbarton.* Department of Social and Economic Research, University of Glasgow, Glasgow.

NORTH, R. C., HOLSTI, O. R., ZANINOVICH, M. G. and ZINNES, D. A. (1963). *Content analysis: a handbook with applications for the study of international crisis.* Northwestern University Press, Evanston, Ill.

NORTHERN REGION PLANNING COMMITTEE (1969). *Outdoor leisure activities in the Northern Region: a survey conducted by N.O.P. Market Research Ltd.* Northern Region Planning Committee.

NUFFIELD FOUNDATION (1947). *Old people: report of a Survey Committee on the problems of ageing and the care of old people.* Oxford University Press, London.

OPPENHEIM, A. N. (1966). *Questionnaire design and attitude measurement.* Heinemann, London; Basic Books, New York.

ORR, J. BOYD (1936). *Food, health and income: report on a survey of adequacy of diet in relation to income.* Macmillan, London.

OSGOOD, C. E., SUCI, G. J. and TANNENBAUM, P. H. (1957). *The measurement of meaning.* University of Illinois Press, Urbana.

PADDOCK, J. (1961). Oscar Lewis's Mexico. *Anthropological Quarterly*, **34**, 129–149.

PARKER, T. (1967). *A man of good abilities.* Hutchinson, London.

PARKER, T. (1968). *People of the streets.* Cape, London.

PARKER, T. and ALLERTON, R. H. (1962). *The courage of his convictions.* Hutchinson, London.

PARKIN, F. I. (1968). *Middle class radicalism: the social bases of the British Campaign for Nuclear Disarmament.* Manchester University Press, Manchester.

PARRY, H. J. and CROSSLEY, H. M. (1950). Validity of responses to survey questions. *Public Opinion Quarterly*, **14**, 61–80.

PARTEN, M. B. (1950). *Surveys, polls, and samples: practical procedures.* Harper, New York.

PATTERSON, S. (1963). *Dark strangers: a sociological study of the absorption of a recent West Indian migrant group in Brixton, South London.* Tavistock Publications, London.

PAYNE, S. L. B. (1951). *The art of asking questions.* (Studies in Public Opinion, no. 3.) Princeton University Press, Princeton.

PEAKER, G. F. (1953). A sampling design used by the Ministry of Education. *Journal of the Royal Statistical Society, A*, **116**, 140–165.

PELZ, D. C. and ANDREWS, F. M. (1964). Detecting causal priorities in panel study data. *American Sociological Review*, **29**, 836–848.

PHILLIPS, B. S. (1966). *Social research: strategy and tactics.* Macmillan, New York; Collier-Macmillan, London.

PIDGEON, D. A. (1960). A national survey of the ability and attainment of children at three age levels. *British Journal of Educational Psychology*, **30**, 124–133.

PIERCE, R. M. and ROWNTREE, G. (1961). Birth control in Britain. Part II. Contraceptive methods used by couples married in the last thirty years. *Population Studies*, **15**, 121–160. [*See* ROWNTREE, G. and PIERCE, R. M. for Part I.]

PLATEK, R., McFARLANE, C. and ROSE, D. (1968). *Continuous social and demographic survey. The sample design.* Continuous Social and Demographic Survey Unit, Department of Statistics, Jamaica.

PODELL, L. and PERKINS, J. C. (1957). A Guttman scale for sexual experience—a methodological note. *Journal of Abnormal Psychology*, **54**, 420–422.

POLITICAL AND ECONOMIC PLANNING (1950). Sample surveys. Part One. Part Two. *Planning* (PEP, London), **16** (nos. 314 and 315).

POLITICAL AND ECONOMIC PLANNING (1952). Poverty: Ten years after Beveridge. *Planning* (PEP, London), **19** (no. 344).

POLITZ, A. and SIMMONS, W. (1949). I. An attempt to get the 'not at homes' into the sample without callbacks. II. Further theoretical considerations regarding the plan for eliminating callbacks. *Journal of the American Statistical Association*, **44**, 9–31.

POPULATION INVESTIGATION COMMITTEE and SCOTTISH COUNCIL FOR RESEARCH IN EDUCATION (1949). *The trend of Scottish intelligence: a comparison of the 1947 and 1932 surveys of the intelligence of eleven-year-old pupils.* (Scottish Council for Research in Education. Publications, no. 30.) University of London Press, London.

PRAIS, S. J. and HOUTHAKKER, H. S. (1955). *The analysis of family budgets: with an application to two British surveys conducted in 1937–9 and their detailed results.* (Cambridge University. Department of Applied Economics. Monographs, no. 4.) Cambridge University Press, Cambridge.

PRINGLE, M. L. KELLMER, BUTLER, N. R. and DAVIE, R. (1966). *11,000 seven-year-olds. First report of the National Child Development Study (1958 Cohort) submitted to the Central Advisory Council for Education (England).* Longmans, London.

PRITZKER, L., OGUS, J. and HANSEN, M. H. (1966). Computer editing methods—some applications and results. *Bulletin of the International Statistical Institute*, **41**(1), 442–472.

RAJ, D. (1968). *Sampling theory.* McGraw-Hill, New York.

REES, A. D. (2nd ed. 1951). *Life in a Welsh countryside: a social study of Llanfihangel yng Ngwynfa.* University of Wales Press, Cardiff.

REISS, A. J. (1961). *Occupations and social status.* Free Press of Glencoe, New York.

RESEARCH COMMITTEE OF THE COUNCIL OF THE COLLEGE OF GENERAL PRACTITIONERS (1962). *Morbidity statistics from general practice. Volume III (Diseases in General Practice).* (General Register Office. Studies on Medical and Population Subjects, no. 14.) H.M.S.O., London.

REX, J. A. and MOORE, R. (1967). *Race, community, and conflict: a study of Sparkbrook.* Oxford University Press, London.

RICHARDSON, S. A., DOHRENWEND, B. S. and KLEIN, D. (1965). *Interviewing, its forms and functions.* Basic Books, New York.

RILEY, M. W. (1963). *Sociological research. I. A case approach. II. Exercises and manual.* Harcourt, Brace and World, New York.

514   SURVEY METHODS IN SOCIAL INVESTIGATION

ROBB, J. H. (1954). *Working-class anti-semite: a psychological study in a London borough.* Tavistock Publications, London.
ROBINSON, J. P. and SHAVER, P. R. (1969). *Measures of social psychological attitudes.* Institute for Social Research, University of Michigan, Ann Arbor, Michigan.
RODGERS, H. B. (1967). *The pilot national recreation survey. Report no. 1.* British Travel Association and University of Keele, London.
RODGERS, H. B. (1969). *The pilot national recreation survey. Report no. 2. Regional analysis.* British Travel Association and University of Keele, London.
ROETHLISBERGER, F. J. and DICKSON, W. J. (1939). *Management and the worker: an account of a research program conducted by the Western Electric Company, Hawthorne Works, Chicago.* Harvard University Press, Cambridge, Mass.
ROGERS, C. R. (1945). The nondirective method as a technique for social research. *American Journal of Sociology,* 50, 279–283.
ROPER, W. F. (1950). A comparative survey of the Wakefield Prison population in 1948. Part I. *British Journal of Delinquency,* 1, 15–28.
ROPER, W. F. (1951). A comparative survey of the Wakefield Prison population in 1948 & 1949. Part II. *British Journal of Delinquency,* 1, 243–270.
ROSE, A. M. (1945). A research note on experimentation in interviewing. *American Journal of Sociology,* 51, 143–144.
ROSE, E. J. B. and associates (1969). *Colour and citizenship: a report on British race relations.* Oxford University Press, London.
ROSENBERG, M. (1962). Test factor standardization as a method of interpretation. *Social Forces,* 41, 53–61.
ROSENBERG, M. (1968). *The logic of survey analysis.* Basic Books, New York.
ROSS, J. A. and BANG, S. (1966). The AID computer programme, used to predict adoption of family planning in Koyang. *Population Studies,* 20, 61–75.
ROSSER, C. and HARRIS, C. (1965). *The family and social change: a study of family and kinship in a South Wales town.* Routledge and Kegan Paul, London.
ROWETT RESEARCH INSTITUTE (1955). *Family diet and health in pre-war Britain: a dietary and clinical survey.* Carnegie United Kingdom Trust, Dunfermline.
ROWNTREE, B. S. (1902, new ed. 1922). *Poverty: a study of town life.* Longmans, London.
ROWNTREE, B. S. (new ed. 1937). *The human needs of labour.* Longmans, London.
ROWNTREE, B. S. (1941). *Poverty and progress: a second social survey of York.* Longmans, London.
ROWNTREE, B. S. and LAVERS, G. R. (1951a). *Poverty and the welfare state: a third social survey of York dealing only with economic questions.* Longmans, London.
ROWNTREE, B. S. and LAVERS, G. R. (1951b). *English life and leisure: a social study.* Longmans, London.
ROWNTREE, G. and PIERCE, R. M. (1961). Birth control in Britain. Part I. Attitudes and practices among persons married since the First World War. *Population Studies,* 15, 3–31. [*See* PIERCE, R. M. and ROWNTREE, G. for Part II.]

Royal College of Physicians (1962). *Smoking and health: a report on smoking in relation to cancer of the lung and other diseases.* Pitman Medical Publishing Company, London.

Rozelle, R. M. and Campbell, D. T. (1969). More plausible rival hypotheses in the cross-lagged panel correlation technique. *Psychological Bulletin,* 71, 74–80.

Rudd, E. and Hatch, S. (1968). *Graduate study and after.* Weidenfeld and Nicolson, London.

Runciman, W. G. (1966). *Relative deprivation and social justice: a study of attitudes to social inequality in twentieth century England.* (Institute of Community Studies Report, no. 13.) Routledge and Kegan Paul, London.

Russell, B. (1927). *An outline of philosophy.* Allen and Unwin, London.

Rutter, M. and Graham, P. (1966). Two surveys of children [abridged]: Psychiatric disorder in 10- and 11-year-old children. *Proceedings of the Royal Society of Medicine,* 59, 382–387.

Sagi, P. C. (1959). A statistical test for the significance of a coefficient of reproducibility. *Psychometrika,* 24, 19–27.

Sainsbury, S. (1970). *Registered as disabled.* (Occasional Paper on Social Administration, no. 35.) Bell, London.

Sampford, M. R. (1962). *An introduction to sampling theory, with applications to agriculture.* Oliver and Boyd, Edinburgh.

Schofield, M. (1965a). *The sexual behaviour of young people.* Longmans, London; (rev. ed. 1968) Penguin Books, Harmondsworth, Middlesex.

Schofield, M. (1965b). *Sociological aspects of homosexuality: a comparative study of three types of homosexuals.* Longmans, London.

Schofield, M. (1969). *Social research.* Heinemann (Concept Books, no. 8), London.

Schuessler, K. F. (1961). A note on statistical significance of scalogram. *Sociometry,* 24, 312–318.

Schulz, T. (1949). Human needs and diets from 1936 to 1949. *Bulletin of the Oxford University Institute of Statistics,* 11, 307–325.

Schulz, T. (1952). Ten years of family surveys. *Bulletin of the Oxford University Institute of Statistics,* 14, 83–95.

Schuman, H. (1966). The random probe: a technique for evaluating the validity of closed questions. *American Sociological Review,* 31, 218–222.

Scott, C. (1959). *The postal services and the general public: an inquiry carried out for the Post Office.* (Government Social Survey, SS286B. Unpublished.) Central Office of Information, London.

Scott, C. (1961a). Research on mail surveys. *Journal of the Royal Statistical Society, A,* 124, 143–205.

Scott, C. (1961b). *The wearing of crash helmets by motor cyclists.* (Government Social Survey, SS277A.) H.M.S.O., London.

Scott, C. (1967). Sampling for demographic and morbidity surveys in Africa. *Review of the International Statistical Institute,* 35, 154–171.

Scott, C. and Jackson, S. (1960). *The use of the telephone for making interview appointments.* Government Social Survey (no. M92), London.

Scottish Council for Research in Education (Mental Survey Committee) (1953). *Social implications of the 1947 Scottish mental survey.* (Scottish Council for Research in Education. Publication no. 35.) University of London Press, London.

SEAL, H. L. (1964). *Multivariate statistical analysis for biologists.* Methuen, London.

SEIBERT, J. and WILLS, G., eds. (1970). *Marketing research: selected readings.* Penguin Books, Harmondsworth, Middlesex.

SELLTIZ, C., JAHODA, M., DEUTSCH, M. and COOK, S. W. (rev. one-volumed ed. 1959). *Research methods in social relations.* Holt, Rinehart and Winston, New York; Methuen, London.

SELVIN, H. C. (1957). A critique of tests of significance in survey research. *American Sociological Review,* 22, 519–527.

SELVIN, H. C. and STUART, A. (1966). Data-dredging procedures in survey analysis. *American Statistician,* 20(3), 20–23.

SENG, Y. P. (1951). Historical survey of the development of sampling theories and practice. *Journal of the Royal Statistical Society, A,* 114, 214–231.

SHAPIRO, S. and EBERHART, J. C. (1947). Interviewer differences in an intensive interview survey. *International Journal of Opinion and Attitude Research,* 1(2), 1–17.

SHAW, M. E. and WRIGHT, J. M. (1967). *Scales for the measurement of attitudes.* McGraw-Hill, New York.

SHEATSLEY, P. B. (1947–48). Some uses of interviewer-report forms. *Public Opinion Quarterly,* 11, 601–611.

SHEATSLEY, P. B. (1949). The influence of sub-questions on interviewer performance. *Public Opinion Quarterly,* 13, 310–313.

SHEFFIELD SOCIAL SURVEY COMMITTEE (Survey Pamphlets) (1931–33).

(1931). *No. 1. A report on a survey of the milk supply of Sheffield; prepared by A. J. Allaway.*

(1931). *No. 2. A report on the housing problem in Sheffield; prepared by A. D. K. Owen.*

(1931). *No. 3. A report on a survey of licensing in Sheffield; prepared by J. N. Reedman.*

(1932). *No. 4. A report on unemployment in Sheffield; prepared by A.D. K. Owen.*

(1932). *No. 5. A report on the development of adult education in Sheffield; prepared by G. P. Jones.*

(1933). *No. 6. A survey of juvenile employment and welfare in Sheffield; prepared by A. D. K. Owen.*

(1933). *No. 8. A survey of transport in Sheffield; prepared by A. G. Pool.*

(1933). *No. 9. A survey of the standard of living in Sheffield; prepared by A. D. K. Owen.*

SHELDON, J. H. (1948). *The social medicine of old age: report of an inquiry in Wolverhampton.* Oxford University Press, London.

SHEPHERD, M., COOPER, B., BROWN, A. C. and KALTON, G. (1966). *Psychiatric illness in general practice.* Oxford University Press, London.

SILLITOE, K. K. (1969). *Planning for leisure: an enquiry into the present pattern of participation in outdoor and physical recreation and the frequency and manner of use of public open-spaces, among people living in the urban areas of England and Wales.* (Government Social Survey, SS388.) H.M.S.O., London.

SIMON, H. A. (1954). Spurious correlation: a causal interpretation. *Journal of the American Statistical Association,* 49, 467–479.

SIMON, H. A. (1957). *Models of man, social and rational: mathematical essays on rational human behavior in a social setting.* Wiley, New York.

SIMON, J. L. (1969). *Basic research methods in social science: the art of empirical investigation*. Random House, New York.

SIRKEN, M. G. and BROWN, M. L. (1962). Quality of data elicited by successive mailings in mail surveys. *Proceedings of the Social Statistics Section, American Statistical Association*, **1962**, 118–125.

SIRKEN, M. G., MAYNES, E. S. and FRECHTLING, J. A. (1958). The Survey of Consumer Finances and the Census Quality Check. *Studies in Income and Wealth, Vol. 23: An appraisal of the 1950 Census Income and data* (pp. 127–168). Princeton University Press, Princeton.

SJOBERG, G. and NETT, R. (1968). *A methodology for social research*. Harper and Row, New York.

SMITH, G. H. (1954). *Motivation research in advertising and marketing*. McGraw-Hill, New York.

SMITH, H. L., ed. (1930–35). *The new survey of London life and labour*. 9 volumes. P. S. King, London.

SMITH, H. L. and HYMAN, H. (1950). The biasing effect of interviewer expectations on survey results. *Public Opinion Quarterly*, **14**, 491–506.

SMITH, J. S. (1958). The 'G' technique of attitude scaling. *Incorporated Statistician*, **9**, 9–16.

SMITH, J. S. (1960). The use of the Guttman scale in market research. *Incorporated Statistician*, **10**, 15–28.

SNEDECOR, G. W. and COCHRAN, W. G. (6th ed. 1967). *Statistical methods*. Iowa University Press, Ames, Iowa.

SOBOL, M. G. (1959). Panel mortality and panel bias. *Journal of the American Statistical Association*, **54**, 52–68.

SONQUIST, J. A. (1970). *Multivariate model building: the validation of a search strategy*. Survey Research Center, Institute for Social Research, University of Michigan, Ann Arbor, Michigan.

SONQUIST, J. A. and MORGAN, J. N. (6th ed. 1970). *The detection of interaction effects: a report on a computer program for the selection of optimal combinations of explanatory variables*. Survey Research Center (Monograph, no. 35), Institute for Social Research, University of Michigan, Ann Arbor, Michigan.

SPENCE, J. C., WALTON, W. S., MILLER, F. J. W. and COURT, S. D. M. (1954). *A thousand families in Newcastle upon Tyne: an approach to the study of health and illness in children*. Oxford University Press, London.

SPENCER, J. C. (1964). *Stress and release in an urban estate: a study in action research*. Tavistock Publications, London.

SPROTT, W. J. H. (1949). *Sociology*. Hutchinson (University Library, no. 34), London.

STACEY, M. (1960). *Tradition and change: a study of Banbury*. Oxford University Press, London.

STACEY, M. (1969a). *Methods of social research*. Pergamon Press, London.

STACEY, M., ed. (1969b). *Comparability in social research*. (Social Science Research Council. Reviews of Current Research, no. 6. Published with the British Sociological Association.) Heinemann, London.

STEINKAMP, S. W. (1964). The identification of effective interviewers. *Journal of the American Statistical Association*, **59**, 1165–1174.

STEMBER, H. (1951–52). Which respondents are reliable? *International Journal of Opinion and Attitude Research*, **5**, 475–479.

STEMBER, H. and HYMAN, H. (1949). Interviewer effects in the classification of responses. *Public Opinion Quarterly*, **13**, 322–334.

518   SURVEY METHODS IN SOCIAL INVESTIGATION

STEMBER, H. and HYMAN, H. (1949–50). How interviewer effects operate through question form. *International Journal of Opinion and Attitude Research*, 3, 493–512.

STEPHAN, F. F. (1948). History of the uses of modern sampling procedures. *Journal of the American Statistical Association*, 43, 12–39.

STEPHAN, F. F. and McCARTHY, P. J. (1958). *Sampling opinions: an analysis of survey procedure*. Wiley, New York; Chapman and Hall, London.

STEVENS, S. S. (1946). On the theory of scales of measurement. *Science*, 103, 677–680.

STEWART, C. (1948). *The village surveyed*. Arnold, London.

STOCK, J. S. and HOCHSTIM, J. R. (1951). A method of measuring interviewer variability. *Public Opinion Quarterly*, 15, 322–334.

STONE, P. J., DUNPHY, D. C., SMITH, M. S. and OGILVIE, D. M. (1966). *The general inquirer: a computer approach to content analysis*. M.I.T. Press, Cambridge, Mass.

STOUFFER, S. A. (1950). Some observations on study design. *American Journal of Sociology*, 55, 355–361.

STOUFFER, S. A. (1962). *Social research to test ideas: selected writings*. Free Press of Glencoe, New York.

STOUFFER, S. A., BORGATTA, E. F., HAYS, D. G. and HENRY, A. F. (1952). A technique for improving cumulative scales. *Public Opinion Quarterly*, 16, 273–291.

STOUFFER, S. A. and others (1949). *The American soldier. Volume I. Adjustment during army life. Volume II. Combat and its aftermath.* (U.S. Social Science Research Council. Studies in Social Psychology in World War II, Vols. I and II.) University Press, Princeton.

STOUFFER, S. A. and others (1950). *Measurement and prediction.* (U.S. Social Science Research Council. Studies in Social Psychology in World War II, Vol. IV.) University Press, Princeton; Wiley, New York.

STUART, A. (1952). Reading habits in three London boroughs. *Journal of Documentation*, 8, 33–49.

STUART, A. (1962). *Basic ideas of scientific sampling*. Griffin (Statistical Monographs and Courses, no. 4), London; Hafner, New York.

STUART, A. (1968). Sample surveys. II. Nonprobability sampling. *International Encyclopaedia of the Social Sciences* (Macmillan and Free Press, New York), 13, 612–616.

STUART, W. J. (1966). Computer editing of survey data—five years of experience in BLS manpower surveys. *Journal of the American Statistical Association*, 61, 375–383.

SUCHMAN, E. A. and GUTTMAN, L. (1947). A solution to the problem of question 'bias'. *Public Opinion Quarterly*, 11, 445–455.

SUDMAN, S. (1965). Time allocation in survey interviewing and in other field occupations. *Public Opinion Quarterly*, 29, 638–648.

SUDMAN, S. (1966). Probability sampling with quotas. *Journal of the American Statistical Association*, 61, 749–771.

SUDMAN, S. (1967). *Reducing the cost of surveys.* (National Opinion Research Center. Monographs in Social Research, no. 10.) Aldine, Chicago.

SUKHATME, P. V. and SUKHATME, B. V. (2nd ed. 1970) *Sampling theory of surveys with applications.* Asia Publishing House, London.

SULLIVAN, M. A., Jr., QUEEN, S. A. and PATRICK, R. C., Jr. (1958). Participant observation as employed in the study of a military training program. *American Sociological Review*, **23**, 660–667.

SUMMERS, G. F., ed. (1970). *Attitude measurement*. Rand McNally, Chicago.

SURVEY RESEARCH CENTER, UNIVERSITY OF MICHIGAN (1951). *Field methods in sample interview surveys*. Survey Research Center, University of Michigan, Ann Arbor, Michigan.

SURVEY RESEARCH CENTER, UNIVERSITY OF MICHIGAN (1969). *Interviewers' manual*. Institute for Social Research, University of Michigan, Ann Arbor, Michigan.

TAYLOR, H. (1970). The power of the polls. *New Society*, no. 390 (19 March 1970), 477–479.

TAYLOR, S. J. L. (1954). *Good general practice: a report of a survey*. Oxford University Press, London.

THOMAS, M. (1969). *The Fire Service and its personnel: an enquiry undertaken for the Home Office*. (Government Social Survey, SS417B.) H.M.S.O., London.

THOMLINSON, R. (1965). *Sociological concepts and research: acquisition, analysis, and interpretation of social information*. Random House, New York.

THOMSON, W. E. (1959). ERNIE—a mathematical and statistical analysis. *Journal of the Royal Statistical Society, A*, **122**, 301–333.

THURSTONE, L. L. (1947). *Multiple-factor analysis: a development and expansion of the vectors of the mind*. University of Chicago Press, Chicago.

THURSTONE, L. L. and CHAVE, E. J. (1929). *The measurement of attitudes: a psychophysical method and some experiments with a scale for measuring attitude toward the church*. University of Chicago Press, Chicago.

TIPPETT, L. H. C. (1927). *Random sampling numbers*. (University College London, Department of Applied Statistics. Tracts for Computers, no. 15.) Cambridge University Press, London.

TIPPETT, L. H. C. (4th ed. 1952). *The methods of statistics*. Williams and Norgate, London.

TORGERSON, W. S. (1958). *Theory and methods of scaling*. Wiley, New York.

TOWNSEND, P. B. (1954). Measuring poverty. *British Journal of Sociology*, **5**, 130–137.

TOWNSEND, P. B. (1957). *The family life of old people: an inquiry in East London*. (Institute of Community Studies. Reports, no. 2.) Routledge and Kegan Paul, London; (abr. ed. with a new postscript, 1963) Penguin (Pelican) Books, Harmondsworth, Middlesex.

TOWNSEND, P. B. (1962a). The meaning of poverty. *British Journal of Sociology*, **13**, 210–227.

TOWNSEND, P. B. (1962b). *The last refuge: a survey of residential institutions and homes for the aged in England and Wales*. Routledge and Kegan Paul, London; (abr. ed. 1964) Routledge and Kegan Paul, London.

TOWNSEND, P. B. and WEDDERBURN, D. (1965). *The aged in the welfare state: an interim report of a survey of persons aged 65 and over in Britain, 1962 and 1963*. (Social Administration Research Trust. Occasional Papers on Social Administration, no. 14.) Bell, London.

TREASURE, J. A. P. (1953). Retail audit research. *Incorporated Statistician*, **4**, 148–159. Also in EDWARDS, F. (1956), *which see*.

TRENAMAN, J. M. and MCQUAIL, D. (1961). *Television and the political image: a study of the impact of television on the 1959 General Election.* Methuen, London.

TUFTE, E. R. ed. (1970). *The quantitative analyses of social problems.* Addison-Wesley, Reading, Mass.

TURNER, M. E. and STEVENS, C. D. (1959). The regression analysis of causal paths. *Biometrics*, **15**, 236–258.

TURNER, R. (1961). Inter-week variations in expenditure recorded during a two-week survey of family expenditure. *Applied Statistics*, **10**, 136–146.

TURNER, R. H. (1964). *The social context of ambition: a study of high-school seniors in Los Angeles.* Chandler, San Francisco.

U.K. BOARD OF TRADE (1969). Foreign travel and tourism in 1968. *Board of Trade Journal*, **197** (27 August 1969), 558–565.

U.K. CENTRAL STATISTICAL OFFICE (May 1968 onwards). *Statistical news. Developments in British official statistics.* [Quarterly.] H.M.S.O., London.

U.K. COMMITTEE ON HIGHER EDUCATION (1964). *Higher education: report of the committee appointed by the Prime Minister under the chairmanship of Lord Robbins 1961–63.* (Command Paper, 2154. Department of Education and Science.) H.M.S.O., London.

U.K. COMMITTEE ON HOUSING IN GREATER LONDON (1965). *Report of the Committee on Housing in Greater London.* (Command Paper, 2605. Ministry of Housing and Local Government.) H.M.S.O., London.

U.K. DEPARTMENT OF EDUCATION AND SCIENCE (1966). *Progress in reading, 1948–1964.* (Department of Education and Science. Pamphlets, no. 50.) H.M.S.O., London.

U.K. DEPARTMENT OF EDUCATION AND SCIENCE (1969). *Statistics of education, 1968. Vol. 2: G.C.E., C.S.E. and school leavers.* H.M.S.O., London.

U.K. DEPARTMENT OF EDUCATION AND SCIENCE and THE BRITISH COUNCIL (1969). *Scientific research in British universities and colleges, 1968–69. Vol. III: Social sciences (including government departments and other institutions).* H.M.S.O., London.

U.K. DEPARTMENT OF EMPLOYMENT AND PRODUCTIVITY (1969, 1970). *Family Expenditure Survey. Report for 1968, 1969.* H.M.S.O., London.

U.K. GENERAL REGISTER OFFICE (1966). *Classification of occupations, 1966.* H.M.S.O., London.

U.K. GENERAL REGISTER OFFICE (1968). *Census 1961. Great Britain. General Report.* H.M.S.O., London.

U.K. INTERDEPARTMENTAL COMMITTEE ON SOCIAL AND ECONOMIC RESEARCH (Guides to Official Sources) (1951–61).
(rev. ed. 1958). *No. 1. Labour statistics: material collected by the Ministry of Labour and National Service.*
(1951). *No. 2. Census reports of Great Britain, 1801–1931.*
(1953). *No. 3. Local government statistics.*
(1958). *No. 4. Agricultural and food statistics.*
(1961). *No. 5. Social security statistics: material collected by the Ministry of Pensions and National Insurance and the National Assistance Board.*
(1961). *No. 6. Census of production reports.*
H.M.S.O., London.

U.K. MINISTRY OF EDUCATION (1950). *Reading ability: some suggestions for helping the backward.* (Ministry of Education. Pamphlets, no. 18.) H.M.S.O., London.

U.K. MINISTRY OF EDUCATION (1957). *Standards of reading, 1948–1956.* (Ministry of Education. Pamphlets, no. 32.) H.M.S.O., London.

U.K. MINISTRY OF HEALTH (1968). *A pilot survey of the nutrition of young children in 1963.* (Reports on Public Health and Medical Subjects, no. 118.) H.M.S.O., London.

U.K. MINISTRY OF HOUSING AND LOCAL GOVERNMENT (1968). *Central Lancashire new town proposal: impact on northeast Lancashire; (consultants' appraisal).* (Robert Matthew, Johnson-Marshal & Partners and Economic Consultants Ltd.) H.M.S.O., London.

U.K. MINISTRY OF HOUSING AND LOCAL GOVERNMENT and MINISTRY OF TRANSPORT (1969). *Teesside survey and plan: final report to the Steering Committee. Volume 1: Policies and proposals.* (H. Wilson & L. Womersley, and Scott, Wilson, Kirkpatrick & Partners.) H.M.S.O., London.

U.K. MINISTRY OF HOUSING AND LOCAL GOVERNMENT and WELSH OFFICE (1969). *Rates and rateable values in England and Wales 1969–70.* H.M.S.O., London.

U.K. MINISTRY OF LABOUR (1961–1967). *Family Expenditure Survey. Reports for 1957–59, 1960 & 1961, 1962, 1963, 1964, 1965, 1966.* H.M.S.O., London.

U.K. MINISTRY OF LABOUR AND NATIONAL SERVICE (1940–41). Weekly expenditure of working-class households in the U.K. in 1937–38. *Labour Gazette,* December 1940, January 1941 and February 1941.

U.K. MINISTRY OF LABOUR AND NATIONAL SERVICE (1957). *Household expenditure, 1953–54: report of an enquiry.* H.M.S.O., London.

U.K. MINISTRY OF PENSIONS AND NATIONAL INSURANCE (1954). *National insurance retirement pensions: reasons given for retiring or continuing at work. Report of an enquiry.* H.M.S.O., London.

U.K. MINISTRY OF PENSIONS AND NATIONAL INSURANCE (1966). *Financial and other circumstances of retirement pensioners: report of an enquiry by the Ministry of Pensions and National Insurance with the co-operation of the National Assistance Board.* H.M.S.O., London.

U.K. MINISTRY OF SOCIAL SECURITY (1967). *Circumstances of families: report of an enquiry by the Ministry of Pensions and National Insurance with the co-operation of the National Assistance Board* [subsequently combined to form the Ministry of Social Security]. H.M.S.O., London.

U.K. MINISTRY OF TRANSPORT (1967). *National Travel Survey 1964: Preliminary report.* Ministry of Transport, London.

U.K. NATIONAL BOARD FOR PRICES AND INCOMES (1968). *Increases in rents of local authority housing.* [and] *Statistical supplement.* (Command Papers, 3604 and 3604–1. National Board for Prices and Incomes. Reports, 62 and 62 (Supplement).) H.M.S.O., London.

U.K. NATIONAL BOARD FOR PRICES AND INCOMES (1970). *Standing reference on the pay of university teachers in Great Britain. Second report.* (Command Paper, 4334.) H.M.S.O., London.

U.K. NATIONAL FOOD SURVEY COMMITTEE (1951). *Urban working-class household diet, 1940–1949. First Report.* (Ministry of Food.) H.M.S.O., London.

U.K. NATIONAL FOOD SURVEY COMMITTEE (1968). *Household food consumption and expenditure. Annual report, 1966. With a supplement giving provisional estimates for 1967.* (Ministry of Agriculture, Fisheries and Food.) H.M.S.O., London.

U.K. ROYAL COMMISSION ON DOCTORS' AND DENTISTS' REMUNERATION (1960). *Report of the Royal Commission on Doctors' and Dentists' Remuneration, 1957–1960.* [and] *Supplement to Report: further statistical appendix.* (Command Papers, 939 and 1064.) H.M.S.O., London.

U.K. ROYAL COMMISSION ON LOCAL GOVERNMENT IN ENGLAND (1969). *Community attitudes survey: England.* (Research Studies no. 9. Research Services Ltd., prepared for the Government Social Survey.) H.M.S.O., London.

U.K. ROYAL COMMISSION ON MEDICAL EDUCATION (1968). *Royal Commission on Medical Education, 1965–68. Report.* (Command Paper, 3569). H.M.S.O., London.

U.K. ROYAL COMMISSION ON POPULATION (1950). The relations between intelligence and fertility. *Papers of the Royal Commission on Population, Volume V: Memoranda presented to the Royal Commission* (H.M.S.O., London), 35–75.

UNITED NATIONS STATISTICAL OFFICE (1949 onwards). *Sample surveys of current interest.* (Statistical Papers, Series C, nos. 2–12.) United Nations, New York.

UNITED NATIONS STATISTICAL OFFICE (1950). *The preparation of sampling survey reports.* (Department of Economic Affairs. Statistical Papers, Series C, no. 1.) United Nations, Lake Success, N.Y.

UNITED NATIONS STATISTICAL OFFICE (1960). *A short manual on sampling. Volume 1. Elements of sample survey theory.* (Department of Economic and Social Affairs. Studies in Methods, Series F, no. 9.) United Nations, New York.

UNITED NATIONS STATISTICAL OFFICE (1964). *Recommendations for the preparation of sample survey reports (provisional issue).* (Department of Economic and Social Affairs. Statistical Papers, Series C, no. 1, rev. 2.) United Nations, New York.

U.S. BUREAU OF THE BUDGET (1952). *Standards for statistical surveys.* Bureau of the Budget, Washington, D.C.

U.S. BUREAU OF THE CENSUS (1963a). *The Current Population Survey: a report on methodology.* (U.S. Department of Commerce. Technical Paper no. 7.) U.S. Government Printing Office, Washington, D.C.

U.S. BUREAU OF THE CENSUS (1963b). *Evaluation and research program of the U.S. Censuses of Population and Housing, 1960: background, procedures, and forms.* (U.S. Department of Commerce. Series ER60, no. 1.) U.S. Government Printing Office, Washington, D.C.

U.S. BUREAU OF THE CENSUS (1964a). *Evaluation and research program of the U.S. Censuses of Population and Housing, 1960: record check studies of population coverage.* (U.S. Department of Commerce. Series ER60, no. 2.) U.S. Government Printing Office, Washington, D.C.

U.S. BUREAU OF THE CENSUS (1964b). *Evaluation and research program of the U.S. Censuses of Population and Housing, 1960: accuracy of data on housing characteristics.* (U.S. Department of Commerce. Series ER60, no. 3.) U.S. Government Printing Office, Washington, D.C.

U.S. BUREAU OF THE CENSUS (1964c). *Evaluation and research program of the U.S. Censuses of Population and Housing, 1960: accuracy of data on population characteristics as measured by reinterviews.* (U.S.

Department of Commerce. Series ER60, no. 4.) U.S. Government Printing Office, Washington, D.C.

U.S. BUREAU OF THE CENSUS (1964d). *Evaluation and research program of the U.S. Censuses of Population and Housing, 1960: accuracy of data on population characteristics as measured by CPS-Census match.* (U.S. Department of Commerce. Series ER60, no. 5.) U.S. Government Printing Office, Washington, D.C.

U.S. BUREAU OF THE CENSUS (1965). *Evaluation and research program of the U.S. Censuses of Population and Housing, 1960: the employer record check.* (U.S. Department of Commerce. Series ER60, no. 6.) U.S. Government Printing Office, Washington, D.C.

U.S. BUREAU OF THE CENSUS (1966). *Atlantida: a case study in household sample surveys. Unit IV, sample design.* (U.S. Department of Commerce. Series ISPO 1, no. 1-E.) Bureau of the Census, Washington, D.C.

U.S. BUREAU OF THE CENSUS (1968a). *Evaluation and research program of the U.S. Censuses of Population and Housing, 1960: effects of interviewers and crew leaders.* (U.S. Department of Commerce. Series ER60, no. 7.) U.S. Government Printing Office, Washington, D.C.

U.S. BUREAU OF THE CENSUS (1968b). *Supplemental courses for case studies in surveys and censuses: sampling lectures.* (U.S. Department of Commerce. ISP Supplemental Course Series, no. 1.) Bureau of the Census, Washington, D.C.

U.S. DEPARTMENT OF AGRICULTURE (1952). *Problems of establishing a consumer panel.* (Marketing Research Report no. 8, Bureau of Agricultural Economics.) Dept. of Agriculture, Washington, D.C.

U.S. DEPARTMENT OF HEALTH, EDUCATION, AND WELFARE: PUBLIC HEALTH SERVICE (1954). *Smoking and health: report of the Advisory Committee to the Surgeon General of the Public Health Service.* (U.S. Public Health Service Publications, no. 1103.) U.S. Government Printing Office, Washington, D.C.; (reprinted 1954) Van Nostrand, Princeton, N.J.

U.S. NATIONAL CENTER FOR HEALTH STATISTICS (1961). *Health interview responses compared with medical records: a study of illness and hospitalization experience among health plan enrollees as reported in household interviews, in comparison with information recorded by the physicians and hospitals.* (Vital and Health Statistics. Series 2, no. 7.) U.S. Department of Health, Education, and Welfare, Public Health Service, Washington, D.C.

U.S. NATIONAL CENTER FOR HEALTH STATISTICS (1963). *Origin, program, and operation of the U.S. National Health Survey.* (Public Health Service Publication, no. 1000, Series 1, number 1.) U.S. Government Printing Office, Washington, D.C.

U.S. NATIONAL CENTER FOR HEALTH STATISTICS (1965a). *Reporting of hospitalization in the Health Interview Survey: a methodological study of several factors affecting the reporting of hospital episodes.* (U.S. Department of Health, Education, and Welfare. Vital and Health Statistics, Series 2, no. 6.) U.S. Government Printing Office, Washington, D.C.

U.S. NATIONAL CENTER FOR HEALTH STATISTICS (1965b). *Comparison of hospitalization reporting in three survey procedures: a study of alternative survey methods for collection of hospitalization data from household respondents.* (U.S. Department of Health, Education, and

Welfare. Vital and Health Statistics, Series 2, no. 8.) U.S. Government Printing Office, Washington, D.C.

UTTING, J. E. G. and COLE, D. E. (1953). Sample surveys for the social accounts of the household sector. *Bulletin of the Oxford Institute of Statistics*, **15**, 1–24.

UTTING, J. E. G. and COLE, D. E. (1954). Sampling for social accounts—some aspects of the Cambridgeshire Survey. *Bulletin of the International Statistical Institute*, **34**(2), 301–328.

VELDMAN, D. J. (1967). *Fortran programming for the behavioral sciences.* Holt, Rinehart and Winston, New York.

VERNON, P. E. (1960). *Intelligence and attainment tests.* University of London Press, London.

VOIGHT, R. B. and KRIESBERG, M. (1952). Some principles of processing census and survey data. *Journal of the American Statistical Association*, **47**, 222–231.

WADSWORTH, R. N. (1952). The experience of a user of a consumer panel. *Applied Statistics*, **1**, 169–178.

WALLIS, W. A. and ROBERTS, H. V. (1956). *Statistics: A new approach.* Free Press, Glencoe, Ill.; Macmillan, London.

WARNER, S. L. (1965). Randomized response: a survey technique for eliminating evasive answer bias. *Journal of the American Statistical Association*, **60**, 63–69.

WEBB, B. (1926). *My apprenticeship.* Longmans, London.

WEBB, E. J., CAMPBELL, D. T., SCHWARTZ, R. D. and SECHREST, L. (1966). *Unobtrusive measures: non-reactive research in the social sciences.* Rand McNally, Chicago.

WEISS, C. H. (1968–69). Validity of welfare mothers' interview responses. *Public Opinion Quarterly*, **32**, 622–633.

WELLS, A. F. (1935). *The local social survey in Great Britain.* Allen and Unwin, London.

WEST MIDLAND GROUP ON POST-WAR RECONSTRUCTION AND PLANNING (1946). *English county: a planning survey of Herefordshire.* Faber, London.

WEST MIDLAND GROUP ON POST-WAR RECONSTRUCTION AND PLANNING (1948). *Conurbation: a planning survey of Birmingham and the Black Country.* Architectural Press, London.

WHITFIELD, J. W. (1950). The imaginary questionnaire. *Quarterly Journal of Experimental Psychology*, **2**, 76–87.

WHYTE, W. F. (2nd ed. 1955). *Street corner society: the social structure of an Italian slum.* University of Chicago Press, Chicago.

WILKINS, L. T. (1949). *Prediction of the demand for campaign stars and medals.* (Government Social Survey, no. 109.) Central Office of Information, London.

WILKINS, L. T. (1952). Estimating the social class of towns. *Applied Statistics*, **1**, 27–33.

WILLMOTT, P. (1963). *The evolution of a community: a study of Dagenham after forty years.* (Institute of Community Studies Report, no. 8.) Routledge and Kegan Paul, London.

WILLMOTT, P. and YOUNG, M. D. (1960). *Family and class in a London suburb.* (Institute of Community Studies Report, no. 4.) Routledge and Kegan Paul, London.

WILSON, E. C. (1954). New light on old problems through panel research.

ESOMAR Journal (European Society for Opinion Surveys and Market Research), no. 1, 87–92.

WITTS, L. J., ed. (2nd ed. 1964). *Medical surveys and clinical trials: some methods and applications of group research in medicine*. Oxford University Press, London.

WOLD, H. (1956). Causal inference from observational data. A review of ends and means. *Journal of the Royal Statistical Society*, A, **119**, 28–60.

WRIGHT, S. (1934). The method of path coefficients. *Annals of Mathematical Statistics*, **5**, 161–215.

WRIGHT, S. (1960). Path coefficients and path regressions: alternative or complementary concepts? *Biometrics*, **16**, 189–202.

YAMANE, T. (1967). *Elementary sampling theory*. Prentice-Hall, Englewood Cliffs, N.J.

YATES, F. (1946). A review of recent statistical developments in sampling and sampling surveys. *Journal of the Royal Statistical Society*, A, **109**, 12–43.

YATES, F. (3rd ed. 1960). *Sampling methods for censuses and surveys*. Griffin, London; Hafner, New York.

YEE, A. H. and GAGE, N. L. (1968). Techniques for estimating the source and direction of causal influence in panel data. *Psychological Bulletin*, **70**, 115–126.

YOUNG, M. D. and WILLMOTT, P. (1957). *Family and kinship in east London*. (Institute of Community Studies Report. no. 1.) Routledge and Kegan Paul, London; (rev. ed. 1962) Penguin (Pelican) Books, Harmondsworth, Middlesex.

YOUNG, P. V. (4th ed. 1966). *Scientific social surveys and research: an introduction to the background, content, methods, principles, and analysis of social studies*. Prentice-Hall, Englewood Cliffs, N.J.

YOUNG, T. (1934). *Becontree and Dagenham. The story of the growth of a housing estate*. Samuel Sidders, London.

YULE, G. U. and KENDALL, M. G. (14th ed. 1950). *An introduction to the theory of statistics*. Griffin, London.

ZARKOVICH, S. S. (1965). *Sampling methods and censuses*. Food and Agriculture Organization of the United Nations, Rome.

ZARKOVICH, S. S. (1966). *Quality of statistical data*. Food and Agriculture Organization of the United Nations, Rome.

ZEISEL, H. (4th ed. 1957). *Say it with figures*. Harper, New York.

ZWEIG, F. (1948). *Labour, life and poverty*. Gollancz, London.

Index of Names and Organizations

Abel-Smith, B., 11, 32
Abernathy, J. R., *see* Greenberg and others (1969a), 329, 330
Abrams, M. A., 39
Abul-Ela, A.-L. A., 328. *See also* Greenberg and others (1969b), 328
Adams, F. G., 326 n
Akhurst, B. A., 38
Alberman, E. D., 28
Alker, H. R., 451 n
Allaway, A. J., *see* Sheffield Social Survey Committee (1931–33), 9
Allen, P. G., 22
Allen, Sir Roy, 59
Allerton, R. H., 37
Allport, G. W., 255
Anderson, C. A., 30
Andrews, F. M., 457, 479
Angell, R., 255
Aronson, E., 255, 271, 274, 302, 349, 376, 408, 438
Atkinson, J., 277, 287, 301, 315, 316
Attwood Statistics, 141, 141 n
Audits of Great Britain Ltd, 24, 248

Backett, E. M., 32
Backstrom, C. H., 39, 52
Baerwaldt, N., *see* Morgan and others (1966), 442, 478
Baggaley, A. P., 377
Bailar, B. A., 408
Bakke, E. W., 31
Bancroft, T. A., *see* Kempthorne and others (1954), 479
Bang, S., 478
Banton M. P., 36
Barr H., 38

Barry, J. W., 437
Bartholomew, D. J., 177, 186
Beamish, P., *see* Kay and others (1964), 27
Bechhofer, F., *see* Goldthorpe and others (1968a, 1968b), 35
Becker, H. S., 252, 255
Beeching, Lord, 59, 484
Bell, C. R., 23
Belson, W. A., 33, 39, 222, 237, 281, 328, 330, 347, 349, 409
Benjamin, B., 20, 60
Bennett, J. W., 255
Benney, M., 34
Berelson, B. R., 438
Berkson, J., 226 n
Bershad, M. A., 381 n, 408, 409. *See also* Hansen and others (1961), 382, 401 n
Beveridge, W. I. B., 236
Birch, A. H., 34
Blackstone, T. A. V., 32
Blalock, A. B., 117, 237, 376, 384 n, 479
Blalock, H. M. Jr., 78, 117, 207 n, 237, 376, 384 n, 459 n, 463, 478, 479
Blankenship, A. B., 408
Blau, P. M., 31, 442, 479
Blomfield, J. M., 27, 139 n, 145
Blumler, J. G., 35, 145
Blunden, R. M., 163, 186, 187
Bogardus, E. S., 377
Bonham, D. G., 28
Bonham, J., 35
Booker, H. S., 389 n
Booth, C., 6, 7–8, 9, 58, 242
Borgatta, E. F., 451 n, 478, 479. *See also* Stouffer and others (1952), 377

Borko, H., 438
Borus, M. E., 408
Bott, E., 23
Boudon, R., 479
Bournville Village Trust, 11
Bowley, A. L., 6, 9, 58
Boyajy, J. S., 437
Brazer, H. E., *see* Morgan and others (1962), 442, 478
Brennan, T., 12, 22
Brillinger, D. R., 208 n
British Broadcasting Corporation, 17–18, 33, 58, 135, 279, 284
British Council, 42
British Institute of Public Opinion (B.I.P.O.), 18, 289, 290. *See also* Gallup Poll, Social Surveys (Gallup Poll) Ltd
British Market Research Bureau (B.M.R.B.), 131, 170, 171, 176, 182, 183, 188 n, 199, 201, 262, 284
British Medical Association, 28, 229, 240
British Museum, 161
British Sociological Association, 417
British Tourist Authority, 33
British Travel Association, 33
Brooke, E. M., 26, 349, 407 n
Brookes, B. C., 78
Brown, A. C., 257. *See also* Shepherd and others (1966), 26, 362
Brown, M. L., 267
Brown, W., 354
Brownlee, K. A., 226 n
Brunner, G. A., 176
Buchanan, C., 59, 484
Bucher, R., 281 n
Buckland, W. R., 54
Burnett-Hurst, A. R., 9
Burt, C., 28, 37
Butler, D. H. E., 35, 145
Butler, N. R., 28. *See also* Pringle and others (1966), 139 n
Bynner, J. M., 375

Cahalan, D., 408
Campaign for Nuclear Disarmament, 35
Campbell, D. T., 215, 216, 218, 224, 224 n, 236, 247, 357, 376, 479. *See also* Webb and others (1966), 255
Campbell, P., 34
Cannell, C. F., 258 n, 269, 271, 274, 276, 302, 346, 349, 408

Cantril, H., 40, 279, 317, 324, 346, 349, 395, 408
Carroll, S. J., 176
Carr-Saunders, A. M., 37
Cartwright, A., 21, 28, 32, 123, 175, 263, 269, 391
Cartwright, D. P., 437. *See also* Katz and others (1954), 302
Cattell, R. B., 377
Cauter, T., 33, 188 n, 240, 464
Central Advisory Council for Education (England), 3, 29
Centre for Urban Studies, University College, London, 12, 21, 22
Chapin, F. S., 236
Chave, E. J., 377
Chilton, R. J., 371 n
Coale, A. J., 437
Cochran, W. G., 78, 80 n, 95, 117, 167 n, 185 n, 186, 187, 224 n, 236, 237, 311 n, 381 n, 382 n, 384 n, 409, 454, 467, 478
Cockburn, C., *see* Donnison and others (1961), 21
Cohen, J., 478
Cohen, W. J., *see* Morgan and others (1962), 442, 478
Cole, D. E., 25, 37, 172, 275, 288
College of General Practitioners, 26
Cook, S. W., 117. *See also* Jahoda and others (1951), 250, 255; Selltiz and others (1959), 39, 60, 215, 236, 255, 257, 302, 327 n, 328, 349, 376, 437, 478
Cooley, W. W., 478
Coombs, C. H., 352 n, 366 n
Coombs, L., 137 n, 239
Cooney, E. W., *see* Brennan and others (1954), 22
Cooper, B., 257. *See also* Shepherd and others (1966), 26, 362
Corlett, T., 14, 15, 145, 159, 161, 170, 171, 173 n, 174, 186, 187, 195, 196, 201, 208, 209. *See also* Donnison and others (1961), 21; Gray and others (1951), 196
Cornfield, J., 226 n
Court, S. D. M., *see* Miller and others (1960), 28; Spence and others (1954), 28
Cox, D. R., 224 n, 232, 237, 455 n
Cox, G. M., 237
Crawford, M. D., 27
Crespi, L. P., 408
Crewe, I. M., 31

Crossley, H. M., 408
Crowther, Sir Geoffrey, 29, 59, 484
Crutchfield, R. S., 408
Cullingworth, J. B., 21
Cushion, A. A., 26
Cutler, S. J., 226 n

Dalenius, T., 210
Dalton, M., 255
Daniel, W. W., 36
David, M. H., 408. See also Morgan and others (1962), 442, 478
David, S. T., 326, 389 n
Davie, R., 28. See also Pringle and others (1966), 139 n
Davies, M., 38
Davies, O. L., 237
Day, D. J., 239
Deming, W. E., 68, 117, 124, 126, 145, 186, 210, 408, 438
Department of Applied Economics (Cambridge University), 25, 288
De Reuck, A. V. S., 26
Deutsch, M., 117. See also Jahoda and others (1951), 250, 255; Selltiz and others (1959), 39, 60, 215, 236, 255, 257, 302, 327 n, 328, 349, 376, 437, 478
Dick, W. F. L., 78
Dickson, W. J., 219, 297 n
Didcott, P. J., see Belson and others (1968), 39
Doby, J. T., 39
Dohrenwend, B. S., 302. See also Richardson and others (1965), 349
Doll, R., 226, 227, 228, 229, 229 n
Donnison, D. V., 21
Douglas, J. W. B., 27, 29, 139 n, 145
Downham, J. S., 15 n, 33, 240, 437, 464, 464 n
Draper, N. R., 478
Duncan, J. A., 349
Duncan, O. D., 31, 418, 442, 458 n, 459, 461, 479
Dunn, J. E., 239
Dunphy, D. C., see Stone and others (1966), 438
Dupeux, G., 35
Durant, H., 18, 408
Durant, R., 11
Durbin, J., 136, 169, 174, 175, 177 n, 178, 178 n, 180, 181, 188 n, 210, 233, 289, 290, 293, 401 n, 424, 425, 426, 427, 476
Duverger, M., 39, 255

Eberhart, J. C., 408
Eckland, B. K., 142
Eckler, A. R., 393, 401 n, 408
Economist Intelligence Unit, 12
Eden, F., 6
Edwards, A. L., 376, 377
Edwards, F., 15 n, 40, 161, 171, 174, 176, 188 n, 200, 209, 301, 392, 437
Ehrenberg, A. S. C., 141 n, 236
El-Badry, M. A., 408
Eldersveld, S., see Katz and others (1954), 302
Emmett, B. P., 145, 186, 223, 237
Erritt, M. J., 25
Essex University, 42
Evans, J. C. G., see Backett and others (1953, 1954), 32
Evans, W. D., 408, 413 n
Eysenck, H. J., 226 n, 229 n, 366, 376

Fasteau, H. H., 437
Feldman, J. J., 408
Fellegi, I. P., 409
Fennessey, J., 451 n, 458, 478
Feber, R., 145, 408
Ferguson, T., 37
Festinger, L., 39, 60, 78, 117, 236, 252 n, 255, 302, 349, 373, 437
Finch, S., see Morton-Williams and others (1966), 32
Finney, D. J., 47 n
Firth, R., 255
Fishbein, M., 376
Fisher, G., 408
Fisher, H., 408
Fisher, R. A., 82, 237
Fiske, D. W., 357, 376
Fiske, M., 302
Fitzpatrick, T. B., 210
Flanders, A., 31
Floud, J., 30, 31
Folkard, S., 38
Forcese, D. P., 39
Ford, P., 9
Forsythe, J., see Ferber and others (1969), 408
Fothergill, J. E., 301, 392, 478
Fowler, F. J., 258 n, 269, 302
Frankel, M. R., 209
Frankenberg, R., 22
Frankland, P., 161, 174, 186
Frechtling, J. A., see Sirken and others (1958), 408
Freedman, R., 137 n, 239, 255

French, J. R. P. Jr., 236
Freund, R. J., 438
Friend, I., 326 n
Fritz, C. E., see Bucher and others (1956), 281 n
Fruchter, B., 377
Fulton, Lord, 31, 484

Gage, N. L., 236, 479
Gales, K. E., 32, 401 n, 464 n. See also Blackstone and others (1970), 32
Gallup, G. H., 345, 349
Gallup Poll, 1, 18, 349, 359. See also British Institute of Public Opinion, Social Surveys (Gallup Poll) Ltd
Galtung, J., 39, 478
Gavron, H., 23
Gee, F. A., 161, 162, 163 n, 186
General Medical Council, 229
Geoffrey, L., 438
Gibbens, T. C. N., 38
Glass, D. V., 5, 20, 31, 39, 54, 185, 418, 442
Glass, R., 11, 12, 13, 21, 22, 36, 39
Glock, C. Y., 7, 145, 255
Goldberg, S. A., 408
Goldstein, H., 145
Goldthorpe, J. H., 35
Goode, W. J., 39, 60, 269, 302, 376, 437, 468
Goodman, L. A., 371 n
Goodman, N., 38
Gordon, D. A., 408
Gottschalk, L., 255
Gowen, J. W., see Kempthorne and others (1954), 479
Gowers, E. A., 320
Graham, P., 26
Gray, A. P., 34
Gray, P. G., 14, 15, 145, 159, 161, 162, 163 n, 170, 171, 173 n, 174, 178, 186, 187, 195, 196, 201, 209, 239, 262, 269, 349, 401, 401 n
Gray, S., 187
Greater London Council, 21, 34
Grebenik, E., 5, 20, 54, 185
Green, B. F., 370, 371 n, 376, 438
Greenberg, B. G., 328, 329, 330. See also Abul-Ela and others (1967), 328
Greenwood, E., 236
Grey, E., 32
Grundy, F., 12
Guest, L., 408
Guilford, J. P., 376, 377

Guthrie, H. W., see Ferber and others (1969), 408
Guttman, L., 366 n, 369, 372, 373. See also Guttman scales

Hadfield, S. J., see British Medical Association (1953), 28
Hadley, R. D., see Blackstone and others (1970), 32
Haenszel, W., see Cornfield and others (1959), 226 n
Hall, J., 418
Haller, A. O., see Duncan and others (1968), 458, 479
Halsey, A. H., 30, 31, 32
Hamilton, J. G. M., see British Medical Association (1953), 28
Hammond, E. C., see Cornfield and others (1959), 226 n
Hammond, P. E., 255
Hansen, M. H., 78, 81, 117, 145, 158 n, 178, 209, 267, 378 n, 381 n, 382, 401 n, 403, 408, 409, 438
Hanson, R. H., 401, 401 n, 408
Harewood, J., 210
Hargreaves, D. H., 30
Harman, H. H., 377
Harris, A. I., 37, 437
Harris, C., 23
Harris, C. W., 215, 236
Hart, C. W., 408
Hartley, H. O., 178, 438
Hatch, S., 32
Hatt, P. K., 39, 60, 269, 302, 376, 437, 468
Hauser, P. M., 145, 408
Hays, D. G., see Stouffer and others (1952), 377
Hays, W. L., 152, 207 n, 478
Heady, J. A., see Backett and others (1954), 32; Morris and others (1953), 27
Heise, D. R., 479
Henry, A. F., see Stouffer and others (1952), 377
Henry, H., 400
Henry, N. W., 377
Hess, I., 177, 209, 210
Heyns, R. W., 252 n
Higher Education Research Unit, London School of Economics, 32
Hill, A. Bradford, 26, 27, 78, 226, 227, 228, 229, 229 n, 237
Hilton J 58

Himmelweit, H. T., 33, 232
Hirschi, T., 478
Hochstim, J. R., 239, 259, 267, 269, 401 n
Hodge, R. W., 384 n, 479
Hodges, J. L., 152
Hogg, M. H., 9
Hole, V., 22
Holland, Sir Milner, 21, 59
Holsti, O. R., 438. See also North and others (1963), 438
Hood, R. G., 38
Horst, P., 377
Horton, M., 239
Horvitz, D. G., 384 n. See also Abul-Ela and others (1967), 328; Greenberg and others (1969a), 329, 330; Greenberg and others (1969b), 328, 329
House, J. W., 13
Houthakker, H. S., 442
Huff, D., 479
Hull, T. E., 438
Hunt, A., 33
Hursh, G. D., 39, 52
Hurwitz, W. N., 78, 81, 117, 145, 158 n, 178, 209, 267, 378 n, 381 n, 401 n, 408, 409, 438. See also Hansen and others (1961), 382, 401 n; Hansen and others (1953), 403
Hyman, H. H., 121, 214, 224 n, 269, 275, 300, 302, 311 n, 385 n, 386, 386 n, 408, 448 n, 478. See also Mosteller and others (1949), 19, 20, 39, 317, 345, 346, 349, 399, 477

India, Cabinet Secretariat, 210
Indian Statistical Institute, 145
Ingram, J. J., see Fasteau and others (1964), 437
Institute for Social Sciences, Cologne, 293
Institute of Community Studies, 23
Institute of Practitioners in Advertising, 174
Institute of Race Relations, 36
Isaacs, S., 243

Jackson, B., 30
Jackson, S., 175
Jaeger, C. M., 408
Jahoda, M., 117, 250, 255, 376. See also Selltiz and others (1959), 39, 60, 215,

236, 255, 257, 302, 327 n, 328, 349, 376, 437, 478
Janda, K. F., 438
Jessen, R. J., 143
Jobling, D., 371 n
John Lewis Partnership, 31
Johnson, N. L., 384 n, 408
Johnston, J., 384
Joint Industry Committee for National Readership Surveys (JICNARS), 16, 163 n, 209, 279
Joint Industry Committee for Television Advertising Research (JICTAR), 17, 33, 248
Jones, D. C., 9, 39, 418
Jones, G. P., see Sheffield Social Survey Committee (1931–33), 9
Jones, P., 196. See also Gray and others (1951), 196
Jones, W. R., 30
Juster, F. T., 326 n, 408

Kahn, R. L., 271, 274, 276, 302, 346, 349, 408
Kalton, G., 78, 454. See also Shepherd and others (1966), 26, 362
Kaplan, A. B., 236
Kapp, R. O., 479
Katz, D., 39, 60, 78, 117, 236, 252 n, 255, 302, 349, 373, 408, 437
Kay, D. W. K., 27
Keele University, 33
Kelsall, R. K., 31, 32
Kempthorne, O., 479
Kemsley, W. F. F., 24, 171, 195 n, 201, 209, 269, 322, 349, 401 n, 407 n
Kendall, M. G., 42, 54, 78, 80 n, 82, 117, 153, 154, 386 n, 401 n, 478
Kendall, P. L., 302, 478
Kenney, K. C., 377
Kerlinger, F. N., 236, 376, 377
Keyfitz, N., 145, 233
Khan, S., 95
King, A., 35
King, A. J., 143
Kinsey, A. C., 23, 78, 311 n, 325, 327 n, 394, 467
Kish, L., 60, 78, 80 n, 89, 92 n, 94, 95, 101, 115 n, 117, 124, 143, 145, 154, 158 n, 165 n, 167 n, 174, 177, 177 n, 186, 187, 198, 199, 202, 203, 203 n, 207, 208, 209, 210, 224 n, 234 n, 236, 274, 398 n, 401, 402, 405, 408, 409, 442, 443, 475 n, 478

Klein, D., 302. *See also* Richardson and others (1965), 349
Kluckhohn, C., 255
Kluckhohn, F. R., 255
Knight, E. M., 13
Knox, E. G., *see* Miller and others (1960), 28
Koch, G. G., 384 n
Koch, S., 377
Kokan, A. R., 95
Kornhauser, A., 324, 349
Krausz, E., 165 n
Kriesberg, M., 438
Kruskal, J. B., 366 n
Kruskal, W. H., 247
Kuenstler, W. P., 437
Kuper, L., 22

Lahiri, D. B., 115 n, 145
Lambert, R., 243
Land, H., 11
Land, K. C., 479
Lansing J. B., 398 n, 409
Lasswell, H. D., 437
Lavers, G. R., 10, 33
Lawley, D. N., 377
Lazarsfeld, P. F., 145, 302, 323, 345 n, 372, 377, 438, 448 n, 478
Lazerwitz, B., 117
Lee, A. M., *see* Katz and others (1954), 302
Lehmann, E. L., 152
Leicester University, 33
Leites, N., 438
Le Mesurier, T. H. F. T., 141 n
Lewis, O., 254 n
Lewis, R. W., *see* Blackstone and others (1970), 32
Lewis-Faning, E., 20, 321
Li, C. C., 479
Liepmann, K. K., 34
Likert, R., 377. *See also* Likert scaling
Lilienfeld, A. M., *see* Cornfield and others (1959), 226 n
Lindzey, G., 255, 271, 274, 302, 349, 376, 408, 438
Lingoes, J. C., 366 n
Little, K. L., 36
Liverpool University, 31
Lock, C. M., 12
Lockwood, D., *see* Goldthorpe and others (1968a, 1968b), 35
Logan, W. P. D., 26, 349, 407 n
Lohnes, P. R., 478

London Borough of Camden, 21
London School of Economics, 31, 32, 39, 135, 262, 289
London Transport, 248
Lord, F. M., 354, 376
Louis Harris (Research) Ltd, 18
Lupton, T., 31
Lush, J. L., *see* Kempthorne and others (1954), 479
Lydall, H. F., 25, 95, 173, 182, 200, 201, 441
Lynd, H. M., 251
Lynd, R. S., 251

McCabe, S., 26
McCall, G. J., 255
McCarthy, P. J., 78, 117, 133, 145, 187, 209. *See also* Mosteller and others (1949), 19, 20, 39, 317, 345, 346, 349, 399, 477
McCracken, D. D., 438
McFarlane, C., 210
McGinnis, R., 234 n, 478
McKennell, A. C., 354, 366, 366 n, 375
Mackenzie, H. C., 34
McKenzie, R. T., 35
McNemar, Q., 349, 384, 478
McQuail, D., 35, 145
Madge, J. H., 39, 236, 253 n, 255, 302
Madow, W. G., 78, 81, 117, 145, 158 n, 210, 378 n, 409, 438. *See also* Hansen and others (1953), 403
Mahalanobis, P. C., 126, 145, 400
Mann, P. H., 39
Mannheim, H., 14, 37, 442
Mannheimer, D., 121
Mark, M. L., 39, 269, 438
Market Research Society, 15 n, 17, 17 n, 236, 282, 285, 286, 287, 302, 376, 417 n, 479
Marks, E. S., 397, 401, 401 n, 408. *See also* Mosteller and others (1949), 19, 20, 39, 317, 345, 346, 349, 399, 477
Marplan Ltd, 18
Marquis, K. H., 231, 302, 322
Marriott, R., 298
Marsden, D., 23, 30
Martin, C. E., *see* Kinsey and others (1948), 311 n, 325, 327 n, 394; Kinsey and others (1953), 311 n, 327 n
Martin, J. P., 32, 38
Massey, P., 24
Mass Observation, 252, 255

Maud, Sir John, 484
Mauldin, W. P., 397, 408
Maxwell, A. E., 377
Mayhew, H., 6, 34, 298
Maynes, E. S., 394 n, 408. *See also* Ferber and others (1969), 408; Sirken and others (1958), 408
Medical Research Council, 27, 226
Melhuish, R. M., 16
Merseyside Area Land-Use Transportation Study, 34
Merton, R. K., 302, 478
Michigan University, 141, 202, 209, 274, 290, 290 n, 291, 302, 437
Miller, D. C., 376
Miller, F. J. W., 28. *See also* Spence and others (1954), 28
Miller, S. M., 30, 250
Millerson, G. L., *see* Belson and others (1968), 39
Millham, S., *see* Lambert (1968), 243
Milne, R. S., 34
Minton, G., *see* Fasteau and others (1964), 437
Monk, D. M., 223
Mooney, H. W., 349, 391, 408
Moore, R., 36
Morgan, J. N., 442, 457, 478
Morris, J. N., 27
Morris, P. J., 26, 38
Morrison, D. F., 478
Morton-Williams, R., 32
Moser, C. A., 60, 130, 131, 134, 135, 137, 145, 172, 188 n, 280 n, 303 n, 349, 390 n, 408, 444
Moss, L., 14, 246
Mosteller, F., 19, 20, 39, 78, 317, 345, 346, 349, 395, 399, 477. *See also* Cochran and others (1953, 1954), 311
Muehl, D., 437
Mueller, E., 326 n
Murthy, M. N., 117, 409
Myers, R. J., 407 n

National Birthday Trust, 28
National Corporation for the Care of Old People, 37
National Foundation for Educational Research, 30
National Institute of Economic and Social Research, 42
National Opinion Polls Ltd, 18
National Opinion Research Center

(N.O.R.C.), University of Chicago, 128, 135, 275, 300, 302, 385, 385 n, 386, 387, 402, 404, 408
Neter, J., 145, 340, 349, 391 n, 394 n, 408
Netherlands Institute of Public Opinion, 359
Nett, R., 39, 254 n, 255
Newsom, Sir John, 59
Newson, E., 23
Newson, J., 23
Nicholls, D. C., 33
Nicholson, J. L., 24, 25, 269
Nisselson, H., 397, 408
North, R. C., 438
Northern Region Planning Committee, 33
Novick, M. R., 354, 376
Nuckols, R., 408
Nuffield Foundation, 28, 33, 36

Ogilvie, D. M., *see* Stone and others (1966), 438
Ogilvie, H., *see* British Medical Association (1953), 28
Ogus, J., 438
O'Leary, E., 38
Opinion Research Centre, 12, 18, 19
Oppenheim, A. N., 327, 328, 349, 376, 418. *See also* Himmelweit and others (1958), 33, 232
Orr, J. Boyd, 25
Osgood, C. E., 373, 374, 375, 377
Owen, A. D. K., *see* Sheffield Social Survey Committee (1931–33), 9
Oxford University Institute of Statistics, 24, 25, 172, 201, 441

Paddock, J., 254 n
Parker, T., 37
Parkin, F. I., 35
Parkinson, P., 188 n
Parks, J. W., *see* Morris and others (1953), 27
Parr, E. A., 239
Parry, H. J., 408
Parten, M. B., 39, 52, 269, 302, 437, 478
Paton, M. R., 437
Patrick, R. C. Jr., *see* Sullivan and others (1958), 250
Patterson, S., 36
Payne, S. L. B., 311, 319, 320, 321, 324, 349

Peak, H., 373
Peaker, G. F., 30, 209
Pear, R. H., 34
Pelz, D. C., 479
Pennock, J. L., 408
Perkins, J. C., 372
Phillips, B. S., 39
Pidgeon, D. A., 30
Pierce, R. M., 21
Pilkington, Sir Harry, 59
Platek, R., 210
Platt, J., see Goldthorpe and others (1968a, 1968b), 35
Plowden, Lady, 29, 59, 484
Podell, L., 372
Political and Economic Planning, 11, 36, 39
Politz, A., 178, 178 n, 179, 179 n, 180, 181
Poll, C., see Morton-Williams and others (1966), 32
Pollins, H., see Brennan and others (1954), 22
Pomeranz, R., 31
Pomeroy, W. B., see Kinsey and others (1948), 311 n, 325, 327 n, 394; Kinsey and others (1953), 311 n, 327 n
Pool, A. G., see Sheffield Social Survey Committee (1931–33), 9
Pools Promoters' Association, 324, 325
Population Investigation Committee, 20, 27, 28, 123, 139, 141, 145, 287
Porter, R., 26
Portes, A., see Duncan and others (1968), 458, 479
Prais, S. J., 442
Price, J., 38
Pringle, M. L. Kellmer, 28, 139 n
Pritzker, L., 393, 408, 438

Quarantelli, E. L., see Bucher and others (1956), 281 n
Queen, S. A., see Sullivan and others (1958), 250

Raffle, P. A. B., see Morris and others (1953), 27
Raj, D., 117, 409
Ramanathan, R., 394 n
Redfield, R., 254 n
Reedman, J. N., see Sheffield Social Survey Committee (1931–33), 9
Rees, A. D., 22, 252
Reigrotzki, E., 293 n

Reiss, A. J., 418
Research Committee of the Council of the College of General Practitioners, 26
Research Techniques Division, London School of Economics, 135
Rex, J. A., 36
Rhodes, E. C., 37
Richardson, S. A., 302, 349
Richer, S., 39
Riedel, D. C., 210
Riley, M. W., 39, 236, 250, 255
Robb, J. H., 36, 250
Robbins, Lord, 29, 30, 32, 59, 165 n, 484
Roberts, C. G., see Morris and others (1953), 27
Roberts, H. V., 78
Robinson, H. L., 145
Robinson, J. P., 376
Rodgers, H. B., 33
Roethlisberger, F. J., 219, 297 n
Rogers, C. R., 302
Roper, W. F., 38
Rose, A. M., 300 n, 302
Rose, D., 210
Rose, E. J. B., 36
Rose, R., 35
Rosen, A. C., 38
Rosenberg, M., 145, 448 n, 454, 478
Ross, J. A., 237, 478
Ross, J. M., 29, 139 n
Rosser, C., 23
Roth, M., see Kay and others (1964), 27
Rowett Research Institute, 25
Rowntree, B. S., 6, 8, 9, 25, 33, 58
Rowntree, G., 21
Rowntree Trust, 21
Royal College of General Practitioners, 26
Royal College of Obstetricians and Gynaecologists, 27, 28, 287
Royal College of Physicians, 226 n
Royal Medico-Psychological Association, 263
Rozelle, R. M., 479
Rudd, E., 32
Runciman, W. G., 35
Russell, B., 253
Rutter, M., 26

Sagi, P. C., 371 n
Sainsbury, S., 22

Sampford, M. R., 78, 117
Schofield, M., 23, 39, 327 n, 366, 372, 391
Schuessler, K. F., 371 n, 451 n, 478
Schulz, T., 25
Schuman, H., 345
Schwartz, R. D., see Webb and others (1966), 255
Scott, C., 175, 210, 239, 246, 259, 261, 262, 263, 265, 266, 269, 305
Scott, W. A., 376
Scottish Council for Research in Education, 28, 29, 123
Seal, H. L., 478
Sechrest, L., see Webb and others (1966), 255
Seibert, J., 40
Selltiz, C., 39, 60, 215, 236, 255, 257, 302, 327 n, 328, 349, 376, 437, 478
Selvin, H. C., 446, 478
Seng, Y. P., 60
Shankleman, E., 15 n
Shapiro, S., 408
Shaver, P. R., 376
Shaw, L. A., see Backett and others (1953), 32
Shaw, M. E., 376
Sheatsley, P. B., 281 n, 349, 408
Sheffield Social Survey Committee, 9
Sheldon, J. H., 36
Shepherd, M., 26, 362
Shimkin, M. B., see Cornfield and others (1959), 226 n
Siegel, P. M., 384 n, 479
Sillitoe, K. K., 33
Silver, A., 35
Simmons, J. L., 255
Simmons, W., 178, 178 n, 179, 179 n, 180, 181
Simmons, W. R., see Greenberg and others (1969b), 328
Simon, H. A., 478
Simon, J. L., 39
Simpson, H. R., 29, 139 n
Sirageldin, I. A., see Morgan and others (1966), 442, 478
Sirken, M. G., 267, 408
Sjoberg, G., 39, 254 n, 255
Smith, B. Babington, 82, 153, 154
Smith, G. H., 327
Smith, H. Jr., 384 n, 408, 478
Smith, Harry L., 386, 408
Smith, Sir Hubert L., 9
Smith, J. S., 377

Smith, M. S., see Stone and others (1966), 438
Smith, P., 237
Snedecor, G. W., 78, 117, 478
Snell, E. J., 371 n
Sobol, M. G., 141 n
Social Surveys (Gallup Poll) Ltd, 18, 282-3, 283 n, 303 n, 304, 304 n, 318, 324, 325, 326, 342. See also British Institute of Public Opinion, Gallup Poll
Sonquist, J. A., 457, 478
Spearman, C., 354
Spence, J. C., 28
Spencer, J. C., 22
Sprott, W. J. H., 486, 487
Stacey, M., 22, 39, 250 n, 251, 255, 417
Stanley, J. C., 216, 218, 224, 224 n, 236
Steinkamp, S. W., 294, 302
Stember, H., 408
Stephan, F. F., 57, 58, 60, 133, 145, 187, 437
Stevens, C. D., 479
Stevens, S. S., 352 n
Stewart, C.. 22
Stock, J. S., 401 n
Stokes, D. E., 35, 145
Stone, P. J., 438
Stouffer, S. A., 236, 369, 373, 377, 442
Stuart, A., 78, 117, 130, 131, 132, 134, 135, 136, 137, 145, 169, 172, 174, 175, 177 n, 178 n, 181, 233, 280 n, 289, 290, 293, 303 n, 321, 401 n, 424, 425, 426, 427, 444, 446, 476, 478
Stuart, W. J., 434 n, 438
Suchman, E. A., 369, 372, 373
Suci, G. J., see Osgood and others (1957), 373, 374, 375, 377
Sudman, S., 128, 135, 137, 145, 175, 239, 269, 273, 302, 430 n, 438
Sukhatme, B. V., 117, 409
Sukhatme, P. V., 117, 409
Sullivan, M. A. Jr., 250
Summers, G. F., 376
Survey Research Center, University of Michigan, 141 n, 202, 209, 274, 290, 290 n, 291, 302, 437
Survey Research Centre, London School of Economics, 39

Tamulonis, V., see Cahalan and others (1947), 408
Tannenbaum, P. H., see Osgood and others (1957), 373, 374, 375, 377

Tavistock Institute of Human Relations, 252
Taylor, H., 20
Taylor, S. J. L., 28
Television Research Committee, University of Leicester, 33
Tepping, B. J., 438
Thaiss, G., 255
Thomas, M., 32
Thomlinson, R., 39
Thomson, W. E., 154 n
Thurstone, L. L., 377. *See also* Thurstone scaling
Tippett, L. H. C., 78, 82, 154
Titmuss, R. M., 12
Tizard, J., 38
Todd, J. E., 239
Todd, Lord, 59
Torgerson, W. S., 366 n, 370, 376
Townsend, P. B., 10 n, 11, 23, 37
Treasure, J. A. P., 15 n, 16
Trenaman, J. M., 35
Trow, M. A., 32
Truman, D. B., *see* Mosteller and others (1949), 19, 20, 39, 317, 345, 346, 349, 399, 477
Tucker, W., 175
Tufte, E. R., 39
Tukey, J. W., 78. *See also* Cochran and others (1953, 1954), 311
Turner, M. E., 479
Turner, R., 349, 407 n
Turner, R. H., 460, 461

U.K. Board of Trade, 14, 21, 59
U.K. Central Office of Information, 13, 262, 305
U.K. Central Statistical Office, 13, 14, 24, 25, 42, 209
U.K. Committee on Higher Education, 29, 30, 165 n. *See also* Robbins Committee, 32, 59, 484
U.K. Committee on Housing in Greater London, 21. *See also* Milner Holland report, 59
U.K. Department of Education and Science, 14, 30, 32, 42
U.K. Department of Employment and Productivity, 14, 24, 59, 209
U.K. Department of Health and Social Security, 14, 240
U.K. General Post Office, 154 n, 246
U.K. General Register Office, 13, 14, 26, 60, 396, 409, 418, 485

U.K. Government Social Survey, 5, 5 n, 13, 14, 15, 18, 21, 25, 26, 31, 33, 42, 131, 145, 161, 170, 171, 176, 195, 196, 209, 210, 246, 262, 266, 277, 278, 281, 284, 285, 287, 288, 289, 290, 301, 303, 315, 316, 392, 414, 416, 437, 485, 486
U.K. Home Office, 31, 32. Research Unit, 38
U.K. Interdepartmental Committee on Social and Economic Research, 42
U.K. Ministry of Agriculture, Fisheries and Food, 14, 25, 59
U.K. Ministry of Education, 30, 209
U.K. Ministry of Health, 25
U.K. Ministry of Housing and Local Government, 13, 14, 34, 159
U.K. Ministry of Labour, 24, 201
U.K. Ministry of Labour and National Service, 24, 58, 171
U.K. Ministry of Pensions and National Insurance, 37
U.K. Ministry of Public Building and Works, 59
U.K. Ministry of Social Security, 11
U.K. Ministry of Transport, 34
U.K. National Board for Prices and Incomes, 21, 32
U.K. National Food Survey Committee, 14, 25, 171, 172, 209
U.K. Office of Population Censuses and Surveys, 5 n, 13, 485. For Social Survey Division, *see* U.K. Government Social Survey
U.K. Post Office, 154 n, 246
U.K. Registrars-General, 21, 190, 229, 418
U.K. Road Research Laboratory, 14
U.K. Royal Commission on Doctors' and Dentists' Remuneration, 32, 269. *See also* Pilkington report, 59
U.K. Royal Commission on Local Government in England, 13. *See also* Maud report, 484
U.K. Royal Commission on Medical Education, 32
U.K. Royal Commission on Population, 5, 20, 28, 54, 185, 321
U.K. Schools Council, 14
U.K. Social Science Research Council (S.S.R.C.), 42, 417, 487. Data Bank, 42. Survey Unit, 487
U.K. Treasury, 13
U.K. Welsh Office, 159

United Nations Statistical Office, 60, 117, 210, 469, 469 n, 475, 476, 479
U.S. Bureau of Labor Statistics, 413 n, 434
U.S. Bureau of the Budget, 52
U.S. Bureau of the Census, 117, 143, 145, 209, 210, 290, 393 n, 396, 396 n, 401, 401 n, 406, 409, 418, 438, 483
U.S. Department of Agriculture, 145
U.S. Department of Health, Education, and Welfare, 226 n
U.S. National Center for Health Statistics, 26, 258, 259, 266, 269, 408
U.S. Social Science Research Council, 477
Upshaw, H. S., 376
Utting, J. E. G., 25, 37, 172, 288

Veldman, D. J., 438
Verner, H. W., see Cahalan and others (1947), 408
Vernon, P. E., 217
Vice-Chancellors' Committee, 32
Vince, P., see Himmelweit and others (1958), 33, 232
Voight, R. B., 438

Wadsworth, R. N., 141 n
Waksberg, J., 145, 340, 349, 391 n, 408
Walker, N., 26
Wallace, W. P., 247
Wallis, W. A., 78
Walton, W. S., see Miller and others (1960), 28; Spence and others (1954), 28
Ward, A. W. M., 263, 269
Warner, S. L., 328, 329
Warren, N., 376
Webb, B., 7, 8, 242
Webb, E. J., 255
Wedderburn, D., 37
Weick, K. E., 255
Weiss, C. H., 406

Wells, A. F., 1, 39
Westergaard, J. H., 21
West Midland Group on Post-War Reconstruction and Planning, 12
Whitfield, J. W., 346
Whyte, W. F., 250, 255
Wilkins, L. T., 14, 246, 385, 442, 464 n, 478
Willcock, H. D., 301, 392
Willett, T. C., 38
Willmott, P., 22, 23
Wills, G., 40
Wilson, E. C., 145
Wilson, G. G., 32
Witts, L. J., 27, 237
Wold, H., 224, 478
Wolfenden, Sir John, 484
Woodward, J., 31
Wright, J. M., 376
Wright, S., 479
Wynder, E. L., see Cornfield and others (1959), 226 n

Yamane, T., 78, 117
Yates, F., 40, 78, 82, 95, 117, 130 n, 137, 143, 153, 154, 186, 187, 210, 254 n, 430 n, 438, 442, 443
Yee, A. H., 479
Young, A., 33
Young, M. D., 23
Young, P. V., 39
Young, T., 11
Yule, G. U., 78, 80 n, 386 n

Zander, A. F., 252 n
Zaninovich, M. G., see North and others (1963), 438
Zarkovich, S. S., 187, 349, 409, 436 n, 438
Zeisel, H., 145, 478
Zinnes, D. A., see North and others (1963), 438
Zweig, F., 34, 56, 298, 443

Index of Subjects

Accuracy
 and bias, 65, 67–8
 definition, 64
 and precision, 64, 67–8
Accuracy checks, 311 n
Acquiescence response set, 345, 362
Additivity, 455, 457, 458
 see also Interaction
Addresses, sampling of, 159–60, 164
Adjustments in the analysis of experiments, 218, 222, 223–4, 448
Administrative districts as sampling
  units, 106, 120, 128, 160, 161, 189,
  190
After-only design, 215, 218
Aided recall, 17, 279, 331, 340
Alpha coefficient of reliability, 354
Alternative hypothesis, 76, 152
 see also Significance tests
Analysis, 439–67
 and causal models, 458–64
 and elaboration, 448–53
 errors in, 437
 and index construction, 464–6
 and regression, 454–8
 reporting of, 472
 sampling in, 436
 statistical description, 439–42
 and statistical inference, 443–7
 see also Tabulation
Analysis of covariance, 451 n, 454,
  457–8
Analysis of variance, 447, 454, 457–8, 472
Anonymity, 261, 266, 275
Appointments for interviews, 175
Area sampling, 102, 118–21, 135, 144,
  158, 273, 396

Asking of questions, 275–9, 293, 294,
  387, 388
 in informal interviewing, 296–300
 uniformity in, 275–6, 296, 388, 400,
  404–5
Association and causation, 211–15, 228,
  229
 see also Causal relationships
Attitude, 299–300, 317, 318, 350–1
 as evaluative factor, 374
Attitude scales, 318, 350–76
 existing scales, 376
 general procedures, 357–8
 Guttman scales, 351 n, 357, 364,
  366–73, 374
 item analysis, 358
 item choice, 357–8
 Likert scales, 351 n, 357, 361–6, 368,
  374
 semantic differential, 357, 366, 373–6
 Thurstone scales, 351 n, 357, 360–1,
  364–5, 368, 374
Attribute, definition, 61–2
Attwood Consumer Panel, 141
Audiometer, 248 n
Automatic interaction detector
  (A.I.D.), 457, 478
Average, 61 n

Balanced repeated replications, 208–9
Before-after designs, 215, 216, 217, 218,
  247
 with control groups, 138, 215, 217,
  218–19
Beta coefficients, 459
Bias, 65, 379
 and accuracy, 65, 67–8

538

in estimation, 65, 71 n, 78
from non-response, 167–9, 181–6, 268
and precision, 67–9
from sampling, 79–80, 82, 84–5
and variance, 381, 384
see also Interviewer bias, Question wording, Response bias
Biased-viewpoint effect, 250
Blanks on sampling frame, 156–7, 158, 159, 163, 169
Blocking, 138, 230, 231
Blocks in area sampling, 118–19
Bracket codes, 418, 435
Buying intentions, surveys on, 326

Call-backs, 170, 176–8, 274, 283
Cameras, use in surveys, 239, 248
Case records, 241–3
Case study approach, 2, 56, 466, 488
Causal models, 458–64, 483
assumptions in, 461–3
testing, 463
Causal relationships, 2–3, 211–14, 228, 229, 441, 447–64
and causal models, 458–64
and elaboration, 448–53
Causation, 211–14, 461–2
Census, definition, 54
Census, Population, *see* Population Census
Census of Production, 59
Cheating, 285, 293, 389–90
Checking of results, 181–2, 268, 294–5, 318, 392, 399–400, 406–7
see also Gross errors, Net errors, Response errors, Validity
Child upbringing, survey on, 23, 31
Chunks in area sampling, 120
Classification questions, 315–16, 417–18
Cluster analysis, 366 n
Clustering, 100–11, 196
cluster sampling, 100–6
and mail questionnaires, 257
multi-stage sampling, 106–11
Cluster sampling, 100–6, 110
precision of, 103–6, 108
see also Multi-stage sampling
Clusters of elements on sampling frame, 156, 159–60
Coders, training of, 423
Coding, 46, 304, 389, 410, 414–28, 433, 434
of answers, 422–3

and content analysis, 414
errors in, 45, 294, 343, 386–7, 412, 417, 423–8, 483
frames, 414–22, 423
by interviewers, 342–3, 386–7, 393, 404, 412, 422
in office, 342, 422–3
of open questions, 343, 416
of pre-coded questions, 50, 343–4, 415
by respondent, 342, 422
variability in, 417, 423–8
Coefficient of reproducibility, 369–71
Collapsed strata, 92 n, 203
Community studies, 22
Comparability of coding frames, 417
Complete coverage
definition, 54
use of, 6, 55, 56, 57, 59–60
Computations, 436–7
reporting of, 472
see also Analysis
Computers, 46, 432–6, 472–3, 483
for analysis, 410, 418, 419, 437, 472–3
for editing, 413, 472
input media, 435
languages, 433
programs for, 46, 47, 419, 421, 429, 433–5, 436
Conditioning in panels, 142–3, 341
Confidence intervals, 73–4, 77, 206
and precision of standard error estimator, 208
Confidence levels, 74
Confidentiality, 241, 266, 275
Consistency checks, 311 n, 394–5, 407, 412, 434–5
Constituencies, as sampling units, 102, 106, 144, 157, 161, 190, 283
Content analysis, 414
Control cards for computer programs, 433
Control effect with observation, 250
Control group, 36, 37, 38, 215, 216, 217, 220–4, 225, 227
Controlled selection, 92 n
Control through measurement, 222, 229
see also Adjustments in the analysis of experiments
Conversational interviewing, 298, 301
Cope-Chat cards, 430
Correlation, 384, 442, 452
partial, 463

see also Association, Causal relationships
Costs, 44, 47, 50–1, 57, 408
and mail questionnaires, 257
and multi-phase sampling, 122, 178
and multi-stage sampling, 101, 108, 109
and quota sampling, 134
reporting of, 471
and sample size, 151
variation between strata, 93, 98, 221
Counter sorter, 431
Covariance, 451 n, 454, 457–8
Covering letter with mail questionnaire, 264–5, 303
Crime, surveys on, 14, 37–9, 328
Cross-product, 451–3
Cross-tabulations, 222
see also Tabulation
Cumulative scales, 361, 367

Data collection, 470, 480, 481–2
decisions on, 41, 44–5, 49
methods of, 238–40
Demographic surveys, 5, 20–1
see also Population Censuses
Depth interviewing, 297 n, 301
Depth of interviewing, 299–300
Descriptive surveys, 2, 4, 211, 486
Designated respondent, 391, 396
Design effect (Deff), 89, 207, 447
for analytical statistics, 209, 447
for cluster samples, 103, 104–5
in fixing sample size, 150
for multi-stage samples, 105–6
for stratified multi-stage samples, 150, 201–2, 206, 209
Diary records, 24, 32, 141, 142, 171, 248, 279, 340–1
personal, 243
Differential scales, 361
Discriminant analysis, 458, 464 n, 465
Disproportionate stratified sampling, 85, 90, 93–7, 123, 191
Disturbing variables, *see* 'Third' variables
Documents, use in surveys, 6, 240–4
Domains of study, 95
Double-blind trial, 216
Double sampling, 121
Dummy variables, 456–7, 458
Duplication of research, 43
Duplication on sampling frame, 155, 157, 164

Editing, 46, 281, 304, 341, 392–3, 410–14
computer programs for, 434–5
Education, surveys on, 3, 14, 27, 28–30, 31, 32
Elaboration, 448–53, 457
Election forecasts, 18–20, 399, 477, 486
Election surveys, 34–5
Endogenous variables, 459, 460
Epidemiological surveys, 27, 226–30
Epsem samples, 81, 111, 112, 113, 114, 160, 163, 164, 443
and area sampling, 119–20
Equal-appearing intervals, method of, 360–1
see also Thurstone scales
ERNIE (electronic random number generating equipment), 154
Estimate and estimator, 65
Estimation of population values, 62, 63, 78, 442–3
and under types of sample
Exogenous variables, 459, 460
Expected value, 65, 68, 69
Expenditure surveys, 14, 24–5
see also Family Expenditure Survey
Experimental designs, 214–15, 220–6, 230–6
Experiments
definition, 224
in pilot surveys, 51
see also Experimental designs, Investigations
Experts as interviewers, 3, 20, 282, 287, 298–9
Explanatory surveys, 2–3, 27, 211
see also Association, Causal relationships, Experimental designs, Investigations
Ex post facto designs, 225
External validity, 220, 233, 234
Extraneous variables, *see* 'Third' variables

Factor analysis, 365–6, 372, 374, 375, 465
loadings, 366
rotation, 365
Factorial designs, 230–3
Factual questions, 276, 277–8, 310, 311, 315–16, 401
Family budget surveys, *see* Expenditure surveys, Family Expenditure Survey

Family Census (Royal Commission on Population), 5, 20, 54, 185
Family Expenditure Survey, 14, 24, 171, 195 n, 201–2, 209, 269, 279, 322, 340, 349
Family life, surveys on, 22–3
Fertility, surveys on, 20–1
Fieldwork checks, 45, 293–5, 389
  see also Checks, Re-interviewing
Filter questions, 325
Finite population correction (f.p.c.), 67, 81, 146
Focused interview, 298
Follow-up methods, 44, 176–8
  for mail surveys, 226–7
  and weighting for non-response, 185–6
Foreign elements on sampling frame, 156–7
Frame of reference for questions, 318–19, 344
Funnel sequence of questions, 346

Gallup Polls, 1, 18
  see also Public opinion polls, Social Surveys (Gallup Poll) Ltd
General Inquirer computer program, 438
General linear model, 458
General practitioner records, 26, 241, 242
Geometric codes, 421
Gross errors, 392–8, 402, 426
  see also Response errors
Guided interview, 298
Guttman scales, 351 n, 357, 364, 366–73, 374
  item choice, 371
  multi-category items, 371
  reproducibility, 369–71
  scalogram, 367–9, 465

Half-open interval, 120 n, 155
Halo effect, 359–60
Hand tabulation, 410, 428–9
Hawthorne effect, 219
  experiments, 297 n
Health, surveys of, 14, 25, 26–8, 258–9, 349, 391
Health services, surveys on, 28, 123, 269
History, as a source of experimental invalidity, 216
Household composition questions, 322, 417, 424, 428

Households, sampling of, 159–60, 164, 197–8
Housing, surveys on, 14, 21–2
Hypotheses, testing of, 4, 62–3, 74–6, 444–7

Identification codes, 419, 431
Inadequate response, types of, 276–7
Income, questions on, 322, 413, 417, 424, 428
Incomplete coverage, 54–5
Inconclusive results, 476–7
Index construction, 464–6
Individual response error, 378–9
  bias, 380, 381, 382
  variance, 380, 381
  see also Memory errors, Response errors
Individuals, sampling of, 163–4, 165, 198–200, 273–4
Industrialization index, 189, 190, 193–4
Inference
  and analysis, see Analysis
  and observation, 253
Informal interviewing, 3, 31, 34, 56, 242, 270–1, 296–301, 482
  in attitude scale construction, 357–8
  in pilot surveys, 348
Instrumentation as a source of experimental invalidity, 217
Intelligence, surveys on, 28–9, 123
Intensity analysis, 372–3
Intensive studies, 2, 3, 56, 488
Interaction effect, 232, 455–6, 457
Internal validity, 220, 233
Interpenetrating sampling, 124
  see also Replicated sampling
Interpretation of associations, 214, 440, 447–64
  and causal models, 458–64
  and elaboration, 448–53
  see also Causal relationships
Interpretation of punched cards, 420, 430–1
Interval scales, 61 n, 352, 360, 364
Interview
  nature of, 271–2
  opening, 274–5, 346
  place of, 270 n, 391
  record sheets, 273
Interviewer bias, 228, 284, 379, 380, 382–3, 385–7
  and expectations, 386–7
  in informal interviewing, 299

and opinions, 386
and personal characteristics, 385–6
and variance, 402
see also Response bias, Response errors, Response variance
Interviewer-respondent interaction, 272, 385
Interviewers
adaptability of, 286
assignments of, 283, 295–6, 401, 404, 405–6
desirable characteristics of, 282, 285–7
errors of, 45, 293, 385–90
expectations of, errors due to, 386–7, 388, 389
instructions to, 50, 275–6, 291–2, 388, 391
matching to respondents of, 406
morale of, 295
number of, 401, 404, 405–6
payment of, 45, 295, 389, 396
reports of, 281
selection of, 41, 45, 282–7, 379, 404
supervision of, 293–4
training of, 41, 45, 50, 272, 275, 277, 283, 284, 287–91, 391, 396, 404, 470
and quality of interviews, 290–1, 404
and refusals, 174–5, 289–90
working conditions of, 295–6
Interviewers' manual, 277, 283, 287, 288, 315
Interviewer variance, 132, 383, 384, 400–3, 405
Interviewing as a method of enquiry, 2, 6, 45, 49, 270–301
combined with observation, 239
combined with self-completion questionnaires, 261–2
compared with mail questionnaires, 257, 258–9, 267
Intra-class correlation
for cluster samples, 104–6
for interviewer variance, 383, 401
Inverted funnel sequence of questions, 346–7
Investigations
definition, 224
examples of, 27, 226–30
Item pool for attitude scaling, 357–8, 360–1, 362

Jack-knife method of variance estimation, 208 n
Judgement samples
definition, 80
and inference, 443–4
see also Quota sampling
Jurors' index, 196–7
Juvenile delinquency, surveys on, 37, 39, 328

Keypunch, 420, 430, 431
Kish selection table, 174, 198–9, 274
Knowledge questions, 277–8, 315

Labour vote percentage, as stratification factor, 190, 196
Latent structure analysis, 372, 465
Leisure, surveys on, 33–4
Length of mail questionnaire, 263–4
Likert scales, 351 n, 357, 361–6, 368, 374
Linearity in regression, 455, 457, 458
Linking procedures for missing elements, 155, 163
Listing in area sampling, 119–20, 121, 273
Lists, sampling from, 83, 86, 163, 164
Literary Digest, 79, 147
Location sampling, 247
Longitudinal studies, 27–8, 29, 38, 137–43
see also Panels
Lottery method, 81, 82

Machine tabulation, 429, 431–2
see also Computers, Unit record equipment
Magnetic tape, 435
Mail questionnaires, 6, 45, 49, 256–69
for appointments, 175–6
bias from non-response, 79, 267–8
combined with interviewing, 261–2
combined with observation, 239
compared with interviewing, 258–9
and interview follow-up, 178, 239
and multi-phase sampling, 122, 123, 269
non-response to, 256–7, 262–9
Main effects, 456
Maps, as sampling frame, 102, 118–21, 135, 158, 273
Marginal associations, 449
Market research, 1, 2, 15–17, 58, 200, 326, 386, 485–6

Mark sensing, 430 n
Master samples, 143–5, 283
Matching, 138, 218, 220–2, 223–4, 227, 230, 232, 235, 236, 448, 453
Maturation as a source of experimental invalidity, 216–17
Mean, arithmetic, 61 n
Mean square error, 69, 383–4
Measurement errors, 378 n, 381 n, 384, 482–3
Measures of size, 112, 114–15
  in area sampling, 119
Memory errors, 45, 134, 140, 142, 225, 245, 310–11, 331, 340–1, 390, 407, 471, 482
Mental health, surveys on, 26–7
Middletown surveys, 251
Migration, surveys on, 21
Missing elements from sampling frame, 154–5, 163
Mortality as a source of experimental invalidity, 218–19
Motivation research, 485
Movers, 157, 162–4, 169, 174
Moving observer, 254 n
Multi-phase sampling, 60, 121–4, 269, 469
  and non-response, 182
  and Population Census, 60, 123–4
  for stratification, 122
Multiple classification analysis (M.C.A.), 457, 478
Multiple comparisons tests, 446
Multiple regression, see Regression
Multiple stratification, 92
  without control of sub-strata, 130 n
Multiple treatment interference as a source of experimental invalidity, 220
Multi-punched columns, 419, 420, 421, 435
Multi-purpose nature of surveys, 469–70
  and multi-stage sampling, 109
  and sample size, 149
  and stratification, 92–3, 95
Multi-stage sampling, 100, 106–11, 189, 190–200
  and area sampling, 118
  and cluster sampling, 105–6, 110
  and multi-phase sampling, 121
  and stratification, 106, 107–8, 110
Multivariate analysis, 432, 436, 440, 442, 465, 466, 483

National Child Development Study (1958 Cohort), 28, 29, 139
National Food Survey, 14, 25, 171–2, 209, 279, 340
National Readership Survey, 16, 163, 174, 279, 323, 330, 331, 347, 409
National Survey of Health and Development, 27, 29, 139–40
Net errors, 392, 398–400, 402, 426
  see also Bias, Checks, Response errors, Validity
Nominal scales, 61 n, 352
Non-contacts, 44, 49, 79, 170, 171, 175
Non-contact sheet, 181
Non-directive interviewing, 297, 298
Non-electors, sampling of, 163
Non-quantified material, use of, 2, 300–1, 437–8, 439, 466, 475
Non-repondents, characteristics of,
  in interview surveys, 172
  in mail surveys, 263, 267–8
Non-response, 22, 44, 49, 58, 79–80, 166–86, 443, 470, 471, 481
  adjustment for bias from, 181–6
  bias from, 167–9, 172–3
  on individual questions, 294
  to mail surveys, 256–7, 262–9
  in panels, 141
  and quota sampling, 134,137, 481
  and sample size, 152, 189
  and sampling error, 186, 481
Non-sampling errors, 384, 482–3
  and replicated sampling, 126, 382–3, 400–1
  reporting of, 473, 476
  and sampling errors, 384, 408, 482
  see also Response bias, Response variance
Normal distribution, 72–3. 77
Null hypothesis, 75, 151–2
Nutrition surveys, 8, 14, 25–6

Observation as a method of enquiry, 6, 31, 44, 49, 244–54
  advantages of, 245–6, 254
  combined with interviews, 239, 254
  combined with mail questionnaires, 239
  limitations of, 247–8
  participant, 23, 30, 36, 38, 245, 249–54
  sampling with, 247
  for studying activities, 246–54
Occupation, codes for, 417–18

Occupations, surveys of, 14, 21, 31–3
Old age, surveys on, 14, 22, 23, 36–7
Open questions, 50, 280, 281, 296 n, 341–6, 390, 412
  coding answers to, 343, 416–17, 426, 427
  and informal interviewing, 296 n
  recording answers to, 343, 389, 412
  and response errors, 389, 390
Opinion questions, 5, 276, 277–8, 310, 315, 316–18, 344, 395 n, 401
Opinions, 316–17
  and attitudes, 318
  counting of, 318, 350
  intensity of, 317, 318
  many-sidedness of, 317, 350–1
  see also Attitude scales, Opinion questions, Public opinion polls, Rating scales
Optical scanners, 430 n
Optimum allocation in stratified sampling
  for means and proportions, 93–5
  for comparisons between strata, 98–9
Ordinal scales, 61 n, 352, 364, 368
'Overheards', 247

Paired comparison experiment, 223
Paired selection sample design, 124, 208, 401, 443
Panels, 27, 35, 137–43, 340
  in market research, 16, 138, 141, 142
  for measuring changes, 138, 144
  in radio research, 17–18, 142
  volunteers, 17–18
  see also Longitudinal studies
Parameter, definition, 62
Partial associations, 449–51
Partial correlation, 463
Participant observation, 23, 30, 36, 38, 245, 249–54
Path coefficients, 459–63
Periodicity and systematic sampling, 83–4
Personal documents, 243–4
Pilot surveys, 47–51, 93–4, 301, 310, 319, 348–9
  and attitude scaling, 365, 375
  and mail surveys, 264
Placebo effect, 216
Political behaviour, surveys of, 34–5
Politz-Simmons method, 178–81
Polling districts as sampling units, 44,

102, 107, 144, 157, 161, 163, 189, 190, 196–7
Population
  coverage, 43, 44, 53–4, 188–9, 470
  definition, 5
  for experimental studies, 234
  survey, 53, 155
  target, 53, 155
Population, surveys on, 5, 20–1
  see also Population Censuses
Population Censuses, 20, 54, 170, 261–2, 418
  and quality check, 396–7, 409
  and sampling, 57, 59–60, 123–4, 166, 436, 481
  see also U.S. Population Censuses
Postcard checks, 293–4
Post-Enumeration surveys, 294–5, 395–8, 482
Post-stratification, 99–100
  see also Stratification after selection
Poverty lines, 8–9, 10–11
Poverty surveys, 1, 5, 7–11, 484
Power of significance tests, 152, 444–5
Precision, 64–74
  and accuracy, 64, 67–9
  and bias, 67–9
  and cost, 80
  and sample size, 71, 85, 146–52
  of standard error estimator, 126, 207–8
  see also Standard error
Pre-coded questions, 280, 341–6, 390
  coding of, 50, 343–4, 415
  order of codes for, 345
  and random probes, 345
  and response errors, 390
Predictions, based on surveys, 245–6, 326, 485
Prestige effects, 246, 311, 327, 379–80, 387, 390, 404
Pre-tests, 47–51
  see also Pilot surveys
Primary sampling units (PSU's), 106
  of unequal size, 111–12
Probability proportional to size (PPS), 111–16, 189, 190, 195, 197
  and area sampling, 119
Probability sampling
  definition, 63, 80
  with quotas, 137
  see also Random sampling
Probing, 271, 276, 277–8, 315, 345, 388–9, 393, 396–7, 404

Processing data, 410–37, 472–3, 483
  coding, 414–28
  computers in, 46, 432–6, 472–3, 483
  editing, 46, 281, 304, 341, 392–3, 410–14, 434–5
  punched cards in, 304, 415, 418–19, 420, 430–1
  tabulation, 46, 410, 419, 428–36, 441, 466
  unit record equipment in, 410, 413, 418, 419, 429, 431–2, 437
Projective techniques, 327–8, 485
Prompting, 278–9, 345
Proportionate stratified sampling, 85, 86–90, 93, 96, 191–2
Prospective design, 225–6, 229–30, 242–3
Psychiatric illness, surveys on, 26–7
Public opinion polls, 18–20, 35, 58, 485
  see also Opinions
Punched cards, 304, 415, 418–19, 420, 430–1
  punching of, 422, 430–1
  verification of, 420, 431
Purposive sampling, 54 n, 80, 85 n
  in experiments, 233

Quality checks, 294–5, 395–8, 482
Quasi-random sampling, 83
Question
  order, 276, 346–7, 388, 390
    in mail surveys, 260–1
    rotating, 347
  wording, 318–31, 340–1, 391
    principles of, 308–10, 318, 347–8
    simplicity in, 260, 304, 319–22
    see also under Questions
Questionnaire
  design of, 45, 303–49, 390, 422, 430
    and pilot survey, 49–50, 310, 319, 348–9
  · examples, 305–7, 312–14, 332–9
  instructions, 292
  length of, 263–4, 309–10, 390, 482
  and recording schedule, 260 n, 303
  in survey report, 470
Questions
  ambiguous, 322–3
  complex, 321–2, 390
  context of, 324–5, 346–7
  embarrassing, 258, 311, 325, 327–30, 390
  hypothetical, 325–6
  indirect, 327–8

leading, 323–5
length of, 322, 388
many-sided, 318–19
memory, 331, 340–1, 390, 471
  see also Memory errors
on periodical behaviour, 330–1
personalized, 319, 326, 327
presuming, 325
vague, 323
  see also Factual questions, Knowledge questions, Open questions, Pre-coded questions, Questionnaire, Question order, Question wording
Quintamensional plan of question design, 345–6
Quota sampling, 17, 18, 54 n, 80, 127–37, 165, 399
  assignments, 129–32, 316, 390
  controls, 128–9, 133–4, 316, 390
  and costs, 134, 136
  experiment on, 135–7
  and non-response, 134, 137, 170, 481
  and random sampling, 127, 131, 133, 136–7
  and representativeness, 130, 131–2, 133, 135–6, 188
  and sampling errors, 132–3, 136, 200
  and speed, 134–5
  and stratified sampling, 127

Race relations, surveys on, 36
Radio listening, surveys on, 17–18, 135, 142
Randomization in experiments, 218, 222–4, 228, 448, 453
Randomized response technique, 328–30
Randomness, 80, 81, 82, 84–5, 116, 152–4
  see also Randomization in experiments, Random numbers
Random numbers, 81, 82, 83, 115–16, 152–4, 195
Random sampling
  definition, 63, 80–1
  importance of, 55–6, 63, 80, 82, 116, 127
  from lists, 82–3, 86, 163, 164
  and non-response, 166–7
  procedures, 81–2
  and quota sampling, 80, 127, 133–5, 137, 188
  and simple random sampling, 80

and stratification, 81
Range for estimating standard deviation, 125
'Rapport', 275, 286, 309, 346, 406
Rare populations, sampling of, 123, 135, 164–5
    by mail surveys, 257, 269
Rateable value, as stratification factor, 193, 195, 195 n
Rating records, as sampling frame, 158–60, 187
Rating scales, 358–60, 362, 373
    errors with, 359–60
    reliability of, 360
Ratio scales, 61 n, 353
Reactive effect
    of experimental arrangements, 219
    of testing, 219
Readership surveys, 16, 163, 174, 279, 323, 330, 331, 347, 409
Recall loss, 340
Re-calls, see Call-backs
Recoding programs, 419 n, 421, 435
Record checks, 384, 393–4
Recorded interviews, 248, 279 n, 281, 288, 289, 299 n, 348, 358, 405
Recording of answers, 279–81, 389, 404
    errors in, 280, 286, 294, 379, 389
    to open questions, 342–3, 389
Recording schedule, 260 n, 303, 304
    see also Questionnaire
Record-keeping, see Diary records
Record system for questionnaires, 414
Refusals, 44, 49, 79, 170, 171, 172, 174–5
    and interviewers' experience, 289–90
    in quota sampling, 134
    see also Non-response
Regional planning surveys, 1, 5, 11–13, 484
Register of Electors, as sampling frame, 19, 46, 48, 91, 123, 159 n, 160–5, 169, 174, 175, 186–7, 190, 197
Regression, 222, 384, 435, 442, 443, 446, 454–5, 457–8, 460, 465, 472
    coefficients, 454, 459
    as a source of experimental invalidity, 217–18
Reinforcement by interviewer, 231–2, 322 n
Re-interviewing, 294–5, 384, 395–8
Relationships, study of, see Causal relationships

Reliability, 353–7, 364, 395 n
    alternate forms, 354
    of coders, 427
    split-half, 354–5
    stepped-up, 354–5
    test-retest, 353–4
Replacement
    and PPS sampling, 115–16
    sampling with, 80, 202
    sampling without, 64, 81, 202
Replicated sampling, 124–7
    and non-sampling errors, 126, 295, 382–3, 384, 400–1, 473
    and quota sampling, 132–3, 136
    restricted, 401
    for standard error estimation, 124–5, 207–9, 443
    and stratification, 127, 207
Report writing, 467–78, 483
    negative findings, 476
    objectivity in, 467
    style, 468
    U.N. recommendations, 469–75
Representativeness, 5, 84–5, 268
    of quota samples, 131–2, 133, 135–6
    see also Randomness
Reproducibility, 364, 369–71
Research, information on current studies, 42
Respondent, designated, 391, 396
Response bias, 380–1, 383–4, 395
    and variance, 381, 384, 402, 403–4
Response errors, 45, 310–11, 378–408, 482
    bias and variance, 378–81, 402
    control and measurement of, 403–8
    correlated, 382–3
    from interviewer, 385–7
    models for, 381–4
    operation of, 388–92
    from respondent, 387–8
    sources of, 385–8
    uncorrelated, 382
Response set, 362, 374
Response variance, 380–1, 382, 383, 384, 395
    and bias, 381, 384, 402, 403–4
Retail audit surveys, 16
Retrospective design, 225, 227, 230
Re-weighting, see Weighting of results
Rotation designs, 143
Rounds of survey, 471
Royal Commissions, use of sample surveys by, 59, 484

ample design, decisions on, 41, 44, 48, 55, 56
  reporting of, 472
  and under types of sample
Sample size, 44, 48, 55, 116, 146–52, 189, 192
  and bias, 146
  for complex sample designs, 150
  and confidence intervals, 147–51
  and non-response, 152, 173
  and population size, 146
  and significance tests, 151–2
  and sub-groups, 148
Sample survey, definition, 54
Sampling
  advantages of, 56–8
  in analysis, 436
  development of, 9, 10, 57, 58–9
  in editing, 413
  for experimental studies, 233–6
  in the field, 60, 197
  future advances in, 480–1
  and inference, 63, 440, 442–7
  in official enquiries, 59
  rare populations, 123, 135, 164–5, 257, 269
  by serial numbers, 166
Sampling distributions, 64, 69–74, 77
Sampling errors, 45, 55, 58, 65–74, 124–6, 132–3, 200–9, 440, 442–7
  for complex samples, 200–9, 443, 447
  presentation of, 200, 443, 471, 475–6
  see also Standard error
Sampling fractions, 81, 146, 191
  in stratified sampling, 85, 88 n, 93, 94, 95, 96, 98, 123, 191
Sampling frames, 44, 46, 48, 90, 154–66, 190, 443, 472, 473–4
  and area sampling, 118, 135, 158, 273
  basic frame problems, 154–8
  in Britain, 158–65
  faults in, 79–80
  and multi-stage sampling, 101, 108, 110
  and quota sampling, 135
Sampling unit, choice of, 44, 100, 105, 106–7, 120, 157, 190
Sampling variance, 66, 203–7
  and bias, 69, 381, 384
  and response variance, 382, 383
  see also Standard error
Savings, surveys on, 25, 172, 201
Scale points, number to use with rating scales, 344, 359

Scales of measurement, 61 n, 352–3
Scale types in Guttman scaling, 368
Scalogram analysis, 367–9
Scalometer method, 359
Secondary analysis, 43
Segments in area sampling, 119
Selection as a source of experimental invalidity, 218
  selection-history interaction, 219
  selection-maturation interaction, 219
  selection-testing interaction, 219
Selection equation, 112–15, 160
Selection of interviewers, *see* Interviewers, selection of
Self-completion questionnaires, 258–9, 405–6
  see also Mail questionnaires
Self-representing primary sampling units, 116, 193, 196, 203
Semantic differential, 357, 366, 373–6
  and factor analysis, 374, 375
  and profile analysis, 375
Sentence completion, 327–8
SETmeter, 248
Sexual behaviour, surveys on, 23–4, 311 n, 325, 327 n, 372, 391, 394
Significance level, 76, 152
Significance tests, 74–6, 151–2, 444–7, 455, 462 n
  and estimation, 447
Simple random sampling, 63, 64–5, 67 n, 78, 80 n, 81
  and cluster sampling, 104–5
  and multi-stage sampling, 105–6
  and stratification, 85, 86, 89
  and systematic sampling, 83
  and unrestricted random sampling, 80–1
Smoking and lung cancer, studies of, 27, 226–30
Social class
  classifications, 279, 417–18, 464
  as quota control, 129, 134
Social mobility, surveys on, 30–1, 442
Social surveys
  definition, 1
  evolution in Britain, 6–39
  in official administration, 1, 2, 3, 14–15, 59–60, 484
  purposes of, 1, 2–4, 43, 469, 483–8
  in social research, 1, 2, 3, 15, 484, 486–7
  subject matter of, 1, 4–5
Sorter, 431

Spearman-Brown reliability formula, 354–5
Sponsorship of survey, 262–3, 392, 471
Spurious association, 214, 450, 453, 462
    see also Causal relationships
Stable correlate matching technique, 222
Standard deviation
    and estimator, 71
    of a proportion, 94, 149
    S, 66–7
    σ, 66
Standard error, 62, 63, 66–7, 68, 69–74
    for multi-stage stratified samples, 200–9, 443
    with replicated sampling, 124–5, 207–9
    reporting of, 473, 475–6
    of standard error, 207–8
    in systematic sampling, 202–3
Standard error of a difference
    between two means, 138, 151, 447
    between two proportions, 75–6
Standard error of a mean
    cluster sample, 103, 104
    disproportionate stratified sample, 97
    multi-stage sample, 109–11
    proportionate stratified sample, 87, 89
    simple random sample, 66–7, 71, 148
Standard error of a proportion
    disproportionate stratified sample, 87 n
    multi-stage sample, 203
    proportionate stratified sample, 87, 89
    simple random sample, 77, 87, 89, 103 n, 147, 200
Standardization as analytic tool, 222, 236, 454
Standardized variables, 459 n
Standard Regions, Registrar-General's, as stratification factor, 190, 191
Statistic, definition, 62
Statistical regression as a source of experimental invalidity, 217–18
Statistical significance, 74–6, 444–7
Statistical sources, 42
Stealing, study of, 39, 328
Stratification, 84, 85–100, 107–9, 110, 189, 190–1, 193–7
    and area sampling, 119
    disproportionate, 85, 90, 93–7, 123, 191

and increased precision, 85, 86–7, 90
and multi-phase sampling, 122–3
and multi-stage sampling, 92, 107–9
optimum allocation, 93, 98
proportionate, 85, 86–90, 93
and purposive sampling, 85 n
and randomness, 81, 85, 92
reasons for, 90
and replicated sampling, 127, 207
without control of sub-strata, 130 n
Stratification after selection, 99–100, 184, 443
    and matching, 222
    and multi-phase sampling, 122
    and re-weighting for non-response, 184
Stratification factors, 85, 87, 90–3, 189, 193, 195, 196–7
Student's 't' distribution, 207–8
Sub-questions, 304, 308, 347, 390
Sub-sampling
    for non-response, 177–8, 267
    see also Multi-phase sampling, Multi-stage sampling
Substitution, 156 n, 169, 172–3
Summated rating scales, 362, 374
    see also Likert scales, Semantic differential
Supervision of fieldwork, 41, 292–5, 404
Survey of Sickness, 14, 26, 349
Survey population, 53, 155, 443
'Sympathy effect', 386 n
Systematic sampling, 83–4, 163, 195 n
    with probability proportional to size sampling, 116, 195
    and standard error, 202–3

Tabulation, 46, 410, 428–36, 441, 466
    computer programs for, 419, 429, 433–4, 435
Tabulator, 432
Tammeter, 248 n
Tape recorders, use in surveys, 248, 279 n, 281, 288, 289, 299 n, 348, 358, 405
Target population, 53, 155
Telephones
    for appointments, 175–6
    for interviews, 137 n, 238–9, 267
Telescoping effect, 340, 407
Television viewing, surveys on, 17, 33, 35, 135, 232, 237, 248
Test factors, 448–55